Project Management Institute

PROJECT MANAGEMENT
CIRCA 2025

Project Management Institute

PROJECT MANAGEMENT CIRCA 2025

Edited by
David Cleland, PhD
Bopaya Bidanda, PhD

Project Management Circa 2025

ISBN: 978-1-933890-96-8

Published by: Project Management Institute, Inc.
                  14 Campus Boulevard
                  Newtown Square, Pennsylvania 19073-3299 USA.
                  Phone: +1-610-356-4600
                  Fax: +1-610-356-4647
                  E-mail: customercare@pmi.org
                  Internet: www.PMI.org

PMI Publications welcomes corrections and comments on its books. Please feel free to send comments on typographical, formatting, or other errors. Simply make a copy of the relevant page of the book, mark the error, and send it to: Book Editor, PMI Publications, 14 Campus Boulevard, Newtown Square, PA 19073-3299 USA.

To inquire about discounts for resale or educational purposes, please contact the PMI Book Service Center.

                  PMI Book Service Center
                  P.O. Box 932683, Atlanta, GA 31193-2683 USA
                  Phone: 1-866-276-4764 (within the U.S. or Canada) or +1-770-280-4129 (globally)
                  Fax: +1-770-280-4113
                  E-mail: book.orders@pmi.org

Contents

Preface

A significant body of book literature in project management has evolved over the last 50 years. This literature has addressed a wide range of approaches to the management of projects, including theory, processes, and principle.

Edmund Gosse (1840-1928) noted that "The Future comes like an unwelcome guest." Unfortunately there has been little literature on what the likely future of project management might be. In order to fill that void, this book will present the likely future of project management in terms of the possibilities and probabilities of how the discipline will be used to manage the tactical and strategic changes that will impact current and forthcoming products, services, and organizational processes.

As the technological, economic, political, legal, and competitive world changes, what strategies should be developed and implemented to facilitate survival and growth? The evaluations are done by professionals who have extraordinary credentials in the use of project management, and are the best qualified to identify and evaluate the likely future changes in their environment.

We believe that this first-of-its-kind book will create awareness of what future changes can be expected in the use of project management. The thoughts contained can be used to facilitate the management of current and future change.

David I. Cleland, Ph.D.
Bopaya Bidanda, Ph.D.
University of Pittsburgh

Introduction

Project management has evolved over many centuries as a means for organizations to deal with change. It was not until the 1950s that the literature began to reflect the evolving theory and practice of this discipline. The proposed book draws from the collective experience of project management leaders from around the world to develop a project management based scenario for the year 2025.

The project management practitioners authoring chapters are knowledgeable experts in the theory and practice of project management. These contributors, drawn from different industries and countries around the world, have written their chapters from a perspective of the likely forces and factors that will influence the probable state-of-the-art in project management for the period circa 2025.

The principal guiding criteria for the chapter authors were: (1) A very brief introduction of the current state-of-the-art of project management in their industry or environment; (2) A general overview of the expected and future technological, economic, social, political, and competitive characteristics of their industry or environment; (3) Identification of current trends in their industry or environment that will likely affect the manner in which project management is used in the future in their environment; and (4) Identification of the major characteristics of project management likely to be found in their industry or environment for the period circa 2025. The authors were given wide latitude in preparing their material and describing their knowledge and the experiences that influenced their foretelling of what the likely appearance of state of both theory and practice of project management in 2025.

The book is organized into five parts as follows:

Part 1 Examples of Projects from Geographic and Industry Applications
Part 2 Project Management Systems Applications
Part 3 Project Management Organizational Applications
Part 4 Project Management in Government
Part 5 Likely Growth of Project Management

Each part brings together for the reader the probable state-of-the-art in diverse environments for the year 2025. It provides the basis for the reader to learn of the varied uses of project management in the present, and how the cultural ambience of the organizations of the future will impact the probable state-of-the-art of project management circa 2025. As readers see what the future of project management may be, they might see how their organizations could be impacted. A brief outline of the parts and chapters follows.

Part 1: Examples of Projects from Geographic and Industry Applications

Several projects are described in this part from different geographic areas. These projects describe how the strategic change management in their particular areas have been initiated and executed to deal with the alteration of the employment of organizational resources to accomplish desired objectives and goals. While there is a central theme of generic project management in these projects, there are provincial characteristics to be found as well.

In chapter 1, Christophe N. Bredillet presents a chapter on the deployment of project management in the Europe of 2025. He makes the key point that the project management discipline will likely continue to grow and is expected to be adopted more and more by companies and organizations, including governments, non-government, business and non-profit organizations and associations. The overall purpose of this chapter is to analyze the contribution of two organizations in the deployment of project management and compare their deployment within the European countries by 2025.

In chapter 2, Alfonso Bucero, PMP, explains that project management is becoming more and more popular in Spain, but is still understood as a tactical set of methods and tools focused principally on the project manager. Very few Spanish organizations spend time and money training their executives in the strategic part of project management and in their critical role as project sponsors. The author points out that the board of directors of many Spanish companies do not see the need of being trained as sponsors. There is a need to develop and train skilled project managers in both the hard and soft skills used in the management of projects.

Raju Rao, in chapter 3, has a vision of India where the role of the project manager is critical in transforming a nation from developing to developed. India has consistently maintained an economic growth of over 9% over the last several years. World Bank reports state that India will be the third-largest economy by the year 2025, although the rapid growth is threatened in terms of environmental issues, sustainability, degradation, infrastructure resource inadequacy, social imbalance, cultural differences and the lack of appropriate managerial skills. The chapter closes with the provocative question: Can project management as a discipline be used to handle these opportunities and threats?

In chapter 4, Brian Kooyman describes how project management will likely change in the Australasian and Pacific Region. The first part of the chapter addresses the geography of the region followed by a review of the current levels of project management and application in the region. Then a summary of the likely developments and changing environments in the region is presented. This is followed with hypotheses on how the region will cope with these changes. The last part of the chapter considers how these hypothetical changes may be managed.

Chapter 5 by Charles R. Franklin, PMP, Naceur Jabnoun, Ph.D., and Shriram R. Dharwadkar, Ph.D, states that project management in the Arabian Gulf region will be impacted by factors which include emerging and rapidly changing technologies, economics as the region's economies make a shift away from their dependency on oil and gas, critical issues in human resources development, and the increasing size and complexity of projects. These will result in new challenges to business in general and projects specifically. Some of the major challenges may be categorized as knowledge management, innovation, business, ethics, and safety. Project professionals of 2025 will have developed new competencies both to meet these challenges and to leverage the opportunities they present.

Part 2: Project Management Systems Applications

In chapter 6, Elaine Bannon and David Pericak say that although external factors change over time, the key personal values and deliverables of project management that deliver excellent results do not. This chapter describes those key elements, how to measure them, and discusses the health of your project management organization and how a high performing team can thrive in time of significant change. It is critical for organization to recognize and deliberately foster these key personal values and core deliverables in order to strengthen their companies in any set of external factors, whether they are deemed challenging or enabling.

Chapter 7 by Janice Lynn Thomas, Jenny Krahn, and Stella George provides insight into the shape of project management research to come. They believe that those most successful in predicting the future are not so much predictors as shapers. What great shapers do is recognize the trends and needs that are about to become important to the world. Shapers support change through innovation. Considering the direction of changes in the world of work, project management is well-placed to shape itself to meet coming needs. The future of project management needs to be innovatively responsive to the leading edge of work.

Chapter 8 by Randall L. Speck focuses on the legal framework for projects circa 2025. The author notes that legal systems inherently resist change and rely on precedents. Statutes, he says, do not change easily or quickly and usually lag behind changes in economic relationships. Legal systems protect parochial, entrenched interests based on territorial jurisdiction. There is the need to develop legal constructs that will promote projects in a global, instantaneous, and transparent environment. Different legal traditions clash as globalization requires cross-border relationships, which also leads to the difficulty of assigning jurisdiction in one locale. The role of government regulations complicates the legal issues.

Stacy Goff admits at the beginning of chapter 9 that prediction is difficult. His chapter hedges that difficulty by applying several scenarios to establish alternative futures for the portfolio, program, and project management software industry. The chapter applies experience of industry veterans, interview results with several product managers of current market leaders, and insights from several more who are involved with changes in the industry's direction. A trajectory scenario traces key project management software achievements of the past

Chapter 10 discusses the likely growth of quality management in projects circa 2025. Sandra K. Ireland explores the history of quality management from original meaning of words through the turbulent "quality revolution" of the 1970s, where a sharp focus changed the thrust of quality from defect correction to defect prevention. This prevention focus is carried forward into the future with suggestions on what will cause changes and where some changes will occur by 2025. All of this is described within the context of projects, the environments that influence project work and organizational changes that meet the quality challenges of 2025.

In chapter 11, Edmund M. Ricci and Beth A. D. Nolan describes scientific program evaluation in a comprehensive framework of concepts and methods. This is used to assess the resources, activities, outputs, and outcomes used in the design and implementation of a time-limited project. Initially the chapter describes current concepts and methods used in scientific program evaluation. While certain aspects of scientific program evolution share similarities with project management, in reality their scope and methods are significantly different. The chapter concludes with suggestions describing how these two intellectual systems should be merged in the future to create a robust framework for monitoring an assessment of all aspects of time-limited projects.

James S. Pennypacker, in chapter 12, presents three vivid scenarios, each an equally plausible, yet very different story, about what might happen to project portfolio management (PPM) in the future. Facts about the future demographics, geographic, and industrial information, along with plausible social, technical, economic, environmental, educational, and political trends are key driving forces in creating these three possible futures. The result will be a surprising look into the future, offering insight into what the general shape of the future of PPM might be, and a framework for dealing with it.

Part 3: Project Management Organizational Applications

In chapter 13, Kam Jugdev, Ralf Müller, and Maureen Hutchinson examine the likely interdependence of strategic and project management circa 2025. The chapter authors view strategy as matching an organization's capabilities to changing market environments to achieve better competitive positions. They note that increasingly, companies are turning to project management to help them be more effective and efficient. The question is posed for the year 2025: What are the likely interdependences between strategic management and project management? To help answer this question, the authors refer to some key concepts in strategy followed by a discussion of trends today as they relate to strategy. The chapter reviews macro environmental factors, and then discusses these factors for the year 2025 to develop perspectives on the links between strategy and project management.

In chapter 14, Howard Bruck, PMP, examines the likely future of financial services circa 2025. He predicts that fierce competition exists on a global scale. The traditional barriers to entry and competition are no longer in play, so he posits that the project management practice for financial services in 2025 will be much more demanding and specialized. The success of projects will be judged for several years after initial completion as the results are not a static solution, but one which will evolve over time. The degree to which the project manager can advise the firm along the way will separate the profitable projects from those that quickly lose their value.

Writing in chapter 15, Belle Collins Brown believes the research and development (R&D) project manager will continue to evolve away from his or her process roots. Future R&D managers must be prepared to face the reality that most of today's work—planning, status tracking, reporting—will be automated into large development systems designed to provide portfolio-level views for an organization's R&D activities. Project managers of the future must develop leadership competencies rather than managerial capabilities alone. Such project managers will no longer be involved in discrete functional entities in "silos" crying out for coordination. Instead they will be part of project-based organizations that require real leadership.

In chapter 16, Hugh Woodward reviews the role of project management professional societies in connecting and networking, circa 2025. Project management professional associations, especially the Project Management Institute, have been growing exponentially since the early 1990s and one is tempted to predict that continued double-digit growth will occur through 2025. He then asks the question of whether the professional association of 2025 will just be bigger versions of what we see today. Demographic trends and technological advancements will continue to affect the way we work, and even the nature of work itself. These trends are likely to impact the project manager's relationship to his or her professional associations. The professional associations will have to adapt, and the resulting organizations will look different than what we have today.

In chapter 17, Richard E. Boyatzis, Mary Fambrough, David Leonard, and Kenneth Rhee look at the emotional and social intelligence competencies of effective project managers. They note that emotional and social intelligence competencies have been shown to distinguish effective from ineffective managers and leaders at many levels in organizations around the world. Using original data from a study of effective versus less effective project managers at the R&D facility of a major government based research organization, they present a model of the competencies distinguishing outstanding project managers is presented. Implications will be discussed for the selection, retention, and development of effective project managers.

In chapter 18, Stephen R. Thomas, Ph.D., P.E., Edward J. Jaselskis, Ph.D., P.E., and Cory McDermott examine the trends likely to affect the future of construction project management. They note that the construction industry is fortunate to have an industry-driven process in place with the specific purpose of identifying trends likely to affect the construction industry. This process is a function of the Construction Industry Institute (CII) Strategic Planning Committee. CII is recognized as the principal construction industry forum for addressing current and future issues because CII members represent the leading owners, contractors, suppliers, and academics that are actively funding, directing, and performing research to improve competitiveness and prepare the engineering and construction industry for the future.

Part 4: Project Management in Government

In chapter 19 Michelle R. Brunswick describes how project management and defense acquisition in 2025 will likely look. The purpose of her chapter is to focus the reader on U.S. Department of Defense acquisition and how it will meet future threats. The chapter has three areas of assessment: Office of Secretary of Defense (OSD) including political atmosphere, the armed forces, and industry perspective. The first section of the chapter is a top-level vision and will address the OSD viewpoint of 2025 considering the political and economic global environment. The second section will narrow in on how the military services perceive the threat. The third section will cover how industry is prepared to meet the future vision of 2025.

In chapter 20, Dorothy J. Tiffany, CPA, PMP, will examine what new frontiers will exist in space exploration. The chapter author asks the obvious question: What does the future hold for space exploration? She believes that some of the most revolutionary changes in project management occurred during the years between 1983 and 2008, and equally important changes will take place over the next few decades. Just as the space hardware and software systems become more complicated, project management techniques matured and grew as well with the building of the International Space Station, Hubble Space Telescope, Phoenix Mars Lander and other trail-blazing missions. That maturation and growth will continue.

In chapter 21, Jonathan Weinstein, PMP, and Timothy Jaques, PMP describe how U.S. state governments are currently using project management. Such governments will face tremendous upheaval in the next 18 years in the scale and scope of the services they deliver to their citizens and the methods by which those services are delivered. The chapter focuses on the key drivers of project management, specifically addressing the types of likely projects, the organizational design utilized, maturity levels, tools, processes, and skills and capabilities required of project teams. The chapter includes the results of interview and focus-groups session with state government project management personnel.

Part 5: Likely Growth of Project Management

In chapter 22, Dr. Hans J. Thamhain looks at the future of team leadership in complex project environments. The author believes that team leadership has become critically important to project performance. The twenty-first century is bringing new technologies, social innovations, and a closely-linked world but also brings constant change, uncertainty, and disruption. This has provided great business opportunities, but also enormous managerial challenge. Team leaders of the future must understand the dynamics of people and organization at all levels, including the cognitive structures that create change and influence decision-making, in order to build and sustain high-performance project teams. This chapter provides an insight into the changing social processes and organizational environments that drive team performance.

Chapter 23 by Storm Cunningham provides insight into important global trends in project management. Four major trends are opening a vast gap between today's project management disciplines/tools and those that will be increasingly needed as this century progresses. These trends are restorative development, integration, engagement, and partnering. The strategic need to plug this gap is already urgent, and presents possibly the best career path for project managers just entering the field. The author argues that by 2025, these four trends will be well-established as the norm. Project managers who aren't intimately familiar with the technical, legal, and managerial challenges of all four will likely find they are obsolete. One of the many outcomes of this confluence of trends will be the ascendancy of program management over project management.

In chapters 24 and 25, David L. Pells provides an examination of new frontiers for project management. An examination is provided of seven new industries where projects and project management will play a significant role, with tremendous potential impact on economies and society. These new frontiers will be nanotechnology (applied across various industries and scientific fields); new energy supplies; humans in space (colonization of the moon, flights to Mars, space tourism, commercialization of space, etc.); climate change and sciences (near space research, development and technologies); economic development, especially in Africa, Asia and Latin America; health and medicines; and global security. Most of this area will require global cooperation, global programs and projects, and application of portfolio, program, and project management models.

The title of chapter 26 by Rebecca Ann Winston, "Why are We Still Conducting Risky Business?" prepares the reader for the challenges coming forth in the next two decades. The author explores the business drivers that will still be operable in the year 2025 that will drive risk management in projects. The exploration begins from the first strategic decisions to initiate the project to how risk will be disseminated in lessons learned. The focus will be on medium to large corporations and government corporations. The author believes that the connection between the business drivers and how risk management should be conducted has been and will continue to be ignored in many areas of project management. The chapter will highlight those areas and the impact on the whole (the net bottom line) when one does not holistically view the impact of the connection between business drivers and risk management within project management.

In chapter 27, Guiping Hu, Lizhi Wang, and Bopaya Bidanda review the likely connection between sustainable manufacturing and project management, circa 2025. Sustainability/sustainable manufacturing has gained popularity in a broad spectrum of societal sectors. Sustainable manufacturing can be viewed as the implementation of a group of projects the product's life cycle evolution process. Therefore, it is important to incorporate the concept of sustainability into the project management process. In this chapter, the authors discuss how to implement and manage projects within the sustainability concept. A case study is utilized for demonstration purposes. In addition, quantitative models are also be discussed to assist decision making problems for stakeholders.

"Project management in a flat world" is the subject of chapter 28. Ozlem Arisoy, Murat Azim, David Cleland, and Bopaya Bidanda note the growing offshoring trend forces companies to transfer their high-cost activities to low-labor rate countries. A systematic project management approach during the process of global sourcing decisions is usually the key driver to success and will likely grow in importance over the next few decades. Offshoring decision-making processes can be considered as large-size projects that impact a company's strategies and future operations. Although these projects can be managed based on the classical project management principles, modifications and extensions are inevitable to support the wide scope of growing globalization.

In chapter 29, Jang Ra focuses on predicting the roles of project managers circa 2025 and using that knowledge to provide better education and training by reshaping the project management curriculum, teaching methods, delivery means, faculty and students. This approach is taken on the premise that future organizations will survive mainly through innovative and successful projects, within a globally competitive environment representing many different cultures and time-zones, and by completing transformation cycles faster than their competitors.

PART 1

Examples of Projects from Geographic and Industry Applications

CHAPTER 1

The Deployment of Project Management: A Prospective View of G8, European G6 & Outreach 5 Countries in 2025

Christophe N. Bredillet

Background

The world is moving fast and turbulently. The Gross Domestic Product (GDP), one of the measures of a country's economy defined as the total market value of all final goods and services produced within a country in a given period of time (Wikipedia, 2008), is used as a development indicator for countries, regions and for global levels. For example, the Economist Intelligence Unit expects for China a real GDP growth in 2008 of 9.8%, less than the 11.9% expansion recorded in 2007, with an expected further slowing to 9% in 2009 (Economist Intelligence Unit, 2008a). The slowdown in India, according to EIU (Economist Intelligence Unit, 2008b), will be relatively shallow, with real GDP growth slowing to 7.7% in 2008-09 and 7.1% in 2009-10. For the U.S., real GDP is forecast to grow by just 0.8% in 2008 and recover modestly to 1.4% in 2009 (Economist Intelligence Unit, 2008c).

The major organizations and governments need more and more to know about the past performances, but also to better predict the future in order to quickly define or re-define their strategies and policies in various domains. This need has been created in the past few decades because of an environment in which international organizations such as the United Nations (UN), International Monetary Funds (IMF), World Bank, or governmental organizations such Energy Information Administration (EIA), Eurostat, Organization for Economic Co-operation and Development (OECD), are developing important standards and frameworks to collect and process the information related mainly to social, financial, economical, environmental, demographic, and technologi-cal domains at the country, regional, and worldwide levels. A look at the publications and databases of these organizations shows the huge amount of information collected, processed. and made available through public means such as the Internet. While there is a great deal of historical data at the major databases, the forecast data is rarely available. Some short-term two-to-three-year projections may be accessible for some domains, but mid- and long-term forecasts are absent or not available to the public.

The project management discipline is a part of this moving world. The United Nations and OECD[1] reported in 2005 that about 22% of the GDP of the economies in transition and developing economies is gross fixed capital formation (United Nations, 2007), which is almost entirely project-based[2]. The professional associations aiming at developing and supporting project management continue to grow globally and regionally. The Project Management Institute (PMI) announced more than 275,000 members by July 2008 (Project Management Institute, 2008) and the International Project Management Association (International Project Management Association, 2007) announces more than 73,000 members by end of 2007. The actions initiated by the educational systems in many countries, and the worldwide certifications programs supported by standards development continue to progress and to contribute to project management deployment (Bredillet, Ruiz, & Yatim, 2008a).

The major trends that characterize the 21st century such as global competition, rapid technological change, short product life cycle, process improvement, the complexity of undertakings, and the focus on quality all require extensive and professional use of the project management discipline (Lientz & Rea, 2002).

As part of this moving world, project management deployment needs not only to be observed, but also to be predicted like any other important social or economical indicator. Business organizations as well as project management professional bodies should have the possibility to predict the project management deployment status in the future. Can we perform a projection of the project management deployment in the future? What will be the project management deployment situation in a given country at a given year, for example? How the countries can be compared in terms of project management deployment in the future?

The purpose of this paper is to suggest a framework that allows the construction of a prospective view of project management deployment in the future. This framework

---

[1] http://www.swivel.com/data_sets/spreadsheet/1004863 - access 6 October 2008
[2] Definition

Gross fixed capital formation (GFCF) is the acquisition, less disposal, of fixed assets, i.e. products which are expected to be used in production for several years:

– Acquisitions include both purchases of assets (new or second-hand) and the construction of assets by producers for their own use.
– Disposals include sales of assets for scrap as well as sales of used assets in a working condition to other producers: New Zealand, Mexico and some Central European countries import substantial quantities of used assets. Fixed assets consist of machinery and equipment; dwellings and other buildings; roads, bridges, airfields and dams; orchards and tree plantations; improvements to land such as fencing, leveling and draining; draught animals and other animals that are kept for the milk and wool that they produce; computer software and databases; entertainment, literary or artistic originals; and expenditures on mineral exploration. What all these things have in common is that they contribute to future production. This may not be obvious in the case of dwellings but, in the national accounts, flats and houses are considered to produce housing services that are consumed by owners or tenants over the life of the building.

In calculating the shares, gross fixed capital formation and GDP are both valued at current market prices.

will then be used to present the prospective views up to 2025 for the G8, G6 and O5 countries presented in a former paper (Bredillet, et al., 2008a).

Project Management Deployment and Forecasting

To be able to build a forecast model that predicts project management deployment, we first need to adopt a tool that measures this project management deployment. This paper relies on the project management deployment definition and the project management deployment index (PMDI) indicator defined in Bredillet, et al. (2008a) and presented below.

Project Management Deployment Index (PMDI)

The measurement of project management deployment is defined as the level or the degree of deployment of project management within a country (or group) by dividing the total number of the project management-certified individuals within this country (or group) by the total population of that country (or group) during a given point in time (a year). The certification figures considered in this paper integrate those from PMI and the International Project Management Association (IPMA). For a given country, the sum of certified individuals from these both organizations is considered. This restriction to PMI and IPMA figures should have a negative impact on the PMDI by lowering its real value, and very serious impact in some countries like Japan and Australia, where other project management certification bodies are operating.

Forecasting

Second, we need to design a forecasting model that fits best to the project management deployment setup. The literature review reveals no studies addressing the project management deployment forecasting topic as per the date of this paper. In economics, for example, an econometric model is used to forecast future developments in the economy, and econometricians measure past relationships between variables and then try to forecast how changes in some variables will affect the future of others. Most forecasters believe that analysts judgment should be used not only to determine values for exogenous (outside of the model) variables, but also to reduce the likely size of model error (endogenous variables unpredicted variations) (Hymans, 2008). Based on historical time series data, the past relationships between the project management deployment and some influencing factors such as the gross domestic product per capita and the national culture dimensions have been studied in Bredillet, Ruiz, and Yatim (2008b) without proposing any forecasting model. The regression model generated with the above-mentioned cultural study could have been used to forecast the values of PMDI in the future, based on the values of GDP per capita and cultural dimensions scores. But we have excluded it because the national culture is generally stable and not changing significantly from one year or one decade to another (Hofstede, 1983). Thus, the variation in PMDI will be only linked to the GDP per capita growth, which is assumed not enough to explain the future predictions.

With the absence of a forecasting model or a theory of how various factors influencing project management deployment interact with each other, we focused in this paper on the trend model derived directly from the past recorded time series of PMDI values, bearing in mind that:

- Any forecast of the project management deployment for such a period of about 20 years is subject to uncertainty and error. This is due to unpredictable changes and events that may take place during this period of time. An example of such unpredictable events is the effect of the new certification exam PMI announced to take place by September 2005. At the end of 2005, the results show 86% growth in the U.S. (PMDI passed from 174 in 2004 to 323 in 2005), compared to 44% in 2004 (PMDI passed from 121 in 2003 to 174 in 2004), and 20% in 2006 (PMDI passed from 323 in 2005 to 388 in 2006).
- Basing our forecast only on the past experience (growth trends) of project management deployment is not enough to carefully predict the future. This past experience should be correctly analyzed with other possible influencing factors to elaborate better forecasting models (NOBE, 2002).

Methodology and Data Choices
Trend model

The proposed trend model is based on PMDI, argued to be a valid measurement tool for project management deployment measurement within a country or a region; and is based on the concept of project management certification process supported by the major project management professional bodies and adopted more and more by the business organizations (Bredillet et al., 2008a).

For this paper, we consider a forecast approach based only on historical past trend data. This presupposes that, in the future, project management deployment will behave the same way as it did during the past recorded years and that the impact of the influencing variables will continue to be exactly the same. This assumption introduces a non-measurable error that may appear in the final forecasting results.

The trend equations have been calculated for each country and the polynomial (degree 2), having goodness-of-fit ($R2$) greater than 96% for all of the considered countries, and have been selected as the trend equations that best represent the trends based on the past recorded data.

The absence of inflexion points in the analyzed data dismissed the possibility of an "S" curve in the near future. This confirmed the general increasing trends of PMI and IPMA members and certified individuals and of the GDP per capita for the considered countries.

Accordingly, we propose the following framework based on the application of the trend equations of the past values of PMDI:

- Select the country or the set of countries that will be the objects of the projection (forecast)
- Select the past period of time for which the PMDI values for the selected countries are known
- Elaborate the trend equation(s) based on the best-fit extrapolation of the past data
- Proceed with the application of the elaborated trend equation(s) to calculate the PMDI values for the projected period of time for each selected country.

Selected Countries

We have selected the following 15 countries to deal with for this study. Apart from their important roles as major economic and social actors on the international market, this selection is dictated by the fact that we have already presented and discussed project management deployment within these countries during the period 1998-2006 (Bredillet, et al., 2008a) and that we have at our disposal the related set of data. These 15 countries are grouped as follows:

- The G8 countries constituted Canada, France, Japan, Germany, Italy, Russia, United Kingdom, and the United States. The selection of these countries was based only on their economic size (about 65% of the world economy) and their presence at the international level as the most developed countries.
- The European G6 countries constituted France, Germany, Italy, Poland, Spain, and United Kingdom. They constitute the largest European countries in terms of population and economic sizes.
- The O5 countries constituted Brazil, China, India, Mexico and South Africa—also called the "emerging powers." The selection of these countries was based on their significant growth rates and economic readiness as the most important developing countries.

Selected Past Period

We have selected the period of 1998-2007 as the past period of time for which we have calculated and reproduced the PMDI data in Table 1. The year 1998 is considered to be the beginning of significant deployment of project management for each of the considered countries. In fact, the data collected from PMI shows a total of 2,537 certified individuals up to 1997, present mainly in the U.S. (2,062) and Canada (282). The data from IPMA (International Project Management Association, 2007) shows a total of 8,123 certified individuals up to 1999, present mainly in U.K. (4,194) and Germany (3,346).

Selected Projection Period

We have selected the period of 2008-2025 as the projection period of time for which we will be calculating the forecasted (projected) values of PMDI for the selected countries.

Data Results

The Trend Equations Model

Based on the past data presented in Table 1, we have elaborated the polynomial (degree 2) trend equation for each selected country. The resulting equations are summarized in Table 2 where x indicates the time (year) and $R2$ indicates the coefficient of determination that reflects the goodness of fit of the equation model.

Based on the polynomial trend equations, we have calculated the projected PMDI in the years 2008 to 2025. The results are shown in Table 3.

The following example illustrates the calculation of the projected PMDI for France in 2008 and 2009:

PMDI(France, 2008)=$0.4924*(2008-1997)^2 - 0.0758*(2008-1997) + 0.3265 = 59.07$

PMDI(France, 2009)= $0.4924*(2009-1997)^2 - 0.0758*(2009-1997) + 0.3265 = 70.32$

The same calculation has been performed to obtain the results of Table 3.

Based on the PMDI definition (PMDI = (the cumulative number of certified individuals) / (the population within a country)), Table 3 allows calculation of the fore-

Table 1.   Project Management Deployment Index (PMDI) – PMI and IPMA data - 1998/2007

Country	Group	1998 PMDI	1999 PMDI	2000 PMDI	2001 PMDI	2002 PMDI	2003 PMDI	2004 PMDI	2005 PMDI	2006 PMDI	2007 PMDI
Brazil	O5	0.14	0.35	0.71	1.37	2.35	4.30	6.87	20.72	24.98	29.45
China	O5	0.00	0.01	0.04	0.20	1.46	4.81	8.61	14.14	21.12	24.46
Spain	G6	0.18	0.35	1.45	3.32	4.76	6.37	8.14	12.69	14.95	20.09
France	G8, G6	1.44	2.37	4.46	6.44	10.60	18.18	25.17	32.77	39.90	47.34
Germany	G8, G6	21.09	41.84	45.19	52.48	63.95	82.94	108.35	143.13	173.81	200.44
India	O5	0.02	0.04	0.09	0.19	0.41	1.26	2.97	8.30	10.44	13.01
Italy	G8, G6	0.09	0.52	1.49	2.63	3.87	6.79	10.80	17.12	24.51	29.44
Japan	G8	0.50	2.32	3.97	6.87	9.63	26.29	53.66	116.01	144.40	165.39
Mexico	O5	0.11	0.47	0.84	1.25	1.61	2.22	3.37	6.38	8.52	9.78
South Africa	O5	1.08	1.46	1.97	2.44	2.99	5.37	8.37	16.76	20.66	26.47
Poland	G6	0.00	0.00	0.05	0.31	0.88	4.48	9.59	17.84	24.13	37.27
Russia	G8	0.00	0.07	0.23	0.65	0.80	1.60	3.22	5.17	7.01	9.24
United Kingdom	G8, G6	38.01	75.93	99.54	125.58	154.24	191.83	225.38	270.41	318.24	367.57
United States	G8	13.00	20.69	35.41	58.00	80.10	121.42	174.63	323.86	388.68	428.74
Canada	G8	17.08	27.91	47.38	75.75	108.17	167.23	227.91	383.26	455.39	514.97
GLOBAL PMDI / SC		2.42	4.39	6.40	9.38	12.97	20.29	29.53	51.41	63.47	71.96

Note: GLOBAL PMDI SC = PMDI for the Selected Countries (SC) = PMDI for the Selected Countries (SC) = Total number of certified for the selected countries / total population of the selected countries

Table 2. Polynomial (2) Trend Equations For The Selected Countries – Based on PMI and IPMA data – PMDI 1998-2007

Country	Linear Trend Equation	
Brazil	$y = 0.5888x^2 - 3.1149x + 3.5853$	$R2 = 0.9601$
China	$y = 0.4671x^2 - 2.3084x + 2.1951$	$R2 = 0.9906$
Spain	$y = 0.2241x^2 - 0.3218x + 0.3695$	$R2 = 0.9936$
France	$y = 0.4924x^2 - 0.0758x + 0.3265$	$R2 = 0.9952$
Germany	$y = 1.902x^2 - 1.4419x + 28.025$	$R2 = 0.9921$
India	$y = 0.2824x^2 - 1.6516x + 1.8863$	$R2 = 0.9719$
Italy	$y = 0.4762x^2 - 1.9788x + 2.2769$	$R2 = 0.994$
Japan	$y = 3.1951x^2 - 15.777x + 16.667$	$R2 = 0.9715$
Mexico	$y = 0.1549x^2 - 0.6253x + 0.9298$	$R2 = 0.9802$
South Africa	$y = 0.4734x^2 - 2.4377x + 3.9409$	$R2 = 0.9852$
Poland	$y = 0.7683x^2 - 4.6654x + 5.5343$	$R2 = 0.9907$
Russia	$y = 0.163x^2 - 0.7932x + 0.8876$	$R2 = 0.9948$
United Kingdom	$y = 1.5709x^2 + 18.197x + 26.114$	$R2 = 0.9983$
United States	$y = 6.0831x^2 - 17.514x + 26.583$	$R2 = 0.9765$
Canada	$y = 6.4986x^2 - 12.888x + 23.195$	$R2 = 0.9855$
GLOBAL PMDI / SC	$y = 1.0329x^2 - 3.8026x + 6.8898$	$R2 = 0.9973$

casted number of certified individuals for each country during the period 2008-2025 considering the population forecasts during this period given by the U.S. Census Bureau – International Data Base. The results are presented here after in Table 4.

The Certified Individuals per country per year = PMDI (Country, Year) * Population (Country, Year).

The Populations of the Selected Countries during 2008-2025 are based on the forecast data from US Census Bureau – International Data Bases.

Results Discussion
Note on S-Time Distance

The conventional statistical measurement and comparisons tools are used for data analysis. We mean that the growth variations are recorded mainly on a time-period basis (generally one year), and comparisons are made among these percentages to evaluate differences between measured units (countries, regions, or socio-economic groups). The current state-of-the-art of comparative analysis is based mainly on some conventional statistical measures which are recalled here after the definitions of the most-used of them. In the following formulation the subscripts (i) and (j) indicate respectively two time-series or units (i) and (j). X indicates the level of the indicator (variable) at time t (Sicherl, 2004c).

Table 3. Projected PMDI 2008-2025 –Polynomial (2) Trend Equation Model

Country	2008	2009	2010	2011	2012	2013	2014	2015	2016	2017	2018	2019	2020	2021	2022	2023	2024	2025
Brazil	40.566	50.994	62.599	75.382	89.342	104.480	120.795	138.288	156.959	176.807	197.833	220.037	243.418	267.977	293.713	320.627	348.718	377.987
China	33.322	41.757	51.126	61.429	72.667	84.838	97.944	111.984	126.959	142.867	159.710	177.487	196.198	215.843	236.423	257.936	280.384	303.766
Spain	23.946	28.778	34.059	39.788	45.965	52.590	59.664	67.186	75.155	83.574	92.440	101.754	111.517	121.728	132.387	143.494	155.050	167.054
France	59.073	70.323	82.557	95.776	109.980	125.168	141.342	158.500	176.643	195.771	215.883	236.981	259.063	282.130	306.182	331.218	357.240	384.246
Germany	242.306	284.610	330.718	380.630	434.347	491.867	553.191	618.319	687.251	759.987	836.527	916.871	1001.019	1088.971	1180.728	1276.288	1375.652	1478.820
India	17.889	22.733	28.141	34.114	40.652	47.755	55.423	63.655	72.452	81.814	91.741	102.233	113.289	124.910	137.096	149.847	163.163	177.043
Italy	38.130	47.104	57.030	67.909	79.740	92.523	106.259	120.947	136.588	153.181	170.726	189.224	208.674	229.077	250.432	272.739	295.999	320.211
Japan	229.727	287.437	351.538	422.029	498.910	582.181	671.842	767.893	870.335	979.167	1094.389	1216.001	1344.004	1478.397	1619.180	1766.353	1919.916	2079.869
Mexico	12.794	15.732	18.979	22.536	26.403	30.579	35.066	39.862	44.968	50.384	56.109	62.145	68.490	75.145	82.110	89.384	96.969	104.863
South Africa	34.411	42.861	52.258	62.603	73.893	86.131	99.316	113.447	128.525	144.550	161.522	179.440	198.305	218.118	238.876	260.582	283.235	306.834
Poland	47.179	60.185	74.727	90.806	108.421	127.573	148.261	170.486	194.248	219.546	246.381	274.753	304.661	336.106	369.087	403.605	439.659	477.250
Russia	11.885	14.841	18.123	21.731	25.665	29.924	34.510	39.422	44.660	50.224	56.113	62.329	68.871	75.739	82.933	90.452	98.298	106.470
United Kingdom	416.360	470.688	528.157	588.768	652.522	719.416	789.453	862.632	938.952	1018.414	1101.018	1186.764	1275.651	1367.680	1462.852	1561.164	1662.619	1767.216
United States	569.972	692.367	826.928	973.655	1132.548	1303.607	1486.832	1682.223	1889.780	2109.503	2341.392	2585.447	2841.668	3110.055	3390.608	3683.327	3988.212	4305.263
Canada	667.758	804.337	953.914	1116.489	1292.060	1480.629	1682.194	1896.757	2124.318	2364.875	2618.430	2884.981	3164.530	3457.077	3762.620	4081.161	4412.698	4757.233
GLOBAL PMDI/SC	90.042	109.996	132.016	156.102	182.253	210.471	240.754	273.103	307.517	343.998	382.544	423.156	465.834	510.578	557.387	606.263	657.204	710.211

Table 4.   Projected Certified Individuals 2008-2025 –Based on Table 3 and Populations Forecasts

Country	2008	2009	2010	2011	2012	2013	2014	2015	2016
Brazil	7,785	9,881	12,243	14,876	17,786	20,977	24,454	28,219	32,276
China	44,319	55,896	68,895	83,348	99,277	116,698	135,618	156,041	177,967
Spain	970	1,166	1,381	1,614	1,864	2,132	2,418	2,720	3,039
France	3,784	4,530	5,347	6,235	7,195	8,227	9,332	10,509	11,759
Germany	19,959	23,432	27,212	31,299	35,690	40,383	45,376	50,669	56,257
India	20,537	26,508	33,322	41,007	49,596	59,117	69,600	81,073	93,566
Italy	2,217	2,738	3,313	3,941	4,623	5,356	6,141	6,977	7,864
Japan	29,242	36,527	44,577	53,376	62,914	73,171	84,130	95,771	108,073
Mexico	1,407	1,750	2,135	2,563	3,036	3,554	4,119	4,731	5,392
South Africa	1,507	1,867	2,264	2,699	3,169	3,676	4,218	4,794	5,405
Poland	1,816	2,316	2,874	3,491	4,165	4,897	5,685	6,530	7,430
Russia	1,672	2,078	2,526	3,015	3,544	4,112	4,718	5,362	6,042
United Kingdom	25,375	28,765	32,368	36,185	40,218	44,469	48,941	53,634	58,551
United States	173,172	212,210	255,655	303,613	356,196	413,502	475,630	542,673	614,726
Canada	22,178	26,935	32,204	37,995	44,318	51,183	58,599	66,576	75,122
GLOBAL	355,939	436,600	526,317	625,257	733,590	851,454	978,977	1,116,278	1,263,468

2017	2018	2019	2020	2021	2022	2023	2024	2025
36,628	41,279	46,230	51,485	57,045	62,910	69,081	75,555	82,335
201,398	226,331	252,759	280,667	310,029	340,813	372,988	406,528	441,410
3,374	3,725	4,092	4,474	4,872	5,285	5,712	6,155	6,612
13,082	14,478	15,948	17,491	19,108	20,799	22,563	24,402	26,314
62,138	68,309	74,766	81,505	88,522	95,809	103,363	111,177	119,248
107,110	121,730	137,453	154,306	172,318	191,520	211,937	233,590	256,504
8,800	9,785	10,819	11,900	13,029	14,205	15,427	16,694	18,007
121,017	134,580	148,740	163,476	178,766	194,589	210,923	227,748	245,042
6,102	6,863	7,674	8,538	9,453	10,422	11,445	12,522	13,653
6,049	6,725	7,432	8,168	8,932	9,723	10,540	11,381	12,244
8,384	9,392	10,451	11,562	12,721	13,929	15,183	16,482	17,825
6,757	7,508	8,291	9,108	9,956	10,834	11,743	12,681	13,647
63,691	69,055	74,642	80,453	86,484	92,735	99,204	105,887	112,781
691,880	774,230	861,869	954,890	1,053,427	1,157,628	1,267,611	1,383,495	1,505,405
84,246	93,954	104,253	115,149	126,645	138,744	151,448	164,758	178,676
1,420,656	1,587,943	1,765,420	1,953,171	2,151,308	2,359,946	2,579,166	2,809,055	3,049,704

Absolute difference between units i and j at time t:

$$Aij(t) = Xi(t) - Xj(t) \tag{1}$$

Ratio between units i and j at time t:

$$Rij(t) = Xi(t)/Xj(t) \tag{2}$$

Percentage difference between units i and j at time t:

$$Pij(t) = [Xi(t)/Xj(t) - 1]*100 \tag{3}$$

According to Sicherl (1998a), existing methods in economics and statistics fail to extract the notion of time embodied in the existing data and to fully use the information content with regard to time.

Comparative analysis based on time-series data does use time as an identifier only to mark the occurrence of events at a given time. It does not incorporate time as an indicator that can be measured and compared. The analysis of disparities among different units (for instance, among different countries) results in a one-dimensional view of the analyzed variable(s) (for instance, per-capita income) that only relies on static measurements losing the dynamic perception of time. The degree of disparities of the studied situation may be very different when incorporating the time measurement to complement the conventional static measurements (Sicherl, 1998a).

Sicherl (2006) derived from the time-matrix presentation of the time series the novel statistical measure, the S-time-distance measure, as the horizontal time difference for a given level L of the variable XL:

$$Sij(XL) = ti(XL) - tj(XL) \tag{4}$$

This statistical S-time-distance (S stands for Sicherl) measure is intended to enhance the analytical framework of the time-series comparisons process by adding a new dimension of analysis: the time dimension (Sicherl, 1998b). Based on existing time-series data, the S-time-distance offers a new perception (time distance) of the data, offering to the comparative dynamic analysis a new and complementary instrument that brings new insights, in addition to static measures and a general presentation tool (Sicherl, 2004g).

This generic concept of time-distance analysis is applied in a variety of domains: economic and social development (Sicherl, 2000, 2001, 2004a, 2004b, 2004e, 2004f), social indicators (Sicherl & Vahcic, 1999), information society (Sicherl, 2005), monitoring implementation of development goals (Sicherl, 2007), and other socio-economic domains (Sicherl, 2004c, 2004d, 2004g). Granger and Jeon (2003) used the concept of time-distance as a criterion for evaluating forecasting models. It is used to analyze a variety of problems "in time series comparisons, regressions, models, forecasting and monitoring, the notion of time distance was always there as a hidden dimension" (Sicherl, 2004g).

Time-distance analysis is a supplementary statistical tool that complements the existing conventional statistical tools.

Current Situation of project management deployment – S-Time Distance 2007

Before proceeding with the presentation of our prospective results, it is important to show the current status of the project management deployment for reference and comparison purposes when exploring the prospective results later on. The current status of project management deployment within the selected countries (SC) is shown in Figure 1 with the S-Time distances recorded in 2007.

More than 14 years mark the gap between the leading and lagging countries (i.e., United Kingdom and Russia). The leading group of countries is United Kingdom and Canada, followed by the U.S., Germany, and Japan, which altogether constitute the five countries recording a lead time versus the average PMDI of the selected countries. All the other 10 countries are recording lag time versus the average, led by France and Poland for the European countries, and by Brazil and South Africa for the other countries. Russia is lagging well behind the average with about six years delay.

Prospective Situation Based on Trend Equations – S-Time Distance 2025

Based on the data elaborated in Table 3, we have calculated and presented in Figure 2 the PMDI S-Time distances in 2025 for all the selected countries.

The project management deployment S-Time distances shown in Figure 2 clearly indicate the very important gap expected to take place in 2025. This gap amounts more than 32 years between the leading and lagging countries (Canada and Mexico). The expected leading countries are Canada and the U.S., recording more than 15 years lead time, versus selected countries' PMDI average—United Kingdom with 12.14 years, Japan with 10.6 years, and Germany with 8.68 years ahead of the selected countries' average. Poland will be recording a lag time of 4.47 years behind the average. France, Brazil, Italy, South Africa, and China are expected to record between 6.96 and 9.11 years lag times behind the average in 2025. India and Spain will be recoding around 13 years, and Russia and Mexico more than 15 years of lag time behind that average.

We should notice also in Figure 2 that the leading countries (Canada, the U.S., U.K., Japan, and Germany) are expected to be the same in 2025 as in 2007, but the ordering will be change significantly. In fact, Canada and the U.S. will overtake United Kingdom, and Japan will overtake Germany. For the lagging countries, Poland is expected to record high performance, passing far before France, and India before Spain. Brazil is expected to enhance its position against Italy, South Africa, and China, while Russia and Mexico will maintain approximately their relative positions.

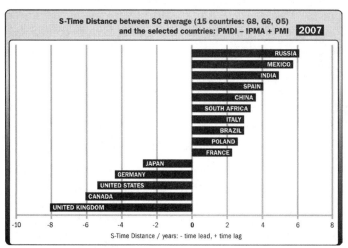

Figure 1.   S-Time Distances Between SC Average & the Selected Countries – PMDI, 2007

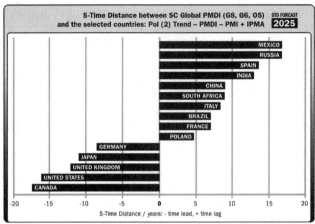

Figure 2.   S-Time Distances Projection Between SC Average & the Selected Countries – Trend Equations - PMDI, 2025

Forecasting, GDP, and cultural factors

We mentioned above – in the "forecasting" paragraph – that based on historical time series data, the relationships between project management deployment and some influencing factors such as gross domestic product per capita and national culture dimensions have been studied in Bredillet, Ruiz, and Yatim (2008b). This led us to develop in this study through stepwise linear regression the following equation:

$PMDI(country, year) =$

$284.46 + 0.004*GDP/Capita(country, year) - 2.156*UAI(country, year) - 1.931*PDI(country, year)$

Where:
- *GDP/Capita(country, year)* is the GDP based on purchasing-power-parity (PPP) per capita in U.S. dollars for the considered *country* at the time *year*
- *UAI* is the uncertainty avoidance index score for the considered *country* at the time *year*
- *PDI* is the power distance index score for the considered *country* at the time *year*

And we noticed above that the national culture is generally stable and not changing significantly from one year or one decade to another (Hofstede, 1983), and thus, the variation in PMDI would be only linked to the GDP per capita growth, which is assumed not enough to explain the future predictions.

If we apply this equation to forecasted GDP per country (NOBE, 2002), we obtain these results in 2025, as shown in Figure 3.

Although probably a bit simple, this approach provides another view of the end result in 2025, with some significant differences compared to the approach used in this paper. As usual in forecasting studies, it is always worthwhile to use different approaches to get a picture of the future and then discuss them with a group of experts. This would lead us beyond the scope of this paper, but the reader has thus the opportunity to think about these results and get an idea of what the most probable future could be.

Prospective Situation Based on Trend Equation – Evolution 2008-2025

After the above global view presentation of the S-Time distances in 2025 for all the countries, we present in this section the dynamic prospective view of the PMDI between 2008 and 2025 for the three groups of countries G8, G6 and G5.

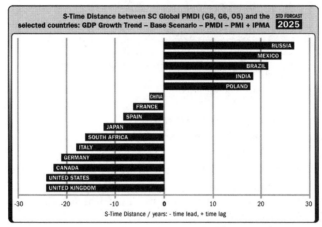

Figure 3.   S-Time Distance between SC Global PMDI (G8,G6, O5) and the selected countries: GDP Growth Trend - BASE Scenario - PMDI-PMI+IPMA, 2025

Prospective Evolution - G8 Countries

Figure 4 shows the dynamic evolution of the forecasted PMDI values of the G8 countries during the period 2008-2025.

Canada and the U.S. constitutes the leading sub-group, reaching a PMDI score of 4,757 and 4,305 respectively. Japan, United Kingdom, and Germany constitute the medium sub-group, having PMDIs between 1,478 for Germany and 2,080 for Japan. The lagging sub-group constitutes France, Italy, and Russia with 384, 320, and 106 respectively.

We can notice the relative low performance of the United Kingdom and Germany compared to Japan within the medium sub-group. In fact, Japan will overcome U.K. in 2019 and continues increasing the gap until 2025. During the period 2008-2025, the gap among the countries of each sub-group is relatively small, but the gap among the sub-groups is important and significantly increases between the beginning and the end of the considered period.

Looking at the performance of the various G8 countries from the perspective of the Period Increasing Ratio (*PIR*), representing the quotient *PMDI* at 2025 divided by *PMDI* at 2008, we can see that Canada for example having a PIR of 7.12 is performing less well than Russia, which will have a PIR of 8.96. Japan will be recording the best performance in term of PIR with a score of 9.05. Table 5 represents the PIR for the G8 countries.

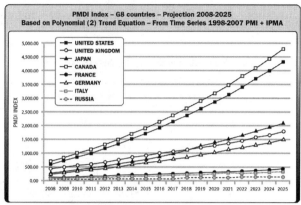

Figure 4.   PMDI Projection of G8 countries – PMI and IPMA - PMDI, 2008-2025

Prospective Evolution – G6 Countries

Figure 5 shows the dynamic evolution of the forecasted PMDI values of the G6 countries during the period 2008-2025.

United Kingdom and Germany will be leading within this G6 group of countries. They constitute the leading sub-group, reaching a PMDI score of 1,767 and 1,478 respectively. Poland, France, and Italy constitute a medium sub-group, reaching a PMDI of 477 for Poland, 384 for France, and 320 for Italy in 2025. The lagging sub-group constitutes Spain, alone recording a PMDI of 167 in 2025.

Poland reaches France in 2103 and continues its progress until 2025 with a difference of 93 points ahead of France. During the period 2008-2025, the gap among the countries of each sub-group is relatively small, but the gap between the leading sub-group and the other two sub-groups is important and significantly increases between the beginning and the end of the considered period.

Table 5.   Period Increasing Ratio (PIR) of the G8
                 countries - PMDI, 2025/2008

Country	Period Increasing Ratio 2025/2008
France	6.50
Germany	6.10
Italy	8.40
Japan	9.05
Russia	8.96
United Kingdom	4.24
United states	7.55
Canada	7.12
GLOBAL PMDI / SC	7.12

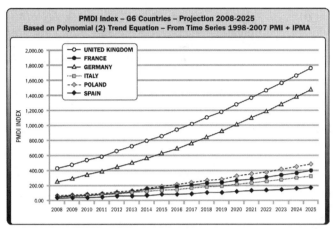

Figure 5.   PMDI Projection of G6 countries – PMI and IPMA - PMDI, 2008–2025

Looking at the performance of the various G6 countries from the perspective of the PIR, we can see the high performance of Poland with a PIR of 10.12, followed by Italy with a PIR of 8.4. France, Germany and Spain have almost the same PIR scores of around 6.5. United Kingdom records a very low performance, with a PIR of 4.24. Table 6 represents the PIR for the G6 countries.

Prospective Evolution – O5 Countries

Figure 6 shows the dynamic evolution of the forecasted PMDI values of the O5 countries during the period 2008-2025.

Brazil, South Africa, and China are leading within this O5 group of countries. They constitute the leading sub-group, reaching a PMDI score of 378, 306 and 303 respectively. While China and South Africa are progressing similarly, Brazil is showing more aggressive performance during the period 2008-2025. India and Mexico constitute the lagging sub-group reaching a PMDI of 177 for India and 105 for Mexico in 2025.

During the period 2008-2025, the gap between the countries is relatively important, except for China and South Africa.

Looking at the performance from the perspective of the PIR we can notice a general high performance of the O5 countries with PIR around 9. Table 7 represents the PIR for the O5 countries.

Limitations

The main indicator used in the present study is the PMDI, which should be carefully interpreted with its limitations of not being fully representative of the full picture of project management deployment and its restriction to the PMI® and IPMA certification program (Bredillet, et al., 2008a).

The time-distance analysis applied within the scope of this paper considers the average of the selected 15 countries and, accordingly, the results obtained are closely linked to this average. Any modification in the list of the studied countries could have implied a modification of the referenced average and consequently could have changed the results, but not the global picture: the order among countries would be the same.

Table 6.   Period Increasing Ratio (PIR) of the G6
            countries - PMDI, 2025/2008

Country	Period Increasing Ratio 2025/2008
France	6.50
Germany	6.10
Italy	8.40
United Kingdom	4.24
Spain	6.98
Poland	10.12
GLOBAL PMDI / SC	7.12

The prospective view presented in this paper should be considered carefully with the following two main reasons:

- The basic values of PMDI used for 2007 have their limitations as not fully representative of the global project management population as mentioned here above. The fact that PMDI values for 2007 are underestimated (we have for instance not considered PRINCE2™ or MSP™ certifications) impacts certainly the prospective values for 2008-2025.
- The trend equation model used in the calculation of the forecasted values should be considered with its limitation of being representative of the historical behavior of the PMDI only. It is assumed that project management deployment will continue behaving the same way as during the past recorded period with no variation in the impact of other influencing factors.

Accordingly, it is important to focus the interpretation of the analysis on the benchmarking and comparison between the countries more than on the absolute values of PMDI for the studied countries. The accuracy of the forecasted PMDI values is limited by the above-mentioned limitations. Furthermore, when some PMDI boundaries or limits are set up and discussed within this paper, they should be seen as comparative tools that help in the cross-countries assessment.

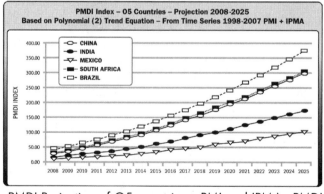

Figure 6.   PMDI Projection of O5 countries – PMI and IPMA - PMDI, 2008-2025

Table 7.   Period Increasing Ratio (PIR) of the O5 countries - PMDI, 2025/2008

Country	Period Increasing Ratio 2025/2008
Brazil	9.32
China	9.12
India	9.90
Mexico	8.20
South Africa	8.92
GLOBAL PMDI / SC	7.12

Conclusions

The paper introduces a framework to forecast project management deployment empirically based on PMDI as a project management measurement indicator (Bredillet et al., 2008a) and the trend equations (see Table 2) estimating the PMDI based on the historical data recorded between 1998 and 2007.

The major 15 economies (i.e., G8, G6, and O5) were used as the experimental setup to apply the proposed framework. The results show important increase of the S-Time distance between the extreme countries (Canada and Mexico) reaching 32 years difference in 2025. The leading countries—Canada, the U.S., U.K., Japan, and Germany—are enhancing their positions from 2007 to 2025, and the lagging countries—Poland, France, Brazil, Italy, South Africa, China, India, Spain, Russia, and Mexico—are deteriorating their positions against the selected countries' average.

The G8 countries will continue to lead the selected 15 countries, with large scores for Canada and the U.S., reaching PMDIs more than 4,300, compared to Japan, U.K., and Germany reaching respectively around 2,000, 1,700 and 1,400. They will be followed by France, Ital,y and Russia reaching scores of 384, 320, and 106 respectively.

The G6 countries will continue to be at the middle of the selected countries. Behind U.K. and Germany, Poland scores 477 before France and Italy. Spain will reach 167 in 2025.

The O5 countries are expected to record significant results, with Brazil at 378, South Africa at 306 and China at 303. India with a score of 177 will overcome Spain in 2025, and Mexico with 104 will have some difficulties in joining the general trend.

Two prospective views based on the time distances and the dynamic evolution of the project management deployment in the considered 15 countries are presented in this paper. These views could be of great interest for the project management professional bodies, researchers, and business and educational organizations aiming to enhance the project management profession academically and practically, and thus potentially impact and answer the economic and social development.

Further studies can follow focusing on the design of a PMDI forecasting model that integrates the impact of possible influencing factors–for instance, among the factors impacting GDP forecasts, which ones have a key impact on PMDI, or is it PMDI which impacts GDP, and if so, which factors? A kind of eggs and chicken problem! Another approach would be to validate the proposed framework and extending its application to other countries or industries. By the way, the current financial crisis will have probably an impact on the future GDP and project management deployment, and it will be of great interest to pursue these investigations in the coming years to better understand the socio-economic factors influencing project management deployment.

References

Bredillet, C., Ruiz, P., & Yatim, F. (2008a). *Investigating the deployment of Project Management A Time-Distance Analysis approach of G8, European G6 & Outreach 5 countries*. Paper presented at the PMI Research Conference.

Bredillet, C., Ruiz, P., & Yatim, F. (2008b). Project Management Deployment: The Role of the Cultural Factors. EDEN Doctoral Seminar: 9 schools of Project Management, Lille, France, 18-22 August 2008.

Economist Intelligence Unit (2008a). China Country Forecast. Retrieved July 7, 2008, from Economist: http://www.economist.com/countries/China/profile.cfm?folder=Profile-Forecast

Economist Intelligence Unit (2008b). India Country Forecast. Retrieved July 7, 2008, from Economist: http://www.economist.com/countries/India/profile.cfm?folder=Profile-Forecast

Economist Intelligence Unit (2008c). USA Country Forecast. Retrieved July 7, 2008, from Economist: http://www.economist.com/countries/USA/profile.cfm?folder=Profile-Forecast

Granger, C. W. J., & Jeon, Y. (2003). A time-distance criterion for evaluating forecasting models. *International Journal of Forecasting, 19*, 199-215.

Hofstede, G. (1983). Cultural dimensions for project management. *International Journal of Project Management, 1*(1), 41-48.

Hymans, S. H. (2008). Forecasting and econometric models. *The Concise Encyclopedia of Economics (CEE)*. Retrieved from http://www.econlib.org/Library/Enc/ForecastingandEconometricModels.html#biography

International Project Management Association. (2007). *IPMA Certification Yearbook 2006* (Version 1.00 ed.): IPMA.

Lientz, B. P., & Rea, K. P. (2002). *Project Management for 21st Century* (Third ed.). San Diego: Butterworth-Heinemann Ltd ISBN 012449983X, 9780124499836 .

NOBE (2002). *Forecasts Of The Economic Growth In OECD Countries and Central and Eastern European Countries for the Period 2000-2040*. New York and Geneva: United Nations.

Project Management Institute, P. (2008). PMI Today Fact File. *PM Today* (September, 2008), 8.

Sicherl, P. (1998a). A new view in comparative analysis. Ljubljana, Slovenia: University of Ljubljana & SICENTER

Sicherl, P. (1998b). Time distance in economics and statistics: Concept, Statistical measure and examples. In A. Ferligoj (Ed.), *Advances in methodology, Data analysis and statistics* (pp. 8). Ljubljana, Slovenia. (see http://www.sicenter.si/td_briefhistory.htm) for instance

Sicherl, P. (1998b), 'Time Distance in Economics and Statistics, Concept, Statistical Measure and Examples', in Ferligoj A. (ed.), Advances in Methodology, Data Analysis and Statistics, Metodološki zvezki 14, FDV, Ljubljana

Sicherl, P. (2000). Development distances in Southeast Europe, *Countdown Project: European Union Enlargement, regionalization and Balkan integration* (pp. 35). Ljubljana, Slovenia: EU-Interreg II/C project coordinated by WIIW Vienna.

Sicherl, P. (2001). New analytical and policy insights on the severity of the gap between USA, Japan and EU in research and development provided by time distance (S-distance) methodology: A brief illustration. Ljubljana, Slovenia: Sicenter Center for Socio-economic Indicators.

Sicherl, P. (2004a). Distance in time distance between Slovenia and the European Union around 2001. In K. H. Muller (Ed.), *Time-distance Analysis: Method and Applications* (Vol. 2a/2004, pp. 81-110). Vienna: Wiener Institute for Social Science Documentation and Methodology (WISDOM).

Sicherl, P. (2004b). Leads and lags between the United States and the European Union. In K. H. Muller (Ed.), *Time-distance Analysis: Method and Applications* (Vol. 2a/2004, pp. 67-80). Vienna: Wiener Institute for Social Science Documentation and Methodology (WISDOM).

Sicherl, P. (2004c). New perspective on the digital divide. In K. H. Muller (Ed.), *Time-distance Analysis: Method and Applications* (Vol. 2a/2004, pp. 45-66). Vienna: Wiener Institute for Social Science Documentation and Methodology (WISDOM).

Sicherl, P. (2004d). TDA: A new perspective in convergence and divergence analysis and in typologies for development indicators. In K. H. Muller (Ed.), *Time-distance Analysis: Method and Applications* (Vol. 2a/2004, pp. 31-44). Vienna: Wiener Institute for Social Science Documentation and Methodology (WISDOM).

Sicherl, P. (2004e). Time Distance As A New Additional Way To Measure And Assess The Overall Position Among And Within Countries. Ljubljana, Slovenia: SICENTER and University of Ljubljana.

Sicherl, P. (2004f). *Time distance: A missing link in comparative analysis.* Paper presented at the 28th General Conference of the International Association for Research in Income and Wealth.

Sicherl, P. (2004g). Time distance: A missing perspective in comparative analysis. In K. H. Muller (Ed.), *Time-distance Analysis: Method and Applications* (Vol. 2a/2004, pp. 11-30). Vienna: Wiener Institute for Social Science Documentation and Methodology (WISDOM)

Sicherl, P. (2005). Analysis of information society indicators with time distance methodology. *Journal of Computing and Information Technology, 13-4-2005*, 193-198.

Sicherl, P. (2006). Measuring progress of societies. Ljubljana, Slovenia: SICENTER.

Sicherl, P. (2007). Monitoring implementation of the millennium development goals in the time dimension. Ljubljana, Slovenia: Socio-economic Indicators Center (SICENTER).

Sicherl, P., & Vahcic, A. (1999). The indicator model for design of development policy and for monitoring the implementation of the strategy of economic development of the Republic of Slovenia. Ljubljana, Slovenia: Center for Socio-economic Indicators (SICENTER).

United Nations (2007). *World Economic Situation and Prospects 2007.* New York: UN.

Wikipedia (2008). Gross Domestic Prodcut. Retrieved 25/5/2008: http://en.wikipedia.org/wiki/Gross_domestic_product#International_standards

Passion, Persistence and Patience: Keys to Convert Project Management Vision to Reality in Spain

Alfonso Bucero, PhD Candidate, PMP

Abstract

A lot of progress may be achieved in the field of project management in Spain in the next decades. Spanish project management has become more and more popular, but it is still thought of as a tactical set of methods and tools focused on the project manager only. I have seen very few Spanish organizations spending time and money on training their Executives in the strategic part of project management. Executives need to be trained in their critical role of project sponsors. Most Spanish executives see project management as a tool, and then they understand that project management is only tactical—meaning it is only for project managers but not for them. Because of that, the boards of directors of many Spanish companies don't see the need of being trained as sponsors. They strongly believe the project manager is either the winner—or guilty, in case of failure.

Organizations need better and better skilled project managers, and they need to develop and cultivate not only hard but also soft skills in them. Enthusiasm must be developed in our future project managers, starting from schools and keeping growing up to universities. We must educate children about the importance of passion (to believe in), and persistence (to insist more than one time to accomplish your objectives), and the need of patience (sometimes, project managers must wait for some things to be successful). Those principles must be cultivated by teachers in school with very young children, teaching them that they must think before acting, and they need to learn about making decisions themselves in different situations. This should continue in high schools, where students must do their first project. There they should learn the need of defining and planning for good execution, as well as the importance of leadership for every professional. Finally, project management should be taught at business schools where junior and senior executives need to work together and support each other through project management discipline. The youngest students must manage projects, but nobody explained to them what a project is. Now the foundation of project management is being taught to principals, but a big change must be achieved in terms of teachers' culture.

For many years, the project management culture has been very locally oriented (Spain-focused). However, we boarded the "Globalization" train some years ago, and that is where we must be. We cannot forget the different cultures and behavior patterns from others. We need more leaders than managers in Spanish organizations—leaders who have enthusiasm, who believe that project management is adding value to organizations, leaders who have a vision and will be able to transform that vision into a reality through people.

Current situation

In the last six years, the project management awareness and practice has been growing very rapidly in response to the needs of Spain. Globalization has been increased and more and more multinational companies have opened subsidiary offices in Spain. Because of that, local companies started up organizational changes and moved forward to a project orientation.

However, it has not been the general approach for all Spanish organizations. Lack of discipline is a generic Spanish characteristic and it also affects to the project management arena. The growth was not accompanied by the development of project management as an important profession.

There are still no concerted efforts from the public sector. Public administration business is very slow in Spain. Bureaucracy is one of its main characteristics. Public administration managers have no interest in project management. Most public administration people see this discipline as an aggression to their power. As they use many subcontractors for managing their projects, they believe that don't need to learn anything about project management. For instance, management people from the public construction sector misunderstand the project manager job.

The private sector is becoming more and more conscious about the need for project management, and they send their professionals to be trained in project management. However, project management is being introduced step by step in public capital firms which have private management systems. Nevertheless, most Spanish organizations believe that project management is only for project managers and they don't understand the strategic part of project management. You can still find companies who think that managing a project is just using a tool like Microsoft project. As they consider that managing a tool is not part of their management responsibility, then those managers don't see anything interesting in project management for them.

What industries or type of projects are the main users of project management in Spain today?

Industries divide between those that follow some methodology in the information technology sector, and general business areas, and the more historically project-based industries that have a more intuitive approach to project management. I am not totally sure one could identify which industries have a greater need for more or better project management. Some Spanish companies are adopting project management as a way of improvement; however, most of companies are now in the very beginning in project management involvement.

I interviewed about 30 Spanish senior project professionals from several industry sectors, and most of them believe the project manager role does not formally exist in Spain. That means the project manager job is not a position in many Spanish companies. The companies consider it a role to be played temporarily by a technical professional, whose primary responsibility is technical but the project management role will be considered additional. Then they do not formalize the project management position. The consequence is that those professionals become frustrated very soon because there are no rules. There is a lack of authority, commitment, and sponsorship.

More and more organizations understand the need for project management, but they don't put many efforts in creating the right environment for project success. Most Spanish companies spend money training project managers, but they don't spend any effort, time, or money training and coaching their executives about the strategic part of project management, and how big the business impact would be if executives knew more about the strategic emphasis needed in project management.

Organizations do not train the rest of the organization about the project management discipline. One of the major troubles I found managing customer projects was dealing with internal people in my organization, such as financial and legal staff. Organizations that do projects must spend time explaining to the different project stakeholders the pieces of the "puzzle." If the only personnel that are trained in that discipline are the project managers, projects will run in trouble and generate a lot of stress for the project managers. All industries are improving their understanding and application of project management techniques. I strongly believe the greatest challenge is upper managements recognition of high-level input at the front end of the project, and much more attention to the interpersonal and soft project management skills.

Universities and business schools are more and more interested in project management today. There are about 17 masters in project management programs offered by different institutions in Spain:

- Universidad Pontificia de Salamanca (Master in project Management)
- Instituto de Estudios Caja Sol (Postgraduate Studies in Project Management)
- Civil Engineering School at Bilbao (Master in Project Management)
- Universidad Politécnica de Madrid (Postgraduate Studies in Project Management)
- Universidad de la Coruña (Master in Project Management)
- Universidad de Castilla la Mancha (Master in Project Management)
- Instituto Europeo Campus Stellae (Postgraduate Studies)
- INSA (Master in Project Management)
- ONLINE Business School (Master in Project Management)
- Fundación UPC (Master in Project Management)
- EOI (Master in Project Management)
- Arquitects School of Madrid (Master in Project Management)
- UAX. ES (Postgraduate Studies)
- LA SALLE Business School (Master in Project Management)
- EAE Business School (Master in Project Management)

Young people have a clearer understanding about the need for project management skills, and they are looking for locally available training.

In terms of professional project management associations, we have three in Spain that are working on expanding the profession, but all three have different approaches and focus:

- AEIPRO (Spanish Project Engineering Organization). This organization started in universities. Their focus is on project engineering for engineering students and post graduates. They continue working very hard and they organize an annual congress. They belong to IPMA (International Project Management Association). They do certification exams according to IPMA levels.
- AEDIP (Spanish Project Management Organization). Its focus is the construction industry. It is a group of companies that deliver project management services in the construction industry. They are very active and they helped PMI in the PMI Global Congress 2006—EMEA in Madrid. They organize frequent events and they created the "White Book of Project Management" in 2007.
- PMI chapters. We have three PMI chapters in Spain (in Madrid, Barcelona, and Valencia). Their focus is the global project management profession and the different practices of the profession in the several industries in the Spanish market.

Some efforts have been made by PMI Spanish chapters to look for synergies among those different associations, but the result has been poor so far. There are more than 1,000 recognized project professionals, in Spain and many more who are unrecognized project management practitioners.

The opportunity of merging efforts is tremendous in our country. The first Spanish chapter was the PMI Madrid Chapter (2003). More than 200 professionals joined that chapter. However the lack of activities and service of this chapter awoke other Spanish professionals, who asked PMI for creation of new chapters. The PMI Barcelona Chapter was born by 2004 and PMI Valencia Chapter by 2006.

Due to a lack of services by the PMI Madrid Chapter, the relationship among the rest of the Spanish chapters was very poor. Fortunately a new board of directors for PMI Madrid Chapter was elected by February 1, 2008. The new management style and enthusiasm is provoking chapter membership growth. Some initiatives like common meetings and events are being planned. Looking at the future, we really look forward to a new atmosphere of collaboration and cooperation for the next decade.

Issues of common global interest

Spanish professionals believe that standardization is a need and that we need "frameworks" like PMI's *A Guide to the Project Management Body of Knowledge (PMBOK® Guide)*. However, the Spanish point of view is that the global project management body of knowledge can only identify high-level generic issues in project management. It is not possible to have a *single detailed* body of knowledge, because countries like Spain will develop and progress ideas in their own cultural style. I believe that while the techniques and applications of project management may be universal, the detailed implementation and approach is a very personal issue. That means that depending on local patterns and behaviors, the processes implementation in

A Guide to the Prjoect Management Body of Knowledge (PMBOK® Guide) may be slightly different. One example is in the procurement area of knowledge. We have different types of contracts in Spain. And in Spain, we have different local languages and cultures by geographical community.

International standards of project management are appropriate in providing a framework or guideline. Since 2007, an international group of professionals is working globally on an ISO (International Organization for Standardization) standard for project management. Representatives from different countries are working in reviewing the *PMBOK® Guide* and how it can be customized according ISO guidelines. In terms of certification, project management certification is of interest in Spain, although professional certification is not totally known in all industry sectors. In fact, business globalization has generated more project management awareness among Spanish professionals. Eighteen Spanish companies are offering project management training programs to get preparation to obtain project management certifications (Certified Associate in Project Management (CAPM)®, Project Management Professional (PMP)SM, and the IPMA certifications). The role of PMI chapters in Spain is crucial to promote the Spanish project manager certification need, and also awareness of that need among Spanish organizations. There is a huge opportunity to get those things happening.

A key issue is how can project management associations around Spain better communicate and cooperate to advance the project management profession?

To ensure greater communication and cooperation, all project management associations should respect the ideas and geographic boundaries of other project management associations. The important thing is for organizations to collaborate and not to develop a confrontational attitude over promoting different ideas of standards and programs. Having a clear spirit of understanding and cooperation, communications could then be established by means of an electronic network and regular meetings. Probably as soon as a project management ISO certification exists, all Spanish associations will be better aligned.

Other suggestions about how project management associations could advance the project management profession in Spain might be:

- Organizing Spanish congresses and events, where all Spanish project management associations might add value to the profession
- Creating a chapter's federation. PMI might support us on those actions
- Selling the need of project management into public administration, getting support from the European Union organisms through public administration dedicated events
- Looking for alliances among Spanish-speaking chapters worldwide, mainly in South America.
- Selling the need of project, program and portfolio management to associations for professional executives, and explaining to them the big business impact that the profession may have

One of the issues I have observed in professional project management associations in Spain is that some members are owners of project management consulting firms, and sometimes the code of ethics is not well respected. Some people mix professional objectives with the business ones.

Expected future

What we need to do, within this general flourishing environment for project management, is to continue to promote best-practice generic standards. In order to avoid confrontational attitudes in the development of standards and programs, we must facilitate all the information and point of views among all Spanish associations, promoting leadership and teamwork. What we don't want to do is to find people saying project management is a state, or process. The way we can best do is by having well respected quality, practices, and professionalism that represent the project management discipline.

I believe we must cultivate the passion. Enthusiasm is contagious among professionals in organizations, associations, schools, and universities. I strongly believe that project leadership is the key for our professional future. Spanish associations must encourage project professionals to develop their leadership skills. We need and we will need more leaders than managers in Spanish organizations. I found some Spanish project management professional organizations that do not use project management practices inside their own associations. It seems to be crazy but I observed that to be the truth. We must select *those project managers who want to be leaders*. Most Spanish companies do not have a project manager selection process in place; however this process is becoming more familiar in some big Spanish organizations now.

The expected future of the profession in Spain is different depending on the industry. For instance, project management professionalism in the IT sector is becoming a fact. The reason is the reaction from of project failures in which organizations did not have a skilled project manager. The big influence that the multinational firms have toward the recognition of our profession will be very helpful to move forward on the profession. Some Spanish project managers from the IT sector believe that a local project management standard like ISO would be very helpful in our country. Spanish organizations need to have standard rules on board, to be able to compete with each other for standard's achievement.

In the construction sector, Spain is living a "boom" that forces Spanish professionals to go out Spain to start to use global management disciplines like project management. Most of the professionals interviewed from the construction sector believe that project management will be a core discipline for the next decades, and something very valuable for this sector. In fact, more and more architects have been trained in the project management discipline during the last three years. Let me give you some examples:

> "*I am an architect and my perception from project management in the construction industry is that it is been expanded in Spain. The interest of professionals about project management in this sector is growing up. The most sad part is the public administration way of operation, characterized by its bureaucracy and slow way of working*" (Miguel Angel Álvarez, Spanish architect and PMI Madrid Spain Chapter Past Vice President).

> "*I am optimistic about the project management profession in Spain. I believe that Spanish organizations think that they do not need to be more efficient to be happier. Public administration, the main project services buyer in all technological environments, still does not believe in project management, and they are introducing very few procedures to move forward. Some relevant public project results show the lack of project management discipline*" (Marc Serer, PhD, and PMI Barcelona Spain Past Chapter President).

"Project management is at the very beginning and not well understood in our society and government. On the other hand, there is huge opportunity to move forward in this profession because the need of traveling and doing business outside Spain" (Felipe Fernández, PMP, Spanish architect and PMI Madrid Spain Past Chapter Secretary).

Project professionals interviewed from saving banks believe that project management will be a core discipline needed for financial organizations. This is because of the need that these organizations have to outsource. They need more and more project managers inside the organization who are well-prepared to manage other external companies doing things and achieving better and lower-cost results. On the other hand, I observed that saving banks spend the money on training project leaders and project managers, but they don't spend any money in coaching executives about project sponsorship, and they usually don't spend any money training technical people on the foundation of the project management discipline. I believe it is one of the reasons that some saving banks organizations in Spain are not as successfult than they could be.

Project professionals from the pharmaceutical industry cannot survive without project and program management. Although they should use it all the time, not all the pharmaceutical organizations interviewed do use it. Project and program managers in those organizations are dealing with internal problems all time because they have a lack of project sponsorship. Their managers are not trained about that. Then the focus is on the project and program manager who will be either champion or guilty. I have lived some real examples of trying to move a pharmaceutical organization to a project-oriented organization. Those companies have some money to be spent and hire some consultants and experts to do it. However, when the consultants leave, most of upper managers are managing the old way again.

The engineering sector in Spain is beginning to be more and more trained in project management, but it is more focused on technical skills development, not on project management skills. This situation has been evolving since three or four years ago, but once more again, engineering organizations train project managers, not executives. Now I have discovered some multinational firms with subsidiaries in Spain that have defined the project manager function as a recognized job in the organization. Nevertheless, once more time they are only focused on training project leaders and project managers and not taking into account the rest of project stakeholders.

Most of professionals interviewed believe project management will be a need in all organizations at any management level. The project management discipline will be evolving to a "managing by projects" discipline. Some advanced companies are starting to do it now, but very few so far.

Current trends

Today, I have observed the most active industry in project management in Spain is the IT and telecommunication sector, but the most emerging is the construction sector. The latter is promoting the profession more and more from universities and business Schools. A 50% growth has been detected from last year in that industry sector. More and more people are getting the PMP certification and are more interested in being better and better trained in project management. Although the project management training focus in Spain has been on hard skills, the main focus since a couple of years ago is project management soft skills development.

Project management professionals want to be more skilled in teamwork, communication, conflict management, negotiation, influence management and politics. Multicultural skills are becoming more and more important because we are moving to a world of globalization in all industries. We manage many international projects, and project professionals must deal with different cultures, patterns, and behaviors.

Some Spanish organizations are starting to define formal project management career paths and need the assessment of project professional associations for that. That fact has grown since a couple years ago when the PMI Global Congress 2006—EMEA took place in Madrid—the 850 project professionals who participated in that congress generated a lot of awareness within our Spanish society.

Project management has not been started yet in schools, and it is one of the focuses of Spanish PMI chapters. Being supported by PMI and the PMI Educational Foundation, many training projects will be started in the near future. For example, only 100 of the 850 PMI Global Congress 2006—EMEA attendees came from Spain.

As a frequent PMI congress attendee, I have observed a growth in the number of attendees to the European congresses in the last three years. We joined 30 Spanish professionals attending to PMI Global Congress 2007—EMEA in Budapest, Hungary. I strongly believe that the focus of PMI Spanish chapters will affect positively to the project management training and education in Spain.

All Spanish chapters are promoting the value of professional certification in Spain very actively. PMI membership is growing in Spain. All Spanish chapters are focused on explaining the importance of project management for better business results to Spanish private and public organizations. We must use the experiences and best practices from other European countries, and obviously from Latin America countries as well.

Global congresses and symposiums are an ideal vehicle of communication and sharing among those communities, however I must sadly say that I have found a very small Spanish group of project practitioners at those events. I hope we, as project practitioners, are able to transmit positive energy and passion for project management to our next generations of project and program managers.

CHAPTER 3

India in 2025
The role of project management in meeting opportunities and threats

Raju Rao

Section 1
India in 2025 – the Vision

Labeled as the "Great Indian Pie," democratic India, with over a billion people and a booming economy, is still known as a developing country—even after 60 years of independence. But that image is fast undergoing a remarkable transformation. It began with liberalization of economy in the early 1990s and since then there has been no looking back. Today India, the world's largest democracy, is the 10th-largest economy and the fourth largest in the world in terms of Purchasing Power Parity. According to World Bank sources, by 2025 India is expected to become the third-largest economy after China and the United States (Jafri, 2006). Interestingly, as shown in Table 1, India's share of world GDP has consistently dipped to very low levels through 1973, but from 2001 it is showing an upward trend, giving rise to speculation that the "Bird of Gold" (McKinsey, 2007) will make a comeback by 2025.

In recent years in India, many organizations and individuals have been involved in future planning and have been looking ahead at scenarios for the year 2020 and 2025. These include prominent persons in public life, such as the former President of India Prof. A. P. J. Abdul Kalam, as well as many state governments, companies, and research organizations. Each study has its own angle, emphasizing the importance of different sectors in the next two decades. Some of most prominent examples of such studies are:

- India's New Opportunity–2020 from the Boston Consulting Group in association with CII and AIMA (2003)
- Book on Vision 2020 by A. P. J. Abdul Kalam and Y S Rajan (1996)

Table 1.   India's share of world's GDP (Adapted from Sabharwal, 2008).

Share of World's GDP - Figures in %						
	India	**China**	**Japan**	**USA**	**Europe**	**Rest of the World**
1 AD	33	27	1	0	14	25
1500 AD	25	25	3	0	21	26
1820 AD	15	33	3	2	27	20
1870 AD	12	17	2	9	38	22
1913 AD	8	8	4	21	39	20
1950 AD	4	5	3	28	31	29
1973 AD	3	5	8	23	29	32
2001 AD	4	7	8	23	21	37
2008 AD	6	13	7	21	19	34

- Various sector-based reports for 2025 from the Planning Commission, Government of India
- India and the World–Scenarios to 2025, from the World Economic Forum (2005)

Figure 1 presents one such set of scenarios. The most optimistic and what we would like to see happen is "India First." Six key areas have been identified to meet it (World Economic Forum--CII, 2005):

- Poverty alleviation – basic needs for all
- Agriculture and rural development
- Healthcare
- Access to education
- Leapfrogging infrastructure constraints
- Effective governance

Based on conditions prevailing now and assuming the same trends will continue, one would expect the scenario of "Getting Stuck" or "Business as Usual" to happen. Therefore, by 2025 it may be realistic to assume that the situation may be somewhere in between these two scenarios. So, we can expect pockets of excellence in some sectors or regions, whereas others could be be lagging behind substantially. It will be a great challenge to reach the goals as envisioned in "India First" instead of being led by the other two scenarios.

Section 2
Opportunities and Strengths
2.1 Availability of Skilled Manpower
The Boston Consulting Group, in its report titled "India's New Opportunity–2020" (2003), indicates that there is a surplus manpower in the region of +47 million in India

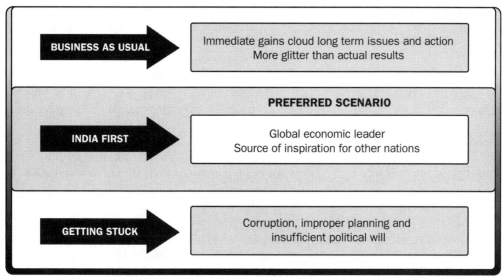

Figure 1.   India and the world: Scenarios to 2025 (Adapted from World Economic Forum—CII, 2005).

as compared to deficits in many of the advanced countries (–17million in the U.S., -9 million to –10 million in Japan and China, and –2 million to –3 million in many countries in Europe). Even within the BRIC (Brazil, Russia, India, and China) and other developing countries, India has an advantageous position in terms of numbers, productivity, English-speaking skills and cost.

Keeping this in mind, two major sources of opportunity could be visualized. One relates to remote education and the other to serving customers within India through tourism of different types (e.g., medical tourism). The success of the IT sector in buoying up the economy in India has spurred planners to consider the availability of a large skilled workforce in the working-group age as an advantage to develop many new opportunities in other sectors. R & D outsourcing has received a lot of attention. This is based on the fact that many multinational corporations such as Microsoft, GE, Cisco, etc., have set up shop here. Contract research is becoming equally attractive going by the trends in the biotech sector and clinical research.

2.2 A Large Middle Class

New research from the McKinsey Global Institute (2007) shows that within a generation, India will become a nation of upwardly mobile middle-class households, consuming goods ranging from high-end cars to designer clothing. In two decades, the country will surpass Germany as the world's fifth largest consumer market. The middle class currently numbers some 50 million people, but by 2025 will have expanded dramatically to 583 million people—some 41 percent of the population. These households will see their incomes balloon to 51.5 trillion rupees ($1.1 billion)—11 times the level of today and 58 percent of total Indian income. A huge shift is underway from spending on necessities such as food and clothing to choice-based spending on categories such as household appliances and restaurants. Households that can afford discretionary consumption will grow from 8 million today to 94 million by 2025. The growth of a large middle class with improved purchasing power will mean substantial investments in manufacturing and energy infrastructure, which in turn will need investments in maintaining the environment.

2.3 A Significant Upper and Upper Middle Class

The other major spending force in India's new consumer market will be what is termed as the global Indians, These could be senior corporate executives, large business owners, high-end professionals, politicians, and big agricultural-land owners. Today there are just 1.2 million global Indian households accounting for some 2 trillion rupees in spending power. By 2025 there will be 9.5 million Indians in this class and their spending power will hit 14.1 trillion rupees, 20 percent of total Indian consumption

2.4 Leveraging Manufacturing Capability

The experience gained by Indian IT companies in providing services to overseas clients could be replicated in the manufacturing sector as well. The global trend by those in the advanced countries to manufacture and source products in low-cost countries (LCCs) is likely to gather strength over the next two decades, particularly in the skill-intensive industries where India has a significant competitive advantage. Studies shows that India could threaten China or replace it as the world's factory and become the hub for this industry. Already just over half of all offshore manufacturing by US companies involves skill-intensive sectors, and that figure could rise to 70 percent by 2015, opening up huge opportunities. India is expected to increase its share in world manufacturing trade from 0.8 per cent now to 3.5 per cent by 2015 . Along with robust domestic demand growth, this is likely to create 25-30 million new jobs in manufacturing and add 1 per cent to India's annual GDP growth rate.

Examples of leading manufacturing companies which have already moved to take advantage of the situation include Nissan, Suzuki, Fiat, Hyundai, BMW, Samsung, Toyota Motor, Degussa, Rohm and Hass, and Nokia, to name a few. Some Indian companies have established a global reputation either through excellence in manufacturing or by global acquisitions. These include Sundaram Clayton, Bharat Forge, Ranbaxy and some companies of the Tata group.

What helps tap some of the opportunities in manufacturing? The availability of low-cost workers with advanced engineering and technical skills and a pool of people with higher educational qualifications and proven track record in quality. Apart from these, other advantages are established raw material bases, a mature supply base and a growing domestic demand.

The sectors that are likely to grow are auto components, specialty chemicals, pharmaceuticals, and industrial electronics. As a result, offshoring to LCCs is expected to increase from the current US$1,300-US$1,400 billion to US$4,000 billion-US$4,500 billion by 2015. Skill-intensive industries will drive most of this increase. In the U.S., for example, the share of skill-intensive industries could rise from 55 to 70 per cent of total offshoring to LCCs.

It is worthwhile at this juncture to compare India and China in the manufacturing sector. While China has been the leader for low-cost manufacture of standard products and those with large volumes, India presents unique advantages in troubleshooting, new product development and higher-end research. While China is considered very good at repetitive work and mass production, India has been found to be comfortable with uncertain situations and Indian companies are able to find solutions to unexpected problems and scenarios (Meredith,2007)

2.5 Agriculture and Food Processing

Since 70% of the Indian population still lives in the countryside, agriculture and food processing is expected to play a much bigger role in India's growth picture. Agriculture still accounts for a sizeable 22% of GDP. India is the second-largest producer of fruits and vegetables in the world and the country accounts for 10% of the world's fruit production, but approximately 43% of the production is wasted because of lack of cold storage facilities and energy infrastructure. Food processing is a key priority area for India and it is only recently that the private sector has started looking at the sector. Just about 1.3% of fruits and vegetables get processed in India, as against 80% in the US, 70% in France, 80% in Malaysia, and 30% in Thailand. Sub-optimal growth of food processing can be attributed to the vicious circle of high unit cost, low demand, low capacity utilization, and outdated technology. In the coming years, considerable development on supply chain management will be required in the food and agriculture sector.

2.6 Infrastructure

India has achieved substantial success in some sectors such as telecom and a concerted effort in the last few years in other areas. A few significant pointers to its importance are the facts that India spends just 6 percent of its GDP on infrastructure, compared to China's 20 percent. To achieve its targeted GDP growth rates, the country will need to invest approximately $400 billion in infrastructure over the next five years. It has been recognized by the government that "The most glaring deficit in India is the infrastructure deficit."(Chidambaram, 2005)

2.6.1 Power

Based on forecasts by McKinsey (2007), the demand for power is likely to soar from 120 GW in 2007 to more than 300 GW by 2017, which will require a generation capacity of about 430 GW. This demand will be driven to a large extent by high growth in manufacturing as well as residential consumption due to a substantial increase in middle class population. This will mean a capacity addition of five- to tenfold more than that being done over the last 10 years in India. To keep pace with the soaring demand, India will need an investment of about US$600 billion by 2017 (McKinsey, 2007). Apart from electric power, there is lot of interest in other forms of energy such as nuclear and wind, solar, and biofuels.

2.6.2 Transport

The aviation industry is growing by leaps and bounds, judging from the number of airlines that have been set up in recent times. This growth has been fuelled by an increase in passenger traffic as a result of an improved economy, proactive government policies, innovative funding mechanisms, etc. So is the case with the railways, a sector traditionally in the red but now turned around. Modernization of many railway stations is on the way. Along with this, many urban metro transport systems are being planned.

2.6.3 Roads and Highways

One of the significant projects undertaken recently in India is the Golden Quadrilateral, which links the north, east, south, and west in India. It is expected that public-private partnership will play a major role in construction of roads and highways. The experience of countries that have gone through this exercise earlier, such as Australia and U.K., will be very useful here.

2.6.4 Housing and Industrial Estates

Residential complexes, particularly in the urban areas, have shown growth in the last few years, and this is likely to continue to keep pace with large middle class with its added purchasing power. Sustained growth in manufacturing and services will also mean more industrial estates, parks, and special economic zones (SEZ).

2.7 Financial Investment

Since the start of liberalization in the 1990s, India has had a steady flow and increase in foreign direct investment (FDI). This has been one of main reasons for economy to grow at near double-digit rates. By 2025, the outlook for the financial sector, especially the capital market, is quite comfortable. There have been plans to upgrade the financial activity in Mumbai to the level of other financial centers in the world such as Hong Kong, Singapore, and New York. The demographic profile with a large percentage of younger people is correlated with a buoyant equity market (Menon, 2008)

2.8 Work Culture

Let us for a moment look at the work culture and infrastructural environment prevalent in India over last several decades and see if it helps in unraveling some of the anomalies and paradoxes that can be observed. It is quite baffling to understand that a land with so much poverty, illiteracy, and bureaucracy can also achieve phenomenal progress and efficiency on certain fronts, presenting the "best of the best" world-class standards in products and services.

One reason for such pockets of excellence is the presence of an educated workforce able to produce goods and services at a cost that is a fraction of that in the advanced countries. A theory that is frequently propounded is that people in India are so much used to facing roadblocks in most of their activities that they become tenacious and resilient, and therefore skilled, in addressing sudden changes and managing crisis situations. This is well-proven by the fact that many Indian entrepreneurs perform exceedingly well outside India, especially in organized business environments, since the home ground serves as a training ground for handling tougher situations.

Section 3
Threats and Weaknesses
3.1 Non-Availability of Appropriate Manpower and Skills

As India's economy moves up the value chain, educating, training, and retaining a talented workforce will be a major growth challenge. Despite its favorable demographics, the talent pipeline is at risk not only in knowledge-driven industries but also in agriculture, construction, and manufacturing. Contrary to the "myth" that India has a large employment pool, there is a massive shortage of skilled professionals (Albright and others, 2007). In surveys, it has been found that only about 15 % of India's engineering graduates are employable and most have to be retrained by their organizations before they can take up responsibilities . The key question is not if "will there be enough people " available but "are these large numbers employable?" (Albright and others, 2007). There is little doubt that in the next two decades education and skills development will be a core issue for meeting the human resource requirements of organizations. Of particular concern is the fact that while many professionals are technically educated, they lack the requisite soft skills required for effective performance. The Indian education pyramid is narrow because it produces more soloists than team members, and their soft skills are not on par with their technical skills. (Brown and Others, 2007) Historically, India has been saddled with an antiquated, government-controlled, syllabus-driven education system which lays more emphasis on rote learning rather than original thinking. While the cost of higher education is low and therefore accessible to many, there is a considerable gap in competency and skills between what is available and what is required, even by present-day requirements. In the next two decades with the explosive growth expected in the economy, this gap will widen, and unless there is a concerted effort by all in industry and government to find solutions, it will be become very difficult to meet the demands of the economy.

3.2 Inadequate Infrastructure

This is easily the weakest link in the India growth story. Infrastructure includes telecommunications, power, roads, airports, ports, housing and industrial estates. It has been often said that one of the reasons for success of the IT industry in India is its non-dependence on conventional infrastructure. The same cannot be said with, for example, manufacturing. This is highly dependent on energy, transportation, and water. Further, only since last few years has it been able to tap overseas markets, and this has stunted its growth.

The current expenditure on infrastructure is about 5% of GDP annually, and this is expected to grow to about 9% by 2011-2012. In monetary terms, India is looking to spend US$500 billion over five years. This investment will provide the necessary infrastructure base for the growth of the manufacturing industry.

Three problems can be identified in this sector:

- Putting in place channels to capture funds available from domestic or foreign investors;
- Addressing skills shortage; and
- Speed of decision-making (Ahluwalia and Others, 2007).

Based on reports, India should spend 12.5% of GDP on infrastructure. In this context, the public-private partnership model can be very successful, and there is a need to empower local self-governments to improve city governance in India, especially as India is likely to witness urbanization on an enormous scale. It needs to evolve an environment where government officials called upon to take policy decisions can do so without fear of retribution. It is expected to implement a unified general tax system in a few years, which will help smooth out regional differences that often act as a hindrance to the seamless functioning of supply chains and distribution channels (Ahluwalia and Others, 2007)

3.3 Insufficient Power

The power sector continues to lag behind inspite of introduction of progressive measures. Impediments include tariff, dependence on imported fuels, shortages, and distribution. (McKinsey,2007). 50% of India still does not have access to electricity and the country's electricity supply must increase five to seven times to sustain 8% future growth. Public-private partnerships are being touted as the means to draw in the US\$75 billion in FDI needed to improve power infrastructure.

3.4 Lack of Institutionalized Innovation

One of the factors responsible for the success of advanced countries has been its emphasis on innovation and entrepreneurial activity. The example of Silicon Valley shows that while substantial research and educational facilities may be available elsewhere, attention is continuing to be drawn there due to the unique environment and culture prevalent. In India, while there is no dearth of entrepreneurial capability, it has not flourished due to lack of institutional support. While the number of patents from India is on the rise, there is still along way to go. In comparison, in other countries, we find a strong commitment to research and product development, either through large funding from philanthropic organizations or by private sector companies.

3.5 Environment and Healthcare
3.5.1 Water Shortage

It is now widely recognized that the world is heading for a water crisis of unusual dimensions in the next two decades. A recent study projected that several countries, including parts of India and China, with a population of 1 billion people, would face absolute scarcity of water by 2025. Although the problems associated with water shortage and water contamination have been acknowledged and solutions identified, the resulting efforts at resolution have been poor. Recognizing this shortage, a World Bank report pointed out that although solutions to the water crisis have been, to an extent, "developed," it is not yet "managed," a situation that has contributed to misuse and scarcity.

3.5.2 HIV / AIDS

The HIV/AIDS epidemic, fueled by co-infection with tuberculosis, is predicted to be a significant drag on India's future economic growth as it continues to affect millions of working-age adults. Businesses are now taking an active role in tackling these infections, but questions remain about partnering with national public health agencies as well introducing greater innovation to address the evolving epidemic.

3.5.3 India vs. Bharat

While discussing development, many Indian researches have made a distinction between "India," which is moving upward in economic terms and is well integrated with the world as shown by the growing numbers of the upper middle class, and "Bharat," which is lower middle class predominantly in the rural and to some extent in the urban areas. "India" has very little difference from the west in terms of consumption or life style. A debate often rages if the benefits of economic development are reaching the poor or if the gap between rich and poor is widening.

The problems of poverty and poor economic development are acute in some parts of India, so much so that despite pockets of excellence, the country as a perceived as poor and overall economic development gets affected. In this context the philosophy of addressing the "bottom of the pyramid" as a consumer (Prahalad, 2005) has some relevance, as unless this group is taken into account, a sustainable overall high growth rate can hardly be achieved.

As Indian incomes rise, the shape of the country's income pyramid is also expected to change dramatically. Over 291 million people will move from desperate poverty to a more sustainable life, and India's middle class will swell by more than ten times from its current size of 50 million to 583 million people. How can a "Pyramid" where the lowest income group are concentrated at the base be converted to a "Diamond" with the middle class occupying a large part of the area (Prahalad, 2005) This could be a challenge. Some significant developments have taken place which give pointers on how the "bottom of the pyramid" market can be addressed and help people move from a lower class to the middle class. These developments are a combination of the use of technology, innovation, and institutional and organizational support. Successful examples include the growth of use of mobile phones, microfinance, cooperative dairying, eyecare, etc

Section 4
Using Project Management to Meet the Opportunities and Threats

Many of the opportunities and threats that are expected in 2025 could either be exploited or met through appropriate projects. While doing so we could be making use of the strengths and overcoming the weaknesses at present and those that are likely next two decades.

These projects can be classified in terms of domains or sectors or in terms of their application. Figure 2 shows an overall picture.

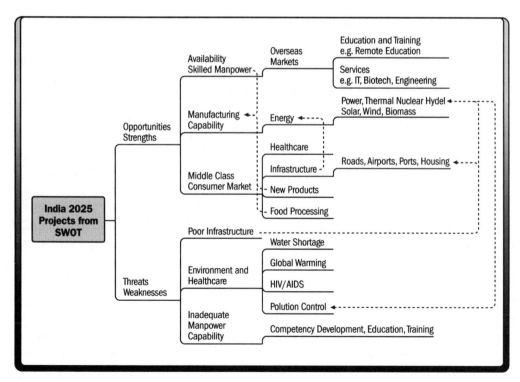

Figure 2:   India in 2025: SWOT (strengths, weaknesses, opportunities, threats) to projects.

	Remote Servicing	"Importing" the customers
Individuals	Tele-medicine E-Learning D-I-Y support	Tourism - medical, adventure, heritage Education – higher education, heritage Nursing homes and retirement services
Corporates	IT and IT Enabled Services Knowledge Process Outsourcing R & D and Contract Research	Tourism – corporate Education - corporate

Figure 3: Opportunity for services--examples. Adapted from India's New Opportunity—2020 (Boston Consulting Group-CII, 2003)

4.1 Utilization of skilled manpower for providing services

Easily, this is likely to be a major area of thrust. The success of the IT and business process outsourcing (BPO) sectors have been instrumental in showing that similar methods could be used gainfully in other sectors. Examples of areas which could be in focus in the next two decades include:

- IT Services (i.e, software development and providing solutions);
- IT-wnabled services and BPO;
- Knowledge process outsourcing;
- Engineering and R&D; and
- Education.

Another way of classifying such future opportunities is shown in Figure 3.

Table 2: Examples of projects from infrastructure: An overview.

Sector	Application or Area	Examples of Projects
Transportation	Railways	Metro rail, modernization of railway stations
	Roads and Highways	Interstate highways, expressway flyovers, village roads
	Airports	Greenfield airports, modernization of existing airports
	Ports	Greenfield ports
Construction	Shopping Malls commercial complexes	Mega malls
	Industrial Estates, SEZ	IT and biotech parks
	Housing complexes	Residential cities
Energy	Thermal, nuclear, hydro, wind, solar, biomass	Power plants, nuclear reactors, jatropha fuel, wind farms, solar panels in remote areas

Applying project management for services

The IT services sector has been one of main users of project management for software development and solutions. This will grow further to meet the increased demand in the next two decades. Since India has become a leading country for providing IT services and solutions on a global scale, one will find increased maturity in project management practices in this sector in terms of best practices, methodologies, and tools. The other sectors like contract research, knowledge process outsourcing, and remote education may apply project management in selective cases. Application in areas like tourism will depend if the concept of project management finds acceptance, since this industry has traditionally not been applying such practices.

4.2 Infrastructure

The infrastructure sector has been very weak for many years, but it is looking up now (see Table 2). Large projects are being set up, for example, the Delhi Mumbai Industrial Corridor (Sharma, 2007) with investment of about US$90 billion over the next five years. This is facilitated by a spurt in financing from overseas along with improved and innovative ways of financing and contracting. The model of public-private partnership has become one of the innovative ways for implementing infrastructure projects and examples of countries where they have found success include Australia and the U.K. Experience here has shown that there is a learning curve involved specific to a country or geography for such projects. In India, such models are being attempted in many areas, particularly for roads/ highways and airports, such as the new airports at Bangalore and Hyderabad and the Bombay - Pune expressway.

Significant investment is expected in the infrastructure sector in the next decade and while it may plateau in the decade after, it will be necessary to evaluate the capabilities and gaps now in order to take adequate steps to reach the vision in 2025.

Applying project management for infrastructure

In the next two decades the contribution of project management to the infrastructure sector will be in the form of project and construction management in each of the domains mentioned above, and program management. Further, infrastructure project management will develop as a separate discipline. Topics like stakeholder management, particularly the interface among organizations implementing projects, political entities, and the government will be important. This sector is expected to face a crunch for manpower resources both technical and managerial, and so competency building and training will be necessary, which is also an area of application.

4.3 Manufacturing

The strong base in manufacturing developed over the period will be used to leverage opportunities especially in relation to overseas markets. This is visible in products like automobile and auto components and consumer electronics. A large middle class will be a driver for products, especially in consumer durables, automobiles and auto components, which will generate demand for other basic products like petrochemicals and plastics.

Applying project management for manufacturing

Installation of new plants, capacity building and new product development are the thrust areas where maximum use of project management is likely. It can also be applied for training and competency development, since this sector will also require large number of people with appropriate technical and managerial skills. Another area of use is for internal projects for cost reduction, quality improvement, plant de-bottlenecking, machinery modification, etc. While formal project management practices have been used so far mainly for capital projects, in the next two decades we could find it being used for other non-traditional areas like internal projects, training, and competency building.

4.4 Environment and Healthcare

In the next decades a growing middle class, substantial increase in manufacturing, and energy installations will have effects on environment and will require increase in healthcare. Below are some of the major areas that have to be addressed.

4.4.1 Water

Water is expected to a major issue all over the world in the next two decades and particularly in India where a shortage is expected due to the large population and substantial economic activity (International Life Sciences Institute –India, 2002). Based on literature and current practices one could identify some examples of projects for water conservation and reuse use:

- Harvesting of rainwater;
- Recycling of municipal and industrial waste water;
- Supplementing fresh water by desalination of sea water in coastal areas;
- Better irrigation methods to improve productivity of water usage; and
- Water treatment and surveillance systems.

The Jaipur Declaration on Water Quality Management - Vision 2025 (International Life Sciences Institute- India, 2002) has recommended that 3% of GDP should be targeted for water development and management, and international institutions such as the World Bank, Asian Development Bank, and WHO should partner in this effort.

4.4.2 Global warming

Since India is expected to have substantial industrial activity, global warming will be an issue and projects either using carbon credit or other mechanisms and technologies will be in focus.

4.4.3 HIV/AIDS

Since indications are that HIV/AIDS will affect a large number of people in India, implementing programs in prevention and rehabilitation will be a major initiative from the government. Already many programs are being implemented both at the state as well as the central government level, and this will only intensify and expand further.

4.4.4 Healthcare

Applying project management for the environment and healthcare

Some of the main areas of application for project management will be for reduction of global warming through projects for carbon trading or other means. Conservation, generation, and distribution of water using newer technologies for water reuse and reduction, desalination plants, etc., will be an area of focus. The incidence of HIV/AIDS is also likely to receive lot of attention and projects for prevention as well as rehabilitation from the government or nongovernmental organizations is likely. Due to increase in purchasing power, healthcare in the private sector is likely to increase in terms of hospitals, diagnostic centers, etc. This is identified as a thrust area by many who have identified the vision in the next two decades for medical tourism and low-cost applications and practice.

Section 5
Bridging the Gap and Next Steps
5.1 Focus Areas

Based on strengths, weaknesses, opportunities and threats in India likely in the next two decades, the areas where project management will find an application have been identified and these are summarized in Figure 2. The figure shows that some thrust areas are there because of positions of strength, and they represent an opportunity (e.g., availability of educated manpower in large numbers, growth in the middle-class consumer market, and requirements of processed food for a large population). For others, thrust areas are there because of weaknesses or threats (e.g., poor infrastructure facilities, water shortages and absence of pollution control systems, inadequate health care , and mismatch or inadequate skills and competencies. From this overall picture, we can identify key areas which could become focus areas where project management will be used. These are shown in Table 3.

Table 3:   Major thrust areas for applying project management.

Five major thrust areas for application of project management Opportunities and Strengths	
Services	Remote education, knowledge process outsourcing, contract research, IT
Consumer market	Products and services - new product development for consumable durable and industrial goods and services, capital projects
Food processing	New product development, capital projects
Threats and Weaknesses	
Manpower	Skills and competency development, education
Environment / Healthcare	Global warming, water shortage, pollution control, capital projects, HIV/AIDS
Infrastructure	Roads/highways, water, energy, transportation, housing

5.2 Project Management in India Today

In India, during the last decade substantial interest has been observed in the application of project management practices and certification. This is seen from chapters being set up mainly by PMI and the project management conferences and seminars being conducted at various locations. In 2005 the first world conference of IPMA outside Europe (in 40 years) was held in New Delhi.

There are seven PMI Chapters in India - New Delhi, Mumbai, Pune, Hyderabad, Bangalore, Chennai, and Trivandrum. IPMA is represented in India by Project Management Associates at New Delhi, which has one Chapter at Pune. The interest in project management certification has largely been from IT industry for PMI-based certification.

In terms of standards development, India is yet to take off as it is highly dependent on standards developed with a base in other regions such as the U.S. and Europe. There is no move as yet either to develop original standards or adapt global standards to local conditions and culture. This is also so because, barring exceptions, most of the universities, business schools, and institutes of management have not as yet been developed as research institutions but have concentrated at providing basic education. One example of an organization working on unifying the various professional bodies in project management is the Indian Project Management Forum.

5.3 Project Management Knowledge, Standards, and Thought processes

India will be a hotbed of activity in the next two decades, and therefore a large number of projects of different types and sizes and in various sectors will be implemented. This is a fertile ground for testing many of the new concepts and practices of project management. This is similar to the experience of the Software Engineering Institute (SEI), which used India's IT industry to successfully test and refine the application of CMM models. Some of the concepts and principles that we can expect to be tried and tested here could be related to program management, crisis and change management, organizational project management, participatory and collaborative project management, etc.

It is inconceivable that the large growth in the Indian economy and resultant needs of project management can be met without an active initiative in either developing or adapting standards and knowledge and conducting research based on local conditions . So this is an area where professional bodies can work in promoting projects and provid-

Table 4:   Project management applications: New areas.

New Areas – Sectors and Industries – Examples	
Tourism – particularly medical tourism	Remote education
Global warming	Nanotechnology
New Areas – Project Management – Examples	
Government	Event management
Projects within manufacturing	Managing by projects in operations
Entrepreneurial activity	New product development
Education and Training	Automobile and Auto components

ing the right environment for advancement of the project management profession in the region, and will form an important area for practitioners in the next two decades.

5.4 New Sectors and Areas for Applying Project Management

The proportion of people using project management as a discipline is increasing nearly exponentially and can be forecast for the next two decades, if not in terms of real numbers but in terms of a trend. Further, two significant developments are likely, namely an emphasis on soft skills and the unpredictable nature of project management getting more readily accepted and being the norm (Barnes,2002). In the Indian context, keeping in mind the large growth and its resultant problems of imbalances will mean many projects in new areas or requiring different methods and processes. Of these, some are required for traditional sectors such as construction or software development, and some for new areas like remote education, medical tourism, development of products using nanotechnology, etc. Project management practice can also be classified as either traditional (i.e., those which have been applied for a long time) or in new areas that are new either in India or being applied for the first time. This is shown in Table 4.

5.5 Looking Ahead

The next two decades are going to be an exciting period for project management in India. Being a country on high growth curve, project opportunities are going to be enormous. Project management professionals all over the world will find very attractive opportunities both in the economic and professional sense.

There is also very good opportunity for testing many of the newer concepts of project management here, and this will help in the expansion and growth of the profession to many non-traditional sectors and areas. As an example, during the last two decades we found the IT sector as a new entrant but now it is fully entranced as a user of project management knowledge and skills. The next two decades will see the emergence of newer sectors and applications, and this may well happen in India since it will have a large number of projects being implemented.

So, far, world over, it is being debated whether project management can be considered as a profession. Hopefully in the next two decades, the projects and its implementation in India will help in resolving this question. .

References

Abdul Kalam, A.P.J.and Rajan, Y.S (1996). *India 2020 – A vision for the new millennium.* India: Penguin Books

Ahluwalia, M.S. and Others (2007). *10% growth – Infrastructure picture.* World Economic Forum - India Economic Summit

Albright, M.K. and Others (2007). *India@Risk: Six global challenges ahead.* World Economic Forum - India Economic Summit

Barnes, M, (2002). *A long term view of project management - its past and its likely future.* 16th World Congress on Project Management - Berlin

Boston Consulting Group - CII (2003). Report of the High Level Strategic Group – India's New Opportunity – 2020 Boston Consulting Group and CII for AIMA.

Brown, J.F. and Others (2007). *Soft infrastructure: What are the skill sets for success in India?* World Economic Forum - India Economic Summit

Chidambaram, P. (2005). Comment by P Chidambaram Finance Minister in Parliament. http://www.indiadaily.com/editorial/1765.asp. India's infrastructure seen getting major boost from federal budget

Gokarn, S. (2002). *Industry in India – A look into the next quarter century.* (part of India 2025 project) Paper submitted to Center for Policy Research. www.cprindia.org

International Life Sciences Institute – India (2002). *Jaipur declaration on water quality management: Vision 2025.*

India Economic Summit (2006). *India: Meeting new expectations preliminary programme.* Report of World Economic Forum. www.weforum.org

Ireland, L. (2006) Project Management: Past, Present, Future- Article www.asapm.org. http://www.asapm.org/asapmag/m_articles.asp

Jafri, S.A. (2006). India will be third largest economy by 2025. Extracted from www.rediff.com 23 Oct 2006 http://in.rediff.com/cms/print.jsp?docpath=//money/2006/oct/23india.htm

McKinsey - CII Report (2002). *Made in India - The next big manufacturing export story*

McKinsey and Co (2007). *Powering India – Road to 2017.*

McKinsey Global Institute (2007). The *"Bird of gold"* - The rise of India's consumer market.

Meredith, R.(2007) *The elephant and the dragon: The economic rise of India and China, and what it means for the rest of us.* New York: W W Norton and Co, Inc .

Menon, S (2008). Outlook bright - 2020 period to be best years for Indian capital markets. : *Economic Times Mumbai,* Jan. 8 2008.

Prahalad, C.K. (2005). *The fortune at the bottom of the pyramid.* Wharton School Publishing. Pearson Education (Singapore) Pte Ltd., Delhi, India

Rediff.com - Article on Lecture by RA Mashelkar - India to be No 1 knowledge hub by 2025 Extracted from http://www.rediff.com//money/2003/dec/06hub.htm.

Sabharwal, J.S. (2008). The return of India and China. *The Economic Times, Chennai,* Jan. 29 2008.

Sharma, S.N. (2007). Delhi-Mumbai corridor gets bigger. *The Economic Times, Mumbai,* Jun. 24, 2007, page 1.

Wheelwright, S.C. and Clark, K.B. (1992). *Revolutionizing product development.* New York: The Free Press.Div of Simon and Schuster Inc.

Wideman, R.M. (2001). *The future of project management.* Vancouver, Canada: AEW Services. www.maxwideman.com . Extracted from http://www.maxwideman.com/papers/future/intro.htm

World Economic Forum-CII (2005). India and the world: Scenarios to 2025. Executive summary

CHAPTER 4

The Likely Future of Project Management in the PACIFIC RIM circa 2025

Brian R. Kooyman

Preamble

The challenge of responding to a hypothetical question that required "crystal ball" gazing into the future is always intriguing and perhaps a bit dangerous. One day after 2025 someone is likely to compare the visions with reality – at least good project managers will do so on the basis of monitoring projects. Like any good project manager, I have endeavoured to spread this risk by seeking the views of experienced project management professionals who contributed to my thought processes in preparing this Chapter. For this I thank them for their valuable contribution and sharing some of the responsibility for my conclusions. These special contributors are:

Dr. Bob Hunt (Macquarie Graduate School of Management – Macquarie University)
Peter Dechaineux (Commodore – retired, Royal Australian Navy)
Dr. Chris Stevens (Transfield Services)
Steven Fischer (BCA & Project Solutions)
Diane Dromgold (RNC Global Projects)
Chivonne Watt (University of Technology – UTS)
Karen Wenham (Tracey Brunstrom & Hammond)
Bill O'Toole (Events Development Specialist)

From the contribution of these people, there were some very different responses to what I expected; these had an impact on the approach I took toward my research for this chapter. Some of these responses were:

- *"My own feeling is that project management competency will become a necessary core competency of organizations (well before 2025). The reason is that with the accelerating rate of change, more and more the important changes in organizations are being carried out through projects, and organizations (and their strategic part-*

ners) need to be able to quickly and effectively form project teams, scope projects, execute, and institutionalize the gains, and then re-deploy the project team members back into the organizations. Few organizations currently possess this ability to a high degree."

- *"The Olympics in Sydney in 2000 established project management as a fundamental tool in the delivery of events. The massive construction and software projects needed to create the Sydney Olympics enabled the engineers and project managers to mix with the event managers. From the Olympics, the other major sport and other festivals adopted project management as their underlying methodology and communication tool - the Commonwealth Games in Melbourne and the Youth Day in Sydney are examples. An indication of the acceptance of project management is found in the University and TAFE (sic Tertiary and Further Education) course, all of these have project management as a core subject in their event management courses."*

- *"In the construction industry there is likely to be more modularization as on-site project management will be more of the management of components arriving 'just in time' for 'slotting' into previously assembled units. The construction industry will become more aligned to what the car industry is now, 2008. Cars are now seen as individual projects as more and more cars are built to a specific specification and NOT in batches of old. These lessons, I think, will evolve and be adopted and adapted to enable competitive advantages to be gained by completing work earlier. Working in a sequential or parallel traditional way no longer works in the IT industry, therefore much more innovation will occur in the traditional PM industries such as construction. As more regional countries see the advantages of project management they, like with technology in general, will skip a generation of 'how to do things' and create a new generation of project management – I suggest that this will be a hybrid of existing management techniques with an 'Asian' flavour utilizing western ideas."*

- *"As major infrastructure projects complete the focus for the resources industry will be portfolio management. Alliance/partnering arrangements are likely to be impacted by the relatively small pool of major players in the domestic construction/engineering industry. This trend may possibly create a number of long-term relationships between design and engineering/construction organizations to the exclusion of others. The long-term adoption of alliance/partnering agreements is likely to depend on the outcome of the first big 'blow-up' and how Government responds to underperforming projects. – Government policies on carbon/emission trading schemes and the impact on project values are likely to come under greater focus in the next ten years."*

It also became apparent that generally there was a limited extent of knowledge of the Oceania region beyond Australia and New Zealand, thus I have taken a substantial part of this chapter in understanding and explaining the region beyond the boundaries of these two better-known nations. In order to try to look into the future, it is fundamental to have a good understanding of what has happened in history and what the current status or situation is, thus much of the chapter attempts to review history and the situation today. As expected, the general results of this research verified a number of my early opinions, however I was very surprised at the extent of variation in the quantum of these opinions. A notable example was the extent of GDP wealth concentrated in the

Australasian region compared to the rest of the Oceania region, a significant difference that raises many social and foreign aid needs. Similarly, climate change is likely to have some very significant impacts that will be influenced again by foreign aid, and by technological developments and advancements from around the world.

BRIAN R. KOOYMAN August 2008

Introduction

The Pacific Rim generally refers to countries and regions around the edge of the Pacific Ocean. There are many economic centers around the Pacific Rim, such as Hong Kong, Singapore, Seoul, Tokyo, Manila, Lima, Los Angeles, Taipei, Ho Chi Minh City, Sydney, Melbourne, Brisbane, Auckland, Santiago, San Francisco, Seattle, San Diego, Portland and Vancouver.[1]

The Pacific Rim extends over many countries and continents which are more expertly addressed in this publication by other authors. For the purposes of this Chapter the geographic area covered has been restricted to what is generally recognised as "Oceania." This region (sometimes called Oceanica) is a geographical and geopolitical region consisting of numerous independent nations, predominantly islands of varying size and levels of development in the Pacific Ocean and vicinity.[1]

The exact scope of Oceania is variably defined as including Australia, New Zealand, New Guinea, and islands that are ethnologically divided into sub regions of Melanesia, Micronesia and Polynesia [1] (refer to diagram 1 below)

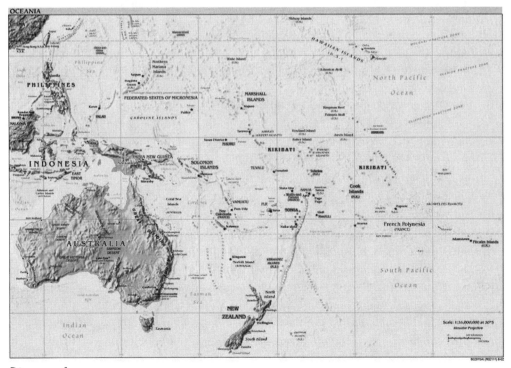

Diagram 1

Therefore, the areas identified for this chapter are as follows:

- **Australasia:** *(Includes Australia and New Zealand)*
- **Melanesia:** *(Includes Bismarck Archipelago, Fiji, Maluka Islands, New Caledonia, New Guinea-and Papua, Norfolk Island, Solomon Islands, Torres Straits Islands, Vanuatu, Flores, Nauru, Sumba, Timor)*
- **Micronesia:** *(Includes Guam, Kiribati, Marshall Islands, Federated States of Micronesia, Nauru, Northern Mariana Islands, Palau, Wake Island (US Territory)*
- **Polynesia:** *Includes American Samoa (US Territory), Anuta and Bellona Island-both in Solomon Islands, Cook Islands, Easter Island–part of Chile, French Polynesia, Niue, Hawaii, Samoa, Tokelau, Tonga, Tuvalu, Wallis and Futuna Islands (French territory)*

1. A History and Background to the Areas of Oceania
1.1 The History and Geography of Oceania
1.1.1 Melanesia:

The original inhabitants of the islands now named Melanesia were likely the ancestors of the present day Papuan-speaking people. These people are thought to have occupied New Guinea tens of millennia ago and reached the islands 35,000 years ago (according to radiocarbon dating). They appear to have occupied these islands as far east as the main islands in the Solomon Islands and perhaps even to the smaller islands farther to the east. [1]

The region began to develop western influence with the discovery by the Dutch navigators in the early 17th Century, and further discovered by Captain James Cook (British Royal Navy) in the late 18th Century. Colonization by European culture occurred during the 19th and 20th centuries by English, French, Portuguese, German and Dutch colonists. The peoples of this region are amongst the most diverse in the world linguistically, genetically, socially and culturally, and it was the European powers who fostered the illusion of "Melanesian culture". Within the "Melanesia"

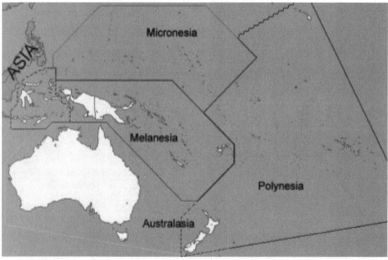

Diagram 2

region, there are countries still seen as part of other cultures, such as Papua New Guinea (the western region of New Guinea) and Western Timor, which are governed by Indonesia from Jakarta. One of the newest nations on the region is East Timor (Timor-Leste), which recently became self governing, being proclaimed a nation on May 20, 2002. [1]

1.1.2 Micronesia:

Micronesia is a region to the north of the region of Melanesia (refer to Diagram 2), consisting of many hundreds of small islands spread over a large region of the western Pacific Ocean. The term "Micronesia" was first proposed by the French explorer Jules Dumont d'Urville in 1831.

Politically, Micronesia is divided into eight nation states and territories. Guam (an incorporated territory of the United States), Kiribati, Marshall Islands, Federated States of Micronesia, Nauru, Northern Mariana Islands (an organised and incorporated territory of the United States), Palau and Wake Island (an incorporated territory of the United States). Much of "Micronesia" came under European domination when the Philippines was colonized by the Spanish in the early 17th century, being part of the Spanish East Indies. However, in the early 20th century the area was divided among three major nations:

- The United States, which took control of Guam following the Spanish-American War of 1898, and colonized Wake Island.
- Germany, which took Nauru and bought the Marshall, Caroline, and Northern Mariana Islands from Spain. Following World War 1, these territories were taken away from Germany and made into League of Nations mandates; Nauru becoming an Australian mandate, the other islands given as mandates to Japan until after World War 11, when its mandates became a United Nations Trusteeship ruled by the United States, and
- Britain, which took the Gilbert Islands (Kirabati)

Currently, all of Micronesia are independent states, with the exceptions of Guam and Wake Island (which are U.S. territories), and the Northern Mariana Islands (which is a U.S. Commonwealth).

1.1.3 Polynesia:

Geographically, Polynesia may be described as a triangle of islands with its corners at Hawaii, New Zealand and Easter Island (near South America).The other main islands included within this triangle are Samoa, Tonga, the various island chains that form the Cook Islands and French Polynesia. [1]

It is considered that the origins of the Polynesian culture spread from New Guinea around 1600 – 1200 BC, moving as far east as Fiji, Samoa and Tonga. Around 300 BC, this new Polynesian people spread from Fiji, Samoa and Tonga to the Cook Islands, Tahiti, the Tuamotus and the Marquesas Islands. Between 300 and 500 AD, the Polynesians settled Easter Island, and around 500 AD settled Hawaii, New Zealand being settled by the Polynesians around 1000 AD. The migration of the Polynesians is considered impressive as they were sailing "sight unseen" over the Pacific Ocean (an ocean covering nearly half the earth's surface) at a time when other cultures rarely sailed beyond the sight of land. [1]

European influence in the Pacific Ocean is predominantly derived from the great English and French explorers in the 18th and early 19th centuries, such as Captain James Cook (RN). Thus many of the islands are linked to France and England, although U.S. influence became significant after the Spanish-American War and World War 11[1]

1.1.4 Australasia:

For the purposes of this article, the category "Australasia" has been used only for the countries of Australia and New Zealand. This is not strictly correct as the term often includes New Guinea – which I have included as part of Melanesia.

Australia is often described as "the world's largest island" or as "the world's smallest continent." Either way, it is a substantial land mass of approximately 7,740,000 sq. km. (2,989,000 square miles), with a population of some 21,000,000 people and is the driest inhabited continent. It is considered one the oldest land masses on the planet and the first human inhabitants are estimated to have settled between 42,000 and 48,000 years ago when there was a land bridge between Australia and South East Asia.

European influence began with the discovery of the west coast of Australia by the Dutch in the early 17th century, and the east coast by Captain James Cook in 1770. Australia was settled by the English in 1788, and developed into 6 colonies, which became a federation in January 1901, and the Commonwealth of Australia was formed.

New Zealand comprises two main land masses, North Island and South Island, as well as numerous smaller islands. New Zealand is geographically located about 2000 km (1250 miles) south east of Australia, has a land mass of approximately 268,700 sq. km (103,740 sq. miles) and a population of 4,268,000 people. New Zealand's topography is significantly different from Australia's, being a recently formed land mass on the edge of what is often called the Pacific "rim of fire" – a geologically active area for earthquakes and volcanoes that stretches from New Zealand to Hawaii and the west coast of the U.S. The vegetation and climate is also radically different from Australia's, being a mountainous and wet region scoured by glaciers, glacial valleys and fjords (Australian's often refer to New Zealand as "the Land of The Long White Cloud"). New Zealand was originally settled by Polynesians in approximately 1000 AD. European discovery occurred with the Dutch explorer Abel Tasman in 1642 and the English explorer Captain James Cook (RAN) in 1769. The country was visited and partially settled by numerous European and North American whaling, sealing and trading ships, until 1840 when the British claimed sovereignty with a treaty with the Maori (the Treaty of Waitangi). In 1907 New Zealand became an independent Dominion and a fully independent nation in 1947. [1]

An Overview of the Current Economic Development of Oceania

The economy of Oceania comprises more than 14 separate countries and their associated economies. On a total scale the region has approximately 35,835,000 inhabitants spread over 30,000 islands in the South Pacific, bordered between Australasia, Asia and the American continents. The region is spread over a vast area equating to more than 25% of the Earth's surface being the Pacific Ocean and thus predominantly water. The region has a diverse mix of economies from the highly developed financial markets of Australia and New Zealand (comparable in maturity to Western Europe economies) to the much less developed economies that belong to many of the island countries in the area. [1]

Many of the smaller Pacific nations rely on trade with Australia, New Zealand and the United States for exporting goods and for accessing other products. Australia and New Zealand trading arrangements are known as Closer Economic Relations, and Australia and New Zealand (along with other countries) are members of Asia-Pacific Economic Co-operation (APEC) and the East Asia Summit (EAS), which may become trade blocs in the future. [1]

The main economic sectors within Oceania are as follows:

- Service Industry: the majority of people living in Oceania work in the service industry which includes tourism, education and financial services. Oceania's largest export markets include Japan, China, the United States and South Korea. [2]
- Manufacturing: the manufacture of clothing is a major industry in some parts of the Pacific, especially Fiji, although this is decreasing. [2]
- Tourism: has become a large source of income for many inhabitants in the Pacific, with tourists coming from Australia, New Zealand, Japan, the U.S. and the United Kingdom. [2]
- Agriculture and Fishing: surprisingly agriculture and natural resources constitutes only 5% to 10% of Oceania's total jobs, but contributes substantially to export performance. It should be noted that the most populous two nations, Australia and New Zealand, are also the most developed and have majority service industries. This dilutes the data from the less developed Pacific Island nations who have major agricultural economies. [2]. Many nations (excluding Australia and New Zealand) are still quintessentially agricultural: for example, 80% of the population of Vanuatu and 70% of the population of Fiji work in agriculture. The main produce from the Pacific is copra or coconut, timber, beef palm oil, cocoa, sugar and ginger. Old-growth logging is exploited on larger islands, including the Solomons and Papua New Guinea. Fishing provides a major industry for many of the smaller nations of the Pacific, although many fishing areas are exploited by other larger countries.
- Natural resources such as lead, zinc, nickel, iron ore and gold are mined across the west of the region, in Australia, New Zealand and the Solomon Islands. Oceania's largest export markets include Japan, China, the U.S. and South Korea. [2]
- International Aid and Charity: The most populous nations of Australia and New Zealand are both highly developed and are large international aid donors to the Oceania region, with the less developed nations still relying on foreign aid for development. In the 2007 to 2008 financial year Australia provided $AU 3.155 billion Australian dollars worth of official development assistance of which $AU 2.731 billion will be managed by AusAID (an Australian government Aid Agency). Every week, each Australian contributes around $2.40 to Australia's aid program, amounting to around 1% of the Australian Federal Government expenditure, compared to the 42% spent on social security and welfare. [2]

Table 1 indicates some interesting statistics in that:

- The two wealthiest countries in Oceania have the lowest population density, i.e. 3.2 for the region compared to an Oceania average of 4.2, Australia being the lowest country in Oceania at 2.5 people per square kilometer.

Table 1   A Summary of the Current Economic Development of Countries in
           Oceania[1]

Australasia	Area (Km2)	Population	Pop'n. Density	Administered By	Gdp ($Us-2007)	% Gdp
Australia	7,686,850	21,050,000	2.5	Sovereign state	$718.400 bill	
New Zealand	268,680	4,108,037	14.5	Sovereign state	$117.700 bill	
Regional Totals	**7,955,530**	**25,158,037**	**3.2**		**$836.100 Bill**	**95.7%**
Melanesia	**Area (Km²)**	**Population**	**Pop'n. Density**	**Administered By**	**Gdp**	**% Gdp**
Fiji	18,270	856,346	46.9	Sovereign state	$3.677 bill	
Indonesia (Oceania part only)	499,852	4,211,532	8.4	Indonesia	N/A	
New Caledonia	19,060	207,858	10.9	France	$6.183 bill	
Papua New Guinea	462,840	5,172,033	11.2	Sovereign state	$14.400 bill	
Solomon Islands	28,450	494,786	17.4	Sovereign state	$0.911 bill	
Vanuatu	12,200	196,178	16.1	Sovereign state	$0.726 bill	
Regional Totals	**1,040,672**	**11,138,733**	**10.7**		**$25.897 Bill**	**2.97%**
Micronesia	**Area (Km2)**	**Population**	**Pop'n. Density**	**Administered By**	**Gdp**	**% Gdp**
Federated States Of Micronesia	702	135,869	193.5	Sovereign state	$0.277 bill	
Guam	549	160,796	292.9	United States	$3.200 bill	
Kiribati	811	96,335	118.8	Sovereign state	$0.206 bill	
Marshall Islands	181	73,630	406.8	Sovereign state	$0.115 bill	
Nauru	21	12,329	587.1	Sovereign state	$0.0369 bill	
Northern Mariana Islands	477	77,311	162.1	United States	N/A	
Palau	458	19,409	42.4	Sovereign state	$0.1577 bill	
Regional Totals	**3199**	**575,679**	**179.9**		**$3.9926 Bill**	**0.46%**
Polynesia	**Area (Km2)**	**Population**	**Pop'n. Density**	**Administered By**	**Gdp**	**% Gdp**
American Samoa	199	68,688	345.2	United States	N/A	
Cook Islands	240	20,811	86.7	New Zealand	$0.1832 bill	
French Polynesia	4,167	257,847	61.9	France	$5.330 bill	
Niue	260	2,134	8.2	New Zealand	$0.0076 bill	
Pitcairn Island	5	47	10	United Kingdom	N/A	
Samoa	2,944	178,631	60.7	Sovereign state	$1.218 bill	
Tokelau	10	1,431	143.1	New Zealand	$0.0015 bill	
Tonga	748	106,137	141.9	Sovereign state	$0.817 bill	
Tuvalu	26	11,146	428.7	Sovereign state	$0.01494 bill	
Wallis and Futuna	274	15,585	56.9	United States	N/A	
Regional Totals	**8873**	**662,457**	**74.7**		**$7.57224 Bill**	**0.87%**
Oceania Totals	**9,008,274**	**37,534,906**	**4.2**		**$873.562 Bill.**	**100%**

- The GDP of the Australasia region is a total of US $836.1 billion compared with the Oceania total of US $873.562 billion, representing 95.7% of the wealth is in Australia and New Zealand.
- Melanesia is next at US $1.041 billion, representing 2.97% of the region's GDP.
- Micronesia and Polynesia combined have a total GDP of US $11.565 billion, representing 1.33% of the region's GDP.

When considering the population levels of each of the regions, a ratio of wealth per capita (based on the above figures as a guide) would indicate the following:

In reference to Table 2, an approximate assessment of the GDP per capita indicates a significant range across many of the nations, from over $34,000 per capita down to $1.048.22 per capita. There are only five nations that are above or near $20,000 per capita; Australia and New Zealand in the Australasia region, New Caledonia in the Melanesia region, Guam in the Micronesia region and French Polynesia in the Polynesia region. There is a significant difference between this level and the next level, which are the Cook Islands at $8,803.04 per capita.

As a result of this significant difference many of the nations are supported by Foreign aid and assistance and are desperately in need of economic support for much needed infrastructure. Other than Australia and New Zealand, the other nations in the top five per capita GDP, are New Caledonia and French Polynesia, strongly influenced by France, and Guam strongly supported by the United States.

1.3 A View of the Current Challenges Facing Oceania

Australasia (including Australia and New Zealand) tend to stand significantly apart in the developed nation or region context, so I have separated the review of the Australasian region from the Melanesian, Micronesian and Polynesian regions, addressing these latter three regions generally as the Pacific Islands region.

1.3.1 The Pacific Islands Region of Oceania

As has been generally viewed and reported,

> "The overall performance of the Pacific Island countries in the course of the past two decades has been poor. The region suffers from high unemployment and joblessness, and government services fail to meet public expectations. Several countries suffer from social or political instability, or serious crime. Some face daunting health or environmental challenges. Without an upturn in economic growth, the future for these countries is at best uncertain and at worst bleak". [2]

The PACIFIC 2020 Report prepared by the Australian Commonwealth Government in May 2006 [2] identifies and refers in much greater detail to nine growth topics, four cross-functional "growth factors," and five "productive sectors."

The Four growth factors are identified as:

- Investment (or capital)
- Labor
- Land
- Political Governance

The first three factors identified above are the traditional "factors of production" – those that are essential for growth whatever the sector. Also identified in the report is

Table 2   Per Capita Wealth[1]

Australasia	Population	GDP ($Us-2007)	GDP Per Capita ($Us)	Ranking
Australia	21,050,000	$718.400 billion	$34,128.27	1
New Zealand	4,108,037	$117.700 billion	$28,651.15	3
Regional Totals	**25,158,037**	**$836.100 Billion**	**$33,233.91**	
Melanesia	**Population**	**GDP**	**GDP Per Capita**	**Ranking**
Fiji	856,346	$3.677 billion	$4,293.83	10
Indonesia (Oceania part only)	4,211,532		N/A	n/a
New Caledonia	207,858	$6.183 billion	$29,746.27	2
Papua New Guinea	5,172,033	$14.400 billion	$2,784.20	14
Solomon Islands	494,786	$0.911 billion	$1,841.20	17
Vanuatu	196,178	$0.726 billion	$3,700.72	11
Regional Totals	**11,138,733**	**$25.897 Billion**	**$3,738.45**	
Micronesia	**Population**	**GDP**	**GDP Per Capita**	**Ranking**
Federated States Of Micronesia	135,869	$0.277 billion	$2,038.73	16
Guam	160,796	$3.200 billion	$19,900.99	5
Kiribati	96,335	$0.206 billion	$2,138.37	15
Marshall Islands	73,630	$0.115 billion	$1,561.86	18
Nauru	12,329	$0.0369 billion	$2,992.94	13
Northern Mariana Islands	77,311		N/A	N/A
Palau	19,409	$0.1577 billion	$8,126.10	7
Regional Totals	**575,679**	**$3.9926 Billion**	**$8,011.35**	
Polynesia	**Population**	**GDP**	**GDP Per Capita**	**Ranking**
American Samoa	68,688		n/a	n/a
Cook Islands	20,811	$0.1832 billion	$8,803.04	6
French Polynesia	257,847	$5.330 billion	$20,671.17	4
Niue	2,134	$0.0076 billion	$3,561.39	12
Pitcairn Island	47		N/A	n/a
Samoa	178,631	$1.218 billion	$6,818.53	9
Tokelau	1,431	$0.0015 billion	$1,048.22	20
Tonga	106,137	$0.817 billion	$7,697.6	8
Tuvalu	11,146	$0.01494 billion	$1,340.39	19
Wallis and Futuna	15,585		N/A	N/A
Regional Totals	***662,457***	***$7.57224 Billion***	***$13,097.66***	
Oceania Totals	***37,534,906***	***$873.56184 Bil.***	***$26,342.46***	

the importance of the quality of institutions or governance in a country for long term economic growth. Thus, political stability is a major consideration.

The five productive sectors are identified as:

- Agriculture   Still provides livelihoods and social security for most people in the region, and in some settings it is an important export earner.

- Fisheries   In much of the region is a basic food source, and in some different countries also provides employment, government revenue and export earnings.
- Forestry   Draws on natural resources and is fundamental to a few of the countries in the region for employment and export earnings. However, a major concern is the devastation occurring to this natural resource, particularly in the natural rainforest areas.
- Mining and Petroleum   Draws on natural resources to a few countries, but creates significant environmental issues.
- Tourism   Is a sector which is developing in a number of the Pacific Island countries, and a sector in which Pacific Islands can compete.

Some of the above sectors offer abundant growth opportunities. Agriculture, fisheries and tourism clearly fall into this category. However, they all involve important management challenges. The logging of natural forests is currently being carried out in an unsustainable way. Unsustainable practices are also a risk for fisheries. Mining is seen as an unsustainable activity, the risk being the extraction of minerals without effective governance. This will not only cause local environmental damage, but also generate prosperity in the short term and do nothing to lay the foundations of long-term growth.

A developing risk to the natural resources of fisheries and minerals/petroleum in the Pacific region's international waters is the encroachment of larger, more developed, and more powerful nations exploiting and claiming these natural resources. This effect is already impacting on the stocks of fish; which to many of the Pacific nations is a food fundamental, as well as a potential source of income. These small islands have very little ability to protest and/or enforce their claims to these resources, due to their relative economic size[2].

Excluding Australasia, the Oceania regions vary enormously in population, wealth, GDP per capita and other social indicators such as literacy, etc. All of these nations are highly vulnerable to external or unforseen shocks – natural (such as volcanic, earthquake, and particularly climate change), political, as well as economic. Many of these countries are experiencing low levels of employment, which in turn is leading to poverty, social and political instability, and crime. This lack of employment manifests itself not only in the unemployed (those looking for work) but also in the large number that withdraw from the workforce altogether. These are the "inactive" – neither working nor studying.

The employment challenge the Pacific Islands are facing is large because of the rapid population growth some countries are continuing to experience. Population growth rates are slowing, but remain high outside of Polynesia. The total population of the Pacific Islands was estimated in 2003 to be 8.4 million, up from 2.5 million in 1950.[2] In the next 50 years, the population of the Pacific Islands may well double, due to rapid growth in Melanesia and Micronesia.

Other than the immediate problem of unemployment or "joblessness," there are other challenges that the Pacific Island countries currently face or will face in the future to 2025. [2]

- Health: The traditional communicable diseases, such as malaria and tuberculosis, are thriving in the Pacific, whilst HIV/AIDS is ravaging Papua New Guinea[2]. However, it is the non-communicable diseases such as cancer and diabetes (now at or exceeding levels in developed countries) that is the greatest burden for many Pacific nations.[2]

- Education: Some countries now have a large number of out-of-school children. Some still have a rapidly growing number of children to educate. In many Pacific Island nations, student performance indicates low levels of literacy and numeracy. [4]
- Environment: A recent report by the World Bank (2006b, p.viii) concluded that *"there is no doubt that disasters in the region are becoming more intense and probably more frequent."* Climate change for the Pacific point to *"more extreme conditions and increased climate variability..."*[4]. Average temperatures are expected to rise by between 1.0 and 3.1^0C. Sea level is expected to rise by between 9 and 90 centimetres by the end of the century. Cyclones are expected to increase in intensity by about 5 – 20 %. For the low-lying atolls, the economic cost would be particularly large. Other pressing environmental problems faced by the Pacific Island nations include waste disposal. In Kiribati, faecal contamination of shellfish because of inadequate sanitation in Tarawa is the cause of outbreaks of diarrhoeal diseases, hepatitis, and sometimes cholera (Nukuro 2000) [2].
- Urbanization: Higher levels of population growth are likely to result in higher levels of urbanization, which will require increased spending on infrastructure from roads to solid waste management, and a lack of jobs is likely to lead to a rise in urban crime and thus adequate police forces to manage such. [2]
- Poverty: Despite poor data, there is now a consensus that poverty is a serious problem in the Pacific Islands. It does not result in malnutrition, as it does in some other areas, but it is reflected in difficulties in meeting basic needs such as adequate shelter and health care. [2]
- Transportation: Due to the extensive distances in the Pacific Island region, the cost of travelling between these nations is extremely expensive for both local residents and for transport of goods and foods. Both air transport and sea transport is limited and expensive. [2]
- Telecoms: The Pacific Islands region is separated over a wide area predominantly consisting of ocean, and as a result the sophistication of telecommunications is very low compared with many other areas around the world. The region lacks infrastructure and the capital to develop more advanced telecommunications systems. [2]

Addressing the factors identified above will preoccupy much of the anticipated development of the Pacific Islands in the foreseeable future, and increase reliance on the more developed nations who have interests or influence in the region. Such nations include Australia, New Zealand, the United States and France, as well as members of ASEAN. The region currently receives aid and assistance, and will continue to need assistance from the United Nations and the World Bank.

1.3.2 The Australasian Region of Oceania

As clearly identified in Tables 1 and 2, a significant proportion of the region's GDP rests with Australia and New Zealand. These two nations are also recognised as developed countries regarding their economies and social infrastructure.

Australia is an extremely large land mass with a comparatively small population. It has a well developed financial industry, a large agricultural and mining industry base for exports, but needs substantial capital for the development of capital infrastructure works to support a larger population and manufacturing base. The cost of labor in Australia is high compared to the manufacturing "powerhouses" of nations nearby, such as China, South East Asia and Indonesia; thus, Australia is limited by population size and the cost of labor. The nation has a high standard of living (by world standards), which has been built on the agricultural industry and over the last four decades by the export of minerals. By far the majority of the population is urbanized living in major cities located on the seaboard of the continent, and is supported by sophisticated health, education, business, and legal systems. The areas of the country outside the cities are sparsely populated, with distance and isolation being the major impediments to development. Australia is often described as the driest populated country in the world, and with the advent of climate change, needs to address the conservation of its environment and water supplies (both natural and man-made).

New Zealand is a smaller nation located approximately 2000 km (1250 miles) to the east of Australia, comprising two main land masses (the North Island and the South Island) and numerous smaller islands. Similar to Australia, New Zealand has a predominantly European background, being a constitutional monarchy with a parliamentary democracy. New Zealand has a modern, prosperous economy, with a relatively high standard of living. The country is heavily dependent on trade, particularly agricultural products, although tourism is playing a significant role in the nation's economy. Like Australia, the country is also predominantly urbanized, with 72.2% of the population living in 16 main urban areas, half living in the four major cities. Similar to Australia, the population is supported by sophisticated health, education, business, and legal systems. New Zealand receives significant rainfall, but has a geology that is subject to volatility, being part of the Pacific "ring of fire," thus is subject to earthquakes.

1.3.3 A Summation of the Current Challenges Facing Each Nation of Oceania

The following series of tables summarises each nation's current status of development and reliance on external assistance. Australasia is included in Table 3A, Melanesia in Table 3B, Micronesia in Table 3C; and Polynesia in Table 3D:

As indicated in the Table 3 series, the **Australasian** region has well-developed economies, sophisticated financial markets, political stability, and is self supporting; the region has a population of over 25 million and a GDP over $(US)836 billion. The individual wealth of the population is substantially higher than any other region in Oceania, and compares well with the rest of the world.

The **Melanesian** region is generally underdeveloped, except for New Caledonia, which benefits from assistance and administration from France. This region significantly lacks infrastructure, health and education facilities, and is unsophisticated in its financial markets. Although it has the second highest population (over 11 million) and the second highest GDP of US $25.9 billion, it has the lowest individual wealth in Oceania. The wealthiest per capita nation is New Caledonia, followed by Fiji, which has political stability concerns to overcome if growth is to be achieved in the future. Other than Fiji, a significant improvement in education is required. As has previously occurred on three occasions in Fiji, this region is becoming more prone to natural disasters such as cyclones (hurricanes), but does not have the resources to manage such events.

Table 3A

Country	Pop'n	Gdp Wealth	Infra-Structure	Political Stability	Self Supporting	Health Rating	Education**	Threats
AUSTRALASIA								
Australia	21 mill.	$ 718.4 bill. $(US)	Good in urban areas, needs development outside urban areas	Stable, sovereign state	Yes	good	High level and high literacy rate. Tertiary education standards high	Lacks human and financial resources to develop infrastructure for transport, roads telecommunications. Isolation makes transport expensive
New Zealand	4.1 mill.	$117.7 bill. $(US)	Good in urban areas, needs development outside urban areas	Stable, sovereign state	Yes	good	High level and high literacy rate. Tertiary education standards high	Lacks human and financial resources to develop infrastructure for transport, roads telecommunications. Isolation makes transport expensive

** – based on literacy rates 2004[2]

Table 3B

Country	Pop'n	Gdp Wealth	Infra-Structure	Political Stability	Self Supporting	Health Rating	Education**	Threats
MELANESIA								
Fiji	0.86 mill.	$3.7 bill $(US).	Limited except for tourist facilities	Republic under military rule	No, receives economic aid	Average, needs development	93% adult pop'n	Political stability and natural disasters will hinder growth. Reliant on tourism
New Caledonia	0.21 mill.	$6.2 bill. $(US)	Locally adequate supported by French influence	Stable under French administration	No, receives economic aid from France	Average, needs development	N/A	Potential for growth through tourism, provided it continues to be supported through France
Papua New Guinea	5.1 mill.	$14.4 bill. $(US)	Very poor and under-developed	Potentially unstable due to high joblessness	No, receives economic aid from Australia and World Bank	Limited, needs development	57% adult pop'n	Political stability, major infrastructure development required to allow growth
Solomon Islands	0.495 mill	$0.91 bill. $(US)	Very poor except for tourist facilities	Sovereign state currently seen as stable-potential ethnic problems	No, receives economic aid from Australia, European Union, NZ and China	Limited, needs development	30% adult pop'n	Major infrastructure development required to allow growth, likely to be through tourism. Needs to improve educational facilities
Vanuatu	0.196 mill.	$0.73 bill. $(US)	Limited except for tourist facilities	Sovereign state currently seen as stable	No, receives economic aid from Asian Devpt. Bank	Limited, needs development	34% adult pop'n	Major infrastructure development required to allow growth, likely to be through tourism. Needs to improve educational facilities

** – based on literacy rates 2004[2]

TABLE 3C

Country	Pop'n	Gdp Wealth	Infra-Structure	Political Stability	Self Supporting	Health Rating	Education**	Threats
MICRONESIA								
Fed States Of Micronesia	0.136 mill.	$0.28.4 bill. $(US)	Limited & basic, viewed as locally adequate	Sovereign state currently seen as stable	No, receives economic aid from the U.S.	N/A	95% adult pop'n	Future growth is tied to U.S support and economic aid
Guam	0.161 mill.	$3.2 bill. $(US)	Locally adequate supported by U.S. influence	Stable under U.S. administration	No, receives economic aid from the U.S.	N/A	N/A	Future growth is tied to U.S support and economic aid. Growth seen with relocation of U.S. forces to Guam
Kiribati	0.096 mill.	$0.206 bill. $(US)	Very poor and under-developed	Sovereign state currently seen as stable	No, receives economic aid from the U.K. and Japan	Limited, needs development	93% adult pop'n	Rising sea levels are a threat to land mass existence. Two atolls have already disappeared
Marshall Islands	0.074 mill.	$0.12 bill. $(US)	Basic, but locally adequate -supported by U.S. influence	Sovereign state currently seen as stable	No, receives economic aid from the U.S.	N/A	92% adult pop'n	Future growth is tied to U.S support and economic aid
Nauru	0.012 mill.	$0.04 bill. $(US)	Very poor and under-developed	Sovereign state currently seen as stable	No, receives economic aid from Australia	Limited, needs development	95% adult pop'n	Faces major problem as phosphate reserves diminish, needs external aid
N. Mariana Islands	0.077 mill	unknown	Locally adequate supported by U.S. influence	Stable under U.S. administration	No, receives economic aid from the U.S.	N/A	N/A	Future growth is tied to U.S support and economic aid
Palau	0.019 mill.	$0.16 bill. $(US)	Limited & basic, viewed as locally adequate	Sovereign state currently seen as stable	Self supporting but receives some aid from the U.S.	Limited, needs development	91% adult pop'n	Future growth is tied to U.S support and economic aid

** – based on literacy rates 2004[2]

TABLE 3D

Country	Pop'n	Gdp Wealth	Infra-Structure	Political Stability	Self Supporting	Health Rating	Education**	Threats
POLYNESIA								
American Samoa	0.069 mill.	unknown	Locally adequate supported by U.S. influence	Stable under U.S. administration	No, receives economic aid from the U.S.	N/A	N/A	Future growth is tied to U.S support and economic aid
Cook Islands	0.021 mill.	$0.183 bill. $(US)	Basic, viewed as locally adequate	Stable under New Zealand administration	No, receives economic aid from New Zealand	Limited, needs development	94% adult pop'n	Future growth is tied to N.Z support and economic aid
French Polynesia	0.258 mill.	$5.33 bill. $(US)	Locally adequate supported by French influence	Stable under French administration	No, receives economic aid from France	N/A	N/A	Future growth is tied to French support and economic aid
Niue	0.002 mill.	$0.008 bill. $(US)	Basic, viewed as locally adequate	Stable under New Zealand administration	No, receives economic aid from New Zealand	Limited, needs development	95% adult pop'n	Future growth is tied to N.Z support and economic aid
Pitcairn Island	47	unknown	unknown	Under U.K. administration		N/A	N/A	N/A
Samoa	0.179 mill.	$1.218 bill. $(US)	Basic, viewed as locally adequate	Sovereign state currently seen as stable	No, receives economic aid from Australia NZ and Japan	Limited, needs development	99% adult pop'n	Future growth is tied to Australian and N.Z support and economic aid
Tokelau	0.001 mill.	$0.002 bill. $(US)	Very poor and under-developed	Stable under New Zealand administration	No, receives economic aid from New Zealand	Limited, needs development	N/A	Future growth is tied to N.Z support and economic aid
Tonga	0.106 mill.	$0.817 bill. $(US)	Basic, viewed as locally adequate	Sovereign state currently seen as stable	No, receives economic aid from Australia & NZ	Limited, needs development	99% adult pop'n	Future growth is tied to Australian and N.Z. support and economic aid
Tuvalu	0.011 mill.	$0.014 bill. $(US)	Very poor and under-developed	Sovereign state currently seen as stable	No, receives economic aid from Australia Japan and U.S.	Limited, needs development	95% adult pop'n	Rising Sea levels is a threat to land mass existence
Wallis & Futuna	0.015 mill.	unknown	Locally adequate supported by U.S. influence	Stable under U.S. administration	No, receives economic aid from the France	N/A	N/A	Future growth is tied to U.S support and economic aid

** – based on literacy rates 2004[2]

The **Micronesian** region is the smallest populated region (approx. 576,000), but is assisted through the foreign aid and economic influence, predominantly from the United States. The region consists predominantly of small island nations in the northern section of Oceania - Pacific Ocean. Distance between the islands is significant, and travel and transportation for exports is difficult and expensive. Infrastructure is limited, and financial markets are unsophisticated. The GDP of the region is the lowest in Oceania, being US $4 billion, but the individual wealth is the third-highest in Oceania, lifted significantly by Guam and Palau who receive aid from the United States. The political stability is generally good, and literacy levels are generally high. However, the region relies heavily on external support economically, and the region is prone to natural disasters, particularly Kiribati, which is under threat due to sea-level increases.

The **Polynesian** region is the second-smallest populated region (approx. 662,000), and is virtually reliant on foreign aid and economic influence, predominantly from the United States. Similar to Micronesia, the region consists predominantly of small island nations spread over a vast area of the eastern section of Oceania - Pacific Ocean. Distance between the islands is significant, and travel and transportation for exports is difficult and expensive. Infrastructure is limited, and financial markets are unsophisticated. The GDP of the region is the second-lowest in Oceania, being US $7.6 billion, but the individual wealth is the second highest in Oceania, lifted significantly by French Polynesia, which receives economic aid from France.

It is apparent that Oceania splits into two distinct spheres of development, one dominated by the developed nations of Australasia, and the second being the under-developed nations of Melanesia, Micronesia and Polynesia. This places a significant responsibility on Australia and New Zealand to provide stability and assistance/aid to the rest of the region. There are some small island nations that are managing reasonably well, but all of these nations rely on external assistance from Australia, New Zealand, the United States, France and the World and ASEAN Development Banks. Should this assistance be withdrawn, these countries would probably face the same problems the other small nations are facing. The small size of these nations in this vast area of ocean also creates unique problems in travel, export, infrastructure development, health, education, and ability to respond and manage natural disasters (particularly in the light of climate change).

2 Current Project Management Maturity in Oceania
2.1 Project Management Maturity Modelling Basis

There are a number of project management maturity models being promoted within the project management discipline at present, and for the purposes of a general maturity assessment for the regions of Oceania, I have adopted the Clifford F. Gray and Erik W. Larson model for this evaluation.

The model indicated in Table 4 is referenced from "Project Management—The Managerial Process", third edition by Clifford F. Gray and Erik W. Larson; ISBN-10:0-07-297863-5; published by McGraw Hill/Irwin -2006). This model is developed from various versions, but endeavours to "focus less on process and more on the state an organization has evolved to in managing projects." This seemed more appropriate for this study than the more specific models available. On this basis the various levels can be described as follows:

Table 4

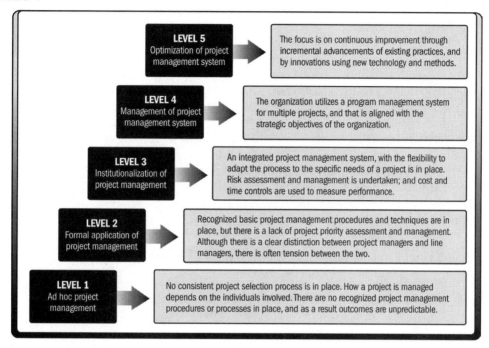

Level 1: Ad hoc project management.

- No consistent project selection or project management process is in place.
- The management of these projects is dependant on the individuals involved, and therefore outcomes are unpredictable.
- Project management training and systems implementation are non-existent.
- Project management practices are not recognised as established policies or procedures.[5]

Level 2: Formal application of project management.

- Recognized project management procedures and processes are utilized, notably for scope definition and work breakdown structures, and with a growing recognition of the need for cost management.
- There is a clear distinction between project managers and line managers, It is understood by each of the respective operatives and the organization.
- There is a lack of project priority assessment or management.
- Quality control is recognized but not integrated into project management systems.
- Project management training is provided in a limited framework. [5]

Level 3: Institutionalization of project management.

- An integrated project management system, with the flexibility to adapt the process to the specific needs of a project.

- An integrated project management framework exists, supported by planning templates, status report systems, and guidelines/checklists for each stage of the project life cycle.
- Project priority assessment and management is based on a formal set of criteria.
- Quality control is integrated as part of the project delivery process, and promoted within the project team.
- Risk assessment is undertaken, technically analyzed, and identified risks are managed.
- The organization undertakes skill-based training in project management, and measures the improvement in organizational skills.
- Cost control is related to time control, and is used to measure and monitor performance based on earned value analysis.
- Sophisticated change control systems are in place
- Cost and schedule tools are developed for each project.
- Project audits tend to be performed only when a project fails. [5]

Level 4: Management of Project Management System.

- Program management systems are recognized and implemented throughout the organization. Projects are selected based on resource capacity.
- Portfolio project management is practiced; projects are selected based on contribution to strategic goals.
- A project priority system is clearly established and practiced.
- Project work is integrated with ongoing operations.
- Benchmarking is part of the practice for continual improvement.
- Project audits are regular occurrences on major projects to ensure lessons learned are implemented on other and future projects.
- Quality initiatives are integrated into project delivery systems to improve the quality of outcomes.
- A tracking system is used to monitor resource usage and performance.
- Organizations at this level often have established a project management office or Center for Excellence. [5]

Level 5: Optimization of Project Management System.

- A project management information system is used that is highly effective in providing information to different stakeholders.
- Has an inherent organizational culture that naturally seeks improvement.
- Shows increased flexibility in adapting the project management process to the specific needs of a each project..
- The focus is on continuous improvement through incremental advancements of existing practices and by innovations using new technologies and methods. [5]

2.2 Assessment of Current Project Management Maturity in Oceania

As described in section 1.3.3, there are two distinct spheres of development and economic maturity in the region, splitting into Australasia and Micronesia, Melanesia, and Polynesia. Assessing each of these regions into Australasia and Pacific Islands (the other three regions, Melanesia, Micronesia and Polynesia, combined), the level of project management skills and maturity is similar to the assessed economic and social assessment. Thus I have assumed that Australasian countries have a measurable project management maturity, but the Pacific Island nations have a Level 1 maturity (i.e., ad hoc) or are reliant on the countries that support them.

A tabulation of this assessment based on the maturity model adopted for this study, and for Australia and New Zealand only, is as follows:

Table 5

AUSTRALASIA			
Country	**Commentary**	**PM Institutes**	**Assessed Maturity Level**
AUSTRALIA			
Generally	Active project management organizations, application within certain industries is mature, but not across all industries. Little evidence of organizational capabilities in project based management.	• AIPM, • PMI Chapters	LEVELS 2 to 3, some industries moving to LEVEL 4
Mining	Professional project managers and program managers, with some mining organizations moving toward project-based management in multiple projects, and becoming aligned to strategic management. Project management is more traditional in this industry, and has been used since the late 1960's.		LEVEL 3
Financial	Limited use of project managers except for relocations or development work, although recent trends indicate a move toward project management principles on an organizational basis		LEVEL1 moving toward LEVEL 2
Engineering & Construction	Professional project managers and program managers, with some contracting/construction organizations moving toward project-based management in multiple projects, and becoming aligned to strategic management. Project management is more traditional in this industry, and has been used since the late 1950's and early 1960's.	Institute of Engineers Australia	LEVEL 3 moving toward LEVELS 4 and 5
Defence	Defence Material Organization (DMO – procurement arm of Defence) is undertaking the development of a strong competency in project-based management (e.g., coaching, audits, health checks, etc.) and traditional project management (complex project management framework). Working jointly with U.K. and U.S. defense organizations to refine and develop this process.		LEVEL2 moving toward LEVELS 3 and 4

(continued)

Table 5 *(continued)*

AUSTRALASIA *(continued)*			
Country	**Commentary**	**PM Institutes**	**Assessed Maturity Level**
AUSTRALIA			
IT & Telecoms	Quite varied and a wide range. Some organizations are currently at developing a system of managing multiple projects and seeking to move to optimize practices through continued improvement. There is a wide range of maturity; the more advanced maturity is used by multinational organizations and Telecom Australia.		LEVEL2 moving toward LEVELS 3 and 4 (and in some cases perhaps LEVEL 5), but the predominant indicator is immature development of individual skills.
Other	The extent of project management application in the foreign aid area is very limited, being used in the employment of contract project managers for individual aid projects, but not on an organizational basis. A similar approach is utilised in response to natural emergencies, although the specific application in response to emergencies is an extremely high level of maturity.		Foreign Aid at LEVELS 1 to 2 Natural Emergencies at LEVELS 2 to 3
NEW ZEALAND			
Generally	Similar levels of maturity as Australia, due to the close relationship between the two countries. Active project management organizations, application within certain industries is mature, but not across all industries. Little evidence of organizational capabilities in project-based management	• PMI Chapter	LEVELS 2 to 3, some industries moving to LEVEL 4
Mining	Limited development of mining in New Zealand, as it is predominantly agricultural and knowledge-based economy. Mining is assessed as limited in project management maturity, due to the small nature of the mining projects.		LEVEL 1 moving toward LEVEL 2
Financial	Limited use of project managers except for relocations or development work, although recent trends indicate a move toward project management principles on an organizational basis		LEVEL1 moving toward LEVEL 2
Engineering & Construction	Professional project managers and program managers with some contracting/ construction organizations are moving toward project-based management in multiple projects. Project management is more traditional in this industry, and is aligned toward Australian companies that also work in New Zealand.		LEVEL 2 moving toward LEVELS 3 and 4

Table 5 *(continued)*

AUSTRALASIA *(continued)*			
Country	**Commentary**	**PM Institutes**	**Assessed Maturity Level**
Defence	Fairly limited as New Zealand has a small defence force and cooperates closely with the Australian Defence organizations through alliances and joint projects such as the ANZAC Frigates project.		LEVEL 1 possibly moving toward LEVEL 2
IT & Telecoms	Similar to Australia, being varied and a wide range of skills. As a result there is a wide range of maturity; the more advanced maturity is used by multinational organizations and on smaller projects		LEVEL2 moving toward LEVELS 3 and 4, immature development of individual skills.
Other	Again, similar to Australia, the extent of project management application in the foreign aid area appears to be very limited. A more mature approach is utilized on response to natural emergencies, although the specific application in response to emergencies is an extremely high level of maturity.		Foreign Aid at LEVELS 1 to 2 Natural Emergencies at LEVELS 2 to 3
PACIFIC ISLANDS (OCEANIA Grouped to include Melanesia, Micronesia and Polynesia)			
Generally	As previously described, struggling to be self supporting, and therefore immature in project management maturity, unless imported through external relationships with more developed nations. Assessed as "ad hoc."	Not aware of any	LEVEL 1 Ad hoc, depends on others

3 Projected Future Economic Growth and Development in Oceania

In order to consider the hypothetical for the future development of project management in 2025, the unique geographical, topographical and socio-economic nature of Oceania needs to be projected forward to a similar time-frame. Thus, the projected growth and a consideration of the potential threats to the area have to be understood prior to projecting project management maturity to 2025.

Identified from Table 6, it is apparent that the region is unlikely to change its overall split into two spheres of influence, one sphere being significantly dominant (i.e., the Australasian region) and the other continuing to struggle for growth, and socio-economic development.

Australasia will increase its GDP wealth to US $1,947.871 billion, an increase of $1,112 billion, and will increase its percentage of the total wealth of Oceania (i.e., from 95.7% to 96.23%).

The Pacific Islands region of Oceania (Melanesia, Micronesia and Polynesia) will increase its GDP wealth to US $14.16 billion, an increase of US $6.6 billion, but has a lower percentage of the overall wealth of Oceania than previously.

TABLE 6

Australasia	Current GDP ($Us-2007)	GDP Growth Rate Per Annum (Assumed)	Anticipated GDP	Increase In GDP	% GDP of Oceania	Pop'n. Increase Per Annum	Rank'g GDP Per Capita
Australia	$718.400 bill	4.4%	$1,699.72 bill	$981.316 bill	83.97%	2.0%	1 (1)*
New Zealand	$117.700 bill	3.8%	$248.155 bill	$130.455 bill	12.26%	1.5%	2 (3)*
REGIONAL TOTALS	**$836,100 bill**		**$1,947.871 bill**	**$1,111.771 bill**	**96.23%**		
Melanesia	**Current GDP ($Us-2007)**	**GDP Growth Rate Per Annum (Assumed)**	**Anticipated Gdp**	**Increase In GDP**	**% GDP of Oceania**	**Pop'n. Increase Per Annum**	**Rank'g GDP Per Capita**
Fiji	$3.677 bill	5.8%	$11.356 bill	$7.679 bill	0.56%	4.0%	9 (10)*
Indonesia (Oceania part)	n/a	n/a	n/a	n/a	n/a	n/a	n/a
New Caledonia	$6.183 bill	4.4%	$14.629 bill	$8.446 bill	0.72%	2.5%	3 (2)8
Papua New Guinea	$14.400 bill	2.9%	$25.508 bill	$11.108 bill	1.26%	3.5%	15 (14)
Solomon Islands	$0.911 bill	5.8%	$2.813 bill	$1.902 bill	0.14%	4.0%	13 (17)
Vanuatu	$0.726 bill	1.1%	$0.904 bill	$.178 bill	0.05%	3.0%	14 (11)
REGIONAL TOTALS	**$25.897 bill**		**$55.209 bill**	**$29.312 bill**	**2.73%**		
Micronesia	**Current GDP ($Us-2007)**	**Growth Rate Per Annum (Assumed)**	**Anticipated Gdp**	**Increase In GDP**	**% GDP of Oceania**	**Pop'n. Increase Per Annum**	**Rank'g GDP Per Capita**
Fed. States Of Micronesia	$0.277 bill	1%	$0.338 bill	$0.061 bill	0.017%	3.0%	18 (16)
Guam	$3.200 bill	3.2%	$6.008 bill	$2.808 bill	0.297%	3.0%	4 (5)
Kiribati	$0.206 bill	1.5%	$0.277 bill	$0.071 bill	0.014%	2.0%	16 (15)
Marshall Islands	$0.115 bill	1%	$0.140 bill	$0.025 bill	0.007%	2.0%	19 (18)
Nauru	$0.0369 bill	1%	$0.045 bill	$0.008 bill	0.002%	1.5%	12 (13)
North'n Mariana Islands		n/a	n/a	n/a	n/a	n/a	n/a

	Current GDP ($Us-2007)	Growth Rate Per Annum (Assumed)	Anticipated Gdp	Increase In GDP	% GDP of Oceania	Pop'n. Increase Per Annum	Rank'g GDP Per Capita
Palau	$0.1577 bill	1%	$0.192 bill	$0.035 bill	0.01%	2.0%	8 (7)
REGIONAL TOTALS	$3.9926 bill		$7.001 bill	$3.009 bill	0.346%		
Polynesia							
American Samoa		n/a	n/a	n/a	n/a	n/a	n/a
Cook Islands	$0.1832 bill	0.1%	$0.187 bill	$0.004 bill	0.009%	2.0%	10 (6)
French Polynesia	$5.330 bill	3%	$9.627 bill	$4.297 bill	0.476%	3.0%	5 (4)
Niue	$0.0076 bill	1%	$0.009 bill	$0.002 bill	0.0005%	2.0%	11 (12)
Pitcairn Island		n/a	n/a	n/a	n/a	n/a	n/a
Samoa	$1.218 bill	5%	$3.232 bill	$2.014 bill	0.160%	3.0%	6 (9)
Tokelau	$0.0015 bill	2%	$0.002 bill	$0.001 bill	0.0001%	2.0%	20
Tonga	$0.817 bill	1.4%	$1.079 bill	$0.262bill	0.053%	2.0%	7 (8)
Tuvalu	$0.01494 bill	3%	$0.027 bill	$0.012 bill	0.001%	2.0%	17 (19)
Wallis and Futuna		n/a	n/a	n/a	n/a	n/a	n/a
REGIONAL TOTALS	$7.57224 bill		$14.163 bill	$6.590 bill	0.700%		
OCEANIA TOTALS	$873.56184 bill		$2,024.244 bill	$1,151.682 bill	100%		

**Note figures in brackets (x) are previous ranking per capita based on Table 2

Overall Oceania will increase its GDP wealth from US $873.562 billion to US $2,024.244 billion, and will increase its population from some 37 million to 55 million over the same period. On average for each region, Australasia's GDP wealth per capita will increase from $33,000 to $52,000, Micronesia has increased from $3,700 to $4,000, and Melanesia from $8,000 to $8,400 and Polynesia from $13,000 to $14,000 per individual.

It is apparent that this wealth increase will increase the region's reliance on the external assistance of the two wealthy countries of Australia and New Zealand, as well as relying on support and aid from the U.S, France, Japan and increasingly China (both of whom will be seeking access to natural resources close to their own homelands). Aid will also be required from other agencies such as the World Bank and the ASEAN Development Bank.

3.1 Assessment of Future Growth for Each Nation of Oceania

However, in assessing the potential for future growth, there are many factors to be considered particularly related to the potential threats identified in Tables 3A, 3B, 3C and 3D. The potential growth areas currently identified by various sources will also have an impact on any consideration for future growth and development. A review on a nation-by-nation basis is as follows:

3.1.1 Australasia

Australia:
Current GDP: US $718,400,000,000 Projected GDP: US $1,699,715,743,227
Current Population: 21,050,000 Projected Population: 31,279,193
Current Growth Areas: Australia has over recent years been enjoying a minerals export boom that has and is currently supporting a strong economy. Infrastructure development is progressing at an increasing rate both through private and public expenditure. The financial sector has a dominant role in the Oceania region and is seen as a continuing significant measure on the world financial scene. The education system is also seen at a well developed and high level, and is sought after in the region with overseas students attending educational facilities in Australia. Although the traditional agricultural markets with Europe have long been closed due to the European Common Market, Australia has developed substantial export markets with the ASEAN countries. Medical research in Australia has been at a high level comparative to its size, and Australian pharmaceutical companies are beginning to seek offshore markets to promote their products. Since the Sydney Olympics in 2000, there has been some increase in tourism, but this tends to fluctuate as Australia is very distant from the wealthier and larger population centers.

Potential Growth Areas: With the closer developing relations between Australia and its neighbors in Asia (particularly China and Japan), South East Asia and closer relations with India, the future for Australian resource exports is likely to continue and perhaps increase. Moving to a knowledge-based economy that utilizes its educational system to encourage research and development, Australia has the potential to improve relationships and trade with larger developed neighbours in the ASEAN region.

Current Threat Areas: Distance and isolation from other developed nations and traditional markets. A small population living in a large land mass, and an environment requiring significant financial and manpower resources to develop. Isolation from other parts of the globe, meaning transport and travel is expensive and time consuming.

Potential Threat Areas: Climate change, which could impact on the already limited water supplies and river systems in the country – thus affecting agriculture and export of food. Small manufacturing base, and if there is a significant reduction in the demand for raw materials and resources, the Australian economy may suffer.

Anticipated Scenario 2025: Australia will continue to increase its population, predominantly by immigration, will significantly increase trade and relations with China, South East Asia, India, and Japan. It will take on a greater financial and assistance role with the less developed nations of Oceania. It will continue to develop and maintain its educational and health systems, particularly in the international arena. It will still be comparatively underdeveloped and will need to spend more on infrastructure for transport, mining and telecommunications. It will need to move more rapidly to a knowledge-based economy, to diversify its exports from raw materials and agriculture. It will be moving toward water and river system conservation and there is already an increase in desalination plants and alternative power sources such as wind and solar.

New Zealand:
Current GDP: US $117.700,000   Projected GDP: US $248,155,287
Current Population: 4.108,037   Projected Population: 5,532,930

Current Growth Areas: New Zealand is already moving more toward a knowledge-based economy, and industrializing some areas particularly food processing, steel fabrication, and wood and paper products. Tourism to New Zealand is also a growth area, but is constrained by distance and the cost of travel. New Zealand has substantial hydroelectric power and sizeable reserves of natural gas.

Potential Growth Areas: Being closely located and aligned with Australia, New Zealand's potential growth is similar to that assessed for Australia, in that it has the opportunity to develop closer relationships with its neighbors in Asia (particularly China and Japan), South East Asia, and India. This provides a much increased market for its export goods, away from the traditional markets of Europe. New Zealand has an excellent educational and health system, and the potential to export these knowledge areas.

Current Threat Areas: Similar to Australia, distance and isolation from other developed nations and traditional markets is a threat. New Zealand has a very small population living on two main islands and still heavily dependent on agriculture. It is isolated from other parts of the globe, meaning transport and travel is expensive and time consuming.

Potential Threat Areas: New Zealand's wealth is predominantly linked to Australia's, thus any economic pressures that Australia faces tends to translate to New Zealand. The New Zealand economy is perceived as successful, although it does currently have a large current account deficit. There has been a significant increase in net foreign debt – predominantly held by the private sector in New Zealand. The country is also prone to earthquakes, being located on the Pacific "rim of fire," and therefore needs to take account of the potential for natural disasters in the futures.

Anticipated Scenario 2025: New Zealand will marginally increase its population, predominantly by immigration. It will significantly increase trade and relations with China, South East Asia, India, and Japan. It will take on a greater financial and assistance role with the less developed nations of Oceania. It will continue to develop and maintain its educational and health systems, particularly in the international arena. It will still be underdeveloped and will need to spend more on infrastructure for transport and telecommunications. It will need to continue to move to a knowledge-based economy, to continue to diversify its exports from predominantly agriculture.

3.1.2 Melanesia
Fiji

Current GDP: US $3,677,000,000   Projected GDP: US $11,355,518,884
Current Population: 856,346   Projected Population: 1,876,360

Current Growth Areas: Fiji has suffered three political coups over the last two decades, and this has severely hampered current growth areas. The country is endowed with forest, mineral, and fish resources and is one of the more developed of the Pacific Island economies. Tourism is also a major growth area but is volatile dependent on the political stability of the nation, and the cost of travel.

Potential Growth Areas: The predominant aim for the government is to develop Fiji into a self-sustaining economy, rather than relying on foreign aid. A major target for Fiji is to achieve self-sufficiency in rice production, cattle farming, fishing, and forestry to help diversify the economy.

Current Threat Areas: The unstable political environment, and coping with a deficit economy, loss of skilled and professional personnel (which has the potential to affect existing educational and health systems), and natural disasters.

Potential Threat Areas: Continued instability affecting tourism and reliability of any export trade. The continuing emigration of skilled and professional personnel. Coping with a potential of increased natural disasters due to climate change.

Anticipated Scenario 2025: In an optimistic approach, Fiji has the potential to grow both its population and its GDP over the next two decades. It needs financial support for development and infrastructure to manage and maximise its natural resources. In the interim, it will continue to require substantial foreign aid and assistance.

New Caledonia

Current GDP: US $6,183,000,000   Projected GDP: US $14,628,817,428
Current Population: 207,858   Projected Population: 340,600

Current Growth Areas: New Caledonia has more than 25% of the world's known nickel resources, and the economy is volatile to the international demand for nickel, the principal source of export earnings. Cultivation is limited, with the country needing to import 20% of its food, and other than nickel, the nation requires substantial support from France and tourism.

Potential Growth Areas: Other than tourism, growth of the economy is subject to the world's demand for nickel, thus fairly limited.

Current Threat Areas: The cost of travel, and the price of nickel.

Potential Threat Areas: The extent of nickel reserves and the continued support from France.

Anticipated Scenario 2025: Tourism is being promoted for New Caledonia, and this has a potential to significantly increase due to the unique nature of the land and ecology. Other than the development of tourist facilities, the current state of the nation is unlikely to change.

Papua New Guinea

Current GDP: US $14,400,000,000   Projected GDP: US $25,507,622,871
Current Population: 5,172,033   Projected Population: 10,291,254

Current Growth Areas: Papua New Guinea is richly endowed with natural resources, but it is difficult to develop due to a rugged terrain and the high cost of developing infrastructure. Agriculture provides a subsistence livelihood for the bulk of the population. Mineral deposits including oil, copper, and gold account for 72% of export earnings.

Potential Growth Areas: The only real potential for growth is in the export of minerals and other natural resources (such as timber), and thus significant investment in the development of infrastructure, including education and health systems.

Current Threat Areas: Political stability, law and order are two fundamentals that make foreign private investment in Papua New Guinea a higher risk for foreign companies. The level of literacy and skills locally in Papua New Guinea also restricts the rate of development. The current economy can be separated into two, a subsistence sector and a market sector. Approximately 75% of the population relies on the subsistence sector, whilst the market sector is dominated by foreign investors.

Potential Threat Areas: The lack of all forms of infrastructure development, from transport, telecommunications, health, education, etc., is a major constraint over the next two decades.

Anticipated Scenario 2025: The scenario for Papua New Guinea is unlikely to change with continued foreign aid required, and development required for social infrastructure from public sources. Natural resources development will continue, subject to foreign investment form private sources.

Solomon Islands
Current GDP: US $911,000,000   Projected GDP: US $2,813,401,605
Current Population: 494,786   Projected Population: 1,084,137
Current Growth Areas: One of the least-developed nations in the world, with over 75% of its labor force engaged in subsistence farming. No notable growth areas.

Potential Growth Areas: Possibly tourism.

Current Threat Areas: Lacks educational facilities.

Potential Threat Areas: Increase in natural disasters such as cyclones.

Anticipated Scenario 2025: Very little change to the current situation with subsistence farming, fishing exploitation and substantial foreign aid required to continue.

Vanuata
Current GDP: US $726,000,000   Projected GDP: US $903,565,692
Current Population: 196,178   Projected Population: 354,319
Current Growth Areas: One of the least-developed nations in the world, with over 80% of its labor force engaged in subsistence farming. No notable growth areas.

Potential Growth Areas: Possibly fishing/marine resources due to a claimed 680,000 square kilometers.

Current Threat Areas: Lacks educational facilities, needs infrastructure development.

Potential Threat Areas: Increase in natural disasters such as cyclones. The fishing and marine resources are being exploited by foreign nations.

Anticipated Scenario 2025: Very little change to the current situation with subsistence farming, fishing exploitation and substantial foreign aid required to continue. There is some potential for tourism to increase, but this is likely from foreign private investment.

3.1.3 Micronesia
Federated States of Micronesia
Current GDP: US $277,000,000   Projected GDP: US $337,992,641
Current Population: 135,869   Projected Population: 245,395

Current Growth Areas: Primarily subsistence farming and fishing. Some islands have high grade phosphate for export. No notable growth areas.

Potential Growth Areas: Possibly fishing/marine resources.

Current Threat Areas: Needs infrastructure development.

Potential Threat Areas: Increase in natural disasters such as cyclones.

Anticipated Scenario 2025: Very little change to the current situation with subsistence farming, fishing exploitation and substantial foreign U.S. aid required to continue.

Guam

Current GDP: US $3,200,000,000   Projected GDP: US $6,008,193,680

Current Population: 160,796   Projected Population: 290,425

Current Growth Areas: Primarily relies on tourism and U.S. Department of Defense installations.

Potential Growth Areas: The transfer of 8,000 U.S. Marine Corps troops (and their dependents) planned to be transferred there in 2010-2014.

Current Threat Areas: Needs infrastructure development.

Potential Threat Areas: Increase in natural disasters such as cyclones.

Anticipated Scenario 2025: Very little change to the current situation with subsistence farming and fishing exploitation and substantial foreign U.S. aid and presence required to continue.

Kiribati

Current GDP: US $206,000   Projected GDP: US $277,452,131

Current Population: 96,335   Projected Population: 143,149

Current Growth Areas: Kiribati has few natural resources, copra and fish representing the bulk of production and exports. No notable growth areas.

Potential Growth Areas: Possibly fishing/marine resources, and tourism.

Current Threat Areas: Rising sea levels are threatening the health and extent of this nation. Needs infrastructure development.

Potential Threat Areas: Increase in natural disasters such as rising sea levels and cyclones.

Anticipated Scenario 2025: Very little change to the current situation with subsistence farming, fishing likely to continue. The nation urgently needs assistance and foreign aid to continue.

Marshall Islands

Current GDP: US $115,000,000   Projected GDP: US $140,321,855

Current Population: 73,630   Projected Population: 109,410

Current Growth Areas: Primarily relies on tourism, marine resources and farming. Also provides U.S. Army installations at Kwajalein.

Potential Growth Areas: Shipping registrations under the Marshall Islands flag, and tourism.

Current Threat Areas: Needs infrastructure development.

Potential Threat Areas: Increase in natural disasters such as cyclones.

Anticipated Scenario 2025: Very little change to the current situation with farming, fishing exploitation and substantial foreign U.S. aid and presence required to continue. There is some potential for tourism to increase, but this is likely from foreign private investment.

Nauru

Current GDP: US $36,900,000   Projected GDP: US $45,025,012

Current Population: 12,329   Projected Population: 16,605

Current Growth Areas: Has traditionally relied on the export of phosphate, but supplies are becoming depleted and this source of income is dramatically slowing.

Potential Growth Areas: Nauru's economy is seriously under threat with financial expertise being sent from Australia to assist in the economy's long-term viability and the uncertainties of rehabilitating mined land.

Current Threat Areas: The future viability of the economy, and environmental recovery.

Potential Threat Areas: Ability to remain viable without foreign aid.

Anticipated Scenario 2025: Very little change to the current situation with subsistence farming, fishing likely to continue. The nation urgently needs assistance and foreign aid to continue.

Northern Mariana Islands

Current GDP: US $N/A   Projected GDP: US $N/A

Current Population: 84,546   Projected Population: N/A

Current Growth Areas: Primarily relies on tourism and U.S. Government subsidies.

Potential Growth Areas: In its position with a free trade agreement, the country may be able to revive its garment manufacturing industry.

Current Threat Areas: Exploitation of cheap labor may force constraints of the free trade agreement.

Potential Threat Areas: Increase in natural disasters such as cyclones.

Anticipated Scenario 2025: Very little change to the current situation with subsistence farming, fishing exploitation and substantial foreign U.S. aid and presence required to continue.

Palau

Current GDP: US $157,700,000   Projected GDP: US $192,423,969

Current Population: 19,409   Projected Population: 28,841

Current Growth Areas: Primarily relies on tourism, subsistence agriculture and fishing, and U.S. financial assistance.

Potential Growth Areas: The most likely area of growth is in the tourism industry.

Current Threat Areas: Needs infrastructure development.

Potential Threat Areas: Increase in natural disasters such as cyclones.

Anticipated Scenario 2025: Very little change to the current situation with subsistence farming, fishing exploitation and substantial U.S. foreign aid required to continue. There is some potential for tourism to increase, but this is likely from foreign private investment.

3.1.4 Polynesia

American Samoa

Current GDP: US $500,000,000   Projected GDP: $US) N/A

Current Population: 68,200   Projected Population: N/A

Current Growth Areas: Primarily relies on tourism, subsistence agriculture and fishing, and U.S. financial assistance.

Potential Growth Areas: The most likely area of growth is in the existing tuna fishing and processing exports to the US, and the tourism industry.

Current Threat Areas: Needs infrastructure development, and diversification of its economy.

Potential Threat Areas: Increase in natural disasters such as cyclones.

Anticipated Scenario 2025: Very little change to the current situation with subsistence farming, fishing exploitation and substantial US foreign aid required to continue. There is limited potential for tourism to increase, but this is likely from foreign private investment.

Cook Islands
Current GDP: US $183,200,000   Projected GDP: US $186,899,018
Current Population: 20,811   Projected Population: 30,924

Current Growth Areas: Agriculture is the main base of the economy, but the economy relies heavily on external foreign aid.

Potential Growth Areas: Encourage tourism, off shore banking and expand fishing and mining industries.

Current Threat Areas: Classic Pacific Islands economic position, limited by a subsistence economy, non-diversified economy, isolation, transport costs and natural disasters.

Potential Threat Areas: Classic Pacific Islands economic position, limited by a subsistence economy, non-diversified economy, isolation, transport costs and natural disasters.

Anticipated Scenario 2025: Very little change to the current situation with subsistence farming, fishing exploitation and substantial foreign aid required to continue. There is limited potential for tourism to increase, but this is likely from foreign private investment.

French Polynesia
Current GDP: US $5,330,000,000   Projected GDP: US $9,626,572,881
Current Population: 257,847   Projected Population: 465,700
Current Growth Areas: Primarily relies on tourism and French military personnel.
Potential Growth Areas: The most likely area of growth is in the tourism industry.
Current Threat Areas: Needs infrastructure development.
Potential Threat Areas: Increase in natural disasters such as cyclones.

Niue
Current GDP: US $7,600,000   Projected GDP: US $9,273,444
Current Population: 2,134   Projected Population: 3,171

Current Growth Areas: Agriculture is the main base of the economy, but the economy relies heavily on external foreign aid.

Potential Growth Areas: Encourage tourism and expand fishing industries.

Current Threat Areas: Classic Pacific Islands economic position, limited by a subsistence economy, non-diversified economy, isolation, transport costs and natural disasters.

Potential Threat Areas: Classic Pacific Islands economic position, limited by a subsistence economy, non-diversified economy, isolation, transport costs and natural disasters.

Anticipated Scenario 2025: Very little change to the current situation with subsistence farming, fishing exploitation and substantial foreign aid required to continue. There is limited potential for tourism to increase, but this is likely from foreign private investment.

Samoa
Current GDP: US $1,218,000,000   Projected GDP: US $3,231,716,605
Current Population: 178,631   Projected Population: 322,627

Current Growth Areas: Agriculture is the main base of the economy, but the economy relies heavily on external foreign aid.

Potential Growth Areas: Encourage tourism, forestry and expand the fishing industry.

Current Threat Areas: Classic Pacific Islands economic position, limited by a subsistence economy, non-diversified economy, isolation, transport costs and natural disasters.

Potential Threat Areas: Classic Pacific Islands economic position, limited by a subsistence economy, non-diversified economy, isolation, transport costs and natural disasters.

Anticipated Scenario 2025: Very little change to the current situation with subsistence farming, fishing exploitation and substantial foreign aid required to continue. There is limited potential for tourism to increase, but this is likely from foreign private investment.

Tokelau
Current GDP: US $1,500,000   Projected GDP: US $2,228,921
Current Population: 1,431   Projected Population: 2,126

Current Growth Areas: Tokelau is noted as having the smallest economy in the world, and is almost entirely dependent on foreign aid. Tokelau has added to its GDP through registrations of internet domain names through its top-level domain (.tk.).

Potential Growth Areas: Through the development of high-speed Internet connections.

Potential Threat Areas: Classic Pacific Islands economic position, limited by a subsistence economy, non-diversified economy, isolation, transport costs and natural disasters.

Anticipated Scenario 2025: Very little change to the current situation with subsistence farming, fishing exploitation and substantial foreign aid required to continue. There is limited potential for Internet revenue to increase.

Tonga
Current GDP: US $817,000,000   Projected GDP: US $1,078,899,909
Current Population: 106,147   Projected Population: 157,714

Current Growth Areas: Agriculture is the main base of the economy, but the economy relies heavily on external foreign aid.

Potential Growth Areas: Encourage tourism, forestry and expand the fishing industry.

Current Threat Areas: Classic Pacific Islands economic position, limited by a subsistence economy, non-diversified economy, isolation, transport costs and natural disasters.

Potential Threat Areas: Classic Pacific Islands economic position, limited by a subsistence economy, non-diversified economy, isolation, transport costs and natural disasters.

Anticipated Scenario 2025: Very little change to the current situation with subsistence farming, fishing exploitation and substantial foreign aid required to continue. There is limited potential for tourism to increase, but this is likely from foreign private investment.

Tuvalu

Current GDP: US $14,940,000   Projected GDP: US $26,983,302
Current Population: 11,146   Projected Population: 16,562

Current Growth Areas: Tuvalu has few natural resources, copra and fish representing the bulk of production and exports. No notable growth areas. Tuvalu, like Tokelau, has added to its GDP through registrations of internet domain names through its top-level domain (.tv.).

Potential Growth Areas: Possibly fishing/marine resources, and tourism.

Current Threat Areas: Rising sea levels are threatening the health and extent of this nation. Needs infrastructure development.

Potential Threat Areas: Increase in natural disasters such as rising sea levels and cyclones.

Anticipated Scenario 2025: Very little change to the current situation with subsistence farming, fishing exploitation and substantial foreign aid required to continue. There is limited potential for Internet revenue to increase.

Wallis and Futuna

Current GDP: US $188,000,000   Projected GDP: US $N/A
Current Population: 15,480   Projected Population: N/A

Current Growth Areas: Primarily relies on subsistence agriculture, fishing rights and French subsidies.

Potential Growth Areas: The most likely area of growth is in the tourism industry.

Current Threat Areas: Needs infrastructure development.

Potential Threat Areas: Increase in natural disasters such as cyclones.

Anticipated Scenario 2025: Tourism is being promoted, along with French Polynesia. Other than the development of tourist facilities, the current state of the nation is unlikely to change, substantial foreign French aid is required to continue.

3.2 An Overview Assessment of Future Growth of Oceania

With the future development and as the global region's become more interlinked in trade blocs (i.e., Europe, etc,) the future for Oceania could lead to either increased unity or separatism. Future issues such as climate change/global warming, pollution, and carbon trading, and the development of wealthier and more powerful neighbors throughout Asia and South East Asia and closer to Oceania for trading, increases the region's viability to become more centralized. It will also be crucial for the development and improvement of prosperity among Oceania nations, many of which are facing a potentially difficult survival.

As is clear from the current assessment and anticipated scenarios for much of the region, the development of Australia and New Zealand will have the biggest single influence over the next 20 years. Many of the Pacific Island nations that are reliant upon foreign aid will continue to need to do so, and those relying on France, the U.S. and other distant nations, are at risk that the aid will continue. The responsibility for assistance and support in the Oceania region will fall more and more heavily on Australia and New Zealand.

In summary the growth of Australia and New Zealand over the next two decades is seen as follows:

Australia: <u>**Anticipated Scenario 2025**</u>: Australia will continue to increase its population, predominantly by immigration, it will significantly increase trade and relations with China, South East Asia, India and Japan. It will take on a greater financial and assistance role with the less developed nations of Oceania. It will continue to develop and maintain its educational and health systems, particularly in the international arena. It will still be comparatively underdeveloped and will need to spend more on infrastructure for transport, mining and telecommunications. It will need to move more rapidly to a knowledge based economy, to diversify its exports from raw materials and agriculture. It will be moving toward water and river system conservation and there is already an increase in desalination plants and alternative power sources such as wind and solar.

New Zealand: <u>**Anticipated Scenario 2025**</u>: New Zealand will marginally increase its population, predominantly by immigration; it will significantly increase trade and relations with China, South East Asia, India and Japan. It will take on a greater financial and assistance role with the less developed nations of Oceania. It will continue to develop and maintain its educational and health systems, particularly in the international arena. It will still be underdeveloped and will need to spend more on infrastructure for transport and telecommunications. It will need to continue to move to a knowledge based economy, to continue to diversify its exports from predominantly agriculture.

Pacific Island Nations (including Melanesia, Micronesia and Polynesia): <u>**Anticipated Scenario 2025**</u>:

In summary for the Pacific Island nations, referring to section 1.3.1 of this report, the PACIFIC 2020 Report identified the four growth areas as:

- Investment (or capital) – will require a greater political governance and improvement in fiscal performance to encourage private investment, may be enticed by raw and natural resources being developed.
- Labour – will require more emphasis to technical and vocational training, thus improving local skill levels.
- Land – is one of the most contentious issues, and land rights and ownership must be resolved to ensure economic improvement and encourage investment.
- Political Governance – will need to stabilise electoral systems, to encourage external investment and local economic stability. [2]

Assuming the above four areas can be encouraged, the PACIFIC 2020 Report identified the five productive and potential growth areas as:

- Tourism
- Fisheries
- Mining and Petroleum
- Forestry
- Agriculture

Other than nations such as New Caledonia (supported by France), French Polynesia (supported by France) and Guam (supported by U.S. influence), the remaining nations are focussed on developing a self sustaining economy over the next two decades. These countries will continue to require external financial and aid support over the period and therefore are unlikely to develop any project management maturity from their current position. Two nations in fact face major survival issues if the climate change predictions are realised, and rising sea levels threaten their existence. This means unique problems for the region and a likely increasing commitment of assistance from Australia and New Zealand. [2]

4 An Assessment of Project Management in Oceania Circa 2025
4.1 Assessment of Future Development of Project Management in Australia

As discussed in section 2.2, Australia has a current project management maturity that varies significantly over a range of industries. However, as tabulated in Table 7 a general improvement and wider application of project management is predicted for 2025.

Key points are:

- Australia will probably still have two project management representative institutes in AIPM and PMI, but hopefully they will be working more closely together for the benefit of project management in Oceania.
- Portfolio and program management will have developed more in industry application, Portfolio Management having the greater potential and likelihood of developing, thus a greater penetration into the financial industry.
- The mining, engineering, and construction industries will continue to flourish with the export of minerals, and are likely to move further forward in maturity. A couple of the larger contracting companies will likely move more into the international market to increase business. The development of Alliance Contracting will impact into the engineering and construction, legal, and financial industries. Infrastructure for transport and environmental needs (particularly water conservation) will need significant development. There will also be a significant increase in "environmental" infrastructure for power generation, and notably water and river conservation.
- Defence will improve its capacity and structure for project management application to achieve greater return on limited resources, and will become more involved in peacekeeping, aid support, and assistance to neighboring Oceania nations due to climate change and other needs.
- IT and Telecommunications will need to be a major growth area over the next few decades due to infrastructure and communications upgrading, thus providing the opportunity to raise project maturity in this industry. This growth is urgently required in Australia and in the Oceania region.
- Probably one of the most significant areas of growth will be the need to increase and improve foreign aid and assistance to other nations in this region. The requirement for the application of project management techniques and optimizing the limited resources (both financial and personnel) in Federal Government agencies such as AusAID will increase as Oceania will require additional assistance from the wealthier countries of Australia and New Zealand. This

Table 7

Australia	Projection	Current Maturity Levels	Projected Maturity Levels - 2025
Generally	Active project management will be required to meet the needs of infrastructure development both within and external to Australia (i.e., more assistance to Oceania nations). Australia needs to develop at a more rapid rate, but will continue to suffer from limited financial and human resources to meet the demand. Australia also needs to maintain and develop its educational system as it moves more toward a knowledge-based economy.	LEVELS 2 to 3, some industries moving to LEVEL 4	LEVELS 3 to 4, some industries moving to LEVEL 5
Mining	Major mining organizations will be utilizing project based management in multiple projects, and aligned to strategic management. Portfolio will be practiced, and project work will be integrated with ongoing operations.	LEVEL 3	LEVEL 4
Financial	Will have moved substantially toward project management principles on an organizational basis. Increased training in project management, and risk analysis will be more formally derived from scope and technical analysis. This will be enhanced by the increased use of public-private partnerships for major infrastructure projects between government and private investment. Alliance contracts will be more regularly used in an effort to reduce contract disputation.	LEVEL 1 moving toward LEVEL 2	LEVEL 2 moving strongly and rapidly toward LEVELS 3 & 4
Engineering & Construction	Professional project managers and program managers, with some contracting/construction organizations will have moved into project-based management in multiple projects, and becoming aligned to strategic management. This will have come about due to the need to expand markets internationally, and being active partners with developers and investors in major infrastructure joint ventures.	LEVEL 3 moving toward LEVELS 4 and 5	LEVEL 4 moving into LEVEL 5, some having moved into LEVEL 5
Defence	Defence will have completed the development of a strong competency in project based management (e.g., coaching, audits, health checks, etc.) and traditional project management (complex project management framework). Working jointly with U.K. and U.S. defense organizations will have improved their current capacity. Increased pressure to provide stability and aid in the Oceania region will also involve defense support and this will increase capacity to manage and prioritize resources, both financial and human.	LEVEL 2 moving toward LEVELS 3 and 4	LEVEL 4 moving toward LEVEL 5

(continued)

Table 7 (continued)

Australia	Projection	Current Maturity Levels	Projected Maturity Levels - 2025
IT & Telecoms	Telecommunications will be a major area of focus over the next two decades, both within Australia and external to Australia throughout the Oceania region. This industry is endeavoring to move more rapidly toward improved project management processes and techniques, and the interrelationship with the large multinational companies and a local highly skilled workforce should provide an opportunity to significantly improve the current levels.	LEVEL 2 moving toward LEVELS 3 and 4 (in some cases perhaps LEVEL 5), the predominant indicator is immature development of individual skills.	LEVEL 3 moving toward LEVELS 4 and 5
Other	As determined in this analysis, there will be an increased dependence on Australia and New Zealand for foreign aid and assistance. This should mean a greater need for good project management, program management and portfolio management techniques to be introduced. The challenge is whether this can occur. A similar approach will be required on response to natural emergencies. However, the need for assistance to nations in Oceania should natural disasters occur, may have to be supported by the defense forces and integrated with the natural disasters authorities. This will require a greater integration of organizations and skills.	Foreign Aid at LEVELS 1 to 2 Natural Emergencies at LEVELS 2 to 3	Foreign Aid at LEVELS 3 to 4 Natural Emergencies at LEVELS 3 to 4

aid will be financial, health, infrastructure, and education, as well as a likely increase in natural disaster assistance.

AUSTRALIA – COMPARISON OF MATURITY LEVELS 2008 to 2025

Based on the above Table 7, a graphical measure of the projected increase in project management maturity levels is indicated below.

Table 8

Industry		Level 1	Level 2	Level 3	Level 4	Level 5
Generally	2008	██	██			
	2025	██	██	██		
Mining	2008	██	██			
	2025	██	██	██		
Financial	2008	██				
	2025	██	██	█		
Enginineering & Construcio'n	2008	██	██	██		
	2025	██	██	██	██	
Defence	2008	██	██			
	2025	██	██	██	█	
IT & Telecoms	2008	██	██			
	2025	██	██			
Foreign Aid	2008	██				
	2025	██	██	██		
Natural Disasters	2008	██	██			
	2025	██	██			

4.2 Assessment of Future Development of Project Management in New Zealand

As discussed in section 2.2, similar to Australia, New Zealand has a current project management maturity that varies significantly over a range of industries. However, as tabulated in Table 9, a general improvement and wider application of project management is predicted for 2025.

Key points are:

- New Zealand may have two project management representative Institutes in PMI and AIPM, but working closely together for the benefit of project management in Oceania.
- Portfolio and program management will have developed more in industry application, Portfolio Management having the greater potential and likelihood of developing, thus a greater penetration into the Financial industry.

Table 9

New Zealand	Projection	Current Maturity Levels	Projected Maturity Levels - 2025
Generally	Similar levels of maturity as Australia, due to the close relationship between the two countries. Active project management will be required to meet the needs of infra-structure development both within and external to Australia (i.e., more assistance to Oceania nations). New Zealand also needs to maintain and develop its education-al system as it continues to move toward a knowledge-based economy.	LEVELS 2 to 3, some industries moving to LEVEL 4	LEVELS 3 to 4, some industries moving to LEVEL 5
Mining	Continuing limited development of mining in New Zealand, as it will continue to be predominantly an agricultural and knowledge-based economy. Mining is likely to remain limited in project management maturity, due to the small nature of the mining projects, although there will be an increased influence from investing companies external to New Zealand.	LEVEL 1 moving toward LEVEL 2	LEVEL 2 moving toward LEVEL 3
Financial	With the continued development of a knowledge-based economy and the need for New Zealand to continue off shore investment, there is likely to be an increased impact and application of project management processes and systems, and the ap-plication of risk management principles on an organizational basis.	LEVEL 1 moving toward LEVEL 2	LEVEL 2 moving toward LEVELS 3 and 4
Engineering & Construction	Professional project managers and program managers, since some contracting/con-struction organizations will have moved into project based management in multiple projects, and becoming aligned to strategic management. Project management in more traditional in this industry, and is aligned toward Australian companies that also work in New Zealand.	LEVEL 2 moving toward LEVELS 3 and 4	LEVEL 3 moving toward LEVELS 4 and 5
Defence	As New Zealand has a small defense force and cooperates closely with the Austra-lian Defence organizations through alliances, and joint projects such as the ANZAC Frigates project. Will probably improve maturity in project management through working relationships with Australian Defence organizations.	LEVEL 1 possibly moving toward LEVEL 2	LEVEL 2 possibly moving toward LEVELS 3 and 4
IT & Telecoms	Similar to Australia, telecommunications will be a major area of focus over the next two decades throughout the Oceania region. This industry is endeavoring to move more rapidly toward improved project management processes and techniques, and the interrelationship with the large multinational companies and a local highly skilled workforce should provide an opportunity to significantly improve the current levels.	LEVEL 2 moving toward LEVELS 3 and 4, im-mature development of individual skills.	LEVEL 3 moving toward LEVELS 4 and 5.
Other	Again, similar to Australia, there will be an increased dependence on Australia and New Zealand for foreign aid and assistance. This should mean a greater need for good project management, program management, and portfolio management techniques to be introduced. Again, similar to Australia, a similar approach will be required in response to natural emergencies. However, the need for assistance to nations in Oceania, should natural disasters occur, may have to be supported by the defense forces and integrated with the natural disasters authorities.	Foreign Aid at LEVELS 1 to 2 Natural Emergencies at LEVELS 2 to 3	Foreign Aid at LEVELS 3 to 4 Natural Emergencies at LEVELS 3 to 4

- The mining industry will continue with limited development of mining. Development in project maturity for this industry is more likely to be generated through international investment in the New Zealand resources.
- Engineering and construction will flourish with the development of more infrastructure (an emphasis is placed on thermal power being developed, due to the nature of New Zealand's natural volcanic environment). There will be a strong influence from large projects which involve international contracting companies, particularly Australian contractors, and this will increase project management maturity in this industry.
- New Zealand has a small defense force and cooperates closely with the Australian Defence organizations through alliances, and future joint projects with Australia's Defence Forces. This will probably improve maturity in project management through working relationships with Australian Defence organizations.
- Similar to Australia, telecommunications will be a major area of focus over the next two decades throughout the Oceania region. This industry is endeavoring to move more rapidly toward improved project management processes and techniques, and the interrelationship with the large multinational companies and a local highly skilled workforce should provide an opportunity to significantly improve the current levels.
- Linked with Australia, probably one of the most significant areas of growth will be the need to increase and improve foreign aid and assistance to other nations in this region. The requirement for the application of project management techniques and optimizing the limited resources (both financial and personnel) in government agencies will increase as Oceania will require additional assistance from the wealthier countries of Australia and New Zealand. This aid will be financial, health, infrastructure and education as well as a likely increase in natural disaster assistance, and would benefit from the two countries coordinating and working together.

New Zealand – Comparison of Maturity Levels 2008 to 2025

Based on the above Table 9, a graphical measure of the projected increase in project management maturity levels is indicated below.

4.3 Assessment of Future Development of Project Management in the Pacific Islands

As previously discussed in section 3.2, the countries of the Pacific Islands region will be struggling to become self-supporting economies and managing with climate change. Thus aid assistance from foreign nations and organizations such as the World Bank, ASEAN Development Bank, etc., will be a major focus until 2025. The potential growth areas are likely to be tourism, minerals and fishery/natural resources, most likely to be developed by private investment and thus a reliance on external and international project management practices, and this is also reflected in nations reliant upon U.S Defense Forces support.

Project management in the Pacific Islands region is likely to remain "ad hoc," i.e., Level 1 maturity.

Table 10

INDUSTRY		Level 1	Level 2	Level 3	Level 4	Level 5
Generally	2008					
	2025					
Mining	2008					
	2025					
Financial	2008					
	2025					
Enginineering & Construcio'n	2008					
	2025					
Defence	2008					
	2025					
IT & Telecoms	2008					
	2025					
Foreign Aid	2008					
	2025					
Natural Disasters	2008					
	2025					

Pacific Islands – Comparison of Maturity Levels 2008 to 2025

Based on the above Table 11, a graphical measure of the projected increase in project management maturity levels is indicated below.

Table 11

Pacific Islands (Oceania Grouped to Include Melanesia, Micronesia and Polynesia)			
	Projection	Current Maturity Levels	Projected Maturity Levels - 2025
Generally	As ascertained in this paper, Oceania is struggling to be self supporting, and is therefore immature in project management maturity, unless imported through external relationships with more developed nations. Assessed as "ad hoc". This situation is not perceived as changing, and therefore remains at Level 1, except where project management skills are imported externally.	Level 1 Ad hoc, depends on others	Level 1 Ad hoc, depends on others

TABLE 12

Industry		Level 1	Level 2	Level 3	Level 4	Level 5
Generally	2008	▓				
	2025	█				
Mining	2008	▓				
	2025	█				
Financial	2008	▓				
	2025	█				
Enginineering & Construcio'n	2008	▓				
	2025	█				
Defence	2008	▓				
	2025	█				
IT & Telecoms	2008	▓				
	2025	█				
Foreign Aid	2008	▓				
	2025	█				
Natural Disasters	2008	▓				
	2025	█				

4.4 Assessment Of The Impact Of International Development In Project Management

Without doubt, there are many nations around the world facing similar problems to the Pacific Islands region and some of the major impacts have a global urgency and are beyond the resources of less-developed nations. The more developed nations will need to address such universal problems such as climate and weather change, natural disasters, renewable energy, global economies, transport demands, health needs, and increasingly rapid technological and communication developments.

All of these demands will increase the potential for the application of project management techniques, as organizations seek more effective levels of management and co-ordination of limited resources. The ability of current project management practices and processes will be tested and must be flexible to the changing needs of new industries and greater responsibility in producing outcomes that are socially and environmentally responsible. Perhaps this is an aspect that is significantly lacking in current project management practices.

New Frontiers for the application of project management could well be driven as follows:

- **Climate Change:** leading to increased emphasis on earth science research and technologies such as geography, geology, geophysics and geodesy, soil sciences, oceanography and hydrology, glaciology, and atmospheric sciences, all potentially resulting in increased satellite surveillance and new infrastructure. [6] [8]

- **Natural Disasters:** leading to increased study of meteorology, climatology, seismology, and many of the sciences listed for climate change. An additional factor will be the development of rapidly deployed emergency services and support in the wake of natural disasters when they occur. Again, all potentially leading to increased satellite surveillance to monitor the planet, and new and more complex infrastructure. [6]
- **Renewable Energy:** leading to research and development of alternative energy sources such as nanotechnology, and further developing known sources such as hydro-electric, solar, tidal, geo-thermal, bio-fuels, nuclear energy, wind, etc. This will also lead to new and complex infrastructure. [7]
- **Global Economies:** leading to more complex financial structures and the need for instant communications around the planet and accessible at all times to all people. The current distribution of wealth around the world is a major imbalance that if not addressed will lead to inadequacies in health and education, famine and political instabilities.
- **Transport Demands:** with the limitation of fossil fuels such as oil, the ability to provide air transport has the potential to become limited, expensive and beyond the reach of many isolated nations and their communities. Alternative means of providing rapid transport of people and goods over large distances will become an urgent need over the next few decades, and requires new technologies and infrastructure.
- **Health Needs:** leading to significant increases in biosciences, biomedical sciences, medical practices, and medical facilities. This will range from the complex advancement of medicine in areas such as organ replacement, cancer research, etc., to the fundamentals of delivering basic good health to less fortunate nations, including clean drinking water, efficient waste disposal, and hygienic environments. This will also require new technologies and infrastructure.

Project management faces the challenge of meeting these different demands of a modern world if it is to significantly contribute. It will move substantially beyond current practices into the future of portfolio management—project and program management are likely to become sub-disciplines if organizations are to respond creatively and effectively to 2025.

REFERENCES

(1) Sourced from Wikepedia
(2) *Sourced from "PACIFIC 2020 – Challenges and Opportunities for Growth"; Report published by AusAID, Australian Commonwealth Government (May 2006)*
(3) *Latest estimates quoted in Duncan, owes and Williams (2005, p.9) indicates at current trends 11% of Papua New Guinea's adult population could be living with HIV/AIDS by 2025*
(4) World Bank 2006c
(5) *"Project Management -The Managerial Process", third edition by Clifford F. Gray and Erik W. Larson; ISBN-10:0-07-297863-5; published by McGraw Hill/Irwin -2006).*
(6) *Sourced from PM WORLD TODAY – Editorial July 2008 "New Frontiers for Project Management: Earth Sciences, Monitoring the Planet &Climate Control"; by David L. Pells*

(7) *Sourced from PM WORLD TODAY – Editorial May 2008 "New Frontiers for Project Management: Future Energy"; by David L. Pells*

(8) *Sourced from PM WORLD TODAY – Editorial February 2008 "Climate Change, What it means for the World of Project Management"; by David L. Pells*

CHAPTER 5

Project Management in the Arabian Gulf Region, circa 2025

Charles R. Franklin, PMP
Project Support & Controls Department, Saudi Aramco, KSA

Naceur Jabnoun, PhD
SSPGE, Ras Al-Khaimah, UAE

Shriram R. Dharwadkar, PhD
Organization Consulting Department, Saudi Aramco, KSA

Abstract

The Arabian Gulf region continues to experience very strong growth, with the largest mega projects in the world being executed amid a vibrant and rapidly growing project management community. Looking ahead toward the year 2025, project management in the region will be impacted by factors which include emerging and rapidly changing technologies, economics as the region's economies make a shift away from their dependency on oil and gas, critical issues in human resources development, and the increasing size and complexity of projects. These will result in new challenges to business in general and projects specifically. Some of the major challenges may be categorized as knowledge management, innovation, business, ethics, and safety.

Project professionals of 2025 will have developed new competencies both to meet these challenges and to leverage the opportunities they present. Developing the needed competencies will require corresponding changes in the systems that are used for creating and maintaining them. Education systems must be more aligned with the needs of industry; knowledge management systems must be developed that enable access to the knowledge that is needed, by whom it is needed, and when and where it is needed. Change will require project professionals to become proactive in working with the educational systems to design the curricula that will provide the training required by aspiring project professionals.

The future of project management in the Gulf region is exciting but the challenges are great. Gulf region project management professionals have the power in their hands to determine the destiny of project management through 2025 by guiding the education and training of the next generation of professionals.

Introduction

Fueled by income from oil and gas production, growth and development in the Arabian Gulf region during the early 21st century has been explosive, with as many as 2,000 projects under way simultaneously worth close to a trillion dollars in total (Emirates News Agency, WAM, 2007). At one point there were unverified claims that almost a quarter of the world's construction cranes were in Dubai, some 30,000. Mega projects, worth billions of dollars each, are in progress throughout the region, and despite the global economic meltdown of 2008-09, it appears that most planned projects are going ahead.

The Gulf region is also a hotbed of project management growth, where some of the most exciting and challenging projects in the world are being executed. The local Project Management Institute – Arabian Gulf Chapter (PMI-AGC) has had prolific growth, from an initial group of less than 20 in the early 1990s to over 4,000 today. Over one-fourth of the chapter's membership holds the Project Management Professional (PMP)® credential. The chapter has quadrupled in size in less than five years.

Today, the courses of the region's largest businesses, the national oil companies, have been steered for two generations by Gulf Cooperation Council (GCC) country nationals rather than western management, and more foreign workers in these companies are being replaced yearly by local citizens. Saudi Aramco now boasts that its workforce is 87% Saudi (Al-Saadoun, 2007).

In the midst of this phenomenal growth, there are critical concerns. The economies of the region, which until recent years were entirely based on oil and gas, must undergo a fundamental shift away from petroleum in order to provide jobs and educational opportunities for those entering the workforce. The thrust of projects as we look ahead to 2025 will be dominated by building and infrastructure projects, rather than the hydrocarbon facilities which have been the rule for many years.

New Challenges to Project Management in 2025

In order to understand the challenges that will be faced by GCC projects in the future, we must first visualize that future and the factors that will drive new challenges. Among these drivers, some major ones are technology, economics, human resources, and project complexity.

Technology

It is impossible, of course, to predict which emerging technologies will mature and gain acceptance so that they produce a significant impact on project management in the future. 64-bit operating systems, for example, have been available for workstations since at least 2005 when Microsoft released a 64-bit version of Windows XP Professional (Microsoft Corporation, 2005). But whereas there was a rush to move from 16-bit to 32-bit operating systems as soon as they became available, there has been no similar exodus from 32-bit platforms to 64-bit technology because there is little perceived performance gain for typical business applications, including those used to support project management processes. Similarly, technologies which automate labor-intensive construction processes such as pipe welding have not been widely adopted by GCC contractors because the low-cost and plentiful supply of Asian labor makes the option economically unattractive.

Nevertheless, technologies which demonstrate a compelling business advantage have been and will continue to be embraced in the GCC region. Some examples of these are 3D laser scanning, geographic information systems, and nanotechnology research. Some growing technology areas that are likely to have impact on project management in the future are discussed in the following sections.

FIATECH and technology development for projects

With the formation in 1999 of FIATECH (Fully Integrated and Automated Technology) (FIATECH, March 2009), a consortium of owner/operators, engineering, procurement, and construction (EPC) companies, academia and technology developers, efforts are being made to pursue coherent strategies for technology development based on a consensus among technology users as to value and priority. "FIATECH is an industry consortium that provides global leadership in identifying and accelerating the development, demonstration and deployment of fully integrated and automated technologies to deliver the highest business value throughout the life cycle of all types of capital projects" (FIATECH, July 2009). FIATECH's Technology Roadmap is comprised of nine elements:

1. Scenario-based Project Planning
2. Automated Design
3. Integrated, Automated Procurement & Supply Network
4. Intelligent & Automated Construction Job Site
5. Intelligent Self-maintaining and Repairing Operational Facility
6. Real-time Project and Facility Management, Coordination and Control
7. New Materials, Methods, Products & Equipment
8. Technology- & Knowledge-enabled Workforce
9. Lifecycle Data Management & Information Integration (FIATECH, June 2009)

Within each of these elements or focus areas, initiatives are in progress to develop technologies which will have global impact on project planning and execution. One example of a major effort is FIATECH's Accelerating the Deployment of ISO 15926 project. ISO 15926 is an international standard that will provide for seamless handover of data among all stakeholders in the facility lifecycle. For project managers in 2025, it means that all facility data will be visible to them in real time and across platforms without the need for conversion or translation.

Knowledge Management

By 2025, knowledge management will be even more critically important than it is today. When speaking of knowledge management, it is useful to describe it in terms of intellectual capital. Intellectual capital is comprised of "the knowledge assets that are attributed to an organization and most significantly contribute to an improved competitive position of this organization by adding value to defined key stakeholders" (Marr & Schiuma, 2001). One component of intellectual capital is human capital, defined as "the skills and know-how of the people in the organization, working individually and in teams" (Dawson, 2000). Human capital belongs to the employee, and when he leaves the company, it leaves with him. One very important aspect of knowledge management is the capture of human capital – the knowledge and experience of valuable company employees – so that it can be transferred to less-knowledgeable employees.

As technologies such as text mining and natural language processing enable knowledge capture from unstructured data contained in document repositories and records of all kinds, the mass of information will require new methodologies for access and retrieval of relevant, timely knowledge for project management decision support when and where it is needed. To be successful in 2025, project managers will require new competencies that enable them to make use of this knowledge, both for themselves and for the development of their project management team personnel.

Other electronic technologies

Several electronic technologies are already leveraging the 3D model developed during a project's design phase as a basis for linkage to construction data, inspection data, and ultimately operations data, and this will be common by 2025. It is possible that cheap 3D scanners may become available which could be permanently mounted around a construction site to provide continuous as-built data for comparison with the 3D model to permit early detection and prevention of construction errors. Communications technologies will make virtual teams the norm, with online meetings among geographically diverse members common. Wired networking will be reserved for servers and network infrastructure, while users will be mobile with wireless notebooks, hand-held computers, and personal digital assistants.

Nanotechnology

Nanotechnology will be much more widespread in 2025, with the potential for enhancing crude oil recovery. One methodology would have nanodevices provide measurement data passively, as markers that can be tracked as they move through an oil formation (Hardage, 2009). Another possibility involves using micro-electromechanical devices that can network with each other to relay temperature, pressure, and other data (Satyanarayanan, 2003). Saudi Aramco, the Saudi Arabian Oil Company, is actively pursuing nanotechnology applications for the petroleum industry through its EXPEC-Advanced Research Center, which has introduced the concept of Resbots, or nanoscale reservoir robots. Deployed into a formation through injection water, they would move through the reservoir recording temperatures, pressures and fluid types until recovered at producing wells and downloaded, enabling more precise mapping of the reservoir than is currently possible (Business Intelligence Middle East, 2008).

In addition to understanding the use of nanotechnology, project managers will need to be aware of its safety risks. Nanodevices may be able to pass through skin, be inhaled, or ingested (National Institute for Occupational Safety and Health, 2008). They could also pass into the water supply or food chain with catastrophic consequences (Oberdorster et al., 2005). There may also be new ethical conundrums related to privacy and security as more sophisticated nanodevices make the possibility of unobtrusive electronic surveillance a threat (Bailey, Newton, & Turney, 2005).

Technology summary

The proliferation of technology will empower project managers with unprecedented access to business intelligence and knowledge, with the caveat that the sheer volume of information will be overwhelming. The creation of systems that can take over the job of sifting through this morass to reveal the relevant nuggets is essential and a challenge that will be discussed further.

It will be a constant challenge for project managers to maintain a current working knowledge of these technologies as the rapid changes accelerate further, and new, as yet unforeseen technologies are engendered as spin-offs from this ongoing development.

Economics

The reality of globalization and the interdependencies among economies were vividly demonstrated by the global economic meltdown of 2008-09. In 2025, it will be impossible to view the GCC – or any other region in the world – in isolation. Despite the effects of the current economic meltdown and recession, the years leading up to 2025 hold great economic potential for the GCC.

The National Intelligence Council (2008) forecasts that "OPEC production in the Persian Gulf countries is projected to grow by 43 percent during 2003-2025. Saudi Arabia alone is expected to account for almost half of all Gulf production..." The McKinsey Global Institute predicts that at $70 per barrel, GCC oil revenues will total $6.2 trillion during the 14-year period from 2008-2022, which is more than triple the amount they earned during the preceding 14 years (de Boer, Farrell, Figee, Lund, Thompson, & Turner, 2008).

However, the National Intelligence Council report (2008) also predicts that by 2025, it is likely that a technological breakthrough will provide a viable alternative to oil and natural gas. The impact of this scenario on GCC economies would be far-reaching, although not immediate, since petroleum-fueled equipment and infrastructure would in no case be phased out immediately.

The specter of the region's economy suddenly losing its fundamental underpinnings has not escaped the oil-dependent governments, and efforts to attract foreign investment have met with some success. Direct foreign investments into the GCC increased from $2 billion in 2001 to over $20 billion in 2005. Planned building and infrastructure projects totaled almost $1 trillion in 2007 and by pre-global meltdown estimates could have exceeded $3 trillion by 2010 (de Boer & Turner, 2007).

GCC governments are also under considerable pressure to create jobs for their burgeoning populations as well as providing training opportunities that will enable them to compete on an equal footing with foreign labor. Saudi Arabia is under the greatest pressure in this regard; although it enjoys 63% of the total oil and gas income among the GCC states, its population has far outpaced its oil and gas production so that its per capita income from petroleum is only one-sixth that of the United Arab Emirates (de Boer & Turner, 2007).

For this reason, mega projects will continue to be undertaken in the GCC, but as the current oil and gas facilities expansion programs are completed, a larger portion of these will be projects aimed at shifting GCC economies away from their dependence on petroleum. In Dubai, such projects have already radically altered its skyline as well as its perception in the rest of the world as it has transformed itself into a global economic and tourist center.

In another example, Saudi Arabia is building six new economic cities in the Kingdom for the purpose of attracting domestic and foreign investment, with desirable living and working conditions for approximately 2.5 million people, at a total investment of about $200 billion (de Boer & Turner, 2007). The attractions for manufacturing will be relatively cheap energy, availability of feed stock for petrochemicals, ready access to sea transportation, and, coupled with the Kingdom's massive investments in education, a pool of skilled labor.

Infrastructure investment in the GCC is expected to exceed $1.3 trillion between 2007 and 2012; in April 2007, the GCC had more than 2,000 active infrastructure projects. (Emirates News Agency, WAM, 2007) With billions of dollars being invested in construction projects in the GCC countries in the years leading to 2025, project activity will continue to be high. However, the project landscape will come to be dominated by building and infrastructure projects rather than hydrocarbon capacity expansion.

Human Resources

The most serious challenges faced by projects in the Gulf region in the coming years are related to population growth, education, and employment opportunities. In the most populous country of the region, Saudi Arabia, the population has exploded from less than ten million in 1980 to more than 26 million today; it is expected to swell to around 34 million by 2025. The burgeoning population of the region includes more than 50% who are under the age of 25 today, and this demographic will likely comprise about 43% of the population in 2025 (United Nations Population Division, 2009).

In the past, the largest employers of citizens in the region were the national oil companies and the governments, but these have long since reached a saturation point, and by 2025 will hardly be a major source of needed job opportunities. Furthermore, although the public education systems have improved greatly over the years, there is a consensus that graduates should be better prepared to enter the work force and be productive. More needs to be done in this area, and it will be a continuous effort to maintain curricula that reflect the changing needs of industry.

Nationalization, used in this sense to describe employment of citizens in place of foreign workers, is a vital effort throughout the Gulf, where it is referred to as "Saudization," "Qatarization," "Omanization," etc., as appropriate to each country. By law, nationalization quotas are required of businesses and must also be incorporated into the provisions of contracts that include labor, along with penalties for non-compliance. Fulfilling these legal requirements creates a unique situation for project management in the Gulf region; it effectively becomes a stakeholder along with government in its efforts to develop its workforce and provide employment opportunities for them.

Despite these requirements, many of these available jobs end up filled by foreign workers because nationals who have the needed competencies may be scarce, and many are unwilling to accept jobs that are typically performed by foreign labor from the Indian sub-continent. These attitudes are changing as the work force accepts that the lucrative and highly respected managerial jobs that formerly were targeted for nationalization have already been filled by nationals and that such opportunities are now rare.

In the short term, Cambridge Energy Research Associates (CERA) projects a 10 to 15 percent worldwide "people deficit" in engineering and project management by 2010. The causes of this deficit are the large wave of new projects in this sector and the aging of the current workforce. With an average age of 51 in 2007, CERA estimates that 50% of today's project workforce will likely retire by 2015, an attrition rate of 6% per year (CERA, 2007). The lack of a skilled workforce is more severe in the Middle East, which will require 35% of the world's projected manpower requirements between 2007 and 2011.

Clearly there will be project professional jobs to be filled as we look ahead to 2025, but the ability of young Gulf region nationals to adequately perform in these slots is dependent on there being educational opportunities and capacity to meet the need.

Project Complexity

For hydrocarbon projects, the key point is that all of the easy-to-recover oil and gas in the Gulf region has been found. Future hydrocarbon facilities will be in even more remote and harsh environments and will be more difficult and more expensive to build. If Saudi oil and gas production moves into the Red Sea, where depths are in the 1,000 meter range, technologies will need to be adapted from other deep water oil production areas like the North Sea and Gulf of Mexico.

For building and infrastructure projects, the defining factor will be size, with entire cities being built rather than simply buildings, roadways, or utilities individually. If recent history is an indication, then future mega projects will be executed on ambitious schedules; King Abdullah University of Science and Technology in Saudi Arabia is one such project. Comprised of a complete university campus, residential buildings, civic buildings, and a marina, the entire project was built in only two years at a cost of $3.5 billion. Classes are scheduled to begin in September, 2009 (Construction Week Online, 2008).

In the UAE, the Burj Dubai (Arabic for "Dubai Tower") recently reached the height of 700 meters. The iconic project developed by the Dubai real estate giant Emaar is currently the highest building the world, and the rumor is that it is planned to be 800 meters tall when complete. Emaar refuses to release the target height of its building due to concern over competition. This status is likely to be fleeting, however. Neighboring Saudi Arabia announced plans for a 1,600-meter-tall building, and Kuwait announced its plans to build a 1,001 meter high building (Al-Arabiya, 2008). Fueled by oil revenues, mega projects are a source of pride in collectivist societies in general, and in the Gulf region in particular.

Looking toward 2025, the trend is towards more such mega projects that are challenging due to design, location, environment, and ambitious schedules. As with the competition for the world's tallest building, at least some of these projects will be driven by national pride as well as other considerations. The project professionals who execute these projects will need solid competencies both in technical areas and in business to see them through to successful completion.

Meeting the Challenges – the Need for New Competencies

Given the forces that will impact projects and project management professionals in the coming years, we should next break out the specific areas in which new competencies must be developed. The major ones are knowledge management, innovation, business, ethics, and safety.

The Knowledge Management Challenge

With the knowledge management efforts that will be fully mature by 2025, project managers will be challenged by an explosion of information that they will be expected to leverage in order to enhance project planning and execution and avoid mistakes. Saudi Aramco's project management organization has a lessons-learned knowledge base in place which has already been recognized by the Construction Industry Institute as one of the most mature in the world. Recognizing that there was a need to focus users on the lessons which were most relevant to their projects and had a high frequency of repetition, Saudi Aramco took it a step further with the introduction of their Pitfall Prevention Tool, which presents users with "a shortlist of common pitfalls with corresponding pitfall avoidance strategies that is based on years of collected wisdom" (Construction Industry Institute, 2009).

Innovations of this type will become more critical as the mass of available knowledge increases, perhaps leading to the development of project management expert systems coupled with neural networks that are able to judge which results are "most like" the natural language meaning of the user's query, rather than simply matching search terms. This would enable an expert system to identify the knowledge that is most relevant to a user's query regardless of its wording, in much in the same way as a human expert would. Using heuristic processing to learn a user's patterns and behaviors, such systems could become a true electronic assistant or adviser, producing the most relevant, valuable knowledge as it is needed.

In the past, it was the one who gave the best answer who was rewarded; with the advent of search engines such as Google™, today's challenge is to ask the best question. Successful project managers in the coming years will not be simply "computer literate," but will embrace the technology and consider it part of their project management toolboxes. For younger professionals, as part of the "Facebook" and "Twitter" generation, their social networking skills will transform easily into communities of practice where ideas are shared continuously rather than twice a year at communications meetings or forums. In fact, a search of www.ning.com, a provider of social networks, yields over a hundred project management-related social networks, with the largest of these having over 10,000 members. It will be a challenge to older project managers to attain proficiency and a level of comfort with these technologies as well.

The Innovation Challenge

Drexler (2009) discusses the qualities that make a society a world-class center of technological innovation, but his points may be applied to a group such as project management professionals as well. Paraphrasing and adapting these to project management as a profession, we must have:

- Drive – professionals who not only do not fear change, but actively support it
- Human capital – a knowledge of our business that enables us to readily understand how new technologies will fit and add value
- Capacity for mobilization – the willingness and wherewithal to pursue new goals, even though success in not assured.

True innovations often occur because someone realizes that a technology intended for one purpose has application in a completely different field. Khalid Al-Falih, president and CEO of Saudi Aramco, has stated that "There are tools and technologies developed in the medical field that may have widespread applications for our business… Just because a new technology wasn't designed with oil and gas in mind doesn't mean it can't be of immense value to us in our operations" (Business Intelligence Middle East, 2008).

Relatively little technology development is likely to be directed solely toward project management needs. However, the challenge to project professionals will be to make themselves widely aware of emerging technologies, even though at first glance they may not appear to have application to projects. In fact, most will not, but it is necessary to compare these technologies' capabilities with project needs in order to detect those that may fit and become the innovative solutions that will add value to project processes. This requires an open mind; those that fear change will not be innovators.

The Business Challenge

The most successful project managers will be those who understand the business of project management as well as the technology. This has taken on new importance following the global economic meltdown of 2008-09, which changed the engineering and construction projects landscape almost overnight from a schedule-driven market where manpower was at a premium to a cost-driven market with more relaxed schedules. Understanding business means having a solid grasp of the flexibility available when negotiating contracts while also understanding allocations of risk which vary depending on the contract type.

The Ethics Challenge

Ethics is defined most simply as understanding right and wrong, justice and injustice, good and bad, and choosing to do what is right no matter what the cost (National Health and Medical Research Council, 2005). As mentioned earlier in this paper, new technologies may bring new ethical challenges. The example given earlier related to the use of nanotechnology, but other examples could be related to genetically engineered microorganisms that could be intended for oil spill cleanup, but which might have poorly defined long-term health risks to personnel, or unknown consequences in the food chain. Some new technologies may represent a threat to personal privacy. In each case, project professionals must examine and weigh the risks against the benefits and be guided by honesty and integrity in determining what is acceptable, even if the right choice is not the most profitable one or the most popular.

The Safety Challenge

Safety should be a project manager's overriding concern above all others. By the time the Panama Canal opened in 1914, it was estimated that a total of 27,500 workmen had died in its construction, mainly from disease and landslides. In 2009, lost-time incidents are not tolerated and even one fatality would be unacceptable no matter the size of the project. In 2025, the ability to track safety infractions in great detail and identify common infractions early, and identify root causes will lead to safer worksites and even less tolerance for incidents.

Developing the Project Managers of the Future
Strategies for Building Tomorrow's Competencies

Development of competencies in any profession requires a combination of education, experience, skills, attitudes, and behaviors (Frame, 1999). Competencies are the product of both learning and doing. As shown in Figure 1 below, there is an interaction between education/training and experience, whereby education provides a context or framework for fully understanding the knowledge gained from experience, while experience, in turn, reinforces the learning acquired by education. Experience is critical, as no one can claim to be competent in an area unless they have actually performed the

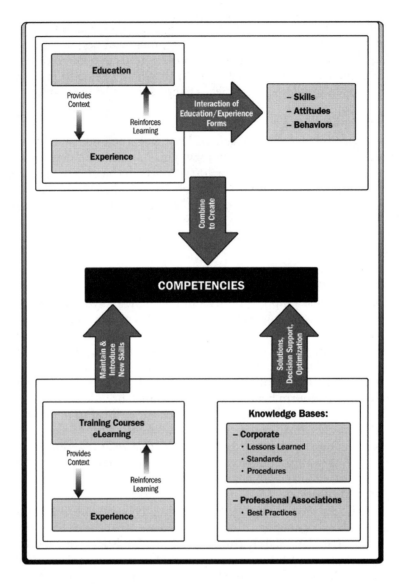

Figure 1

work involved. This interaction leads to skills, attitudes, and behaviors which become part of the tacit knowledge for a particular competency, and all of these factors – education, experience, skills, attitudes, and behaviors – comprise a competency. The cycle is repeated in order to maintain competencies as technologies and practices change.

Per Turner and Huemann (2000), it is also important to differentiate between the terms "education" and "training." From the Oxford English Dictionary, education is defined as:

Structured extended programs to impart knowledge and develop competence

And training is defined as:

Short courses to develop specific skills.

Education, then, includes formal courses of study at the secondary school and university level, while training includes in-company courses, those provided by training companies, and those provided by professional organizations such as PMI. Training courses may be used to introduce new skills and help maintain the currency of a competency as technologies and practices change. Knowledge management, with knowledge contained in corporate knowledge bases and industry knowledge repositories such as PMI, the Construction Industry Institute (CII), and others provides the ability to draw on the collected wisdom of others for decision support, solutions to special problems, and best practices.

Development of GCC project professionals in the coming years will require strategies related to education, training, and experience. Additionally, knowledge management's place in building competencies and providing just-in-time learning will be addressed.

Education for project professionals

Preparation for a successful project professional in the GCC in 2025 will begin as early as public school, with the development of attitudes toward work and the prerequisites for careers in applied science, including science, mathematics, and communications. Although public education in the GCC countries has improved greatly, it is still widely regarded as not being in alignment with the requirements of industry. According to de Boer and Turner (2007), "young GCC nationals face a future of underemployment or no employment at all; the educational system has failed to prepare them for the rigors of working in the private sector."

The key to change in this situation will be the active participation of industry, and specifically project professionals, with the GCC ministries of education to determine the curricula required to prepare young people to fill the jobs. A number of countries have incorporated basic project management into their public school curricula, teaching these skills to students as young as 16 (Turner & Huemann, 2000). This author has recently taught skills such as work breakdown, scheduling, resource allocation, and designing processes for quality assurance to a 15-year-old Boy Scout. These are organizational skills that will be valuable to young people no matter what professions they pursue.

At the university level, it will again be up to GCC project professionals to drive the creation of degree programs that will prepare young people to fill jobs currently held by foreign workers. As of 2009, Al-Faisal University in Riyadh offers a bachelor's degree in project management, and King Saud University, also in Riyadh, offers a master's degree in project management. King Abdullah University of Science and Technology, presently under construction, will be a world-class university on Saudi Arabia's west coast and will provide curricula that will support project management needs. A number of U.S. universities have also set up campuses in Qatar and the UAE, including George Mason, Texas A&M, and American University. There are currently 60 universities in the UAE alone. Most of these universities offer business degrees that cover the project management subject.

To reiterate, GCC project professionals, perhaps acting through professional associations such as PMI, must be proactive in promoting project management education and assuring that public school and university curricula fulfill the requirements to prepare young people to enter the profession.

Structured experience programs

As mentioned above, education and experience go hand-in-hand and are vital components in developing competencies. Typically, project personnel accumulate experience in a haphazard way, depending on where they land in the project landscape, often thrown into a job with no preparation and little direction from busy colleagues. They have no choice but to learn on their own. To develop well-rounded project personnel with the right competencies, a structured approach is required that provides real experience in the needed areas.

Some companies such as Saudi Aramco are already creating competency maps for various project management specialties. These maps define the needed competencies and the combinations of education and experience required to master each one. Key to the success of such a program is measurement and evaluation to ensure that goals are met, and a periodic assessment of the competency map itself to maintain its currency.

Continuing Education

Continuing education in the form of training courses and conferences is vital in order to maintain competencies in a rapidly changing world. The increasing availability of online courses means that project professionals can maintain their competencies even from remote locations and, depending on the design of the eLearning course, on their own schedules. The downside of at-your-own-pace or asynchronous training is the lack of interaction with colleagues, but many courses are instructor-led or synchronous courses with participation from the class.

As the technology improves, eLearning will change. Social learning, which involves media tools such as blogging, micro-blogging, RSS feeds, social networking, and collaboration tools, is one direction for this technology, but the face of eLearning in 2025 is unknowable at this point. The things of which we can be certain are that it will continue to evolve, and that it will provide powerful options for learning over the coming years, eventually becoming the norm for most of our training. Capitalizing on this technology for training project professionals and maintaining their competencies should be a critical part of the overall development strategy.

Knowledge Management

To reiterate what has already been discussed here, knowledge management, and particularly the capture of knowledge held as human capital by highly trained and experienced professionals, is critical to assuring that this expertise is transferred to younger developing professionals. However, it is important to note that simply capturing knowledge into a vast repository has little value unless that knowledge is accessible when, where, and by whom it is needed. Emerging technologies for knowledge management will facilitate this, and interface technologies from other disciplines, such as gaming, may put a friendly face on such a system. By 2025, project professionals may rely on expert systems as assistants or advisers when answers are needed.

Professional Associations and Certifications

The Project Management Institute is a primary professional association for project professionals in the GCC, where membership in the Arabian Gulf Chapter has grown from less than 20 it its inception in the early 1990s to over 4,000 in mid-2009, quadrupling its numbers in the past five years. Of these members, over one-fourth or 1,339 hold the PMP certification.

PMI-AGC provides numerous training courses at locations throughout the Gulf region to enable project professionals to continue their development. PMI certifications are also being incorporated into competency maps developed by Saudi Aramco to define the roadmap for development of its project specialists. As the profession becomes more complex, we can expect that there will be an increasing tendency to specialize in certain areas, and this is already being recognized by PMI as specialist certifications are being added. This specialization is likely to continue in the coming years.

Although the Construction Industry Institute had limited its membership to owners, EPC companies, and suppliers with a presence in North America, they have recently expanded their scope to allow membership for companies abroad as well. Saudi Aramco and the Saudi Chamber of Commerce have approached them with a proposal to sponsor a chapter in Saudi Arabia. Barring that, the plan is to set up a Saudi institute modeled along the same lines as CII. Other project management-related associations in the GCC include the Arabian Association of Cost Engineers and the Society of American Value Engineers (SAVE International), which provides certifications for value engineering specialists.

Looking ahead to 2025, we expect that other engineering and project-related associations will extend their presence to the Gulf region, and their importance will grow as the number of professionals and specializations increases. This will certainly be beneficial to the professional development of the workforce.

Conclusion

The defining characteristic of the Gulf region is change. The GCC countries have come a very long way in a relatively short span of time, being transformed from a mainly agrarian culture with sparse population to become the primary supplier of the world's most valuable commodity. They have undergone significant growing pains in the process and will continue to do so as their populations have outstripped their infrastructures, educational systems, and employment opportunities.

The practice of project management in the region is heavily affected by these factors and will continue to be so during the coming years. Because of nationalization, coupled with its inclusion in contracts, project management has become a partner with government in its efforts to develop its workers. The challenge to build fully competitive professionals is a driving force for project management which is unique to this region, and which will continue to play a major role into 2025.

In summary, as we look ahead to 2025, the outlook for project management in the Gulf region is bright but the challenges are great. However, these challenges will be met by educated, tech-savvy project professionals, more and more of whom will be GCC citizens standing shoulder-to-shoulder with their peers throughout the world.

References

Al-Arabiya. (2008, March 13). *Saudi tower to dwarf Burj Dubai: report*. Retrieved August 9, 2009, from Al-Arabiya web site: http://www.alarabiya.net/articles/2008/03/13/46879. html#002

Al-Saadoun, H. (2007, February 4). *Saudi Aramco's Experience in Preparing the Workforce for the Future*. Retrieved August 10, 2009, from Saudi Management Association web site: http://www.sma.org.sa/pdf/44/5.pdf

Bailey, P., Newton, G., & Turney, J. (2005, June 1). *Big Picture on Nanoscience.* Retrieved August 1, 2009, from Wellcome Trust Web Site: http://www.wellcome.ac.uk/stellent/ groups/corporatesite/@msh_publishing_group/documents/web_document/ wtd015798.pdf

Business Intelligence Middle East. (2008, March 7). *Business Intelligence Middle East.* Retrieved August 1, 2009, from BI-ME Web Site: http://www.bi-me.com/main. php?id=18067&t=1&c=36&cg=4

CERA. (2007, October 4). *Engineering Talent Squeeze - "People Deficit" - likely to cause further delay in some oil & gas production projects through 2010.* Retrieved August 9, 2009, from CERA web site: http://www.cera.com/aspx/cda/public1/news/pressReleases/ pressReleaseDetails.aspx?CID=9006

Construction Industry Institute. (2009, July 28). *2009 CII Annual Conference Presentation Abstracts.* Retrieved August 2, 2009, from Construction Industry Institute web site: https://construction-institute.org/AC/2009/abstracts.cfm

Construction Week Online. (2008, December 4). *King Abdullah University of Science & Technology.* Retrieved August 9, 2009, from Construction Week Online web site: http://www.constructionweekonline.com/projects-19-king_abdullah_university_ of_science_technology_kaust/

Dawson, R. (2000). Knowledge capabilities as the focus of organisational development and strategy. *Journal of Knowledge Management , 4* (4), 320.

de Boer, K., & Turner, J. M. (2007, January 1). *Beyond Oil: Reappraising the Gulf States.* Retrieved August 2, 2009, from McKinsey Quarterly web site: http://www. mckinseyquarterly.com/Beyond_oil_Reappraising_the_Gulf_States_1902

de Boer, K., Farrell, D., Figee, C., Lund, S., Thompson, F., & Turner, J. (2008, January 1). *The Coming Oil Windfall in the Gulf.* Retrieved August 3, 2009, from McKinsey Global Institute web site: http://www.mckinsey.com/mgi/reports/pdfs/the_ coming_oil_windfall/Coming_Oil_Windfall_in_the_Gulf.pdf

Drexler, E. (2009, August 6). *Asia and the elements of innovation.* Retrieved August 6, 2009, from McKinsey Digital web site: http://whatmatters.mckinseydigital.com/ innovation/asia-and-the-elements-of-innovation

Emirates News Agency, WAM. (2007, October 5). *Infrastructure projects in UAE exceed US$300b.* Retrieved August 9, 2009, from UAE Interact web site: http://www. uaeinteract.com/docs/Infrastructure_projects_in_UAE_exceed_US$300b/25248. htm

FIATECH. (2009, June 5). *Capital Projects Technology Roadmap Overview.* Retrieved August 1, 2009, from FIATECH Web Site: http://fiatech.org/tech-roadmap/ roadmap-overview.html?start=3

FIATECH. (2009, March 6). *FIATECH History.* Retrieved August 1, 2009, from FIATECH Web Site: http://fiatech.org/history.html

FIATECH. (2009, July 29). *FIATECH Home Page.* Retrieved August 1, 2009, from FIATECH Web Site: http://www.fiatech.org

Frame, J. D. (1999). *Project Management Competence: Building Key Skills for Individuals, Teams, and Organizations.* San Francisco: Jossey-Bass Publishers.

Hardage, B. (2009, March 20). *Possible Nanotechnology Applications in Petroleum Reservoirs.* Retrieved August 1, 2009, from American Association of Petroleum Geologists - Search and Discovery: http://www.searchanddiscovery.net/ documents/2009/40396hardage/index.htm

Marr, B., & Schiuma, G. (2001). *Measuring and managing intellectual capital and knowledge assets in new economy organisations.* (M. Bourne, Ed.) Wokingham: GEE Publishing.

Microsoft Corporation. (2005, April 25). *Microsoft Raises the Speed Limit with the Availability of 64-Bit Editions of Windows Server 2003 and Windows XP Professional.* Retrieved August 1, 2009, from Microsoft.com: http://www.microsoft.com/presspass/press/2005/apr05/04-25Winx64LaunchPR.mspx

National Health and Medical Research Council. (2005, December 8). *Keeping Research on Track.* Retrieved August 9, 2009, from National Health and Medical Research Council web site: http://www.nhmrc.gov.au/publications/synopses/_files/e65.pdf

National Institute for Occupational Safety and Health. (2008, February 1). *NIOSH Publication No. 2008-112: Safe Nanotechnology in the Workplace.* Retrieved August 1, 2009, from CDC-NIOSH Web Site: http://www.cdc.gov/niosh/docs/2008-112/

National Intelligence Council. (2008, November 1). *Global Trends 2025: The National Intelligence Council's 2025 Project.* Retrieved August 1, 2009, from National Intelligence Council Web Site: www.dni.gov/nic/NIC_2025_project.html

Oberdorster, G., Maynard, A., Donaldson, K., Castranova, V., Fitzpatrick, J., Ausman, K., et al. (2005). Principles for characterizing the potential human health effects from exposure to nanomaterials: elements of a screening strategy. *Particle and Fiber Toxicology , 2* (8).

Rafique, M. (2008, February 28). GCC construction tops at $1 trillion. *Arab News .*

Satyanarayanan, M. (2003). Of smart dust and brilliant rocks. *Pervasive Computing* (October-December), 2-4.

Turner, J. R., & Huemann, M. M. (2000). Current and future trends in the education in project managers. *Project Management - The Professional Magazine of the Project Management Association Finland , 6,* 20-26.

United Nations Population Division. (2009, March 11). *The 2008 Revision Population Database.* Retrieved August 6, 2009, from United Nations Web Site: http://esa.un.org/unpp/index.asp?panel=1

PART 2

Project Management Systems Applications

CHAPTER 6

The Constant Evolution of Timeless Management

Elaine Bannon
David Pericak

Fast forward to 2025. Competitive Vehicle Development is 24 months start to finish versus a norm of 36 months today. Physical based testing and validation has been nearly eliminated. The vehicle styling is reviewed by design studios around the world simultaneously using holographic imaging technology. Employees have the flexibility to work from a number of locations (e.g. home, work, satellite locations). And they have the responsibility to pull it all together – on time, with quality, meeting all financial metrics and all customer expectations.

In the future, global project management teams will be the norm rather than the exception. The engineering team could be in Germany, the design studio in Italy, the manufacturing facility in Brazil, and the home office in Detroit. In order to manage the diverse cultures, multiple time zones, longstanding work practices, and an aggressive timeline for delivery, a framework of core values and deliverables will be essential to thrive in the constant and evolutionary global business environment.

Experience may give you a "gut" feeling of your current project management team's health and performance. You know some of the staff of your organization very well and have established relationships with them. Others are less familiar – as this is a global team and your monthly travel only allows so much relationship-building in person. It is important to keep a feedback-rich environment that nurtures continual personal coaching. Also important is to track your key metrics and to know when to intervene to ensure the highest levels of excellence. You need to keep things running smoothly to achieve results that yield higher levels of company performance and morale for everyone—even in the face of the most challenging of external factors.

While external factors—such as environmental, political, and technological, to name a few—are constantly changing, the key core values and deliverables of project management that drive excellent results are timeless. This chapter will describe those key core values and core deliverables, how to foster them, and how a high-performing team can thrive in times when some external factors can be challenging. It will describe how to leverage a diverse personality-rich team and ensure that it is driven by a set of clear core values. It is critical for organizations to recognize and deliberately foster these key personal values and core deliverables in order to strengthen their companies in any set of external factors – whether they are deemed challenging or enabling.

> **Key Takeaway**: Whether it is 10 or 100 years in the future – if you do not possess the core values and core deliverables that ensure high performing teams – you will fail.

Defining the Core Deliverables

Managing the core deliverables of any project is the reason project management exists. They are timeless in nature and impervious to external factors as the framework of the system to deliver them must also be. Core deliverables are defined as a project meeting:

- Customer Expectations;
- Quality Objectives;
- Financial Targets; and
- Timing.

Delivery of the core deliverables must be "owned" by the project management team, as opposed to the team simply tracking and reporting the progress of others. Ownership is the overarching operational core value whose importance will be described later in this chapter.

Defining the Core Values

Core values are defined in two parts: operational and personal. Both are key to the success of a highly successful project management team. The operational values will set up the basics for any team to function at a competent level; however, the personal values will foster delivery at world-class levels of excellence.

Operational Core Values

Operational core values (OCV) are the guiding principles that shape the behavior of the project management team. They are teachable points of view that ensure the longevity of the organization, regardless of the individuals within it. The absence of them will significantly reduce the efficiency and effectiveness of the team, as they are the common ground in times of uncertainty or change.

For something to qualify as an OCV it must meet one or more of the following criteria:

- It is essential to delivery of products customers want to buy and buy again;
- It is something that can be applied in any circumstance and environment and is independent of the project or issue type;
- It is timeless and impervious to external factors; and

- It is something that everyone can understand regardless of culture, knowledge base and/or experience level.

Operational core values form the foundation of the team's day-to-day activities, and consistently drive clarity to those important elements of a highly executed project. The OCVs are defined in the automotive industry as the following:

1) Communication
2) System Engineering
3) Validation/Verification
4) Attribute Balancing
5) Managing the Details
6) Voice of the Customer
7) Ownership

Let's take a moment to better understand the meaning behind each OCV.

- **Communication**: Methods of communication may change, but the basic principle does not. This is one operational core value that can never be overdone. It can be frustrating at times that one may think he or she has communicated a given direction or message, and yet some members of the team have not received the message or have misinterpreted it. Good communication includes confirmation that the intended message has been heard or received accurately. Realizing this will help in developing and maintaining good communication over time.
- **System Engineering**: The majority of organizations have engineers working on a component level. Some may be complex, such as engines and instrument panels, while others are fairly straightforward. One thing is clear: A system mindset where each engineer routinely manages a full interior, for example, is not innate in every person. Project managers must bridge the gap between the component and system-level mindset. It is this ability to see the system as the customer will see it and experience it that is key to success. As well, the ability to keep that system vision in front of the total team at all stages of project implementation is critical to delivering excellence.
- **Validation/Verification**: Delivering a vehicle customers want to buy and buy again has a lot to do with exceptional verification and validation confirming an outstanding product with high quality. Technically, validation methods have become more nimble over time through increased use of CAD/CAE tools versus physical vehicle testing. The essential value of the project manager is confirming that verification/validation of the complex vehicle system is robust and mimics customer usage throughout the product development process. It is the key enabler to keeping a project on track to the originally specified timing plan, since robust verification will reduce the need for multiple design/product changes.
- **Attribute Balancing**: Each vehicle attribute is represented by a group of engineers, designers, manufacturing personnel, marketers, finance analysts, etc. They all have very good reasons why their attribute needs top priority and cannot deviate from the "rulebook" in any way. In the context of an automobile, they include ride and handling, styling, weight, and after-tax return on sales (ATROS), among many others. Since a vehicle is a complex system, attribute balancing means ensuring that each individual attribute is optimized within a total vehicle system to best meet customer expectations. Balancing should

never be looked at as a compromise. On the contrary, attribute balancing done well is all about optimizing – as stated above. Everyone, including the end customer, benefits from this holistic approach. We define it as value.

- **Managing the Details**: This should not be confused with micro-management. As a project manager's role is to deliver the core deliverables, it is critical to understand the completeness and correctness of them throughout the entire product development process. This includes tier I/II/III suppliers, internal engineering, manufacturing, purchasing, etc. As an example, taking a supplier's final production-ready component as acceptable for mass vehicle production without any due diligence (review of final test results/walk of supplier's manufacturing facility) would be far too risky to the project's robust completion. The devil is in the details and a great project management team will get to know the devil. When managing a project, to trust the data is to know the data.

- **Voice of the Customer**: Being the voice of the customer means standing up for their wants and needs even in the face of internal objectives that, on the surface, could sub-optimize the overall product experience. Keeping ahead of the competition in providing high levels of customer satisfaction from a new vehicle introduction along with improving their experience over time in an established product is key to automotive project management. Experience in a given vehicle nameplate with delivery of multiple product updates over a given time period is essential. Meeting with the customers of our products to discuss their experience, along with ongoing review of external feedback sources such as Customer Reports, J. D. Powers, Yahoo! Auto, Edmunds.com and Kelly Blue Book (to name a few), are required to methodically enhance the vehicle experience.

- **Ownership**: Ownership is the overarching value that effects the outcome of the operational core values as illustrated in Figure 1. It is required by each member of the team to deliver at the highest levels of excellence and cannot be understated. The leader of the project needs to ensure ownership is clearly communicated as such and must role-model this behavior.

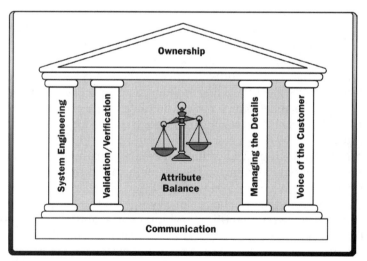

Figure 1.   Operational core values.

> **Key Takeaway**: Ownership is the overarching operational core value. Less successful project management teams do not view their role as delivery of the project, and with lack of ownership find themselves with suboptimal results at project completion.

Personal Core Values

Personal core values (PCV) are those behaviors in people that are integral to high performing project management teams. They represent the essential qualities in people that enable the delivery of a project at world-class levels, resulting in vehicles people want to drive. For a vehicle design to be emotive, it must be developed with a passion for the product that is derived from a strong set of personal core values. PCV's must be role-modeled by the leaders of the team through their day-to-day actions.

Behaviors that qualify as PCVs in the automotive industry (and arguably in any industry) meet one or more of the following criteria:

- Essential to healthy human relationships;
- Simple in nature;
- Enabling you to be honest with yourself;
- Enabler to optimize a complex system;
- Enabler to optimize the customer experience at all times in the development process; and
- Enabler to develop alternative solutions and challenge long standing norms.

The PCVs are defined in the automotive industry as the following:

1) Integrity   5) Creative
2) Tenacity   6) Decisive
3) Listener   7) Common Sense
4) Open Minded

Below we outline the common definition, as defined by Webster's dictionary, of each PCV as well as our interpretation of them in the automotive project management context.

- **Integrity**: *The quality or state being of sound moral principle, uprightness, honesty and sincerity.* It is the basis of accurate communication throughout the product development process. Representing the health of the deliverables accurately, rather than not employing "theatrical license" to make the deliverables appear better/worse than they actually are, is key to delivering the project for the good of the company. Representing the point of view of the customer requires steadfastness toward this end, upheld with the highest level of integrity.
- **Tenacity**: *The quality or state of being persistent.* Attribute owners who advocate for their position without an eye on the total system and general bureaucracy can get in the way of achieving the core deliverables. It is key to be persistent in the stated goals to ensure the project is of the highest possible quality. However, persistence should not be confused with stubbornness or lack of open-mindedness.

- **Listener**: *To make a conscious effort to hear, attend closely so as to hear.* Key to achieving the highest level of project development and execution is to always listen to your team and your customer. It is easy to become dictatorial in a leadership position and, even if you are listening to people, they will not see that quality in you and potentially keep great ideas or suggestions to themselves. One must be overt in asking team members as well as the customer base for the product for their opinions. One ensures good listening by repeating key points that the person you are listening to has articulated.
- **Open Minded**: *Having a mind that is open to new ideas, free from prejudice or bias.* You can be a great listener; however, that does not always translate into being open-minded about what you are hearing. The ability to truly internalize suggestions and act on them, including course corrections, is critically important to delivering a high quality outcome. It is a sign of an extremely mature leader.
- **Creative**: *Having or showing imagination in artistic or intellectual inventiveness.* In this context, creativity is the ability to take the standard operating process and finding new, efficient ways of delivering within it. Like an intellectual artist, it is the ability to see a complex system execution that has a major issue and getting the team to a brilliant optimized solution.
- **Decisive**: *Having the quality of decision; showing determination or firmness.* Easy decisions can be made by anyone, but it is the difficult decisions that require a person with the ability to use the data available, knowledge to know if the data is sufficient, and character to make the tough call. A good decision maker will use the 80/20 rule, having 80% of the data, to make the decision. This is key so as not to get "bogged" down in every small detail.
- **Common Sense**: *Ordinary good sense or sound practical judgment.* At times during the development and delivery of a project, "gut" calls are required to break a roadblock or course correct. Even if the data suggests otherwise, your experience/common sense may appropriately require you to challenge or better understand the data before proceeding. The balance of utilizing data, listening to customer wants and interpreting this to achieve the highest quality outcome does take sound practical judgment.

> **Key Takeaway**: Integrity is the most important of the personal core values. Without a strong core of personal integrity that drives you to optimize for the good of the corporation and customer, all of the other core values will be less effective and/or compromised

Fostering Core Values

Does your team understand core values? What value system do they possess? It is rare when we take time out to discuss with our team the basic principles of a value system and why it is important to the delivery of a well-executed project. This initial discussion needs to take place, along with an openness to revisit these core values at any time with the entire team or individually. The group needs to understand and believe in the culture and values they will encounter when working on your project management team. We need to enable our team to thrive within this well-understood culture.

The first step in fostering the core values is to lead by example. The impact that the leader has on the larger group cannot be underestimated; one must always be aware of his or her actions as they are constantly under scrutiny of the team. It is not only what you say, but what you do that will communicate to others the health of your personal core value system.

Additionally, one must understand each individual's value system, including their strengths and challenges with it. With this assessment, the leader can work with the individual to assimilate into the broader core value system as defined by the PCVs and OCVs.

A healthy organization will have a formal and only a formal leader. An unhealthy or compromised organization will have both a formal and an informal leader. You need to be able to determine if your organization has an informal leader, and if so, how to return your team to health by returning to the basics of the core values as described in this chapter. This will enable your team to always operate to its highest potential. If not, communication will begin to deteriorate and decisions will be sub-optimized. So, how can you gauge your leadership health? Let's begin by defining what is meant by formal and informal.

A formal leader is the organization's named head of a given project. The personnel announcement is sent to the entire organization via e-mail, clearly stating his or her position and scope of responsibility.

The informal leader; however, may or may not always exist. If your team has an informal leader it is due to the inability of the formal leader to clearly communicate and exhibit the core value system as described here. Without this and a clear set of core deliverables, a team will try to enable themselves to "get the job done" and will informally migrate to the person on the team that will enable them to do so. This may or may not be the formal leader. If it is not, work will get done, but the core deliverables will be compromised. The formal leader will still be operating at some level and will typically, in the presence of an informal leader, sub-optimize the outcomes of the deliverables.

The formal leader is not typically aware of the presence of an informal leader. The following describes the warning signs of when an informal leader has been chosen by the team.

- Your team no longer solicits your advice, guidance, and help in resolving issues on a regular basis;
- Your team does not talk to you in one-on-one situations regarding the health of the core deliverables or any suggestions they have to improve overall team effectiveness;
- You find out that decisions normally involving you have been made without your knowledge; and
- You find out that key communications within the team are occurring without your knowledge.

Remember, clarity and consistency of leadership style, including a well communicated core value system, is necessary to the high performance of the team.

> **Key Takeaway**: A healthy organization will have a formal and only a formal leader. An unhealthy or compromised organized organization will have both a formal and an informal leader. It is important to acknowledge this possibility and recognize the warning signs for awareness and potential action as required.

Influence of External Factors

External factors that affect the automotive industry change over time. They have influenced, to a greater and sometimes lesser extent, the type of vehicles we develop to meet customer expectations. They influence what we do; however, they do not influence how we do it. In other words, the core values and core deliverables of the project remain the same. They are timeless. To better illustrate this point, let's take a look at the external factors that were the most influential on the U.S. automotive industry during a span of time from about 15 to 20 years ago and looking forward to 2025.

Recall the Gulf War, the dot.com boom, and the major inroads the Japanese automotive industry made in their global presence. Back in the early 1990s, the external factors with the most impact to the U.S. automotive industry were political unrest, information technologies, and global competition. These external factors influenced the industry to focus on lean manufacturing principles to help make its operations more efficient against a growing foreign threat. The information technology boom brought with it greater flexibility for global communications as well as greater access for customers to compare vehicle products on their own personal computer. The Gulf War, as most wars do, provided leaps in new technologies that ultimately found their way into customer products. An example of this is the global positioning system (GPS) navigation systems that are, to this day, becoming increasingly more sophisticated.

Today, global competitors are making more and more inroads to the U.S. automotive industry's volume share. Brand image and perceived quality differences in the vehicles continue to erode market share. In addition, increasing concerns over global warming, the current state of fuel efficiency in our vehicles, and the race among the automotive industry's manufacturers to develop the most efficient and compelling strategy, are changing the shape of vehicles to come. Ultimately, the manufacturer that develops the most fuel efficient, environmentally friendly product will arguably develop the new barrier to entry for all other manufacturers.

The U.S. automotive industry's profitability was primarily based on the sale of large sport utility vehicles (SUVs) and trucks. The realignment of customer trends towards smaller, more fuel-efficient vehicles created an aggressive retooling of our products and assembly plants. And the movement to leverage global engineering, supplier, and manufacturing resources is key to delivering healthy bottom line profits to the original equipment manufacturers (OEMs).

All of this is progressing under an increasingly difficult global political climate. Continued unrest in the Middle East and that effect on the current prime source of automotive fuel, oil, is challenging the ongoing stability of all automotive OEMs. Will the current landscape of OEMs survive into the future, or will there be increasing mergers and partnerships?

Fast forward to 2025. We have settled on a few forms of fuel that are both efficient and environmentally friendly. The automotive OEMs that have survived are stable and profitable. Countries considered to be world powers have increased from today. With that, political priorities have shifted to safe sources of food supply and those countries that have developed effective technologies to protect human beings from the effects of global warming. In this time, vehicles and their associated technologies have evolved from today's norm to fit these key external factors.

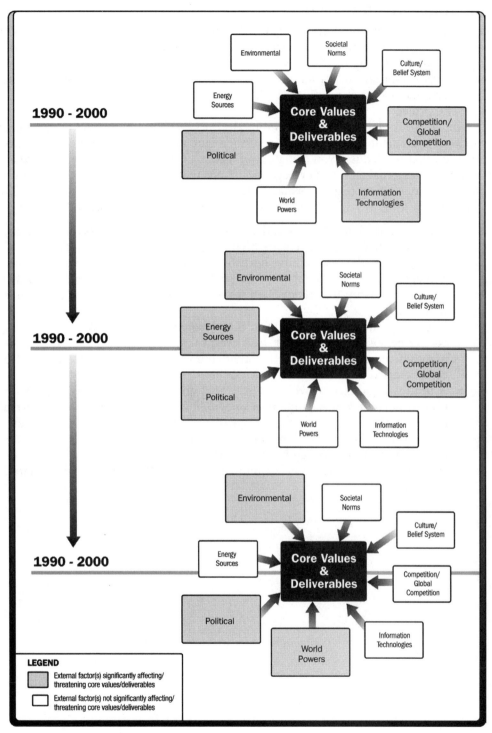

Figure 2.   External factors influencing the U.S. auto industry over time.

Conclusion/Key Takeaways

So, what do we mean by "The Constant Evolution of Timeless Management"? The world will continue to evolve and external factors, as previously described, will continue to change the way in which we do business. However, the "how" of managing complex vehicle programs, at its core, will never change. They key is ensuring that the external factors never modify the core values or deliverables required to deliver a successful project.

Don't let yourself get off track by embracing the latest "trendy" project management process improvement. The principles described here are timeless and the only course correction ever needed is if you deviate from them. Let's be clear—do not fear change driven by the external factors. Leverage the change that can enable your core value system to be more efficient (e.g., information technology).

If you take away anything from this chapter, you should remember the following:

- Whether it is 10 or 100 years in the future – if you do not possess the core values and core deliverables that ensure high performing teams, you will fail.
- Ownership is the overarching operational core value. Less successful project management teams do not view their role as delivery of the project, and with lack of ownership find themselves with suboptimal results at project completion.
- Integrity is the most important of the personal core values. Without a strong core of personal integrity that drives you to optimize for the good of the corporation and customer, all of the other core values will be less effective and/or compromised
- A healthy organization will have a formal and only a formal leader. An unhealthy or compromised organization will have both a formal and an informal leader. It is important to acknowledge this possibility and recognize the warning signs for awareness and potential action as required.
- Do not fear change driven by the external factors. Leverage the change that can enable your core value system to be more efficient (e.g., information technology).

CHAPTER 7

Shaping the Future of Project Management Research

Janice Lynne Thomas, Athabasca University
Jenny Krahn, University of Calgary
Stella George, Athabasca University

"The only way to predict the future is to have power to shape the future." Eric Hoffer (1902-1983)

"The future is here. It's just not widely distributed yet." William Gibson (1948 -)

So far, each chapter has presented a future-oriented vision of the shape of project management practice in the year 2025. Each chapter lays out a significant research agenda and identifies questions to be addressed as we move towards that future. This chapter sets out to define what project management research will look like in 2025 by identifying the historical and contextual influences at play today that will shape this future. Our focus is not so much on identifying the future questions for project management research to address in the future (though some of those will be identified too), but more on predicting what the field of project management research could look like (in terms of methods, academic standing, and practical impact), given the trajectories of current project management research and trends in the future of work.

Predicting the future has often been described as a fool's game. We all know about many famous quotes, particularly about information technology, that have been proven ludicrous with the benefit of hindsight. At the same time, many seemingly impossible predictions have been proven true. Often the difference is that those that were proven true were made by someone who had a background and vested interest in, and some power to influence, the outcome predicted. At the same time predictions often serve to provide direction and motivation for moving in a particular direction. It is the premise of this chapter that it is time to make some predictions about the future of project management (project management) research to begin a dialogue aimed at shaping this future.

Project management research in the future will grow from the foundation of current project management research, stimulated by the needs of project management practice as embedded in the future world of work. Before we can predict the future, we need a strong grounding in the present. As both practitioners and academics, we need to make sure that we understand what we know about project management (not just what we think we know), and what we need to learn. The shape of project management research in the future will be built on prior research and will need to be appropriate to the current trends in the practice of project management and the world of work. Reviewing existing project management research within engineering, management, and project management since 2000, we can determine the recent focus of investigations and provide a platform for moving project management research forward. However, understanding the past so that we avoid reinventing it alone is not enough. We must also review others' attempts to look forward to understand how changes in the context of work and organizations are likely to change how we manage and what we research. We must also think about the future practice of project management.

This chapter is laid out in five additional sections. The first presents the current state of project management research by examining existing reviews and criticisms of project management research and practice. The second surveys recent project management literature in three areas of publication (management, engineering, and project management). The third section presents emerging trends in the nature of work that can be expected to impact project management practice in the future. The fourth section explores different future visions of the role project managers will fill in organizations in the future. The final section discusses the likely impact of these global trends on the future of project management research. We conclude by offering some predictions about project management research by the year 2025. We present these predictions as a starting point for dialogue on the future of project management research rather than as certainties.

Evolution and Trends in Project Management Research

Project management research has evolved from a fairly concentrated focus on developing tools and techniques for management control to a much more varied interest in how project management operates within organizations. Project management research began largely as a search for tools to support project work in the 1950s and 1960s (Cleland, 2004; Stretton, 1994a). Much of the focus at this time was aimed at developing scheduling and tracking tools. Early research in project management tended to focus on improving specific individual tools and techniques of project management, or on understanding how various project management tools and techniques support project effectiveness or performance. With the spread of project management practices from engineering into information systems projects and new product development in the 1980s, interest grew in how projects were differentiated and whether different types of projects required different tools or techniques (Shenhar & Dvir, 1996). In the 1990s, the focus of both practice and research tended to dwell on the importance of teams, people, social skills, communication, partnering, and alliance formation to the success of projects (Thamhain, 1996). By the early 2000s, the focus had changed yet again from single projects to integration of project management concepts into organizational management. Interest focused on gaining executives' attention (Thomas, Delisle, Jugdev, & Buckle, 2002) organizational project management maturity (see, for example, Jugdev &

Thomas, 2002; Mullaly, 2006), selecting the right projects, and the links between strategy and project management (Milosevic & Srivannaboon, 2006; Morris & Jamieson, 2005). In project management publications, authors have considered a wide range of topics individually, such as how to plan projects effectively, develop strong schedules, and many others. Recently, the focus in project management literature has shifted from performing project management to integrating it into the organization. Papers on project management maturity (see, for example, Mullaly, 2006) and linking project management and strategy (see, for example, Milosevic & Srivannaboon, 2006; Morris and Jamieson, 2005) have become common.

Other papers have considered the relationship among project elements. Authors have examined a wide range of relationships between project management elements, such as the way in which the level of standardization of project management elements impacts project effectiveness (Milosevic, Inman, & Ozbay, 2001) and the impact of project leadership on project performance (Jiang, Klein, & Chen, 2001; Odusami, Iyagba, & Omirin, 2003), which may include the development environment in which an information technology project is delivered or elements of team composition in construction. Another paper linking project management concepts considered the impact of goals on the way in which decisions are made on a project (Abdel-Hamid, Sengupta, & Swett, 1999). In some cases, the topics being related in the literature do not compare two topics specific to project management. For example, Maya, Rahimi, Meshkati, Madabushi, Pope & Schulte. (2005) argue that in order to most effectively collect lessons learned from projects, a culture change is required. Thus, we see other management literatures (organizational learning, culture, organizational behavior, organizational theory, and complexity among others) having an impact on research in project management.

We are by no means the first to suggest that there is something to learn from understanding the evolution and topic trends emerging from the growing body of project management literature. Over the past 10 or 15 years, several authors have attempted to make sense of the evolution of project management research and practice (Betts & Lansley, 1995; Crawford, Pollack, & England, 2006; Kloppenborg & Opfer, 2000; Morris, 2002; Morris, Jamieson, & Sheppard, 2006; Morris, Patel, & Wearne, 2000; Pinto; 2002; Stretton, 1994a, b, c; Themistocleous and Wearne, 2000; Urli & Urli (2000); Zobel & Wearne, 2000). All in all, a great number of studies have sought to categorize and explore our learnings with respect to project management.

The most recent contribution to this literature (Crawford, Pollack, & England, 2006) presents a consolidated review of seven key studies reviewing project management literature over the period 1983 – 2003 (The articles introduced above: Betts & Lansley; Kloppenborg and Morris; Morris Patel & Wearne; Themisocleous & Wearne; Urli & Urli (2000); Zobel & Wearne). The authors note how difficult it is to perform an integrative comparison of quality detailing areas of contradiction as well as consistency across the literature. Their work adds to the trend prediction by use of a computational analysis method, keyword analysis, on five-year sections of the two leading project management journals (*Project Management Journal* and *International Journal of Project Management*). They suggest "Project Evaluation and Improvement and Strategic Alignment are both increasing in their significance to the field" (Crawford et al., p. 183), and note interesting trends in quality management and interpersonal issues. "Although both these topics have been found by previous studies to be of significance, and increasingly so, this study found a decrease in their significance...although these topics may be important in managing projects well, the significance that is placed on these topics may have peaked" (Crawford et al., p. 183). The authors also note decreasing interest in scope management, finalization and marketing.

Articles examining project management topics and the potential future of project management focus on topics as wide-ranging as the demands that project managers may face (Barnes & Wearne, 1993) to the current challenges that are facing those in project management today (Shenhar & Dvir, 2007). Others suggest that specific topics will be of interest for research in the short or long term. In one case, a government research network in the United Kingdom proposes future research directions based on their review of what is being produced by the network as well as the needs they perceive in the practice of project management (Winter, Smith, Morris, & Cicmil, 2006). While this group made many recommendations about future directions for project management—and those interested really should read the entire Special Edition of the International Journal of Project Management for November of 2006—one of the principle findings with respect to the usefulness of research to practice is that for research to be useful it must be based on the actuality of what is done in projects and not what academics or others believe should be done (Cicmil, Williams, Thomas, & Hodgson, 2006). Again, the authors heavily critique the current state of project management research and make numerous suggestions for improving both relevance and rigor.

Some indication of topics of particular importance in the future of project management may be reflected in increased focus on emerging topics such as leadership agile teams and increasing focus on team and individual creativity and complexity. These are the focus of sponsored project management research arising from practical needs (See www.pmi.org/resources/pages/current-research.aspx). These topics are developing in response to external stimuli, which may make them to some extent indicators of changes in direction in terms of how the field of project management will change in the next ten years. The characteristics of projects are another factor that will impact the field of project management. The level of project uncertainty can increase the level of challenge on a project, particularly in a rapidly changing project environment with competing demands. Authors recommend that in this situation, project managers should recognize heuristics and take appropriate action (McCray, Purvis, & McCray, 2002). Project complexity has led to a higher need for integrating components of a project by the project manager and necessitated that they have a higher level of cognitive complexity to support their effective leadership (Thomas & Mengel, 2008). The level of innovation on projects impacts the management style of the project manager (Shenhar & Dvir, 1996) and the number of locations for a project has consequences for the project (Evaristo & van Fenema, 1999).

In some cases these emerging topics, as well as more traditional project management topics, are linked with external forces that have promoted their introduction and use. This gives us a first look at how external forces, or global trends that are external to project management, may be shaping past and future trends in project management. Some examples are Jaafari (2003), who considers the impact of a complex society on the field of project management and the changes that will be necessary to a field that is based on a static environment. The Sarbanes-Oxley Act has also had an impact on some projects in such areas as increased formalization and longer project duration (Leih, 2006). Changes in organizations are impacting the way in which projects are managed. In Ives (2005) review, he found that there is considerable organizational change but little related to the effective fit of projects into organizations (his study is limited, as it includes in-depth interviews of only four people). Within the organization, other factors also impact project management such as the influence of business strategy on projects (Srivannaboon & Milosevic, 2006).

Finally, it is also prudent to note that there have been many criticisms leveled against this body of research as well. Meredith (2002) conducted a review of the articles published in *Project Management Journal* for the years 1995 - 2001. He found that two-thirds of these articles were of low academic rigor. In addition, others (Cicmil & Hodgson, 2006; Thomas 2000a, b; Winter, Smith, Morris, & Cicmil, 2006) have strongly made the case that overreliance on positivist methods, modern epistemological assumptions and normative motivations have left project management practice and research struggling to get beyond reported best-practice compilations. Their suggestions for how to do that include improving the rigor of application of all research methods, more detailed and constructive reviews of articles before publication, greater use of reflective practice, action research, and qualitative research designed first to understand what is really happening on projects. Shenhar and Dvir (2007) criticize project management research for having little, if any, impact on the teaching or preparation of project managers. Raising the quality, rigor, and relevance are all firmly stated goals necessary for improving the academic standing and practical credibility of project management research.

Review of Project Management Research Topics in Three Disciplines

We set out to explore the extant literature on project management in three academic disciplines: management, engineering, and project management. However, the scant nature of the management literature identified as project management made it uninformative to compare to the other two publication areas. Thus, we present this section in two parts. First we examine the management literature explicitly identified as project management research. Then we present he findings of our study of the two foremost engineering management journals of the day, *IEEE Transactions on Engineering Management (IEEE)* and the *Engineering Management Journal (EMJ)*, and the two journals dedicated explicitly to project management research and practice (the *International Journal of Project Management (IJPM)* and the *Project Management Journal (PMJ)*.

Exploring Project Management Within Management

The results of searching for references to project management in the abstracts and citations held in ABI-INFORM for key management journals show few project management-oriented publications in management literature. We found only 63 publications categorized as project management over the last seven years (summarized in Table 1). The majority of these articles were in the *Harvard Business Review* (24 articles) or in *Management Science* and *Decision Sciences* (29 articles). Most of the articles published in *Management Science* or *Decision Science* tended to be highly mathematical in method and focused on scheduling or risk analysis. Articles published in the less academic journals, (e.g., *Harvard Business Review*) focused on managers rather than professionals, and were often written by consultants and based on survey or survey-like methods. There were very few articles aimed at theory development.

Table 1:   Project management articles within management literature.

Journal	Number of Articles	Year							
		2000	2001	2002	2003	2004	2005	2006	2007
Management Science	22	2	4	4	4	1	2	2	3
Decision Sciences	7				1	1		1	4
Academy of Management Journal	0								
Organization Science	4	1		1	1	1			
Organization Studies	4			1		3			
Administrative Science Quarterly	1			1					
Academy of Management Review	1					1			
Strategic Management Journal	1						1		
Academy of Management Executive	0								
Sloan Management Review	0								
Harvard Business Review	23		2	5	5	3	2	1	5
TOTALS	63	3	6	11	11	10	5	4	10

Our findings suggest that there has been little coverage of project management as a topic within mainstream management literature, with no trend towards increasing its coverage. And yet, there are many articles published every month on topics such as risk, teams or team leadership, management of new product development, or change. All of these are likely talking about some aspect of project management.

The recently published research monograph by Kwak and Anbari (2008) supports this assertion. They reviewed a wider body of management and business journals (18 in total) over the period of 1980 to 2000, and used a broader set of search terms (e.g., searching on topics like teams, risk, etc instead of just project management). Using this broader set of search terms, they found that there was an increase in project management articles in these journals of 12% over the period. Although the current areas of interest in project management literature and management research literature are different, Kwak and Anbari predict that relevant knowledge will be integrated into project management and go further to suggest that project management"...must embrace and apply them (allied disciplines) as part of project management" (p. 64).

These two analyses of the management literature on project management raise two important concerns for the future of project management research. First is the question of what is the domain of project management research? if all these topics are covered in other management disciplines, then how does project management research contribute unique insights to the literature? Second is the question of the preparation of project management researchers. If project management research is intricately related to these other management disciplines (such as organization behavior, organization theory, operations management, and others), how can project management researchers contribute to this literature unless they are thoroughly grounded in the base disciplines to ensure that project management research is not simply reinventing work that has been done already in other disciplines? Studying project management at a doctorate level may not be good preparation for studying some specific topics in project management if the student is not required to cover the foundations in management literature for the study of that topic. Perhaps these are the first questions that have to be answered to explore the future of project management research if project management is to find a home alongside the other management disciplines.

Comparing Project Management within Engineering and Project Management Journals

We set out to explore the extant literature on project management in the two foremost engineering management journals of the day, *IEEE Transactions on Engineering Management (IEEE)* and the *Engineering Management Journal (EMJ)*, and the two journals dedicated explicitly to project management research and practice (the *International Journal of Project Management (IJPM)* and the *Project Management Journal (PMJ)*. Our purpose was twofold: first, to understand what differences there may be in the topic coverage in these two arenas, and between the reviews conducted earlier and this one, particularly with respect to any differences between the two arenas of publishing studied; and second, to identify existing or emerging trends in this research that would allow us to speculate on what project management would look like by 2025.

The ABI-INFORM database was searched for all published items from *PMJ*, *IJPM*, *IEEE*, and *EMJ*, within the period 01/01/2000 – 12/31/2007 (performed in November 2007 and updated in May 2008). Each result set was saved into an EndNote 9.0.1 database engine. A second search of *IEEE* and *EMJ* returned results for all publications containing "project management" within the abstract and citation; Table 2 shows many fewer *IEEE* (PM) and *EMJ* (PM) items. A keyword count was performed, using EndNote's internal subject bibliography tool, The count identified prominent keywords present in each of the journals. Table 2 indicates the number of papers in which each keyword was used for each journal database

An additional search using the subcomponent terms from the Centre for Research in Managing Projects (CRMP) /A project management BoK categories (Morris, 2002)

Table 2:   Comparison of Engineering and Project Management Journals

	PMJ	**IJPM**	**IEEE**	**EMJ**	**IEEE (PM)**	**EMJ (PM)**
Published Items	328	548	347	212	53	60
Articles	236	500	326	182	51	54
Book Reviews	92	48	21	30	2	6
Total keywords	317	529	510	356	109	124
*Prominent Keywords	22	29	32	43	31	42

*used in >= 2.5% of papers

Table 3:   Categorization overview, after CRMP/APM.

Category	Subcomponent
General	Project management; program management; portfolio management; project context
Strategic	Project success criteria; strategy/project management plan; value management; risk management; quality management; safety/health and environment; ethics
Control	Work content and scope management; time scheduling phasing; resource management; budgeting cost management; change control; performance management; information management
Technical	Design, production and handover management; requirements management; technology management; estimating; value engineering; modeling and testing; configuration management
Commercial	Business case ; marketing and sales; financial management; procurement; bidding; contract management; legal awareness
Organizational	Lifecycle design and management; opportunity; design and development; production; handover; project evaluation review; organization structure; organizational roles
People	Communication teamwork leadership decision-making; negotiating and influencing; conflict management; project management competency development; personnel management

(Table 3) was performed on the EndNote database of each journal and the results ranked per category. Analysis of keywords on a year-by-year basis for each of the four journals (and the two project management journal sets from *IEEE* and *EMJ*) did not indicate any particular trend within the 2000-2007 period.

Engineering management, engineering project management and project management literature was categorized using the BoK categories (shown in Figure 1 below). Both the engineering project management articles and the overall set of engineering

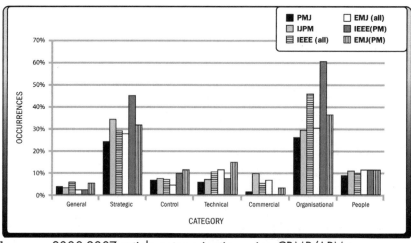

Figure 1:   2000-2007 article categorization using CRMP/APM terms.

management articles show the same focus as those in the project management litera-ture. If anything, the engineering project management articles, particularly those in *IEEE*, appear to be leading these trends.

Morris' study (2002) categorizing the project management literature from *IJPM* and *PMJ* (including PMI's *PM Network* magazine) over the 1990s provides a similar data set. A cross-decade comparison based on Morris' 1990s data and our 2000-2007 data, illustrated in Figure 2 below, shows more interest in strategic and organizational issues in the 2000s than the 1990s. The 2000s demonstrate an accompanying trend away from articles focusing on general project management and control.

Although it is clear that trend insights are influenced by how researchers look for trends, there are some common changes in topics of publication between what was pub-lished in the 1990s and what was published in the 2000s. As per Kwak and Anbari's (2008) review, our review of management literature found many important and in-sightful project management articles that are not categorized as project management literature and so would never be found by one searching only for project management research. The majority of the articles in the management journals that were classified as project management were either practically oriented problem or consulting research or highly empirical and usually mathematical modeling approaches to "hard" operations management-type topics.

This failure to use a common categorization system that allows research to be effec-tively categorized and found makes it difficult for future research to build from a solid foundation on prior research. There is very little difference in focus of recent project management research published in engineering and project management journals over the period 2000-2007. Engineering and project management literature exhibits virtually the same trends away from general and control techniques to a focus on organizational,

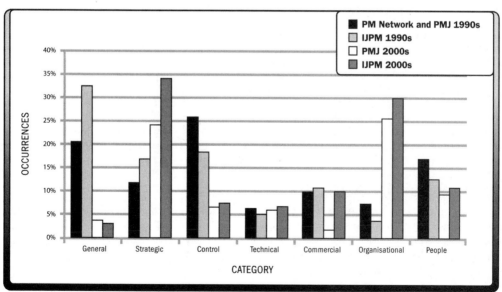

Figure 2:   1990s vs. 2000s project management CRMP/APM categorization in PMJ and IJPM.

strategic, and decision-making topics since 1990. In addition, Meredith's (2002) view that there is a static, low level of research quality in this body of literature is supported by this review of the management, engineering, and project management literature. We encountered very few theoretical research papers in our review of this literature. One additional finding of note is the insight we came to in looking at these papers that some authors took advantage of the relative isolation of these research fields to publish very similar articles in both realms – thus counting the research papers twice in the publication game. Review processes need to be improved to both strengthen the quality of the papers submitted and to eliminate this illegitimate practice of double publishing. These challenges in terms of the rigor of the foundation, the research methods, and the reviewing processes must also be addressed by project management research by 2025 in order to give this work credibility within the body of management literature.

Having reviewed where project management research sits today and identified a number of critical questions that need to be addressed in moving the research domain forward, we turn now to an exploration of the trends and changes in the world of work that are predicted for the period up to 2025. Exploring these trends will help us illuminate the types of research that will be necessary by the year 2025, and thus the future of project management research. Questions include: How will the emerging global changes in the nature of work and organizations impact how projects are managed? Will research done today be capable of preparing project managers for tomorrow's world? As we think about how to move the future of research forward, we need to remember that the roots of both practice and research are firmly embedded in solving the problems of the work world.

Trends and Tendencies in the World of Work

There are many factors that influence the world of work and how it may change in the future. Clearly there is much interaction between influencing factors. World demographics (both of working age and overall population size), technology, and political attitudes are fundamental factors. For business, we are interested in them and their influence on organizational structure and internationalization. What happens in the world over the next 17 years influences the research that will occur to inform the following 25 years. This section provides a brief overview of key trends futurists expect to impact the world of work between now and 2025. Readers interested in this topic are referred to the futurists who wrote the cited literature for a fascinating review of possible futures. In this section, we have focused on three areas where changes are most likely to impact the management of projects and therefore the topics of research required to support project management: Workforce demographics, technological innovation, and organizational structures.

Workforce Demographics

Two important demographic trends are likely to impact the world of work over the next few decades. First, the world's population is aging. World population will climb to 9 billion by 2043, but the growth rate will fall from between 1% and 2% (held consistently through 1960 to 1990s) to 0.5% in 2050 (U.S. Census Bureau, 2008): we are having fewer children and living longer. The effect of this world population slowdown has been seen in the western workforce already. However, the aging population effect is not just a European or North American phenomenon but could also be felt in China shortly as a side effect of the one-child policy (since 1979). Table 4 illustrates the projected aging of the workforce over the next several decades.

This aging of the work force has a number of implications for work and projects. For years, the world economic growth has depended on a growing relatively wealthy workforce to drive the economic engine of consumption. Until recently, the concern was that we would not have enough new workers to make up for the retirement of the wealthy "baby boomers" who would now have time to spend their accumulated wealth. Emphasis was placed on how to entice the new generation workforce into the workplace and keep them. Today the impact is likely to shift to how we will afford to look after all the retirees; given the reduced economic wealth both they and their countries will have to spend because of the recent economic meltdown in the fall of 2008. It is highly likely today that people will retire later and that there will be fewer jobs for entry-level people.

Now organizations and projects are likely faced with the challenges of accommodating aging workforces with high accumulations of vacation time, possibly greater likelihood of serious illness, and different and perhaps unique motivations. Work-life balance is likely to be of increased importance as workers of all ages will likely have less interest in long, intense work days. All ages will want balance but for different reasons: Baby boomer's children don't want to be absent parents, younger generations are more likely to move if not satisfied, and senior experienced workers have more bargaining power and less stamina.

The second major demographic shift will be a continued shift in population to the east. By 2030, India is expected to have a population of more than 1.53 billion (18% of the expected world population). In comparison to China's population, which is expected to be at its peak of 1.46 billion (and will begin to drop in subsequent years), India will be the most populous country in the world. Combine these population trends with western immigration trends, the need for both skilled and unskilled labor in western

Table 4: World population in 2008, 2025, and 2050, within standard working age.

Age	2008	% of 2008	2025	% of 2025	2050	% of 2050
20-24	580,567,629	15.44%	590,572,324	12.94%	631,084,971	12.10%
25-29	535,051,158	14.23%	581,133,256	12.73%	629,588,354	12.07%
30-34	496,269,808	13.20%	572,765,961	12.55%	627,424,459	12.03%
35-39	489,558,772	13.02%	577,922,372	12.66%	616,554,686	11.82%
40-44	446,157,545	11.87%	523,993,263	11.48%	588,211,602	11.28%
45-49	374,765,642	9.97%	474,497,174	10.40%	555,510,679	10.65%
50-54	341,389,644	9.08%	459,414,198	10.07%	538,135,095	10.32%
55-59	282,383,265	7.51%	423,405,496	9.28%	519,944,253	9.97%
60-64	213,940,038	5.69%	359,845,470	7.89%	508,988,580	9.76%
total	3,760,083,501		4,563,549,514		5,215,442,679	

Source: U.S. Census Bureau, Population Division

countries and the move to outsource jobs to places where the workers are (like China and India), and this will result in significantly higher levels of cross-cultural differences in the work force. Migration from these high-population growth areas to lower-population countries will change the role of immigrants and minorities in the western workforce and the role of outsourcing to workforces outside of the parent country. Groups that are currently in the minority may soon find themselves in the majority. Accommodating differences in everything from work weeks to holiday schedules will be only the least of the challenges in managing such a multifaceted workforce.

Technological Innovation

The computer and telecommunications revolution over the last 20 years has directly impacted how work and projects are managed. Virtual working environments are almost the norm today. Despite the increasing prevalence of this mode of work, many questions remain to be answered in how virtual projects and teams can best be managed. In many ways, it has been this explosion in computer and communication technologies that has allowed work to move to a 24/7 global basis in many industries and on many projects and led to the resulting concerns with cross-cultural and virtual management (Williams, 2007). Research into how technology, virtual communication, time zones, and distance impact the delivery of projects will continue to be very important over the next 20 years. In addition, other trends in working and backlashes to some of the current technology-enabled work tendencies are likely to shape research agendas in the years to come.

Stone (2007) suggests that living with continuous partial attention will become the reality and opportunity of living and working with handheld electronic devices. This reality will create at least two significant challenges for project managers that will drive future research. The first challenge will be to understand how project managers (and team members) will cope in a world where they are expected to be available to answer questions and handle situations from all sides at any point in time. Research into this topic—particularly around work-life balance (Lindgren and Packendorf, 2006)—is beginning to be seen and will increase in importance over the next decades. The second challenge is more tentative at present, but prognosticators are starting to see evidence of a backlash to the accessibility of technology and the sensory overload it can bring with it (Penn & Zalesne, 2007). Combining this microtrend with the demographic changes and expected changes in motivations in the workforce suggests that intense project work may be increasingly difficult to staff and motivate. Research into how to manage people rebelling against living with continuous partial attention will become increasingly important to improving effective project management.

A second area where technology is set to change the work world is in the area of automated information/knowledge tracking. New technologies and computer processing power have made the capture and analysis of large sets of data available for automatic assessment of work activities. For example, Microsoft has patented technology that can track time knowledge workers spend on various computer tasks over the course of the day (Mostrous & Brown, 2008). In addition, there are many commercially available applications to track computer time spent on different types of work, and some can be covertly deployed through networks. These technologies may very soon eliminate the need for manual time-tracking and automate some components of effort tracking and reporting. But beyond simple time tracking, this may also allow the real-time updating of status of tasks, indicators arising, issues, etc. to be flagged to the project management, or by the program manager or sponsor of a project. *Algorithms in the Attic* by Michael Schrage (2007) indicates that known algorithms now can be applied both to automate decisions and assist in decision-making more widely in the business world due to more advanced computing power. Already being applied in retailing to "efficiently sift through the mountains of data that are now being collected" (Schrage 2007, p. 8) it is easy to see how data-review management could be applied in many other management fields. This sort of technology will raise management challenges around the psycho-social impact of surveillance and its legality, privacy issues, control and possibly mental health impacts, as well as the role of the project manager. There will be little need for a technocrat processing, analyzing, and making decisions based on time data if the computer can do this aspect of the job.

Prognosticators observing these changes in technology (Karoly, 2004) suggest that in the coming 10-15 years, we will see increasing work impacts of technological change, both in terms of synergies across technologies and employee skills sets, and change of organization forms and employee relationships. These changes are expected to increase the importance of flexibility and learning in organizations and individuals to respond to international and technological changes. This leads us to questions of how work will be organized to support these demographic and technological trends.

Organizational Structure

Malone (2004) concisely described the future of work as following his observations about the social organization of our world: business organizations imitate real life. He observes an amazing pattern and variety of organizational forms ranging from increased independence (individuals or small businesses) to centralization (kingdoms or corporate hierarchies), through to decentralization (democracy or networks/business groups). Others contribute to the discussion about the future of work and organizations by suggesting that formalization of an employment economy, commodification and motivations to work, and a move to globalization are not a natural inevitable process—they can be part of the picture but are not necessarily required to be (see, for instance, Hamel, 2007). Other futures of employment are: information and knowledge society; form of the flexible work organization; post-bureaucratic management; and non-capitalist (community). The future of work centers around ways to organize work to allow for these types of employment and to include greening of the organization.

One emerging form of work organizing, open source type democratic networks, is receiving an increasing degree of attention today (Tapscott & Williams, 2006). This form of organizing has been used to create free encyclopedias online (Wikipedia), develop open source software (e.g., Linus and Moodle) and invite donations of free expertise (such as a mining company example in Tapscott's book). These networks work because they are used to review and adapt refined versions of an existing main thing. It is suggested today that this approach will not work for new products or new development efforts–however this assertion has yet to be tested. In these fluid communities, who plays the role of project manager, how is the project managed, and is there such a thing as start and end dates?

This open-source approach fits somewhat into a growing concern with self-organizing systems and other complex human systems. Research into how taking these concepts seriously is likely to impact project management is beginning to appear (Cicmil,

Table 5:   Impact of global trends on project management and future of project management research.

Future of work – ideas	Impact on Project Management	Future Demands on project management Research
Workforce Demographics		
Aging of the workforce Shift of population to east Continuing high immigration in west Global employee resource pool. International operations and communications. Ongoing education flexibility to allow in business changes of direction/production.	Teams, leadership, negotiation. Control mechanisms established and shared through standard accreditation in process and tools. Increasing use of distributed work teams, including team members of various cultures and work motivations around the world. Strategic project management as project improvement. Motivating different age groups.	People, communications, and people management is more complex must be supported by project management. Sophisticated control mechanism to unify international working teams. The position of project management in global organizations working on projects indifferent industries and project types. Challenges of using increased standardization while facilitating greater flexibility in workforce.
Technology		
Virtual working environments. Automated time/task tracking. Easy access to standardized project management methodologies. Continuous partial attention. Technology backlash.	Control mechanisms use technology available. Information management as control. Project management tools widely available. Extended tools for supporting project management available but less widely used. Increased resistance to technology.	Increased work on work tracking tools and automated project planning. Psycho social impacts of increased technological surveillance and connectivity.
Organizational Forms		
Decentralized organizations. Networks of smaller operational units within an organization or that work in collaboration to form temporary (long and short term) organizations. Collaborative self-organizing work structures	Increasing use of temporary organizational structures (projects). Enterprise-wide systems integrating project management into organization management systems. project management as a discipline of management, integration with corporate strategy. Standardized reporting frameworks. More varied and numerous project stakeholders on many projects. New project management approaches for non-hierarchical and non-organizational projects.	When is project management appropriate/effective? When can VALUE be yielded from project management? Autonomous action – different models of project management responsibility. Legal support for autonomy and flexibility.

Cooke Davis, Crawford, & Richardson, 2009). However, the open-source approach is still more organized than what self-organizing seems to be related to. It seems that what we might be missing from our picture are implications originating in the fine grain details of the future way we work; the social epidemic phenomenon discussed by Gladwell (2000) in his book *The Tipping Point*. What are the dynamics of having ideas and motivators accepted by a group of independent individuals such that you create a "tipping point" that drives the project forward? Duncan J. Watts (2007) claims that ideas are spread by volume of ordinary people signed up—witness the 2008 U.S. election and the impact on voting. Consideration needs to be given to the fact that it may be more that the specialist group that "tip" the network of influencers within the masses. The challenge for project management is, therefore, to know how its masses will respond to the ideas of the specialists within the domain, and how to enroll these masses in the objective of interest. One could view project management as always having been part of Malone's (2004) decentralized business organization. In essence, the devolved responsibility of business actions within project teams if they have autonomy to act is already part of Malone's future.

In order to realize these visions of alternative organizations, we return to Karoly's (2004) suggestion that the workforce will require greater flexibility and openness to change and adaptability. However, there also is the question of what affects the ability and willingness of individuals to be autonomous? The legal system's impact on an individual's desire to take risks and manage creatively and flexibly will also need to be explored. The role of standardization in an individual's perception of how to act; it's not just project management maturity but the maturity and mastery confidence of the project manager. Finally, we come back to the matter of control. How do you "manage" these independent, autonomous contributors who are not necessarily paid by the organization attempting to produce the product? And how do individuals come to earn a living from participation in stimulating knowledge-sharing activities they are passionate about?

These trends in demographics, technology and organizational forms will all impact the future of work and the practice of project management in many ways already discussed in earlier chapters.

Evolving Role of Project Managers

Each of the trends influencing the world of work discussed above will have serious implications for the role of project managers within the work world. Krahn and Thomas (2008) address the changing nature of the project manager's role: "As the project environment becomes more complex and projects become larger, there are also a larger number of more powerful stakeholders on projects. This fact, combined with the trend toward project managers having less authority and more accountability, will make the project manager's role more challenging." They consider the range of project manager roles as options for the future: project manager as certified technician; project management as profession; all "managers as project managers" where project management is an unremarkably usual tool and mindset for any manager and project management enables collaborative free enterprise. In particular, one idea that seems in synch with the current, more leading-business edge is that a project manager is to all intents and purposes acting as CEO of a temporary organization. Table 6 summarizes the implications for project management and project management research of each of these potential roles.

Implications for project management research in the change in role of project managers varies quite widely with scenario, extending from further entrenchment of project management as a sector-specific tool right through to complete integration of project management

Table 6: Impact of alternative future roles of project management on future of project management research.

Scenario	Evidence and Implications for Project Management	Implications for Project Management Research
Project Manager as Certified Technician		
	Technical experts: Ongoing recognition of the importance of a technical background relevant to the project: Increased certification, formalization of tools, processes, practices, project management career paths, project management offices. Often provided by organizations. Implies increased responsibility without accountability or authority. Increased competition for services, products as recognition of a real market in this field. Formalized field of study, subgroups dedicated some focus by recognized fields of study.	Experts temporarily crossing over from other fields (total quality management, engineering, accounting, cost control, risk, human resources). Continued separation of project management from management research. Continued separation of sector-specific journals. Focus on efficiency and marketing of project management and project management products as research topics. Possible separation of project management subtopics into own fields or research.
Project Management as Profession		
	Professional associations certify competent project managements as professionals. Project managers seen as trusted advisors and senior managers in their own right, Higher quality project management. Cost project management increases. Project management at professional level largely outsourced or divisional zed (like accounting, law, engineering). Increased accountability and legal activity, contracts, liability insurance. Not all projects need professional project management. Tools customized and tailored to individual organizations or projects through the professional judgment of the project manager.	Increasingly held accountable for both body of knowledge and results. More practitioner led research by expert project managements (similar to medicine). Stronger interest in metrics to measure project management effectiveness. Legal and contractual research required. Responsibility and accountability defined within professional terms. Separation between theoretical and practice-based research more defined. Theoretical project management becomes part of management research.
Managers as Project Managers		
	Project management becomes standard management tool (with administrative support from a project management office). No longer differentiated as project management. Tied in with strategic planning – seen to be competitive advantage. The largest, most complex projects managed separately from organization as a temporary organization. Project management taught in core of MBA programs. May not move project management forward as this is not seen as a separate field.	Research topics: human resources, governance and organizational structure to clarify role compression and confusion of responsibilities and the project as temporary organization. Project management part of mainstream management literature.

(continued)

Table 6: Impact of alternative future roles of project management on future of project management research. *(continued)*

Project Management as Peer Collaboration

	Virtual and distributed project management (and project team) to support complex worldwide projects of distributed project teams (employees with flexibility). Control, responsibility and accountability by peer pressure and personal integrity. Decentralized decision making; communication challenges. Agile methods, trial and error, learning by doing become much more acceptable methods of project management. Tools for sharing both accountability and information are available.	New research field, virtual management, containing project management, technology and organization management. Field for project management will contain: people (communication, motivation, management), project management tools (IT, technology and virtual environments), temporary organizational structure, distributed governance, legal, contractual liability. Cultural research to support communication and outcome expectations.

Source: extended from Krahn and Thomas 2008

research within the management research domain a new field of research that supports the management of global virtual collaboration. With a change toward professionalization of project management, project management research will both have to become part of theoretical management literature and create a space for good quality practitioner (manager)-led research in a similar way that medicine is both underpinned by theory and practical discussion of methods, techniques, and process. A good question raised by Krahn and Thomas (2008) is what will make project management a desirable field in which to work. The increasing complexity and changing face of project work that they envision is something that project management research needs to consider, and prompt discussion is called for about the change needed in how we think about the practice of project management.

Predictions for Project Management Research in 2025

Science fiction writers and even some theoretical physicists suggest that there is no one future that can be accurately predicted but that each and every small decision today triggers and extinguishes some of a set of possible futures. For that reason, given all the changes happening in the both the world of work and of project management, we do not claim to be able from this review of trends and changes to accurately predict what the future of project management will look like by the year 2025. Instead we provide three predictions as a potential vision of what the future could hold for project management by 2025. These potential future states are offered as a foundation for both discussion and action.

By 2025, we predict that project management will be recognized as:

- An important cross-disciplinary research area making unique contributions to the management academic discipline;
- The source for practical and scientifically rigorous knowledge about managing projects necessary for, and driving, practice; and,
- Responsible for clarifying project management's role as a strategic facilitator, not a control process.

In order to attain this vision, there will need to be changes in both the research undertaken and the attitudes and activities of practitioners, professional associations, and educational institutions. Key changes we identify for these two groups are summarized in Table 7.

Table 7: Predictions for the future of project management research

By 2025, we predict that project management will be recognized as an important cross-disciplinary research area making unique contributions to the management academic discipline.	

Implications	**Research:**
	Contribute to the understanding of projects by clearly aligning new research with past research across disciplines through shared terminology, common models of categorization, etc.
	
	Ensure that project management research is founded on earlier management literature – eliminate reinventing the wheel.
	
	Researchers will need a thorough grounding in the base disciplines in order to do more than descriptive research.
	
	Clearly delineate what project management research's unique contribution is to the management literature.
	
	Eliminate republishing of similar studies and findings in different journals.
	
	Increase ease of knowledge transfer:
	    Consistent application of keywords;
	    Editors agreeing on and enforcing common use of keywords; and
	    Knowledgeable reviewers who can recognize new from recycled knowledge.
	
	Increase in problem-based research grounded in theory.
	
	Rigorous application of scientifically valid research methods.
	
	Research into the presence or absence of context specificity in research findings—what can be usefully generalized.
	
	Practice:
	Training and professional standards founded on a common body of knowledge recognized as applicable to project management.
	
	Decreasing variance across audiences in the use of project management constructs.
	
	Education of project managers recognized as cross-disciplinary, ongoing, reflective and practice learning, education.

By 2025, we predict that project management will be recognized as the source for practical and scientifically rigorous knowledge about managing projects necessary for, and driving, practice.	

Implications	**Research:** Movement away from overreliance on survey- and interview-based atheoretical research. Movement to critically applied action and interpretive research involving both practitioners and researchers. Conceptualizing new tools and techniques and testing them in practice. Empirically grounded, evidence-based, theoretically conceptualized discipline from which best practices can be derived. Resurgence in people management, project quality and risk research to support changes in work. Human resources research into the variance in motivations (in particular, views on quality of life) within project teams, and the motivational effects on team and subsequently project, performance. Researchers must address the topics of critical importance to practitioners in a way that addresses the scientific requirements of "owning" the research agenda.

(continued)

Table 7: Predictions for the future of project management research *(continued)*

<table>
<tr><td rowspan="8" style="writing-mode: vertical">Implications</td><td>

Topics to be covered include:
    Project teams;
    Managing temporary organizations;
    Work-life balance in temporary work assignments;
    Application of new technologies;
    Managing "open source" self organizing projects;
    Developing new technologies to track project time and effort against objectives;
    Appropriate and ethical use of such technologies;
    How to implement such technologies to reduce resistance; and
    How to synthesize, report, use and understand such data.

People-based research to support leveraging of technology and human resources legislation for virtual working occurring in practice settings.

Practice:
Participation in applied research:

Testing new tools and techniques in conjunction with researchers - critically applied action and interpretive research.

Technology to be commercialized and widely introduced.

Best practice refinement and agreement between researchers and experienced practitioners.

Professional organizations responding to all (novice through to master) project managers' needs via research knowledge transfer.

</td></tr>
</table>

By 2025, we predict that project management will be recognized as responsible for clarifying project management's role as strategic facilitator, not control process.

<table>
<tr><td rowspan="4" style="writing-mode: vertical">Implications</td><td>

Research:
Increase in research on the "soft" challenges of project management, including decision-making, communications, team building, virtual teaming, dealing with uncertainty and complexity

Further elaboration of the value project management brings to organizations and its role in delivering strategic initiatives.

Topics to include:
    The new "old boy" network, virtual social networking, peer collaboration;
    Implications of cultural differences in key working relationships;
    Top management decision-making;
    Human resourcing issues involving personal personnel expectations;
    The role of hierarchy in decision-making and issue resolution;
    Issue resolution process in virtual projects; and
    Differing motivational approaches for differing ages and cultures.

Practice:
Immediate information availability and automatic synthesis of project data. Many of the traditional control activities of project managers (collecting and interpreting information, status reporting, etc.) will be automated or delegated to an administrative function.
Workers to accept this level of intrusion in their lives.
More options available for virtual working.

Increased numbers of networked peer collaboration projects involving large numbers of stakeholders.

Invest in competency development in people skills such as communication and e-communication.

</td></tr>
</table>

(continued)

Table 7:	Predictions for the future of project management research *(continued)*
Implications	Movement from naïve application of tools and techniques to sophisticated mastery and adaptation of technical and political skills. Recognition that planning only gets you started—intuition, creativity, resilience, motivation, and leadership get you finished.

Conclusions

We started by laying out the trends in project management research that have been observed to date and the global and micro trends and predictions about the world of work that are likely to influence the future of project management. We stopped then to think about how these trends are likely to influence the future of project management and the role of project managers. Next, we examined some potential alternate futures of project management and considered how these different futures are likely to impact project management research. Finally, we presented some predictions about what project management research could look like by 2025.

We recognize that predictions are risky business. Predictions of the potential impact of workforce demographics not been terribly successful in the past. Karoly (2004) tells of a U.S. commission on the Year 2000 established in the late 1960s to build predictions about workforce needs based on identified structural changes already underway and extrapolation of these trends. The prediction was not useful in the end, as history can often turn on unforeseen events. But often the course of change can be proposed. However, a follow-up study correctly anticipated some important trends such as the communications revolution and global communication infrastructure, as well as population and educational changes (and demands). What escaped their view was the role women and minorities would play in the workplace and the global interconnectedness of business: perhaps this is partly due to not knowing the actual nature, that is, how much technology would change the employment profile. In our case, the financial crisis in the fall of 2008 substantially impacted some of the demographic workforce trends discussed in this chapter, as concern shifted from problems of managing and retaining the interest of the younger generations at a time of labor shortage to managing older ready-to-retire older workers who could no longer afford to retire as the global economic slowdown reduced the demand for labor around the world.

However, Einstein said that the problems of tomorrow will not be solved by the tools of today. Likewise, the future of project management research is unlikely to be totally predicted by the research and practice of today. It will be inextricably tied to the changing future of work, organizations, and project management itself. It will require us to think very differently about what we do as either practitioners or researchers.

We admit to an ulterior motive here. We are not so much interested in trying to predict the future from past trends. We are more interested in shaping the direction and efforts of those of us who will have an influence on this future. We hope that the presented background and discussion, combined with the chapters that make up the rest of this book, stimulate thought and foresight about what the future of project management needs to be and which work can make it happen.

We have never suggested that we know what the future will bring. Our aim in writing this chapter was to explore the trends impacting project management research and present some speculations about what project management research will look like in 2025. We conclude by posing two thought-provoking questions we find ourselves asking with respect to the future of project management in general and project management research in particular.

The first and foremost of these questions is, "What is project management research's unique contribution to the management literature?" What can we add that is not simply a restatement of other management disciplines findings in a unique setting? An alternate way to ask this question is to ask "What do we really know about project management and what do we need to know to move it forward in practice and research?" Projects today fail at a ridiculous rate. Why is this so? If project management in the future is going to continue to look much like project management of the past, how is this likely to change? Does it need to? What future is there for a failing management methodology? What is the purpose of project management if it is not to complete successful projects? What does the study of project management add to the body of management knowledge that is not already contributed by other management disciplines?

The second question of importance is, "Who will shape the future of project management research?" In considering this question we must answer a number of other important questions: Who is currently investing in designing the future of project management (consultants, associations, researchers, practitioners)? Who is best situated to invent the future? For whom will this future be advantageous? What are we doing to ensure that the future of project management is a fruitful one?

We hope that the review of all the changes occurring in the workforce has opened up your eyes to the fact that the future of project management is likely to be quite different from today. If you accept that this is the case, we hope that this chapter provides fertile ground for launching questions. For ourselves, our exploration of these trends has brought us to realize how avoiding the cost of being wrong before predicting the future limits both our ability to shape it and our ability to prepare for all the potential futures we can imagine.

Acknowledgements: This chapter results from an ongoing research project exploring the future of project management. Earlier versions of these ideas were presented as a PMI Southern Alberta Chapter keynote address developed by Jenny Krahn, Ph.D., and Janice Thomas, Ph.D., in November of 2007, and subsequently written up and presented to the Project Management Institute's Biannual Research Conference in July of 2008.

References

Barnes, N. M.L, Wearne, S. H. (1993) The future for major project management. International Journal of Project Management. Kidlington: Aug 1993. Vol. 11, Iss. 3; p. 135

Betts, M., & Lansley, P. (1995). International Journal of Project Management: a review of the first ten years. *International Journal of Project Management, 13*(4), 207-217.

Cetron, M. J., & Davies, O. (2003). Trends shaping the future: Technological, workplace, management, and institutional trends. *The Futurist, 37*(2), 30-43.

Cicmil, S., Cooke Davis, T., Crawford, L., & Richardson, K. (2009, in press). *Impact of complexity theory on project management.* Hoboken, New Jersey:Wiley Publishing.

Cicmil, S., & Hodgson, D. (2006). New possibilities for project management theory: A critical engagement. *Project Management Journal, 37*(3), 111-123.

Cicmil, Sveltlana, Terry Williams, Janice Thomas, Damian Hodgson (2006) Rethinking Project Management: Researching the actuality ot projects. International Journal of Project Management. Kidlington: Nov 2006. Vol. 24, Iss. 8; p. 675

Cleland, D. I. (2004). The evolution of project management. *IEEE Transactions on Engineering Management, 51*(4), 396-397.

Crawford, L., Pollack, J., & England, D. (2006). Uncovering the trends in project management: Journal emphases over the last 10 years. *International Journal of Project Management, 24*(2), 175-184

Evaristo, Roberto, van Fenema, Paul C.(1999) A typology of project management: Emergence and evolution of new forms International Journal of Project Management. Kidlington: Oct 1999. Vol. 17, Iss. 5; p. 275

Gladwell, M. (2000) The Tipping Point. Little, Brown and Company, USA

Hamel, G. (2007). *The future of management.* Boston, MA: Harvard Business School Press.

Ives, M.(2005) Identifying the Contextual Elements of Project management Withing Organizations and their Impact on Project Success Project Management Journal. Sylva: Mar 2005. Vol. 36, Iss. 1; p. 37

Jaafari, Ali (2003) PROJECT MANAGEMENT IN THE AGE OF COMPLEXITY AND CHANGE Project Management Journal. Sylva: Dec 2003. Vol. 34, Iss. 4; p. 47

Jiang, J., Klein, G., & Chen, H. (2001). The relative influence of IS project implementation policies and project leadership on eventual outcomes. *Project Management Journal, 32*(3), 49-55.

Jugdev, K., & Thomas, J. (2002). Project management maturity models: The silver bullet of competitive advantage? *Project Management Journal, 33*(4): 4-14.

Karoly, L.A. (2004). *The 21ˢᵗ century at work: Forces shaping the future workforce and workplace in the United States.* Santa Monica: RAND, Labor and Population.

Kloppenborg, T. J., & Opfer, W. A. (2000). Forty years of project management research: Trends, interpretations and predictions." In PMI Research Conference, PMI, 41-59.

Krahn, J., & Thomas, J. (2008). Applying formalized curiosity: Exploring trends driving the future of project management. PMI Research Conference in Warsaw, Poland, 13-16 July 2008.

Kwak, Y.H and Anbari, F. (2008) Impact on Project Management of Allied Disciplines: Trends and Future of Project Management Practices and Research PMI, Penn

Leih, M.J. (2006) The Impact of the Sarbanes-Oxley Act on IT Project Management JITTA : Journal of Information Technology Theory and Application. Hong Kong: 2006. Vol. 8, Iss. 3; p. 13

Lindgren, M. and Packendorff, J (2006) What's New in New Forms of Organizing? On the Construction of Gender in Project-Based Work. The Journal of Management Studies. Vol 43(4) p841.

Gordon E McCray, Russell L Purvis, Coleen G McCray.(2002) Project management under uncertainty: The impact of heuristics and biases Project Management Journal. Sylva: Mar 2002. Vol. 33, Iss. 1; p. 49

Malone, T.W. (2004). *The future of work.* Boston, MA: Harvard Business School Press.

Maya, I., Rahimi, M., Meshkati, N., Madabushi, D. et al. (2005) Cultural Influence on the Implementation of Lessons Learned in Project Management Engineering Management Journal. Rolla: Dec 2005. Vol. 17, Iss. 4; p. 17

Meredith, J.R. (2002). "Developing project management theory for managerial application the view of a research journal's editor" In D. P. Slevin, D. I. Cleland, & J. K. Pinto (Eds.),*Proceedings of PMI Research Conference 2002.* Newtown Square, PA: Project Management Institute.

Milosevic, D., Inman, L., & Ozbay, A. (2001). Impact of project management standardization on project effectiveness. *Engineering Management Journal, 13*(4), 9-16.

Milosevic, D., & Srivannaboon, S. (2006). A theoretical framework for aligning project management with business strategy. *Project Management Journal, 37*(3), 98-111.

Morris, P.W.G., & Jamieson, A. (2005). Moving from corporate strategy to project strategy. *Project Management Journal, 36*(4), 5-19.

Morris, P.W.G., Jamieson, A., & Shepherd, M. (2006). Research updating the APM body of knowledge 4th edition. *International Journal of Project Management, 24*(6), 461.

Morris, P. W. G. (2002). Forty years of project management research. In D. P. Slevin, D. I. Cleland, & J. K. Pinto (Eds.), *The frontiers of project management research.* Newtown Square, PA: Project Management Institute.

Morris P.W.G, Patel M.B., & Wearne, S.H. (2000). Research into revising the APM project management body of knowledge. *International Journal of Project Management 18*(3), 155.

Mostrous, A., & Brown, D. (2008) Workers wary of office spyware. Reprinted from *Times of London* in *Calgary Herald*, Jan. 16, 2008. p 1.

Mullaly, M 2006. Longitudinal analysis of project management maturity. *Project Management Journal, 37*(3), 62-74.

Odusami, K. T, Iyagba, R. R. O., & Omirin, M. M. (2003). The relationship between project leadership, team composition and construction project performance in Nigeria. *International Journal of Project Management, 21*, 519-527.

Penn, M.J., & Zalesne, E.K. (2007). *Microtrends: The small forces behind tomorrow's big changes.* New York: Twelve.

Peterson, E. R. (2004). Seven revolutions: Global strategic trends out to the year 2025. *Multinational Business Review, 12*(2), 111-119.

Pinto, J.K. (2002). Project management 2002. *Research and Technology Management, 45*(2), 22-37.

Schrage, M. (2007) HBR List: Breakthrough Ideas for 2007. Harvard Business Publishing. http://harvardbusinessonline.hbsp.harvard.edu/b01/en/common/item_detail.jhtml;jsessionid=QYZN0FFM4CPH0AKRGWDSELQBKE0YIISW?id=R0702A&_requestid=32452

Shenhar, A. J., & Dvir, D. (1996). Toward a typological theory of project management. *Research Policy, 25*(4), 607-632.

Shenhar, A., & Dvir, D. (2007). Project management research: The challenge and opportunity." *Project Management Journal, 38*(2), 93-99.

Stone, L (2007) HBR List: Breakthrough Ideas for 2007. Harvard Business Publishing. http://harvardbusinessonline.hbsp.harvard.edu/b01/en/common/item_detail.jhtml;jsessionid=QYZN0FFM4CPH0AKRGWDSELQBKE0YIISW?id=R0702A&_requestid=32452

Stretton A. (1994a). A short history of project management: part one the 50s and 60s. *Australian Project Manager, ,14*(1), 36-37.

Stretton A. (1994b). A short history of project management: part two the 1970s. *Australian Project Manager, 14*(2), 48.

Stretton (1994c). A short history of project management: part three the 1980s. *Australian Project Manager, 14*(3), 65.

Srivannaboon, S., Milosevic, D.Z. (2006) A two-way influence between business strategy and project management. International Journal of Project Management. Kidlington: Aug 2006. Vol. 24, Iss. 6; p. 493

Tapscott, D., & Williams, A.D. (2006). *Wikinomics: How mass collaboration changes everything.* New York: Portfolio.

Thamhain, H.J. (1996). Enhancing innovative performance of self-directed engineering teams. *Engineering Management Journal, (8)*3, 31-40.

Themistocleous G., & Wearne, S.H. (2000). Project management topic coverage in journals. *International Journal of Project Management, 18*(1), 7-11.

Thomas, J.L. (2000a). Making sense of project management. Ph.D. dissertation, University of Alberta.

Thomas, J.L. (2000b). "Making Sense of Project Management" Published in *Projects as business constituents and guiding motives,* Eds: R. Lundin, F. Hartman, & C. Navarre

Thomas, J., Delisle, C., Jugdev, K., & Buckle, P. (2002). *Selling project management to senior executives.* Newtown Square, Pennsylvania: Project Management Institute.

Thomas.J, Mengel, T.(2008) Preparing project managers to deal with complexity - Advanced project management education International Journal of Project Management. Kidlington: Apr 2008. Vol. 26, Iss. 3; p. 304

Urli, B., & Urli, D. (2000). Project management in North America, stability of concepts. *Project Management Journal, 31*(3), 33-44

U.S. Census Bureau, Population Division, ,http://www.census.gov/ipc/www/idb/world-popinfo.html. Accessed May 28, 2008.

Watt, D.J HBR List: Breakthrough Ideas for 2007. Harvard Business Publishing. http://harvardbusinessonline.hbsp.harvard.edu/b01/en/common/item_detail.jhtml;jsessionid=QYZN0FFM4CPH0AKRGWDSELQBKE0YIISW?id=R0702A&_requestid=32452

Williams, C.C. (2007). *Rethinking the future of work.* Basingstoke: Palgrave Macmillan.

Winter, M., Smith, C., Morris, P., & Cicmil, S. 2006. Directions for future research in project management: The main findings of a UK government-funded research network. *International Journal of Project Management, 24*(8): 638

Zobel, A. M., & Wearne, S. H. (2000). Project management topic coverage in recent conferences. *Project Management Journal, 31*(2), 32-37.

CHAPTER 8

How Project Managers Will Interface With The Law and Lawyers In 2025

Randall L. Speck

Abstract

The substantive legal system is typically averse to change. Reliance on precedent and the inertia that characterizes most legislative processes tend to perpetuate the status quo, particularly over periods as short as a single generation. Nevertheless, globalization, technological advances, and stakeholders' self interest may accelerate that progression as applied to projects. Private agreements on applicable legal rules may largely control bilateral relationships by 2025, and multinational arrangements may provide more consistent regulatory rules as they affect projects. On a structural level, disputes will continue to arise. They may be resolved in 2025; however, by the parties ceding decision-making authority to artificial intelligence systems as independent arbiters that will assess the facts from an electronic repository that compiles all project records, analyze those facts within an agreed-upon legal framework, and determine binding liability and possible damages. Project managers will also have their own expert systems to assure compliance with legal requirements on a real-time basis and will consult lawyers only for exceptional cases that fall outside the parameters of standardized legal rules.

Introduction

The legal world rarely takes radical leaps that propel it in dramatically new directions. Because the law is largely about preserving expectations and avoiding uncertainty, it changes incrementally and sometimes only imperceptibly over a period as short as a generation. Thus, much of the fundamental legal framework for project managers in 2025 will likely be quite familiar. Governmental regulation will continue to dictate standards for a wide range of project elements (e.g., assurance of worker safety and minimum compensation, protection of the environment, promotion of competition, and security of intellectual property). Project stakeholders' rights will remain subject to a variety of local, national, and transnational legal regimes. Project disputes will still arise and require managers to devote scarce resources to their resolution. The legal overlay on projects will be more complex than ever, but may provide little additional certainty or predictability. In short, project managers will face many of the same daunting legal challenges in 2025 that they face today.

Nevertheless, the legal landscape will evolve in ways that could provide opportunities for an astute project manager. Despite a proliferation of governmental regulations, managers may, ironically, have more freedom and flexibility. Globalization will affect the law by stimulating extra-governmental rules and standards that transcend national borders. Technology will dictate instantaneous, round-the-clock reactions to changing circumstances, but will also permit a small cadre of legal advisors to operate as an integral part of the project team and to focus on exceptions that cannot be addressed through standardized rules. Stakeholders may claim newly enfranchised legal rights that could be impaired by a project continents away, but effective project managers may anticipate and preempt those claims. A broad variety of dispute resolution mechanisms will give project managers an array of tools to keep their projects on track without crippling disruptions or costs. Although much will be familiar in 2025, changes to the legal milieu could enable perceptive project managers to plan and execute their projects with fewer risks and greater efficiency.

On a micro level, the interactions of project managers and the legal resources on their project team may be significantly transformed by 2025 in three respects. First, technology will make the law much more accessible to non-lawyers. Standardized procedures will let project managers and their staffs tap directly into legal knowledge systems to address routine issues without having to rely on their lawyers. Second, information technology will integrate legal requirements with the projects' physical criteria to ensure compliance with applicable standards. Automated checks will ensure conformance to required codes and identify potential deviations that warrant additional attention. Third, by 2025, standardization will have created routine solutions to most repeatable legal issues that projects face, so that project managers will limit their need for legal advisors to exceptional circumstances. Nevertheless, those nonconforming situations will be so significant that they will dictate the project's success or failure, and project managers must devote disproportionate attention and resources to identifying and addressing those legal concerns.

The Legal System's Inherent Resistance to Change

The legal system is structured to dampen radical shifts, so that it would be unreasonable to expect a sea change within the relatively short horizon of 2025. Recent experience supports that guarded expectation. Although there have been dramatic technological and globalization advances in the past 16 years, the legal context has evolved only modestly. There have long been predictions of a new world order that would simplify the rules governing commercial relationships or that would revolutionize the ways that legal services are dispensed. Of course, there have been incremental adjustments in the last two decades—primarily to assimilate substantial advances in communications and computerization—but the fundamental legal core remains largely intact.

This aversion to change is not surprising given the historical development of Western legal traditions and the need to preserve and protect reasonable expectations.

The U.S. and English legal systems are firmly grounded in the principle that precedent governs the development of common law as it will be applied to modern circumstances. This reliance on past decisions to determine contemporary issues begins with the way courts construe laws. In U.S. Constitutional law–and even the interpretation of federal or state statutes–courts attempt to tease out the original drafters' intent. Thus, in deciding parties' current rights, courts may try to decipher what the Founding Fathers meant when they approved the Bill of Rights in 1789 or what a New Deal congress intended when it enacted the backbone regulatory statutes that guide much of today's administrative law in the United States. This reliance on legislative intent, when strictly enforced–as it typically is–tends to preclude radical shifts to conform the law to current circumstances.

Moreover, precedent generally controls when a court is confronted with a case that is analogous to those it has decided before. Western courts have recognized the value of continuity and predictability. When a legal ruling has been tested over time and used to arrange orderly business relationships, courts are loath to disrupt those established norms, even in the face of challenges demanding a different outcome. Judge-made law is designed to react slowly in order to avoid disrupting commercial or personal relationships that may have been structured in reliance on an established order.

Legislatures are also typically slow to modify statutory law, despite occasional pressures to adopt a more abrupt course change. On the federal level, any bill that attracts significant opposition may be delayed or defeated by the threat of a potential presidential veto or congressional rules that favor inaction over action. In state legislatures, the inability to address regional or even global issues (e.g., climate change, outsourcing, intellectual property protections) make comprehensive reform difficult and unlikely.

On a more fundamental level, legislatures and courts are generally predisposed to protect and preserve the status quo. Legal systems tend to reflect the existing political and economic interests and are structured based on maintaining their territorial jurisdiction. Thus, any material change that would disrupt existing relationships or detract from the authority of a particular state or nation to control transactions within its borders will probably be viewed unfavorably. While incremental modifications can effectuate modest shifts that could affect project relationships and responsibilities over time, the basic legal framework in 2025 may not look significantly different from today.

That is not to say that the legal system does not warrant a major overhaul to address issues that project managers will likely face by the end of the first quarter of the twenty-first century. Technology now permits instantaneous, world-wide access to information, making it possible to create virtual project teams that may be scattered through several countries with no ties to a particular territorial jurisdiction or its parochial laws. By 2025, project managers will likely draw their human, capital, natural, and creative resources from multiple countries with diverse legal traditions and substantive laws. Projects may also impact the environment, economies, health, safety, and welfare of nations and their citizens far removed from the project's physical location. To the extent that the legal system does not address key issues arising from globalization, technological advances, and modern business needs, pressures will mount for a more efficient, fair approach tailored to the new environment.

Defining Legal Relationships Among Project Stakeholders
Remote Stakeholders May Have Rights That Affect Projects

By 2025, the straightforward project in a fixed location with a defined impact limited to its immediate area and industry will have become increasingly rare. The inability of projects to function as independent islands will become even more pronounced, and projects are likely to expand their reach in two directions.

First, their scope will encompass multiple disciplines and business sectors. For instance, many projects that now give only a slight nod to environmental impacts will have those concerns thrust on them by 2025. Every project will face the need for energy-efficient solutions, limitations on carbon emissions, and economies that consider material's full lifecycle. Moreover, as critical resources become more scarce, the need for sustainability will drive project decisions as never before. Consequently, a large proportion of projects will need to consider recycling technologies, waste disposal, and efficient reuse as part of their design and implementation, thereby implicating previously remote bodies of law.

Second, by 2025, many more projects will extend their reach geographically well beyond the borders of a particular legal regime. Much of the project team will be virtual, located for convenience and economy, not driven by the need for physical proximity. Thus, the project may be designed in India, fabricated in China, assembled in Mexico, installed in Minnesota, and managed from England. Moreover, even localized projects will have significant cross-border effects. For instance, a project to develop a uranium mine in Uzbekistan may have (a) environmental implications for nearby countries that could receive pollutants from mining operations, (b) antitrust consequences in the United States if there are alleged conspiracies to control uranium prices, (c) human rights effects in England if there are alleged labor abuses, and (d) worldwide geopolitical repercussions if the uranium is intended to go to potentially hostile countries for weapons. While the immediate project contacts might be exclusively with Uzbekistan, the effects may be felt much more widely.

Historically, courts confer legal jurisdiction based on the place with the primary contacts. By 2025, this construct may no longer have meaning for many projects, and courts will need to develop alternative methods for determining the applicable law. Indeed, the relevant law may vary, depending on the interests affected. It might be appropriate in the Uzbek uranium mine hypothetical, for example, to apply the law where the effects occur, so long as those effects were reasonably foreseeable, in which case multiple national laws would pertain. In order to protect the project from potential liabilities, therefore, the manager may need to assume the perspective of widely scattered stakeholders who could seek redress for remote alleged injuries. By anticipating those possible claims, the manager can prepare accordingly and take anticipatory steps.

The absence of a clear geographical locus for projects may also create conflicts when radically different legal traditions clash, as they will more frequently in 2025. For instance, Western law has long held that claims have a definite shelf life and cannot be pursued after the expiration of a specified statute of limitations. These rules are intended to give parties a sense of repose based on assurance that they will not be required to defend stale claims where the evidence may be difficult or impossible to compile. In contrast, Islamic law – controlling in some Muslim countries – may not recognize the extinguishment of a claim based on the lapse of time. Thus, while a project may be considered fully concluded after expiration of the applicable statute of limitations, with no more liability for claims, a party seeking compensation under Islamic law may still seek redress in a Muslim jurisdiction. Without a common understanding of governing rules, this potential uncertainty may discourage projects in countries with conflicting or inadequately defined legal customs.

Legal Rules That Transcend Geographical Boundaries

By 2025, the need for project predictability and the increased costs of uncertainty will undoubtedly trump desires to preserve traditional legal rules that are closely tied to a specific geographical location. Developers may forego beneficial projects (e.g., infrastructure expansions, resources exploitation, outsourcing to an economic labor force) if the legal structure creates unacceptable risks. As pressures increase to pursue those otherwise desirable projects, managers will seek new legal frameworks that can accommodate twenty-first century demands. Some of those procedures have already begun to emerge.

Unlike state-to-state relationships, which must be governed by treaty and require strict protections of sovereignty, private relationships are largely controlled by the parties' agreements. If the parties agree, they can skip over the niceties of determining legal jurisdiction and simply declare what legal rules will apply. Of course, not all stakeholders are parties to the relevant project agreements, so not everyone can be assembled under the same legal tent, but a definitive understanding at the start of the project about the relevant legal standards can provide the certainty necessary to proceed. Two approaches will likely prevail by 2025.

First, the Westernization – and Americanization – of applicable law has already begun to germinate in much of the world and is likely to grow. For commercial relationships, more parties will likely adopt the familiar conventions of Western common law that have been refined over centuries and are now extremely well codified. These legal constructs have an advantage over a more static framework because they are not frozen in time but will develop slowly in predictable and acceptable ways. Western common law also reflects efficient commercial relationships in developed economies, so that it will be suitable to a variety of projects, from rudimentary to the most sophisticated. Using this established legal platform, project managers will be able to define clear obligations and responsibilities.

Of course, by 2025, other legal systems may be in the ascendancy and could rival Western common law as the arbiter of choice. By dint of its size alone, China will play a prominent role in future projects, and may exercise sufficient dominance to insist that its projects proceed under its own set of laws. Such a development will have serious ramifications for projects accustomed to Western precepts. Chinese law is not well understood in the West and does not engender the same confidence in impartiality and fairness. Those impediments to widespread acceptance are unlikely to dissipate fully by 2025. Thus, unless China assumes a completely dominant economic position that permits it to dictate project development terms–which is a plausible scenario–Western law is likely to provide the organizing basis for most projects.

Another possibility, however, is the more widespread recognition of an international private commercial law–*Lex Mercatoria*–that is not tied to any country's law or legal tradition but reflects merchants' needs and experience. The Unidroit Principles Of International Commercial Contracts, most recently codified in 2004 (available at http://www.unidroit.org/english/principles/contracts/principles2004/blackletter2004.

pdf), could provide a starting point for a more comprehensive set of detailed rules, but several factors make its widespread adoption somewhat problematic. The current principles are extraordinarily general and, for that reason, not very valuable in a practical project setting.

For instance, the Unidroit Principles are satisfactory to establish simple procedural conventions (e.g., Article 1.12, how to compute time, or Article 1.10, when a person receives actual notice), but leave some important issues completely unresolved (e.g., the measure of damages), or provide no more than a simple bromide that will not help project managers to do their jobs (e.g., Article 5.1.3, "[e]ach party shall cooperate with the other party when such co-operation may reasonably be expected for the performance of that party's obligations"). These gaps may be filled by 2025, however, by refinements that provide greater precision and direction, particularly through the accumulation of arbitration awards or other interpretations that apply the Principles.

PMI itself may develop a vehicle by 2025 that would clarify the requirements for reasonable project performance and–if widely accepted for this purpose–could provide a binding standard that project stakeholders could use to structure their legal relationships. PMI's *A Guide to the Project Management Body of Knowledge (PMBOK® Guide)* already captures key elements of "reasonable project management," the foundation for many determinations of legal accountability. If expanded and focused to address key legal issues that are likely to arise (e.g., what planning, control, and reporting mechanisms are necessary in specified circumstances, when responsibility to third-party stakeholders arises, how disputes should be resolved), the *PMBOK® Guide* may be used in conjunction with standards like the Unidroit Principles to create a comprehensive paradigm to guide legal decisions relating to projects. Such a regime will give project managers greater certainty and predictability, knowing that the project's legal obligations will be dictated by the same values used to manage the project.

The Role of Government Regulation

Of course, no matter what the parties agree about how they will handle their bilateral arrangements, they will remain subject to potentially overlapping, inconsistent, or confining governmental requirements. Governmental regulation is both a blessing and curse for projects. Some projects would not be feasible without regulatory support to secure rights of way, exclusive franchises, or favorable financing arrangements. On the other hand, regulators may insist on environmental, safety, or aesthetic standards that complicate the project, delay its completion, and increase its costs. From the project managers' standpoint, however, the most important aspect of regulation is the degree to which it is predictable and certain (i.e., sound planning can proceed so long as the rules are clear and consistent). On that score, the regulatory framework by 2025 should be rationalized to support projects more effectively.

The current hodgepodge of administrative requirements that affect projects must give way to streamlined and coordinated processes and standards. Even relatively localized projects must often traverse standards set by multiple local jurisdictions (e.g., towns, counties, water districts), with comprehensive state and federal overlays. Projects with multinational impacts face even more complex, diverse, and often contradictory requirements. Because projects cannot proceed when stymied by inefficient and inconsistent rules, governments will by 2025 develop more sophisticated mechanisms for coordination and harmonization.

These trends are already well advanced. The European Union is an obvious example where sovereignty concerns have been suppressed in favor of promoting common development and commercial interests. As a result, projects in the EU can rely on more uniform rules (e.g., relating to environmental protection, wages, working conditions, health and safety, antitrust, and intellectual property), thus permitting managers to plan more effectively and to use resources more efficiently, without regard to national borders. Similar tentative–but much less comprehensive–efforts were taken with the North American Free Trade Agreement, which included a limited spectra of common rules for environmental and labor issues.

By 2025, the demand for consistent standards will produce a much wider consensus on at least the core regulatory rules. The most fruitful area for such standardization may be with regard to environmental controls. Regardless of current disparities between developed and developing countries, by 2025, worldwide concerns about global warming, resource depletion, air and water quality, habitat destruction, and species extinction should lead to relatively uniform criteria for developing manufacturing, energy production, and infrastructure projects. Because environmental degradation anywhere in the world affects multiple countries, projects will likely face similarly stringent constraints whether they are located in China, India, Germany, Brazil, or the United States. Even if a few countries remain outliers in 2025, the public pressure on international companies to conform to the world's environmental norms will tend to bring all projects into line. This widespread uniformity will give project managers greater ability to standardize designs and implementation procedures because they will no longer require tailored approaches to fit individual country disparities.

Other dynamics are likely to produce greater uniformity in health and safety regulations. Concerns about the spread of food-borne or communicable diseases in a worldwide economy will require common standards for food production, transportation, marketing, and distribution. Drug development, manufacturing, and labeling will necessarily become more consistent country to country in order to allay growing fears about counterfeit or contaminated medicines. Health authorities will impose uniform tracking systems to permit them to trace disease outbreaks to their origins. Each of these areas will create opportunities for project managers to build replicable systems that will comply with a regularized set of legal directions.

Similarly, project managers will likely face much more uniform labor rules by 2025. Even today, customers and shareholders sometimes demand to know whether companies follow minimum standards for worker compensation and employment conditions. This trend will likely continue so that by 2025, many more projects will be expected to meet a threshold level for worker treatment. That is not to say that this standard will necessarily provide a dramatic improvement relative to current requirements. Disparities in minimum wages and mandatory benefits will certainly persist, but the gaps between countries may be narrowed because of the greater ability of labor to compete worldwide (i.e., average minimum wages in developed countries may fall relative to those in developing countries). Countries or project developers are also likely to establish similar floors for worker safety and exposure to hazardous materials, permitting project managers to use comparable tracking and control systems on all projects.

Regulation of scarce resources will also likely constrain project managers, and in this arena, differences between countries may have intensified significantly by 2025. As hydrocarbon fuels and critical raw materials become more depleted, those countries blessed with these natural assets will undoubtedly attempt to hoard them and maximize their value. Controls on their exploitation and development may severely limit project managers' ability to manage their costs or schedules because the availability of vital raw materials and fuels may be dictated by uncertain and uncontrollable events. A major challenge for project managers will be to assure the necessary supply of these resources in the face of governmentally imposed restrictions on their production or distribution.

Finally, by 2025, intellectual property rules will become an even more significant factor for project managers. Patents and copyrights are currently a patchwork of individual countries' acceptance and recognition. Notoriously, countries like China have been slow to enforce intellectual property rights, perhaps to give their own fledgling industries an opportunity to develop unencumbered by limitations on the use of new technologies and innovations. Indeed, European copyright and patent holders raised comparable complaints about the infant United States for its similar *laissez faire* approach through the beginning of the nineteenth century. As other economies mature, however, they will also recognize that creativity should be a highly valued commodity, and they are likely by 2025 to acknowledge the importance of protecting intellectual property. Consequently, countries will cooperate to enforce patents, permitting project managers to rely on their own intellectual property but also requiring them to avoid infringing on any other worldwide rights. In concert with such a more uniform enforcement regime, however, project managers will likely be able to rely on comprehensive data systems that track patents and identify potential infringement and areas for possible new innovation.

Dispute Resolution

If current trends persist, 2025 could see a proliferation of project-related disputes. As noted, the law will be more accessible than ever, so that any stakeholder will be able to use readily available resources to pursue a perceived injury by raising a colorable claim. Self-taught claimants will be ubiquitous, but for those who seek professional counsel, law schools will oblige by producing an abundance of new lawyers anxious to test their mettle. Contractual counterparties will be acutely aware of their rights and will not hesitate to exercise them. As today, projects may succeed or fail based on their ability to manage and contain disputes at every stage of the project.

By 2025, however, the current arsenal of dispute resolution mechanisms will have proved to be entirely deficient for project purposes. Lawsuits in government-run courts, traditional arbitrations, and third-party mediations simply take too long, create too many uncontrollable risks, tie up too many project resources, and create too many unproductive constraints on project decision making. Each of the steps currently used to settle disputes—finding the facts, apportioning liability, and calculating damages—creates delays and risks that, if current trends persist, the project managers of 2025 will find unacceptable.

At the fact-finding step, the traditional approach requires a period of "discovery" when each side spends months or years rummaging through the other's records and the collective memories of their respective employees to construct a plausible story that will support a purported claim or defense. Lawyers may review millions of electronic documents and interview dozens of witnesses. Even the threat of such invasive discovery can spawn counterproductive limitations on communications that may adversely affect project efficiency or trigger ill-advised settlements simply to avoid intolerable litigation expenses.

After each side has painstakingly assembled its side of the facts, someone must go through the messy process of deciding which party has the better of the argument. Legal rules guide this determination, but if those principles invariably provided a clear, unassailable answer, there probably would have been no dispute in the first place. Consequently, the determination of liability is often a gamble. Each side takes a risk, and the outcome may rest on unpredictable and uncontrollable factors (e.g., the happenstance of where the dispute will be heard, the identity of the judge or arbiter, or the skill of the individual lawyer). When a tidy profit or devastating loss may turn on the outcome of a dispute, project managers will seek to avoid such exposure.

Finally, if there is liability, someone must decide the value of the injury, if any. Of course, quantifying physical injury is notoriously problematical, but even purely monetary losses may be difficult to calculate because damages are usually estimated by postulating an alternative history from what actually transpired (i.e., what costs or profits would have occurred if some aspect of the project had been handled differently). Experts may opine and lawyers may hypothesize, but divining a precise dollar amount of reparations will always entail at least as much art as science. Project managers are justifiably loath to entrust their fate to such an imprecise process.

By 2025, project managers will no longer abide multi-year disputes that devour project resources, cast a persistent shadow over the project's results, and create undesirable risks. The first step in liberating projects from the tyranny of distracting disputes will likely be to eschew public processes in favor of tailored, private resolution mechanisms. Arbitration and mediation may often disserve project needs, however, because experience has shown that the parties' lawyers can hijack those mechanisms and, in most respects, replicate the flaws of traditional litigation. Once discovery procedures and multiple rounds of evidence and briefing have been grafted onto arbitration or mediation, they become only marginally more attractive and may have few advantages.

Project managers will need more cost-effective, risk-reducing solutions, and may turn to modeling and probability analyses that will significantly shorten the process and increase predictability. In this projected scenario, the "arbitrator" for the majority of disputes may be a sophisticated computer program that identifies the salient facts, applies predetermined legal rules, assigns liability, and calculates any damages. Projects have an advantage over the random legal relationships reflected in other types of disputes (e.g., a slip-and-fall or auto accident) because most of the affected parties have agreed at the beginning of the project to a common set of objectives. In the same way that parties now agree to arbitrate disputes, this core agreement can form the basis for a comprehensive dispute prevention/resolution mechanism that takes full advantage of 2025 technology.

For example, just as the parties agree to a wide range of essential project-related issues at the outset, they could consent to route project records through a third-party, independent, secure data processor. By applying an agreed set of legal parameters–whether a particular jurisdiction's laws or some extra-territorial standard–the third party would assess potential legal liabilities in real time. The data processor would use artificial intelligence technology to identify risks and to assign probabilities based on the law and any uncertainty about the facts. Any party could ask the third party for a confidential assessment of the potential legal ramifications of its actions, and the third party could offer confidential, unsolicited advice to a party that has taken or is about to take an action that conflicts with the agreed legal rules. Any party may request that the third party provide a binding legal determination based on its contemporaneous evaluation of all the project files.

This approach to dispute resolution integrates determinations of potential legal liability with a project manager's ability to control the project as it progresses. The third-party data processor will have comprehensive access to project files, eliminating the need for after-the-fact discovery. The computer program will alert project managers to incipient disputes at a point when corrective action can be taken and before the any significant damages accrue. The fact that project records will be comprehensively collected and independently assessed against legal criteria may also have a prophylactic effect by encouraging project personnel to document their decisions more accurately and ensure that they are adequately supported. Any deficiencies will be identified immediately to permit timely correction. The parties may raise a dispute at any point with an assurance that the issue will be resolved promptly based on the agreed criteria and without disrupting the project.

Aside from lawyers' obvious concern that they might be replaced by automated jurists, project managers might raise questions about how this 2025 dispute resolution scheme will decide cases that turn on credibility (i.e., when equally knowledgeable sources offer conflicting facts). Even then, however, the parties may permit the independent program to decide these intractable issues based on objective factors such as consistency with other evidence, historical credibility of the source, or probabilities. Granted, cross-examination of witnesses sometimes dramatically elicits truths that might otherwise escape detection. Given human fallibility, however, a judge, jury, or arbitrator might just as often misinterpret the witness's sweaty palms or cracking voice as intended deception when it was no more than nervousness in a stressful situation. A dispassionate computer program of 2025 vintage will likely make no more mistakes–and probably many fewer–than a human fact-finder. Even if the parties chose to limit the third-party program's ability to decide irreducible credibility questions, automated dispute resolution mechanisms can substantially reduce the contested issues and facilitate a quicker resolution.

Project Managers' Interaction With The Law

Rather than first killing all the lawyers, as Dick the butcher suggested (William Shakespeare, The Second Part of King Henry the Sixth act 4, sc. 2), by 2025, project managers may merely make them obsolete for many day-to-day functions. Today, the proliferation of legal issues heaped on project managers' plates almost dictates keeping a lawyer constantly at hand to anticipate problems or to offer counsel for timely solutions. As a transition mechanism between now and 2025, lawyers will undoubtedly play an increasingly significant role as part of the project team and will be as closely integrated as engineers, accountants, or other project professionals. Technology is likely, however, to reach a point when specialized computer programs and databases will provide the necessary legal advice for all except the most significant, bet-the-project problems.

Many legal resources are already easily available on-line, and that trend will continue. Beyond a simple hunt-and-peck attempt to decipher those resources, however, expert legal systems tailored to particular industries or types of projects will let managers and their staffs conduct queries to address specific issues. Some project lawyers are extraordinarily skilled and have specialized knowledge that gives their advice particular weight, but not every lawyer can boast that level of focused expertise. It will be possible by 2025, however, to capture that relatively exceptional capacity to benefit a broader range of projects. Project managers will be able to draw on all of the usual building blocks that contribute to legal advice (e.g., statutes, regulations, codes, court decisions, and treatises), but will also be able to use computer systems to tap the analytical skills necessary to maneuver through the legal maze to achieve the project's objectives.

Even more significantly, the project's physical and technical systems will be linked with formal requirements to ensure that each element satisfies all legal obligations. For instance, as design elements of a construction project are completed, they will be compared with building-code specifications, and any deviations will be highlighted and corrected or justified in real time. Project labor agreements, employee schedules, and payrolls will be vetted against all labor laws, regulations, and internal company policies to assure conformity. Project communications will be matched automatically with relevant contract specifications to ensure consistency. Expert legal systems will monitor most routine project procedures for any deviations and identify exceptions that cannot be readily corrected to meet legal requirements and may require further attention.

Standardization will make most legal advice routine and highly mechanized. By segregating a relatively small number of non-conforming exceptions, however, the project manager will be able to focus on those legal issues that truly warrant a more sophisticated analysis. At that point, the project manager may call on specialized project lawyers for assistance. Although the number of law firms may have dwindled to a few mega firms by 2025, as some predict, managers will continue to rely on personal relationships with individual lawyers who are steeped in projects' distinctive needs and can provide advice tailored to a project's particular problems.

Conclusion

The legal system evolves slowly, and project managers should not expect a radical substantive transformation within the relatively short time span until 2025. Nevertheless, there are actions that project stakeholders are like to take that will help them to control the legal framework. First, rather than relying on public laws to control their relationships, parties will more frequently turn to private rules that they can tailor to the project's circumstances and the parties' expectations. Second, government regulation will likely transcend geographic borders and provide more uniform standards for key issues that affect projects. Third, the structures for dispute resolution may change most radically with the advent of artificial intelligence systems that can assume many of the adjudicative functions currently performed by judges, jurors, or arbitrators. Finally, project managers will likely have much greater, highly automated access to legal advice that will identify and correct deviations from permissible standards on most routine matters. Project managers will resort to lawyers with special project-specific expertise only in those exceptional circumstances where expert judgment can add significant value.

CHAPTER 9

Visions For the Project Management Software Industry

Stacy Goff, PMP

A. Chapter Introduction

This chapter identifies visions of the future for the project management software industry. It hedges the difficulty of making these predictions by applying two groups of scenarios to establish possible futures for the portfolio, program, and project management software industry. The chapter's audiences include project management practitioners, managers, executives, and key stakeholders in project-oriented or project-involved enterprises, and executives and product managers in project management product or services organizations. This chapter applies the experience of industry veterans, interview results with executives of project management Software market leaders, and insights from other key individuals who are involved with changes in the industry's direction. We appreciate the contribution of ideas, predictions and visions of these individuals, giving credit to their specific citations with end-notes A-F, where we provide more information about them. Still, Microsoft visionary Ludo Hauduc[D] cautions that some of these predictions may be too naïve, or a bit too much like science fiction for some readers.

Trajectory scenarios trace key project management software achievements of the past and present to project a likely future. *Discontinuity* scenarios probe the game-changing disruptions from apparently unrelated or unseen impacts upon project management through 2025 and beyond. An example of an apparently unrelated impact is the rise of virtual worlds over the last several years, with a potential for far-reaching project impact. Both the trajectory and discontinuity sets of scenarios are relevant as project management practice continues to advance through 2025 and beyond. Indeed, an increasing number of project management software vendors have visions and plans for continuing that advancement. Yet, few enterprises (where enterprises include government agencies and corporations) take advantage of the power of all the portfolio, program, and project management Software tools they already have. Adding more features and capabilities will not be the driver for advancement. The challenge of the next several decades is to maximize our benefits from proper use of the tools that exist today, *and then* to add the project management competences needed to embrace the advancements to come. If you are prepared to suspend the reality of now for just a while, please read on.

B. Leaders and Laggards: The Gap Widens

Figure 1 shows a list of 10 project management functions that benefit from automated support. It is part of a larger list assembled by the author in 1980 while designing a project management methodology. That design included the roles of the project manager and key stakeholders, documenting project processes and activities, and citing the extent to which then-current automated support (running mostly on mainframes and minicomputers) helped manage projects. Since that time, the list has been the basis for evaluating the usefulness of a wide range of project management software.

The list is still useful today for evaluating a project management software suite, *and* for evaluating the extent to which any enterprise or project team is leveraging their software. For example, some project-oriented enterprises use a range of desktop tools, content management systems, and project or portfolio software, together with databases, to implement the entire list. Others use only desktop tools, barely covering items 1-3. Their schedules are "good enough to get executive approval" but are seldom used as a baseline for tracking purposes. The challenge for the project management software industry: *The majority of the existing market is still not effectively using 20-25 year-old technology!*

To help explain this perplexing situation, where for some the future arrives slowly, examine the innovation adoption curve shown in Figure 2. Originally popularized by Everett M. Rogers[2], this standard bell-shaped curve with two standard deviations and a further breakdown on the left identified five groups by their technology adoption patterns: innovators, early adopters, early majority, late majority, and laggards. Using this curve as a guide, it is the innovators and early adopters that we call leaders, those who have made significant progress against our 1980 list of project management functions. Clearly, project management software vendors must either increase their audience or improve the market penetration of their tools, or both, to realize their potential. Which will they do? The answer is one of the purposes of this chapter.

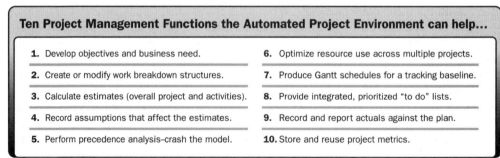

Ten Project Management Functions the Automated Project Environment can help...

1. Develop objectives and business need.	**6.** Optimize resource use across multiple projects.
2. Create or modify work breakdown structures.	**7.** Produce Gantt schedules for a tracking baseline.
3. Calculate estimates (overall project and activities).	**8.** Provide integrated, prioritized "to do" lists.
4. Record assumptions that affect the estimates.	**9.** Record and report actuals against the plan.
5. Perform precedence analysis–crash the model.	**10.** Store and reuse project metrics.

Figure 1: Ten project management functions of the automated project environment, by ProjectExperts; used with permission[1].

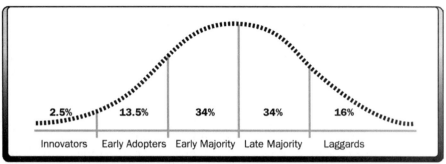

Figure 2:   Innovation adoption curve.

C: The Trajectory Scenarios: Past, Present, and Future

The Trajectory scenarios trace a small but relevant handful of key project management Software achievements of the past and present, and then project a likely future from those achievements. Featured scenarios for the past, present, and future in this section include project scheduling tools, the microcomputer revolution, automated project guides, virtual teams and social networks, portfolio management, emergence of real-time timesheets, capture and sharing of project knowledge, information leveraging into project intelligence, and the absorption of project management software into enterprise systems. One challenge of making predictions based on trends is the surprises that occur, but that is the purpose of the discontinuity scenarios section that follows.

Trajectory C1, Learning From The Past: 1960s and Project Scheduling Tools

In 1968, a young Fortran programmer integrated a new Calcomp 30" continuous-roll plotter with a 32KB IBM 360 Model 30 computer. After adapting road design software to work with the new operating system and plotter, he wrote a project schedule-plotting program. At first his motivations did not involve project management, but rather intrigue with the challenge of producing an up-to-1000-activity precedence diagram with a minimum number of lines crossing. The program input punched cards, and used Julian dates and 7/5 algorithms to approximate weeks. When donated to the Calcomp User-Group Library, this program challenged the survival of two companies' similar commercial programs. Their programs required the user to manually locate the activities on a grid, and his program calculated and deduced the optimum location. Thus, from the earliest days of commercial project management software, innovation leapfrogged and challenged the project management software industry[3].

C1a. 1980s: The Rise of Microcomputer-based Project Management Tools

Microcomputers began to arrive in the enterprise by the late 1970s but did not produce notable benefits at first. When the Apple Lisa computer came out in 1983, it included an innovative project management software package. For those who did not have access to mainframes or minicomputers with powerful workstations and high-end project management software, it was the first time they could "crash the model" (perform precedence analysis and see the cost and schedule impacts) *in real time*. This was an era of massive platform change, as mainframe and mini-computer applications jumped from their format to this emerging new microcomputer platform. In a portent of things to come, visionary Joel Koppelman[E] saw the opportunities of the personal computer (PC) platform, and co-founded a new company, Primavera, to develop for that platform. He emphasized combining processing power with ease of use. Existing industry standard tools (at least in oil, aerospace and construction) such as Artemis also migrated to the new PC. New applications caught on, including SuperProject, Timeline, Harvard Project Manager, and others at the midrange. At the low end, there emerged MacProject and others. The market was booming and broadening at the same time. This broadening aspect, with project management Software reaching many more people, was a key outcome of the microcomputer revolution, benefiting from the ubiquity of the personal computer: You could manage your project on your desktop—or on the road. Such a concept!

C1b. Intelligent Project Guides

Two project management methodologies, SDM/70 and Arthur Anderson's Method One, emerged in the late 1970s and early 1980s to significantly influence project management practices. Both were for information technology (IT) projects, in part because of that application area's need for improvement, and in part because that need was recognized with available funding. This is proof that the market often leads the tools. Each methodology had strengths and weaknesses. Their strengths included strong support for better project management practices. Their weaknesses included adding unneeded overhead to projects, and their lack of scalability to projects of different sizes than their design targets. They spawned a series of more scalable alternatives, and some project management consultancies booked engagements to downsize the monolithic efforts to something more usable for smaller projects[4]. The net result of these efforts, when well-adapted, was more consistent project management processes, and higher levels of project success. Concurrently, the enterprise was moving from "big bang" multi-year projects to medium ones that delivered business results within a year (where feasible). That scaling down was also key to extending the reach of project management software to people who were *part-time project managers.* The ultimate scaling: one consultancy[5] published, marketed and trained tens of thousands in small project management, with Co-Pilot: Small Project Guide® as a *universal project method* for any project from 8-360 hours of effort.

In 1987-1988, Ed Dante[C] developed Project Bridge[6], a powerful "front-end" planning tool that supported ABT's Project Workbench and other popular scheduling software. Project Bridge was a key achievement in moving project management software beyond scheduling and tracking functions to supporting the development of reusable project plans. It used key project attributes to select a project path, establish traceable estimates, help manage risk, and then scale a reusable project schedule template to serve as an 80% complete cost and schedule portion of a plan. The templates were pre-loaded with activity estimates and contained all key needed project roles, so all the Project Manager needed to do was to fill the roles and fine-tune the plan for the distinctive aspects of the project. The tool offered a way to model and measure the impact of insufficient support, and perform multiple viable project plan and schedule scenarios. While this method was focused on IT, it could work across the enterprise with the addition of customized project kits. Now, competent project managers had a credible tool to show executive managers the cause-and-effect relationship between adequate project support and success. Ed sold his product to ABT, marketer of Project Workbench, and the combination of Bridge and Workbench made a good project management scheduling tool into a much more powerful project management tool, *"the combination of which was lethal,"*[c] that dominated the midrange project management software market for years.

Trajectory C2. *The Present:* Assessing Where We Are

After 40 years, we in the project management software industry have not made much progress—neither in increasing the size of the market nor in increasing the penetration of our 10 project management functions into enterprises. In fact, while it is clear that the innovators and early adopters have advanced significantly, the late majority and laggards have barely moved. This is reflected on the revised version of the innovation adoption curve, shown in figure 3, overlaid by each group's estimated implementation of the 10 project management functions. To explain the scale, innovators, at left, now apply all 10 project management Functions. Laggards, at the right, only apply three of them. This is unfortunately the case, despite huge investments in tools, processes, and training. And where in 1980 there was perhaps a 10-year gap in adoption rates between leaders and laggards, today that gap is approaching 25 years! Thus a prediction: unless something changes, the average enterprise in 2025, even with innovation, market pressures and significant effort, will still be struggling to adopt today's leading technologies!

What is holding back the successful adoption of needed functions? Here is one perspective: Many companies begin to improve their project management processes by finding and buying promising new technology. project management consultants frequently get a call for help *after* the decision to purchase and implement the new technology. By then, it is often too late to maximize the investment's benefit. Technology can help, but only if it is the last step in a sequence that prepares the organization for beneficial change. Based on the work of the author[7], successful project management methods improvement always considers the right factors, executed in the right sequence:

1. Enabling Policies;
2. Responsibilities;
3. Processes; and
4. Technology.

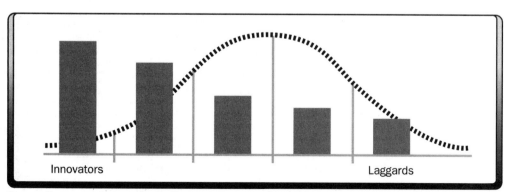

Figure 3:   Innovation adoption curve and 10 project management functions.

Thus the first step is *not* to explore the technology, but to identify the enabling policies, that set the stage for beneficial change. Here is an example of a policy: All projects of a certain size and greater shall have a viable project plan, with a schedule that is staffed, has precedent relationships for each activity, and that the team will use as a baseline for tracking.

Next, identify the stakeholders, their roles, and responsibilities. The third step: identify the processes, supported by detailed procedures, where needed. Finally, and only last, specify the requirements and identify the technology needed to enable, support, and accelerate the improvements. Any gap in this proven sequence dooms the improvement effort if not to failure, at least failure to fulfill its potential.

Identifying Problems, and Seizing Opportunity

Besides the problem of inappropriate sequence of implementation, today's enterprises and today's project management software vendors are well-aware of the problems they are trying to solve. The most common project, program, and portfolio management problems encountered today are listed in Figure 4 (your list may vary, and it does depend on the industry). Innovators who manage project-oriented enterprises have overcome these problems, and apply project management software to extend their competitive edge over the rest. On the other hand, Ron Brown[B] points out that most of these problems are all symptoms of a greater set of problems. For example, many enterprises are trying to manage projects using an operations mentality, a sure sign of a company that has not made the leap to a project-oriented enterprise.

Today's project management Software Status Summary

Even with our progress of the last 40 years, the project management software industry of today has barely penetrated its recognized market. And, that recognized market is still less than 5% of the world's population. This is the case even with the "mainstream-

---

Common Project Problems

1. Inconsistent prioritization of project efforts.

2. Changes in priority that affect project momentum.

3. Conflicts between "real work" and project work for project participants.

4. Too many projects run in too short a time with too few team members.

5. Incomplete project plans and poor tracking against them.

6. Lack of clear, agreed-upon project success criteria.

7. Failure to capture project intelligence in lessons learned, issues, risks and assumptions.

8. Competition, not cooperation, in organizations that are driven by operational accomplishment rewards.

9. A re-invent, rather than reuse mentality, and no rewards for changing this pattern.

10. Failure to develop project stakeholder competencies, especially sponsors and resource managers.

Figure 4:   Common project problems; used with permission of ProjectExperts.

Figure 5:   5% market penetration.

ing" of project management in the 1980s mentioned earlier, as increasing numbers of knowledge workers became part-time project managers or team members. This is the case despite an increasing chorus of voices joining in since 1986, saying that the majority of society's work is project-oriented, and the majority of that work is not treated as projects, just more work to be done by the end of the week, or end of the month, between perceived more-important process or support work efforts. The untapped market potential is huge. Half the world's population or more should be the project management software market. But perhaps we are getting ahead of ourselves.

Trajectory C3. *The Future:* Scenarios Bloom Through 2025

In addition to other changes, it will be the continuation of trends that solve the problems users of project management software face today. This section explores advancements that can be expected based on the trajectory extending from the present through 2025 and beyond. These advances will both increase the market's size, and increase the penetration of it. Undoubtedly many other interesting innovations will also occur; these are merely samples.

C3a. *Project Portfolio Management*

Project portfolio management (PPM) has been around for years, and it will continue to increase its functions and audience for the foreseeable future. According to PMI's *The Standard for Portfolio Management*, PPM is *the centralized management of one or more [project] portfolios, and involves identifying, prioritizing, authorizing, managing, and controlling projects, programs, and other related work, to achieve specific strategic business objectives*[9]. Separating the PPM business functions from the technology is difficult but important. It is difficult because few organizations have identified a job classification and clear responsibilities for a portfolio manager. Instead, in many companies, portfolio management is administered by a part-time committee of managers and/or executives, with support from staff. It is important because of the need to implement technology *last*, only after planning enabling policies, responsibilities, and processes. The key to PPM is that although every organization does it, some just don't do it well.

As Ron Brown[B] points out, PPM is not a project function, but an enterprise function. So the first step in maximizing a portfolio is to decide how each project relates to enterprise strategies, operations, and a multi-year funding process. On the technology side, tools for PPM first emerged in the 1980s, with a focus on aggregating cross-project plans for their common resource use. Many of the high-end project management software tools supported that aggregation, either with additional modules, or within the tools themselves. Soon PPM vendors began adding prioritization, risk management, dashboard indicators, and portfolio tracking functions. Today there many PPM vendors, many of them having only marginal penetration in their market. But given continued investment, plus feedback from the innovators and early adopters, some of the vendors will see a massive increase both in their market breadth and in their penetration midway between this writing and 2025. But what are the features that will cause these increases? Looking at a few examples can help answer that question. In researching this chapter, we interviewed a handful of key executives from leading PPM vendors, including some with whom you are familiar, and some you should be.

Our selection of leaders includes (among others) those involved with Microsoft's Enterprise Project Management Solution, Primavera's P6, Spider Project software from Russia, and Delta Group's Proconsul. Each has their strengths, and many of the features they currently offer will be the in-demand functions of the 2025 project-oriented enterprise. For example:

- A more-complete enterprise portfolio that integrates the management of projects with operations and business functions—with the knowledgebase and information from all areas—for improved executive decision-making;
- Cash flow and human resources management across the enterprise, including the prioritization, modeling and provisioning of project, process, and on-demand support staff (often the bottleneck in today's enterprise[b]);
- Multi-year workplace projections, and the budgeting to support them, including capital investments needed;
- Modeling and simulation to show the trade-offs between combinations of proposed efforts—and their benefits;
- Calculation of net present value of planned initiatives, plus follow-up to assure that benefit realization occurs;
- Inclusion and key consideration of otherwise-separate project management activities and tools within the portfolio, including parametric estimating and risk management; and
- Process and template reuse and metrics capture for improved estimating, bidding, risk management, and project performance.

To a great extent, this partial list of features shows the future of project management. It is also the present. In a déjà vu way, Ed Dante, mentioned in the section C1 Past Trajectories with his innovative Project Bridge, reappears here with his newest effort, Proconsul®. And outside the United States, Spider is seeing increasing uptake from construction to petroleum, to other serious project-oriented industries. Microsoft's suite solution does a stellar job of targeting the roles and information demands of unique stakeholders. And the progeny of the original PC-based Primavera solution is still a preferred leader for many enterprises, significant in that none of their first-decade competitors remain today.

C3b. Collaboration: Virtual Teams and Social Networks

A range of innovations (some of which have been on the scene for some time) promise to improve the adoption rate and increase the size of the project management software market—if one is flexible in identifying what that market is. One such innovation is the combination of virtual teams (project teams that are not co-located) with social networks. Bringing together the tools that support this collaboration and communication reaps great results for those who apply them. Starting with voice over Internet protocol (VOIP)-based Skype conference calls and web-conferencing, and supported by wikis or SharePoint sites for content management, some of the tools are known for their flexibility and power, others for their accessibility and ease of use. Increasingly, teams combine those tools with free or fee-based social networks[8] that help virtual teams to work together, research together, network together, relax together (where that is within the boundaries of the culture), and achieve together. This movement is viral rather than planned, and that in itself is a boost: This is not just another change that is mandated from above. The net result is a *massive increase* in the size of the market audience that uses project management software. And, imagine what this can do for market penetration in the 10 project management functions!

C3c. Mastery of Real-time Time Tracking

Time tracking has long been a frustrating factor for project teams; too many team members view time sheets as one of their greatest scourges. This is exacerbated for any person who works on multiple projects, and who has ongoing work responsibilities, plus frequent interruptions for customer support or other causes. And then managers wonder why the project cost numbers are so unreliable! To repeat our policies, responsibilities, processes, and technology sequence; *enabling policies* are essential to save time wasted in tracking ineffective assignments. For example, *in large[10] projects, the core team members shall be full-time-assigned and their other responsibilities covered by others. In medium projects, core team members shall be at least half-time assigned (with the timing established in advance); and their interruptions from ongoing responsibilities shall be handled by others.*

Here is the breakthrough: The next release of your calendaring system does more than accept and notify you about project assignments, due dates, ongoing work responsibilities and other scheduled events. *Under your control* (an *essential* privacy requirement), it also records all your activities against those and all other events during your day. Your unified phone system, calendar, and car link with your PCD (personal communication device, a cell phone-sized supercomputer) to collect and maintain your activity information. They also track your interruptions, recording them with their charge number and the context of the interruption, so later you can reduce the unnecessary ones. At the end of your day, summary information "pops up" for your review, complete with all needed charge numbers. After your approval, all information brokers, including project cost, status, and earned value, activity completions, and payroll, receive postings in the right locations, with the right codes. Working late? Your PCD also records that information. On holiday? Your PCD reports in, and logs your time, at your option.

Significant advances result from real-time tracking: it drives the need to develop honest schedules that the team actually tracks against, abandoning the too-frequent trick (in some enterprises) of developing a schedule that is only good enough to get an executive approval. From this advancement, the penetration of project management software increases significantly. Earned value management becomes much more useful, as the window of currency moves from one month after the work to one day; plus, the information is now much more accurate and reliable. Managers make better decisions much faster, and project success rates soar. Of course, all this is mostly for the back half of the innovation curve: The innovators and early adopters solved this problem years ago.

C3d. Capture and Reuse of Project Knowledge

In the 1970s, most companies realized that literally thousands of homegrown pay-roll or general ledger systems had been developed, and started buying their commodity software, rather than writing yet another costly system. That same realization contin-ued in the 1980s for project players cited in the past trajectories section: You only really need to develop the same project schedule, and to a great extent, the same project plan, once. All successive similar projects should merely reuse the materials as templates. Af-ter all, most of your organization units repeat the same six-to-nine projects over and over, 80% of the time; the only difference is their scale, plus several key and distinc-tive attributes. That reuse potential also applies to the product documentation: require-ments, test plans, even training templates all contain reusable project knowledge. As content management systems increase in both power and ease of use (both increases are essential), the information reuse goes beyond the clever few to the mainstream many.

There exist challenges to reuse: first is a lack of incentive to reuse project material. The incentives set up by some enterprises (note the enabling policies) include rewarding not only those who reuse materials, but also those who *produce* reused materials. This incents those who produce the materials to internally market them to others. Other challenges include the selfish departments that discourage sharing outside their group, because others may instead receive the scarce performance bonuses from the enter-prise pool. Add the issue of tagging the content with the right searchable attributes so template-shoppers can easily screen for the most relevant works by project size, disci-plines, and strategy or approach. The last issue is the greatest one: Even with tagging and attributing there are still over a dozen template candidates; which one is best? Ludo Hauduc[D] asserts that a user ratings method, as is used at Amazon, NewEgg or eBay, will nicely fill that knowledge gap.

Innovators and early adopters are already doing much of this: They prosper with this use. But as the early and late majorities also adopt the approach, an open market emerges for the exchange of these *project catalysts*, first within professional societies, then industry groups, and then worldwide. A role of *project knowledge broker* emerges, as enterprising salespersons bring together knowledge buyer and seller—and profit from it. Schools and government agencies are the first to plunge into this new information-is-knowledge economy, because they are less-often competitors. Some enterprises block the sharing of knowledge that could be competitive advantage, but after just a few years, most see that the benefits of shared knowledge far outweigh the risks. As this market matures, it results in another massive increase in market size and in penetration of the project management software market.

C3e. Dashboards and Project Intelligence

Project dashboards have been around since the 1980s, but aside from the leaders, too many enterprises were basing them on poor tracking against even poorer project plans. Even worse, many focused on easy-to-measure trailing indicators, rather than more actionable leading ones. The resolution of that long-standing time-tracking problem mentioned earlier opened the door for much smarter project information management. Project information that is rear-view mirror shows where we were last week—or last month. You would never drive a car based on reports that you drove off the road last Thursday, but for too many projects, that has to suffice. A car's dashboard is in front of you so you can glance at your indicators without taking your attention from the road ahead. This helps explain the need for leading indicators, rather than just trailing ones. As explained by the author in an article[11], *Project Levers and Gauges*, cost and time are trailing indicators. By the time you see them "go red," it is too late to fix them. Scope and the right talent are leading indicators. Action taken on leading indicators shows up (much later) on the trailing ones. But what do most project management software tools track? Mostly trailing data on time and cost. This insight opens the door to project intelligence to those who act on it.

If data is important and information is very important, how do you use them? Effective managers make decisions based primarily on information. Data is useful in identifying the amplitude of the impact, but one cannot make a decision based just on data. As presented at the IPMA 2005 World Congress[12], the best source of actionable project information is constantly in front of us: Assumptions, risks, issues, failures, and lessons learned are *all the same information, at different points in time*. And they are recurring from phase to phase in one project, and from project to project. This is proof that they are more-often lessons recorded than lessons learned. In addition to improving actionable project information, the other scenarios also contribute: they contribute real-time tracking and Enterprise-wide portfolios of projects, programs, *and* operations. Enterprise dashboards are now relevant, accurate, timely, and essential. Intelligent project practices proliferate, project communications improve, decisions are smarter, and adopting enterprises thrive. The project management software market increases audience and penetration once again.

C3f. Project Management Absorbed into Enterprise Systems

These trajectory scenarios seem to be soaring; how could it get any better than this? Depending upon your point of view, this may be as good as it gets. As inspired by Vladimir Liberzon[F], most of today's project management software functions get absorbed by one of the enterprise software management domains. The fight is between ERP, CRM, SCM, and PLM. The rationale is this: it is all enterprise data, and as we move towards virtual enterprises, with CEO, a procurement staff, and a program management office—with everything else a project contract—the requirements change. The challenges of flowing project data and information, first one direction, then the next, and keeping it all current while reducing duplication and accelerating access to it, just breaks too many processes. The latest challenge begins when project-oriented enterprises focus on their program/project systems, and flow all data from there to payroll, to payables, general ledger, and others. The only back-postings are for depreciation, additional overheads that are not customer-billable, and vacation accrual. Between new transparency and regulatory requirements and increasing back-and-forth flow of data between systems, by the early 2010s we will see a monster data management problem. Just as industries run in cycles, the cycle of centralized management systems comes back into vogue.

Enterprise resource planning (ERP) has the longest ties to the project management software, having served it well for years as a separate Enterprise service. And with its absorption of all the human resources functions, it already has all the information about people, their competences, and qualifications. Customer relationship management (CRM) points out that ERP just covers overhead functions, while CRM is all about the customer, *whom projects serve.* Supply chain management (SCM) opines that without the supply chain, no one is going to get anything done, and besides, once every enterprise is a virtual corporation, SCM is the last service remaining. And the engineers in Product lifecycle management (PLM) point out that adding the other enterprise project competences to their portfolio would be the easiest integration of all. PLM eventually wins with the argument that the project life cycle was really just a small part of the inspiration-to-retirement product life cycle they manage. But shed no tears for the project management software industry: Entrepreneurial as they are, the vendors soon become the spokespersons and visionaries for the engineers and product managers with whom they are partnered. With this move (which takes some time), the market size and penetration of the project management Software industry increases again.

Impact of the Trajectory Scenarios

The trajectories grow the project management software market, and increase penetration of it. For the project management software vendors in 2025, there is a combination of the same patterns of the past: We see some new players that establish innovations, some larger, well-known players that continue to serve, and too many familiar players that cannot survive. But project management software of 2025 (based just on trends) still has far to go to fulfill its potential (see figure 6). Of course, there are many

Figure 6:   40% of 2025 market.

other candidate scenarios that will have impact, beyond our slim sample. For example, we have not even gotten into the existing simulation software that will be able to simulate your entire project execution, proving or disproving your assumptions, risks, and strategies. Still, it will take more than useful tools for project and portfolio managers, teams, and managers, to realize the promise of project management. Fortunately, one does not predict the future just based on past trends. For example, many of us figured in January 2000 that we might be able retire comfortably by 2002, given the trends at that time in retirement accounts in the U.S. stock market. We must also explore the discontinuity scenarios to understand more about the possible state of the project management software industry in 2025.

D. The Discontinuity Scenarios Transform the Industry

Kurzweil's *Age of Spiritual Machines*[13] inspired some of the content in this section. This section has two parts: *Near-term scenarios* that reflect the first half of the time between now and 2025, and the *longer-term scenarios* that reflect through 2025 and beyond. And where Rogers' innovation curve was an important visual for understanding the project management software market for the trajectory scenarios, something a bit different is essential for the discontinuity scenarios. We refer you to *Crossing the Chasm*[14], where Geoffrey A. Moore adapted Rogers' innovation curve to illustrate the unique difficulties of organizations in adapting to discontinuities. The challenges of discontinuities are multiple. They come out of nowhere. When they work, their impact can be game-changing, both for those who adopt them, and those who avoid them. And the majority of discontinuities fail; we all remember those attempted by others, and conveniently forget those we tried that failed. In this section we introduce the Disrupt-O-Meter to summarize the impact of these discontinuity scenarios, based on feasibility, cost-effectiveness, and disruptiveness.

D1. Near-term Discontinuity Scenarios

Scenarios in this group may be only partly outrageous. Most discontinuities are outrageous, you know. These may occur in the period between our publication date and 2017; they have their roots in accomplishments outside the project management software industry over the last 20+ years. Although coming from outside, they will have impact by helping to resolve two problems facing project management software vendors. To grow their market, they must:

1. Increase the functions to increase penetration in their market, while also increasing ease-of-use.
2. Increase the market size, by broadening the audience from project specialist tools to general population tools.

The gains for project management vendors from the project management software trajectory scenarios, as described in the previous section, are often only incremental. At the same time, the benefits for the innovators and early adopters are significant. The discontinuity scenarios offer both greater risk and greater reward for both groups—if they happen. Those that do will have profound impact on the market, and upon the success of organizations managing projects. But here is a warning: even these near-term discontinuities may be disconcerting for those who have difficulty letting their imagination roam.

D1a. Near-Term Scenario: Gloria Gery's Electronic Performance Support Systems

In 1991 Gloria Gery published her book, *Electronic Performance Support Systems*[15], based in part on her experiences in helping a major insurance company improve the efficiency and effectiveness of staff performance. Moving far beyond classroom training, her approaches dealt with the fact that most of the real learning and skill-building occurs on the job, not in the classroom. Her concept, which forms the foundation for today's performance management, was to provide just-in-time coaching, examples, or tutorials for knowledge workers. Perhaps her work inspired Microsoft's Clippy, that paperclip that kept pestering you until you figured out how to turn it off. But that is all background information. Let's extrapolate Ms. Gery's concepts forward to a possible future. Do you have your imagination circuits triggered and ready?

Monday morning when you arrive at work (your home office, time-shared cubical at headquarters, or your favorite coffee shop) your PCD (personal communications device) presents you with a prioritized list of your actions for today, the week, and the next month. You review, modify, and approve the list, then start your first activity. Your PCD has multiple ways for you to interact: digital paper that displays and records your updates (for interactive work), a personal viewer that attaches to your glasses or earphone and displays the equivalent of a 30-inch monitor, or a small projector that pops out of your PCD and can project an up-to 8 foot display on the wall (it only runs 4 hours on a charge without the solar panel). Based on a combination of Ms. Gery's efforts and your enterprise knowledgebase, an "Intelligence Agent" (IntellAgent) layer between your hardware and your operating system assures that your every action is monitored, coached, critiqued, improved, and researched on the web for citations or disagreements with your theme. When you encounter a stumbling block, your IntellAgent records what information or inspirations you need, and goes out in search of them. When you are awaiting information or approvals from others, your IntellAgent interacts with theirs to deliver what you need to complete your efforts. And because project work relies so much on research and innovation, your IntellAgent doubles your results in half the time. Feasible? Absolutely! Cost-Effective? Definitely! Disruptive? Definitely!

D1b. Near-Term Scenario: Bonnie O'Neil's Rule-Based Databases

In the early 1990s a database consultant named Bonnie O'Neil was inspired to establish the first real innovation in databases since Codd's relational revolution: Rule-based databases. Ms. O'Neil worked with a group of database luminaries, together with database vendors, to establish a new standard for the use of databases with business rules. This idea, with the resulting standard, eased the implementation of data warehouses and the potential for data conversions, as well as solving the information management challenge of the preceding 30 years: *"Separate the business rules from the logic, and make them accessible to the customer."* And what does this have to do with the project management software industry? It established the foundation for a transformation in the way Enterprises collect, manage, use, reuse, and store project information—after all, the most valuable project information is primarily business rules.

This particular discontinuity began with the Hedge Funds using business rules with neural networks (self-learning networks of computers working concurrently to solve wicked problems) to game the U.S. stock market, often by selling short in derivatives. This discontinuity then proceeded to the project world. As mentioned in the trajec-

```
┌─────────────────────────────────────┐
│         Disrupt-O-Meter             │
│  ┌───────────────────────────────┐  │
│  │  100    100    100            │  │
│  │ Feasibility Cost-Effect. Disrupt.│ │
│  └───────────────────────────────┘  │
└─────────────────────────────────────┘
```

tory scenarios, most project decision-making is based primarily on information, with supporting data. Much of that information is recurring risks/issues/failures (and successes) and lessons learned. The final link: Those can all be expressed as business rules in your business rules enterprise engine device, a massively parallel neural net workstation. A simple example: *If* there is a freeze in Florida in March, *then* the cost of orange juice will go up by 25% in June. Add a consequences engine, and you no longer need a Monte Carlo simulation module to model 1,000 instances of a risk/threat, you can merely search your active project histories. Need to bid a project? Add your selection of competitive strategy (Win on price, win on prior record, win on business development relationships) and your workstation will prepare your bid as specified in the request for proposal, then coach you through the project delivery when you win the contract. Feasible? Probably! Cost-effective? Probably! Disruptive? Definitely! Thanks Ms. O'Neil!

D1c. Near-Term Scenario: Collaboration Impacts From Virtual Project Worlds

This discontinuity scenario also has its roots in the past. You may recall the adventure games from the early 1980s. The idea was to navigate a virtual environment (using up/down/left/right arrow keys), overcome challenges or puzzles, and find the gold. Primitive, but engaging, they were. Today's manifestations consist of virtual communities where you immerse in three-dimensions and engage in interaction and discovery. Second Life is our favorite, although it is only one example. How does this scenario affect project management software? We'll tell you in a bit, after we complete our transaction for a new wardrobe for our avatar: we didn't like the corporate-issued version.

OK, follow closely: Projects are virtual, because the product does not yet exist. It is a vision, ideally held by an enterprise executive who will serve as project sponsor or champion. The project manager works with that sponsor to flesh out the vision in a simple project charter, then create a likely team. That team further fleshes out the vi-

```
┌─────────────────────────────────────┐
│         Disrupt-O-Meter             │
│  ┌───────────────────────────────┐  │
│  │   80     80     100           │  │
│  │ Feasibility Cost-Effect. Disrupt.│ │
│  └───────────────────────────────┘  │
└─────────────────────────────────────┘
```

Disrupt-O-Meter

100	100	100
Feasibility	Cost-Effect.	Disrupt.

sion with business objectives, preliminary scope, approach, effort, cost and duration estimates, and a next phase or next stage plan. Your executive group funds and approves the effort—and it is still all in your imagination!

This entire set of transactions could take place between avatars in Second Life, or any of the similar virtual worlds. The advantages include no need for travel time to distant locations. Technology limitations, such as sharing a document at a face-to-face meeting, are already being solved through SharePoint or other online community tools. And while research at Purdue University and other places has shown how the avatars can respond to all your body movements using sensors in your clothing, other research determines participant mood and satisfaction with meeting proceedings by "watching" facial expressions and eye movements. The finishing touch: those personal viewers mentioned earlier are superseded by a three-dimensional holographic environment in which you and your project team plan, execute and close out even your most complex projects—at least those that produce soft products. You'll still have to be "onsite" for the hard-product ones to pave a road, build a skyscraper, or run clinical trials. At least for now. Feasible? Definitely! Cost-effective? Definitely! Disruptive? Absolutely!

D1d. Near-Term Scenarios: Changing Requirements from Governments

The near-term scenarios presented so far benefited the innovators and early adopters. But looming is *Son of SarbOx*, the next round of government regulation. Expensive, stringent and ineffective regulations enacted by the United States and other nations to deter corrupt enterprises were relaxed to increase productivity and revive struggling world economies after the 2008 crash. Then, a new wave of populist-oriented re-regulation strikes. Its basis is the need for greater enterprise transparency, coupled with legislative and voter anger over perceived excess pay and profits in some industries, plus the necessity for struggling governments to replace taxes lost by economies in chaos. This new legislation enacts regulations and taxes that cause a new era of centralization in all enterprises. Even not-for-profit organizations having revenues above a certain level are affected. Draconian information monitoring and reporting requirements stifle any enterprise activity that contains unmanaged risk, or poor transparency, or both. Most projects in many enterprises are curtailed or eliminated, causing them to degrade services or fail. Enterprises that intelligently and consistently apply our 10 project management functions continue unscathed. And the project management consultancies that specialize in developing organizational project management competence cannot fulfill all the demands for their services.

The affected enterprises' trauma only lasts four years, but in that time entire industries are gutted. First-world countries become third-world. Resource-rich and ag-

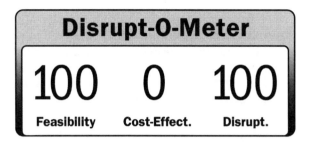

Disrupt-O-Meter

100	0	100
Feasibility	Cost-Effect.	Disrupt.

ricultural economies thrive (nations in Africa send food and economic aid to the US), but most of the services, knowledge and financial industries take years to recover—and the gap between project oriented enterprises and those that are not continues to grow. Governments on all continents gently nurse their struggling economies back to health, eliminating corporate and capital gains taxes, and establishing worldwide flat taxes. Out of the chaos, Phoenix-like, a new world economy gradually emerges, even stronger than former ones at their peak: This is the new project intelligence economy—in more ways than one. Feasible? Absolutely! Cost-effective? No way! Disruptive? Yes!

D2. Longer-Term Discontinuity Scenarios

Now we move from the short term scenarios to longer-term ones; our samples are few, compared to the potential for many discontinuities. Again, two threads are consistent: increasing support for project management functions in existing markets, and growing the market. As we move closer to a project-oriented culture, the latter will have the greatest impact.

D2a. Longer-Term Scenarios: IntellAgent-Facilitated Meetings Improve Effectiveness

Do you spend a significant amount of time in meetings? Is that your most productive time? Whether it is a cross-functional managers' meeting, a staff meeting, a project team meeting, or a facilitated project kick-off meeting, too many meetings today waste your time. Worse, they are not the type of event that generates stakeholder passion for more such meetings. Despite John Cleese's definition of the problem and the solution over 30 years ago in his popular video, *Meetings, Bloody Meetings*[16], today's meetings are worse, not better. Many enterprises could save massive amounts of money and make huge productivity improvements just by making their meetings more effective.

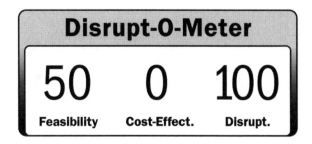

Disrupt-O-Meter

50	0	100
Feasibility	Cost-Effect.	Disrupt.

Imagine a time when your personal communication device's IntellAgent could prepare you for all your meetings, coach you through your key talking points, and help you complete the needed follow-up. Voice recognition captures and categorizes all comments. Using recorded knowledge and processes, the IntellAgent learns how to improve your processes, interactions, and the results of each session. It adds new topic processes as meetings evolve them. Need a SWOT (strengths, weaknesses, opportunities, threats) analysis? Your IntellAgent does a better job than you can in guiding the process. This capability exists today, but does not reach critical mass until longer-term because of participants who see their power being eroded. For an early example of such a future, see www.BeyondTeam.com. Feasible? Eventually! Cost-effective? Definitely! Disruptive? Yes!

D2b. Longer-Term Scenarios: Plug and Play Project Plans

The concept of reuse took longer than expected to achieve adoption. project management software leaders, reinforced by project intelligence brokers, institutionalize the profitable exchange of vital project information, processes, and metrics. One obvious business driver is the brokers who profit from bringing buyers and sellers together. Another unexpected driver (for some) is the emergence of project management competence as the new taxonomy for project management, rather than focusing upon knowledge. The roots of this scenario go back many years: the *Project Manager Competency Development Framework*—Second Edition, published by PMI in 2007, and the IPMA Competence Baseline for Project Management (with many corresponding national competence baselines) popularized the demand for performance-competence in project management practices, building on the knowledge foundation.

The consequence: No more reinventing the wheel. If it has been done before, you can license a reusable, tailorable project management plan, you can adapt it for your current project's attributes, link it to your enterprise strategies and see the majority of the risks you will encounter (threats *and* opportunities). All of this is tuned for your project by (once again) your IntellAgent. The new competence taxonomy establishes the needed framework for concurrent interaction of multiple elements, allowing modeling and simulation of project scenarios as a dynamic way to plan, monitor and control projects. Leveraging other scenarios in this chapter, alerts "pop up" with possible paths, and consequences of actions taken. Project managers, project management office consultants, and executives spend more time evaluating consequences of action (or inaction) and less time trying to sort out data. Feasible? Yes! Cost-effective? Definitely! Disruptive? Yes!

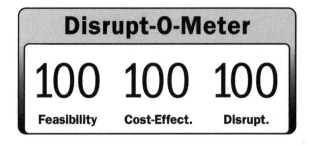

Disrupt-O-Meter

50	50	100
Feasibility	Cost-Effect.	Disrupt.

D2c. Longer-Term Scenarios: Socket To Me and the Wisdom Tooth

Our last disruptive scenario is just several small steps beyond the preceding one. By 2020 or so, Kurzweil[13] predicts that computers will catch and exceed humans in processing power. Coupled with massive storage and the ability to tap larger networks when needed, this new technology leverages our earlier scenarios to reach new markets. The first innovation is the *Socket to Me* chip. Capable of storing the knowledge, business rules and project intelligence of more than 1,000 project experts, the chip is powerful, yet very small. Now the differentiator between enterprises and between project management practitioners is not their years of training and knowledge, but their ability to harness, reuse and apply the encapsulated intelligence of others. Of course, the prior steps of learning to capture and use project intelligence, plus the project management competence taxonomies and tagging for easy reference, were prerequisites to this advancement.

The chip is located in a new socket near the base of the spine (a freeway to the brain), runs off body electricity, and can be swapped in the socket based on the nature of the work you perform. There is only one known disadvantage: it depends on your willingness and ability to be a life-long learner. Two successive releases appear, and further miniaturization and speed prompts a new location for the chip. The distance from the base of the spine is now the greatest barrier to performance. The third generation, much faster, much smaller chip, called the **Wisdom Tooth**, is implanted in the open slots in your upper jaw—and has direct access to the brain. But the disruption is not as far-reaching as imagined. As observed by guest expert Ludo Hauduc[D], knowledge alone does not accomplish all the needed results: *"Everyone knows the notes, but there is only one Mozart"*. Religious experts are concerned about the societal impact, amid fears that we are trying to become god-like. Those concerns are quelled when people who were active in the movements of the 1970s observe that we have finally figured out how to *tap their cosmic consciousness*. Feasible? Perhaps! Cost-effective? Maybe! Disruptive? Yes!

D3. Summary of the Discontinuity Scenarios

It is difficult enough to predict the impact on market penetration and market size of any one of these discontinuity scenarios. To predict the compounded impact of any two or three (or more) would be impossible. Yet they all range from quite feasible to just perhaps so. Clearly, they will not only vastly grow the market for project management Software, they will also demand higher levels of use of the functions the software delivers. They will require other changes, for those companies that survive. And because the market leaders *"are great people filled with great ideas"* (a quote from Joel Koppelman[E]), new functions will continue to increase the gap between the leaders and the laggards.

Figure 7:   80% of potential market by 2025.

E. Implications of the Project Management Software Industry Scenarios

Based on assertions made in this chapter, the reader might assume that that majority of enterprises are troglodytes—ancient, backward, slow-moving entities. On the contrary, those Enterprises that are not among the project management software innovators or early adopters have carefully chosen their market position. They are often the leaders in their marketplace (or government-space) *based on excellence in their ongoing business processes.* This excellence may come from combinations of procedure efficiency, customer focus, financial management brilliance, ability to attract and keep talent, or other factors. And while project-oriented enterprise leadership and process-oriented excellence are not mutually exclusive, enterprises must manage them differently. For example, "Starve the process" is a typical approach in a process-oriented enterprise. Use statistical control to track the process quality and only intervene—adding needed resources or funding—when the defect rate exceeds bounds. In a project-oriented enterprise, you "Feed the project." If you instead starve the project of needed funding or resources, you delay delivery, may hamper needed scop e and quality, and significantly delay or eliminate benefit realization. This is a completely different mentality, and method of operation. The integration of a program/project portfolio with financials, operations, and all other enterprise aspects, is a huge first step in bringing together multiple strengths, while balancing them all.

The Project Management Software Vendors. Many project management software vendors have burst on the scene with novel ideas, then either established their niche, got absorbed by larger enterprises, or died out. As the project management software market broadens and deepens, we see a flood of great new ideas and players, just as we saw in the roaring 1980s. At the same time, consultancies also thrive, in part just because of the massive growth in the size of the market. Of course, both vendors and consultancies must have their differentiating competences.

The Practice of Project Management. The practice of project management has changed from the late 1970s, when the majority of projects had full-time, experienced project managers. By the mid-1980s, project management was often an added "spare-time" assignment for roles ranging from business analysts to programmers to engineers. It was expected to take no time (if it did, that was treated as overhead), and no training or experience. With the emergence of project management competence in the 1990s, championed by nations (Australia, New Zealand, and South Africa) and professional organizations (such as International Project Management Association), most enterprises began to realize that the trained, experienced, competent (and proven so) full-time practitioner was the key to their project and program success. That built the foundation for the transformation of the practice of project management in the 2000s, resulting in great increases in project success over the next 20 years. Still, as identified by guest expert Ludo Hauduc[D], both practitioners and their enterprises will need to change old habits (specifically around reuse and improving collaboration effectiveness) to maximize those increases.

Executive Transformation: The greatest project management challenge for many executives is to get timely, actionable project management information. Over the last 20 years, enterprise executives have been increasingly frustrated by the lack of visibility into an increasing proportion of their enterprise portfolio, that of projects. Many have responded by inserting more layers of middle managers between them and "the problem." As described in *"Let's Cure the Dumbing-Down of Project Management"*[17] changes occurring today will improve visibility, especially into leading indicators of project success. Couple that with the integration of projects and programs, operations, and financials in one true enterprise portfolio management system (with better plans and honest status tracking). Add the prediction by guest expert Dr. Kraft Bell[A] that the software will present the needed information in the style, format, and level of detail needed by each individual executive: They can achieve piercingly clear vision into their entire domain, enabling better decisions, faster. But with some, the damage has been done; as predicted by one of our experts, Ron Brown[B], many disgusted executives will retire before the needed and actionable information—and delivery systems—are available.

Enterprise Change Management: It is not just project practitioners and executive managers who will see change. Entire organizations will change their structures, their strategies, their prioritization processes, and their reward systems. As the practice of project management becomes the universal core management discipline, the enterprise learns to manage change as well as it manages the status quo today. De-Taylorizing[18] the enterprise reverses the de-skilling of assembly-line process workers. We will broaden the skill, experience, discretion and rewards for talent, and accelerate the flow of actionable information. The enterprise collaborative network blows away the rigid inflexible, information-thwarting power-seeking old hierarchy. The nearly-trite call of the 1970s, "Information Is Power" is reborn and partnered with "Competence Leads Success." Those who demonstrate competence have the power to apply it. Those who do not have the option of gaining it—or to retire. It costs the enterprise less to pay them to leave, than to keep them on. Energized talent soars in mutual project successes.

Societal Impacts: As mastery of project management and its related practices begins by age seven (when students begin working in teams), project management becomes a core competence for all disciplines. Its value-add is clearly perceived by all who desire beneficial change. Clear understanding of the need for scalability allows adaptation of different methods or emphasis for projects of varying size or complexity. Highly complex projects, such as major disaster recovery, use appropriate project management approaches, thus accelerating rescue of those affected, and recovery from economic impact. As basic knowledge, experience, and wisdom become commodities, innovation, interpersonal skills and communication effectiveness become the differentiator between nations, industries, and individuals. And what is the role of the project management software industry in all this change? Merely the catalyst, available for the ready reagents of the willing enterprises.

F. Reference Information
Chapter Contributors: Guest Talent Interviewees

This chapter benefited from the insights of the people, listed in alphabetic sequence below, who participated in interviews to contribute their vision, insight and time. We cite them for their "sound bites" with end note references A-F in the text. We also blended into this chapter many of their opinions, predictions, concerns, and respect for the practice and practitioners of project management. We very much appreciate their comments and their perspective.

[A] **Dr. Kraft Bell** is a visionary, yet practical consultant on business strategy, IT alignment, project management, and cultural change. Dr. Bell was vice president and distinguished analyst for Gartner, as the resident expert on corporate strategy, the business value of IT, and a keynote speaker on enterprise change management at Gartner's portfolio, program, and project management conferences. Dr. Bell is valued by top IT, corporate, and government executives for actionable advice that insures viable business strategies, enterprise change, and issue resolution. Dr. Bell has spent 25 years working with executives and teams in medium and large-sized firms in the United States, Europe, and Japan on enterprise, project, process, and change management. He is now CEO and executive consultant for RKB Strategic Change Consulting, as well as vice chairman and chief change officer for a transformational start-up with an industry-changing, integrative solution that delivers the highest quality at lowest total usage cost.

[B] **Ron Brown** speaks in this chapter for visionary executives of enterprises that are customers of project management software vendors. Mr. Brown is a senior executive and consultant with extensive business and program management experience. He has served in the following industries: applications software; information technology; technical and systems software, internet software and services; and medical laboratories and research. He has worked for or completed engagements with Fortune 5000 companies, including HP, AT&T, Procter & Gamble; and Exxon. Mr. Brown's significant experience at the Executive and Enterprise level brings a unique mix of business perspective and program management experience to challenging technology-change initiatives. He is a certified Project Management Professional (PMP®) and is a member of PMI, *asapm®*, and CTEK. Ron has a MBA in information and operations management.

[C] **Edmund Dante** is president and CEO of Delta Group International (DGI), providers of the enterprise portfolio management tool Proconsul*. Dante brings a history of project management Software tools innovation to our chapter. Prior to establishing DGI, Mr. Dante founded Princeton Management Sciences, which developed and marketed Project Bridge in North America as well as Europe with The Hoskyns

Group, a major consulting group in London. Project Bridge was acquired in 1990 by Applied Business Technology, where Ed continued to evolve and promote the capabilities of the product, renamed Project Bridge Modeler. After Project Bridge, he developed The Enterprise Process Continuum (EPC). EPC became the Platinum Process Continuum (PPC), which was acquired by Computer Associates in 1999. Mr. Dante's latest tool, Proconsul*, extends his vision of the complete project and process portfolio management tool to include projects *and* operations in the portfolio. See Proconsul at proconsulonline.com.

[D] **Ludovic Hauduc,** general manager, is responsible for product development and strategic direction of the Microsoft Project Business Unit. Ludovic has been involved with the Microsoft Project team since 1994. Prior to this role, he led the development team for Project Pro/Std, Project Server, and Project Portfolio Server. Mr. Hauduc holds a BS in computer science from ESIGELEC, an electrical engineering school based in France. His insights for this chapter that we especially appreciated focused on the sociological and enterprise changes needed to benefit from today's and tomorrow's project management software. He cited the need to change old habits, and recognize and reward those who do so. See Microsoft's enterprise project management solution website by starting at: office.microsoft.com/project.

[E] **Joel Koppelman** co-founded Primavera Systems in 1983 with the vision of creating project management software for the IBM PC and revolutionizing the way people plan and control projects. Today, after 25 years of consecutive growth and profitability, Primavera is a Global Business Unit of Oracle, having been acquired in October 02008. The company is a leading provider of project, program, and portfolio management software in the world and its nearly 600 employees offer industry-specific solutions to customers in 85 countries. Mr. Koppelman co-authored the PMI best-selling book *Earned Value Project Management* with Quentin Fleming. Among his other activities is the funding, through the PMI Educational Foundation, of a unique project management approach for complex projects, such as in disaster recovery. See Primavera.com.

[F] **Vladimir Liberzon** is the architect of Spider Project. He has been involved in project management since 1975. He first developed project management software for mainframe computers in the USSR in 1978. Mr. Liberzon is a mathematician and developed many of Spider Project's algorithms. Today he is a well known project management consultant and trainer and serves as vice president of the PMI Moscow, Russia Chapter. Spider Project was originally presented in 1993 at exhibitions in Russia and Germany. Even in 1993, it had many advanced features including skill scheduling, parametric estimation of activity durations, resource-constrained scheduling optimization, etc. Since then its development has been continuous and today it is powerful project portfolio management software with many unique functions. As of 2008 Spider Project is in use in 22 countries. See Spider Project at (English website version): spiderproject.ru/aboutus_e.php.

End Notes

[1]The author's company, ProjectExperts, has used this list of 10 project management functions to evaluate project management Methods Improvement needs and to perform project management effectiveness analysis for over 28 years. Used with permission of ProjectExperts.

[2]Rogers, Everett M. *Diffusion of Innovations*. Free Press of Glencoe, 1962.

[3]The source of this saga about the scheduling software? That young Fortran developer is the author of this chapter.

[4]Many buyers of these powerful tools contracted with consultancies that helped them scale down from their design targets to the much-smaller-projects those buyers more often managed. This demonstrated early understanding that "one size doesn't fit all."

[5]That consultancy is ProjectExperts, of which the chapter author is owner and president.

[6]The author collaborated with Ed Dante during 1987; both were working on similar concepts, and benefited from each other's insights. This chapter focuses on Ed's achievements, rather than ours, to avoid self-promotion. Our IT methodology product, The Project Guide, with Plan By Example*, continues to serve from 1985 through today.

[7]*project management Methods Improvement Plan* is a methodology for improving project management processes. It helps increase success with all new project management methods. A copy is available at: ProjectExperts.com.

[8]There are many popular social networking sites as of this writing; Ning, a recent venture, is more business-friendly than others, while still having enough of the same features so younger generations embrace it. See Ning.com.

[9]*The Standard for Portfolio Management*. Project Management Institute, 2006.

[10] In 1983, the author classified projects by size, established minimum staffing requirements for each size range, set the ideal duration, and identified the primary roles of the project manager. A white paper that explains the size ranges and key success factors for each, *The Successful Project Profile*, is available at the ProjectExperts.com website in the *articles* section. Note that other organizations have their own preferred size ranges and rationales.

[11]"Project Levers and Gauges" is available in the *articles* section at the ProjectExperts.com website.

[12]"*Risk Management: Key to Project Intelligence*," presented at the IPMA 2005 World Congress in India, is available in the *articles* section at the ProjectExperts.com website.

[13]Kurzweil, Ray: *The Age of Spiritual Machines*. Penguin Books, 1999. This book predicts key changes in computer and societal development decade-by-decade, predicting how computers will have caught up, then surpassed human processing speed and capacity by the year 2020 or so.

[14]Moore, Geoffrey A,: *Crossing the Chasm*. Collins Business, Revised edition 2002.

[15]Gery, Gloria: *Electronic Performance Support Systems*. Gery Performance Press, 1991.

[16]*Meetings, Bloody Meetings* is available for personal use through most libraries, or for commercial use through johncleesetraining.com. Although it was originally produced in 1976, it is still totally relevant and useful today.

[17]"Let's Cure the Dumbing-Down of Project Management" is available in the *articles* section at the ProjectExperts.com website.

[18]The term *de-Taylorizing* refers to reversing the de-skilling of processes instituted by Fredrick W. Taylor, the father of scientific management. His scientific approach to optimizing manufacturing and other repeatable processes revolutionized mass production in the early 1900s. But some feel the process went too far. The quality movements of the 1980s began the re-enrichment of knowledge workers' (including project managers') jobs.

CHAPTER 10

The Likely Growth of Quality Management in Projects Circa 2025

Sandra K. Ireland, MBA, PMP

"It takes less time to do things right than to explain why you did it wrong."
Henry Wadsworth Longfellow

Introduction to Quality in Projects

Over the past few decades, project quality has made significant improvements through a variety of programs that brought a sharper focus on two factors. First, there is a sharp focus on meeting the customer's requirements. Second, there is a concentration on preventing defects in products and services rather than identifying and fixing problems. Both of these initiatives have changed how quality management is viewed and treated since the 1960s when quality just meant "inspect and repair defects" in products.

At one time in the 1990s, there were more than 37 different programs with similar goals. Perhaps the most well known or recognized is TQM – or Total Quality Management. Six Sigma Quality programs have also grown in popularity where the objective is to reduce defects to less than 2.8 defects per billion operations. All programs, however, had a form of defect prevention and reduced reliance on inspection for quality metrics. Prevention of defects has proven to reduce costs as well as give greater customer satisfaction.

Quality management in projects has evolved today to a system of planning, assurance, control, and continuous improvement. This system is the generic approach to achieving quality goals and has been tailored to meet specific industry and project requirements. Each component is defined in the following:

- Quality Planning – identifying relevant standards for application to the work and designing the product to meet the customer's requirements. This involves anticipating the form, fit, and function of the product that meets the customer's requirements and establishing a blueprint to work with for constructing the product.

- Quality Assurance – evaluating the overall project performance on a periodic basis to build confidence that the construction of the product meets the standards selected during planning. This may include reviews of the product's technical development on a periodic basis to assure the work meets the customer's requirements.
- Quality Control – tracking specific work results to determine compliance with the selected standards. This includes inspection and testing of materials, components, and systems to verify that the standards are being met.
- Continuous Quality Improvement – identifying and implementing incremental changes to procedures, practices, processes, materials, and operations for more effective project results. Continuous quality improvement may span several projects under which ongoing project improvements would feed new project efforts, to include planning, assurance, and control.

Quality Management Definitions and Evolution

Current definitions of project quality management have evolved and are understood from a contemporary basis within different industries, organizations, and countries. Professional organizations have to some extent promoted definitions that are similar in intent, if not in precise wording.

The history of the word *quality*, however, has evolved from people and animals to products and services. According to the Oxford English Dictionary (OED), the word *quality* was coined circa 1290 with specific reference to people or animals. Circa 1290, *quality* referred to a person's character, disposition, nature, capacity, ability, and skill. When a person was said to be a quality person, it meant the individual possessed good disposition and could be trusted.

The OED goes on to suggest that by 1374, quality meant the nature, kind, or character of something, which could be people, animal, or product. By 1579, the definition included "to rate [assess] at a certain quality," meaning something rare. In 1867 the definition of quality added such words as attribute, property, character, or special feature.

Today, the meaning of quality as recognized by the OED is "the essential character of something [such as a product] or nature of something." It may include an inherent or distinguishing characteristic or property. Most often, quality refers to the level or degree of conformance to a customer's requirement. Variance from the customer's requirements detracts from quality.

The second part of quality management is the term *manage*. Again, the OED provides a history of the term and its meaning. Coined circa 1490-1500, *manage* referred to the handling of horses, which evolved in 1561 to train or direct a horse. By 1579 the meaning expanded to "carry on a war or business" and subsequently in 1609 "to control or direct the affairs of a house or institution." Today, the meaning evolved "to direct or control the use of [something] and to make submissive to one's authority."

One may use *manage* today in the context of control and direction of the quality of a project's product through active measures designed to achieve the customer's requirements. Active measures would include planning for quality, periodic assessments of progress toward the build of the product, testing, and demonstrating that the product meets the customer's requirements through a program designed to prevent defects. Continuous improvement of the quality process is inherent in directing a quality program.

Conditions that Dictate Changes in Quality Management for Projects by 2025.

> "The most damaging phrase in the [English] language is: 'It's always been done that way.'" - *Rear Admiral Grace Hopper, USN*

Quality management involves working within an environment and the contextual relationship with other factors of projects and project management. Quality management must adapt to these changing factors as projects are implemented from the present time to year 2025. Some areas to consider are described below. How these trends will affect quality management will be explained in the section entitled "Conditions that Dictate Changes in Quality Management for Projects in 2025."

- **Energy Resources.** Shortage of energy-producing fuels and the resultant escalation of the price of these fuels will be transferred to the cost of projects. Electrical energy prices will continue to rise with greater electricity consumption. Solar power and wind power may offset the demand for greater electricity needs, but not to the extent needed to lessen hydroelectricity and nuclear power plants to meet greater demands The demand for gasoline, ethanol, and diesel fuels to operate vehicles and generators will continue to expand with the resultant price increases.
- **Human Resources.** The demand for human resources with the requisite skills in project management will increase. These individuals and teams must not only be knowledgeable in the practice of project management, but must also be competent in modern project management. Competence means the right blend of knowledge, skills, abilities, and behavioral attitude to perform in a project environment.
- **Material Resources.** New materials are emerging with properties of greater strength, less weight, and greater durability. Composite materials, such as those used in stealth aircraft, offer more possibilities with perhaps greater challenges for shaping to the required form in a reasonable time. The disposition of these new materials as waste products or disposal of end products and the end of their useful lives must meet environmental requirements. Countries such as Canada, with vast material resources, will have a major role in supplying large projects.
- **Client Involvement in Projects.** Clients have become savvy about projects in the past few decades and will express a greater need for insight into the processes used–both managerial and technical. This need for visibility into project management activities will not decrease in the future, but should increase to the extent that clients will have access to information from planning through implementation. Clients will influence the direction and rate of change for projects.
- **Global Warming Affect.** Adverse changes to the environment dictate changes to the manner in which projects are accomplished when the ecosystem is affected. In the United States for the past three decades, for example, there has been no new nuclear energy power plants built. The trend is to supplement fossil fuel power plants and hydroelectric dams for electric power by nuclear fuel power plants. Some electrical power, in limited supply, will be available from wind turbines and solar panels. The project's product must be environmentally friendly as well as the processes required to build the product.

- **Global Competition for Project Resources.** The world continues to evolve from a *national* economy to a *global* economy under which large projects and programs will be planned and implemented across many national borders. Human and material resources will vary in quality and quantity for projects, depending upon the education and experience within a country. Countries with large populations, such as India and China with more than a billion people each, will be tapped to be global players in large projects requiring a significant number of staff. There will be resource-poor nations that can, in some fashion, participate in minor roles of all size projects.
- **Aging U.S. Population.** People in the United States are living longer – and it can be assumed that those project participants will also show growth in a full range of ages. The experience base for projects will grow, but there will be a tendency to "do things as they have always been done." Thus, growth in project techniques can be stunted through the reliance on experience more than seeking new, more efficient and effective ways of performing tasks.
- **Information Processing.** The ability to process information is increasing at a geometric rate. In relative computing power growth, it can be said that the computing power in 1960 was rated at 100, and by 2025 the computing power will be rated at 100,000,000 – or a million times more powerful in 2025 than in 1960, a span of 65 years. Automation of various business processes provides data that can be used to track the quality metrics throughout projects and organizations. The focus will be on analyzing that data, via automated methods, to make informed improvements to the quality management processes.
- **Global Competition.** As the world changes through technological advancement, the availability of broadband communication service, combined with the increased computing power, with positively affect the potential for international projects. Alliances will be developed with foreign companies to pursue projects. Projects will be comprised of product components that can be compartmentalized, developed, tested and then integrated. Project components can be outsourced through foreign companies. Organizations will seek mutually beneficial relationships with companies in other countries to change the way that that business is conducted.

Whereas the above-listed conditions are perhaps the major conditions that will influence the future of quality management in projects, and how quality and quality management are addressed in future years, these are considered to have the primary external influence. Technology can offset some of the negative impacts, but it will take more original thinking and perhaps a strategic outlook to compensate for the changes in the next two decades.

Considerations of the internal impact to projects may be the differentiation between size and complexity. In contemporary literature, size is often addressed as "bigger means more difficult in managing." Size, however, may not be the challenge, but rather project complexity may prove to be the real challenge. Projects with greater complexity prove to be more challenging to manage in terms of the technical and business aspects. A brief discussion of the situation is appropriate here.

- Project size will often influence how project quality is viewed. Figure 10.1 illustrates five project sizes and is representative of the work that medium to large

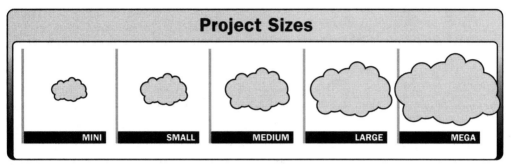

Figure 10.1: Project sizes.

organizations would encounter. Smaller projects have the visibility into the construction from start to finish with relatively few changes – if the original design accurately meets the customer's requirements. Medium, large, and mega projects typically do not provide that visibility from start to finish, even with detailed planning. Size is most often not the determining factor of project quality – it is project complexity defined as managerial and technical complexity.

- Managerial complexity is defined as the number and relationships of the managing elements and the number and relationships of the performing elements. Figure 10.2 depicts an example of a situation under which there are several "managing organizations," that is, several project owners with some degree of influence on how the project will be prosecuted. A single managing organization is the simplest solution and complexity increases when two or more managing organizations become involved. This is true even when the managing organizations are structured in partnerships or consortia, for example.

- Further to Figure 10.2, the number of performing organizations increase complexity because of integration issues, number of contracts awarded, and frequency of contact between the project manager and the performing organization's lead. It is a managerial function to select the project performers to conduct the work on the project.

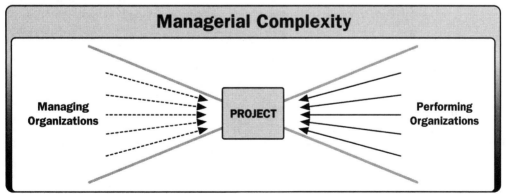

Figure 10.2: Managerial complex projects.

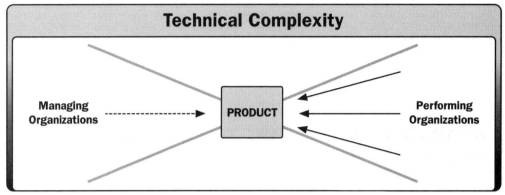

Figure 10.3:   Technical complex products.

- Technical complexity, on the other hand, focuses on the product and the technical ability of the performing organizations to resolve the challenges associated with product. Technical complexity, as depicted in Figure 10.3, can result from too few performing organizations to engaging performing organizations that lack the technical "know-how" to solve the problems. Technical complexity often results from specifying requirements that have not previously been resolved through technology.
- Combining complex managerial situations for the project and complex technical situations for the product can create an overwhelming business model. Figure 10.4 depicts the combination of complexity for the project and product with several managerial organizations overseeing the construction of a product by several performing organizations. The multiple relationships and difficult technical challenge can have devastating consequences on the success of the project.

It is not necessarily the size of the project that can impact project quality, but it is more likely the complexity of the project and product. Managerial complexity has the potential to raise conflicting requirements–both managerial and technical–that cannot be

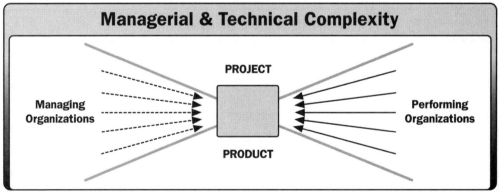

Figure 10.4:   Composite managerial complex project and technical complex product.

resolved easily by the project manager. This can result in unclear specifications to meet requirements as well as significant delays in the business side of projects (i.e., schedule slippage and added cost). Work may be started before all issues are resolved and plans are in place.

Again, size does not relate to product construction technical feasibility. In fact, many new products being designed use micro pieces that are only visible under a microscope. Take computer chips that contain millions of bytes of instructions and are smaller than a human fingernail. Space-based satellites must be constructed to operate in a cold environment, and the environment may be friendly or hostile depending upon the product's purpose. Highly technical products may push the state-of-the-art to meet their functional purpose, which adds complexity to the build cycle.

In the future, project managers will need to address both managerial complexity and technical complexity more thoroughly to plan the project to meet customer's requirements. Designing a management structure that minimizes perturbations and delays in the project's progress will be essential to optimize the project execution and product design.

The Future of Quality Management in Projects

Change is inevitable, progress is optional. Unknown

Although 2025 is less than two decades in the future, dramatic changes are suggested because of the changing environment in which projects are managed. As the availability of resources are both reduced and prices increased, organizations will need to seek new and better methods of overcoming these obstacles. Energy sources and project staff will be perhaps the most expensive items applied to fulfill the customers' requirements.

Energy sources, such as gasoline, diesel fuel, and electricity, prices will continue to escalate with the resultant additional costs to projects. New sources of energy such as fuel cells will be emerging, but there will probably be a heavy reliance on the traditional energy sources. Quick fixes for the energy challenge are not envisioned in the next 25 years.

Project staffs will become more knowledgeable and project-competent through a wider interest and application of project management in organizations. Training and education will become widespread and better. Quality management in projects will be embedded in training of project management, rather than being considered separate and distinct from core project management functions. More emphasis will be on building products and services that meet the customer's needs.

Organizations will work to integrate the project management process with keen emphasis on quality, under which all stakeholders understand the customer's requirements and work toward satisfying those requirements. Some potential changes to improve quality are:

- More time and effort will be spent understanding the customer's requirement at the front of the project before work starts on the product. Collaboration with the customer on the basic design and subsequent changes will be initiated only after customer approval. In most instances, a good understanding of the product will be obtained, with all the nuances associated with product, while some projects will not have that clear a definition because of their nature. By necessity, these projects with unclear paths to completion will prove most challenging to deliver the right products.

- Organizations will conduct a three-day project rehearsal exercise to familiarize and indoctrinate the staff and selected stakeholders with the critical aspects of the project. The rehearsal exercise will touch on major elements of the project and emphasis such areas as the required quality levels to be achieved. Weaknesses will be identified in staff competence as well as product design flaws for correction prior to start of the project. It is anticipated that a three-day rehearsal exercise will result in better quality for the product and a savings of project time. This investment should result in less rework and waste of resources to ensure completion of the project on time and at the least cost.
- Computer simulations will be useful for both product design and staff skill requirement definition. Computer simulations will also be used to train the project staff in specific processes and principles of quality management. Computer simulations will be augmented by specific requirements for each project and its product.
- Organizations will be challenged through lack of critical, competent staff to implement projects to achieve the customer's needs the first time. These organizations will seek to hire certified project management staff that can demonstrate a high degree of competence in all aspects of project management with specific emphasis on the quality function.

Quality tools will be used to measure and resolve defects, where defects are defined as anything that adversely affects the customer. Defects, defined in this context, require some correction to align the product with the customer's need, which may include repair, rebuild, remake, or other consumption of resources. Too many corrections can lead to an excessive consumption of resources that will negatively impact the cost for the customer and can lead to customer dissatisfaction.

As an example, the Pareto chart is a useful tool to identify the impact of defects by ranking those in order of defect frequency. Recognizing that 80 percent of the issues will be included in the first 20 percent of defects, one can work on eliminating those high-frequency defects as a priority. This does not, however, take into consideration the cost to the project for each defect. Sophisticated application of the existing tools will change the way that defects are addressed. The Pareto chart will be used to integrate the cost association with each defect category by multiplying the number of defects times the cost to correct. The more costly defects, because they impact price of the product, will be corrected first rather than the most frequent defect.

This function is illustrated in Figures 10.5 and 10.6, where Figure 10.5 is a typical Pareto chart that shows the most frequent defects starting from the left side. As a general rule, the first 20 percent of the numbered defects will encompass 80 percent of the total defects. This is typically the approach taken to rank the defects by frequency rather than by importance to both the customer(s) and the performing organization.

Figure 10.6 is an example of how the impact of cost per defect can change through multiplying the number of defects by the cost of the defects. The frequency of the defects is shown in the light gray bar and the cost of the defect is shown by the dark gray bar. Note that defect number 5 is the most costly, with defect number 3 being the second-most costly. These costs of defects, if allowed to continue, must be passed along to the customers because the performing organization must operate at a profit.

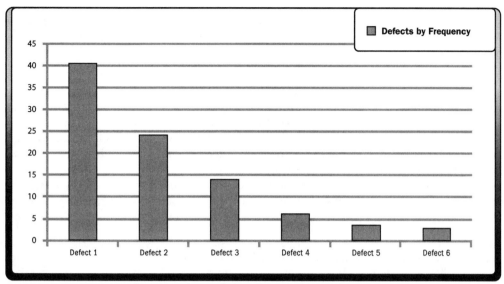

Figure 10.5: Typical Pareto chart (defect frequency).

The capability to electronically format and store quality-related information will be significantly greater for projects, both as single project entities and as organizational business building blocks. This expanded capability will facilitate and ease the application of critical data to achieve continuous improvement of product quality in projects. As information processing power increases, there is an opportunity to improve quality management. Some of the areas to consider are:

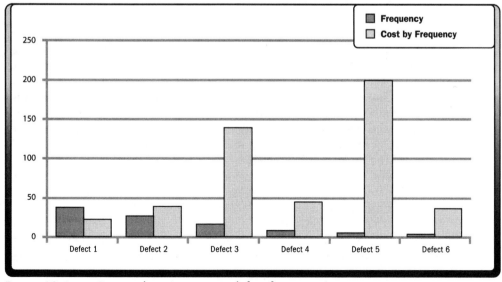

Figure 10.6: Pareto chart (cost times defect frequency).

- Quality Planning–Electronically store standards for easy and ready access. For projects, there will be many standards that can be stored in electronic form. This will provide a foundation for applying information from the standards (e.g., work flow, process times, expected results, actual results).
- Quality Assurance–Use the expanded information processing power to assess the progress of quality against the standards and specifications. Leverage the data that are available on the standards to perform quality assurance reviews and provide valuable information on the emerging results.
- Quality Control–Track inspection and test results for product components as well as construction of the product in process. Compare data between projects to see if better results are being achieved on the current project.
- Continuous Quality Improvement–Establish automated electronic processes to transition the data into information that can be used to solve quality problems. Identify and highlight problem areas for evaluation to obtain opportunities for improvement.

In the world market economy, competition is the driver that causes the demand for higher levels of quality. Projects are negatively impacted when the needed levels of quality cannot be achieved. Scarce resources bring a sharp focus on their efficient and effective use while working to meet the customer's needs. Opportunities provided by international competition will be critically assessed by senior management.

- Quality Planning
    - Standards–The quality standards must be clearly documented for the international project in written form during work as well as during training. Evaluate the situation to ensure that the standards are well-understood by the entire project team. Misunderstood quality standards will negatively impact the project.
    - Requirements–Ensure that the project quality requirements are understood. Project quality requirements must be clear and direct. Subtle nuances may not be obvious to project workers in a foreign country. An additional challenge is that requirements are dynamic and tend to change until they are well-documented and baselined. At that point, they may continue to change, but perhaps not as often. Quality management professionals of 2025 will play an important role in conveying the quality requirements at the outset of the project.
- Quality Assurance–The overall project technical performance needs to be continuously tracked throughout the project life. Success in quality assurance can be accomplished by establishing clear standards, establishing automated processes for tracking those standards, and reviewing the data captured to track and control the project performance.
- Quality Control–Quality control is required to ensure validation of components and materials used in the project. Consistent tracking and testing will need to be conducted to actively control the technical aspects of the product.
- Continuous Quality Improvement–Opportunities for continuous quality improvement will be presented through the collection of defect data and formatting that data into understandable information. Organizations will learn over time what defects occur most frequently for correction. It will also provide the

pointers to defects where interest and emphasis needs to be placed to prevent future defects.

Mature workers in the project team will bring a wealth of knowledge about international projects. They, however, will tend to rely on formerly proven concepts that worked well in domestic projects, but not in international projects. There may be a tendency to continue to perform project work in the formerly successful manner that does not apply well in an international environment. These seasoned project participants can make a contribution to the international project arena if they are willing to try new techniques for managing foreign contractors. There may be a leaning toward "we've always done it this way."

The Future of Quality Management Professionals in Projects (QMPP)

Quality management professionals, preparing for 2025, need to expand their competences to meet the evolving customer demands. Whereas changes are anticipated based on the past three decades of quality management in projects, some general areas of change are expected. Below are some topic areas for consideration by the quality management professional:

- Required to be fully competent in project management functions and have a keen insight into customer needs;
- Aware of the skills needed for projects and ensure the best effort is made to match skills to job requirements;
- Competent in advanced information processing to provide insights on quality management solutions;
- Able to analyze data and identify new ways to look at information to get insights needed for continuous improvement actions;
- Remain open about new ways to analyze quality management processes—new tools, techniques and views will be there if you are open to finding them; and
- Be able to define quality training requirements and oversee the conduct of quality training.

Quality management professionals will take the lead in planning quality initiatives, to include participation in project rehearsal sessions that identify quality strengths and weaknesses in projects. They will create solutions for those identified defects, both in product and process. Quality management professionals will assume a greater role in all aspects of project planning and implementation, as well as determining corrective actions needed to deliver a product or service that meets the customer's requirements.

In Summary

Quality will continue to be an important aspect of the products and services provided through projects. It is anticipated that there will be more projects used to perform the work of organizations and that the importance of quality management in projects will grow accordingly. All stakeholders will have a role in delivering quality products and services to customers.

While project quality management has grown rapidly and evolved in the United States over the past few decades, it will continue in this trend to meet customer requirements through a defect prevention program – rather than a test-and-fix-defects program. The prevention orientation will anticipate quality needs and plan to meet them during the implementation phase. Organizations will build on quality improvement through better practices, procedures, and processes.

The introduction of new technology will aid in improved quality management practices for the quality management professional and give greater visibility into the results of work performed. Expanded computer capabilities will allow for capturing more data to be formatted for analysis to identify repetitious defects. The repetitious defects will then be addressed through a continuous improvement process.

The most significant improvements will be made through the education and training of quality management professionals, project stakeholders, and project practitioners. It is anticipated that large projects will have two- to three-day project rehearsal sessions that simulate the project build process. These sessions will identify strengths and weaknesses in the quality process for correction prior to project start. The quality management professional will play a leading role in the rehearsal sessions.

Bibliography

Cleland, David I. and Lewis R. Ireland (2004). *Project Manager's Portable Handbook*, 2nd Ed., McGraw-Hill, New York

Cleland, David I. and Lewis R. Ireland (2007). *Project Management: Strategic Design & Implementation*, 5th Ed., McGraw-Hill, New York

Coates, Joseph F., John B. Mahaffie, and Andy Hines (1997). *2025: Scenarios of the US and Global Society Reshaped by Science and Technology*, Oakhill Press, North Carolina

Fern, Edward J. et al (2003). *Six Step to the Future*, Time to Profit, Inc., Mission Viejo, California

Friedman, Thomas L. (2007). *The World is Flat – A Brief History of The Twenty-first Century*, Release 3.0, Picador, New York.

Imai, Masaaki (1986). *Kaizen: The Key to Japan's Competitive Success*, McGraw-Hill, New York

Ireland, Lewis R. (1991). *Quality Management for Projects and Programs*, Project Management Institute, Newtown Square, PA

Lassettre, E.R., (1991). *2021 AD: Vision of the Future*, National Engineering Consortium

Oxford English Dictionary, 2nd Ed. (2008). Oxford University Press, Oxford, England

Senqupta, Kishore, Tarek K. Abdel Hamid, and Luk N. Van Wassenhove. "The Experience Trap," *Harvard Business Review, February* 2008, pages 94-101.

Snowden, David J. and Mary E. Boone. "A Leader's Framework for Decision Making," *Harvard Business Review, November* 2007, pages 1-8

The American Heritage Dictionary, 2nd College Ed. (1985) Houghton Mifflin Company, Boston, MA.

CHAPTER 11

The Future Integration Of Scientific Evaluation in Project Management

Edmund M. Ricci
Beth A. D. Nolan

Practical life cannot proceed without evaluation, nor can intellectual life, nor can moral life, and they are not built on sand. The real question is how to do evaluation well, not how to avoid it. (Scriven, 1991)

Introduction

Scientific program evaluation is a comprehensive system of concepts and methods which is used to assess the design and implementation of a program or project. While certain aspects of scientific program evaluation share similarities with professional project management, these perspectives have not been effectively combined in the project management or program evaluation literature. We anticipate that project managers will more fully incorporate scientific evaluation methods into the project management process by the year 2025.

In this chapter we first present some of the basic components of evaluation science and then illustrate their utility by describing their use in a project that has recently concluded its initial 5 year period. The chapter will conclude with suggestions describing how these two intellectual systems could be merged in the future to create a robust framework for designing monitoring and assessing all aspects of time limited projects. This new integration of scientific evaluation with project management could result in a more efficient and cost effective application of project management methods.

We will use the terms program and project management interchangeably when referring to time limited programs or projects, although evaluation methods are also routinely applied to programs and projects which have a very long or unspecified timeframe. The term project management is commonly used in the private sector; governmental and voluntary agencies typically use the label program management.

Background

The essence of program evaluation was described by John Koskinen in testimony to the Committee on Government Reform and Oversight of the Congress of the United States. Koskinen (1997) identified several questions that program project managers should be prepared to answer. The general question, "What are we getting for the money we are spending?" can be expanded into three: "What is your program...trying to achieve? How will its effectiveness be determined? How is it actually doing?" (or How did it perform?). The specialty of scientific evaluation has emerged in the United States and globally to provide methodology for answering these questions.

Scientific program evaluation is based upon a comprehensive framework of values, assumptions, concepts, and methods which can be used to describe and assess the resources, activities, outputs, outcomes, and costs associated with a program or project. While certain aspects of a scientific program evaluation framework are similar to professional project management concepts and methods, in reality the purpose, scope, and methods of the two specialties are somewhat different.

Although descriptions of scientific evaluations can be found in professional journals and unpublished technical reports from the early part of the 20th century onward, the field has evolved rapidly in the United States and internationally from the 1960s onward. The methodology was initially described as a comprehensive framework in a book titled *Evaluation Research*, published in 1967 by the Russell Sage Foundation. In this book the author, Edward Suchman, drew a distinction between "evaluation" and "evaluative research."

> In our approach we will make a distinction between "evaluation" and "evaluative research". The former will be used in a general way as referring to the social process of making judgments of worth....while it implies some logical or rational basis for making such judgments, it does not require any systematic procedures for marshaling and presenting objective evidence to support the judgment..... "Evaluative research" on the other hand, will be restricted [to refer to] the utilization of scientific research methods and techniques for the purpose of making an evaluation...evaluative research refers to those procedures for collecting and analyzing data which increase the possibility for "proving" rather than "asserting" the worth of some social activity (Suchman, 1967, p. 7)

Suchman went on to describe and apply "...principles and procedures that man has developed for controlling subjectivity--the scientific method...for their applicability to the ...process of evaluation" (Suchman, p. 12). While numerous reports of the application of scientific methods to assess individual projects or programs can be found in the fields of public administration and the various human services prior to 1967, Suchman's book signaled an important change in that he described in detail a comprehensive framework of concepts and methods for the application of scientific methods to the evaluation of projects and programs. In this chapter, when we use the term *evaluation,* we are referring to the process in which scientific methods are applied to examine all aspects and components of a project or program.

Following the 1967 publication of *Evaluative Research*, there appeared a huge outpouring of methodological books and articles through the 1970s and 1980s, and this continues to the present (Chelimsky & Shadish, 1997; Cook and Campbell, 1979; Patton 2002; Shadish, Cook, & Levitan, 1991; Wholey, 1983; Wholey, Hatry, & Newcomer, 2004). Courses and training programs in universities, peer-reviewed journals dedicated to publishing evaluation studies, and the formation of the American Evaluation Association in 1985 all were part of the process of professionalization of the emerging specialty of evaluation. Evaluation has emerged as an important activity in the domains of public and private administration and management. The field of evaluation has continued to evolve as a professional specialty as it has added the accoutrements of university graduate training and standards of practice and ethics which have been defined by the leadership of the American Evaluation Association.

Further, evaluation science has become a global enterprise. The first International Evaluation Conference was held in Vancouver, Canada in 1995. Five country-based evaluation associations and 1,600 evaluators representing 66 countries and 5 continents met to address an agenda that included global issues in evaluation, lessons learned from past evaluation practice, and descriptions of the changing characteristics of evaluation (Chelimsky et al., 1997).

Basic Assumptions for Program/Project Evaluation

We believe that evaluation studies are based upon an underlying set of basic values, and assumptions, which inform the process of scientific evaluation. It is useful to briefly explicate these assumptions, especially in order to examine their coherence with the assumptions and values underlying project management. The authors of this chapter have identified 10 assumptions of scientific evaluation to include the following:

1. Evaluation is a basic function of management;
2. Evaluative data and analysis should be used in decision-making about programs or projects;
3. The methods used to evaluate a program or project should be understood by the individuals who are being evaluated;
4. All groups that have a stake in the results of an evaluation study should be represented on a committee (stakeholder group) that serves in an advisory role to the evaluation team;
5. Evaluation should be directed toward improvement and positive growth, and thus became a constructive force in the management of a program or project;
6. Evaluations should be balanced in that good performance should be clearly described as well as areas for improvement;
7. The least expensive evaluation design that will meet the needs of the stakeholder group and decision makers should be used so as not to draw excessive resources from the actual implementation of the program or project;
8. Evaluation research relies upon the scientific method and standards, but these cannot be considered and applied without recognizing the political and ethical aspects of each evaluation study;
9. Scientific evaluation should be viewed as one tool of management. It should not replace management judgment based upon experience and intuition; and
10. Evaluation is one component of a decision system which includes needs assessment, policy formulation, program or project design and implementation, and, of course, evaluation.

We believe that the above-stated assumptions, and the values embedded in them, form the basis for the approach to evaluation, and are equally important to scientific program evaluation in project management as they are to the traditional application of scientific program evaluation. The approach to evaluation is described in the next section.

Components of an Evaluation Framework

There are two important and distinguishable purposes for evaluation research; one more "academic" in nature, and the other more suited to the practical project management world. Some evaluation studies are designed as scientific experiments in order to vigorously test the various effects of an intervention conducted as an organized program or project. Such studies add to the knowledge base of a profession by providing evidence for the use of a particular approach or program. When conducted within the rules for experimental science, strong evidence is obtained to support or reject the continued use of the intervention. Experimental studies have come into widespread use in the public and human sectors as professionals, the public, and governmental leaders have become more pressured to spend money wisely.

Other evaluation studies have a much different aim. These studies are conducted of programs or projects as they are designed, organized, and executed. They are called *managerial evaluations* in that they assess the need, structure, process, outcomes and costs of programs or projects while using the methods of science to do so. *It is the approach taken to conduct managerial evaluations which has the most relevance for the field of project management.*

As defined by Øvretveit:

> *Managerial evaluations are made for managers and supervisory boards to monitor or improve the performance of services or policies, or to check that agreed changes or projects were implemented as intended. Their purpose is to ensure accountability, value for money and performance improvement.* (Øvretveit, p. 35)

Before more fully describing the principles and concepts used in evaluation, it should be noted that experimental and managerial evaluations share certain important characteristics. Each uses systematically obtained data, applying at least minimal standards of validity and reliability to their collection and interpretation. Each must resolve ethical issues concerning confidentiality of information and the admonition to do no harm to participants who are functioning according to established rules of behavior. There are also legal and contractual issues concerning the use and dissemination of evaluative reports which constrain both types of evaluations. Many of these methodological, ethical, and procedural issues are identified in a document that defines standards of practice for evaluators. We will refer to this document later in this chapter.

From this point on, we will be focusing on evaluation from the managerial perspective. There are two ways to describe an evaluation framework within a managerial perspective. One approach is to examine the building blocks of an evaluation study. Among the most important building blocks (or categories of evaluation, as Suchman (1967) referred to them) are structure, process, outcomes, costs, and need (see Figure 1). The *structure* of a program or project includes the staffing, funding, other resources and materials available to be used by program staff and the formal organization of personnel. *Process* refers to the planned and actual day–to-day behavior, communications, interactions, and decision-making of those who are involved in the project. *Outcomes* refer to results or effects achieved by the project team. The category of *costs* is used in the standard accounting or audit framework or in terms of the relationship between costs and benefits. *Need* for the project is usually a quantified description of a state of affairs in an organization or community that serves as a justification for the project. Evaluation can determine the extent to which a program or project actually addresses the defined need.

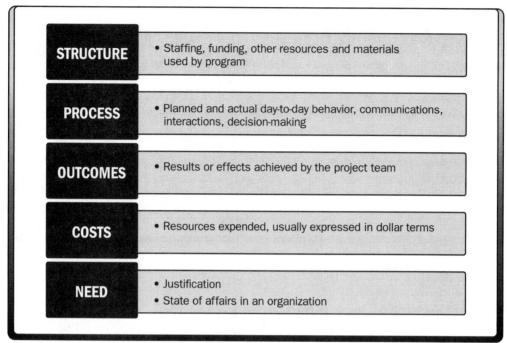

Figure 1:   Building blocks of scientific program evaluation.

A second approach is contained in the concept of a "logic model." A logic model is a way of showing how the *resources* dedicated to a project, and the <u>activities</u> required to implement a project result in certain *outputs* which in turn lead to short-term, intermediate- and long-term *outcomes*. A logic model is thus: 1) a detailed plan for the project; 2) a set of implied hypotheses in the form of "if-then" statements that are also implied, which reveal the "theory" of the project and the connections among the components, and 3) a guide for evaluation (McLaughlin & Jordan, 2004).

Logic models (see Figure 2) are valuable tools for the design, management, and evaluation of a program or project. They require that managers clearly conceptualize and specify program or projects resources, activities, outputs, and expected outcomes and as such provide a basis for process and outcome evaluation. When reading a detailed logic model, one obtains a clear picture of how the project's resources activities and outputs will lead to specific effects (outcomes). In the next section, we illustrate the utility of these ideas by describing an evaluation study of a five-year project.

We can identify basic elements of evaluation categories and logic models in project management (especially process and cost assessment and logic model inputs and outputs/outcomes). Indeed, at any point in the project, project managers can produce the Earned Value Analysis (EVA), for example, as a measure of the project's process. This is an excellent example of a process measure. At the same time, professional evaluators expand upon and embed these ideas in scientific methods, and thus, their impact upon the design, development and management of projects and programs can be significant.

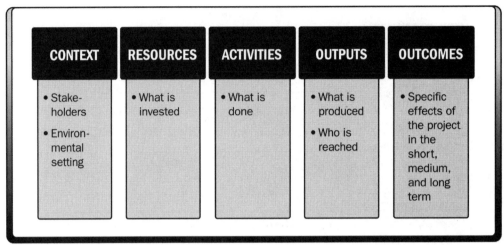

Figure 2: Logic model.

A Brief Description of a Managerial Evaluation

Beginning in 2002, the National Cancer Institute (NCI) of the National Institutes of Health (USA) provided funding for a novel demonstration project of an advanced telecommunications system that the developers named TELESYNERGY®, TELESYNERGY® is a very high-end teleconferencing system that is designed to be used by hospitals for video conferencing and video/voice consultation for the treatment of cancer patients. The long term goal of the Cancer Disparities Research Partnership (CDRP) Project is to use the TELESYNERGY® system to improve the timeliness and quality of cancer treatment and thereby reduce cancer related health disparities in African American/Black, Hispanic/Latino, Native American, elderly and low-income groups. The basic idea for the project was to use a modern telecommunications system to encourage and facilitate communication and collaboration among hospitals (National Cancer Institute, 2002).

The CDRP Program has had five components: (1) planning, developing and conducting radiation oncology clinical research; (2) planning, developing, and implementing and nurturing partnerships between community hospitals and academic cancer research institutions actively involved in NCI-sponsored cancer research, (3) establishing a compatible telemedicine system (TELESYNERGY®) at each CDRP grantee institution and its primary partner to augment partnerships; (4) supporting a "patient navigator program" to facilitate access to radiation oncology services, including clinical trials, by addressing barriers (e.g., financial, geographic, and cultural) that can have an impact on the receipt of timely cancer care by patients from target populations; and (5) conducting community outreach activities to increase knowledge and awareness of cancer and the availability of local treatment and clinical trials research.

In Figure 3, we show a portion of a logic model for one component of the larger project in which the TELESYNERGY® telecommunications system has been used by a set of hospitals in an attempt to improve communication, coordination, and collaboration among the professional staffs of these hospitals and with patients and community residents. The new technology was designed and configured to allow for consultation

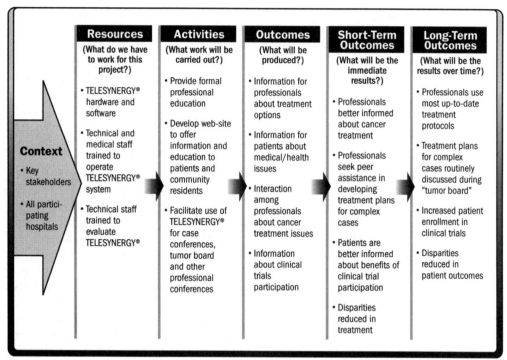

Resources	Activities	Outcomes	Short-Term Outcomes	Long-Term Outcomes
(What do we have to work for this project?)	(What work will be carried out?)	(What will be produced?)	(What will be the immediate results?)	(What will be the results over time?)
• TELESYNERGY® hardware and software	• Provide formal professional education	• Information for professionals about treatment options	• Professionals better informed about cancer treatment	• Professionals use most up-to-date treatment protocols
• Technical and medical staff trained to operate TELESYNERGY® system	• Develop web-site to offer information and education to patients and community residents	• Information for patients about medical/health issues	• Professionals seek peer assistance in developing treatment plans for complex cases	• Treatment plans for complex cases routinely discussed during "tumor board"
• Technical staff trained to evaluate TELESYNERGY®	• Facilitate use of TELESYNERGY® for case conferences, tumor board and other professional conferences	• Interaction among professionals about cancer treatment issues	• Patients are better informed about benefits of clinical trial participation	• Increased patient enrollment in clinical trials
		• Information about clinical trials participation	• Disparities reduced in treatment	• Disparities reduced in patient outcomes

Context
• Key stakeholders
• All participating hospitals

Figure 3

about specific patients, professional continuing education, and the education of patients and community residents about cancer treatment and prevention. In Figure 3, we have reproduced only one section of the complete logic model that was prepared to guide the implementation and evaluation of the telecommunications project (Ricci, Schenken, & Herron, 2006).

The logic model describes the *resources* (a specialized telecommunications system, including hardware, software, and staff); *activities* (professional education, website, and case conferences in which patient treatment options are discussed); *outputs* (increased quality and quantity of information and educational opportunities about cancer treatment and prevention); and *short- and long-term outcomes* (well-informed professionals and patients, resulting in better decision-making about the treatment and prevention of cancer, improved treatment plans and quality of care, resulting in improved patient outcomes in the targeted population).

The entire TELESYNERGY® Project was initially a five-year demonstration of the feasibility of linking several hospitals that had no previous history of collaboration on an ongoing basis. The components of a TELESYNERGY® system are all "off-the-shelf" in nature, and allow a robust and comprehensive type of medical communication. It can be used to communicate with all conventional types of videoconferencing systems. With a variety of additional inexpensive input and output options, the system can be linked to provide information to any laptop/desktop system in the world that can link to the Internet, providing a wide base of versatility and capability for medical professionals and lay populations alike.

The main objectives for TELESYNERGY® video conferencing in radiation oncology have been to: 1) promote participation by attending physicians, nursing staff, and oncology support staff in weekly meetings during which complex patients are discussed; 2) provide opportunity to earn continuing medical education credits; 3) enhance the quality of medical care; 4) offer special topic learning sessions to reinforce understanding by healthcare personnel in how to resolve complex diagnostic and treatment issues; 5) provide on-site and distance learning opportunities for healthcare, community advocates, patient groups; and 6) interact with major health care centers and universities to promote quality in care, quality in education, and equity for all socio-economic and minority groups.

In spite of the many positive outcomes associated with the use of the TELESYNERGY® system, numerous technical and political barriers made it very difficult to actually implement such a system in the real world of medical care. It was therefore decided to incorporate an ongoing "managerial evaluation" into the design and implementation of the project. The evaluation was formalized by identifying two individuals as the "evaluation team." The evaluation team members functioned as ongoing observers of the project implementation team and they collected and analyzed data on a monthly basis in order to document and analyze all aspects of the performance (process, outputs, and outcomes) of the project. Each year, the evaluation team prepared a written assessment of the execution of the project using both quantitative and qualitative indicators of process (activities and outputs) and outcomes. The evaluation team also helped clarify and clearly specify the activities and expected outcomes in a format that allowed for quantitative measurement.

As the evaluation data were studied by the members of the implementation team, adjustments were made frequently in the activity set in order to make it more likely that the outcomes identified for the project were reached. In each of the five years during which the TELESYNERGY® project operated, the evaluation team produced a report in which each major component of the project was rated as being excellent, good, fair, or poor.

The criteria used to arrive at the ratings were:

1) *Excellent:* All activities identified in the logic model were carried out, and creativity was displayed in expanding the activity set when presented with an opportunity to do so; all short term and intermediate outcomes were achieved.

2) *Good:* A majority of activities defined in the logic model were carried out, and the most important short-term and selected intermediate-term outcomes were achieved.

3) *Fair:* Although much activity was undertaken, key activities instrumental to defined outcomes were neglected and only a few short-term outcomes were achieved,

4) *Poor:* Very little progress was made in addressing the defined set of activities, and no short-term or intermediate outcomes resulted.

The evaluation team met with the TELESYNERGY® project implementation team at the start of the project, and the two teams collaboratively prepared a table showing in great detail the process (activities) and outcome measures and the quantitative indicators and data sources for each. We show in Table 1 a sample of these measures, indicators, and data sources to illustrate the manner in which the evaluation team con-

Table 1:   A Sample of Telesynergy® Process and Outcome Measures, Indicators and Data Sources

Planned Processes	Indicators	Data Sources
1. Develop TELESYNERGY® programming for professional development, support of project goals and investigations, mentor communications, minority community outreach and education programs	• Descriptive data showing program team	• Interviews conducted by program evaluation
2. Promote creative use of TELESYNERGY® system for clinical quality control, initiatives, peer review and treatment in radiation oncology.	• Program evaluator rating	• Descriptive data of actual use highlighting creative applications
3. Develop staff training for the operation of the system and medical staff training on system use as a teaching and communication tool.	• Staff knowledge and skill	• Observation assessment
4. Measure technical problems encountered in the operation and use of the system; logistic problems associated with the use of the system, solution to the problems and procedural changes appropriate to eliminate future repetitions of difficulties.	• TELESYNERGY® presentation assessment (NCI form) and descriptive chronology of critical process elements for each presentation	• Evaluator database; log form

Outcomes	Indicators	Data Sources
1. Temporarily increasing numbers of TELESYNERGY® Oncology related programs a. Professional development and education b. Patient support related programs c. Community outreach issues and materials development	• Count by type presentations	• Log of participation & presentation and use of DVD recordings
2. Increase in participation of member hospitals in network produced TELESYNERGY® productions will increase each year of the program	• Count of programs by mechanism/Web/TELESYNERGY®	• PROJECT Records
3. Increase in participation of member hospitals in network produced TELESYNERGY® productions will increase each year of the program	• Count of participants in related specialties who attend programs for cancer-related presentations	• Attendance logs by physician specialty

ceptualized and monitored the implementation of the project. Evaluation data were summarized annually and were provided to all stakeholders, including the funders. In some cases, a decision could be made to do so more frequently (e.g., semiannually or quarterly). However, had a serious barrier emerged to implementation of the project plan, the evaluation team would have promptly communicated with the stakeholders concerning the nature of the problem, and suggestions for overcoming the barrier would have been made and discussed with the stakeholders.

The following is a quote from the evaluation section of the 5th-year annual report to NCI and other stakeholders. This is provided to illustrate the scope and the perspective provided when a scientific evaluation framework is applied to assess a project. This summary report is quite positive, indicating that the project did achieve its planned outcomes; however the annual evaluation reports for project years one through four (not shown here) contained commentary concerning unaccomplished as well as accomplished tasks and outcomes, with suggestions for keeping the project on target.

> *The Evaluation Team's overall assessment of the implementation phase of the TELE-SYNERGY®/PROFESSIONAL DEVELOPMENT/WEBSITE components of the ROCOG Program is "excellent plus."*
>
> *As described elsewhere in this report all implementation (programmatic) goals have been met. This is an impressive accomplishment given the numerous political, administrative and technical barriers that impeded the process. These have been overcome through a clear and persistent focus by Dr… on implementation and ex-*

tensive and sophisticated negotiation by key stakeholders. The TELESYNERGY® system has been fully operative and used for professional development and other project activities (e.g. video conferencing with mentors). An expanded streaming video system for "distance" education has been added. There has been a constant and aggressive push to use the technology for outreach to both professional and lay audiences and this continues to be a high priority.

The Evaluation Team ...has been highly impressed with: 1) the intensity of effort to encourage the utilization of the technology to achieve project goals; 2) the availability of streaming video for use by all partners; 3) the development of a "Technical Tool Kit" for support of project activities, 4) enhancements to the base hospital, 5) the use of the TELESYNERGY® system to support interactions with mentors, and 6) the increased use of the TELESYNERGY® system to provide "continuing medical education."

A number of initiatives have come to full fruition during Year 05, namely: 1) institutionalization of the Thoracic Tumor Conference, and new Tumor Boards which have recently expanded with the installation of their new telecommunication system with new educational programs now endorsed and planned buy both partner facilities; 2) the addition of new TELESYNERGY® systems in all participating hospitals and conversion to video over IP for all 4 systems using the new Tandberg Edge 95 CODEC's; 3) as noted in the "TELESYNERGY®/Professional Development / Web Site" section of this report here has been significant improvement and acceptance of the TELESYNERGY® system usage both in terms of extramural use and for intramural Tumor Board, newly added fall of 2007 Thoracic Tumor Conferences and other activities. In the previous 12 months, the numbers of sessions and measurable results of activities have risen dramatically also there has been a slowly rising increase in program usage with new listings for the hospital systems. The Evaluation Team comments that all relevant process and technical issues have been successfully addressed by Dr. ... and his colleagues. This is a remarkable achievement given the resistance to technical change we encounter generally as attempts are made to change the health care system,

The Evaluation Team notes the very favorable outcome data showing aggregate TELESYNERGY® system use (223 total number of sessions, 15291 system "on time" minutes, 4650 session attendees and 21 average attendees per session). Also notable is the number of individuals who are accessing the project website. Although the average of 5-6 visits per day is considered low by Dr... and his colleagues, the Evaluation Team judges the number to be appropriate for this stage in development of the website. With additional streamlining and simplification the use of the website will most likely increase (ROCOG Year 05 Progress Report, 2008).

It should be obvious that all stakeholders would find this final assessment of value for several reasons: 1) it shows that the funds were well spent and that the project goals were achieved; 2) the full report provides a basis for expansion or continuation of the project; and 3) another set of hospitals could use the complete set of evaluation reports to replicate the project or to adopt the TELESYNERGY® system to meet their unique needs.

The Future Integration of Project Management and Evaluation Research

This case study reveals the manner in which the evaluation process produced useful information for the stakeholder group. There are several reasons for project managers to incorporate managerial evaluation concepts and methods as they design and implement time-limited projects. Increased competitive pressures and funding limitations are being experienced by both public and private organizations. These pressures and constraints have created a need for even more careful planning, monitoring, and assessment throughout each project to assure that goals are reached, within or under budget, within the projects' timeframe.

Logic models, as used in evaluation science, are important planning tools in that they require a careful and detailed specification, in advance of the initiation of a project, of the resources and activities required to produce the outputs, and products needed to obtain the project's desired outcomes.

As noted by McLaughlin and Jordan (1999, pp. 65-72):

> Program managers across private and public sectors are being asked to describe and evaluate their programs in new ways. People want managers to present a logical argument for how and why the program is addressing a particular customer need and how measurement and evaluation will assess and improve program effectiveness...
>
> The logic model describes the logical linkages among program resources, activities, outputs... and short, intermediate and longer term outcomes. Once this model of expected performance is produced, critical measurement areas can be identified.

The assessment of structure, process, and outcomes while a project is being implemented can provide managers with information about: 1) the extent to which a project team is being "faithful" to the project plan (often referred to as program fidelity); 2) barriers that emerge to prevent adherence to a plan and time schedule; and 3) the extent to which short- and longer-term outcomes are achieved, and, if not, where breakdowns or shortfalls are occurring.

In the future, armed with such information, project managers will be better able to: 1) make informed mid-course adjustments in project activities if necessary; 2) have a rational and defensible approach to revise budgets when a shift in resources is required; and 3) determine whether or not the desired short-term outcomes are being achieved, because if they are not, the longer-term (usually the most important) outcomes will not be achieved. In this situation, a major restructuring of resources and activities may be necessary.

Within a traditional project management framework, the concepts and processes related to quality planning, quality assurance quality control, and project network diagrams are comparable in a certain sense to the notion of a logic model with clearly defined resources, activities, outputs, and outcomes. While the project management and program evaluation frameworks seem to converge around these ideas, we believe certain important differences exist.

First, by placing evaluation research within a scientific framework, very high standards of data collection, analysis and reporting are implied. Second, while some form of evaluation should be conducted by project management, scientific evaluation standards call for separation of evaluation activities in order to assure objectivity. Separation of evaluation activities can be achieved by either establishing an "evaluation unit" within the project, or by having a unit outside the project, to conduct the evaluation. The third difference is that scientific evaluation sets certain standards for data collection, analysis, and timely reporting to all project stakeholders on a fixed time schedule. Fourth, scientific evaluation must follow the standards defined by the profession of evaluation. These standards relate to the feasibility, accuracy, propriety, and utility of evaluation.

Feasibility requires that the evaluation be realistic, prudent, diplomatic, and frugal. Accuracy requires that the evaluation reveal and convey technically accurate information. Propriety and utility include the expectation that the evaluation serves the information needs of intended users. An understanding of and adherence to these standards insures that evaluations will be of the highest quality and will actually be used to improve project management (ANSI, 1994).

One additional way in which evaluation will be merged with project management relates to the need for project managers to examine the long-term impact of a project upon the larger entity (organization or community) within which it operated. Professional evaluators do this routinely by, first by conceptualizing a future state in terms of "long term objectives," and second, examining the context of the project (as in the "context" section of the logic model). Long-term objectives as identified in logic models used by evaluators predict a state of affairs 3-5 years beyond the completion of a project. Such a long-term examination can provide information about the impact of the project (both positive and negative) upon such factors as value added, environmental quality, health status, transportation issues, quality of life, and the sustainability of the project.

With regard to the greater context section of the logic model, companies of the future will be required to be responsible stewards in their communities. Project managers executing their clients' requests will therefore be required to address these stewardship expectations. For example, in building a shoe factory, project managers may provide a better outcome for their clients if they propose additional ventilation systems or examine alternative tanning technologies that reduce the smell associated with leather production. Using scientific evaluation techniques takes into account the larger impact on a community by systematizing the community and stakeholder needs and expectations.

The current climate of program efficiency and data-based reporting are established components of any governmental, academic, or private-sector project. Although difficult economic times considerably restrain activities considered ancillary to any project, we believe that, in the future, managerial evaluation components involving systematic, fact-based reporting on projects will be considered critical activities necessary for effectiveness and efficiency. Further, we expect that formal project management techniques will more and more be used by the governmental and volunteer sectors of society. These sectors are already heavily committed to scientific evaluation. Therefore a merger of project management and evaluation frameworks will naturally occur. In the private sector, we expect that evaluation science will be introduced by the cohort of individuals who are now receiving training in business and engineering schools but who are simultaneously earning degrees in schools of public administration, public health, social work, or education, where students are fully exposed to frameworks for scientific evaluation. This merger can only bring about a greater possibility to "...meet or exceed stakeholder needs and expectations" (Preparing for the Project Management Professional (PMP) Certification Exam, 2001; p. 2).

References

American National Standards Institute (1994). *Program evaluation standards, 2nd edition*. Thousand Oaks, California: Sage.

Chelimsky, E., & Shadish, E.R. (eds.) (1997). *Evaluation for the 21st century*. Thousand Oaks, California: Sage.

Cook, T.D., & Campbell, D.T. (1979). *Quasi-Experimentation: Design and analysis issues for field settings.* Chicago: Rand McNally.

Herron, D. *ROCOG Year 05 Progress Report* (2008). UPMC Mckeesport/ROCOG Radiation Oncology Minorities Outreach Program (5U56CAI05486-05). Prepared for National Cancer Institute, NIH, Department of Health and Human Services.

Koskinen, J.A. (1997). Office of Management and Budget testimony before the house committee on government reform and oversight hearing. February 12, 1997.

McLaughlin, J., & Jordan, G. (1999). Logic models: A tool for telling your program's performance story. *Evaluation and Program Planning, 22,* 65-72.

McLaughlin, J., & Jordan, G. (2004). Using logic models. In Wholey, J., Hatry, H., & Newcomer, K. (eds.), *Handbook of practical program evaluation* (Second edition), San Francisco: Jossey-Bass.

National Cancer Institute, National Institutes of Health, Department of Health and Human Services (2002). CDRP (Cooperative Planning Grant for Cancer Disparities Research Partnerships), RFA-CA-03-018.

Newell, M. W. (2001). *Preparing for the project management professional (PMP) certification exam.* AMACOM, division of the American Management Association: New York.

Øvretviet, J. (1998). *Evaluation health interventions.* Maidenhead: Open University Press.

Patton, M.Q. (2002). *Qualitative research and evaluation methods* (3rd edition). Thousand Oaks, California: Sage.

Ricci, E., Schenken, L., & Herron, D. (2006). *A comprehensive outcomes-based planning and evaluation program for assessing TELESYNERGY® and other videoconferencing approaches in radiation oncology.* Philadelphia, PA: ASTRO.

Scriven, M. (1991). *Evaluation thesaurus.* London: Sage.

Shandish, W., Cook, T., & Levitan L. (1991). *Foundations of program evaluation: theories of practice.* London: Sage.

Suchman, E. (1967). *Evaluation research.* New York: Russell Sage.

Wholey, J., Hatry, H., & Newcomer, K. (eds). (2004). *Handbook of practical program evaluation* (Second Edition). San Francisco: Jossey-Bass.

Wholey, J. (1983). *Evaluation and effective public management.* New York: Little, Brown.

CHAPTER 12

Project Portfolio Management Circa 2025

James S. Pennypacker

Effective project portfolio management has become a significant factor in the long-term strategic success of project-oriented organizations. Its growth and acceptance as a management practice can be attributed to its link to business policy and organizational strategy. Project portfolio management (PPM) is concerned with more than the advanced mathematical modeling of business, more than the mechanics of formal project planning systems. At its best, it is concerned with the role of top management and key decision-makers in creating purposeful project investments and in formulating and implementing goals and objectives.

Business Organizations in 2025

As we enter the next few decades, the decentralization of management will be evident in most organizations as the speed of business continues to accelerate. By 2025, FuturOrg – the name we'll use for the successful enterprise in the coming decades — will no longer exhibit the command/control ways of the past. FuturOrg will, however, be organized with a cascading portfolio structure that reaches out to multiple delivery channels while controlling projects and programs, creating value both for customers and the organization. FuturOrg will, in reality, be a conglomeration of small businesses, each with their own portfolios, operating budgets, profit making strategies, suppliers, delivery channels....

FuturOrg employees will work in small business units – many of them either virtual or co-located at the business-unit level. As competition and customer demand increases, the time it takes people to make decisions and implement them must shorten. The bottom half of the organization – the FuturOrg business units -- must make tactical decisions and implement them. This requires an agile corporate structure that provides them with accurate and timely information on projects, programs, resources, etc., in order to make effective decisions. It also requires a robust, yet agile, clearly articulated corporate strategy to insure their decisions are in alignment. This means that senior management and executives have to concentrate on market and business analysis to quickly respond to market conditions and make changes in product and business strategies.

Certain individuals will either have their feet in both halves of the organization – strategic and tactical—or they will move constantly from one half to the other. But because business is now so closely tied to quickly changing customer needs, there are no longer long-term goals and objectives, visions, and missions. There are just projects, results, and benefits. Decisions will be made through consensus building. Strategies will be lean – guiding and aligning the organization, yet capable of quickly adapting to new conditions. And because of this, information must be transparent and distributed widely for effective decision making. The culture of FuturOrg will be one of problem-solving, innovation, creative work environments, agility, trust, and transparency.

Project Portfolio Management Defined

A project is a "temporary endeavor undertaken to create a unique product, service or result" (*PMBOK® Guide,* 2008) within defined parameters. The parameters are typically scope, time, and cost. Examples of projects include designing a new automobile, implementing a new customer service process, changing an organization's structure from functional to matrix, modifying an enterprise information system, and starting a new business. Projects must compete for an organization's scarce resources because there are usually more projects to choose from than there are resources to support them all. But projects are essential to an organization—they are the prime investment in the organization's future.

Project management is the "application of knowledge, skills, tools, and techniques to project activities to meet the project requirements" (*PMBOK® Guide,* 2008). The science of project management is knowing how to use the various project management tools, such as the work breakdown structure, network diagrams, Gantt charts, resource histograms, etc. The art of project management is knowing when to use the various tools and under what circumstances.

A portfolio is a range of investments. Synonyms include "collection," "aggregation," "variety," "accumulation," "multitude," "assortment," and "ensemble." Therefore, a project portfolio is a collection of projects that, in the aggregate, make up an organization's investment strategy.

Project portfolio management is, therefore, the "centralized management of one or more portfolios, which includes identifying, prioritizing, authorizing, managing, and controlling projects, programs, and other related work to achieve specific strategic business objectives" (*The Standard for Portfolio Management,* 2008). It seeks to answer the questions, What should we take on? and What should we drop? It requires achieving a delicate balancing of strategic and tactical requirements.

Project portfolio management often requires determining what is possible (Do we have the capability, the resources?) and what is needed (Does it make good business sense?). Balancing capability and need generally results in defining the best that can be achieved with the limited resources available, rather than attempting to find the perfect solution (which in a perfect world, would include infinite resources). When used effectively, PPM ensures that projects are aligned with corporate strategies and priorities and optimizes resource allocation. It is the practice that bridges the gap between the executive decision process and project execution.

Although project portfolio management is practiced at multiple levels of an organization –business units like corporate divisions or functional units like IT–and these practices are similar, we will focus on enterprise project portfolio management, which concerns the most critical, strategic projects, programs, and portfolios, as well as those that must be integrated across multiple organizational levels.

PPM at FuturOrg

PPM at FuturOrg features fundamental practices that include linking strategy to project prioritization and selection, and balancing the organization's portfolio to achieve the best results. Also included is a process for assessing new project opportunities, communication, and review processes for the portfolio; portfolio tracking and reporting; and continual portfolio realignment. FuturOrg applies these fundamental processes as a standardized approach to creating and managing their diversified portfolio of projects. The stakeholders for the PPM process include financial management, senior business executives, and ultimately the stockholders of the organization, as well as employees, vendors and customers. At FuturOrg, PPM offers a holistic view of all the work taking place and work planned for.

We can best understand how PPM works at FuturOrg by looking at two factors: PPM phases and PPM components.

PPM Phases

Project portfolio management at FuturOrg comprises five phases: portfolio inventory, analysis, planning, tracking, and review and replanning. These phases are dynamic, iterative, and ongoing, and must be managed artfully, depending on project life cycles as well as organizational and environmental issues, such as budget cycles and a rapidly changing marketplace.

Initial project requests enter the portfolio inventory, where project data is captured and organized for portfolio analysis. The inventory includes active projects, proposed

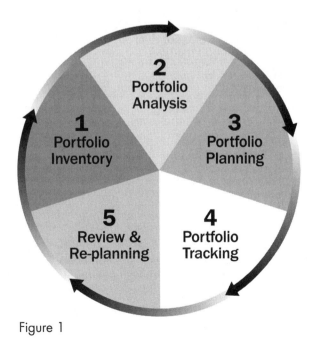

Figure 1

projects, and projects that are on hold or delayed. The inventory will have information about all projects in the portfolio, including schedule and cost estimates, budgets, dependencies, strategic initiatives, expected benefits, risk, relative priority, value, and ranking. The inventory will also have information about available resources, roles, costs, skills, and other needed organizational information.

The portfolio is analyzed periodically, reviewing projects for their fit, utility, and balance: Do the projects fit the organization's strategy? Do they have value? How do the projects relate to each other and how can the project mix be optimized? Portfolio analysis is crucial to prioritizing the portfolio and maximizing the value to the organization, given its resource constraints. FuturOrg prioritizes projects based on a variety of criteria, including financial, technical, strategic alignment, marketability, and risk. Interactions among the projects in the portfolio are considered, including interdependencies, competition for resources, and timing. A variety of decision-making techniques and tools are used to help formulate the problem and facilitate the analysis of alternative solutions. Through multiple iterations, trade-offs are considered and final adjustments made to arrive at the optimal project portfolio.

Once projects are selected and initiated, they enter the project planning phase. Here resources are allocated and projects are scheduled. This project management process is integrated with the portfolio planning process, where resource allocation and schedule decisions are made taking into account the whole portfolio of projects.

In tracking the portfolio of projects, metrics are captured to assess the performance of each project. And these projects must pass through decision-gate evaluations to determine whether or not to continue with the project, to put it on hold, or to kill it altogether.

Reviews of the project portfolio involve a reverification of the projects' critical success factors—including resource availability and the continued validity of the business case—with the business sponsors. In addition, shifting business, technology, and market conditions can rearrange priorities. The decisions made in response to these shifting conditions often result in a realignment of the project portfolio, which may or may not affect other projects in the portfolio. Replanning may be required, including changes in resource allocation and scheduling.

This iterative nature of portfolio optimization requires that project reviews, program reviews, and portfolio reviews are held on a regular basis. These reviews provide a forum for studying the alternatives and help to build organizational buy-in for the portfolio. Integrating project management and project portfolio management is necessary for developing an optimal project portfolio.

In summary, at FuturOrg, we:

- Identify all project work
  - Document dependencies for each
  - Document high level schedule for each
  - Determine resources required for each (rough order of magnitude estimate)
  - Determine total investment (total cost, rough order of magnitude estimate)
- Rate each on business value and on risk and prioritize accordingly (considering dependencies)
- Rank according to priority, then review and adjust as needed
- Determine which can be done based on available resources
- Notify requesters of status (especially of those projects that fall "under the line")

- As new requests are received prioritize them similarly then evaluate and communicate any impact
- Use the data for:
  - Authorizing the "best" projects
  - Resource planning
  - Annual budget planning

PPM Components

At FuturOrg, six components are essential in developing an effective organizational portfolio management environment: portfolio governance; project opportunity assessment; project prioritization and selection; portfolio communications management; portfolio and performance management; and portfolio resource management.

Portfolio Governance

Portfolio governance addresses the organizational and decision-making processes used to manage and review the portfolio of projects. It includes the assignment of decision rights and accountability that encourages desirable behavior. It requires that those steering the organization be alert to all aspects of the internal and external environment and have risk plans in place in event of an emergency. It includes establishing and maintaining the structure and procedures, and roles and responsibilities, for conducting the ongoing assessment and improvement of the portfolio. In addition, such a framework helps workers and teams understand the actions they need to take to deploy and execute the organization's strategy. And it ties everyone in the organization together around consciously chosen purposes. The portfolio governance component ensures that the projects undertaken by FuturOrg are aligned with its vision, strategy, and objectives. This component has two fundamental areas of focus: governance structure and process.

Governance Structure: The Strategic Project Office

FuturOrg has established a Strategic Project Office to oversee its project management practices across their organizations. The SPO, a relatively small, strategic group, connects the executive vision with the work of the organization. Its strategic functions include assessing and promoting project management maturity, creating a project culture, integrating processes and systems enterprise-wide, ensuring enterprise-wide project quality, managing resources across projects and portfolios, and project portfolio management.

The SPO owns the project portfolio management process at FuturOrg. It ensures that the organization's projects are linked to strategic plans. It facilitates the activities of the Portfolio Review Board in the prioritization and selection of projects, and typically is intimately involved in resource allocation decisions. The SPO also coordinates tracking of the current portfolio, analyzing portfolio performance, and is instrumental in administering the decision process for all projects. The SPO ensures that the organization's project portfolio continues to meet the needs of the business, even as these needs continue to change over time. It serves as the critical link between business strategy and execution of tactical plans.

Governance Structure: The Portfolio Review Board

FuturOrg's Portfolio Review Board has the formal authority for prioritizing and approving projects that cut across multiple functional departments. It is a team of executives from across the organization who insure that the portfolio of projects are optimized to meet FuturOrg's goals. The board's policies and procedures are well-documented: each project investment or proposal is evaluated by the board based upon the current decision criteria, primarily alignment with business strategy, market need, risk, and technical capability to deliver. The board also reviews the complete portfolio monthly to ensure that any changes in organizational objectives, market conditions, or project performance effect the decision to continue with any particular projects

Governance Process

FuturOrg's governance process is described at a high level by the organization's governance document: it first defines how strategy is made, and then how that results in the evaluation of ideas, their justification, approval and prioritization, the commissioning of projects and programs, the roles of the departments in those programs, and of the personnel on those projects.

The following process steps show how decisions are made in the management of the organization's portfolio:

- Assess Project Opportunities
  - If Reject, discard or replan
  - If Accept, incorporate into budgeting process, develop project management plan, and add to portfolio
- Review Portfolio (analyze portfolio, prioritize portfolio, select projects)
  - If Kill, discard or replan
  - If Hold, hold until next portfolio review cycle
  - If Continue (existing projects only), continue with project execution until next portfolio review cycle
  - If Authorize (new projects only), go to project execution
  - If Project Complete, close out project and realize benefits
- Execute Projects (or continue executing)
- Review Portfolio ...

Project Opportunity Assessment

Project opportunity assessment at FuturOrg focuses on the processes for identifying business needs that may be satisfied through the development of a solution(s) achieved by a project or projects. It includes processes and procedures for understanding and defining high-level business needs, crafting potential solution concepts, and harnessing the organizational resources to articulate these concepts as suggested projects.

Processes such as opportunity identification, business case development, project approval, post-implementation project review, and lessons learned are refined and consistently applied across the enterprise. Project portfolio management processes are continually assessed and improved, with a particular emphasis on supporting management decision-making during opportunity assessment activities. The Portfolio Review Board is active in the analysis of cost-benefit, schedule, and risk data. Post-implementation reviews validate actual results for comparison to initial data, and the information is used for process improvement efforts.

Opportunity Assessment typically includes a screening step to eliminate project ideas that do not provide real value to the organization. Business cases for proposed projects are completed and compared; the business case is then used in the Project Prioritization and Selection process.

At FuturOrg, an important link between Opportunity Assessment and Project Prioritization and Selection is to insure that all current projects or programs are identified, budgets are established (estimated dollars and human resources), and start and end dates for these initiatives are defined.

First, the organization collects all initiative or project ideas. This constitutes a regularly refreshed pipeline of ideas for business innovation and improvement, so they can be truly prioritized from a strategic perspective. Which projects can be considered strategic? Generally, they are the projects that support innovation, organizational improvement, or mandated corporate or regulatory priorities. Project plans associated with those projects are collected, including resources allocated, budgets, earned value information, and sponsor information. Justifications for each project are determined.

Future projects or programs are also forecasted and added to FuturOrg's potential portfolio of work. Implementing this forecasting process effectively requires the participation of the business sponsors, managers providing the staffing for the projects, subject matter experts associated with each project or program, and often a liaison group that ensures that the portfolio meets the business needs of the organization.

Some of the standard practices at FuturOrg for assessing opportunities include:

- A project charter is used to identify and initiate all projects.
- Roles and responsibilities for identifying project opportunities and initiating projects are clearly defined.
- Formal communication is provided back to each requester identifying the current status of a project opportunity or initiated project.
- An organization-wide, documented process is used to define the business value of a project. The process includes a standard business case that is integrated with project management processes, financial and accounting practices, and other business processes.
- There is a process for examining the fundamental cost, benefit, schedule, and risk characteristics of each project before they are funded and combined with other projects into a portfolio.
- The Portfolio Review Board ensures that the cost-benefit-schedule-risk data and other required data are validated for each project within its span of control.
- Information from post-implementation reviews is used to learn from past projects and assist in the assessment of current opportunities.

Project Prioritization and Selection

FuturOrg's project prioritization and selection processes are used to review potential projects, prioritize these candidates based on sound decision-making criteria, and select the ones that provide the optimum value to the organization within its given resource constraints. It links prioritization and the selection of projects to FuturOrg's strategies, and establishes a framework for systematically evaluating the business value of all projects, and the project portfolio in total.

The framework that FuturOrg uses to evaluate projects has three fundamental areas of focus: fit, utility, and balance.

To assess Fit, the first area of focus, FuturOrg reviews those opportunities that have been identified to determine if they are truly in line with the corporate strategic direction. This first step includes the identification and initial screening of projects before more in-depth analysis is conducted. What is the project? Does the project fit within the focus of the organization and the business strategy and goals?

To assess Utility, the second area of focus, FuturOrg further defines the project (if needed) and analyzes the details surrounding its utility. The utility of a project captures its usefulness, its value, and is typically defined by costs, benefits, and associated risks. Why should this project be pursued? What is the usefulness and value of the project? Since the projects in the portfolio vie for resources and funding, somehow a decision has to be made on which ones to select. To help in the decision-making process, common decision criteria have been created, and each project is measured against the criteria. Since most decisions are based upon multiple factors, each criterion is weighted to establish its relative importance. This helps identify what is most significant to FuturOrg, and allows the company to calculate a score for each project using its value for each criterion and applying the relative weights.

To assess Balance, the third area of focus, FuturOrg looks at the mix of projects in the portfolio in the selection process. Which projects should be selected? How does the project relate to the entire portfolio, and how can the project mix be optimized? FuturOrg's selection process optimizes the portfolio, not just the individual projects. The selection process is not only based on ranking individual project financial returns, but it also takes into account the inter-relationships between projects.

Some of the standard practices at FuturOrg for prioritizing and selecting projects include:

- Roles and responsibilities are clearly defined for prioritizing the portfolio of projects.
- A flexible prioritization scheme exists for ranking the portfolio of work based on agreed upon criteria. The prioritization scheme is supportive in aligning project strategy with business strategy and business unit/functional goals.
- A process exists for periodically updating the prioritization scores and business value of the portfolio of work.
- The Portfolio Review Board assigns project proposals to a portfolio category.
- The Portfolio Review Board approves the core project portfolio selection criteria, including cost-benefit-schedule-risk criteria, based on the organization's mission, goals, strategies, and priorities.
- The project portfolio selection criteria are distributed throughout the organization.
- The project portfolio selection criteria are reviewed using cumulative experience and event-driven data and modified, as appropriate.
- There is a process for comparing worthwhile projects and then combining selected projects into a funded enterprise-wide portfolio.
- The Portfolio Review Board examines the mix of proposals and projects across the common portfolio categories and makes selections for funding.

Portfolio Communications Management

FuturOrg has standard portfolio communications management processes for collecting and sharing information on each project in the portfolio, summarizing and reporting this information in a manner that enables FuturOrg to make strategic portfolio decisions. When properly executed, portfolio communications management helps FuturOrg make rational and unbiased decisions, with full knowledge of each projects' value to the portfolio, and balance this projected value with resource constraints.

Communication processes, techniques, and tools are used in conjunction with senior management's insight, knowledge, and decision-making ability to optimize the project portfolio. Senior management uses the information collected to select the appropriate projects and to communicate portfolio performance to relevant stakeholders. Because review and communication is so important to the process, FuturOrg carefully plans project portfolio reviews. These reviews provide a forum for studying the alternatives and help to build organizational buy-in for the selection of projects.

Of course, the business environment is constantly changing, and things may not unfold as originally planned: a competitor introduces a new product, the chief scientist makes a key breakthrough elsewhere, legislation is enacted causing industry-wide upheaval, or technology advances and matures. The original selection may no longer the best. So, adjustments must be made building a better path for the future. This is the art of PPM—doing the right thing, selecting the right mix of projects, and adjusting as time evolves and circumstances unfold.

Some of the standard practices at FuturOrg for portfolio communication include:

- The project list covers the entire organization and portfolio information is available to all business units for their use as they participate in FuturOrg's project management and portfolio management processes.
- Detailed information is tracked for each project. Information includes descriptive and performance information, resource estimates (high-level), business value, status (e.g. potential, active, hold, cancelled, completed, next milestone, etc.), project categorization, and cost and schedule information.
- Each project is categorized to ensure that investments are balanced to meet the enterprise's goals and objectives (e.g., by program, functional area, strategic vs. tactical, etc.).
- Project portfolio information is audited to validate the data and assumptions.
- Project investment information is available on demand to decision-makers and other affected parties.
- Historical asset inventory records are maintained for future selections and assessments.
- Portfolio information is communicated across and down the organization through meetings and other communication processes.
- A process exists for aggregating portfolio-level information for review and evaluation of impact to investment balance.
- Risk information is also be tracked for each project/work opportunity.

Portfolio Performance Management

Portfolio performance management allows FuturOrg to evaluate the performance of the portfolio of projects and their relative value to the organization. It allows management to evaluate the portfolio of projects, analyze different portfolio scenarios, and replan for changes in strategy or financial budgets. This includes evaluating the business value actually realized by each project, program, or initiative; and using that information for repositioning the organization's project portfolio.

Processes and standards guiding portfolio performance management are institutionalized, portfolio reviews are conducted regularly, and portfolio analysis is conducted to ensure the appropriate balance of project investments. The enterprise portfolio review board provides project oversight through regular portfolio progress reviews. The enterprise portfolio review board prioritizes projects using defined criteria. There is an emphasis on maintaining the performance of a balanced portfolio–monitoring the actual progress and delivery projects against their investment and planned benefit.

Some of the standard practices at FuturOrg for managing the portfolio's performance include:

- An organization-wide Portfolio Review Board monitors the performance of the projects in the portfolio by comparing actual cost-benefit, schedule, and risk data to expectations.
- Organizational standards and institutionalized processes exist for analyzing and reporting on the enterprise portfolio (roll-up includes business units, functional units, project categories, etc.).
- Organizational standards involve the use of consistent data fields, common definitions, and standard business rules.
- There is a process that builds upon the project oversight process by adding the elements of project benefit and risk management to the control process activities.
- There is a process for evaluating portfolio performance and using this information to improve both current project portfolio management processes and future portfolio performance.
- There is a process for analyzing and managing the succession of identified project investments and assets to their higher-value successors.
- Reports are developed on trends at all levels of the organization's portfolio. Aggregate performance data trends are analyzed.
- The interdependency of each investment with other investments in the project portfolio is analyzed.
- The Portfolio Review Board directs special reviews of projects that have not met predetermined performance standards and ensures that corrective actions are developed and tracked.

Portfolio Resource Management

Portfolio resource management includes the processes that allow FuturOrg to effectively assign the appropriate resources to successfully execute the projects in the portfolio. It helps to ensure that FuturOrg's resources are allocated properly to meet the business needs. It also provides management with information for forecasting future resource requirements.

Resources include capital, expenses, staff, time, or anything that is consumed in the planning and execution of a project. Once FuturOrg prioritizes its projects, it must decide how to assign these limited resources to the projects. FuturOrg applies two approaches in allocating resources, depending on the availability of information. In the first approach, they arrange projects in descending order of priority and fund projects starting with the highest priority moving down the prioritized list until all resources are consumed. Essentially, this technique can be visualized as drawing a cut-line under the final project where resources are fully expended.

Another method used for allocating resources strives to optimize benefits to FuturOrg, but it requires a significant amount of data for forecasting results accurately. It involves allocating resources to the group of projects that yield the highest total benefit within the current resource constraints. FuturOrg uses complex cost-benefit analysis and linear programming to assess these portfolios.

Another consideration in resource allocation is the importance of allocating resources across a diversified portfolio. Portfolio theory advocates investment in a diversified portfolio to reduce risks and maximize expected return. Additionally, FuturOrg invests in a variety of different types of projects, which are often very difficult to compare with each other with respect to business benefits. For example, comparing investments on infrastructure or projects that are targeted at "keeping the business running" are difficult to compare with strategic projects that may provide new markets to FuturOrg. Therefore, an important consideration in the resource allocation process is to define and use different investment categories to help align the total portfolio of investment with the needs of the enterprise.

Some of the standard practices at FuturOrg for managing the portfolio's resources include:

- The enterprise Portfolio Review Board oversees the portfolio to ensure resource continuity across projects.
- A resource-pool management process exists that captures skills sets, availability, and knowledge management across the organization.
- Enterprise and business unit resource analysis and reporting occurs on a scheduled basis to ensure that the organization maximizes its potential productivity and effectiveness in realizing the objectives of the projects and financial drivers for the portfolio.
- Project priorities are established by the enterprise Portfolio Review Board and business unit leaders are expected to optimally assign resources based upon resource skills and established project priorities.
- Resources other than people are also contained in the overall resource pool. Equipment, hardware, software licenses, and specialty teams (such as testing) are included in this category to ensure that all constraints are tracked.
- Portfolio resource management functions are executed with an enterprise perspective.
- Resource assignment is based upon resource skills and project priorities. Resource pools are managed and contain all types of resources.

The Importance of PPM to FuturOrg

Applying effective project portfolio management practices is standard practice in 2025. All organizations, large and small, must select and manage their investments and execute their projects wisely to reap the maximum benefits from their investment decisions. In particular, project portfolio management enables FuturOrg to:

- Provide an agile structure for selecting the right projects and eliminating wrong ones
- Allocate resources to the right projects, thus reducing wasteful spending
- Align portfolio decisions to strategic business goals to meet frequently changing market conditions

- Use resources more efficiently
- Provide improved accountability and the ability to demonstrate adherence to corporate governance requirements
- Base decisions on logic, reasoning, and objectivity by having accurate and timely information on the organization's portfolio
- Create ownership among all personnel by involvement at the right levels in the workplace
- Establish avenues for individuals to identify opportunities and obtain support
- Help project teams understand the value of their contributions.

FuturOrg PPM Self-Assessment Tool

The following quiz is used by FuturOrg's Strategic Project Office to continuously improve its PPM practices. Answers to the quiz quickly reveal how well the company is managing the project portfolio.

- Does the portfolio reflect and support the business's strategy?
- Is each project consistent with business strategy?
- Does the breakdown of project spending reflect the strategic priorities?
- Is the economic value of the total portfolio higher than what we've spent on it?
- Once projects start, what is the chance they'll ever be killed?
- Are projects being done in a time-efficient manner?
- Are project success rates and profit performance results consistent with expectations?
- Is the project portfolio heavily weighted to low-value, trivial, small projects?
- How are opinions of senior people and key decision-makers in the business captured in order to make project decisions?
- Have we considered what the right balance of projects for the new product portfolio is?
- Are there redundant projects being performed?
- Have all the projects in play been justified on solid business criteria?
- And of those that were approved, are they still justified?
- Do the managers and team members know where the projects they are working on fit into the priority ranking that best supports the business?
- Are there enough resources to get the work done; and if there are not, what trade-offs need to be made?
- Which projects make the most money?
- Which have the lowest risk?
- Which have subjective value, in terms of community image or internal morale?
- Which are not optional—projects dictated by regulatory requirements, for example?

References

Project Management Institute (2008). *A Guide to the Project Management Body of Knowledge (PMBOK® Guide)*—Fourth Edition. Newtown Square, PA: Project Management Institute.

Project Management Institute (2008). *The Standard for Portfolio Management*—Second Edition. Newtown Square, PA: Project Management Institute.

Section 3

Project Management
Organizational Application

CHAPTER 13

Future Trends in Project Management: A Macro-Environmental Analysis

Kam Jugdev
Ralf Müller
Maureen Hutchison

Abstract

Strategy is about matching an organization's capabilities to the changing market environment to achieve better competitive positions. Increasingly, companies are turning to project management to help them be more effective and efficient. In the year 2025, what will the project management landscape look like? This chapter discusses recent trends in project management and the relationship between project management and strategy. The chapter then reviews macro-environmental factors (i.e., demographic, economic, political-legal, ecological, socio-cultural, and technological) and presents an assessment of future trends in project management. The chapter concludes with some pragmatic trends and our hopes for the future of project management. Gazing forward, the future looks bright.

Introduction

What will the project management landscape look like in the year 2025? What are the interdependencies between project management and strategic management? This chapter discusses recent trends in project management and the relationship between project management and strategy. The chapter then reviews macro-environmental factors (i.e., demographic, economic, political-legal, ecological, socio-cultural, and technological) and presents an assessment of future trends in project management. For this assessment, we drew from the collective experiences and insights of colleagues worldwide to gather different viewpoints on project management in the year 2025. The chapter concludes with some pragmatic trends and our recommendations for the future of project management.

Recent Trends in Project Management

What does it take for a company to remain competitive? It takes entrepreneurship, innovation, nimbleness, and core competencies. A company's competitive advantage can vanish in the blink of an eye as rivals innovate and create new, better, or different services and products. It is a constant struggle for companies to develop, let alone maintain, a competitive advantage. Since business success depends on competitive advantage, there is a heightened interest in the role that project management plays in helping companies to sustain competitiveness.

To academically assess recent trends in the field, we used the ABI INFORM library database and the key subject search terms "project management," "trends," and "changes" to find papers on this topic. Our search unearthed four key academic papers that examined trends in project management at the macro level. Pinto (2002) examined trends in the context of research and development projects. He indicated that there is a move towards more project-based work and that other advances in the field pertain to risk management methodologies, scheduling techniques, control practices, use of project management offices, cross-functional team work, and Internet/web-based technologies to enhance virtual teamwork. In the same year, Kloppenborg and Opfer (2002) reviewed the research literature in project management from 1960 to 1999. In the 1990s, the main trends included publications on human resources, team building, leadership development, and motivation. Jugdev and Müller (2005) reviewed the changing understanding of project success over the last 40 years and predicted that, in the future, judgments on project success will include an even broader set of criteria than today and would span the entire product life cycle (not just the project life cycle). More recently, Crawford, Pollack, and England (2006) reviewed trends covered in the *Project Management Journal and International Journal of Project Management* from 1994 to 2003. Overall, they found that there was an increase in the prevalence of papers on the topics of project evaluation and improvement, risk and costs, relationship management, resource management, and time management.

Project management is an experiential discipline learned by showing others how to use and apply tools, techniques, and practices. Two themes that we draw from these papers on trends in project management are, first, that the emphasis on practices to control projects remains and will continue to be relevant; and, second, that there is an increase in the number and types of papers on the interpersonal dimensions of project management. This is supported by the growing interest in leadership studies since 2006, following an initial study funded by the Project Management Institute (Turner & Müller, 2006).

Specific to the topic of strategy and project management, Crawford et al. (2006, p. 183) noted that "alignment has been found by the other studies to be increasing in significance. This suggests that Strategic Alignment could form a progressively dominant aspect in the field."

Project Management and Strategy

Project management is valued in strategic terms when a clear connection is made between how efficiently *and* effectively a project is done and how the project's products and services provide business value. However, if project success is defined only in terms of time, cost, and scope—and the links to product or service value are missing—then project management is perceived as providing tactical (operational) value, and not strategic value. The Project Management Institute's *PMBOK® Guide* describes project management tactically as a way of conducting work (i.e., tools, techniques, and practices) in relation to an organization's policies (Project Management Institute, 1986, 1996, 2000). A more recent version claimed to have "strengthened the linkages to organizational strategy" (Project Management Institute, 2004, p. 316) and identified projects (not their management) as an important means to implement strategy, but no evidence is provided to support this statement. Project management methodologies have spoken to the strategic importance of projects, with the majority of methodologies suggesting that project goals and scope be derived from an organization's strategy or business opportunity (e.g., projects in controlled environments [PRINCE 2]) (Office-of-Government-Commerce, 2008).

The awareness that project management can be linked to strategy is evolving. For example, recent empirical research applied the Resource-Based View from strategy to project management to assess the discipline as a source of competitive advantage (Jugdev & Mathur, 2006; Jugdev, Mathur, & Fung, 2007; Mathur, Jugdev, & Fung, 2007). These studies indicate that intangible resources within the discipline, such as tacit knowledge sharing and know-how, are more apt to be sources of competitive advantage than tangible resources are.

The growing body of research in the program and portfolio management domain is also strengthening understanding of the link between strategic management and project management (Project Management Institute, 2006; Stawicki & Müller, 2007). Project management governance pertains to the processes and procedures used to ensure the coordinated interaction of organizational strategy, portfolio, program, and project management through appropriate policies, standards, and frameworks. According to the Association for Project Management (2008), governance involves effective and efficient management through sponsorship practices. Successful companies simultaneously balance both program and portfolio management as part of their governance structure (Blomquist & Müller, 2006). A recent study of European companies found that most of the companies used their strategy to define the goals and scope of their projects and programs (Morris & Jamieson, 2005). These companies also used portfolio management techniques to select and prioritize those projects, creating maximum benefits for the organization. Morris and Jamieson (2005) describe the relationship between project management and strategic management as consisting of five interacting elements: organizational strategy, portfolio management, program management, project management, and governance.

Figure 1 shows the relationship between a company's strategic management and project management practices as a delivery circle (solid-line arrows) and a control circle (dotted-line arrows) (Müller, 2009,). The strategy determines the strategic goals, which, in turn, define the goals of the portfolios, programs, and projects. The scope of individual projects and programs are determined by business cases (which stem from the company's strategy). This delivery circle is shown by solid arrows. Project management offices (or related structures) help with information flow to the various levels of the organization to control the alignment of strategy and capabilities (Hobbs & Aubry, 2007). For example, the project management office aggregates project performance information for the portfolio manager, who then reports this to upper management levels of the organization so that they, in turn, can refine the strategy. This control circle is shown by the dotted line arrows.

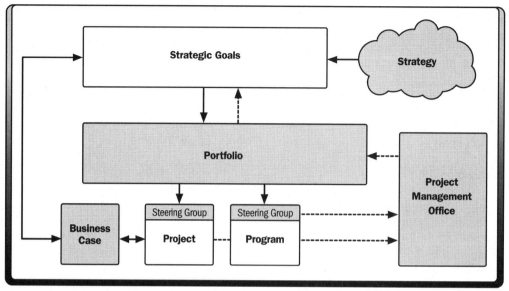

Figure 1   The relationships between strategy and project management

Project, program, and portfolio managers have an additional role in that they interact with upper management to contribute to the formulation and implementation of organizational strategies. However, while there are pockets of project management practices within industry sectors that may exemplify excellence in terms of the processes in Figure 1, not all companies have matured to this extent.

In summary, this section outlines some of the evolving relationships between project management and strategic management, as strengthened through portfolio and program management. In the next section, we discuss strategic management and macro-environmental factors as they pertain to project management.

Strategic Management and Macro-Environmental Factors

Developing organizational strategies is one of the biggest challenges that companies face in a competitive environment. Managers address numerous challenges such as the reduction of trade barriers across international markets, industry deregulation, increasing pressures from social and natural environments, and competition from rival firms. Furthermore, organizations are evolving into increasingly complex and technology-driven systems. To respond to such challenges, organizations require complex, specialized structures and detailed processes that are also flexible and nimble, so that they may simultaneously respond to the external environment and develop appropriate internal capabilities.

Companies also need to relate their strategy to their company's values, vision, and mission in order to align short-term targets with long-term goals. The strategic management process includes a clear elaboration of the firm's reason for existence: its mission. The company then defines the vision for its future: that is, what the company wants to be. Thereafter, the company conducts an internal and external analysis, and uses this information to design strategies that are implemented to help it achieve a competitive advantage. An overall approach to assessing both internal and external environments is the strengths, weaknesses, opportunities, and threats (SWOT) analysis.

The external environment approach is based on an analysis of other firms and industry factors; this approach explores a company's position relative to other firms. Several techniques help organizations analyze the external environment: for example, Porter's five forces framework (Porter, 1996) examines potential entrants, buyers, suppliers, substitutes, and industry competitors; competitor analysis (Grant, 2007) systematically gathers information about rival firms to try to predict what choices rivals will make and how rivals will react to environmental changes.

Several techniques that help organizations analyze the internal environment. These include value chain analyses, which assess activity costs through the various organizational departments/processes in a systematic manner; and a resources assessment, such as the Resource-Based View of the firm (Barney, 2007). In the Resource-Based View, specific resources that meet all four criteria—that is, resources that are valuable (help companies make a profit), rare (unique), inimitable (difficult to copy), and have strong organizational support (Barney, 2007)—are sources of sustained competitive advantage. Typically, these resources are knowledge-based intangible resources. Resources that are only valuable and rare (not inimitable), and have organizational support, are sources of temporary competitive advantage. Resources that are valuable and have organizational support are sources of competitive parity. The Resource-Based View offers a powerful explanation of firm performance; however, in order to assess strategic management and project management circa 2025, we need to look at strategy from a broader perspective.

A macro-environmental assessment involves understanding those factors external to the company that are generally viewed as being uncontrollable by the firm. Thus, managers should constantly monitor the local, regional, national, and international demographic (D), economic (E), political-legal (P), ecological (E), socio-cultural (S), and technological (T) environments. Such an analysis is sometimes referred to as a DEPEST analysis (Grant, 2007). The DEPEST framework represents the main macro-environmental factors and is not an exhaustive list. Often, textbooks will refer to fewer factors and label them PEST or other variations of the DEPEST acronym. A brief overview of each factor follows:

- *Demographic factors and trends* relate to the size, distribution, and growth rate of groups of people.
- *Economic factors and trends* relate to economies, including data on the labor force, such as employment rates, income, infrastructure, rate of inflation, and gross domestic product.
- *Political-legal factors and trends* relate to domestic and international government activities, policies, laws, regulations, litigation, court decisions, and political unrest.
- *Ecological factors and trends* relate to energy, product reusing and recycling, and protection of biological bases, along with food and water quality.
- *Socio-cultural factors and trends* relate to groups of people and their numbers, characteristics, lifestyles, consumer preferences, purchasing power, group behaviors, growth projections, attitudes and ideas, values and beliefs, religion, families, health, crime patterns, and education.
- *Technological factors and trends* relate to scientific and technological innovations that affect the development of new products and services.

These external factors do overlap somewhat, and trends specific to one factor can have implications for the other factors. By conducting such an analysis of the macro-environmental factors, organizations can more easily identify how external factors impact those internal to the organization, and how project management principles can reduce risks and add control measures to ensure organizational success and generate greater competitive advantage.

A Strategic Assessment of Future Trends in Project Management Using the DEPEST Factors

As part of data collection for this book chapter, we e-mailed 40 practitioner and academic colleagues, and invited them to share their insights about which macro-environmental factors would be relevant to project management in 2025, and how project management will change in the future. Our request was sent in December 2007, and replies were received from eight colleagues for a response rate of 20% (potentially impacted by the holiday period when our request was sent). The following summarizes responders' insights on the types of projects they think will prevail in the future. In this section, we used the term "project management" in a broad context to include program and portfolio management.

Demographics

Communicating in multiple languages on projects will compound project complexity in the future, and demand for multicultural and multilingual capabilities will grow. As developing countries improve their economies and standards of living, they will not necessarily want to use English as the language of commerce. Based on projected statistics, the greatest population growth in Canada will be from immigration, suggesting that workers will influence multilingual preferences as well (Statistics Canada, 2005). The ability of baby boomers (individuals born between 1946 and 1964) to adapt to the changing workforce will have an impact on their employability in future years. By 2025, baby boomers will be well into their retirement years and may be increasingly in demand for their wealth of project and functional experience. With baby boomers' growing need for healthcare and leisure activities, there will be a tremendous growth of construction projects for hospitals, retirement homes, and nursing homes, as well as projects that involve hospitality, travel, second home development, and entertainment.

Economics

By the year 2025, certain countries (e.g., Brazil, Russia, India, and China) will continue to develop their economies and standards of living. Globalization will mean more distributed and multicultural and perhaps multilingual project team work, all of which will contribute to project complexity. As retiring baby boomers turn their attention from their careers to their true life vocations, many may travel and do volunteer work in developing countries. We may see an increase in the number of social projects as current baby boomers and the Internet generation (or Net Generation, defined as those born after 1987) continues to focus on projects that are aligned with their strong social values, green ethics, and belief in certain moral causes.

Political-Legal Factors

Geopolitical unrest will continue, especially in the Middle East and developing countries, as will the wars on terrorism. These trends will fuel the demand for specialized project managers in such areas as high technology, military technology, information technology, and security-oriented projects. Defense projects may increase in size and scope, and it may become harder to address related procurement and logistics needs.

Ecological Factors

Energy, climate, and environmental issues will continue to evolve as pressing matters for countries. This increased ecological focus will draw on the strong environmental and social values of the wave of Net Ggeneration workers (Tapscott, 1998) who will be mid-career circa 2025. As we continue to reduce our carbon footprint, we will also see an increase in the number of new and alternate energy/sustainable development projects (e.g., wind and solar). Ecological factors also include protection of biological bases and food and water quality. For example, we will see more desalinization projects to increase fresh water supplies and projects related to agricultural development.

Socio-cultural Factors

Collaborative and social networking software, such as Facebook, MySpace, and others, along with forums, wikis, and other online areas where individuals come together and discuss issues, solve problems, or connect, will have an impact on the tools and work practices of the future, particularly given the value these social tools have for today's youth, who will lead the organizations of the future. Increasingly, project management will be taught at the undergraduate level, and even at grade school using progressive learning platforms.

Gen-Xers and Gen-Yers have different attitudes towards work-life balance and management in general, as compared to baby boomers. Gen-Xers are those individuals born after the baby boom generation, from the 1965-1982 time period (but not yet of the Net Generation). Gen-Yers are those individuals born after Gen-Xers, from the 1983-1997 time period (and are part of the Net Generation). Gen-Xers and Gen-Yers want to maintain and enjoy their personal time, and many expect that they will have multiple jobs and careers in their lifetime. This will influence how managers and project managers ensure effective communication and project productivity as various generations work together. Gen-Xers and Gen-Yers see themselves as intellectual capital in the form of knowledge workers. Independent of age, location, or origin, the Net Generation is accepting of diversity, given that values are placed on what one knows and has to say, rather than on where one's from, what one looks like, and where one lives (Tapscott, 1998).

The number of people who emigrate from developing to developed countries will continue to rise and many will fill existing job vacancies. Whereas some project managers will be training lower-skilled individuals for certain roles, other project managers will be hiring very well-qualified and educated individuals from other countries.

Technology

Project managers with at least some exposure to technologies such as metallurgy, materials, nanotechnology, microelectronics, biotechnology, pharmaceuticals, and software development will be in demand. An aging population will also require greater emphasis on pharmaceutical research and development, along with technology enhancements to extend the health and wellness of baby boomers approaching their golden years.

Projects will be even more distributed and involve virtual teamwork. Technology will be more tightly integrated with project activities through the use of tools such as video conferencing, collaborative software, and distributed document management. New knowledge workers will demand highly collaborative technology to meet their needs. Analytics involves examining business data for patterns to use the information gathered to improve business performance. As software tools and techniques mature, more companies will use analytics to assess project progress and issues, and to predict outcomes based on the data. We will also see a growth of business intelligence projects across industries.

In thinking about interactive computer-based games and the advances made with the technology involved, we note that both the young and older generations thrive on activities that are intriguing, challenging, involve all the senses, allow participants to take on new roles, and are fun (e.g., Nintendo Wii®). Research on the Net Generation shows that this group of individuals sees work as blending into play, and vice versa (Tapscott, 1998). Project management software tools and techniques will have to be more interactive, user-friendly, and engaging. For example, project management software of the future may well allow extensive scenario planning, role playing, and verbal data entry.

Concluding Thoughts: Pragmatic Trends and Our Hopes for Project Management

Based on the above and our collective experiences in project management as practitioners and academics, we suggest that the following future trends may emerge in project management. We also include some of our hopes for project management practices and education. Although we will see some incremental changes to the project management landscape in the year 2025, more dramatic changes to the field will take longer, in part because we currently lack a cohesive and global approach to project management. Charting aspects of such change, we have a number of project management associations that for the most part are country specific; educational institutions and training bodies also contribute to and shape changes in the field.

With the breadth of global changes outlined in our DEPEST analysis reflecting the types of projects that may be done in the year 2025, the external demands on project managers to meet the triple constraint (time, cost, and scope), along with managing expectations, will continue. To meet these demands, organizational leadership must recognize the resources that are required for successful project management and must offer necessary support, given project management's impact on organizational strategy and success. We anticipate that there will be exciting advances regarding use of business intelligence for project selection and scoping, and technology-based productivity tools for project management staff, especially for workers in distributed environments. The key will be to ensure that the project fits intended markets, project tools fit the project requirements, and thus all fit the organization's strategic goals.

As the use of project, program, and portfolio management continues to grow, and as project sponsors and senior managers learn more about project management processes, the skills required to be effective, and the interdependencies between project and business success, some executives will appreciate the value of project management beyond project deliverables and focus more on project management at the strategic level. Others may take longer to appreciate the contribution of project management because we still lack measures to assess the value of the discipline in the language of business (e.g., financial measures such as returns on investment). Over time, project management should become an essential skill for practitioners and executives. This will help to reduce the prevailing incidence of "accidental" project management practices if executives invest in the appropriate training, resources, and support for staff.

Although we do not anticipate that project management will become a profession in the true sense of the word by the year 2025, we are quite confident that it will be a requisite skill set in a variety of sectors. We expect there to be a growing trend towards positioning project management education for grade school students. The demand for training and education in project management will continue. We anticipate an increased focus on project management topics such as stakeholder management, leadership, governance, and program and portfolio management. In particular, human resources management will take center stage because of the highly collaborative workforce and reliance on knowledge workers within a matrix type of project- or team-based organization. Our hope is that project management associations and educators will move beyond the project management bodies of knowledge to address broader learner-based outcomes.

We expect the project management associations to continue to flourish and to provide their individual body-of-knowledge guides to the public. We may see the growth of more industry-specific certifications (e.g., construction project management). Our hope is that the project management associations will make efforts to establish a global set of standards and body of knowledge, rather than compete for members in different locales. Our hope is also that the global standards and body of knowledge will involve project manager competencies of the behavioral nature and that certification exams will meaningfully demonstrate both theoretical and applied knowledge versus rote memorization content. Following on the values of the Net Generation, who place a high value on knowledge rather than association or hierarchy, individuals may choose to develop their own communities of practice and abandon more formalized approaches to project management.

In the year 2025, the breadth of project types will continue to increase as exemplified in our DEPEST analysis. Project management will continue to be an experiential discipline, learned best by practicing, mentoring, and job shadowing. We noted earlier from our review of trend papers that the emphasis on practices to control projects remains and will continue to be relevant and that there will be an increased focus on the interpersonal dimensions of project management. The emphasis on practices to control projects pertains to knowledge that helps us learn what to do. There is a role for each of us to play in helping each other to learn how to do project management more effectively. Our hope is that project management associations, educational institutions, and companies applying project management will introduce communities of practice into their project management scope of practice to enhance collaborative practices such as knowledge sharing. Ensuring that project knowledge is created, acquired, captured, shared, and used is even more important when we consider that over 80% of workplace learning occurs informally versus formally (Livingstone, 2002). Given our analysis and research, the future of project management appears to be bright.

Acknowledgements: The authors would like to thank the colleagues who took time from their busy schedules to reflect on the topic of project management in the year 2025 and share their insights with us. Our chapter could not have been written without their contributions. The authors would also like to thank Athabasca University and Umeå University for their support and Dr. Lisa LaFramboise for her editorial services.

References

Association for Project Management. (2008, March 21). Association for Project Management. Retrieved May 15, 2008, from http://www.apm.org.uk/

Barney, J. B. (2007). *Gaining and sustaining competitive advantage* (3rd ed.). Upper Saddle River, New Jersey: Prentice-Hall.

Blomquist, T., & Müller, R. (2006). Practices, roles and responsibilities of middle managers in program and portfolio management. *Project Management Journal, 37*(1), 5266.

Crawford, L. H., Pollack, J., & England, D. (2006). Uncovering the trends in project management: Journal emphases over the last 10 years. *International Journal of Project Management, 24*(2), 175–184.

Grant, R. M. (2007). *Contemporary strategy analysis: Concepts, techniques, applications* (6th ed.). Malden, Massachusetts: Blackwell Publishers.

Hobbs, B., & Aubry, M. (2007). A multi-phase research program investigating project management offices (PMOs): The results of phase 1. *Project Management Journal, 38*(1), 74–86.

Jugdev, K., & Mathur, G. (2006). Project management elements as strategic assets: Preliminary findings. *Management Research News, 29*(10), 604-617.

Jugdev, K., Mathur, G., & Fung, T. (2007). Project management assets and their relationship with the project management capability of the firm. *International Journal of Project Management, 25*(6), 560-568.

Jugdev, K., & Müller, R. (2005). A retrospective look at our evolving understanding of project success. *Project Management Journal, 36*(4), 19-31. Reprinted in 2006 by *IEEE Engineering Management Review.*

Kloppenborg, T., & Opfer, W. (2002). The current state of project management research: Trends, interpretations, and predictions. *Project Management Journal, 33*(2), 5-18.

Livingstone, D. W. (2002). *Mapping the iceberg*: NALL Working Paper # 54 – 2002.

Mathur, G., Jugdev, K., & Fung, T. (2007). Intangible project management assets as determinants of competitive advantage. *Management Research News, 30*(7), 460–475.

Morris, P., & Jamieson, A. (2005). Moving from corporate strategy to project strategy. *Project Management Journal, 36*(4), 5–18.

Müller, R. (2009,). *Project Governance.* Aldershot, UK: Gower Publishing.

Office-of-Government-Commerce. (2008). PRINCE 2. Retrieved January 17, 2008, from http://www.ogc.gov.uk/methods_prince_2.asp

Pinto, J. K. (2002). Project management 2002. *Research Technology Management, 45*(2), 22–37.

Porter, M. E. (1996). What is strategy? *Harvard Business Review, 74*(6), 61–78.

Project Management Institute. (1986). Project management body of knowledge. *Project Management Journal,* 17(3), 15–102

Project Management Institute. (1996). *A guide to the project management body of knowledge (PMBOK® Guide).* Newtown Square, Pennsylvania: Project Management Institute.

Project Management Institute. (2000). *A guide to the project management body of knowledge (PMBOK® Guide)* (2000 ed.). Newtown Square, Pennsylvania: Project Management Institute.

Project Management Institute. (2004). *A guide to the project management body of knowledge (PMBOK® Guide)* (3rd ed.). Newtown Square, PA: Project Management Institute.

Project Management Institute. (2006). *The standard for portfolio management* (1st ed. Vol. 1). Newtown Square, PA: Project Management Institute.

Statistics Canada. (2005). Population projections: 2005 to 2031. *The Daily.* Retrieved March 13, 2008, from http://www.statcan.ca/Daily/English/051215/d051215b.htm

Stawicki, J., & Müller, R. (2007, June 18-20). *From standards to execution: Implementing program and portfolio management.* Paper presented at the 21st International Project Management Association World Congress.

Tapscott, D. (1998). *Growing up digital: The rise of the Net Generation.* New York: McGraw-Hill.

Turner, R., & Müller, R. (2006). *Choosing appropriate project managers: Matching their leadership style to the type of project.* Newton Square, Pennsylvania: Project Management Institute.

CHAPTER 14

Project Management Circa 2025

Challenge of Managing Financial Services Projects

Howard Bruck, PMP

Trends in Financial Services

The financial services industry is vital to the world economy. We have come to rely on these businesses to execute billions of diverse and complicated transactions every minute of every day just to meet our most fundamental needs. The significant problems this industry is currently facing magnifies the need for financial services firms to operate efficiently, identify and fix the root causes of the current issues, and execute more effective levels of risk management and services delivery.

As the economy continues towards a larger focus on services and information, financial firms will be called upon to better manage their roles, achieve higher levels of quality, maintain the integrity of the global system, and endeavor to achieve ever-increasing efficiencies. Three specific trends that will significantly influence financial services over the next 20 years are advances in information technologies, globalization of the marketplace, and stricter regulatory requirements.

To a large degree, financial services are based on sophisticated information systems and integrated business processes. The projects to implement and maintain these systems and the associated supporting business processes are large, expensive, time-consuming, and demand very a high degree of accuracy.

Financial services firms are among the most opportunistic in taking advantage of advances in technology primarily because the underlying product or service is rooted in data and information processes. The current balance of a bank account is simply the sum of transactions represented as data on storage devices. The overwhelming volume of equities-trading transactions occur between computers running sophisticated software programs without human interaction. Credit ratings of millions of individuals and businesses are calculated on a daily basis, as disparate systems across many industries and geographies interchange massive amounts of data. Thus, financial services firms are continually looking to leverage technology to deliver compelling services and improve profitability.

Like many industries, financial services firms have been involved in significantly large mergers, creating companies with diversified capabilities and global reach. These mergers have allowed firms to enter markets with broad product offerings utilizing existing infrastructure and resources. Brand names like Citibank, UBS, and HSBC are as well-known in foreign markets as they are in their country of origin. Improvements in telecommunications and travel, as well as trading partnerships like the European Union and the North American Free Trade Agreement, continue to promote expansion of multinational financial services practices. Advances in technology, primarily the universal access to telecommunications and the Internet, also provide small, innovative firms with the capability to quickly participate in the global financial services environment, often by identifying new niches and product lines. The trend towards globalization will continue rapidly as physical, technical, and administrative barriers are broken.

The first two trends, advancing technology and globalization, as well as the current collapse of the financial markets, become drivers for the third trend—a stricter regulatory environment. By their very nature, financial services transactions are susceptible to intentional fraud, unwarranted risk-taking, and unintentional errors, leaving very large monetary value at risk. To protect the public, governments and non-governmental agencies have instituted strict regulations and a strong auditing environment. Even with these structures in place, news of incidents involving fraud, data theft, and lapses in proper controls continue. While we are still diagnosing the root causes of the current financial services collapse, it is clear that the regulatory compliance and audit control environment will continue to grow and play a more influential role, with firms being challenged to meet these demands effectively and efficiently.

These three trends will be the impetus for a long series of large and complex projects that will be undertaken by global and niche financial services firms. These projects will require industry-specific experience and new skills.

State of Project Management in Financial Services

Many of the leading financial services firms have realized that project management is an essential discipline for their future success. It is becoming more common for the large firms to have dedicated project management offices led by highly qualified senior executives. More and more skilled practitioners are in demand. Even small and mid-sized firms recognize this need and have either assigned qualified employees or acquired consultants dedicated to manage projects. Many financial services projects are implemented between a firm and one or more providers. It is the common practice of these vendors to include project management support as a specific deliverable. The level of formal project management skills and methodologies seems to be getting more mature, with the importance of projects being delivered on-time, on-budget, and within requirements.

Effective project management is the result of expertise in three areas—skills unique to project management, mastery of general management capabilities, and experience pertinent to a specific application area, such as financial services. As we examine the trends in the business, and the projects that support them, new and specific application areas are becoming essential for project managers in financial services. Globalization and the ability to manage the complexity inherently involved with diverse workforces, cultures, languages, and geographic constraints will affect all industries, including financial services, and will not be examined in this piece. Neither will we focus on advances in information technology, which appear as a significant component throughout business projects.

However, there are trends that continue to show up as important components in projects in financial services. The first is working in an ever-stricter regulatory and compliance environment during both the project phase and throughout the life of the resultant product. The second is a focus on creating new business processes that are highly efficient, controlled, and measurable using techniques like business process management and automated workflow. The third, which combines and maximizes the opportunities in globalization, vendor management, and process efficiency, is business process outsourcing. Each of these requires the financial services project manager to have a deep understanding of how the specific application works, is planned for, and implemented.

Trend 1: Regulatory and Compliance Environment

Over the past several years, there have been many well-publicized failures of management control at large organizations. The issues at UBS, Countrywide, and Merrill Lynch are still being diagnosed, but clearly demonstrate a lack of proper credit risk management and improper management accountability. The multibillion-dollar losses racked up by a rogue trader at Societe General have been attributed to a lack of internal controls and proper oversight. The home mortgage crisis resulted from insufficient management among financial services firms trying to leverage too much high-risk debt.

As a result of these issues, there has been a significant increase and focus on the regulatory and compliance aspects of management. Managers of publicly traded U.S. firms have dedicated a significant amount of time and resource to comply with the Sarbanes-Oxley Acts of 2002. Commonly referred to as SOX or section 404, this law mandates that a firm's operating processes should be well controlled, and must be both documented and tested on an annual basis by an outside audit firm. Table 1 shows some of the agencies regulating business in the United States.

Government agencies, as well as industry-specific self-governing bodies, have all stepped up their focus to insure that management understands and implements best practices, adheres to the letter and spirit of laws and regulations, and establishes the policies and procedures to protect investors, consumers, and employees. Financial services firms have been among the most scrutinized in this area. The current problems in financial services will surely result in the call for more effective controls and monitoring. All this will have a significant impact for project management.

Project management itself is being recognized as an important aspect of good management practices. Projects are the mechanisms by which much new capital is expended at large firms. As such, auditors are very interested in seeing how much care and resources are dedicated to insuring that these projects are properly managed using industry standards and best practices.

Table 1   Partial list of U.S. financial services regulatory agencies

Organization	Charter	Scope
Federal Reserve Board	Federal	Banks
Office of Controller of the Currency	Federal	National Banks
Federal Deposit Insurance Corporation	Federal	State Banks
Securities and Exchange Commission	Federal	Investment Firms
Fin Industry Regulatory Authority	Industry	Securities Firms
Office of Thrift Supervision	Federal	Credit Unions
AI of Certified Public Accountants	Private	Public Companies
Insurance Regulators	State	Insurance Providers
State Banking Authorities	State	State Banks
Federal Trade Commission	Federal	Credit Providers
PCI Security Standards Council	Industry	Credit Card Industry
FFIEC	Federal	Banking
Securities Investor Protection Service	Industry	Investment Firms

It is becoming the standard to see project management offices at large financial services firms. Auditors are looking for several things from a project management perspective, including: 1) Validating that there is a standard practice for project management across a firm; 2) Verifying that the standard practices are being executed consistently; and 3) Confirming that the project management process keeps senior management sufficiently informed on project performance and risk issues. Lack of formal project management practices, especially at large, publicly held financial services firms, is an audit and control concern.

Projects often involve the internal organization along with third-party suppliers and services firms. As part of the increased focus on internal controls and best practices, auditors and regulators have increased their scrutiny on the vendor-selection process. The project management literature, including *A Guide to the Project Management Body of Knowledge (PMBOK® Guide)* (PMI, 2004), has devoted much attention to the vendor-selection processes. This becomes especially problematic when the project involves the installation of a third-party vendor to take over an entire operation such as business process outsourcing.

The audit and regulatory environment is placing an even greater emphasis on long-term vendor management. This is to address the outdated thinking that "if a vendor fouls up, then it's their problem." As evidenced particularly in the Enron case, even though much of the lack of control was due to faulty work by the CPAs from the auditors at Arthur Andersen, the Enron executives were held directly accountable. In response, many regulations have been put in place to specifically outline the need for formal vendor management practices. The impact for project management is that including vendor management and ultimately preparing the organization for an ongoing process must be part of new projects that have a significant vendor portion.

Specifically, projects that have a large vendor involvement, in terms of financial expenditure or risk exposure, will need to demonstrate that a vendor due-diligence process has been executed. Project managers should be completing thorough documentation about the vendor selection process and the project management processes used.

A third area of keen interest for the examiners is data security. Financial services firms, along with the healthcare industry, have seen a significant increase in the amount of formal legislation and regulations on data security. With financial services being heavily reliant on information systems, most projects involve data, technology, and related processes. Project managers, while not necessarily information security experts, must be aware of the data security regulatory environment. They must include sections of the project plan to ensure that proper data security controls are used during the project itself, and that the resultant systems have provisions for long-term data-security procedures.

A final note for project managers regarding the regulatory and compliance environment is to establish good documentation procedures. External auditors and examiners work primarily with documentation. As such, the project manager can facilitate a smooth audit, and subsequently save the organization money, by organizing and presenting the relevant project management work in an easy-to-use fashion. This in itself will help to demonstrate that the projects have indeed been executed with the proper care and detail.

Trend 2: Business Process Management

In their landmark book *Reengineering the Corporation*, Hammer and Champy (1993) argued that legacy business processes can only be optimized by completely rebuilding a business function from the customer's perspective and then identifying the steps necessary to deliver that desired product or service. This method dramatically changed the way successful firms, and their consulting partners, approached projects. Rather than looking to use projects to optimize discrete functionality within an established business process, project execution started with a complete rethinking of the product or service delivered to the end customer.

This has lead to a focus on a particular expertise called process analysis or process engineering. Wal-Mart and Dell are most notable for reengineering their physical supply chains and driving dramatic efficiencies in their industries. Financial services firms work primarily with information, not physical goods, and their processes are often quite unique. For commercial banks, the process of underwriting a loan involves the gathering, transferring, and analysis of information across more than a dozen functions. Opening an account with a brokerage firm requires many steps to complete, due to the numerous regulatory requirements and internal control points. Servicing an insurance claim consists of a detailed series of tasks used to protect against fraud and meet internal and regulatory audit requirements. Business process engineering is to financial services as supply chain management is to manufacturing and distribution firms.

Financial services firms continually execute projects to introduce new services or optimize existing ones. Process engineering is often a major component of these projects. While process engineering has a focus on efficient analysis and design, new technologies have been created to support this effort. In particular, a software segment called business process management (BPM) continues to emerge as an essential tool used to develop and support complex processes, especially those involving movement of documents, and complex routing based on human and/or system-generated decision points.

BPM tools from the leading companies such as Pegasystems, Savvion, and Lombardi appeared on the market in the 1980s. These systems help process engineers design, run, and analyze the efficiency of business functions. The tools have steadily improved over the past 20 years and have recently seen a dramatic increase in deployment. Project managers working on financial services projects will need to understand BPM and the supporting technology as firms look to management projects that create processes that are efficient and auditable.

In the business process design phase, process engineers use BPM tools to graphically map each step and identify 1) what information is needed to perform the function; 2) what decisions are to be made; 3) how long should each step take; and 4) what should be done after the activity is completed. The design tools are also used to document how exceptions to the routine process are to be handled. Process engineers use the tools to simulate the working process and work with the business operations team to adjust and finalize the new design before implementation. A sample BPM design is shown in Figure 1.

A new process can utilize BPM software to drive the execution of the process. Information enters the BPM software at an entry point. For example, a customer can complete an online application for a residential mortgage. That completed application enters the BPM software where several automated processes can be initiated. Credit scores can be automatically obtained from reporting bureaus, application fees can be debited from the applicant's bank account, and recent home sales prices can be obtained from third-party services.

Based on business rules, defined in the BPM, the application will be delivered to the next appropriate step. Some applications might be immediately rejected and automated notification sent to the customer; others might be sent to a particular credit analyst group either by geography or size of loan request. The BPM tools will monitor the process every step of the way and provide management with the ability to see where in the process any particular application is, or how the whole process is running. Finally, BPM tools provide reports on historic process execution so engineers can analyze the current process and change it to improve efficiency.

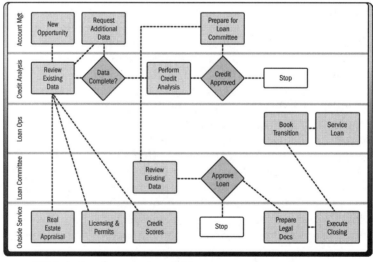

Figure 1   BPM design for commercial loan process

Projects that involve the implementation of business processes, especially those involving the flow of information and decision-making, will utilize BPM methods and technology. Project managers on these initiatives will need to understand the activities, people skills, quality control aspects, and risk management components associated with BPM.

Trend 3: Business Process Outsourcing

The financial service industry continues to participate in the growth of large, multinational firms. Over 20% of the 2008 Fortune Magazine's Global 500 companies can be categorized in the financial services sector. The modern financial services firm is highly diversified, offering services in dozens of areas and selling hundreds of specific products. These products are often further differentiated across countries to meet local preferences and regulatory requirements. Innovations in technology and product development create rapid introduction of new specialized services. Products are then specially configured or mass-customized by clients themselves.

As the large financial services firms become even larger and periodically merge with each other, mid-tier regional providers and smaller niche organizations also play an important role. These firms focus on specific customer needs or address unique situations. It is also quite common for product innovations to originate at this level. While not necessarily trying to compete head-to-head with the largest providers, the small to mid-sized financial services firms often strive to provide their customers with products in multiple areas. One goal of the modern financial services firm is to gain customer "wallet share" by providing services across a wide product range.

Traditionally, delivery of a particular service was performed primarily by the firm itself. This required the company to develop and market the service, as well as create the operational infrastructure to deliver the service and keep it current to changing market trends and regulatory requirements. An alternative method would be to enter into a reseller or partnership agreement with a specialty provider. In this case, the end-customer purchases the service from one firm and the delivery would come from the direct provider. This partnership relationship would usually be evident to the customer, and the product characteristics would clearly be driven by the direct service provider. This disjointed delivery can cause confusion and disruption for the end-customer.

Three specific issues emerge from either the traditional in-house model or the reseller outsource model for the financial services firm: 1) Challenge to be the low cost provider; 2) Inability to have detailed product focus; and 3) Disintegration of the service for the end-customer. The firms that cannot overcome all three of these challenges lose customers and profitability. To address these issues and take advantage of the global services markets, the industry has turned to a new model called business process outsourcing (BPO).

A business process outsourcing organization provides expertise in the delivery of a product and service, but acts as an extension of the firm, rather than simply a reseller of its own products and services. Because the BPO firm can focus on the operational execution of a particular service, it can develop an infrastructure designed specifically for low-cost delivery and high-quality production. This often means strategically locating the work to take advantage of labor, energy, or other geographic advantages as well as streamlining corporate overhead to achieve cost optimization. From a customer perspective, the objective for the financial service firm is to deliver a fully integrated set of solutions in which the customer is not necessarily aware that the underlying service may be delivered by a third party. This is shown in Figure 2.

For financial services firms, becoming a "full-service provider" and obtaining a large "wallet share" requires the capability to provide many services in a highly competitive environment. The growing trend for both large and small firms is to utilize business process outsourcing to achieve the optimum cost structure and product diversity, while maintaining an integrated solution from a customer perspective. The leading business research analyst firms continue to see BPO growing, especially in financial services.

The project to introduce a product or service to be delivered by BPO has several significant elements that need special attention and expertise. Because this business model is still relatively new to both the project management profession and industry in general, the best practices are only beginning to be evaluated and documented.

On a traditional project, the result of the work is the delivery of a product at some point in time. The generalized objective of the project manager is to guide the initiative through its phases in order to meet the specifications of the product description on time and within the identified budget. At the end of the project, one can measure the results and determine if the product description was met. Subsequently, the success of the product in the marketplace is not a project concern, but one of product management.

Conversely, a project to implement a BPO arrangement will result in the creation of a "product" that will be delivered over the life of a specified contract, often five to seven years into the future, and usually with the intention of lasting for several more contract renewals, since the cost and disruption of switching vendors is often undesirable. What is particularly unique about this situation, especially in financial services, is that the stakeholders all can be assured that the product delivered on day one will require

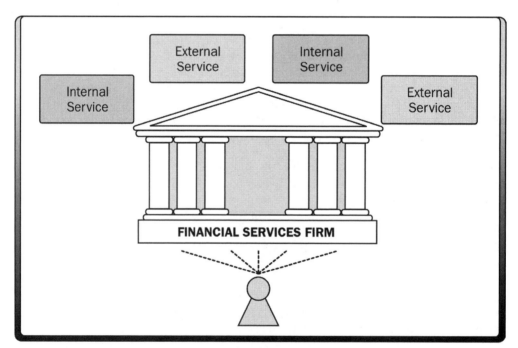

Figure 2   Unified service perspective to the customer

significant, but as of now unknown, changes in order to meet future regulatory requirements, competitive pressures, product differentiation, and customer demands.

Three specific areas where these types of projects will require new thought leadership and expertise are: 1) vendor selection; 2) preparing the Financial Services to support a BPO relationship; and 3) subsequent projects that extend or fundamentally change the original body of work. These three areas are significantly different from a typical project because BPO relationships seek to create a seamless extension of the financial services firm and must anticipate many unknown changes that will occur over the life of the relationship. As such, there are now two goals for these projects: to smoothly introduce the BPO deliverable into the organization, and to ensure that the relationship remains mutually beneficial over many uncertain years into the future.

The project management literature addresses the vendor management selection process in some detail. The *PMBOK® Guide* (PMI, 2004) devotes several sections to the methodology of selecting and contracting suppliers and vendors. Traditionally, suppliers and vendors are called upon to deliver goods or services to fairly detailed requirements and to a timeframe in the relatively near future. In a project to implement a BPO arrangement, especially in financial services, the challenges and risks associated are somewhat unique in that the requirements can be clear for the initial delivery, but will most certainly change over the life of the program. Specifically these changes will be due to regulatory requirements, competitive pressures, and cost structures that are highly unpredictable. As such, the vendor selection process is difficult, but perhaps one of the most important challenges of the project. The five specific challenges unique to selecting a BPO partner are: 1) identifying qualified candidates; 2) determining how your competitors may be using the same vendors; 3) ensuring the partner can comply with industry standards, regulatory requirements, and audit certifications; 4) negotiating service-level agreements that are constructed to ensure product delivery meets requirements; and 5) developing contracts that are constructed with the ability to appropriately adjust for future product changes.

The traditional vendor selection process is well-defined in the project management literature; the practices are quite mature, including the request for proposal (RFP) process, vendor conferences, and reference checks. All of these practices are appropriate for selecting a BPO provider. However, because the relationship with the vendor will last for many years, more scrutiny and discipline must be applied.

One objective in selecting a BPO provider is to find the firm that can implement the transition and then maintain the service at the level required to meet the needs of the hiring company, with the caveat that these needs will likely change dramatically over the life of the contract. Furthermore, while the contract may originally be set for a period of say five years, it is usually desirable to remain with the same provider at contract renewal time, so the selection must provide an analysis of how likely the BPO provider will still be acceptable at contract end. In a business climate with many mergers and acquisitions, the evaluation process must consider whether the company and management team that is originally installed will have the same corporate structure when the contract ends.

An interesting aspect of utilizing a BPO solution is that it is highly likely that some of firm's direct competitors will be using the same providers. In this case, the BPO has knowledge of proprietary information like pricing, account lists, and customer data. The resources performing the work may also be doing so for a direct competitor. Therefore it is imperative that the vendor selection process examines how a BPO handles this situation and what sort of warrantees they are willing to write into a contract to protect a firm from misuse of proprietary information, and how well the firm's management team educates and controls its human resources to protect its clients' information.

The effort to comply with regulatory requirements for public companies, and especially for financial services firms has continued to increase. These requirements cover a broad range of functional areas from information systems and data to operations and customer interaction. The regulators have recognized the more significant role that third-party vendors and business process outsourcing firms are playing. In particular, the regulators and audit firms have stressed the need for firms to put into place formal vendor management programs. This, in turn, creates the need for evaluation of a BPO's internal processes to meet regulatory requirements. For a vendor evaluation tool, the audit firms have created the SAS-70 audit program which evaluates an outsource services provider's ability to control processes and data. Thus, reviewing a potential BPO's internal processes and reviewing a qualified auditor's SAS-70 report can help the project team evaluate a vendor's ability to meet regulatory requirements.

The goal of a BPO project is to use technology and people to create a new process that will serve the business for many years. There are not a lot of physical deliverables in a BPO project and the end product is difficult to examine on a moment-by-moment basis. However, the deliverables ultimately are a service that can be measured and evaluated over a period of time. Therefore, a critical component of the BPO project is to very clearly define the items that should be measured to determine whether the service being provided is meeting the requirements. This is formally captured in a set of service-level agreements (SLA) that becomes an important part of the vendor selection process and ultimately integrated into the formal legal contracts. Additionally, the project must include activities to prepare the organization to manage the SLA to insure that the vendor is delivering the services according to the terms of the contract.

A critical deliverable in the project to implement a BPO relationship is the contract between the financial services firm and the organization providing the service. In addition to the normal issues with contracts, special attention must be made to arrange for the significant changes to the service that are likely to occur. These changes can be the result of advancements in technology, product innovations driving competitive pressures, or through regulatory requirements. It must be assumed that the service being originally contracted for will likely change several times before the arrangement is concluded. Without specific terms governing how changes are handled, the financial services firm will have little influence over quality controls, timeliness of delivery, or pricing parameters for requested changes. Therefore, the procedures for handling changes to the service over the life of the contract must be specifically drawn out. In fact, new variations of existing methodologies like comparative pricing, or cost-plus profit margin are being used to handle future change request pricing proposals.

The appropriate place to address the concerns raised in the preceding sections is on the RFP process of vendor selection. The RFP process gives the financial services firm the opportunity to ask direct questions and obtain direct answers (such as those shown in Table 2) that not only are important for vendor selection, but as a basis for contract negotiation. In particular, issues specific to a BPO project should be identified in the RFP.

It is clear that firms will continue to leverage third-party service providers, and the business process outsourcing model provides an effective model in which to structure such programs. Manufacturing firms have utilized strategic sourcing of physical mate-

Table 2   RFP questions for business process outsourcing.

Describe the methodology for pricing and implementing additional or modified services requested over the life of the contract.
Describe how the service analyzes and meets ongoing regulatory requirements.
Do you have a SAS-70 Type II report? Who is the auditing firm? Can you provide a SAS-70 Type II report annually at no additional cost?
Provide a disaster recovery plan. How frequently do you execute a D/R test? Can you provide the results of the D/R test at no additional cost?
Provide your standard service level agreements, including remediation criteria and penalty structure. (i.e. system performance, uptime...)
Describe all the unplanned downtime incidents you have experienced since January 2004.
Describe any customer data security breaches since January 2004.
How many financial services firms are running this solution? Provide the policies and procedures used to maintain data privacy between the financial services firms.
How many new installations of this service did you complete in 2005 and 2006?
How many existing installations of this solution transitioned off in 2005 and 2006?

rials and leveraging third-party vendors to execute discrete portions in a manufacturing supply chain. These are well established practices. Financial firms, being information and services oriented, utilize business process outsourcing to achieve similar results.

The projects to implement a BPO require specialized knowledge and skills that are just beginning to be uncovered. New project management practices will need to develop as the practice continues to grow and change.

Project Management in the Financial Services Firm in 2025

In the year 2025, project management will be an important role in financial services firms. It will become a core competency within the more successful organizations, because shorter product life cycles, continual innovations, and a changing regulatory environment will mean the number and scale of projects will increase. Companies that are effective and efficient at project execution will beat competitors to market and be more profitable.

Project portfolio management will become a more influential area, primarily focused on analyzing project financial impact, instituting more formal risk management programs, and validating project performance over time. As project-based financial modeling becomes more sophisticated, companies will be able to put more credibility in managing a portfolio of projects based on financial impact. More importantly, employee compensation programs will be focused more on longer-term results. Management performance will be evaluated on how well a project's result performs to the expected return on investment over the full life of the project. Internal and external auditors will more closely scrutinize a firm's project management practices, with a focus on risk management capabilities.

To provide broad product sets and deliver services globally, financial services firms will enter into more vendor relationships and utilize business process outsourcing and off-shoring. Project management practices will evolve specifically to handle these situations. Firms will expect higher levels of project management support and performance from their vendors.

Financial instruments and the rate of transaction processing will become more sophisticated and occur at an even faster pace. Data security will continue to be a never ending chase to keep ahead of intentional and accidental lapses. The potential losses from fraud and human error will become more important to control as nearly all financial transactions will occur in cyberspace. Project management will be called upon to insure that all the right pieces are in place.

Compensation for project management will be more directly tied into actual results. Objective performance measurement systems will be implemented to support such programs. The project management departments will grow and will have their own specialized functions like project financial analysis, project risk management, and vendor management experts. There will be senior management positions within project management that will work closely with the chief operating officer, internal audit group, and chief information officer.

The project management profession will need to continue advancing its practices and capabilities to meet ever more complex and evolving needs. The value of project management to financial services firms will ultimately be measured by financial analysis of the results delivered.

Bibliography

Bennhold, K. Paris Bank's Managers Are Blamed in a Scandal. *New York Times*, May 23, 2008.

Feig, N. The Rise of the Business Analyst and Other Emerging IT Roles. *Bank Systems and Technology*, January 1, 2007

Feig, N. Business Process Management Moves Beyond Workflow to Business Optimization. *Bank Systems and Technology*, June 21, 2007

Greenhouse, L. Justices Reject Auditor Verdict in Enron Scandal. *New York Times*, June 1, 2005.

Hammer, Michael, and James Champy. *Reengineering the Corporation: A Manifesto for Business Revolution*, New York: HarperBusiness, 1993.

Implementing SOX 404 - An Introduction, McGladrey and Pullen Certified Public Accountants. http://www.mcgladrey.com/Resource_Center/Audit/Articles/Imple mentingSOX_AnIntroduction.html

Levinson, M. Project Management - When Failure Is Not an Option. *CIO*, June 1, 2006.

Prahalad, C.K. and Hamel, Gary. 1990. The Core Competence of the Corporation. *Harvard Business Review*, 68(3), 79–87.

Project Management Institute (PMI). (2004). *A guide to the project management body of knowledge (PMBOK® guide)* (3rd ed.), Newtown Square, PA: Author

Ranganathan, C. & Balaji, S. (2007) Critical Capabilities for Offshore Outsourcing of Information Systems. *MIS Quarterly Executive*, 6, 147–164.

Santosus, M. Why You Need a Project Management Office, CIO, July 1, 2004.

Sing, T. Major Trends in BPO –What You Need to Know, *Gartner Teleconference*, June 29, 2006. http://www.gartner.com/teleconferences/asset_152735_75.jsp

Wheatley, M. The Global Risk Factor, *PM Network*, April 2009

CHAPTER 15

The Coming Evolution of the Research and Development Project Manager

Belle Collins Brown

Abstract

Over the next two decades, the position of the research and development project manager will continue to evolve away from its process roots. Future project managers must be prepared to face the reality that most of today's work – planning, status tracking, reporting – will be automated into large development systems designed to provide portfolio-level views for an organization's research and development activities. In order to provide value in the coming decades, project managers must grow to be leaders, rather than managers, because the organizations they serve will no longer be siloed functional entities crying out for coordination. Instead they will be project-based organizations that require real leadership.

Increasing requirements for subject matter expertise in project management

As process knowledge becomes more automated and tool-driven, subject matter expertise will become more of a requirement for research and development (R&D) project managers in the future. No longer is the idea of organization and scheduling a foreign concept understood only by those deemed "process worshipers." These concepts have become a well-established part of the project life cycle. Project managers, in turn, are following a more formalized approach, as many companies require more standardized methods for managing projects. This is due, in part, to the popularity of project management tools and certifications, and increased implementations of well-established and proven methodologies like Six Sigma methods and PMI standards. As these key areas become more standardized, other areas begin to stand out as key to project success. The discipline of project management will evolve into a more organized area of practice, and process knowledge will become more understood, lending itself to become more automated and efficient.

Traditional areas such as project risk and scheduling are prime opportunities for modeling using well-defined formulas and tested strategies. In many environments, the results of these formulas can be tracked and tested against the outcomes of projects and measured for success or failure. Tools to support these practices will continue to evolve into well defined aids to the project managers who will use them in general practice. However, as these tools become more common in the workplace, project managers will need to hone their skills in a way that adds value to a specific environment. Managing process flows and timelines will no longer be the tedious tasks of the past, often requiring numerous meetings and manual tracking. The role of tomorrow's R&D project manager will require more strategic participation to help guide teams to successful development of new products and technologies.

Project managers have long been tasked with identifying and bringing together project stakeholders, facilitating communication, and removing barriers to success. However, these areas have taken somewhat of a back seat in the past to more finite and measurable areas like scheduling and risk analysis. While these more measurable areas are in part attributable to project success, many projects emphasizing these as most critical still fail. Areas like innovation and inspiration have often been ignored by project teams that seek to avoid conflict and move projects forward on an established path. However, in a world of technological innovation, companies strive to find ways to inspire teams to go beyond the established paths and create the competitive edge. It is in this environment that future project managers will soar. It will be the R&D project manager's role to provide inspiration and leadership to move projects in a clear direction for success at a higher level of ownership. Not only will they be responsible for the traditional paths of initiation, planning, execution, and the like, but also for providing strategic direction to align projects to corporate objectives.

Increased impact of corporate objectives on project direction

As companies move more towards aligning product development strategies with overall corporate objectives, there will likely be a trend towards aligning projects accordingly. The overall goal in this approach would be to shift project direction from independently driven project goals to something more overarching or globally reaching. For example, instead of creating a lower-power product, the product would now "go green" to meet the new corporate objective of becoming more eco-friendly. Or, in another case, a project could have a two-year timeline to meet new company international shipping requirements and adhere to a new global trade agreement instead of its previous goal of adding requirements to project plans as regulated by local law.

We see examples of this often in packaging as well. As we become more aware of landfill populations and chemical contamination, we have seen a big shift in product packaging to being "100% recycled." And in areas of high pollution, we see a shift to hybrid cars and the use of biofuels. These examples all trend toward larger goals of companies to protect the environment as a whole by pushing objectives downward into product development. By doing so, companies are encouraging, if not forcing, the management of projects to adhere to these corporate objectives by managing to a new set of requirements that may not have been scoped as part of the original project plan. In fact, in some instances, these objectives may introduce additional costs into the project that would not have been perceived as acceptable in the past.

The idea that small increases in spending now will have greater reward later has become the premise of many global product campaign strategies. Not only will project managers be required to understand how to develop and plan for products within their normal arenas, but they will more increasingly be required to comprehend how projects will impact the longer term objectives set by companies. This will require a better understanding of the project's connection to its surrounding globally themed partners.

Managing vs. leading projects at a portfolio level

By approaching projects from a more global view we can begin to see how projects tie together to form a cohesive set and communicate an overarching theme. Not only could we have a most efficient product A within its class, but it could also integrate seamlessly with the most efficient product B in a different class. And bundled together with products C &D, we now have an overall message of "most efficient" across several product classes, giving us a "most efficient" solution for the targeted customer base.

In this scenario, the project manager's view would now encompass a wider range of dependencies that may or may not be under his immediate control. This will require a level of communication and coordination that has not traditionally been scoped as part of the project plans of the past. In another instance, a company might require a series of projects that are tightly coupled and managed by the same team. For example, an R&D project budget may include development of a complete set of products from now until the year 2015, a whole portfolio. The project manager would be responsible for the initial product delivery and several subsequent enhancements or updates to the products planned out to 2015. In this case, the project manager's view would span the entire portfolio and require a longer planning process that would include requirements for future project pieces. Dependencies for such a portfolio could easily include things like expected lifetimes of components, availability of parts, or simply technology freshness. Any of these attributes could impact the life cycle of one or more of the project deliverables.

Additionally, portfolios could be periodically reviewed to ensure product freshness and profitability. Project managers would be required to understand the business of portfolio management to be effective in this role. Companies are finding great success in managing projects this way. A study performed by the Center for Business Practices showed that companies that use a project portfolio management (PPM) system find greater success than with traditional project management methods. From a portfolio level, we begin to see the evolution of a product or set of products that will need to be managed at a greater level of forward thinking than in traditional projects. Lessons learned from one project of the portfolio can now be transitioned into future projects with project manager and teams maintaining the knowledge to progress without committing the same mistakes of the past. At this level, project managers and teams need to be empowered to make decisions based not only on new project requirements but also on prior experience.

In R&D environments that are portfolio-based, project managers may find themselves with greater leadership responsibilities than that of traditional project management. Not only must they manage the processes needed to deliver the initial products, but also use knowledge gained along the way to assess the future of other portfolio pieces. With increasing organizational compression, project managers will be asked to play a more critical role in the direction and overall outcome of the projects they lead. The impact could be immediate or long term. For example, the success or failure of a first release of a planned group of products could ultimately decide the fate of those planned for the future.

Project cost could also impact long-term project decisions. By providing direction and leadership along the way, project manager's can help direct the development process in ways that may immediately impact the product or those in the future. By being placed in a position of leadership, project managers can make critical decisions along the way without fear of backlash from those stakeholders whose interests they represent. Traditional management, on the other hand, involves the day-to-day tasks of those processes established in the approved project plan with little or no flexibility to change the direction of the project without prior stakeholder approval. As the roles evolve, qualities of good leaders will stand out as critical to skill sets required of future project managers.

Good leadership characteristics may include:

- Relying on others with experience or expertise;
- Soliciting participation in project planning;
- Willing to listen to new ideas and incorporate them in the project plans;
- Inspiring and coaching at every phase of the project;
- Anticipating changes in project direction; and
- Empowering team members to make decisions.

Teams of the future will become powerhouses of knowledge tasked with assessing project viability within portfolios, defining project scope, project implementation, and transitioning to the next phase of the portfolio. These teams will requires leadership beyond today's scope of the traditional project manager, and those who seek to step into these roles will emerge as the leaders of tomorrow.

Project management tool development in the portfolio management space

R&D is a little different than other disciplines in that the tools often need to be broad instead of deep. The idea is not that "one tools fits all" but that tools should be flexible enough to lend themselves useful across a wide range of projects. A tool that is too deep in its ability to document and track milestones may require inputs that are not applicable in all product environments. For example, a tool that specifies a detailed product delivery system may require manufacturing process flows and regulatory specifics. However, if a future product is outsourced to a third-party vendor, the project team may only be responsible for tracking the handoff to the vendor and not the specifics of the vendor's process as part of the overall project tracking tool. In this case, the tool may become useless if critical tool tracking requirements cannot be captured as part of the plan.

With the emergence of computer-based tools used in project management, the industry has seen a rise in the use of more standardized tools for almost all phases of the project life cycle. These standardized tools allow project managers to transfer skill sets across projects, groups, companies, and industries. Such tools have become the baseline for many project management reporting techniques used across many industries. We see evidence of this in increasing requirements for project managers to have specific tool experience such as Microsoft Project, TurboProject, SureTrack Project Manager, and many others. These tools provide a wide array of uses while allowing the creation of very detailed and specialized reporting.

However, if only used at the highest levels of abstraction, the drawback to these tools could be in the nature of the standardization. If only high-level timelines and milestones are inherent in the tool itself, project details must be captured for each new project regardless of its similarity to an existing project. This, in turn, could lead to errors and missed project components.

A scenario like this could be resolved by creating templates that would comprise the critical mass of timelines, milestones, and resources required for particular types of projects. But that would, in turn, require management of its own to keep the templates updated and communicated to the project teams and thus possibly decreasing the templates' usefulness as effective tools. This is where subject-matter expertise would reign. Project managers who are skilled in the areas in which they manage are more likely to be able to realize maximum benefits from such a tool by refining its capabilities to the exact needs of the teams.

Recently, more specialized reporting tools have emerged and are used on custom projects. These can be customized for a company's specific environment or a particular industry segment. Tools used in industries such as oil refining and space exploration have been well known to be very specialized and complex. If tools are too complex in their nature to be easily understood, they are not likely to be used as standards for implementing new large-scale project initiatives. Requiring new project teams to learn the complexity of an existing tool to start a new project may not be worth the time and effort required, especially if the tool will then have to be modified to meet the specific needs of the new project. Customization to this level at each project initiation would be a costly and time consuming endeavor. Its impracticality would inevitably negatively impact overall project performance.

While these tools serve a very specific purpose in their current environments, they can rarely be used without major modification in future projects. Furthermore, they can likely not be used as a metric to compare against. Projects tools with high levels of complexity that pertain only to a specific project's goals can limit the amount of value gained when trying to leverage for future project initiatives. Tools that are broader in scope allow for more flexibility without imposing a stringent learning cure on teams at each new project initiation.

Other areas of the R&D environment also suffer from too much complexity in tools. For example, testing and bug-tracking systems often require updates and refinements to meet the needs of evolving technological changes to the existing environments. As technological advances are made, these environments must adapt their old ways of doing business to accommodate the changes. Testing of areas not traditionally captured and documented may now see improvements in the ability to monitor and alert teams of pending failures. The tool would now be required to show that these areas have now been documented as tested and perhaps indicate more detailed levels of reporting.

Defect tracking systems have also shown similar levels of complexity in the amount to details they can document for projects. Tracking systems can now attach very detailed logs or reports for defects found during testing or manufacturing and perhaps provide links to additional details or other projects that have seen similar failures. With this level of detailed tracking ability, how can these R&D projects abstract themselves to a broader level of tool usage?

To answer this question, we can again look to our subject matter expertise. By applying expertise to a common tool, project managers can create an environment for managing processes that is easily understood by those familiar with the tool itself and the project environment. By using common terminology to describe defect trends and timelines, project managers can effectively use the tool to not only manage the project work but also to communicate information to others that can be easily understood.

In the world of R&D, innovation also poses its own set of challenges for tool usage. As R&D project managers, we are constantly tasked with introducing new and innovative ways of developing and managing projects to align ourselves with evolving technological changes.

How then can such broad tools be applied across R&D projects that require innovation at every turn to meet ever changing technological advances? While we seek to minimize learning curves and limit the use of ineffective tools, we also seek to standardize the process of innovating. We seek to push teams to work efficiently yet effectively, to adhere to the process but make improvements, to deliver products sooner yet stay competitive, to do more work faster but spend less money. To do so would require a well-oiled process machine that could continue to move projects forward and inject imperative knowledge into the process as lessons are learned without disrupting the work or breaking the process model overall. This inherently defines the role of the "future" R&D project manager. We should seek to innovate and compete while maintaining the processes and tools that provide us with the most useful and effective ways of delivering the best of the best.

Organizational trends in the R&D community

There are many trends that will emerge in the R&D project management community over the next several years. The following describe trends identified that will impact organizations globally in the near future and will continue for many years to come.

Blending project management methodologies into other traditional management areas will become more pervasive as companies realize the importance of managing at every level of the company's organization. Project management will become a requirement for managers on a day-to-day basis, with leaders emerging as heads of project based organizations much like CFOs or CEOs. The Chief Project Officer would define policies at a company level that would trickle down at every level.

Certifications will continue to play an important role in the R&D organization in the future. More specialized levels of certifications will emerge that will be based on demonstrated expertise within a defined area combined with common project management practices.

Subject matter experts will emerge as project managers no longer honing their skills in private but continuing to innovate while leading and inspiring teams to deliver the next best technologically based products.

Virtual teams will play an increasing role in the R&D organization. As companies seek to leverage skills sets from globally based teams, organizations will rely more and more on those team members to play pivotal roles in the successes of projects regardless of geographic locations.

Portfolio level management will continue to play a key role in linking corporate objectives project implementation. By grouping products and projects together based on characteristics that align to corporate goals, companies will continue to redefine the way we make decisions that start at the project level and determine the futures of our companies and customers alike.

Empowering teams to make strategic decisions will become increasing more popular. Teams that are rich in expertise and experience will emerge as driving forces for project success models. By choosing the right people with the right knowledge and the right experience and coupling them with the right leadership, organizations will continue to thrive and grow as powerhouses of process and innovation.

Impact of diverse workforce on project management

Today's work environment has evolved into a melting pot of teams that not only consist of many levels of skill sets but also include team members from many disciplines across business divisions, companies, and countries. With increasing inclusion of third parties in the product development cycles, project managers are now faced with leading teams that span the globe. The virtual team is fast becoming the norm. Improvements in collaborative tools now allow us to communicate and share virtually in a way that has long been a laboriously manual process. Partner participation in these teams creates a new set of standards that must now be incorporated into team meetings. For example, when working with internal teams, we often find ourselves using product code names and acronyms that are synonymous with company policy. However, when including third parties and partner companies in meetings, care must be taken to either explain or avoid using such terminology. The same can be true within cross-divisional teams. Many terms and acronyms are used only with certain company segments or business units. When working at the portfolio level, teams often include members from other divisions. This too can cause communication barriers within the team. Project managers must now lead these teams in such a way that allows for productive communication without resulting in confusion or too much sensitive information flowing to the wrong team members. If not managed correctly, these barriers could lead to team division and miscommunication.

Co-development of products is also increasing. As companies seek to reduce costs, they will often negotiate with partners to co-develop and sell products. In some cases products will even exhibit dual branding emphasizing the partnership between two companies. One or both companies could then sell and profit from the products sales. By engaging in such endeavors, teams are now being comprised of internal and external team members. Care must be taken to carefully understand the limits of the working agreements that are in place, and project managers must ensure that team members remain within those guidelines at all times.

Language can also play a key role in virtual teams. Team members rely heavily on conference calls and e-mails to conduct day-to-day business, and effective communication can go a long way in the success of the project. Maintaining a consistent form of communication void of local lingo and company jargon can help build team participation and inclusion. Managing such a workforce diaspora can be critical to achieving useful goals. As virtual technology continues to improve, companies will continue to utilize resources around the globe and project managers will become the glue that keeps successful teams moving forward regardless of location, language, or culture.

As leaders, project managers also seek to minimize distractions and to redirect actions of those who tend to limit positive progression of our projects. By doing so we often find ourselves dealing with small cells of people deemed troublemakers or "organizational cockroaches," workgroups that seek to destroy organizational harmony. They tend to exist in perpetuity, accomplishing nothing of consequence, and yet continue to exist no matter how many times you try to kill them. These cells could consist of long-time employees who want to do things the old way or team members who have no vested interest in the outcome of the project. Unlike ants who always work as a team, cockroaches feed on destruction and lack any sense of unity, and instead are willing to relish the death of one of its own in order to gain more for themselves. The cockroach mentality can be detrimental to a team, and the responsibility lies on the project manager to minimize the intrusions by those who have little regard for team unity. Future project managers will have increasing power to select teams based on criteria driven by project needs and less on the sheer availability of resources. Key to this will be the ability of the project manager to assess individuals and build teams that are not only staffed for technical skills but also for team cohesiveness.

Our relevance as project managers lies in our ability to drive our teams to success, avoiding the mundane and providing inspiration to those who seek to follow in our footsteps. We can no longer rely only on "the process" to guide our successes. We must be proficient in building teams, leading teams, fostering communications globally, and inspiring those around us to become passionate about the work we do. We must pursue excellence in all aspects of our careers and incorporate lessons learned into our working mentality for the future. If we strive to empower the right people with the right knowledge to drive the right projects, we can ensure ourselves that we can effectively govern our paths for success in an ever changing world.

Chapter summary and conclusion

The role of the future R&D project manager will evolve into one that not only encompasses the ideologies of the past but will incorporate strategy, innovation, passion, and leadership as integral parts of the day-to-day activities of the project team. Project managers will have vision into corporate strategy and be empowered to make decisions that will move teams toward aligning project goals to global corporate initiatives. Project teams will consist of not only those who dwell within our close knit silos but also those who emerge as valued contributors regardless of geographic location. Project teams will take advantage of familiar tools and transform them into useful mechanisms for specialized projects. The portfolio level will become the view from which project managers will make project decisions, and the impact of project success will be felt at higher levels than ever before. We will seek subject matter expertise while holding on to our fundamental process knowledge, and will transform the organizations that we serve into ones that incorporate the principles of project management in all aspects of the R&D community.

Bibliography

Arbinger Institute (2000). *Leadership and self deception*. San Francisco, CA: Berrett-Koehler

Archibald, Russell D. *Major project management trends in the next five years*. PM Forum. org.

Cabanis-Brewin, Jeanette (2009). *Project portfolio management is your friend*. The Developer.com

Center for Business Practices (2003). *Project portfolio management: A benchmark of current business practices*. Glenn Hills, PA. Center for Business Practices.

ESI International (2009). *Top 10 project management trends in 2009*. Press Release, ESI International

Rees, Fran (2001). *How to lead work teams*. San Francisco, CA: Jossey-Bass/Pfeiffer

CHAPTER 16

Connecting and Networking Circa 2025: The Role of Professional Associations

Hugh Woodward

Introduction

Project management professional associations have been growing exponentially, along with the profession, since the early 1990s. When I joined the Project Management Institute in 1992, it boasted less than 9,000 members. By the end of 2007, membership had swelled to over 250,000 (Project Management Institute, 2008b). Other associations experienced similar, although less dramatic growth.

Similar growth has occurred in certification. PMI's Project Management Professional (PMP)® designation had been awarded to just 800 project managers at the beginning of 1992. At the end of 2007, total active PMP® credential holders exceeded 267,000. (Project Management Institute, 2008b).

The services offered by these associations have expanded with their membership. PMI was conducting an annual conference, which it called Seminars/Symposium, in 1992. The international project management association (IPMA) hosted a similar conference once every two years. PMI published a magazine, *PM Network*®, and a quarterly journal. The standard known today as *A Guide to the Project Management Body of Knowledge (PMBOK® Guide)* was published in a 3-ring binder. Chapters had emerged in several cities, mostly in North America, and were beginning to host events for their membership. The best arranged perhaps eight dinner meetings per year, and some form of training for the PMP certification exam.

By 2007, the opportunities to connect and network with other project managers had ballooned to a plethora of choices, available almost any day of the year. PMI was hosting four annual conferences, now called global congresses, and a bi-annual conference focused on research into project management. IPMA's World Congress was an annual event. And dozens of other associations were also hosting annual conferences, as were many PMI chapters and specific interest groups. PMForum's calendar of events for

2008 listed no less than eight conferences in June alone: in the United Kingdom, United States, France, Turkey, and Canada (PMForum, 2008). The topics were equally diverse: Women in Project Management, Earned Value, Strategy and Project, and Innovation in Architecture, Engineering and Construction. And these association-sponsored conferences were just part of a bigger picture, which included events conducted by for-profit companies, in-house conferences for employees of large corporations, and virtual events conducted via the Internet.

And so what can we expect in the next 20 years? Will the project management associations continue to see double-digit growth in membership, attendance, and certification? Will the professional associations of 2025 be just bigger and busier versions of what we see today? Or are there fundamental trends that are likely to affect the way project managers think about membership in professional associations, and what they expect their associations to provide.

We will seek to answer these questions by examining the reasons people join, and leave, associations, and by looking at the trends that affect association membership, especially trends driven by fundamental changes in the economic and social environment. But first, we will need to look at the landscape today (in 2008).

Project Management Associations in 2008

The Project Management Institute (PMI) is currently the world's largest project management association, by far, with over 250,000 members. PMI was conceived in January 1968, while Ned Engman and Jim Snyder waited out a snowstorm at the Three Threes Restaurant in Philadelphia, but formally established October 9, 1969, at the American Hotel in Atlanta, Georgia, during a two-day seminar entitled Advanced Project Management Concepts conducted by the Department of Continuing Education of the Georgia Institute of Technology (Wideman, 2001). PMI initiated its PMP certification program in 1984, which after a decade of slow but steady growth suddenly accelerated in the early 1990s and boasted 267,000 active certificants by the end of 2007. PMI subsequently added two additional certifications: Certified Associate in Project Management (CAPM)® and Program Management Professional (PgMP)®.

The first international association of project managers was not PMI, but the International Project Management Association (IPMA), formerly called INTERNET, which was founded in 1965 (International Project Management Association, 2008a). IPMA held its first conference in 1967 in Vienna, Austria, with an attendance of 400. Unlike PMI, IPMA is really a network of 45 national project management associations, with a combined membership of over 60,000. IPMA member associations offer a four-level certification program:

- Certified Projects Director
- Certified Senior Project Manager
- Certified Project Manager
- Certified Project Manager Associate

IPMA's certification is based on the IPMA Competence Baseline, an assessment of the competencies required at each level (International Project Management Association, 2008b).

The largest of IPMA's member associations is the United Kingdom's Association of Project Management (APM) with over 16,500 individual and 450 corporate members

(Association for Project Management, 2008a). APM was formed in 1972 as an IPMA (then INTERNET) association and initially named INTERNET UK. APM also publishes a compilation of the theory and practice of project management, the APM Body of Knowledge. The fifth edition was published in 2006. APM operates locally through "branches" located throughout the UK and Hong Kong.

The other 44 member associations are similar, although smaller and performing at various levels of maturity. The Russian project management association, SOVNET, for example, was founded in 1990 and officially registered as an IPMA member association in February, 1991 (Voropaev & Voropaeva-Cates, 2007). Although SOVNET has only 600 members, it has published a national competency baseline and offers the full IPMA four-level certification program, with now more than 700 certificants. SOVNET organizes a national conference approximately once every two years, and hosted the IPMA World Congress in 2003 with over 350 delegates from 40 countries.

In addition to PMI and IPMA, there are other unaffiliated associations, most notably in Japan and Australia. The Project Management Association of Japan (PMAJ) was formed in 2005 by the merger of the Project Management Professionals Certification Center (PMCC) and the Japan Project Management Forum (JPMF) (Project Management Association of Japan, 2008). JPMF was founded in 1998 as a division of the Engineering Advancement Association of Japan (ENAA) to promote project management in Japan. Like many other project management associations, PMAJ publishes a standard, Project and Program Management for Enterprise Innovation (P2M), maintains a certification program, and conducts regular conferences and educational events.

The Australian Institute of Project Management (AIPM) was formed in 1976 as the Project Managers' Forum and similarly maintains a set of standards: the National Competency Standards for Project Management, and a related certification program: RegPM (Australian Institute of Project Management, 2008a). AIPM also operates locally through chapters in each Australian state and territory, and conducts an annual conference, regularly drawing over 450 delegates.

The development of project standards and certification programs, and even awards programs, has largely followed the growth and proliferation of project management associations, but two additional trends are worth considering as likely to influence the evolution of project management associations.

The first is accreditation. PMI recognized the importance of accreditation as early as 1982 in a landmark report entitled "Education, Standards and Accreditation", and established its first accreditation program in 1985. The program languished for many years, however, with just two accredited institutions: the University of Quebec and Western Carolina University. Finally, a revised and more robust program, the PMI Global Accreditation Center for Project Management, was established in 2001, and by mid 2008, 18 institutions had achieved accreditation for one or more degree programs, with 13 others in various stages of the application process.

No other major project management association has an accreditation program, but some IPMA member associations, notably APM, are exploring the concept and one has initiated a fledgling program. SOVNET operates a program for Russian educational institutions and certification centers. Three organizations, State Academy of Specialists in the Investment Sphere (GASIS), Tekora, and IT Academy had achieved accreditation by April 2007, with others in the application process (Voropaev & Voropaeva-Cates, 2007).

The second of these two recent but important trends is advocacy. National association project management associations have long recognized the importance of establishing a strong relationship with their national government. The IPMA structure evolved in part to facilitate such relationships, and they are actively pursued by many of its member associations. APM, for example, maintains a formal relationship with the UK Office of Government Commerce (Association for Project Management, 2008b). It was the primary driver of a failed attempt to establish a legally recognized national association of PMI chapters in Canada in the 1990s and clearly one of the strengths of the IPMA system.

Project Management South Africa (PMSA) cites the need "for a national body to work with … the South African government in developing effective project management within South Africa" as a reason for its establishment independent of PMI in 1997 (Project Management South Africa, 2008). And PMSA has since been involved in a number of initiatives, including:

- Formation of a project management standards-generating body;
- Contribution to and communication of the local project management standards and national qualifications;
- Contribution to the development of the Construction Professions Act;
- Liaison and observer status on the Project Management Chamber in the Services Sector Education and Training Authority (South Africa); and
- Discussions on the establishment of an education and training quality assurance body for project management under the Services Sector Education and Training Authority (South Africa).

AIPM likewise has a strong relationship with the Australian government, having partnered with the Australia National Training Authority (now part of the Department of Education, Science and Training) to develop National Competency Standards for Project Management (NCSPM) (Australian Institute of Project Management, 2008b). AIPM's RegPM qualification is aligned with the NCSPM.

PMI did not view advocacy as important until around 2002. As an individual-member organization, PMI traditionally focused on its relationship with individual members and with meeting their needs. A "corporate member" program established in 1994 was little more than a group billing arrangement that introduced an array of administrative problems and was abandoned a few years later. However, in the early 2000s, as the PMI Board of Directors was grappling with its strategic plan, it began to realize the real customers of its work were in fact the companies that employed its members. In short, PMI could train, certify, and develop its members, but it was all of no value unless the employers of those members were able to recognize and convert their new skills to profitable use. Thus was born PMI's envisioned goal: "Worldwide, organizations will embrace, value and utilize project management and attribute their success to it." An extensive advocacy program soon followed, which PMI describes as:

> "PMI empowers its members by providing them with the credentials, knowledge and skills they need to succeed. These practitioners in turn become catalysts for organizational transformation; generating business results through effective project management.
>
> In addition to supporting the professional development of project managers, PMI educates those outside the profession about how project management creates success." (Project Management Institute, 2008a).

With this background, it is time to turn our attention to the future. What will the project management associations look like in 2025?

The Changing Way We Live

In his book *Microtrends*, Mark Penn (2007) cites a prediction by U.S. President Lyndon Johnson that 95% of Americans would live in cities, and then adds: "This just proves how hard it is to make assumption about what America will look like fifty years from now – while you're focused on a few big trends, other microtrends seep in and upset your expectations." He could easily have made the same comment about predicting the state of project management associations 20 years from now.

The simple approach is merely to extrapolate. PMI will continue to grow by 30% a year, as will the number of PMP and PgMP credential holders. But this was the mistake made by President Johnson, and more famously by the 18th-century British economist, Thomas Robert Malthus (Naik, Fuhrmans, Karp, Millman, Fassihi, & Slater, 2003). In 1798, Malthus predicted widespread famine due to two observed and intersecting trends: population tends to grow exponentially while food supply grows only arithmetically. Of course, his prediction was soon proven wrong, interrupted by two factors he failed to recognize: the industrial revolution and the impact of technology on agricultural yields.

It is impossible to predict discontinuities with any degree of certainty, of course. Who could have predicted the opening of the Berlin Wall on 9 November 1989 or Al-Qaida's attack on the World Trade Center on 11 September 2001? Yet, both had a profound impact on the way we work and connect with each other, as did a host of other events largely unforeseen but now recognized as earth-shattering: the invention of the telephone, the Japanese attack on Pearl Harbor, the launch of Sputnik, the invention of the microprocessor, and the economic rise of China, to name a few.

However, there also underlying, irreversible shifts that affect our lives and the way we work, and those we can analyze. Consider, for example, population and demographics.

The current population data is surprising, given the 20th century predictions of an explosively overpopulated world gripped by Malthusian famine (Naik, et al., 2003). The world's population is still growing, but the rate of growth is slowing. Birth rates are down, not just in North America and Western Europe, but throughout the world. The United Nations Population Division is now predicting that the world's population will level off at about 9 billion by mid-century.

More importantly, population growth varies considerably between regions of the world. Generally, only the Middle East and Africa is now sustaining a population growth of over 2% (United Nations, Department of Economic and Social Affairs, Population Division, 2007). Much of Eastern Europe is facing declining population, as is Japan, while the United States, Canada, Australia, and Western Europe are maintaining a growing population only through high levels of immigration. The immigrant population of the United States, for example, is 13%, while that of Germany, France and the United Kingdom is 12, 10 and 9%, respectively. Almost 20% of Australia's 21.3 million inhabitants are immigrants.

The net effect of these population trends, in the context of this chapter, is that the workforce is undergoing significant change. While the traditional industrial economies of North America and Europe are dealing with a declining and aging workforce, millions in Asia, and now the Middle East and Africa, are looking for opportunity. The unemployment rate in North America and Europe inevitably rises and falls with normal business cycles, but the unmistakable long-term trend is that the countries of these regions are not growing their workforce fast enough to sustain their standard of living. The situation is even worse if we consider the people with advanced technical skills necessary to drive an economy based on technology. Thomas Friedman (2005), in his book *The World is Flat*, points out that the scientists and engineers who were motivated to go into science by the threat of Sputnik in 1957 and the inspiration of U.S. President John F. Kennedy in 1961 are reaching their retirement years. Half of America's scientists and engineers are aged 40 years or older, and the average age is steadily rising.

Fortunately, the technological advancements of the past few decades have opened a vast new source of labor: the rest of the world.

The technology that allows a call center employee in Bangalore to fix a problem on my personal computer in Cincinnati, or even in a hotel in Warsaw, is the result of a myriad developments, but two in particular stand out: the invention of the Web browser in 1993, and the construction of a global network of fiber optic cable in the late 1990s.

The Web browser was a by-product of a National Science Foundation (NSF) project to build software that would enable scientists to use supercomputers that were in remote locations, and to connect to them by the NSF network. While engaged in this effort, Marc Andreessen, and a team of computer scientists at the National Center for Supercomputing Applications based at the University of Illinois, developed a software tool to allow researchers to "browse" each other's research. Andreessen quickly realized the potential of the browser, and partnered with Jim Clark, the founder of Silicon Graphics, to commercialize the application. They established Mosaic Communications in mid-1994, and by December, the company, renamed Netscape, released its first commercial browser.

Although the first commercial installation of a fiber-optic system was in 1977, the boom was triggered by the dot-com bubble and the Telecommunications Act of 1996. The Act, which deregulated telephone service in the United States, enabled new telephone companies to come online and compete with the giants: AT&T and the Baby Bells, and coincidentally to build infrastructure. By chance, this was the period the Internet boom was doubling the demand for bandwidth every three months and the stock market boom was generating virtually free capital. The result was a building frenzy. Almost $1 trillion was invested in just five years through Global Crossing and other infrastructure companies. But it stopped as suddenly as it started. Global Crossing, which had been founded in 1997, filed for bankruptcy in January, 2002 with $12.4 billion in debt.

The result, however, was a global highway that allowed the creation of a seamless global commercial network and an inexpensive way to move digitized information around the world. The cost of a long-distance telephone call dropped to a fraction of what it had been in the 1990s. Data transmission was virtually free.

I often reflect that when my mother emigrated from Scotland to Australia in 1922, her cousins stood on the dock in Edinburgh and cried because they knew they would never see her again, and likely would never again hear her voice. But just 78 years later, in 2000, I was able to stand beside the tiny cottage on the bank of the Firth of Forth, where she was born, and call her at her home in Tasmania, literally on the other side of the world. The telephone connection was as clear as if she had been in the next room, but cost less than a dollar. If she had had camera-enabled phone (80-year-olds do not tend to be early adopters of new technology), I could have sent her a photograph, instantly, for a grand total of 15 cents.

These recent technological advancements clearly help families stay connected, but they have an even more profound effect on business, changing not only the way businesses connect, but the way they work.

The Changing Way We Work

One of the most obvious changes is globalization: the increasing irrelevance of geography and national boundaries. Companies based in North America and Europe are not only offshoring because they can, but because they must. There are simply not enough qualified workers in their home countries to sustain their business competitively.

Thomas Friedman (2005) describes the phenomenon as the "triple convergence": new players, on new playing fields, developing new processes and habits for horizontal collaboration. He points out that "the creation of a global, Web-enabled playing field is allowing for multiple forms of collaboration – the sharing of knowledge and work – in real time, without regard to geography, distance, or…even language." Further, "the emergence of a large cadre of managers, innovators, business consultants, business schools, designers, IT specialists, CEOs and workers" are getting comfortable with, and developing, the sorts of horizontal collaboration and value-creation processes and habits that take advantage of this new, flatter playing field. And simultaneously, 3 billion people entered the playing field: the peoples of China, India, Russia, Eastern Europe, Latin America and Central Asia, without having to leave home to do it."

This same "triple convergence" is also eating away at another time-honored tradition: job security. It is not just the availability of cheaper labor elsewhere that is driving this change. It also relates back to demographics and technological advancement. As the technology changes, the work people do changes too. And specialized firms find ways to perform whole business functions much more efficiently than they can be done in-house at large corporations. And so while whole departments are disappearing, new ones are being created just as quickly, but someplace else. Sometimes the functions are transferred to other companies, and often to other parts of the world.

The Procter & Gamble Company once handled accounts payable at hundreds of individual sites around the world, essentially anywhere purchases could originate. Today, accounts payable has been consolidated into just three sites: San Jose, Costa Rica: Newcastle, U.K.; and Manila, Philippines. At the same time, they outsourced most IT functions to Hewlett Packard and some employee services to IBM. Jones Lang LaSalle manages the facilities of some of the world's largest corporations 20% cheaper they can do it themselves. Toshiba outsources to UPS not just the shipping of computers from customers to repair centers and back, but the repair itself. Virtual assistants, working half a world away, can answer the phone, schedule appointments, and even assemble a PowerPoint presentation, all while we sleep.

In this rapidly changing environment, companies like General Motors and Procter & Gamble that used to offer, and even encourage, lifetime employment can no longer afford to do so. To compete, they must be ready to outsource, offshore, reinvent their supply chain, close or sell a business, or acquire a new one, at short notice. It is not that jobs are going away. They are just changing. And workers must be ready to adapt too. This is why many human resource experts are predicting today's college graduates will switch jobs as often as once every five years. Knowledge workers, including project managers, will find themselves constantly seeking and preparing for their next job.

Finding a new job necessitates having verifiable qualifications, not just academic, but the proven ability to deliver results, perhaps in roles unconceived just a few years ago. And increasingly, those qualifications must be globally portable. It is those 3 billion new players that are causing the challenge. Suddenly, I am no longer competing with my fellow graduates from Lehigh University, or even MIT and Caltech. I am competing with graduates of Moscow State University, and the Indian Institute of Technology Delhi, and the Huazhong University of Science and Technology. An MBA from a prestigious U.S. university will no longer guarantee a six-figure salary. I must be able to prove I can enhance the profitability of the company I am seeking to join.

The same technologies that enable offshoring also allow nontraditional workplace accommodations, particularly working from home. According the U.S. Census Bureau (2004), 4.2 million Americans worked in a home office in 2000, a 23% increase from 1990 and almost a 100% increase from 1980. An additional 20 million reported working from home "sometimes." Incredibly, stay-at-home workers work longer hours, putting in an average 44.6 hours per week, compared to just 42.2 hours contributed by full-time on-site workers. They gain these additional hours by not having to commute, of course, but there is also an element of guilt or fear about not being instantly available. Although I thought nothing of leaving my on-site office for an hour or more for lunch, when I first started working from home I rarely left my "office" for more than a few minutes lest I missed a call from my boss or a customer.

Working from home is made possible by laptops, high-speed Internet access, Blackberries, cell phones, and videophones, but it is motivated by the high cost of commuting, both from the suburbs to the city, and from suburb to suburb. Its incidence, therefore, is only likely to accelerate as average commuting time increases and the cost of fuel rises. It is especially attractive to single parents, dual-career couples with young children or aging parents, and people who routinely connect with colleagues in other parts of the world, therefore needing to work late in the evening or during the night. As demographic trends drive the competition for workers with advanced technical skills upward, companies will be forced to offer more and more flexibility in accommodating these needs.

Demographic trends and technological advancements will continue to affect the way we work, and even the very nature of work itself, increasing the pressure on both companies and employees to "perform," disrupting the time-honored relationship between employers and employees, all but eliminating the traditional limitations of geography, and transforming the way we look at qualifications. Importantly, they are also irreversible. We will never return to the way we worked in, say, 1995, because nobody can uninvent the Internet. There will certainly be new inventions that cause new discontinuities. And there will inevitably be political events, or natural or manmade disasters, that cause regional or even global perturbations, but for the most part, the "good old days" are just that: the "good old days."

Changes in the way we work inevitably causes changes in the way we connect, and that in turn shapes the way we associate, or at least want to associate, with colleagues. The dramatic changes caused by demographics and technological advancement are, therefore, sure to be reflected in changes of a similar magnitude in what people expect of their associations. And so we can now draw some well-reasoned conclusions about what project managers will expect, indeed demand, of their associations in 2025?

The Changing Way We Connect

First, and perhaps foremost, they will expect community. Human beings have had an innate need to be part of a community since the dawn of time. It has been shown to be one of the reasons people join gangs (National Crime Prevention Council, 2008), as well as a motivation to join clubs and organizations with positive purpose. It is also a need that is not fading with the changing way we work. If anything, many workplace trends are increasing the need for professional associations that can provide an enduring sense of community. Corporations once met that need. When lifetime employment was a reality, workers could proudly identify with the company throughout their careers and well into retirement. My father still proudly displays a set of coasters bearing the logo of the insurance company from which he retired more than 20 years ago, even though the company no longer exists. But in an age where workers switch jobs every two to four years, or find themselves with new employers through acquisitions or divestitures, corporations no longer provide an enduring sense of community.

Stay-at-home workers especially need a way to build community with people doing similar work, or in the same profession. As Mark Penn (2007) poignantly states in *Microtrends*, they need a "virtual water cooler that keeps people connected to their colleagues – not just an insta-message kind of way, but in a collaborative, shared-space, easy-collegiality kind of way." It is the same need that has caused to people to congregate for centuries, around the campfire, in the town square, in the pub, or around the water cooler.

More and more, this implies local communities, the kind where people can congregate frequently without having to travel long distances. Company-sponsored travel to conferences and training events is likely to be increasingly restricted as rising energy costs and security concerns drive the cost of travel skyward. There have been energy crises in the past, of course, most notably in the 1970s and 1980s, but they were soon forgotten and travel recovered. But in 2001 and since, companies have increasingly responded to each successive crisis by accelerating the adoption of virtual meeting technology, technology that simply did not exist in the 1980s. And, so even if energy prices were to decline to, say, 1995 levels (a very unlikely scenario); it will still be easier and cheaper to stay home and conduct a virtual meeting. I noticed the early signs of this inclination very soon after the terrorist attacks of 11 September 2001. Before then, sales people wanting to see me would invariably suggest a date when they were to be in the area, or if I appeared to be especially interested, would offer to make a special trip to my office in Cincinnati. After 11 September 2001, they simply sent me a WebEx link.

Project managers do not just want congregate, of course. They want to network. And by networking, they usually mean connecting in ways that will help them find their next job. As a PMI chapter president, I was amazed to see our membership growth accelerating in 1993 during an economic slowdown. Why were people joining an association and spending their money to attend chapter meetings when they had just lost their jobs? The answer, of course, lies in the question: They had just lost their jobs. This need is only likely to become more acute in the next 20 years. Project managers will expect their associations to be 21st-century job fairs. But just organizing traditional job fairs will not address the need. The World Wide Web has long since obsoleted their usefulness. Nor will providing bulletin boards to post resumes and job openings address the need. Today's young people are in a different world. As Andrea Coombes (2008) writes in the Wall Street Journal's Career Journal, job seekers "often go directly to companies' career sites, where smart employers offer search tools that let students plug in a few words so relevant job postings appear. College grads also tap social-networking sites such as Facebook and MySpace to find more information about specific companies." Similarly, project associations will need to find new ways to help members find meaningful employment, ways that are comfortable to the Gen Y generation (those born after 1980).

Project managers in 2005 will also be looking to their professional associations to provide verifiable credentials. Further, these credentials must verify the project manager's ability to perform and to produce results, not just demonstrate a knowledge of project management theory and practice. IPMA and AIPM address this by certifying "competency," specifically by using a combination of examination, interviews, and references to benchmark against competency standards. PMI has shied away from using the word "competency" because of legal liability in the United States, but nevertheless has gradually tightened its experience requirements and use of references to verify that the people it designates as PMP credential holders can actually manage projects. Employers will undoubtedly require even more rigorous testing in the future.

Associations are likely to be also under pressure to provide industry-specific credentials. PMI and other associations have long held that project management is a generic skill, applicable to projects in all industries. But employers are not buying it. They habitually demand experience in their specific industry. And so, predictably, the instances of project managers transferring seamlessly from one industry to another, say IT to construction, are rare, even 50 years after the invention of PERT/CPM (program evaluation review technique/critical path method). Employers will, therefore, undoubtedly want to verify that a job applicant is not just proficient in project management, but that the applicant is proficient at project management in their specific industry.

Accreditation will continue to be an important function of project management professional associations, although driven more by a demand from academic institutions than practitioners. In the same way that worldwide competition is forcing practitioners to prove their capability, it is forcing academic institutions to demonstrate their adherence to certain standards. A prospective client in the United States may be unimpressed when a project manager cites an engineering masters in project management degree from Shanghai Jiao Tong University, but would be reassured to know the program is accredited by PMI's Global Accreditation Center.

Finally, project managers will expect their associations to conduct advocacy, as most professional associations do currently to some extent. Project managers, like all other professionals, want their work and contribution to be valued, and advocacy is an important element in any comprehensive strategy to build a positive image. But unlike the advocacy generally practiced in the 1990s, the focus of advocacy in 2025 will be corporations, not national and local governments. As companies globalize, local standards and requirements inevitably diminish in relevance. Global companies simply avoid onerous requirements in one geographic region by moving the work elsewhere, just as they move manufacturing and business processing to cheaper locations. Thus, whether or not the United Kingdom or Russia, or even India, recognizes project management as a profession matters little. What does matter, however, is that IBM and BAE and Saudi Aramco understand what project managers can contribute, and pay accordingly.

Connecting and Networking in 2025

When I was asked to write this chapter, I wondered if all the associations that exist today would still be operating in 2025, or whether there would some consolidation. It was a return to a subject that occupied much of my attention during my two terms as PMI Chair in 2000 and 2001. Many countries, including the United States, have two competing project management associations, and sometimes many more, if we count the project management divisions of other scientific and industry associations. Some association leaders argue this is healthy; others that it is dysfunctional. But can it continue? More importantly, can the differing standards and certifications promulgated by these organizations survive in a global marketplace increasingly characterized by horizontal collaboration?

I still find that question as perplexing as I did in 2001. In a world increasingly characterized by globalization, the inherent value of national associations will diminish. On the other hand, the association that best provides community and networking at a local level will be the association of choice for project managers in that locality. This does necessarily imply a plethora of local associations. The same need can just as easily be met with a network of effective chapters and branches, a model already established by PMI, APM, and other large associations.

An easier-to-answer question is: What will the successful associations be doing in 2025? The answer to that is quite evident. They will be meeting the needs of their members and prospective members. They will be providing a sense of community, with an emphasis on enabling their members to congregate physically, even in a world characterized by frugal travel budgets. They will be providing opportunities to network, and facilitating the process of finding jobs in a world characterized by disdain for lifetime employment and traditional approaches to job seeking. They will be providing verifiable credentials, differentiated by industry. They will likewise be verifying the quality of academic programs, not necessarily through traditional accreditation programs, but certainly in ways that allow employers to judge that an individual's academic qualifications are adequate. And they will effectively advocate for project managers with every entity likely to impact their careers, but especially with large corporations and prospective employers.

The associations that are performing these tasks with excellence in 2025 will undoubtedly grow and prosper. The others will inevitably fade away.

References

Association for Project Management. (2008a). *Our mission.* Retrieved September 7, 2008, from APM web site: http://www.apm.org.uk/page.asp?categoryID=1

Association for Project Management. (2008b). *Alliances.* Retrieved September 7, 2008, from APM web site: http://www.apm.org.uk/Alliances.asp

Australian Institute of Project Management. (2008a). *Overview.* Retrieved September 7, 2008, from AIPM web site: http://www.aipm.com.au/html/about.cfm#overview

Australian Institute of Project Management. (2008b). *National competence standards for project management.* Retrieved September 7, 2008, from AIPM web site: http://www.aipm.com.au/html/ncspm.cfm

Coombes, A. (2003, January 24). *Graduates alter recruiters' jobs.* Retrieved September 7, 2008, from the Wall Street Journal web site: http://online.wsj.com/article_print/SB121192296359924017.html

Friedman, T. L. (2005). *The world is flat: A brief history of the twenty first century.* New York: Farrar, Straus and Giroux.

International Project Management Association. (2008a). *History.* Retrieved September 7, 2008, from IPMA web site: http://www.ipma.ch/about/Pages/History.aspx

International Project Management Association. (2008b). *ICB version 3.* Retrieved September 7, 2008, from IPMA web site: http://www.ipma.ch/certification/standards/Pages/ICBV3.aspx

Naik, G., Fuhrmans, V., Karp, J., Millman, J., Fassihi, F., & Slater, J. (2003, January 24). Global baby bust. *The Wall Street Journal,* pp. B1, B4.

National Crime Prevention Council. (2008). *Straight talk about youth gangs.* Retrieved September 7, 2008, from NCPC web site: http://www.ncpc.org/programs/teens-crime-and-the-community/publications-1/adult2-pdf

Penn, M. (2007). *Microtrends: The small forces behind tomorrow's big changes.* New York: Hachette Book Group USA.

PMForum. (2008). *Project management events calendar.* Retrieved June 24, 2008, from the pmforum.org web site: http://www.pmforum.org/events/index.htm

Project Management Association of Japan. (2008). *History.* Retrieved September 7, 2008, from PMAJ web site: http://www.pmaj.or.jp/ENG/index.htm

Project Management Institute. (2008a). *Advocating the profession.* Retrieved September 7, 2008, from PMI web site: http://www.pmi.org/AboutUs/Pages/Advocating_Profession.aspx

Project Management Institute. (2008b, February). PMI Fact File. *PMI Today,* 18 (1), p. 6.

Project Management South Africa. (2008). *Profile.* Retrieved September 7, 2008, from PMSA web site: http://www.pmisa.co.za/page.aspx?ID=15

U.S. Census Bureau. (2004*). Journey to work: 2000 (C2KBR-33).*

United Nations, Department of Economic and Social Affairs, Population Division (2007). *World population prospects: The 2006 revision, Highlights, Working paper no. ESA/P/WP.202.*

Voropaev, V. & Voropaeva-Cates, M. (2007). *Integration of Russia into the global project management community.* Retrieved September 7, 2008, from the pmforum.org web site: http://www.pmforum.org/library/second-edition/2007/PDFs/Voropajev_Cates-4-07.pdf

Wideman, M. (2001). *Project Management Institute in the beginning...* Retrieved September 7, 2008, from Max's Project Management Wisdom web site: http://www.maxwideman.com/papers/pmi/intro.htm

CHAPTER 17

Emotional and Social Intelligence Competencies of Effective Project Managers

Richard E. Boyatzis, Mary Fambrough, David Leonard, and Kenneth Rhee[1]

A t some point in their lives and organizations, everyone works in teams or small groups. In many work settings, these teams are formed around specific tasks and objectives defined as a project. The manager of these teams is the project manager. In this sense, project management is one of the elemental forms of management in our society, and will continue to be for a least the next 25-50 years.

While so much depends on the talent of these managers, relatively little formal research has been published on the competencies that distinguish effective project managers. Much of the competency research has been done by consultants and not been published. Most of the research has focused on tasks and role requirements or general style.

The concept of competency-based human resources has gone from a new technique to a common practice in the 36 years since David McClelland (1973) first proposed them as a critical differentiator of performance. Although some companies began using competencies in identifying outstanding performers and training in the 1970s, the practice spread in the 1980s and 1990s. Initial projects were driven by the desire to make better selection or promotion decisions, or to drive the design of training and development programs. Today, the use of some form of competency-based human resource management is typical in most large companies (Boyatzis, 2008).

A project manager is often in a "player-coach" role. That is, he or she has to mix the talent of the individual contributors working on the team while continuing to be an individual contributor. The competencies distinguishing outstanding individual con-

[1]Richard Boyatzis is Professor in the Departments of Organizational behavior, Psychology and Cognitive Science at Case Western Reserve University; Mary Fambrough is Professor in the California School of Professional Psychology; David Leonard is faculty in Duke Executive Education; and Kenneth Rhee is Associate professor at Northern Kentucky University.

tributors (e.g., scientists, trainers, salespersons, etc.) are somewhat different from those distinguishing outstanding managers and leaders. Except for sales managers or sports team coaches, the clash and conflicts of these two sets of competencies are more apparent in the role of project manager than any other.

This distinction is evident when looking at one of the underlying motives that drives effectiveness of sales or engineering, called Need for Achievement (McClelland, 1985). This unconscious motive helps people be effective individual contributors, but gets in the way when they reach middle-level or executive management when another motive, the Need for Power, becomes key to effectiveness performance (McClelland & Boyatzis, 1982). In the project manager role, a person must be doing both roles, and so must engage somewhat competing drives. This was further illustrated by Spreier, Fontaine, & Malloy, R. L. (2006) when they described how Need for Achievement can create a focus on the task or objectives and exclude awareness of the people who need to be led and motivated to do the complete work of the organizational unit. For project managers, the person must focus on tasks, objectives and deliverables, but he or she must also manage and inspire others to work toward their shared objectives.

The important role the project manager plays in successful projects has been known for a long time. Avots (1969) cited "the wrong man is chosen as project manager" and "management techniques are misused" as two of several reasons why project management fails. Along the same line, Wilemon and Cicero (1970) found that project managers' "abilities in managing the varied interrelationships in the project environment are thus critical to him in terms of his effectiveness as a manager" (p. 282). More recently, Gillard and Price (2005) summarized five clusters consisting of ten management competencies largely based upon Boyatzis' work on competencies (1982): goal and action management, leadership, human resources management, directing subordinates, and focus on others.

Interestingly, more often than not, the majority of literature on project management remains silent on the importance of leadership style and competencies of project managers on success of projects (Turner and Muller, 2005). However, several recent studies on project management (Anderson and Tucker, 1994; Berger, 1996; Jiang, Klein, and Chen, 2001) began to cite the importance of the human factor, such as project leadership and teamwork in the management of successful projects. Furthermore, Weber and Torti (2004) described the multiple roles played by the project manager including coach, entrepreneur, politician, friend, and marketer and the importance of skills pertaining to those roles in project manager's success. The increase in the use of projects in organizations these days raises the importance of the selection and development of effective project managers, and the current study tries to redress the deficiency.

What is a Competency?

A competency is defined as a capability or ability. It is a set of related but different sets of behavior organized around an underlying construct, which we call the "intent." The behaviors are alternate manifestations of the intent, as appropriate in various situations or times. For example, listening to someone and asking him or her questions involve several behaviors. A person can demonstrate these behaviors for multiple reasons or to various intended ends. A person can ask questions and listen to someone to ingratiate him or herself or to appear interested, thereby gaining standing in the other person's view. Or a person can ask questions and listen to someone because he or she is interested in understanding this other person, his or her priorities, or thoughts in a situation. The latter we would call a demonstration of *empathy*. The underlying intent is to understand the person. Meanwhile, the former underlying reason for the questions is to gain standing or impact in the person's view, elements of what we may call demonstration of *influence*. Similarly, the underlying intent of a more subtle competency like Emotional Self-Awareness is self-insight and self-understanding.

This construction of competencies as requiring both action (i.e., a set of alternate behaviors) and intent called for measurement methods that allowed for assessment of both the presence of the behavior and inference of the intent. The earliest competency studies were conducted in 1970 through 1974. They used tests to assess competencies. A major breakthrough occurred in 1974 with the development of the Behavioral Event Interview (Boyatzis, 1982). This was a modification of the critical incident interview (Flanagan, 1954). It was adapted using the inquiry sequence from the Thematic Apperception Test and the focus on specific events in one's life from the biodata method (Dailey, 1971). The Behavioral Event Interview, or Critical Incident Interview, allowed for inductive discovery of relevant competencies in a setting or job role. This appeared particularly relevant in the 1970s and 1980s when many jobs and organizations were being studied for the first time. It also appears useful when first conducting competency studies in a country or culture.

Later, as more and more studies were completed, patterns could be observed of competencies that repeatedly appeared to distinguish outstanding performers. This allowed for the development of generic competency models. These generic models provide the basis for developing "informant (i.e., others') assessment" of a person's competencies demonstrated through 360-degree assessments, assessment centers, or simulations. The latter two sources of information about a person's behavioral patterns required coding by reliable coders (Boyatzis, 1998).

The anchor for understanding which behavior and intent are relevant in a situation emerges from predicting effectiveness in that situation. The construction of the specific competency is a matter of relating different behaviors that are considered alternate manifestations of the same underlying construct. But they are organized primarily, or, more accurately, initially, by the similarity of the consequence of the use of these behaviors in social or work settings.

A theory of performance is the basis for the concept of competency. The theory used in this approach is a basic contingency theory adapted from Boyatzis (1982), as shown in Figure 1. Maximum performance is believed to occur when the person's capability or talent is consistent with the needs of the job demands and the organizational environment (Boyatzis, 1982). The person's talent is described by his or her values, vision, and personal philosophy; knowledge; competencies; life and career stage; interests; and style. Job demands can be described by the role responsibilities and tasks needed to be performed. Aspects of the organizational environment that are predicted to have important impact on the demonstration of competencies and/or the design of the jobs and roles include culture and climate; structure and systems; maturity of the industry and strategic positioning within it; and aspects of the economic, political, social, environmental, and religious milieu surrounding the organization.

Research published over the last 30 years or so shows us that outstanding leaders, managers, advanced professionals and people in key jobs, from sales to bank tellers, appear to require three clusters of competencies (i.e., behavioral habits) which can be

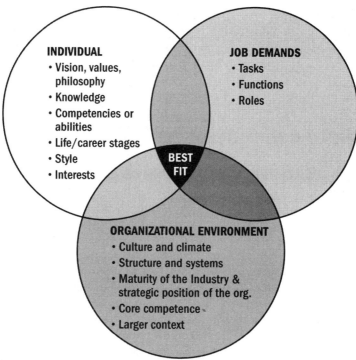

Figure 1.   Theory of Action and Job Performance: Best Fit (maximum performance, stimulation, and commitment) = Area of Maximum Overlap or Integration

thought of as *threshold* competencies and three clusters of competencies as *distinguishing outstanding performance.*[2] The threshold clusters of competencies include:

1) expertise and experience is a threshold level of competency;
2) knowledge (i.e., declarative, procedural, functional and metacognitive) is a threshold competency; and
3) an assortment of basic cognitive competencies, such as memory and deductive reasoning are threshold competencies.

There are three clusters of competencies differentiating outstanding from average performers in many countries of the world (Boyatzis, 1982; Boyatzis, 2006a; Bray, Campbell, & Grant, 1974; Campbell, Dunnette, Lawler, & Weick, 1970; Goleman, 1998; Goleman, Boyatzis, & McKee, 2002; Howard & Bray, 1988; Kotter, 1982; Luthans, Hodgetts, & Rosenkrantz, 1988; Thorton & Byham, 1982; Spencer & Spencer, 1993). They are:

1) Cognitive competencies, such as systems thinking and pattern recognition;
2) Emotional intelligence competencies, including self-awareness and self-management competencies, such as emotional self-awareness and emotional self-control; and

---

[2] A special issue of the *Journal of Management Development* was devoted to original studies of the link between competencies and performance in a variety of organizations in February, 2008.

3) Social intelligence competencies, including social awareness and relationship management competencies, such as empathy and teamwork.

Competencies are a behavioral approach to emotional, social, and cognitive intelligence.

Competencies and Intelligence as Behavioral Manifestations of Talent

While other interpretations of "intelligence" are offered in the literature, we believe that to be classified as "an intelligence," the concept should be:

1) Behaviorally observable;
2) Related to biological and in particular neural-endocrine functioning. That is, each cluster should be differentiated as to the type of neural circuitry and endocrine system involved;
3) Related to life and job outcomes;
4) Sufficiently different from other personality constructs that the concept adds value to understanding the human personality and behavior; and
5) The measures of the concept, as a psychological construct, should satisfy the basic criteria for a sound measure, that is, show convergent and discriminant validity (Campbell & Fiske, 1959).

An integrated concept of emotional, social, and cognitive intelligence competencies offers more than a convenient framework for describing human dispositions. It offers a theoretical structure for the organization of personality and linking it to a theory of action and job performance. Goleman (1998) defined an "emotional competence" as a "learned capability based on emotional intelligence which results in outstanding performance at work." In other words, if a competency is an "underlying characteristic of the person that leads to or causes effective or superior performance" (Boyatzis, 1982), then: (a) *an emotional, intelligence competency is an ability to recognize, understand, and use emotional information about oneself that leads to or causes effective or superior performance;* (b) *a social intelligence competency is the ability to recognize, understand, and use emotional information about others that leads to or causes effective or superior performance;* and (c) *a cognitive intelligence competency is an ability to think or analyze information and situations that leads to or causes effective or superior performance.*

If defined as a single construct, the tendency to believe that more effective people have the vital ingredients for success invites the attribution of a halo effect. For example, person A is effective, therefore she has all of the right stuff, such as brains, savvy, and style. Like the issue of finding the best "focal point" with which to look at a photograph, the dilemma of finding the best level of detail in defining constructs with which to build a personality theory may ultimately be an issue of which focal point is chosen. The separate competencies, like the clusters, are, we believe, the most helpful focal point for description and study of performance.

Several studies of competencies of people in project management roles have been done, but few have been published. In a study of project managers (called team leaders) of drug development teams in a major pharmaceutical company, Boyatzis, Esteves, and Spencer (1992) found that the effective drug development teams produced drugs with full FDA approval in almost half the time of most other teams that resulted in the companies almost doubling their time under patent protection—a huge impact on their bottom line. Those project managers showed significantly more (as compared to their less-effective counterparts): Emotional intelligence (EI) competencies of Achievement Orientation, Initiative, Flexibility, and Self-Confidence; social intelligence (SI) competencies of Empathy, Influence, Networking, and Team Leadership. They also showed significantly more cognitive competencies of Systems Thinking and Pattern Recognition. Comparable findings appeared in project managers of software development project managers in studies conducted for two technology companies (Boyatzis, 2008). This pattern of an assortment of EI, SI, and cognitive intelligence (CI) competencies being key to effectiveness was further validated in a study of leaders in an international consulting company (Boyatzis, 2006a). This was relevant because most of their work was delivered in client teams. In the study of the leaders of the consulting firm, it was further shown that tipping points could be identified as the frequency of use of the competency that "tipped" a person into outstanding and effective performance.

In a closely related study to this one, Dreyfus (2008) looked at the competencies differentiating the outstanding versus average performing middle-level managers in the same lab studied in this paper. These people were the managers of these project managers. She reported that outstanding managers of project managers showed significantly more (as compared to their less-effective counterparts): EI competencies of Initiative, Accurate Self Assessment, Self-confidence, and Flexibility; SI competencies of Developing Others and Team Leadership. This was a government-based research laboratory. Because all of these managers had PhDs and had come up the ranks of bench scientist to project manager to middle-level manager, they all topped the scales on the cognitive competencies. But again, we see an assortment of competencies being needed for effective performance from EI and SI clusters.

Design and Methods

A concurrent validation study was conducted on project managers in a major research and development (R&D) laboratory which is part of a U.S. government agency. The agency was asked to generate a list of all staff in project manager roles. It was determined that regardless of official title, the role reported to a middle-level manager. Those studied by Dreyfus (2008) had to manage projects directly connected to the scientific and/or engineering work of the lab. Administrative and support functions were excluded. They had to have managed at least one previous project and have been a project manager for at least two years (not necessarily continuously). The list contained 210 names.

To obtain a performance measure, nominations were used to determine effective performance (Boyatzis, 1982; Boyatzis, 2008; Luthans et al., 1988). Nominations have been shown to be more effective than ratings and a rigorous approach to assessing effectiveness (Lewin & Zwany, 1976). As the bosses of the project managers, the middle-level managers were sent and asked to complete nomination forms. The nomination form asked them, "On the lines below, please list the names of the project mangers, if any, at XYZ that you consider to be highly effective (e.g., superior or outstanding) in their role as project manager. PLEASE RETURN THIS FORM EVEN IF YOU CHOOSE TO LIST NO NAMES." The forms bore no identification as to whom they were from and were mailed back to the first author at Case Western Reserve University. The forms from the middle-level managers were on blue paper.

Each project manager was given a packet of similar nomination forms. One was on yellow paper for them to complete on their peers (and project managers could include themselves). Also in the packet were five green nominations forms to be given to various project team members. Each nomination form was accompanied by a self-addressed, stamped, return envelope to the first author.

31% of the peer nomination forms, 23% of the subordinate nomination forms, and 51 % of the boss nomination forms were returned. Nominations for each project manager were tallied. To be identified as a superior performer, a project manager had to receive at least one boss nomination, two peer nominations, and two subordinate nominations. This revealed 17 project managers as superior performers—8% of the eligible population. To identify the sample of average performers, a random sample of 17 project managers was selected from the list of project managers receiving no boss nominations, no peer nominations (not even their own), and no subordinate nominations.

Fourteen of the 17 superior performers agreed to participate in the study. Of the three who declined, one was retiring. The other two declined because of extensive travel schedules. Of the first 17 identified as average performers, one was dropped because he had only been a project manager for one year and eight others declined to participate due to busy travel schedules. More project managers were randomly selected from the sample who received no nominations from any source. To obtain a sample of 15 willing to participate, 11 more had to be solicited.

Of the 29 project managers (i.e., 15 average and 14 superior performers) who agreed to participate in the study, one was female. The rest were male. Only one was African American. Nationalities of those who participated included Asian, Central American, and Western European, as well as from the U.S. The two sub-samples were the same age (46 and 44 for average and superior performers, respectively). They had the same years of education (18 and 17), the same years of work experience (23 and 24), years employed by this organization (19 and 21), the same years in a project manager role (11 and 9) and the same salary pay level (GS 13 and 14). Statistical analysis with Mann Whitney U tests showed non-significance in each of these comparisons.

One of the superior performer's audiotapes failed, so information for the Critical Incident Interview coding was not available. Of the External Assessment Questionnaire (EAQ) data from others, Several bosses did not complete the EAQ resulting in a sub-sample of 13 average and 12 superior performers. Among the Peers, unless more than 2 completed the EAQ, the results were not used in the analysis. Insufficient Peers completed the EAQ, so one average and two superior performers were dropped from the analysis. For the same reasons, data from subordinates was reduced by four average and one superior performer.

To assess the competencies, a Critical Incident Interview, also called the Behavioral Event Interview, was used (Boyatzis, 1982; Flanagan, 1954; McClelland, 1998; Spencer & Spencer, 1993). In this interview, a person is asked, "Tell me about an event, recently, in which you felt effective as a manager." In a style similar to a journalistic interview, the interviewer lets the respondent tell the story with minimal probes. Along the way, the interviewer may ask: What led up to the situation? Who was involved? What did each person say or do? What were you thinking or feeling? What was the result or outcome of the event? Once an effective incident is elicited, then the interviewer asks the same question but about an ineffective event. There is an attempt to elicit two to three effective events and two to three ineffective events. The interview usually takes about an hour to an hour-and-a-half, and is audio-taped. The interviewers were blind to the performance group of the people they were interviewing. Names were given to the interviewers in alphabetical order.

The audiotapes were coded for known competencies: EI competencies, including Efficiency Orientation, Planning, Initiative, Self Control, Attention to Detail, Flexibility, and Self-Confidence; SI competencies, including as Empathy, Persuasiveness, Developing Others, Group Management, Networking, and Negotiating; and CI competencies, included Systems Thinking and Pattern Recognition. A competency score was calculated as the sum of the number of incidents in which any of the behavioral indicators of a competency were shown. Another score was computed as the diversity or complexity of the behavioral indicators shown across the incidents in a person's interview. While the former measure is interpreted as the strength of the competency (i.e., the likelihood a person will use it in various situations), the latter measure of complexity is interpreted as the breadth or variety of how a person may demonstrate or express a competency.

Inter-rater reliability among the three coders for each of these competencies were calculated on sub-samples. They ranged from .70 to .96, with a mean of .89. Interviews were also examined for other possible competencies using the method of thematic analysis (Boyatzis, 1998). All competencies discovered were minor variations of existing, generic ones. The data from the new variations were incorporated into the existing competencies. Coding was also done blind to the performance group of the project manager who was interviewed.

Since many of the generic competencies had been identified in other competency studies, a form of assessment was chosen to allow for easier data collection. The method used was a multi-source feedback assessment, often called a 360. The test used was called the Self-Assessment Questionnaire (SAQ) and the version for others to complete was the EAQ. The boss of each project manager in the study, as well as an assortment of their peers and subordinates, were asked to complete the EAQ on each project manager in the sample. It was developed by Boyatzis in 1990 for assessment in an MBA program and competency research projects based on the results of many competency studies, including Bray, Campbell, and Grant (1974), Boyatzis (1982), Kotter (1982), , Luthans et. al. (1988), Howard and Bray (1988), and Thorton and Byham (1982). The data reported in this study was collected in the 1990s. Studies using this test have been reported in Boyatzis, Cowen and Kolb (1995), Boyatzis, Leonard, Rhee & Wheeler (1996), Boyatzis, Stubbs, and Taylor (2002), Boyatzis and Saatcioglu (2008), and Williams (2008). A variation of the questionnaire was used in the studies reported in Boyatzis (2006a). It was also the basis for the Emotional and Social Competency Inventory (ESCI) developed by Boyatzis and Goleman (Boyatzis and Sala, 2004).

The EAQ and SAQ each had items divided into 16 competencies. They were: Emotional Intelligence competencies of Efficiency Orientation, Planning, Initiative, Attention to Detail, Self-Confidence, Self Control, and Flexibility; Social Intelligence competencies of Empathy, Persuasiveness, Networking, Negotiating, Group Management, Developing Others, and Oral Communications; and Cognitive Intelligence competencies of Systems Thinking and Pattern Recognition. Because each scale had a different number of items, the totals are not comparable across competencies, so average item scores were used. Cronbach alpha's showed appropriate reliability in previous studies (Boyatzis, et. al., 2002; Boyatzis and Saatcioglu, 2008; Boyatzis and Ratti, in press).

Given the literature on self versus other assessment of behavioral frequency (Taylor, 2006), it was decided to use only the average of the boss, peer, and subordinate assessments. Each of the assessments were computed as the sum of the item scores. The self-assessment was discarded from analysis.

Results

Analysis of the 360 results showed that bosses saw superior performers demonstrating significantly more Planning than average performers. In bosses' views, superior performers showed near significantly more Efficiency Orientation and Group Management, as shown in Table 1. Peers saw superior performers demonstrating more Efficiency Orientation, Planning, Attention to Detail, Empathy, Negotiating, Group Management, Developing Others, Systems Thinking, and Pattern Recognition than average performers. In peers' views, Superior showed more Persuasiveness at a near-significant level. Subordinates saw superior performers showing more Efficiency Orientation, Planning, Self-Control, Empathy, Persuasiveness, Group Management, and Systems Thinking than average performers. In subordinates' views, superior showed more Self-Confidence and Pattern Recognition at a near-significant level.

In the results from the coding of the Critical Incident Interview, superior performers showed significantly more Planning, Group Management, Developing Others, and Self-Confidence than average performers, as shown in Table 2. Superior performers showed near significantly more Empathy than average performers. The breadth of the competency indicators a person was using showed that superior performers showed significantly more breadth of Planning, Initiative, Self-Confidence, Persuasiveness, Group Management, Developing Others, and Pattern Recognition.

Discussion

To summarize the findings, superior performing project managers showed or used more of these competencies than their average-performer counterparts, as summarized in Table 3:

1) Emotional Intelligence Competencies: Planning, Self-Confidence, Efficiency Orientation, Attention to Detail, and Self-control;
2) Social Intelligence Competencies: Group Management, Empathy, Persuasiveness, Developing Others, and Negotiating; and
3) Cognitive Intelligence Competencies: Systems Thinking and Pattern Recognition.

The pattern found in the other studies reviewed of project managers and their bosses showed that an assortment of EI, SI, and CI competencies are needed to be an effective project manager.

One of the limitations of this study was the small sample size. Unfortunately, due to the small sample size, multivariate analysis such as multiple regression was not appropriate.

Another possible explanation might be that the 360 is more comprehensive than the critical incident interview. In other words, the 360 may have allowed people to articulate more behavior seen and therefore demonstrated by various managers. Because it is

Table 1. Others' Views of Competencies Demonstrated by Outstanding (n=12) versus Average Project Managers (n=13)

Competency	Mean Boss's Views n=13 n=12			Mean Peers' Views n=14 n=12			Mean Subordinates' Views n=11 n=13		
	Ave.	Superior	z¹	Ave.	Superior	z	Ave.	Superior	z
Efficiency Orientation	8.9	9.8	-1.5+	7.4	9.0	-1.9*	7.1	9.1	-2.22*
Planning	10.8	12.8	-1.9*	9.7	12.3	-2.1*	9.0	12.0	-3.02**
Initiative	5.9	5.9	-.03	5.0	5.8	-1.2	4.9	5.7	-1.2
Attention to Detail	4.3	5.0	-1.15	4.0	4.9	-2.0	4.5	4.3	-.18
Self-Confidence	3.8	4.0	-.4	3.8	4.2	-.86	3.4	4.3	-1.55+
Self Control	6.1	6.0	.00	5.4	6.0	-.86	5.2	6.1	-1.66*
Flexibility	4.2	4.9	-1.01	4.1	4.7	-1.01	4.0	4.2	-.20
Empathy	8.6	9.3	-1.0	8.5	9.8	-1.83*	8.1	9.4	-1.78*
Persuasiveness	10.2	10.4	-.4	10.0	11.3	-1.35+	8.8	11.3	-2.23**
Networking	6.5	5.4	-1.2	6.1	6.3	-.29	6.0	6.0	-.09
Negotiating	6.0	5.8	-.2	5.2	6.9	-2.55**	6.0	6.9	-.82
Group Management,	10.9	12.4	-1.43+	9.7	12.6	-3.11***	10.3	12.2	-1.60*
Developing Others	6.9	7.8	-.7	6.4	7.7	-1.83*	6.9	7.9	-1.05
Oral Communications	13.4	14.5	-.8	13.6	14.7	-.80	142	139	-.43
Systems Thinking	4.2	3.6	-.8	2.7	3.92	-2.55**	2.8	3.7	-1.86*
Pattern Recognition	6.3	5.9	-.4	5.7	7.5	-1.99*	5.7	6.6	-1.37+

³Mann Whitney U tests were performed due to the small sample size. Significance levels of one tailed tests are indicated by: + means near significant; * p<.05; ** p<.01; *** p<.001.

Table 2. Behavioral Demonstration of the Competencies in Work Samples from Critical Incident Interviews by Outstanding (n=13) versus Average Project Managers (n=15)

Competency	Average Performer	Superior Performer	z^2
Efficiency Orientation	2.47	2.62	-.19
	2.33	2.69	-.71
Planning	1.27	1.92	-1.63*
	1.53	2.77	-2.23**
Initiative	.87	1.15	-1.08
	.53	1.08	-1.65*
Attention to Detail	.40	.69	-.80
	.40	.62	-.77
Self-Confidence[3]	.20	.77	-2.96**
Self Control	.33	.31	-.52
	.27	.31	-.17
Flexibility	.20	.39	-.73
	.20	.39	-.73
Empathy	1.40	1.92	-1.54+
	1.80	2.23	-.86
Persuasiveness	2.80	2.77	-.31
	2.53	4.08	-2.16**
Networking	.73	.77	-.20
	.53	.77	-.89
Negotiating	.27	.54	-.47
	.33	.38	-.23
Group Management,	.27	.77	-1.99*
	.40	1.15	-1.98*
Developing Others	.40	1.00	-1.61*
	.40	1.08	-1.78*
Systems Thinking	.67	.92	-.79
	.53	.62	-.43
Pattern Recognition	1.73	1.77	-.34
	1.33	2.23	-2.11*

[For each competency, the first line of numbers are mean strength. The second line is complexity or breadth.]

[4]Mann Whitney U tests were performed due to the small sample size. Significance levels of one tailed tests are indicated by: + means near significant; * p< .05; ** p<.01; *** p<.001.

[5]Self-Confidence is not coded per incident but once for the entire interview. Therefore, the breadth code was inappropriate.

Table 3.   Summary of Competencies Distinguishing Outstanding from Average
Project Managers

Emotional Intelligence Competencies		
Planning	from all 3 sources	in Critical Incidents from work
Self-Confidence	from 1 source (subordinates)	in Critical Incidents from work
Efficiency Orientation	from all 3 sources	
Attention to Detail	from 1 source (peers)	
Self-control		from 1 source (subordinates)
Social Intelligence Competencies		
Group Management	from all 3 sources	in Critical Incidents from work
Empathy	from 2 sources (peers and subordinates)	in Critical Incidents from work
Persuasiveness	from 2 sources (peers and subordinates)	in Critical Incidents from work
Developing Others	from 1 source (peers)	in Critical Incidents from work
Negotiating	from 1 source (peers)	
Cognitive Intelligence Competencies		
Systems Thinking	from 2 sources (peers and subordinates)	
Pattern Recognition	from 2 sources (peers and subordinates)	in Critical Incidents from work

a recall of specific incidents at work, it is possible that the Critical Incident Interview (or Behavioral Event Interview) does not provide as comprehensive a sample of a person's behavior as the 360. By only sampling four-to-six incidents, some of the manager's behavior may not be involved in those incidents.

The Critical Incident Interview has been referred to as a more conservative assessment tool. If someone shows a competency in the interview, they are likely to have it as part of their repertoire. If a person does not show a competency in the critical incident interview, we cannot contend they do not have access to this competency, or that they use it less frequently and it did was not relevant in the particular incidents sampled (Boyatzis, Stubbs, & Taylor, 2002; Spencer & Spencer, 1993). Discriminant validity studies of each of these two forms of competency assessment will help to clarify the extent to which the 360 is more comprehensive or not.

Equally possible is that the 360 reminds informants of other behavior, and again, portrays a more comprehensive view of the manager's behavior. If this is a factor, then it may also arouse social desirability and result in an escalation of assessments. Construct validation studies on 360s and other forms of evident behavior evaluations, like coded critical incident interviews, will help to determine the degree to which this is a source of contamination of the results.

Concluding Thought

The typical pattern of promoting the best individual contributor to be the Project Manager, as a reward for a job well done, is condemning the organization to lackluster performance and dwindling innovation. As we understand and document the impact of competencies on effectiveness of Project Managers specifically, we move closer to being able to refine our research and conduct studies looking for precise causality. With such research results, we also equip ourselves to help identify potentially effective project managers for hiring or examining scientists and others for potential promotions to Project manager roles. Similarly, knowing the important competencies helps us to design development programs, developmental opportunities, and other activities that can help people develop and nurture the competencies to be outstanding Project Managers. These findings and future research on emotional and social intelligence competencies will help expand the effectiveness of getting the right people into Project Management jobs or developing people in the best way to be effective Project Managers

References

Anderson, S. D. & Tucker, R. L. (1994). Improving project management design. *Journal of Management in Engineering, 10*(4), 35-44.

Avots, I. (1969). Why does project management fail? *California Management Review, 12*(1), 66-72.

Berger, L. (1996). Emerging role of management in civil engineering. *Journal of Management in Engineering, 12*(4), 37-39.

Boyatzis, R.E. (1982). *The competent manager: A model for effective performance,* New York: John Wiley.

Boyatzis, R.E. (1998). *Transforming qualitative information: Thematic analysis and code development.* Thousand Oaks, CA: Sage.

Boyatzis, R. E. (2006a). Using tipping points of emotional intelligence and cognitive competencies to predict financial performance of leaders, *Psicothemia, 17,* 124-131.

Boyatzis, R.E. (2006b). Intentional change theory from a complexity perspective, *Journal of Management Development, 25*(7), 607-623.

Boyatzis, R.E. (2008). Competencies in the 21st century, a special issue of the *Journal of Management Development.*

Boyatzis, R.E., Cowen, S.S., & Kolb, D.A. (1995). *Innovation in professional education: Steps on a journey from teaching to learning.* San Francisco: Jossey-Bass.

Boyatzis, R.E., Esteves, M.B., & Spencer, L.M. (1992). Entrepreneurial innovation in pharmaceutical development. *Human Resource Planning, 15*(4). 15-30.

Boyatzis, R.E. & Ratti, F. (in press). Emotional, social and cognitive intelligence competencies distinguishing effective Italian managers and leaders in a private company and cooperatives. *Journal of Management Development*

Boyatzis, R.E., Leonard, D., Rhee, K., & Wheeler, J.V. (1996). Competencies can be developed, but not the way we thought, *Capability, 2*(2), 25-41.

Boyatzis, R.E., and Sala, F. (2004). Assessing emotional intelligence competencies. In Glenn Geher (ed.), *The measurement of emotional intelligence*, Hauppauge, NY: Novas Science Publishers, 147-180.

Boyatzis, R.E. & Saatcioglu (2008). A twenty year view of trying to develop emotional, social and cognitive intelligence competencies in graduate management education. *Journal of Management Development, 27*(1), 92-108.

Boyatzis, R.E., Stubbs, L., & Taylor, S. (2002). Learning cognitive and emotional intelligence competencies through graduate management education. *Academy of Management Journal on Learning and Education, 1*(2), 150-162.

Bray, D.W., Campbell, R.J., & Grant, D.L. (1974). *Formative years in business: A long term AT&T study of managerial lives.* NY: John Wiley & Sons.

Campbell, J.P., Dunnette, M.D., Lawler, E.E.III, & Weick, K.E.Jr. (1970), *Managerial behavior, performance, and effectiveness,* McGraw-Hill, New York.

Campbell, D.T., and Fiske, D.W. (1959). Convergent and discriminant validation by the multitrait- muiltimethod matrix. *Psychological Bulletin, 56,* 81-105.

Dailey, C.A. (1975), *Assessment of lives: Personality evaluation in a bureaucratic society,* San Francisco: Jossey-Bass.

Dreyfus, C. (2008). Identifying characteristics that predict effectiveness of R&D managers. *Journal of Management Development. 27*(1), 76-91.

Flanagan, J.C. (1954), The critical incident technique, *Psychological Bulletin, 51,* 327-335.

Gillard, S. & Price, J. (2005). The competencies of effective project managers: A conceptual analysis. *International Journal of Management, 22*(1), 48-53.

Goleman, D. (1995), *Emotional intelligence.* New York: Bantam Books.

Goleman, D. (1998), *Working with emotional intelligence.* New York: Bantam Books.

Goleman, D., Boyatzis, R.E., & McKee, A. (2002), *Primal leadership: Realizing the power of emotional intelligence.* Boston: Harvard Business School Press.

Howard, A., & Bray, D. (1988), *Managerial Lives in Transition: Advancing Age and Changing Time.,* New York: Guilford Press.

Jiang, J., Klein, G., & Chen, H. (2001). The relative influence of IS project implementation policies and project leadership on eventual outcomes. *Project Management Journal, 32*(3), 49-55.

Kotter, J.P. (1982), *The general managers.* NewYork: Free Press.

Lewin, A.Y. and Zwany, A. (1976). *Peer nominations: a model, literature critique and a paradigm for research.* Springfield, VA: National Technical Information Service.

Luthans, F., Hodgetts, R.M., & Rosenkrantz, S.A. (1988), *Real managers.* Cambridge, MA: Ballinger Press.

McClelland, D.C. (1973), Testing for competence rather than intelligence, *American Psychologist, 28*(1) 1-40.

McClelland, D.C. (1985), *Human motivation,* Glenview, IL: Scott, Foresman.

McClelland, D.C. (1998). Identifying competencies with behavioral event interviews. *Psychological Science, 9,* 331-339.

McClelland, D.C. & Boyatzis, R.E. (1982), "The leadership motive pattern and long term success in management", *Journal of Applied Psychology, 67*(6), 737-743.

Spencer, L.M. Jr. & Spencer, S.M. (1993). *Competence at work: Models for superior performance.* New York: John Wiley & Sons.

Spreier, S.W., Fontaine, M. H., & Malloy, R. L. (2006) Leadership Run Amok: The Destructive Potential of Overachievers. *Harvard Business Review,*

Taylor, S. (2006). Why the real self is fundamental to intentional change, *Journal of Management Development, 25*(7): 643-656.

Thornton, G.C. III & Byham, W.C. (1982), *Assessment centers and managerial performance,* New York: Academic Press.

Turner, J. & Muller, R. (2005). The project manager's leadership style as a success factor on projects: A literature review. *Project Management Journal, 36*(1), 49-61.

Weber, S. S. & Torti, M. T. (2004). Project managers doubling as client account executives. *Academy of Management Executive, 18*(1), 1-12.

Wilemon, D. L. & Cicero, J. P. (1970). The project manager-Anomalies and ambiguities. *Academy of Management Journal, 13*(3), 269-282.

Williams, H. (2008). Characteristics that distinguish outstanding urban principals. *Journal of Management Development. 27*:1, 36-54.

CHAPTER 18

The Likely Future of Project Management in the Construction Industry Circa 2025

Stephen R. Thomas, Ph.D., P.E.
Associate Director, Construction Industry Institute

Edward J. Jaselskis, Ph.D., P.E.
Professor, Iowa State University

Cory McDermott
Graduate Research Assistant
Iowa State University

Abstract

In order to prepare for the future, we need to identify and be acutely aware of emerging trends that will have a significant impact on both industry and project management. Such an effort will require the collective input of those with the most at stake: the major players in the industry, including owners, contractors, suppliers, governmental entities, academia, and others.

Although many groups within the various industry sectors have processes in place for strategic planning to prepare them for the operating environment of the future, the construction industry is fortunate to have an industry-driven process in place with the specific purpose of identifying trends likely to affect the industry. This process is a function of the Construction Industry Institute (CII) Strategic Planning Committee. CII, an organized research unit of the University of Texas at Austin, is often recognized as the principal construction industry forum for addressing current and future issues. This is because the members of CII represent the leading owners, contractors, suppliers, and academics that are actively funding, directing, and performing research to improve competitiveness and prepare the engineering and construction industry for the future.

CII has recently identified emerging and longer-term trends that are expected have major impacts on the future of the construction industry and these same trends are likely to impact other industry sectors as well. The institute continually examines each individual trend to identify potential research projects that when funded and executed will provide best practices to improve the likelihood of successful projects and improve industry performance. One of the recent research projects executed by the CII Global Project Controls and Management Systems research team reviewed current project management practices and in the process identified 13 drivers of the changing environment.

This chapter presents these drivers and emerging trends and suggests likely changes for project management as it adapts to the evolving environment.

Introduction

To understand the future of project management, it is useful to review its origins. Although the building of the Egyptian pyramids and the Panama Canal were engineering and construction projects requiring management, project management as a discipline first appeared in the 1950s. The impetus for its emergence is often attributed to large and complex projects that required more rigorous management tools for planning, scheduling, analysis, and control. The 1970s and the arrival of the computer signaled a new platform for the automation of these management tools. Government programs are often credited for developing project management's early concepts, and the construction industry has been recognized for its early adoption.

A look at the first textbooks on project management reveals chapters that address scheduling, budgeting, and resource allocation. One could also find Gantt charts and network diagrams such as the critical path method (CPM) that integrate with budgets to produce cost curves. Resource loading of activities enabled the creation of histograms, which led to leveling and constraining algorithms. Today's project management textbooks address behavioral management, information technology, risk management, decision analysis, and financial analysis. The project manager now is becoming a systems integrator, and virtually all industries have turned to project management as essential for survival in a rapidly changing and complex environment.

As a discipline, project management will continue to evolve. To better appreciate the direction and nature of this evolution, it is useful to examine the environment and trends, some already evident and some still emerging to drive further changes. Such an effort can best be accomplished with the collective input of those with the most at stake: the major players in the industry, including owners, contractors, suppliers, governmental entities, academia, and others.

Although many groups within the various industry sectors have processes in place for strategic planning for the operating environment of the future, the construction industry is fortunate to have a proactive, industry-driven process in place with the specific purpose of identifying trends likely to affect the industry. This process is a function of the Construction Industry Institute (CII), an organized research unit of the Cockrell School of Engineering at The University of Texas at Austin. CII is often recognized as a principal industry forum for addressing current and future issues. This is because the members of CII represent the leading owners, contractors, suppliers, and academics, participants who are actively funding, directing, and performing research to improve competitiveness and prepare the industry for the future.

The CII Strategic Planning Committee (SPC) monitors industry trends and business drivers for updates to the CII Strategic Plan. In addition, CII sponsors 16 to 20 research teams annually that operate throughout North America and that are chaired by industry and facilitated by academic researchers. The CII research teams investigate a wide range of project management issues confronting the construction industry. Fortuitously, one of these teams recently completed research on global project controls and management systems (GPCMS) and identified a number of trends that are currently influencing project management and are likely to shape its future.

This chapter first presents the emerging trends and broad themes identified by CII that are driving the evolution of project management. It then supplements this material with trends identified through the GPCMS research, providing a comprehensive look at both the current environment and construction project management in the future.

Near-Term Impacts on Project Management

Each year the CII Strategic Planning Committee identifies key issues and trends that have the potential to affect CII members. Its findings are analyzed to assess the impact on the CII Strategic Plan. These issues and trends also provide valuable insight in identifying drivers of project management change. The most recent SPC work identified emerging trends that are arguably already upon us and are likely to have impacts within the next three to five years. The committee also noted "blue sky visions" of forces or practices that may have impacts 15-20 years in the future (CIIa, 2008). The emerging trends with near-term impacts are discussed in this section; the broad themes identified in the Blue Sky Visions process are provided in the next section, often quoting near verbatim from the 2008 CII report. Given the nature of emerging trends, their impacts frequently can be estimated quantitatively; however, impacts of the longer-term blue sky visions are nearly impossible to quantify, and can include issues such as the ramifications of emerging economies, states of technology, or even overarching social concepts.

Emerging Trends

The year 2008 was characterized by tremendous economic swings, under which energy and commodity prices escalated at unprecedented rates only to fall even faster before year's end. Such short-term gyrations create their own issues for project management and can actually cloud trends, even disrupting in the near-term drivers that recently have been evolving. Working through this state of affairs, the CII Strategic Planning Committee identified four key drivers impacting project management in the construction industry. The following paragraphs discuss these drivers and offer expected corporate strategy trends that will likely follow.

Workforce and Human Capability: Labor Shortages

Workforce issues are certainly not new to the construction industry. However, they do continue to represent a key component in the analysis of nearly all other emerging trends. Even with the current conditions of economic uncertainty, workforce shortages have remained pervasive. While the credit markets have caused the delay or even cancellation of many projects and alleviated some near-term labor issues, many underlying factors continue to impact workforce availability. The declining availability of skilled craft labor and management professionals has an impact on the training of unskilled labor and the transfer of knowledge from retiring professionals to the next generation. Recruiting nontraditional demographics and using new technologies to retain workers are now common practices in the project environment. At higher levels, organizations are now often involved with issues such as immigration and utilization of undocumented workers.

Sustainability Considerations

Sustainability considerations vary dramatically by sector and location, but nearly all industry sectors have reported at least some sustainability impacts in recent years. The recent spike in global energy prices brought sustainability to the forefront of virtually all projects. Whether it is energy or commodity prices affecting a project's profitability or the desire to produce a carbon-neutral project, sustainability is increasingly a concern for today's project manager. As society reacts to address climate change, project managers are likely to be faced with ever-increasing megaprojects to meet energy demands as well as new population centers, new transportation systems, and new sources of potable water. The increased emphasis on sustainability will require project managers to have greater appreciation for environmental and life-cycle cost issues to ensure the viability of projects.

Global Growth and Interconnectedness

The drive towards a global economy has been affecting the construction industry since the late 1980s. Then, global issues were primarily the concern of those companies working internationally. In more recent years, however, globalization has affected local markets and projects as shown in commodity price pressures, labor competition, outsourcing of engineering, and the emergence of virtual project teams. While the 20th century saw increases in the global transfer of products, the 21st century is experiencing dramatic increases in the transfer of knowledge resources. The virtual project team, with offices connected daily from remote locations around the world, works continuously and provides the project manager with new opportunities and challenges.

The Need for Productivity/Efficiency Improvement Methods

This driver is largely a response to the three previously discussed. While productivity and efficiency have always been integral components of continuous improvement, the need in today's environment is more critical than ever. Workforce shortages, sustainability pressures, and increasing global competition all can be mitigated through improvements in productivity and efficiency. While the industry has been slow to adapt new technologies for productivity improvement, it currently shows great interest in this area. If CII is a forum demonstrating industry interest on the subject, one simply needs to a look at where it has been placing its research dollars. CII has funded continuous studies over the past 10 years to improve both engineering and construction productivity, and has also funded research to learn from other industries that excel in modularization and preassembly, as well as industrial engineering techniques and sustainability. To be effective in this changing environment, project managers will have to be knowledgeable on such topics.

Corporate Strategy Trends

A number of corporate strategy trends were identified by the CII Strategic Planning Committee in its report, but given the rapid change in 2008, corporations are likely adjusting these strategies. Nevertheless, these trends are briefly presented here.

The four corporate strategy trends indentified are: engineer-procure-construct (EPC) contractors more selective of projects pursued; changing risk structures; increased use of joint ventures; and increased use of public, private, partnership (PPP) contracts. While the first trend–contractors being more selective–reflects the "contractors market" evident in recent years, the recent abrupt tightening in credit markets is already mitigating its impacts. Changing risk structures, while also related to the period of the contractor's market, may also be a response to other market factors such as the boom in large energy sector projects and interest in the last two trends identified: increased use of joint ventures and PPP contracts. Both of these trends present an environment for more equitable sharing of risk or at least new opportunities to address this risk. Management of risks at the project level will likely require greater skills than previously identified in project management texts.

GPCMS Emerging Trends

The purpose of CII's Global Project Controls and Management Systems Research Team was to review modern project management practices and specifically the established principles of project controls and management systems (PCMS) to determine if they are still valid. The research team concluded that the principles of PCMS functions that were established in the 1960s and 1970s are still valid today; however, the environment in which modern day construction projects operate has changed dramatically and PCMS needs to adapt accordingly (CIIb, 2008). The team further identified 13 drivers of the changing environment, and these are summarized in Table 1. While these drivers overlap somewhat with the SPC trends presented, most supplement the findings already presented and warrant discussion for a broader understanding of the emerging project environment. This discussion is provided in the following sections, often quoting near verbatim from the CII GPCMS team research report.

Sophistication of IT

Information technology (IT) has become increasingly sophisticated. Among several positive benefits, IT now enables the project team to deal with massive amounts of information, speeds the entry and dissemination of PCMS data, and offers the opportunity for innovative discovery and exploration (e.g., through business intelligence tools) as well as integration with other project management and corporate IT systems (e.g., 4D

Table 1:   Drivers of the changing environment.

Sophistication of Information Technology	Graying of PCMS Professionals
Project Complexity	Contractor Specialization
Speed of Project Execution	Increase in Regulatory Oversight
Recognition of Changes	Distribution of Project Risks
Changing Owner Involvement	Virtual Project Teams
Globalization	Labor and Material Availability and Price Elasticity
Outsourcing	

CAD, accounting). A key negative aspect is that IT can place a focus on data entry and create an over-reliance on computing tools, leading to less time and experience in the interpretation of PCMS output for management decisions.

Project Complexity

Project complexity has increased exponentially since the late 1980s. The increase in project complexity has many dimensions: megaprojects, designs that approach the physical limits of materials and equipment, construction in remote locations, partnerships, data integration requirements, and various project delivery systems and contracting strategies. Globalization and outsourcing also contribute to project complexity. As owners and contractors venture into new territories, geographical, social, and political factors add to the complexity of the project.

Speed of Project Execution

The demand for faster project execution speed has increased tremendously. Today's projects rarely have sequential project phases. Fast-tracking – the practice of overlapping project phases, notably design and construction – is common. The pressures for faster project delivery have led to several changes in traditional practice. First, the procurement and subcontract process starts earlier in the project–the owner often needs to order long-lead items to ensure delivery. Second, the popularity of design-build (DB) and EPC have increased. These trends have driven the need for earlier staffing of project teams.

Recognition of Changes

Change management is one of the greatest challenges to PCMS. As organizations lower the barriers behind reporting changes, increased emphasis is placed on the performance of the PCMS change control system. Everyone becomes responsible for the identification of change, and the number of reported changes increase. This lessening of barriers for bringing changes forward results in a more timely change management system; however, increased recognition of changes requires the project team to be more knowledgeable regarding contract types and project delivery systems.

Changing Owner Involvement

Many industries have seen a shift in owner organization direct involvement. This started with a general downsizing of owner engineering, construction, and PCMS teams and a resulting shift of responsibilities to the contractor(s). This contributed to the popularity of alternative project delivery systems such as design-build and EPC, and the contractor had to increase the number and capabilities of people assigned to the project because in many cases these individuals became essentially the leaders of the project. The pendulum may be swinging back to some degree since a number of owners, at least before the recent collapse of the financial markets, reported more hiring of personnel as they address shortages of professionals approaching retirement.

Globalization

The CII research team identified globalization as a key driver of changing environment. Globalization requires companies to learn how to work within an international setting with people that have different cultures, skill sets, and language capabilities. The trend towards globalization has had tremendous influence on project management. Specifically noted in the GPCMS research, contracting, and execution preferences vary greatly around the world. Constructing or operating outside the United States may require U.S.-based owners and contractors to develop relationships with other governments and their citizens, which may require additional resources. Personnel from international sites and those assigned to international sites also may require additional training and supervision to comply with company standards and best practices. Globalization also affects how the PCMS information technology system is deployed.

Outsourcing

For projects, outsourcing comes in many forms. It may include engineering design, procurement services, construction management, construction, and planning functions. Specifically for PCMS, outsourcing can be thought of in several ways, including: 1) outsourcing of owner PCMS requirements to independent third parties; 2) contracting PCMS resources to supplement owner organizations; and 3) requiring the delivery organization (contractor) to deliver against defined project planning, estimating, scheduling, cost control, progress tracking, and reporting requirements. Each approach involves project PCMS risk to be considered by the project manager.

Graying of PCMS Personnel

This trend refers to the general aging of the PCMS work force in terms of demographics and skill sets and is a part of the overall workforce and labor shortages previously discussed. Many events, such as cut backs on hiring in the early 1990s, led to a shortage of PCMS personnel. As many experienced PCMS personnel are on the verge of retirement, knowledge retention and transfer are especially important. Many believe that the wide adoption of IT and its continuing evolution have led to technology-focused training programs, which often undermine, if not neglect, the analytical skills needed in interpreting project information.

Contractor Specialization

As owners strived to pass more risks on to contractors, contractors focused on their core competencies and looked for ways to assign risks to others. This significantly increased the number and responsibility of project players as well as the complexity of project management. Execution specialization also diluted PCMS expertise and increased interfaces and responsibilities. As noted by CII, however, some rebalancing of risk among owners and contractors may occur.

Increase in Regulatory Oversight

The regulatory bodies, including environmental, safety, security, and financial agencies, are becoming greater influences on projects. Lawyers are omnipresent on modern projects due to significant increases in cases arising from personal injury, liability, and traditional construction disputes. Failures to obtain on-time, appropriate permits and comply with them throughout the project can have significant impacts on project cost and schedule. The PCMS must make sure all regulatory oversight needs are captured and put into the schedule to ensure compliance.

Distribution of Project Risks Among and Within Organizations

Increase in project complexity, changing owner organization direct involvement, and globalization contributed to a rise of project-risk recognition and management. Due to the shift between owner's and contractor's markets, allocation of risk shifts. Many project delivery methods such as EPC and DB, contracting strategies such as fixed-price, and financing strategies like Build-Operate-Transfer provide frameworks for such shifts of risk. These risks also are increasingly being shifted among key suppliers and vendors. While the CII research team viewed risks shifting in the direction of the contractor, much of its data were collected over the past several years and may not reflect trends in the current market. Regardless, the lesson here is that markets are dynamic and with them there will be continual changes in contracting structures that affect risk. As projects get larger and more complex, greater interest in risk management at the project level will be highly likely.

Virtual Project Teams

Virtual project teams are an evolving reality as noted in the previous discussion on global growth and interconnectedness. Technology developments have enabled virtual communication and led to virtual performers on project teams. Global projects and outsourcing practices require project personnel to collaborate electronically. Beyond globalization, accommodation to the current workforce has also increased the number of domestic virtual performers–people who work from home. Having a large number of virtual performers creates unprecedented challenges, requiring standardization of procedures and methodologies, efficient interface management and data transmission processes, and recognition of location differences in language, terminology, and cultural standards.

Labor and Materials Availability and Price Elasticity

In recent years, labor and material availability and price elasticity have been topics of interest in the industry. This is the result of multiple factors, including global material demand, disaster relief resource-pull, and immigration policy, among others. This trend calls for adjustments to the current PCMS to increase forecasting capabilities to better integrate changes in availability and price of labor and materials.

These current trends that drive changes in project management are broadly felt across many project functions. However, given the scope of project controls functions, it is likely that they impact PCMS as much as any other project processes. *Some* of the main implications of the trends are an increased number of interfaces that must be managed and the need for early and team-wide planning and alignment for effective project management.

While the discussion thus far has been on trends that currently or soon will affect project management, CII has identified a number of broader themes that are likely to impact project management over the longer term. Though these themes overlap the trends in some manner, they attempt to address the changing environment at a higher level and provide context for the emerging trends. These themes should continue through 2025 and will likely produce additional trends for the project environment.

Themes Likely to Affect Project Management in 15-20 Years

CII's Strategic Planning Committee produced five broad themes or drivers that provide context for individual, lower-level emerging trends. These themes, which are depicted in Figure 1, define the current state, but at a higher level, establishing a context for discussion of both emerging trends and visions of the project environment for the next 15-20 years (CIIa, 2008).

It is impossible to analyze any of these themes in isolation. The following paragraphs present and discuss these themes that are defining the future.

Rapid and Accelerating Pace of Change

The one theme that is persistent throughout the entire process is the ever-increasing pace of change. A host of factors contribute to this rapid pace, including the constantly increasing demand for resources perpetuated by the global economy and the continuous development of new technologies. These technologies are developed rapidly because of advancements in communication and collaboration. This development occurs throughout the world, bringing the global community into closer contact and impacting the physical environment and global social structure in ways that are almost impossible to fully comprehend. In turn, problems are encountered that necessitate the development of new technologies. This whole process is a feedback loop that acts as a spiral to generate accelerating change.

Complex Model of Interdependence

Nearly all aspects of human society are increasingly interconnected. The same specialization that allows for the greatest efficiency is one of the main contributing factors to this extremely complex model of interdependence. It is highly unlikely that any one individual can fully understand all the products, processes, and theories he or she utilizes

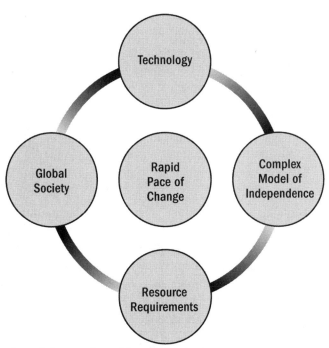

Figure 1:   Broad themes from blue sky visioning process.

in a given day. It is through this lens of interdependence that visions of the future must be analyzed.

Technology

As noted in the GPCMS research, technology or more specifically, IT has become much more sophisticated, and advances in IT serve as enablers of the rapid pace of change and contribute to the complex model of interdependence. Some of the most critical questions needing solutions regard how individuals and organizations can best use and manage this abundance of information. The state of advancing technology most certainly is an underlying theme that will affect how projects are managed in the future.

Global Society

Among other factors, advances in technology have given rise to what is now known as the global economy, which is but one result of the globalization trend identified by the GPCMS research. It is now possible to interact and coordinate with team members from around the globe on a single project. Face-to-face meetings are being supplemented with video conferences and virtual meeting spaces. Some may be more or less affected than others, but no one is completely sheltered from the implications of this new global society.

Resource Requirements

Global interaction stimulates growth and the resulting growth increases global demand for resources. Global collaboration contributes to overall improvements in the standard of living, increasing the demand for raw materials to provide goods and services to new consumers. The new demand tends to severely strain sources of supply that have already been stretched.

A number of intermediate ideas or medium-depth themes flow from these broad themes. These intermediate themes can be thought of as derivatives of the five drivers previously presented. These changes may already be underway, but it will be years before their impact on project management is fully realized.

Medium Depth Themes

The CII report identified seven medium depth themes that, while not as pervasive, are expected to have significant impact on project management over the next 15-20 years. While most of these themes are relevant to project management in general, the reader should be aware that CII views project management in the all-encompassing sense as construction engineering and project management. These themes are presented in Table 2 and are discussed below:

Changing Roles of Project Managers to System Thinkers

The role of the project manager has changed tremendously within just the last generation. Well beyond the basic skills of scheduling, budgeting, and resource management of prior generations, today's project manager needs to think in much broader terms. The project manager needs to think in multidisciplinary terms, have technical skills well beyond those of previous generations, and, most importantly, have greater interpersonal and multicultural skills. The project manager needs to be system-oriented and view the project from a much higher level. The successful project manager in this era

Table 2: Medium-depth themes (CIIa, 2008).

Changing Roles of Engineers to System Thinkers
Era of "Insufficient Plenty"
New Levels of Global Sustainability
Decreasing Significance of Individual Governments vs. Private Global Corporations
Seamless Flow of Global Ideas for Solutions to Problems
Heightened Awareness of Global Security Issues
Comprehensive Energy and Infrastructure Solutions

will have an operational knowledge of risk management and the issues of sustainability. This "systems" view of the project manager by CII is consistent with findings published by the American Society of Civil Engineers in *The Vision for Civil Engineering in 2025*, published in 2007. ASCE noted that "in 2025, civil engineers will serve as master builders, environmental stewards, innovators and integrators, managers of risk and uncertainty, and leaders in shaping public policy" (ASCE, 2007).

"Era of Insufficient Plenty"

The concept of an "Era of Insufficient Plenty" was offered by John Voeller, the noted chief information officer of a major U.S. engineering company, during his keynote address to a meeting of the University-Industry Demonstration Partnership sponsored by The National Academies in 2008. As he noted in the presentation, "For over a century, developing countries have experienced a period of plenty where what they needed could be bought or accessed, for a price...how to innovate and produce in a time where you may not be able to get what you need at any price either by it no longer being available anywhere or by artificial limits on access." This, defined by Voeller, is the "Era of Insufficient Plenty" (Voeller, 2008). Today and in the past, with enough money any resource can and could be obtained. In this "Era of Insufficient Plenty," some of today's resources will be unavailable at any price.

New Levels of Global Sustainability

Depending on the severity of future resource needs, global sustainability could take on a dramatic new meaning. There may be a world where most everything is reused and little is wasted or thrown into landfills. One such presentation of this new sustainability is presented in *Cradle to Cradle* (McDonough & Braungart, 2002). The authors not only describe sustainable solutions, they present a potential business case by which these systems may be implemented. Although identified by CII as an emerging trend, at present sustainability is not fully embraced by society because sustainable systems often are not economically competitive with traditional systems, and thus the full impact of sustainability may not be appreciated. If regulatory measures are implemented in such a way that make sustainable options economically competitive to traditional methods, the drive toward sustainability will have a true business incentive and rapid change may occur. With the Clean Air Act of 1990, a limit for sulfur dioxide (SO_2) emissions was established and a market for SO_2 emerged. If such a system is implemented for other types of emissions and environmental effects, dramatic changes could occur.

Decreasing Significance of Individual Governments vs. Private Global Corporations

In many cases, the influence of national and regional governments is limited by geographic boundaries. Conversely, some private corporations have true global influence. Some business entities have operating revenues larger than the GDP of entire nations. According to the International Monetary Fund, in 2007 Wal-Mart had more revenue than the GDP of Austria. As the world moves toward global economic interconnectedness, some individual governments may be less able to regulate business activities of companies operating within their boundaries. Corporations are able to direct production resources away from the jurisdiction in which regulations are imposed. The individual government, when faced with the possibility of losing production from such corporations, may be reluctant to impose such types of regulation. In the future, political, economic, and technical solutions will continue to be increasingly intertwined.

Seamless Flow of Global Ideas for Solutions to Problems

With increasing collaboration made possible by instant worldwide communication, project managers will have greater access to resources to solve problems. Solutions may come from those with the best ideas rather than from traditional sources. Web communities are connecting customers and suppliers in profound ways. For example, Mfg.com is an online community where users can submit orders to fabrication shops in order to create specialized parts. Yet2.com provides a platform that is "focused on bringing buyers and sellers of technologies together so that all parties maximize the return on their investments." These are examples of groundbreaking collaboration. While apparently lagging on this drive toward mass collaboration, the industry may see major gains by experimenting with a more collaborative approach to idea sharing.

Heightened Awareness of Global Security Issues

Since 11 September 2001, the world has entered a new era regarding global security issues. Despite the heightened awareness of security issues in general, the impacts have not truly been experienced at the project level within the construction industry. Following the 9/11 attacks, the National Institute of Standards and Technology (NIST) funded through CII a significant initiative to define security practices to improve lifecycle project security for capital facilities (CII, 2004). While findings of the study were well received, industry has moved slowly to implement these practices as it is often difficult to make a business case for the cost of implementation, particularly on a first-cost basis. As globalization and interconnectedness continue, it is reasonable to expect that security will increase in importance and impacts on project management will increase as well.

Comprehensive Energy and Infrastructure Solutions

A final theme identified in the CII blue sky report was the expectation that the world community will eventually present a comprehensive energy and infrastructure solution to meet future needs. While tremendous obstacles exist for the development of programs, 2008 offered a preview of scenarios to be expected if the world community continues to ignore the problems. Energy prices escalated to all time high and then, even more quickly, plummeted as governments and companies reacted to address the crisis. The current environment is not conducive to economic and national security, and one must expect that the world soon will be forced to address these issues in a more holistic manner. As this happens, many larger megaprojects are likely to be developed that will certainly challenge the management skills of the most adept team.

PROJECT MANAGEMENT CIRCA 2025

The previous sections discussed the emerging trends and broader themes that provide context for the changes expected to influence the future of project management for construction. This section details some of the specific ways the construction industry is expected to react to those changes.

Table 3 compares present-day construction project management to the changes envisioned by the year 2025. The table is organized into four sections for convenience of

Table 3: Construction industry project management, present day and in 2025.

Construction Project Management - Present	Construction Project Management - c2025
The Project Manager	
• Reactive problem solver • Emphasis on technical knowledge • More project (internally focused)	• Proactive system integrator • More emphasis on interpersonal skills/ communication • Greater awareness of broad public issues
Proximity of the Project Team	
• Mostly onsite management • Often regionally focused	• Centralized command center • Global team
Project Delivery	
• Non-standard, local design • BIM/4D/5D primary for coordination and planning • LEED certification within some building sectors • Onsite fabrication • Labor intensive • Paper documents • Fragmented attempts at productivity and efficiency improvement through largely uncoordinated "Lean" and "Workface" initiatives	• Standardized design tailored for local codes • More BIM/4D/5D for integrated information/ collaborative management • Sustainability programs for most industrial construction projects • Major improvements in supply chain management/standardizing of supplier relationships • Advanced project execution methods to include greater use of modularization and preassembly, industrial engineering techniques that institutionalize "Lean" and/or "Workface" planning concepts • Significant improvements in productivity driven by many of the topics above and as well as acceptance of standardized metrics for monitoring improvements
Organizational Structure/Corporate Strategy	
• Adversarial relationships • Fragmented industry • Project-based metrics (planning through start-up)	• More use of joint ventures and public-private partnerships • Collaborative partnerships in a global setting (less competition due to volume of work to be performed) • Significant changes in risk structure and contracting strategies • Program and portfolio management metrics to include life-cycle and sustainability metrics

discussion: The Project Manager, Proximity of the Project Team, Project Delivery, and Organizational Structure/ Corporate Strategy. The overview here is a simplified snapshot of present and future. These changes represent an aggregation of input from many project management professionals. The actual future state of project management will evolve from progressive change in a fragmented industry that is historically resistant to change. Although the visions summarized in this section represent ideas voiced by many professionals, the reader should appreciate that there is no consensus vision and that Table 3 is simply a synopsis by the authors.

The Project Manager

Throughout history, the management of construction projects has been challenging due in part to the uniqueness of each project. Even when the design and layout of the project are similar, key variables such as location, site conditions, contract type, and stakeholders change. Many have come to view the project manager as being reactive rather than proactive. Project managers encounter unforeseen issues on projects and react to them as effectively as possible. In this role, they have become extremely adept. The project manager is responsible for key decisions that impact most stakeholders of the project team. In the future, however, project managers will be expected to be more proactive system integrators with more interpersonal skills to augment their technical skills. They will be expected to demonstrate greater awareness of broad public issues likely at the international level. They also will be expected to manage in a multicultural environment and therefore will require a greater understanding of the differing cultures of the stakeholders.

Proximity of the Project Team

Although project teams have grown more global, most still operate from onsite management and are often regionally focused. As technology for virtual meetings continues to improve, the cost of travel will increase and project management resources will become even more scarce. It is thus easy to envision the scenario where project managers will operate from a central location or command center where they can manage multiple projects. A tiered project management system might result, in which "super project managers" manage less skilled project managers who oversee and lead daily onsite operations. This centralized model also allows flexibility to accommodate older workers who may be looking to continue their careers but in less strenuous ways. In order to allow this transition, new technologies must be developed and organizations that can embrace and effectively implement these technologies will gain competitive advantage. In 2025, a significant portion of construction project management may be conducted from command centers similar to the Mission Control Centers used by NASA as depicted in Figure 2. Not only will the project management command center require major advances in communication technology, it will also require major advances in virtual models and integrated information management to support multiple projects with ever greater amounts of information.

Project Delivery

As project teams are increasingly spread across the globe, many developments are changing the way future projects will be executed. While most projects still utilize non-standard designs and suffer tremendous inefficiencies due to interoperability issues,

Figure 2.   NASA mission control center vs. future project management center (source: NASA.gov).

advancements finally are being made to address these issues. It appears that owners are warming to the concept of standard designs and advancements in automation, and integration technologies are furthering Building Information Modeling (BIM) concepts within non-building, industrial construction environments. As these technologies mature, contractors who can offer savings in these areas will have a significant competitive advantage. A 2004 NIST study quantified and gave visibility to the cost of interoperability within the U.S. construction industry. NIST placed the annual cost of the lack of interoperability in the U.S. capital facilities market based on 2002 data as approximately $15.8 billion (NIST, 2004).

Interest within CII has also increased for the adaptation of BIM concepts to the larger industrial construction sector. CII last year partnered with the Charles Pankow Foundation to jointly fund research investigating the applicability of BIM systems for industrial construction. Other strides have been made in advancing the implementation of BIM/4D/5D into the construction industry. A recent publication by McGraw-Hill describes the construction industry as being "in the midst of an unprecedented revolution" (McGraw-Hill Construction, 2008). A large-scale move toward BIM/4D/5D, in particular for industrial construction, would represent a step-change in the way construction projects are delivered. As these concepts become adopted by more participants within the industry, its application will likely have major impacts for construction project execution.

While characteristics of project execution vary significantly among industry sectors and particularly with the sophistication of the contractor, a generalization of the current construction environment would describe it as typically using onsite fabrication with rather minor use of preassembly or modularization techniques. It tends to be labor intensive with little use of automation or robotics, especially when compared to manufacturing. It also continues to rely heavily on paper documents, given the lack of implementation of BIM/4D/5D systems, as previously noted. These shortcomings contribute to productivity and efficiency issues.

Sustainability within the construction industry in general is still in its infancy. While the building construction sector has made progress through acceptance of the LEED (Leadership in Energy and Environmental Design) certification program, for now the program is still largely voluntary. For the larger industrial construction sector, interest in sustainability continues to grow and as global growth and development continue, it will likely emerge as a significant issue for most projects.

Project execution in 2025 should reveal considerable advancements from the current state. Given the interest in modularization and preassembly, and current research into adapting techniques from other industry sectors such as industrial engineering and shipbuilding, it is likely that the construction industry will achieve significant gains in project execution. CII currently is funding research on the adaptation of industrial engineering techniques to investigate a broad range of tools and techniques to determine if they can likely bring improvements for the constructed project. Shipbuilding has been identified as an industry with a number of characteristics similar to construction; however, sectors of that industry have experienced significant production improvements using techniques that may have potential within the construction industry. CII has its second research initiative underway at present to examine the possibility of adapting these techniques to the construction industry.

Construction industry interests in automation and fully integrated processes should be fully evident by 2025 as BIM/4D/5D concepts become commonly used. Advances in technology should allow for the cost-effective development and adaptation, despite the fragmented nature of the construction industry. Full implementation of BIM/4D/5D systems should enable design data to be seamlessly integrated with schedules and cost control systems for efficient project execution and later to support operations and maintenance.

Finally, interest in "lean" techniques or related "workface" planning concepts, as it is known in many sectors, should take hold by 2025, and the industry should begin to realize productivity improvements more common within other industries. By this time, standard metrics for measuring engineering and construction productivity will be widely accepted, further enabling productivity improvement.

Organizational Structure/Corporate Strategy

In order to accommodate many of these predicted changes to construction project management, new organizational structures need to emerge. These structures usually evolve from corporate strategies in response to changes in the environment in which projects are executed. The current environment of adversarial relationships within a fragmented industry is likely to change as a plethora of megaprojects emerge to support global growth. The abundance of projects and shortage or contractors capable of delivering these projects will encourage greater use of joint ventures and likely greater use of public-private partnerships for the funding and execution of projects. Collaborative partnering should be common in 2025. Such relationships will alter contracting strategies, delivery methods, and risk structures. New metrics will also evolve that address performance at the portfolio level, rather than individual project level, to reflect the new structures by which these projects are managed.

Conclusion

The visions put forth here provide a glimpse of what project management might look like for the construction industry in 2025. Even though these visions represent the collective wisdom of many experienced industry professionals, no "crystal ball" is available through which to view the future. Many of the changes are almost certain to transpire, in that some of the broad blue sky visioning and medium-depth themes define an evolving state or characteristics of the environment that collectively the global society can influence, but an individual nation, in reality, has little control. Socio-political unrest or some catastrophic event of political terrorism could alter the evolution of the global environment and slow, if not reverse, many of the emerging trends. Short of such an event, project management for the construction industry in 2025 will likely resemble that provided in this chapter, and industry stakeholders are already late in preparing for the new era.

Acknowledgements

This discussion on construction industry project management circa 2025 would not have been possible without valuable input from dozens of construction industry professionals. Much recognition is given to CII for providing valuable insight into the expected future of the construction industry. In particular, thanks are offered to the members of the CII Strategic Planning Committee who reviewed and made additions to the work conducted by the Emerging Trends and Blue Sky Task Force. Appreciation is offered to members of the CII Global Project Controls and Management Systems Research Team, and especially to all of the CII Board of Advisors members who responded to the 2007 Emerging Trends Validation Survey. Additional thanks are given to Jim Ankrum, Virgil Barton, Mark Buehler, Winnie Callahan, Buddy Cleveland, Michael Davis, Alex Delli Paoli, Brad Dickson, Patricia Galloway, Clair Gill, Rodney Hill, Jack Hockey, Ric Jackson, Jim Mcgrath, David Molda, Peter Moore, Kris Nielsen, Nelson Norden, William Pender, Wayne Pettis, Wendy Quattrone, Sarah Slaughter, Rob Smith, John Voeller, and Tom Will for allowing themselves to be interviewed by CII. Many of these people also attended a special CII workshop on the Future of Project Management in October 2008 to further discussions on the topic. Other members of that workshop not noted above deserving recognition include P. Mickey Collins, Stephen Cabano, John Fish, Aivars Krumins, Richard Stephenson, Melissa Herkt, Jerry Eyink, Mark Palmer, Ed Ruane, Ron Campbell, Bryson Edmonds, Jack Dignum, Bob Maxman, Paul Campbell, Vern Owens, Gary Steinmetz, Harold Helland, and Russell Conda. Finally, appreciation is extended to Rusty Haggard who served as technical editor for this chapter.

References

ASCE. (2007). *The vision for civil engineering in 2025*. 9-10.

CII. (2004). Best practices for project security. CII BMM2004-10.

CIIa (2008). Emerging trends & blue sky report. *CII SPC*, September, 2008, 7-24.

CIIb (2008). Global project controls and management systems. RS244-1, 10-14.

McDonough, W., & Braungart, M. (2002). *Cradle to cradle: Remaking the way we make things*. New York: North Point Press.

McGraw-Hill Construction. (2008). *BIM, Building information modeling*. Chicago: McGraw-Hill.

NIST. (2004). Cost analysis of inadequate interoperability in the U.S. capital facilities industry. GCR 04-867.

Voeller, J. (2008). Innovation in an era of insufficient plenty. Keynote address: National Academies Workshop, April 2008.

PART 4

Project Management in Government

CHAPTER 19

U.S. Defense Acquisition 2025

Michelle R. Brunswick

"The greatest strength of our armed forces is the initiative and adaptability of our people."

—U.S. Deputy Secretary of Defense Gordon England
MILCOM 2006 Conference

The "Sergeant York" was the last straw. It was a tracked antiaircraft weapon system that cost the U.S. taxpayers $1.8 billion, but never successfully completed testing and was ultimately cancelled (Biddle, 1996). The U.S. Congress had enough of interservice rivalry and poor performing weapon systems.

It passed the Goldwater-Nichols Department of Defense Reorganization Act of 1986, making the most sweeping changes to the U.S. Department of Defense (DoD) since its creation in 1947 by the National Security Act (National Defense University, 2008). The Goldwater-Nichols Act restructured the procurement process for the services into a joint procurement process with joint implementation requirements.

Just seven years later at "the last supper" held by then-Secretary of Defense Les Aspin, former Deputy Secretary of Defense William Perry told leaders of industry the Cold War was a success. The United States had won and the peace dividend would mean a reduction in DoD procurement. The DoD could no longer support the diverse defense industrial base. This led to the industrial downsizing of the 1990s, causing significant personnel losses across both government and industry, and a massive consolidation effort on the part of industry.

The results of these two major events over the last two decades have led to the defense acquisition process we have today. What actions will drive defense acquisition in 2025? This chapter, which focuses on DoD acquisition and its evolution through 2025, has three sections: the Office of the Secretary of Defense (OSD), the acquisition process and the industry perspective.

The first section describes a top-level vision. It addresses the OSD perspective relating to threats, politics, weapon systems, and research. The second section narrows in

Research Questions

1. What will we be defending in 2025?
2. How do you feel the national security strategy will change over the next 18 years?
3. What do you think the effect of the political climate is on acquisition?
4. What is industry's role with the government 2025?
5. How do you see the industrial base changing between now and 2025?
6. How do you see industry's ability to deliver weapon systems in 2025?
7. What are the changing roles of the prime and sub-prime contractors between now and 2025?
8. How will the acquisition process change by 2025?
9. How will the DoD and the services organize their acquisition workforce by 2025?
10. What do you think the workforce challenges will be in 2025?
11. How will changes in the economy, in resources and technology affect industry over the next 18 years?
12. What challenges will Program Executive Officers face in 2025?

on the acquisition process, as well as the organization and workforce. Finally, the last section addresses industry's role and the industrial base, including the challenges in a global economy and the relationship between the prime and sub-prime contractor.

The future is a tenuous thing to predict. Just 20 years ago, how many would have predicted the current state—the collapse of the former Soviet Union, the emergence of global terrorism as a grave threat, or a lean expeditionary military force? To research these and other questions, and develop a rational vision for the future direction of defense acquisition, I consulted individuals who are on the pulse of the changing acquisition arena. I sought opinions from a cadre of government and industry experts listed under "project participants" starting on page 324. Throughout the chapter, comments provided by project participants are noted with an asterisk[*]. From this culmination of interviews and research material, I formulated the conclusions set forth in this chapter.

My gratitude is extended to all the project participants, with special thanks to my research assistant, Captain Renae Barnes, USAF. Without their knowledge, insight, and input, this chapter would not have been possible.

The DoD acquisition enterprise is managed by a professional workforce made up of several functional career fields, but for the purposes of this chapter it will relate directly to the project management professional.

Section 1
Office of the Secretary of Defense
Threats 2025

> *"What we do know is that the threats and challenges we face abroad in the first decades of the 21st century will extend well beyond the traditional domain of any single government agency."*
>
> —Secretary of Defense Robert Gates
> Kansas State University Lecture, November 2007

Future threats to the United States drive DoD's acquisition process, but we do not do a good job of predicting the next threat, as is evidenced by our history, which shows that DoD prepares for the war just fought. Seventeen years ago, the United States was celebrating the end of the Cold War and the nation's military posture was based on a known threat—the Soviet Union. The United States had a defensive policy to deter communist expansion. Conversely, today's threat is the global war on terrorism. The United States must quickly respond and then project a threat posture anywhere in the world.

Another significant threat to the United States that is seldom mentioned is a weakened economy. The health of the U.S. economy is joined to the health of other countries' economies by globalization. The need for the United States to maintain a strong economy is vital to third-world countries since a recession in the United States could destabilize less-developed regions. The defense budget and the U.S. economy are inextricably linked. Defense spending is related to a robust economy and a strong gross national product. The Soviet Union's collapse was an economic collapse, not a military confrontation. A strong economy enables strength and perhaps is our the best means of defense for the U.S.

The current strategic and economic outlook of the U.S. gives us pause to question: What will the environment look like in 2025? Former U.S. Air Force Chief of Staff General T. Michael Moseley captured a plausible scenario in his white paper dated December 29, 2007.

> The future strategic environment will be shaped by the interaction of globalization, economic disparities and competition for resources; diffusion of technology and information networks whose very nature allows unprecedented ability to harm, and potentially paralyze advanced nations; and systemic upheavals impacting state and non-state actors and, thereby, international institutions and the world order (Moseley, 2007).

A speech given on January 26, 2008, by Secretary of Defense Robert Gates identifies solutions to Moseley's white paper.

> In the Afghanistan and Iraq campaigns, one of the most important lessons that has been learned, and to a large extent re-learned, is that military success is not sufficient. Our efforts must also address economic development, institution building, the rule of law, promoting internal reconciliation, good or at least decent governance, public services, training and equipping indigenous security forces, effective strategic communications and more. These so-called soft capabilities along with military power are indispensable to any lasting success (Gates, 2008).

Predicting the exact threat, whether it be asymmetric warfare or war with a near-peer, is not a realistic task. Instead, officials should seek to understand how the United States can prepare, respond and engage all threats. In the same speech, Gates references future activities that will require the involvement of the entire U.S. Government, including all agencies and departments (Gates, 2008).

Deputy Secretary of Defense Gordon England made a similar reference in a speech stating, "We do live in an interconnected world, and the net-centric requirement is not just internal to the Department of Defense. More and more, we have to have interconnections with a broad range of partners. In the U.S., we need those partnerships to include federal, state and local agencies" (England, 2006).

When we look at this information, it is not just about fighting with joint forces, interagency or coalition partners. All these different components need to be integrated so they complement each other. In 2007, Gates stated, "We also need to be thinking about how to integrate our government's capabilities in these areas, and then how to integrate government capabilities with those in the private sector, in universities, in other nongovernment organizations, with the capabilities of our allies and friends—and with the nascent capabilities of those we are trying to help." This, in essence, will drive the acquisition process, pending its transformation in the political arena.

Politics

"In my judgment, the Department today is overburdened with rules, regulations and legislation that limit effectiveness."
> —Deputy Secretary of Defense Gordon England
> Statement Before the House Armed Services Committee, June 2007

With each new administration, national security priorities and policies are reprioritized based on national security threats pertaining to economic, political or social events. National security decision-making among policy makers determines the budget Congress authorizes for the Department of Defense. Currently, pressure to reduce the defense budget and defense programs continues seemingly unabated as entitlement programs and national debt expenditures consume more of the federal budget. Over the long run, this will undoubtedly affect the Department of Defense and its weapon systems of the future.

Lieutenant General John L. "Jack" Hudson, USAF, Commander, Aeronautical Systems Center, summarized, "National priorities are set by our political leadership; Congress appropriates and authorizes, and this will not change—national security strategy will still flow down to military strategy and then to each of the services. Acquisition will still be expected to procure and sustain the systems we need to execute our national military strategy. A lot of it depends on the overall level of spending that is set by the political leadership."*

Congressional legislation has direct control over the costs for defense weapon systems. Former Under Secretary of Defense for Acquisition, Technology and Logistics Dr. Jacques Gansler stated at an Industrial College of the Armed Forces symposium, "There's a trade-off between regulations [of the industrial base] and market forces [that shape our industries], and we walk a narrow line between the two. I'm worried that perhaps we're going too far now in the direction of regulation as a result of the reactions [to scandals, concerns about the integrity of the system]. The pendulum swings between these two positions on a cycle, if you consider the history of the industrial base" (ICAF, 2005).

Missile Defense Agency Deputy for Acquisition Management Katrina Wahl reflected this same sentiment when she said, "Change is a constant struggle, but the process may not change into something better. We need to target opportunities that require Congressional relief."* Both Gansler and Wahl are addressing the need to find a solution between the two extremes—deregulation and excessive regulation. The DoD will have legislative oversight; the question is to find the "sweet spot"—the right amount of legislation, focusing on the right areas of concern that can only be balanced by Congress.

Lieutenant General George Muellner, USAF (Ret.), former President of Advanced Systems for the Integrated Defense Systems for the Boeing Company, summed it up best when he wrote:

The political climate will continue to apply pressure on the acquisition process. It is highly unlikely that Congress will reduce their scrutiny and interaction as their budget responsibilities are unlikely to change. Therefore, the pressures to have well-executed acquisition programs despite budget and requirements instability will persist. These pressures will be reflected by continued OSD scrutiny and involvement. These are a fact of life in a democracy that must continually make resource trade-offs due to limited resources with competing demands.*

Weapon Systems

"What the Department is seeking is timely synchronization and integrated delivery of capabilities—and to do it within projected costs and on schedule. The approach is to identify gaps and seams, to eliminate redundancies except by design, and to make sure that solutions are completely interoperable."
—Deputy Secretary of Defense Gordon England
MILCOM 2006 Conference

Future threats to the United States and the evolving political environment determine the type of weapon systems the Department of Defense develops. With a constrained defense budget, DoD can ill afford to invest in the research and development of aging technology. The Department of Defense needs to focus on a future military strategy based on information dominance. This is a shift from past single-use platform weapon systems, such as ships, planes, tanks or missiles to a system-of-systems approach (ICAF, 2005).

With the system-of-systems approach, the DoD will purchase fewer highly sophisticated systems. Rex Reagan, a senior acquisition manager at BearingPoint, Inc., commented that with the system-of-systems approach, there will be improvements in commonality and inter-service capability. "Multiple services must be able to employ a weapon, system, material, or any service provided without pronounced adjustments or modifications."*

Gansler concurs that the DoD is transitioning from a platform-based approach to a system-of-systems approach, but he is concerned that budgeting is still done by platforms or mission area needs.* This disconnect needs to be addressed and solved.

Research

"The greatest long-term threat to America, and to our close friends and allies, is falling behind in science and technology."
—Deputy Secretary of Defense Gordon England
MILCOM 2006 Conference

It must be emphasized that the U.S. defense strategy is based on technological superiority (ICAF, 2005). "Yet, the two major DoD accounts that fund acquisitions—R&D and Procurement—have been falling relative to the overall DoD budget" (Spring, 2005).

Former Deputy Secretary of Defense Dr. John J. Hamre wrote, "There is a deep bias in our budgeting system favoring current expenditures against long-term expenditures. This bias is toward operations and against investment. Money that would have been set aside for research and development is going towards personnel and operations supporting the war in Iraq and Afghanistan."* Wahl further elaborated that the DoD is eating its seed corn—its long lead seed corn—and if the DoD continues this engagement, it could potentially limit government and industry's pursuit of new technological advancements.*

The DoD, once the driver of technology, has become a receiver of technology. Commercial-sector developments have outpaced military development, forcing the military to work with industry to capture and use commercial developments, either as whole entities or components of larger systems. These commercial products pose security concerns because they have dual usage and were developed using open-systems architectures. Lieutenant General Ted Bowlds, USAF, Commander, Electronic Systems Center, provided the microprocessor as an example. A platform's mission computer will have its lineage traceable to a commercial processor, such as the Intel dual-core found in commercial laptops.*

Unless Congress and DoD increase R&D funding for long-term expenditures, the weapon systems of tomorrow will become dependent on commercial, dual-use products, which are equally available to adversaries.

Section 2
Acquisition Process

> *"We must have well-identified requirements, adequate funding and robust processes utilized by trained personnel that can execute the program."*
>
> —Keith Ernst
> Former Acting Director, Defense Contract Management Agency*

The acquisition community has an adequate process in place. However, certain aspects of the process prevent it from working properly. One major disconnect illustrated by Deputy Under Secretary of the Air Force for Space Programs Gary E. Payton relates to the three distinct DoD acquisition areas, commonly referred to by acquisition practitioners as the "Big A." The first element is the requirements generation and validation piece, which

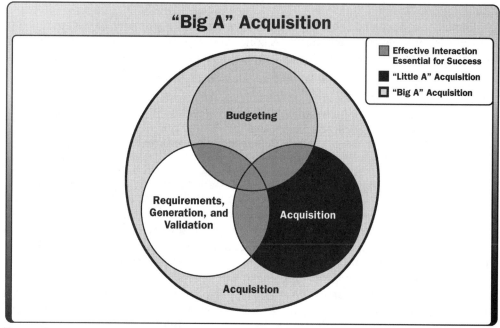

Figure 1.

is designed to validate a requirement independent of cost and schedule. The second area is the actual acquisition of the weapon system. The last area is budgeting.*

The DoD needs to redesign the "Big A" process to create a fully integrated and well-functioning system. Lieutenant General Lawrence P. Farrell, Jr., USAF (Ret.), President and CEO of the National Defense Industrial Association, believes one person should be held accountable for the acquisition process.* The Government Accountability Office (GAO) Report on Best Practices recommended that, "DoD establish a single point of accountability at the Department level, with the responsibility, authority and accountability for ensuring that portfolio management for weapon system investments is effectively implemented across the Department" (Sullivan, 2007).

Requirements Process

Within the requirements process are two components. The first is the DoD's overall requirements generation and validation element addressed under "Big A." The DoD is approving more new programs than fiscal resources can support. This problem is compounded by the highly complex and interdependent programs that are commanding larger budgets than past programs (GAO, 2007).

The second component—the need for stable requirements—relates more directly to the acquisition process or "Little A." Unless the DoD can get control of the requirements process, it will be difficult, if not impossible, to deliver affordable and effective weapon systems.

"Additions or modification of requirements almost always lead to cost and schedule growth" (Meier, 2008). An example of a program suffering from uncontrolled requirements growth is the Space-Based Infrared System High (SBIRS-High). The SBIRS-High program was originally estimated at $3.2 billion in 1996, and then underfunded in 1997 with $2.6 billion. In March of 2002, the program escalated to $6.2 billion, which was primarily attributed to inadequately defining requirements up front and not controlling additional requirements (DoD, 2003). A current cost estimate for the program is now $10.64 billion (Smith, 2005). Rear Admiral William Hunter Hilarides, USN, Program Executive Officer for Submarines, provided a very simple mathematical example when he illustrated requirement changes during the different phases of development. He stated that the cost starts at $1 on the shop floor, it increases to $3 once the ship is completed but still on the shop floor, and escalates to $8 once the ship is in the water.*

To limit cost growth, the DoD should establish an early program baseline and maintain it throughout the acquisition process (Meier, 2008). This means accepting less capability delivered more rapidly, as opposed to the 100 percent solution. Additionally, the government will have to get better at cancelling non-performing programs early on in the process.

Technology Maturity

Another longstanding problem with the acquisition process is programs beginning development with immature technologies. The GAO reported that of the programs assessed, only 15 percent entered development with demonstrated high levels of technology maturity, causing many programs to experience significant growth in development cost. "In the case of the Army's Future Combat System, nearly 2 years after program launch and with $4.6 billion invested, only 1 out of the more than 50 critical technologies is considered mature, and the research and development cost estimate has grown by 48 percent" (Schinasi, 2005). Representative Heather A. Wilson (R-NM) advised, "Aim for only one miracle per program" (Taubman, 2007).

Many technology issues are traced to attempts to push state-of-the-art technology into the acquisition process before it is mature. This results in cost and schedule growth as well as program cancellation (Meier, 2008). DoD should focus more on incremental development. The acquisition process needs more evolutionary steps versus quantum leaps in technology capability. An evolutionary product development process defines the individual increments on the basis of mature technologies and incorporates them into feasible designs that are matched with firm requirements.

Funding

When there are problems with oversight, requirements or technology maturity, cost growth is a natural occurrence. For a program to be successful, it must have stable funding. Unfortunately, as former Acting Director, Defense Contract Management Agency Keith Ernst described, DoD pays for poorly performing programs by expropriating funds from other programs. This type of action destabilizes the other programs and reduces the overall buying power of the defense dollar. This forces the military services to reduce planned quantities or capabilities in order to stay within a new, reduced budget. An example is the reduced number of the F-22A Raptors. * According to the GAO, "As costs escalated in the program, the number of aircraft the Air Force planned to buy was drastically reduced from 648 to 183" (Sullivan, 2007). Additionally, Nicholas W. "Nick" Kuzemka, Vice President, Program Management Corporate Operating Excellence & Program Management, Lockheed Martin Corporation, said funding instability on complex weapon systems causes renegotiation and re-baselining of the plans, schedule and integration. This has a ripple effect through the supply chain.*

Oversight

To counter this ripple effect, there is a need for strong procedural oversight within the acquisition process. The GAO concluded that DoD policy provides for a series of early reviews focused on the acquisition process. Unfortunately, these reviews are often skipped or are not fully implemented (Sullivan, 2007).

The GAO also reported that successful product developers ensure that a high level of knowledge is achieved at key junctures in development so resources and needs match, product design is stable, and the production processes are mature (Schinasi, 2005). The GAO concluded in its High-Risk Series, "DoD has written into policy an approach that emphasizes attaining a certain level of knowledge at critical junctures before managers agree to invest more money in the next phase of weapon system development. This knowledge-based approach results in evolutionary—that is incremental, manageable, predictable—development and inserts several controls to help managers gauge progress in meeting cost, schedule and performance goals" (GAO, 2007).

GAO concluded that "DoD has not been employing the knowledge-based approach, discipline has been lacking, and business cases have not measured up" (GAO, 2007). There should be a more structured review of programs both prior to program approval and after program initiation that emphasizes fact-based decision making.*

Organization and Workforce

"The organization is only as good as the people you put in it."
—Ralph J. DiCicco, Jr.
Acting Director, Air Force Acquisition Center of Excellence*

A review of the acquisition process indicates that it is the people that make all programs work. However, the last decade has brought significant changes within the acquisition workforce. To ensure a continued robust and vital workforce on into 2025, these changes need to be addressed.

Workforce Mix

The first area to address is the acquisition workforce mix. DoD currently has a mix of military, government civilians and contractors. The trick is to get the right mix of the three. Over the last decade, the acquisition workforce converted many military positions to government civilian positions, effectively severing the connection between the acquisition process and the end user. The military understands the use of a system and the requirements, so military personnel must have operational as well as acquisition experience. The government civilian workforce provides stability, knowledge management and a technology base. The need is to balance the government workforce with that of the contractor workforce, using the contractors as shock absorbers with the ability to expand and contract to meet DoD's needs.

According to Acting Director, Air Force Acquisition Center of Excellence Ralph J. DiCicco, Jr., a prevailing concern among acquisition leaders is that the downsizing of the government workforce over the last decade has given contractors increased program management responsibilities along with inherently governmental functions. Unfortunately, the contractor has many of the same issues as the government relating to retaining experienced personnel.* Gansler summed it up best when he said the government needs to maintain the role of the manager and the contractor needs to maintain the role of the doer.*

Former Comptroller General of the United States David M. Walker is also worried about the high percentage of contractors performing government-related work. He stated that, "Agencies need to consider developing a total workforce strategy to meet current and future human capital needs, and address the extent of contractor use and the appropriate mix of contractor and civilian and military personnel. I have also noted that identifying and distinguishing the responsibilities of contractors, civilians and military personnel are critical to ensure the contractor roles are appropriate" (Walker, 2008).

Each service has its own acquisition process, resulting in duplication and inefficiency. The DoD may need to look at a type of joint "purple" workforce in acquisition, as opposed to each service having its own acquisition workforce competing for DoD funding. This consolidation will be driven by a smaller workforce and a reduced DoD budget.

According to Kuzemka, the current joint programs are not able to streamline the requirements process across the services. For example, the Joint Strike Fighter Program Office has a requirements board where the different services convene. However, after a joint decision has been made at this board, each of the services is still required to go through its individual approval channels. He believes the acquisition process should shift towards a more integrated activity that will be more effective than today's joint programs. The solution is to merge the approval channels for each service, thereby developing one approval channel for all services.*

Force Development

"We are losing our competence as a government to be an effective buyer."
—Former Deputy Secretary of Defense Dr. John J. Hamre*

A major challenge to government as well as industry is attracting, training, and maintaining intellectual capital. The downsizing of the 1990s resulted in the loss of an entire generation of program managers. This is true for the government program offices as well as the contractor. It will take at least 10 years to redevelop the workforce. To cultivate an experienced cadre of acquisition professionals, government and industry must challenge and invest in program managers.

Experience

Farrell stressed that program management is a profession just like any other profession, and it must have upward visibility and mobility. The Department must re-professionalize the program management career field by providing personnel with formal education and practical experience.*

The best way to gain experience is to challenge the workforce by moving them from program to program and giving them growth opportunities to gain a broad experience base from a wide range of programs with increasing levels of responsibility. The greatest challenge to developing experienced program managers is the decrease in DoD weapon system procurement. One solution to this shortage is to rotate DoD program managers with program managers in other U.S. government agencies and industry and vice versa.

Training

DoD and industry must capture their corporate knowledge and include it in their standard business practices. According to William "Bill" Kaplan, Chief Knowledge Officer, Acquisition Solutions, 20 percent of the knowledge in an organization is information you can search for in books, regulations or manuals. The remaining 80 percent of the knowledge resides in experience, insight, and lessons learned. This corporate knowledge is the why and how to do things, knowing what works and what doesn't work. The cost associated with failing to capture and use corporate knowledge is the expense of additional training and loss in productivity and competitive advantage.* To enhance knowledge transfer, a strong mentorship program should be implemented.

Allison Stiller, Deputy Assistant Secretary of the Navy, Research, Development, and Acquisition, Ship Programs, noted that the government needs to capture the knowledge in each program office and establish a partnership with industry to enhance and encourage knowledge-sharing. There needs to be knowledge-sharing among the various services and with industry to capitalize on lessons learned. This type of government-industry forum could initiate the joint or "purple" perspective.*

To ensure a steady stream of qualified personnel and increase collaboration among industry, educators and training institutes, the DoD should accept certification and credentialing by professional societies, such as Project Management Institute (PMI), National Contract Management Association (NCMA), and others as DoD equivalents.

Accepting internationally established and recognized organizations and processes will reduce parochialism and duplication in the current system.

Tools

To maximize the capabilities of a shrinking acquisition workforce, tools such as design software and office automation must be leveraged and increasingly emphasized. According to Payton, the workforce of today is more capable than the workforce of 30 years ago because of the tools employed in the work environment to make them more productive. He further commented that Air Force Academy cadets of today are more advanced as compared to when he was at the Academy pursuing the same degree. Cadets of today can build, launch, and control satellites, and they will enter the workforce with these skills. The workforce will only continue to improve and become more productive over time.*

With fewer highly skilled workers, DoD must tear down bureaucracy and build up efficiencies in its processes through the use of tools. Muellner stated that risk-management and systems engineering tools, along with networked communications, should enhance transparency of the acquisition process. This will provide a better understanding of intended and unintended consequences of resource and requirements changes. These tools allow full transparency and real-time reassessment of the risk profile.* Hilarides elaborated on his belief that modular designs are less people-intensive and result in rapid insertion of technology. By using three-dimensional design tools, the government can essentially operate weapon systems in virtual reality and verify that the design meets all the specification requirements prior to building.*

The development of highly sophisticated simulations and war-gaming will reduce costs and allow weapon systems to be tested as a system-of-systems versus as individual platforms. Hudson said there must be improvement at arranging and executing high-fidelity complex netted simulation scenarios, such as F-15s with AWACS, space assets, and bombers. This allows the practice of scenarios that are difficult to arrange and expensive to conduct in a test environment.

Section 3
Industry Perspective

> "Change is relentless … I'd say in a single word "more." We see more foreign ownership of U.S. assets … more export from U.S. companies into the global marketplace … more global supply … more (international) partnering … the global threat and the nature of warfare are changing…."
>
> —Mark H. Ronald, President and Chief Executive Officer,
> BAE Systems North America, Inc.
> Dwight D. Eisenhower National Security Series Symposium, June 2005

Acting Deputy Under Secretary of Defense for Industrial Policy Gary A. Powell said in a letter he sent to the U.S.–China Economic and Security Review Commission:

> DoD research, development, and acquisition, and associated policies and program decisions play the major role in guiding and influencing industry transformation by focusing market demand across a broad spectrum of industry segments to meet emerging and projected DOD requirements. First, the Department's weapon system acquisition policies and decisions shape the technological

and programmatic focus of industry. Second, decisions made on mergers and acquisitions involving defense firms continue to shape the financial and competitive structure of the industry. Third, DOD evaluations and assessments of sectors or specific industry issues help identify future budgetary and programmatic requirements. Finally, the Department incorporates industrial base policies into its acquisition regulation and strategies on an ongoing basis to promote competition and innovation (Powell, 2005).

Industry is reshaping itself to respond to significant changes in military missions, acquisition processes, and workforce. As illustrated by Kuzemka, three pillars of the acquisition process lead to flawless execution: funding stability, requirements stability, and contractor/industry performance. Industry does not have control over funding or requirements stability. It only has control over the contractor/industry performance pillar of the acquisition process. If DoD can create a more stable environment, then industry can improve.*

Industry's Role

"I see industry's role with the Government in 2025 to be an integrated solution provider."

—Frederick C. Payne
Vice President and Global Program Management Director, Ricardo plc.*

Industry and government need to work hand in hand to define what the defense industrial base will be in 2025 and how they will work together. The relationship between the government and industry should shift from an adversarial relationship to a teaming partnership. It is imperative for government and industry to understand each other's business models and have more open dialogue to exchange information.

Industry must focus on the implementation of team strategy. The government will continue to rely on industry, both as the producer of sophisticated weapon systems and as a provider of services. With the shrinking defense budget and the reduction of new weapon systems, industry will have fewer weapon systems to design, develop, and manufacture. Former Commander, Air Force Materiel Command General Lester L. Lyles recommends that industry do more development and planning such as prototyping, as well as modeling and simulation. This will keep the DoD and industry engaged in acquisition, allowing technology and the industrial base to stay current.*

Industrial Base Changes

"We have to find a way to do acquisition with a more consolidated industrial base."
—Chris Deegan
Director, Cost Engineering and Industrial Analysis, Naval Sea Systems Command*

The industrial base will reshape, consolidate, and take on new entrants. Two factors are driving the changes—reduction in programs and fewer available defense dollars. Steve Goo, Vice President of International Operations for Boeing Integrated Defense Systems, said domestic mergers will start to decline as compared to the last two decades, but international mergers and acquisitions will increase.*

Colonel August J. Caponecchi, USAF (Ret.), President Emeritus, Tactair Fluid Controls Inc., wrote that this contraction will create more effective programs by eliminating duplication, and enhancing commonality and interoperability, such as the F-35 program. "Less duplication means fewer opportunities and therefore places a downward constraint on the number of companies that can economically survive in the military procurement sector." An example is the recent decision by Lockheed Martin and Boeing to team up on the next-generation bomber. By combining their R&D resources, they position themselves to block any competitors. *

George Guerra, Vice President for HALE (High Altitude Long Endurance) Systems, Northrop Grumman Corporation, said the companies that survive will make key strategic acquisitions. Those companies able to respond to specific needs will be identified and targeted for mergers and acquisitions. Some companies will change what their core competencies are and adapt to U.S. defense needs.* Many companies will form teaming arrangements on major programs.

Frederick C. Payne, Vice President and Global Program Management Director, Ricardo plc., said, "The consolidation of today will probably revert to specialist-based industries that will be brought together to provide specific solutions to fast-paced operational needs. The specialist-based industries will be able to provide nimble and specific solutions for rapid deployment." Tom Bowler, Vice President of Programs, Bath Iron Works, said we must do more than sustain the industrial base; we must make it a competitive one as well.*

The potential is real that the industrial base will have single suppliers for components. Bowlds said this will lead to the introduction of many non-traditional suppliers, who have not previously been associated with defense work. "This will come about because of the increased use of commercial products and the reduction in resources for the development of unique military solutions."* To ensure competition, the government may have to scrutinize future consolidation, teaming and partnership efforts to enhance innovation and prevent a single defense contractor situation.

Role of the Prime and Sub-Prime Contractor

> "The shift is already underway with prime contractors and sub-prime contractors having closer working relationships. Contractor teams will align themselves early on in the acquisition process with common goals and objectives, and they are willing to share the fee."
> —George Guerra
> Vice President for HALE (High Altitude Long Endurance) Systems,
> Northrop Grumman Corporation*

Caponecchi wrote that the prime contractors will require major sub-prime contractors to design and manufacture major subsystems primarily at their own expense. The subcontractor will be liable for the proper performance of the subsystem through the development cycle and certification of the weapon system with all changes financed by the subcontractor.*

Prime and sub-prime contractors will need to have seamless integration. Kuzemka commented that in order for the prime/sub-prime team to collaborate and communicate more effectively, common systems must be used. Currently, Northrop Grumman and Lockheed Martin have a tremendous amount of business with subcontractors, but each sub-vendor has its own system of tools and processes. The trend will be for the prime contractor's systems and processes to be adopted by the sub-prime. However, when a prime contractor has key partners that are also prime contractors or large sub-prime contractors, it may be difficult to force those partners to adopt the prime contractor's tools and processes, thus leading to interface issues. These issues cause a problem with timeliness, meshing of requirements data, configuration control, risk resolution, flow down of requirement changes, labor hours, and overall performance. Over the next 15-20 years, the industry will move to greater integration of contractors, partially caused by consolidation of industry and more joint ventures.*

The challenge with consolidation and joint partnerships is for the government to have visibility into sub-contractors' performance. Missile Defense Agency Executive Director Dr. Patricia Sanders provided the following example: Lockheed Martin, Raytheon, and BAE are all developing a different type of missile. However, they are all buying the same internal part from Honeywell. Honeywell is essentially providing a component that performs the same fit, form, and function. The only difference is the magnitude of cost. Additionally, if an issue arises with the component, it may not be transparent to all the companies. This highlights that the prime contractors may be diverse; however, sub-vendors typically are not. Few primes are building those components for which they were originally contracted. Greater supply chain transparency is a prerequisite to understanding industrial-base vulnerability.*

There must be a balancing act for the DoD on how many primes and sub-primes can consolidate and partner to ensure there is not a compression of the vendor sub-tier base, narrowing the playing field and subsequent competition. Technology is created and innovation is achieved in the sub-prime and sub-tier vendor base.

Industry's Response to Market Forces

> *"Industry supporting defense is reshaping itself to respond to significant changes in military missions. Major defense firms are responding by reducing excess capacity, streamlining processes, and revamping supplier relationships."*
> —Acting Deputy Under Secretary of Defense for Industrial Policy Gary A. Powell
> Letter to U.S.–China Economic and Security Review Commission, August 2005

According to Muellner, "Industry will respond to the market-driven environment. The days when a major company would 'bet the farm' on a new design or major technology shift are gone. Wall Street rewards and punishes very rapidly, and long-term investment profiles are not highly rewarded. Industry is not likely to make significant long-term investments given the instability and return on investments offered by defense programs. Emerging technologies offer opportunities, but they will be matured in a risk-sharing environment across industry, focusing more on near-term projects."*

Muellner further elaborated, "One area that should be addressed is the impact of emergent systems engineering tools that provide more transparency of risk profiles and risk-mitigation activities. These tools facilitate a more holistic approach to program management that includes the entire value-stream from the requirer to the acquirer to industry to the tester. All of these players must be involved with the activity from start to finish."*

Hudson added that industry's use of modeling and simulation will improve their ability to produce products in the predicted time with the predicted performance. A benefit of this will be a reduction in the amount of hours the government must conduct operational testing and evaluation. The key is to develop a way to identify which tests can be replaced by modeling and simulation and which ones require an operational assessment.

Kuzemka identified that the technical paradigms will evolve, leading to industry's improved responsiveness and advancement along the curve of flawless execution. Industry will develop leading parametric indicators designed to highlight deficiencies and incorporate earned value management principles. This product will be superior to the current lagging indicator of the earned value system of today. All of this will enhance industry's ability to deliver to government expectations.*

Global Economy

"We need to get the best technology at the best price."
—Lieutenant General Lawrence P. Farrell, Jr., USAF (Ret.)
President and CEO, National Defense Industrial Association*

The industrial base will continue to shrink, and concern that the supplier base may dwindle to a sole-source scenario is real and troubling. Globalization of the defense industrial base will apply the competitive force needed to ensure companies continue to innovate and strive for price reduction.

Caponecchi said "The Department must be prepared for more global involvement in the manufacturing of the components going into weapon systems. This will require a major cultural shift in thinking about how to produce military hardware [coupled with] national security concerns regarding the dependence on foreign suppliers for critical military components. However, this is the direction lean commercial manufacturing is taking us."*

The government must balance globalization with security and fair business practices. According to Professor Jerry Emke, Chair of the Defense Acquisition University's Transformation Efforts, "Civilian and military technologies and users are increasingly becoming comingled and at some point it will be impossible to disentangle the two. This will result in the loss of our ability to control access to the design-related information, to availability of technology, and ultimately raise grave security considerations" (Emke, 2008).

A fine line must separate legislative protectionism from globalization. There should be no barriers for overseas competitors who comply with U.S. laws, thus allowing for an open and fair playing field for all companies agreeing to procurement integrity, International Traffic and Arms Regulations (ITAR), and security requirements.

Defense components are a relatively small portion of sales for U.S. defense contractors. Payton said the government comprises 7% of industry's space business revenue and many of the subtiers are divesting from government contracts towards more profitable markets. The subtier components are bound by legislation such as ITAR that increases the cost of domestically manufactured products and disadvantages the U.S. supplier.* To remain competitive, U.S. firms must be allowed to expand and compete in the global marketplace. The United States must monitor export legislation that is detrimental to defense firms while ensuring security.

Conclusion

"Buy the right thing, the right way, with the right process."
—Dr. Jacques Gansler
Former Under Secretary of Defense for Acquisition, Technology and Logistics *

Project Participants

Lieutenant General Ted Bowlds, USAF, is the Commander of Electronic Systems Center at Hanscom Air Force Base, Massachusetts. The center's mission is to acquire command and control systems for the Air Force. The organization is comprised of more than 12,000 people located at six sites throughout the United States. ESC manages more than $3 billion in programs annually. Bowlds provided comments via e-mail February 24, 2008.

Tom Bowler is the Vice President of Programs at Bath Iron Works and has been actively involved in the DDG 051, DDG 1000 and DDG Life Cycle Program since 1997. Prior to joining Bath Iron Works, he was President of the American Shipbuilding Association, the national trade organization representing the six largest private sector shipyards in the United States. I interviewed Bowler February 4, 2008.

Colonel August J. Caponecchi, USAF (Ret.), is the President Emeritus, Tactair Fluid Controls Inc., as well as a member of the Board of Directors for Tactair Fluid Controls Inc., and St. Joseph's Hospital Health Center, Syracuse, NY. Caponecchi completed his USAF career in Washington, DC with senior assignments at the State Department as a member of the Arms Control and Disarmament Agency working on the Strategic Arms Limitation Treaty (SALT) talks with the Soviet Union; and at the Pentagon, as Special Assistant to the Deputy Chief of Staff, RD&A. Caponecchi provided written comments via e-mail February 14, 2008.

Colonel Ralph J. DiCicco, Jr., USAF (Ret.), is currently Acting Director, Air Force Acquisition Center of Excellence, Office of the Assistant Secretary of the Air Force for Acquisition, Washington, DC. The Center is a selectively manned organization chartered to transform Air Force acquisition into a capability-based system with speed and credibility. It creates a sense of urgency and instills innovation and change to redefine how the Air Force procures affordable, effective weapon systems for the war fighter. I interviewed DiCicco March 28, 2008.

Christopher S. Deegan, SES, is the Director, Cost Engineering and Industrial Analysis Division serving as the Naval Sea Systems Command (NAVSEA) focal point for cost engineering and industrial base analysis. Deegan is the only comptroller employee to be recognized by the Association of Scientists and Engineers as "NAVSEA Engineer of the Year." I interviewed Deegan April 3, 2008.

Keith Ernst, SES, was the Acting Director, Defense Contract Management Agency (2006-2008). Ernst was responsible for leading and managing over 10,500 civilian and military leaders, managers and technical experts to perform worldwide acquisition life cycle contract management for Department of Defense weapon system programs, spares, supplies and services. I interviewed Ernst March 7, 2008.

Lieutenant General Lawrence P. Farrell, Jr., USAF (Ret.), is the President and CEO of the National Defense Industrial Association (NDIA)—the largest defense association in the United States. Prior to his retirement from the Air Force, he served as the Deputy Chief of Staff for Plans and Programs. He serves on the boards of Global Healthcare Exchange, Advanced Technology Institute, and the National Center for Defense Manufacturing and Machining. I interviewed Farrell February 19, 2008.

James M. Gallagher, PMP, is the founder and President of Togra Associates, which is a project management consulting and training organization. He served on the Defense Acquisition University Board of Visitors from 1997 to 2002 and the Project Management Institute Board of Directors from 2001 to 2006. He retired from the Senior Executive Service in his first career in the Air Force acquisition community at Wright-Patterson, AFB, Ohio. Mr. Gallagher provided written comments via email February 18, 2008.

Dr. Jacques S. Gansler is the Vice President for Research at the University of Maryland. He holds the Roger C. Lipitz Chair in Public Policy and Private Enterprise in the School of Public Policy. Previously, Gansler served as the Under Secretary of Defense for Acquisition, Technology and Logistics from 1997 until January 2001. I interviewed Gansler March 5, 2008.

Michael C. Gass is the president and CEO for United Launch Alliance (ULA). Gass is the principal strategic leader of the organization and oversees business management and operations. Before joining ULA, he served as Vice President and General Manager of Space Transportation for Lockheed Martin Space Systems Company. I interviewed Gass February 19, 2008.

Steve Goo is Vice President of International Operations for Boeing Integrated Defense Systems (IDS), a $32.1 billion business unit with more than 71,000 employees who provide space, defense, intelligence and communication products and services for military, government and commercial customers around the world. In this position, he is responsible for improving and integrating the company's growing international business. Previously, he was vice president of IDS Program Management & Business Excellence and led company-wide efforts designed to achieve peak performance. His focus included developing and deploying program management best practices, developing current and future program managers, performing independent assessments of IDS programs, and participating in proposal reviews. Goo provided written comments via e-mail April 28, 2008.

George Guerra is the Vice President for HALE (High Altitude Long Endurance) Systems and Deputy Integrated Product Team Leader for the Unmanned Systems market segment in the western region of Northrop Grumman Corporation's Integrated System Sector. His career has been dedicated to advancing unmanned systems technology and capabilities. Before joining Northrop Grumman, he worked for General Dynamics-Convair. Guerra provided written comments via e-mail February 10, 2008.

Dr. John J. Hamre is the President and CEO of CSIS. Before joining CSIS, he served as the 26th U.S. Deputy Secretary of Defense. Prior to that, he served as the Under Secretary of Defense (Comptroller). In 2007, Secretary of Defense Robert Gates appointed Hamre to serve as the chairman of the Defense Policy Board. Hamre provided written comments via e-mail March 1, 2008.

Rear Admiral William Hunter Hilarides, USN, is the Program Executive Officer for Submarines. Since becoming an Acquisition Professional, he has served as the Director, Advanced Submarine Research and Development and as the Conversion

Manager and subsequently the Program Manager for the SSGN Program. I interviewed Hilarides April 15, 2008.

Albert C. "Al" Hoheb is the Principal Engineer, Learning System Center, for the Aerospace Institute at The Aerospace Corporation, a Federally Funded Research and Development Center in El Segundo, CA. Hoheb is the Senior Advisor to the Space and Missile Systems Center (SMC) and other DoD, Intelligence Community and Civil/Commercial organizations for space systems acquisition education. Hoheb provided written comments via e-mail February 1, 2008.

Lieutenant General John L. "Jack" Hudson, USAF, is Commander, Aeronautical Systems Center, Wright-Patterson Air Force Base, Ohio. As ASC Commander and Program Executive Officer for aircraft procurement and modernization, he leads the Air Force's Center of Excellence for Development and Acquisition of Aeronautical Systems. The organization comprises more than 11,000 people located at 39 sites throughout the world. ASC manages more than $19 billion in programs annually. Hudson provided written comments via e-mail April 7, 2008.

Colonel William S. "Bill" Kaplan, USAF (Ret.), is the chief knowledge officer at Acquisition Solutions and is responsible for the development and implementation of the company's knowledge management strategy. Acquisition Solutions, Inc., is a specialist acquisition consultancy supporting government agencies in the procurement of best value products and services. I interviewed Kaplan February 12, 2008.

Colonel Nicholas W. "Nick" Kuzemka, USAF (Ret.), is Vice President, Program Management Corporate Operating Excellence & Program Management (OE&PM), Lockheed Martin Corporation. He is responsible for Lockheed Martin program management policy, processes, tools, training and performance business rhythm/reporting. I interviewed Kuzemka March 6, 2008.

General Lester L. Lyles USAF (Ret.), was the Commander, Air Force Materiel Command, at Wright-Patterson Air Force Base, Ohio. The command conducts research, development, test and evaluation, and provides acquisition management services and logistics support necessary to keep Air Force weapons systems ready for war. He was responsible for executing $30 billion annually and managing 82,000 personnel in operational locations throughout the United States. I interviewed Lyles April 7, 2008.

Lieutenant General George Muellner, USAF (Ret.), retired from the Boeing Company as the President of Advanced Systems for the Integrated Defense Systems business unit with responsibility for developing advanced concepts and technologies, and executing new programs prior to their reaching the System Design and Development phase. Prior to his retirement from the Air Force he was the Principal Deputy, Office of the Assistant Secretary of the Air Force for Acquisition, Washington, DC. Muellner provided written comments via e-mail February 27, 2008.

Frederick C. Payne is Vice President and Global Program Management Director, Ricardo plc. Mr. Payne is responsible and provides guidance for the global Ricardo project management community, ensuring effective and appropriate application of the Ricardo Project Life Cycle Process Framework and the development of project managers through training and certification programs. In his role immediately prior to joining Ricardo, he was the corporate director of program management, responsible for the direction, coordination and stewardship of policy, processes and project management development for over 5000 Project and Program Managers within BAE Systems. Payne was named a "Power 50" project management leader by the Project Management Institute in 2005. He chaired the PMI Global Corporate Council 2006 – 2007. Payne provided written comments via e-mail May 2, 2008.

Gary E. Payton is the Deputy Under Secretary of the Air Force for Space Programs, Washington, DC. He provides guidance, direction and oversight for the formulation, review and execution of military space programs. This includes oversight of all space and space-related acquisition plans, strategies and assessments for research, development, test, evaluation and space-related industrial base issues. He retired from the Air Force with the rank of Colonel after more than 23 years of service. I interviewed Payton March 27, 2008.

Rex Reagan is a senior acquisition, financial and business manager with a successful track record in budget development, implementation, contract administration and program management. He is a Commander in the Navy Reserve (Supply Corps) with more than 20 years' experience and a manager with BearingPoint, Inc., a management and technology consulting firm. Reagan provided written comments via e-mail March 7, 2008.

Lieutenant General Richard V. "Dick" Reynolds, USAF (Ret.), is a Senior Manager with BearingPoint, Inc. He is also a principal of The VanFleet Group, LLC, an aerospace consulting company, and serves as an Outside Director for Apogee Enterprises, Barco Federal Systems, the National Museum of the United States Air Force, and the Museum Foundation. I interviewed Reynolds April 15, 2008.

Dr. Patricia Sanders, SES, was the Executive Director for the Missile Defense Agency (MDA). In this position, she served as the MDA Director's senior advisor on matters related to all Agency operational and management functions. Sanders served as a key interface to the Office of the Secretary of Defense (OSD), the services, andmembers of Congress. I interviewed Sanders March 19, 2008.

Allison Stiller, SES, is the Deputy Assistant Secretary of the Navy, Research, Development, and Acquisition, Ship Programs. She is responsible for executive oversight of all naval shipbuilding programs, major ship conversions and nuclear refuelings, and the maintenance, modernization and disposal of in-service ships. I interviewed Stiller January 24, 2008.

Katrina Wahl, SES, is the Deputy for Acquisition Management at the Missile Defense Agency. She develops acquisition and contracting policy for the Agency's procurements, develops direction and guidance for the Ballistic Missile Defense System (BMDS), assesses performance by program managers against direction, and provides assistance to comply with directions and guidance. I interviewed Wahl February 29, 2008.

The Goldwater-Nichols Act (1986) was developed at a time when there were 20 prime contractors competing yearly for multiple new programs. There were large production runs of aircraft (585), combat vehicles (2,031), ships (24) and missiles (32,714). The threat was well known and DoD had stable strategic planning (DoD, 2006).

Then in 1993, the famous "last supper" occurred and the defense industrial base that defeated the Soviet Union was reduced to six prime contractors competing for fewer and fewer programs each year. A reduction in the number of production runs for aircraft (188), combat vehicles (190), ships (8), and missiles (5,072) occurred. Now, the threat is unpredictable and world dynamics have changed due to globalization (DoD, 2006).

President Eisenhower had vision when he said, "A vital element in keeping the peace is our military establishment. Our arms must be mighty, ready for instant action" (Eisenhower, 1961). The legislative, acquisition, and industrial changes occurring today are defining the future of defense acquisition, which is the vital element supporting the U.S. military establishment. Congress, DoD and the defense industry must work together to ensure a safe and secure future for the United States, its allies, and coalition partners. As Dr. Norman R. Augustine, the retired Chairman and Chief Executive Officer of the Lockheed Martin Corporation wrote, "[U.S.] military forces may be called upon to fight outnumbered, to fight at great distances from home, and to win with very few casualties. Only with a properly functioning defense acquisition process can this be possible" (DoD, 2006).

How can this "properly functioning defense acquisition process" be achieved? The obvious problems of a smaller and less experienced acquisition workforce, and the deficiencies of the acquisition process must be resolved, and all must adapt to a declining budget. Recognition of these problems is the first step to their solution; incorporating recommendations is the second. According to Lyles, the acquisition process can go one of two ways. It can get more bureaucratic and stringent or it can embrace solutions from various studies to improve the whole process. After listening to all the participants in this project, I believe the initiative, talent, and adaptability of the U.S. government and industry team will succeed in providing an acquisition process that meets the demanding requirements of our ever-changing world.

References

Biddle, Wayne. (1996, September). How much bang for the buck? – inadequate field testing of weapons, *Discover*. Retrieved May 5, 2008, from http://findarticles.com/p/articles/mi_m1511/is_v7/ai_4376702

Department of Defense (DoD). (2006, January) Defense Acquisition Performance Assessment Report. Retrieved May 26, 2008, from www.acq.ods.mil/dapaproject

Department of Defense (DoD). (2003, May). Report of the Defense Science Board/Air Force Scientific Advisory Board Joint Task Force on Acquisition of National Security Space Programs, Office of the Under Secretary of Defense for Acquisition, Technology and Logistics. Retrieved April 28, 2008, from http://stinet.dtic.mil/oai/oai?verb=getRecord&metadataPrefix=html&identifier=ADA429180

Eisenhower, Dwight D. (1961, January 17). President Eisenhower's farewell address to the nation. Retrieved May 23, 2008, from http://mcadams.posc.mu.edu/ike.htm

Emke, Jerry. (2008, March-April). Transformation: Climate change, demographics, technology and globalization. *Defense AT&L, 37*(2), 35–37.

England, Gordon R. (2006, October 25). Deputy Secretary of Defense. MILCOM 2006

Conference, Marriott Wardman Park Hotel, Washington, DC. Retrieved January 20, 2008, from www.defenselink.mil/speeches/speech.aspx?speechid=1059

England, Gordon R. (2007, June 26). Deputy Secretary of Defense. Statement for the Record on DoD Management Before the House Armed Services Committee, Washington, DC. Retrieved February 2, 2008, from www.defenselink.mil/speeches/speech.aspx?speechid=1163

Gates, Robert M. (2008, January 26). Secretary of Defense. Center for Strategic and International Studies: Washington, DC. Retrieved February 15, 2008, from www.defenselink.mil/speeches/speech.aspx?speechid=1211

Gates, Robert M. (2007, November 26). Secretary of Defense. Manhattan, Kansas, Landon Lecture, Kansas State University. Retrieved January 20, 2008, from www.defenselink.mil/speeches/speech.aspx?speechid=1199

Government Accountability Office. (2007, January). High-risk series: An update. GAO-07-310. Retrieved January 28, 2008, from www.gao.gov

Industrial College of the Armed Forces (ICAF). (2005, June 2). The U.S defense industrial base, national security implications of a globalized world. Dwight D. Eisenhower National Security Series Symposium. Industrial College of the Armed Forces: Washington, DC. Retrieved January 20, 2008, from www.eisenhowerseries.com/events/05-07/index.php

Meier, Steven R. (2008, March). Best project management and systems engineering practices in the pre-acquisition phase for federal intelligence and defense agencies. *Project Management Journal, 39*(1), 5, 61–63, 65, 67.

Moseley, T. Michael. (2007, December 29). U.S. Air Force Chief of Staff. The nation's guardians: America's 21st century Air Force. U.S. Air Force white paper. Retrieved January 15, 2008, from www.af.mil/shared/media/document/AFD-080207-048.pdf

National Defense University. (2008). NDU Online Library. Goldwater-Nichols Act. Retrieved May 10, 2008, from www.ndu.edu/library/goldnich/goldnich.html

Powell, Gary A. (2005, August 22). Acting Deputy Under Secretary of Defense for Industrial Policy. Letter in response to questions from the U.S.-China Economic and Security Review Commission. Retrieved March 2, 2008, from www.acq.osd.mil/ip/docs/china_economic_and_security_review_commission_8-22-05.pdf

Schinasi, Katherine V. (2005, November 15). Managing Director, Acquisition and Sourcing Management, Government Accountability Office. DoD acquisition outcomes: A case for change. GAO-06-257T. Retrieved January 15, 2008, from www.gao.gov

Smith, Marcia S. (2005, November 25). Military space programs: Issues concerning DoD's SBIRS and STSS programs. CRS Report for Congress, Order Code RS21148. Retrieved May 22, 2008, from www.google.com/search?hl=en&q=CRS+report+for+congress%2C+order+code+rs21148+25+nov+2005

Spring, Baker. (2005, October 19). Congressional restraint is key to successful defense acquisition reform. *The Heritage Foundation Leadership for America*. Retrieved March 31, 2008, from www.heritage.org/research/nationalsecurity/bg1885.cfm

Sullivan, Michael J. (2007, March). Director, Acquisition and Sourcing Management, Government Accountability Office. Best practices: An integrated portfolio management approach to weapon system investments could improve DoD's acquisition outcomes. GAO-07-388. Retrieved January 15, 2008, from www.gao.gov

Taubman, Philip. (2007, November 11). Failure to launch: In death of spy satellite program, lofty plans and unrealistic bids. *New York Times*. Retrieved May 5, 2008, from www.nytimes.com/2007/11/11/washington/11satellite.html?hp#step1

Walker, David M. (2008, March 11). Comptroller General of the United States, Government Accountability Office. Defense management: DoD needs to reexamine its extensive reliance on contractors and continue to improve management and oversight. GAO-08-572T. Retrieved March 28, 2008, from www.gao.gov

CHAPTER 20

New Frontiers in Space Exploration Project Management

Dorothy J. Tiffany, CPA, PMP

"The consequences of our actions are so complicated, so diverse, that predicting the future is a very difficult business indeed."
  J. K. Rowling (1965 -), *Harry Potter and the Prisoner of Azkaban*

"Our imagination is the only limit to what we can hope to have in the future."
  Charles F. Kettering (1876 – 1958), U.S. electrical engineer and inventor

What does the future hold for project management in space exploration? Predicting the future is difficult, and predicting the future of space exploration project management is no exception. However, if we can imagine new processes, tools, and ideas to improve project management, then we can begin the task of making those improvements as we enter the next frontier of space exploration.

In a recent unscientific poll of project managers, the question about changes in the future of project management netted the response that nothing has changed in project management for many years, and nothing is likely to change in the future. Project managers make their decisions based on their knowledge, instinct, and past experiences, and have been quite successful. In their opinion, there is no need to change that model.

At first glance, it seems the project manager poll might have valid conclusions: that management in the space exploration industry has not changed much over the last 25 years, and that project management processes, people, and tools will remain relatively constant in the future. As the French novelist Alphonse Karr wrote in the late 1800s, the more things change, the more they stay the same. However, some of the most revolutionary changes in project management occurred during the years between 1983 and 2008, and equally important changes will take place over the next few decades. Just as the space hardware and software systems became more complicated with the building of the International Space Station, Hubble Space Telescope, Phoenix Mars Lander, and many other trail-blazing missions, project management techniques matured and grew as well. That maturation and growth will continue.

In 1996, project management became a recognized profession with increasingly organized ideas and processes, as evidenced by the publication of the first edition of PMI's *A Guide to the Project Management Body of Knowledge (PMBOK® Guide)*. An explosion of new technologies, tools, and processes permeated project management practices and ideas as the 21st century began. The shifts in the way the space exploration community managed its complex projects were so substantial that the processes, tools, and people of 25 years ago are now scarcely recognizable in today's workplace. At the same time, the shifts were so gradual, and yet so all-encompassing, that the changes were barely recognized as they were happening.

From Past to Present

Prior to 1983, project management existed without the World Wide Web, fax machines, e-mail, cell phones, laptop computers, Power Point™ presentations, and enterprise-wide management systems. Present-day project teams almost would not know where to start without these indispensible tools, as evidenced by the fact that work comes to a halt when the email server goes down or the cell phone company experiences a disruption of service. And yet, project managers functioned very effectively without these modern tools not so long ago.

In the early 1980s, the most advanced project management tool was the "war room", which consisted of a dedicated conference room with elaborately hinged or sliding wall panels covered with cost, schedule, and technical trend charts reporting the status of the project. These hinged walls could be flipped to reveal more panels and charts behind them, allowing for a complete picture of the status of the project. Project support specialists and engineers updated hand-drawn and typed status charts with multi-colored adhesive tape pre-printed with solid, dashed, and dotted lines that represented the project plan and actual trends. Each month, the tapes were gently cut with utility knives and delicately placed on the charts with tweezers. The "war rooms" were the epicenter of project knowledge and status. Project managers used this information, along with their common sense and many years of experience, to make important project decisions. The present-day versions of these "war rooms" are the project collaborative website and the ubiquitous slide shows. The information is still basically the same, but the method of conveying the information has changed.

In the past, analysis of project alternatives for budget, schedule and other resources was done by hand, using adding machines and large main-frame computers. Earned Value Management Systems (EVMS) existed, but in a more primitive state than the current automated and integrated project management tools. Project plans were usually hand-written or typed records. Planning and scheduling tools were so complicated and labor intensive that specialists were required to input the schedule data into main-frame computers. Budgets were recorded with black and red pencils on multi-columned and lined paper, popularly called "railroad pads." Again, the form and function of these processes has remained relatively the same, although the computer handles the computing instead of the adding machine, the laptop does the job of the main-frame, the spreadsheet has replaced the railroad pad, and computer software has been simplified so that everyday project practitioners can master the applications. Reports also look much more professional than they did in the past.

Many of the current automated systems can trace their heritage to these humble beginnings. With the introduction of the low-cost, mass-produced computer, the processes and reports used in the past for project management control and status were converted into computer-enabled and generated reports and records. The personal computer was first marketed by IBM in August 1981 and became a standard for the project office by the mid-1980s. More than any other change, the computer has influenced the way project managers plan and manage their projects, communicate project status, train their new team members, and archive their project information.

Along with the introduction of the computer, a new and diverse labor force was changing the face of project teams. The work force of the late 1970s and early 1980s was male-dominated, with informal mentoring systems that provided the young project team members with the right experiences and contacts to make them successful project managers. Formal project management training was largely not available (Chapman, 1973, p. 113). The title of Richard L. Chapman's book, *Project Management at NASA: the system and the men*, suggests the gender bias prevalent in the space industry at that time. Chapman was commissioned to study the U. S. National Aeronautics and Space Administration's (NASA) project management to determine which attributes contributed to project success, how good project managers were selected and developed, and finally, whether any of his findings were transferable to other industries. The selection of the title, referring to the project management community in the masculine gender, was not an oversight. The project manager of the time was invariably male. As Chapman put it, "The study focuses on both the structure and the men, but principally through the perceptions of those men." (Chapman, vii) As recently as the early 1980s, the aerospace project management field was dominated by men. Relatively few female project managers existed—most female and minority professional employees generally held support roles. Female secretaries answered phones, kept the boss's calendar, and typed all reports and correspondence on typewriters.

Fast-forward to the project management team today and the most remarkable demographic characteristic is the diversity of the workforce. Now, a significant portion of the project management workforce is female, and diversity in a broader sense is normal. The demographics of project management in the aerospace industry will continue to evolve as the workforce becomes more global and, thus, even more diverse.

A Look to the Future

The changes over the past 25 years might have come in gradual steps; the changes over the next 15 years will not be as gradual or subtle. The project management community is poised for a period of extraordinary productivity, efficiency, and integration, due to technological advances. Even greater changes will come as a result of globalization, collaboration, innovation, and the changing composition and location of the workforce.

The Technological Advances

Future advances in automated tools will allow for an unprecedented explosion of productivity for project teams. Advances in cell phones, computers, and new integrated devices under development will allow the entire project team to access and report project status with unparalleled efficiency, speed, and accuracy. Collaborative tools and websites will become the most common means for communicating with team members about the status of the project. Professional online social networks, now in their infancy, will become increasingly important as tools facilitating the identification of potential team members and specialists, as well as solutions to problems. Since much of the work done by the team will be in "virtual" offices, advances in collaborative technology and communication will be some of the most striking productivity enhancers. Rather than relocating team members to a central location, or even commuting to work each day, the project team will be able to tap resources through these new technologies, any time of the day or night.

Advances in tools will also have a major impact on improving project performance with respect to decision analysis and the assessment of risk impacts. New tools will be developed to allow the project team to simulate virtually every project management and engineering decision. These simulations will be built using advances in the technology used for the current generation of games, adapted and enhanced to apply to practically all situations that might arise in the typical project. The game-building genius behind Grand Theft Auto™ and Wii's Fit™ will be unleashed on project management simulation development to produce platforms to train and enable project managers to fully understand decision ramifications. The goal of these models will be to fully integrate cost, schedule, risk, and technical information to give the project team the opportunity to test-run both strategic and tactical decisions, and analyze the cost, schedule, and risk impact of their various decisions alternatives.

The new hardware and software solutions for projects will go far beyond the present state of the industry by developing new ways to do business and communicate, rather than just rely on automating the hand-generated, paper-based tools of the past. Just as Google™, Monster.com™, and craigslist™ completely changed the way information was researched, jobs were filled, and items were sold, the new hardware and software solutions will change the way documents are created, accounting data is recorded, and results are presented to stakeholders. Much of the new software and simulations will be developed open source.

As Tapscott and Williams (2006) state in *Wikinomics: How Mass Collaboration Changes Everything*, "New forms of mass collaboration are changing how goods and services are invented, produced, marketed and distributed on a global basis" (p. 10). Much as Linux and Wikipedia were developed by a community of practice, the project management community will see a surge in collaboratively developed solutions to project management problems. Every project team will have a unique collaborative website and wiki. Even the traditional project management tool vendors will get into the act, and capitalize on the consulting, training, and service aspects of the tools, rather than holding copyrights and patents for the software. In this way, the tools will benefit from a larger, global pool of expertise in the development of capabilities, allowing the tool to develop faster and enhancing capabilities that all users might need. In other words, the tool development will be driven by the user community rather than individual software developers. Instead of new ideas coming from tool vendors, they will come from the project management user community. This "wiki-style" tool development will also enhance the interoperability among different applications and greatly expand the breadth and depth of each tool. There will be no final product in this type of development, and the evolution of these new software solutions will greatly improve productivity, ensure that all project management tools collaborate in ways that are not possible today, and eliminate proprietary software code restrictions.

The Organizational and Process Changes

Advances in tools, and even the manner in which technology evolves, will have a profound impact on the organizations and processes involved in project management in the future. These new processes and organizational relationships will require changes in how projects are managed. The project manager will have far less control of the entire project and will have to manage through influence and relationship-building. Rather than the current paradigm of reviewing project progress by using "dashboards" that summarize data, the project manager will move towards a "steering wheel" concept in which the project manager is actively involved in using technology to aid the project management process. Project managers will find that collaboration and managing through influence will dominate the project control processes. However, as Preston Burch, NASA's Hubble Space Telescope Program Manager at the Goddard Space Flight Center said, "Managing a project is sort of like driving a car down the street. If you had six people in the car and they all had one hand on the steering wheel, that would be a great scenario for a car accident. So there can only be one driver of the car, just like there can be only one project manager" (Bursch, 2007).

Customers will become an increasingly integral part of the project management process. They will not only establish the initial requirements and provide project funding, but will also provide valuable input into product designs, risk mitigation, and problem resolution. This participation, on almost a daily basis, will result in more efficient and effective decision-making. The customer will no longer be just "waiting in the wings" for the final product. This new relationship has already begun to develop, but will take time to fully mature into a more productive work dynamic. The project manager and customer have a natural tendency to want to control the project direction and decisions, and this new paradigm of working closely together will take some practice and mind-shifts in some of the more control-oriented managers.

Along with more direct customer involvement, the space exploration project management community will experience more teaming, partnering, and joint ventures among government agencies within the U. S., with companies and academic institutions, and with foreign governments. Innovative incentives will become available for individuals or companies to develop technologies needed for space travel, resulting in new ways of contracting for the resulting technology and services.

Traditional forms of contract instruments will experience an evolution to new types of agreements to accommodate the change in acquiring technologies through open sourcing and collaborative relationships. Many components of the project procured through blanket agreements with the project's home organization will involve multisourcing. Multisourcing is a strategy to provide for the activities of a project through a variety of sources, including both internal and external, to optimize the cost, schedule, and effectiveness of the activities. Rather than merely treating the components of a project as separate deliverables, multisourcing will maximize on the concept of "make/ buy" decisions to arrive at the optimum, integrated method of achieving all project activities.

In addition to new ways of acquiring materials and services, project managers will also find better ways to manage the activities during and after acquisition. Full integration of the cost, schedule, and technical baselines will be achieved more smoothly than it is today with the emergence of truly integrated management systems. This means that the project team will have the ability to understand the impact of all changes and problems to the cost, schedule, and quality of the project. The use of earned value management will be more widespread with the advent of the requirements from the U. S. Office of Management and Budget (OMB) and the Government Accountability Office (GAO), along with the realization by project teams that the data provided by EVMS is invaluable in forecasting the magnitude of cost and schedule overruns.

Risk management will be fully integrated with the earned value management process, and this integration will result in more informed decisions by the project team. Although projects are currently assessing the impact and probabilities of negative risks and problems on the project baselines, the concept opposite of risk (i.e., opportunity), has not been fully exploited. Increased emphasis on opportunities available to projects will result in new processes, procedures, and decisions that have not been explored in the past. Project teams will explore within the organization (supply chain, process, technology, and new markets) and beyond the organization (customers, competitors and complementors, emerging technologies, influencers, thought shapers, and political, legal and social forces) for new opportunities to reduce cost, improve the final project, or deliver early (Bekefi, Epstein, & Yuthas, 2008).

Since risk management will play an increasing role in project management, some of the most revolutionary changes in tools and processes will take place in this area. Computer-based simulation of risks, problems, and decision options will be key components of the project management process in the future. As discussed earlier, the use of models to forecast complex inter-relating factors will greatly benefit the project team—and allow for optimum choices when faced with multiple options. Since the project team members will consist of many younger workers who were raised on sophisticated simulation games, the progression from games to work problem-solving will be a natural fit. These employees will feel very comfortable with the simulation process and will openly embrace this new way of doing business.

Another area of significant change will be how a project archives and uses historical information. Data will be collected routinely and stored in sophisticated, user-friendly databases, allowing the project team to search for lessons learned on prior projects as well as provide a basis for cost and schedule estimates. The database will not only include the raw data, but will also house analysis of the data so that it is more relevant to project teams. For instance, cost and schedule data will include the impact of changes on project baselines. Also, the results of any decisions made will be detailed for future reference. In this way, the project team can use the data more intelligently and make accommodations in their projects for the changes and problems experienced in the past. These databases will also include video and audio stories from past project teams about the failures and triumphs they experienced, to be downloaded and listened to during commutes and travel. In this way, project historical information will come alive and stimulate more senses than just reading spreadsheets or reports. Since all data and historical information will be at the project manager's fingertips in a manner that makes it easy to retrieve knowledge and lessons from prior projects, performance will improve in delivering the scope and quality requested by the customer within cost and schedule commitments. These databases of information will help the project team avoid mistakes made in the past.

The Political Environment

Most U.S. space exploration is currently funded by the federal budget process. If there is competition for superiority in space, as in the 1960s, or an economic incentive to explore space, more countries will commit resources for space exploration. Already, we are seeing the initial signs of broader interest in space and new sources of funding as private companies and some countries investigate and even invest in space tourism and space transportation. If the various national space agencies and global corporations increase their collaboration and partnering in their quest to explore space, the governments will have less incentive to put scarce resources into this discretionary activity, leaving fewer resources for space exploration. The current trend is towards increased partnering, which is likely to continue over the next 15 years. With fewer resources available for space exploration, the remaining government projects will face increasing competition for the scarce funds and a demand for increased transparency in their project status. Figure 1 shows NASA's budget as a percentage of the U.S. federal budget since NASA was formed. In the early years, the NASA budget was higher due to the race for space and the absence of the large entitlement programs such as Medicare and Medicaid. After the Apollo Program, the NASA budget decreased dramatically and now remains flat, except for inflation adjustments. This trend is not likely to reverse without a substantial change in public sentiment regarding space travel.

The space exploration community will also have to face a perception of non-relevance among the Generation Y or Millennials, a generation born between the years 1977 and 1997. In a February 2008 briefing by Mary Lynne Dittmar at the Third Annual Space Exploration Conference and Exhibit, the results of interviews with 367 people aged 18 to 25 indicated NASA is irrelevant to 51% of the Generation Y population (Figure 2). This data and results from similar surveys suggest that the space exploration project managers of the future will spend more time marketing and defending their projects.

Given the significant changes in the political environment, projects will also find much more emphasis on cost and schedule reporting and forecasting based on performance. To respond to these customer demands, projects will need to improve methods of

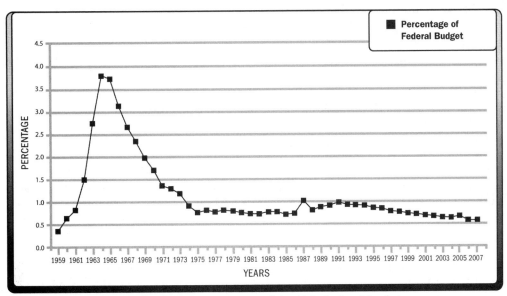

Figure 1:   NASA funding as a percent of the U.S. federal budget.

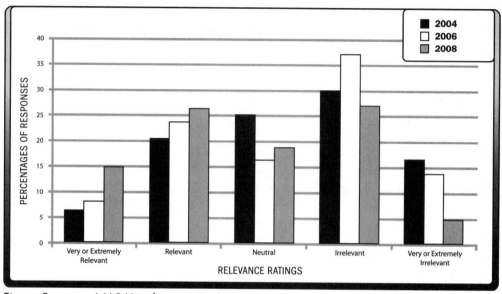

Figure 2:   NASA's relevance to Generation Y.

predicting problems, cost overruns, and schedule slips. Integrated management systems and simulation software will assist the project manager in improving cost, schedule, and technical performance, and with developing mitigation plans to resolve predicted and real problems and risks. Independent integrated cost and schedule assessments will become increasingly widespread. Having an optimistic baseline is fine, but an unrealistic or "success-oriented" baseline will no longer be acceptable. With a "success-oriented" baseline, or one that is under-bid, the flexibility and opportunity to mitigate problems and risks is removed from the project team's control. All that remains is for the project to execute precisely to the baseline plan, or overrun the cost and schedule.

Additionally, the customer base will shift from government programs to commercial ventures. Hence, space exploration projects will have an increasingly difficult time getting funded for the sake of science objectives or pure exploration. Future missions will need to develop a credible business case and aggressively manage their resources, expectations, and outcomes based on a profit or economic motive, not just an altruistic benefit to society.

Ironically, much of the impetus for improving cost and schedule performance will come from the funding government oversight agencies, such as the Office of Management and Budget (OMB) and the General Accounting Office (GAO) in the United States. The managers and analysts in these oversight agencies have become more sophisticated in their understanding of project management and are not satisfied with the status quo. Each year, these agencies, along with Congress, tighten the control on federal agencies and require increased transparency in project status as well as improved performance against project baselines. Projects that fail to meet their commitments will be subject to termination. While termination has been used as a threat in the past, project managers will find that these terminations will increasingly become reality for underperforming projects.

Ultimately, the increased surveillance and accountability to OMB, GAO, and Congress will drive project teams to find better ways of establishing control and reporting status against their baselines through new technology and processes. Project teams will also have incentive to bid the job at a reasonable cost and schedule, and will aggressively work to the baseline plan. Project organizations with a history of performing in line with their commitments will be rewarded with more work, while those failing to meet their commitments will not continue to receive project approvals. The practice of underbidding contracts and projects will result in terminations based on poor performance.

The Global Economy

In the future, space projects will not be influenced just by the sponsoring country and its budget limitations and policies. Increasingly, the global economy will affect where projects are located, who supplies the materials and components, and how the work is organized. The emerging markets of Brazil, Russia, India, and China will have a larger influence on project management, and more manufacturing will occur in these countries. Already these nations are changing global availability of scarce resources, production philosophies, and quality control verification. But no matter what, these countries will have an increasing influence on the economy and business practices of the current aerospace countries.

Chinese consumers will fuel the fastest-growing and largest economy on earth for products ranging from food, electronics, and raw materials and will have a workforce capacity to accommodate many of their own demands. The rest of the world economies will compete for all resources in ways that are still unimaginable. The people of the emerging economies are also going to find innovative ways to meet consumer demands that will surprise and most likely surpass the innovators and project managers of the United States and other Western countries.

Since the project managers of the emerging countries do not have the same model for managing the megaprojects of the space exploration community, they will find new and often cheaper ways to build their hardware. The United States, which currently tries to protect technology advances and secrets, will find itself on the outside looking in at the lower cost and more imaginative ways to access space.

A prime example of this ingenuity is the Indian automobile industry's Nano by Tata. The Nano is the least expensive production car in the world and debuted at US$2,500. The Western automobile manufacturers will not be able to achieve this feat with their current design, development, and marketing models. Just as the Tata Nano is revolutionizing the automobile industry, at least in some parts of the world, so too will India, China, and other growing economies find revolutionary ways to produce space hardware and manage projects.

The Physical Environment

Not only will the global or macro playing field change, the local or micro environment will also change. Because of the realities of the global economy and an increased desire to balance work and home life, "virtual" teams will completely change the way they currently operate. There are two types of projects in the space exploration community: 1) projects that build hardware on-site, and 2) projects that procure and manage the activities of others. The first type of project will continue to have physical office space much as they do now, with the exception that telecommuting will increase in popularity for team members that do not have to "touch" the hardware daily. The other type of project will evolve into a more virtual office concept, using new technology to improve productivity.

High energy prices, along with increased environmental awareness, will cause one of the biggest changes in the way project managers interact with their project teams. Increasingly, team members will work from home, both to save on commuting costs and reduce emissions from automobiles. Fortunately, this "virtual office" concept will be possible with the technological advances that have already been developed and are continuing to evolve. Team members will meet regularly in a central physical office, typically a conference room to handle problems that need face-to-face interaction. All other transactions will occur via encrypted websites, phones, e-mails, and new collaboration devices. The need for individual offices will be greatly reduced, if not eliminated, due to the decentralization of the team. In addition to environmental and cost advantages, the project manager will also find that this virtual office concept opens up a greater field of candidates to the project team. Since communication will predominately be through technology rather than in person, the project manager can hire team members living in other states, and even other countries, so that the best candidate will be selected for each position.

Project travel will also change considerably. Rather than frequent status meetings requiring extensive travel to other parts of the country or world, project managers will rely more on web-based tools to conduct meetings with distant vendors and customers, share files, and view each other on high-definition video feeds. The change in the travel paradigm will enable team members to become more productive, spending less time in airplanes and at airports, as well as give the team members the opportunity to balance work and home life more effectively. The project will also realize a savings from the elimination of much of the cost of travel.

Project managers will not immediately be comfortable with this new distributed office paradigm. They will have a hard time understanding what their team members are working on and will question the efficiency of this new arrangement. Project managers are accustomed to being in control, and the success of the virtual office concept will rely on their ability to release some of that control. Some will do better with this arrangement than others. In the long run, however, the technology that will allow for instant collaboration, communication, and data transfer will make most of the project managers comfortable with the virtual office concept.

A discussion on the physical environment of project team members in space exploration would be incomplete without acknowledging that some of the project team will be in space. The astronauts are vital members of the project team, ensuring that project requirements are met in space. Much energy will be spent on ensuring availability of the best possible collaboration, communications, and advanced technology for these valuable team members. However, with the exception that their hardware and software must have greater redundancy and reliability than their counterparts on Earth, the astronauts are just other telecommuting members of the team, who require the same considerations and capabilities as the other team members, plus a few more specialized capabilities, such as being able to communicate from Mars.

The People

Whereas the workforce has changed over the last 25 years from a white, male, homogeneous labor force to a diversity of races, genders, and religions, the next 15 years will bring even greater change in the project team composition. Truly global and diverse teams will become the norm. Additionally, a new generation (see Figure 3) will inherit the space program.

The workers that have dominated project teams for the past 15 years have been predominantly baby boomers, born between the years 1946 and 1964. This generation was focused on "having it all" and working long, hard hours. They grew up in a relatively orderly world and learned early to combine their efforts to achieve social programs, while maintaining their individuality. As this generation of project managers retires, their replacements will come from Generation Y, sometimes known as the Millennial generation. These new managers are the most highly educated of all U.S. generations to enter the workforce, and grew up in highly structured environments with a multitude of activities. Since this generation grew up multitasking, they will expect to do the same in the workplace. They will not accept the ways of the baby boomers and will find innovative and more flexible ways to accomplish their assignments. They will also expect to have more information at their fingertips, challenge the status quo, and put their own careers ahead of the interests of the organization (Kroeger, 2005). According to a group of Generation Y employees and managers within NASA, their life experiences have made them "easily bored, have short term career perspectives, focus on personal success, and extremely independent" (Skytland & Fitzpatrick, 2008). Without passing judgment on which group will manage projects better, suffice it to say they will manage differently.

Finally, with the departure of the experienced baby boomers from the workforce, the much less-experienced Generation Y managers will need a lot of training and shared lessons from the departing leaders. Even though new processes and tools will be used in the future, the new leaders will need to understand the mistakes of the past to make sure

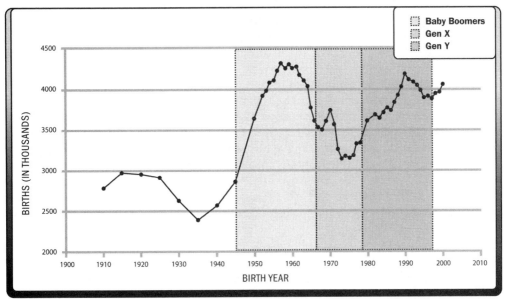

Figure 3:   Changing demographics of the U.S. workforce (Skytland & Fitzpatrick, 2008).

they do not happen again. The static demand-driven nature of current lessons-learned databases prevalent in many aerospace organizations will give way to supply-driven collaborative environments that "suggest" areas that project management teams can explore to mitigate risk, leverage scarce resources, or perform work more efficiently. In other words, the lessons learned will come to the teams, rather than the teams searching out the lessons, much like the micro-marketing done by Apple™ iTunes™ or Amazon.com™, with suggestions of books and music that the user may find interesting to buy. The programming within the lessons-learned databases will predict which data points are important to a team, based on the integrated management system reports and simulations run by the team members.

Training, consulting, and mentoring will play a large role in developing future project managers. Much of this training will be computer- and simulation-based, and will be embraced by the generation of project managers that grew up with video games, iPods™, and cell phones.

Prepared for the Future

New technologies, processes, and relationships will shape a future as different from today's management of projects as today's management techniques are different from those of the past. The future of space exploration project management will rely on the innovations and ideas of the people involved in the space program. They will dream what can be possible, and then go about the task of making it happen.

As Scott Horowitz, the former astronaut and NASA associate administrator for the exploration systems mission directorate said in the PM Challenge 2007 video, "People ask me, having flown on the shuttle four times, what makes the shuttle go up? And a lot of people will say, 'well it's those big, giant, solid rocket motors and those space shuttle main engines and all that flame and propellant that makes the shuttle go.' And it's not. That's not what makes the shuttle go. It's the blood and sweat and the dedication of thousands of people that make this very complex machine fly" (Horowitz, 2007).

The next generation of project managers will take space exploration project management into new directions. While the tools, processes, global economy, and physical environment will all play key parts in changing the paradigms of project management, in the end, the people managing the projects, along with all the factors that influenced their backgrounds and training, will be the most important part of the equation. This thought was conveyed best by Steve Cook (2007), NASA's director of the Exploration Launch Project Office at the Marshall Space Flight Center, "Everything we do is about people. It's about the people that make human space flight successful." And it is the people that will make the new frontiers in space exploration project management successful as well.

Disclaimer: The ideas and opinions expressed in this chapter reflect the opinion of the author and not those of NASA or of the U.S. Government.

References

Bekefi, T., Epstein, M. J., & Yuthas, K. (2008). Creating growth: Using opportunity risk management effectively. *Journal of Accountancy,* June 2008, 72-77.

Burch, P. (2007). *NASA Project Management Challenge 2007 video.* Retrieved from YouTube website, http://www.youtube.com/watch?v=foj6uiZeIvg.

Chapman, R. L. (1973). *Project management in NASA: the system and the men.* Washington, DC: US Government Printing Office.

Cook, S. (2007). *NASA Project Management Challenge 2007 video.* Retrieved from YouTube website, http://www.youtube.com/watch?v=foj6uiZeIvg.

Dittmar, M. L. (2008). *Gen Y and Space Exploration: A Desire for Interaction, Participation and Empowerment.* Retrieved from NASA website, www.nasa.gov/pdf/214675main_ Dittmar.pdf.

Horowitz, S. J. (2007). *NASA Project Management Challenge 2007 video.* Retrieved from YouTube website, http://www.youtube.com/watch?v=foj6uiZeIvg.

Kroeger, L. (2005). *Managing in a Multiple Generation Work Environment.* Obtained from Lin Kroeger, www.pwdconsulting.com.

Project Management Institute. (1996). *A guide to the project management body of knowledge.* Newtown Square, PA.: Project Management Institute.

Rowling, J. K. (1999). *Harry Potter and the prisoner of Azkaban.* London, England: Bloomsbury Publishing.

Skytland, N., & Fitzpatrick, G. (2008). *Generation Y Perspectives.* Retrieved from NASA website, www.nasa.gov/pdf/214672main_KPainting-GenY_rev11.pdf.

Tapscott, D., & Williams, A, D. (2006). *Wikinomics: How Mass Collaboration Changes Everything.* New York, NY: Penguin Group.

CHAPTER 21

State Government —Project Management 2025

Jonathan Weinstein, PMP
Tim Jaques, PMP

1.0 Introduction

The state government environment is unlike any other project environment. Bound together across a myriad of constituencies and programs, state governmental agencies serve as the essential middle layer of a government (see Figure 1), performing key functions for the citizenry that neither the federal government nor the multitude of localities can perform. State governments face enormous challenges in the coming years. With increased populations, infrastructure demands, and program needs, state governments will be challenged over the next 15 years to deliver services that are relevant and cost effective.

Project management in state government is different. State governments represent an enormous marketplace of ideas, interconnected stakeholders, underserved populations, priorities, requirements, and agendas. With budgets in the billions, government projects involve a broad spectrum of disciplines, including construction, health services, the environment, technology, policing and defense, and more. They must contend with legislative agendas and schedules, budgets, state workforce size and capabilities, the authorities of individual agencies, and more. A few trends that will effect state government operations, common with most other industries, include the aging population and the shift in the workforce toward younger, more transient people.

1.1 Key Assumptions:

There are a host of trends that will shape the government project management environment in 2025, including:

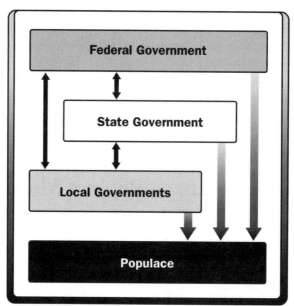

Figure 1:   The layers of government in the United States.

- Project management will become increasingly defined and strategic, to the point where states are maintaining detailed project reporting processes at the executive level. Just as the technology function has evolved toward a centralized role over the past 40 years, project management will continue its evolution up the management chain.
- The volume of information available to project managers will continue to increase. The access to and integration of that information will be improved through the use of more effective technologies such as data mining and business intelligence. These tools will be ubiquitous and used as everyday tools. The emphasis for project managers will be on front-end information management and decision-making.
- Tools employed by project managers in the state government environment will be radically different. Improvements in technology, connectivity, and project management practices will contribute to the emergence of a new type of government project manager in 2025. The public will have access to more data and some familiarity with using business intelligence tools to view and better understand that data. Web 2.0 makes the use of the Internet ubiquitous to most citizens accessing services from the government; similarly the evolution of eGov to the next iteration, eGov 2.0. By 2025, we will be discussing versions 3.0 or beyond.
- The "hyper-connectivity" that is the norm today will continue to evolve in state government. Many more state employees will work from their homes in 2025. These organizations will utilize all means of electronic and inter-personal connectivity–Internet, mobile devices, and online communities. As 2025 nears, use of these tools will be prolific across all elements of the personal, corporate, and

government environments. Social networks (on- and off-line) will be prolific and then consolidate to primary networks for public and private interactions.

- Governments tend to be evolutionary versus revolutionary. Compared to some industries where dramatic change is essential for survival, there is no competition to take over state government's services and "products." Historically, change in government organizations is akin to steering a giant ship and not a sports car.
- A shift from stove-piped, politically structured organizations to organizations structured to align with functions and services will continue to increase. In 2025, state government organizations may reflect how its citizens are organized around specific issues like welfare benefits.
- Political, budgetary, and public pressures to improve efficiency in delivering services to citizens will force the lines between federal, state, and local jurisdictions to become more and more transparent to citizens. The result will be tighter integration and connectivity between programs, allowing citizens to have a single point of entry into the "government" at *any* level and access *all* services and benefits, emphasizing continuity and flow of services.
- The foundations of project management within the government environment will remain fundamentally unchanged. Elements like the project management lifecycle, governance, portfolio management, and earned value analysis will be refined and will experience improvements as a result of technological improvements. The most significant changes in government project management will be the introduction of new skills and techniques and shift in emphasis toward the "softer" side of managing people and building coalitions and communities around projects or programs.

1.2 A Concept of the Future

To provide the essential backdrop for this chapter, we'd like to describe what a citizen's interaction with the government will look like in 2025. Imagine a future where the citizens of your state logon to their "MyState" home page. They have instant access in one place to every byte of their information and relevant state services they utilize. In this session, John Q. Public...

- Pays for his daughter's tuition at the state university...and checks her grades, even reads her most recent paper on the recent presidential election in 2024.
- Speaking of elections, he casts his vote in the local elections for mayor and city council.
- "Tags" the deed and property drawings for his house, on file with county clerk, to be forwarded to the architect designing the addition to his home. The architect will "return" the drawings to the county inspectors for approval.
- Checks to see where his son is currently located. A quick click shows he's driving (over the speed limit) a couple miles away on his way home.
- Checks the real-time traffic pace for his trip out later.
- Confirms his appearance for jury duty.
- Verifies the amount of his upcoming tax bill.
- Determines the status of legislation pending in the state senate on a pending tax increase.

- Renews his license.

- ...and more.

This example is a means of illustrating the possibilities that technology offers, but more importantly it reflects a trend in the state government arena to increase the ability of its citizens to access and utilize services in the most efficient and cost effective manner. The citizen's perspective shown here is meant to open the dialogue about what project management in 2025 will need to be like in order to meet the expectations of its citizens.

2.0 Project Management in 2025

Much like construction or technology, governmental project management will evolve into a specialized field within project management. The structures, skills, and competencies required to effectively operate will be specifically geared toward public service. As information and data become more available through front-end tools, project managers will need special clearances and access levels to successfully execute a project. There will be far more project managers in state government service, but the role will also become more delineated across those roles. Executive program managers will drive the execution of the highest level strategies for state agencies. These prognostications should be seen in the light of history. Figure 2 below illustrates the transformation of project management from its administrative roots to its vibrant current state, and beyond. A description of some key drivers that precipitated this evolution follows.

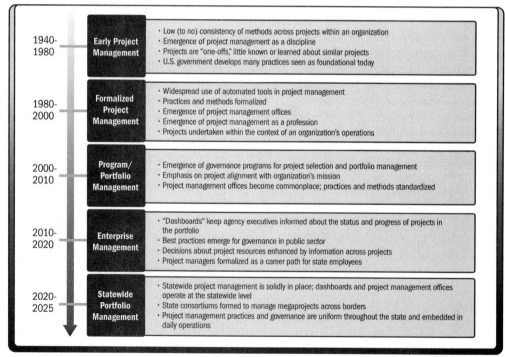

Figure 2:   The transformation of project management.

Consider that government project managers in 2025 will have been involved with formal project management processes since their early years. They will have learned to communicate, work, and manage using technology and Web-based services. As a cohort, the newest project managers today in state government will most likely to be willing and able to be early adopters of the latest and greatest tools and techniques for getting things done.

Leadership will become even more important in 2025 than today as the level of cross-organizational, cross-jurisdictional, and cross-sector integration and consolidation will continue to increase.

The impact of drivers like hyper-connectivity and social networking on the project management environment in 2025 will shift the project management environment and will be most visible in the relationship between the state government and its customers, the citizens. There will be a convergence of the interests of project stakeholders. Citizen "issue communities" built around the hot issues of the day will have complementary "communities of practice" in the state government.

3.0 Managing Projects in 2025

"The more things change, the more they stay the same." This adage best summarizes the state of public sector project management in 2025. The past century of management and organizational advances has supported a massive amount of change undertaken to both the theory and application of project management. Yet despite the very real progress in areas like earned value, scheduling, resource management, and sponsorship, project management will continue to focus on humans introducing change and all the inherent heavy lifting that come with getting other humans to change. Whether it is a new way of paving roads, or new methods for delivering vaccinations through public health, the human capacity to invent and innovate, and also to resist change, will continue as ever.

Improvements in estimating techniques highlight how tools have changed, yet project management has stayed the same. In the old days, estimating techniques for construction projects involved poring over supply schedules, vendor catalogs, and building a cost plan with a small army of clerks. Today, the typical construction planning process involves consulting extensive parametric data sets and leveraging simulation models to evoke a realistic set of assumptions about cost and schedule. These tools evaluate materials, labor, indirect costs and other data against a host of factors including structural complexity, square footage, weather, supply chains, and more. Tools help to quickly compute massive amounts of data through use various simulation techniques, like Monte Carlo, the assumptions are validated and refined. Yet, underlying the latest generation of tools is a project that must be planned, managed and completed by people, as it was done 10, 20, even 80 years ago.

State governments are currently in the throes of widespread adoption of the first generation of formal project management. Many states have methodologies, but inconsistently apply those methodologies. Higher-level project processes, like program and portfolio management, remain in the early phases of maturity for most state governments organizations. By 2025, project management will have matured in the state government arena across most aspects of project management, including organization, lifecycle phases, processes, tools and techniques, and roles. In each of these areas, the theory and application of project management will evolve between today and 2025.

Across all states, the level of maturity is uneven today, and will remain that way into the foreseeable future. Some states will evolve an enterprise approach to managing projects and portfolios, while other states will take longer to move from the tactical form of project management into something higher. At a high level of granularity, statewide maturity can be classified into three categories—tactical, strategic, and enterprise. As Figure 3 shows, tactical is the lowest level of project management, strategic level introduces higher level functions, and enterprise results in truly coordinated project management.

In many state governments today, project management is disaggregated. Individual agencies pursue the implementation of more formalized project management processes on their own, with little coordination across entities. Agencies that have matured this capability have project management offices and a compliment of people and tools. For most state governments, there is little that binds the agency-level project management processes together, except for a statewide methodology. Yet very few states have a significant statewide project management presence today. And you will be hard-pressed to find a state with the capacity to manage resources at the enterprise level.

Many state governments today maintain a statewide project management office (PMO) whose primary function includes:

- Supporting statewide projects with project managers and or consultative expertise;
- Maintaining the project management methodology;
- Evaluating agency-level tool purchases; and
- Project management training and mentoring programs.

Agency-level PMOs are common, and they serve much the same function as the statewide PMO, except that the scope tends to be limited to the agency. The services listed above

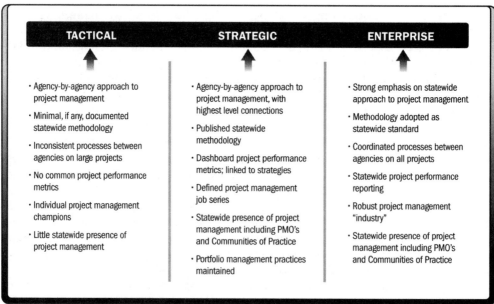

Figure 3: State government project management maturity scale.

underscore the major assumption of PMOs today: they operate as agents of change. Because project management is in its formative years in state government, PMOs are called up to introduce, educate, model, and train good project management.

Unlike the typical Engineering or Human Resources department that has been around for many years and exists to fulfill specific needs, the PMO is still seen as a new entity, an intruder, and a direct affront to budgets everywhere. Because of the resistance to adopting full-scale project management practices, PMOs fill a necessary void in delivery of project management and act as change agents for the adoption of project management practices.

By 2025, formal project organizations will exist within state agencies as an accepted, ongoing business unit. The project management organization of 2025 will be an extension of today's project management offices. But the future state of project management organizations promises a more robust organization, with larger staff and ownership of the project resources across the agency. The PMO circa 2025 will leverage the latest tools to interact with hyper-connected stakeholder groups, much like today's use of the latest tools. But the heavy lifting will not have diminished—at the heart of these PMOs, humans will be acting as agents of change because that is what projects are all about.

In state governments today, project managers and sponsors come into the field from other careers. Most of today's senior project managers evolved from informal project management into certified project managers with a well-defined skill set. In 2025, many agency employees will have been in contact with some sort of formal project management throughout their careers. Project managers and team members in 2025 will have progressed with the benefit of formal methodologies and tools that were absent a generation ago. The familiarity with project management will serve to integrate project management more seamlessly into the various layers of the organization.

In 2025, the project management *organization* will have extended beyond the basic functions seen today and assumed primary responsibility for maintaining the enterprise portfolio of projects for the state. PMOs of the future will have accountability for most major statewide projects, and the core project personnel that oversee the projects. There will be a direct line authority for the success of projects, and there may be PMOs reporting directly to the executive branch of government.

Despite recent advances in the tools and techniques associated with project management, the major pillars of planning and managing projects have remained unchanged. Take the Gantt chart. Developed in 1917 by Henry Gantt, the Gantt chart provided a graphical representation of effort over time. The Gantt is widely used in state governments because it makes for an excellent executive reporting vehicle. Early Gantt charts showed bars on a graph much like today. It was not until much later that task relationships were added to the charts.

Gantt charts gained widespread popularity with the proliferation of Microsoft Project. The beauty of the Gantt chart lies in its ability to show a large amount of information in simple graphical form. An every-day, run-of-the-mill Gantt shows high-level deliverables, milestones, and project phases. But it also includes the length of time for completion of activities and work packages. The Gantt also depicts planned effort, actual progress, and critical relationships between activities. To obtain this much information outside of a Gantt usually involves relying on opaque columns and rows that in their totality fail to "paint the picture," which a Gantt so eloquently does.

Henry Gantt developed the chart in the formative years of modern management theory as a way to improve productivity. Using his chart, managers could plan sequences of tasks, evaluate the efficiency of those plans, and even reward employees for their efforts. The essential function of a Gantt chart, to depict activities in a certain sequence, is a time-tested standard of project management that will remain unchanged into the foreseeable future. Despite great leaps in digital tools, the basic notion of understanding work effort, over time, will persevere.

One arena where great advances are promised is in the area of tools. Today, state governments are beginning the widespread adoption of business intelligence, workflow automation, and content management. This trend will continue, and the reliance of state agencies on these technologies will increase as public demand for information increases. With business intelligence capabilities ripening across the public sector, project managers will be faced with a host of new information from which to generate estimates and project deliverables. The development and implementation of the tools themselves will consume many thousands of project hours between today and 2025. In addition to these tools, the maturation of Web 2.0 technologies will mean that social networks will evolve from the current, inchoate state to where they become very real and influential platforms for public policy discourse. Project teams will use social networking tools in the development of projects, and as a means to communicate with stakeholders and coalitions.

In the future, project schedules, budgets, and deliverables will be created through the use of business intelligence (BI) tools that use a broad set of information. IT projects will begin to leverage the same types of estimating techniques that have long matured in the construction industry, using commercial-grade estimating data sets and tools.

A new breed of project management tools will embrace automated workflow and make today's process of completing templates seem old-fashioned and clumsy. Project information will be maintained in BI-ready data stores and will be viewable through a variety of lenses, including reports, interactive forums, and "mashups" (combinations of disparate data into an integrated tool). New tool interfaces will auto-fill much of the information that is today gotten only through the completion of templates. Project charters, scope statements, budgets, and schedules will be populated automatically.

One advance will be the decrease of the work breakdown structure (WBS) as a stand-alone deliverable. Historically, the WBS has served as a mid-point between identification of deliverables and the creation of a project schedule. While the underlying need for a WBS will not change, the WBS itself will be subsumed into more robust project scheduling interfaces. The trend of minimizing the WBS has already begun, in that often it is bypassed in favor of development of the schedule. Tools today allow for the work breakdown to instantly be viewed as a schedule. WBS strict constructionists will revile at the notion.

Project input and reporting interfaces will evolve to where the need for the forms that are used today is eliminated. State governments will begin adopting new technologies that streamline the creation of charters, scope documents, and schedules. With newer, "intelligent" interfaces, project managers will spend less time creating forms and more time searching for the right predecessor project to use as a baseline of information. Next-generation content management and automated workflow systems will drive the creation of project deliverables. There will be robust resource management technologies that maintain the resource pool in real time.

In addition to Gantt charts, public sector project managers will use other advanced graphical reporting schemas to process and correlate large amounts of information.

4.0 Structures and Processes, Circa 2025

Project management in the government sector in 2025 will evolve from the structures and organizations commonly found today. As shown in Figure 4, the prominence of individual efforts, team-based structures, and basic PMO "formations" in project management today will expand to reflect organizational constructs that are more "coalition" and "state-wide" oriented. Structures and processes associated with enterprise project management (EPM), project/program management, and governance will become increasingly commonplace in public sector organizations in 2025.

Today, there is an emerging constellation of services and organizations that, when combined, form a standard for enterprise-wide project management in the public sector. The enterprise, or agency, usually includes all organizations that fall under the auspices and authority of the most senior leader. By 2025, EPM in the public sector will be commonplace. EPM will become the standard at many state government agencies. While the evolution from traditional project management to its enterprise-oriented successor will not be a dramatic battle to the end, the result may be truly transformational. The goal of most EPM programs can be simply stated as "the right projects, done right." That is, the right mix of projects as selected by a formal selection process, coupled with talented project teams armed with the right tools.

In many resource-constrained organizations, managers must choose the most effective investment strategy for implementing EPM. The investment will involve a multi-year, multi-faceted commitment to creating a full-fledged project management capabil-

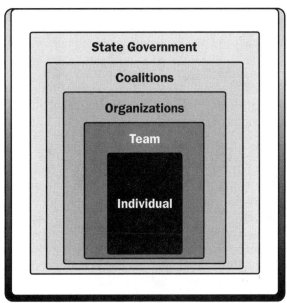

Figure 4: Context of project management structures

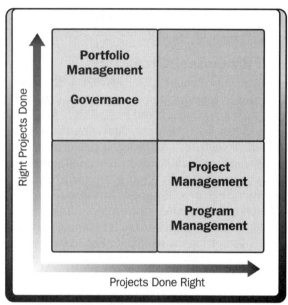

Figure 5: The two basic paths toward enterprise project management.

ity. An organization cannot go from disparate, unorganized project management to EPM overnight, or even over a couple years.

EPM champions should evaluate the two basic paths toward EPM: improving the quality of project execution ("Projects Done Right") and improving the project selection processes ("Right Projects Done") (see Figure x). The first path will take an organization toward standards for projects and programs, implementing training, communities of practice, lessons learned and best-practices reviews, and more. The goal of getting "projects done right" is to have projects come in on time, on budget, and meetings all quality standards. This path will improve projects and programs at the lowest level. With better reporting and estimating, improved project management will increase an executive's insight into each project, making the project more transparent. This approach can be focused within one area of the agency, such as a division. This approach does not address the issues associated with solving the same business problem multiple times through multiple projects, which is where the second path is effective.

The second path, "right projects done," will move the organization toward formal project selection processes, portfolio management, and is, by nature, a top-down endeavor. The shift toward an enterprise perspective is in its formative stages today, taking hold in parts of organizations such as the technology units where project management maturity is typically higher. While this approach can be employed within a discrete part of an agency, one has to consider that enterprise project management is about . . .well . . .the enterprise. The goal of having the right projects done should address making sound project selections for the entire agency, not just a piece of it. Effective project selection processes seek to understand the root business problem or opportunity and to establish a strategy for addressing the root cause. For example, if the root problem is that not enough information is available to staff to troubleshoot help-desk tickets, developing two solutions for help-desk tickets probably will not resolve the problem very effectively. Yet this happens all the time in the public sector. Adjoining divisions solve the same business problem multiple times simply because the project origination process was insufficient to cross-organizational boundaries.

Getting the right projects done involves creating effective portfolio management processes, but the portfolio should exist under the umbrella of governance. Governance is not, strictly speaking, a project management process. Governance is a management process that goes beyond projects, aligning the organization's resources and efforts against the highest-level strategic goals. The implementation of governance processes is akin to the evolution of project management offices—once established within a specific part of an organization, typically IT, now rising to the highest echelons in government organizations. Public-sector experience with governance over the next few years will contribute to the establishment of agency-wide and ultimately, statewide governance structures that will support decision-making by the governor and his or her cabinet in effectively spending the taxpayers' dollars and efficiently delivering the services they demand. Increased access to information by the public will contribute to greater scrutiny on how the government works (or doesn't work), which will, in turn, compel the need for strong governance structures.

The two paths to implementing EPM – top down and bottom up – are less about the direction of the change, and more about the costs and benefits that each path brings to the organization. The path of increased alignment (top down) calls for investments in portfolio management tools, resource management, executive reporting, and governance. Investments in this arena should yield a better portfolio and improved consensus among management as to which projects rank highest and why. This path requires a high degree of executive buy-in to the investment and resulting value of project management. The bottom-up path will result in improvements to the execution of projects and programs, hence the path of increased competency. This path calls for investments in training, PMO design and development, schedule and estimating tools, and methodologies.

Increased "accountability" of government will lead to increased verification processes. The current and emerging structures and processes in the project management arena can be a critical component to improving the level of trust citizens have in their governments. The project audit function will continue to evolve and mature in state governments, and will become a formalized audit function by 2025. This will be necessary to ensure that projects maintain effective documentation and adherence to standards. The audit function will, in and of itself, be a driver of improvements to project management in state government.

As the capability for getting "projects done right" and the "right projects done" matures, public-sector organizations will adopt techniques and tools that are solidly in the private sector today. In particular, resource management and planning, commonly associated with enterprise resource planning (ERP) and business process automation software and practices, are emerging in the public sector to support efforts to improve governments' operational effectiveness and provide greater public access to services via the Web. Significant improvements in project management by 2025, fueled by the structures, processes, and practices discussed in this chapter will support more effective management of public-sector resources, in particular the assignment, utilization, and development of government employees. Program and portfolio management activities are at the epicenter of efforts to introduce resource management practices. With the maturity of project and portfolio management organizations and the implementation of statewide governance practices, government agencies, and ultimately a state's political leadership, will see a commensurate improvement in the effective planning and utilization of increasingly finite human and budgetary resources.

5.0 The Profession of Public-Sector Project Management in 2025

The growth of the project management profession is illustrated by the meteoric growth in membership in the Project Management Institute (over 260,000 as of June 2008, according to www.pmi.org) and the increasing variety of training and certifications available to practitioners. The discipline of project management is not likely to go the way of some fads that have come and gone (and come again) into the business of management (remember total quality management?). This trend of formalization and institutionalization through certification, advanced degrees, and continuing education indicates that the project management profession as a career path in the public sector, particularly in state governments, will continue to grow and become more specialized in the future.

The next generation of public sector employees, in general, will reflect two key trends: 1) the increasing mobility and desire for a variety of professional experiences among the workforce; and 2) the sector's hiring practices, which are subject to budgetary and efficiency pressures forcing periods of limited or no hiring of "new blood." The evolution of the discipline, practices, structures, and processes in project management in the public sector described in this chapter suggests that the public sector needs to improve its capacity to think "outside the box," testing new ideas and making bold decisions related to the management, visibility, and accountability for executing the people's business. No longer can the public sector operate as it has for decades; simply delivering the "products and services" the government believes are best for its constituents. Rather, governments' effectiveness will depend on its increasing ability to apply knowledge and skills from a coalition built from multiple sources, including academia, business and its citizens.

Skills and Competencies

Future state government managers and leaders, today's high school and college graduates, will have grown up in a hyper-connected world. They will bring a new set of skills, capabilities, personalities, and work methods to the workforce. Today's government managers and leaders must start now to create an appropriate environment that accommodates and leverages these emerging skills and capabilities. In short, the skills and competencies required by project management practitioners, teams, and executives will significantly evolve by 2025.

The project manager in 2025 will reflect a merger of competencies from specific areas of project management to the areas of "general" business management, such as business process execution, personnel development, budgeting, procurement, and contracting. As shown in Figure 6, the project manager in 2025 will interface with a wide range of stakeholders and sources, as shown in the graphic. Conversely, senior managers will be required to possess and practice core project management skills and competencies. The executive sponsor in 2025 will have to do more than agree that project management is important or valuable. They will have to be actively involved in projects through their

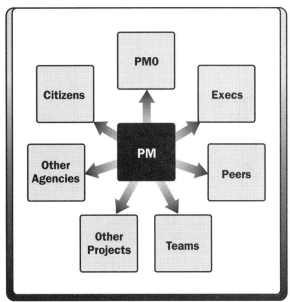

Figure 6:   A wide range of relationships for the project manager of 2025.

participation in the emerging core structures of program management, portfolio management, and governance.

Coalition building is one skill likely to be essential in 2025 that is not common among today's project management practitioners and project participants. Executing a project like the one described earlier in this chapter that provides citizens with a single, comprehensive point-of-entry to access information and services from the state will require levels of cross-organizational cooperation and coordination not often found in the silo-structures of many of today's state governments. While some level of co-operation and information-sharing occurs today, the formation of functional, task-or outcome-oriented coalitions of government agencies, non-profit organizations or interest groups, and individual citizens will be the norm in 2025. The proliferation of online social networks offers a glimpse into the possibilities for project management as we complete the first quarter of the 21st century.

With increased specialization in project management, the project manager of 2025 will see greater opportunities in sub-disciplines. Specialization, stemming from the knowledge and expertise requirements in particular fields, will drive the industry toward increased granularity of the project manager role. Today, the profession is beginning to recognize horizontal specialization in project management, for example with scheduling and risk management certifications. As other fields continue to increase in complexity (for example construction, technology, drug development, and manufacturing), vertical expertise will emerge as a prerequisite for success. In state government, project manager requirements will reflect this trend in both contracted project managers and state staff.

Characteristics of the primary project management roles and their associates skills and competencies circa 2025 are outlined in Table 1. Some of the documented items may seem more appropriate in the private sector environment. However, the adoption and refinement of skills and competencies not typically found in the government will be a hallmark of the period leading to 2025 in the area of public sector project management.

Table 1:   Skills needed by role in 2025.

Role	Characteristics and New Skills & Competencies for 2025
Project Team Member	• Can rapidly apply information from a myriad of sources • Adept at a broad source of technologies, mostly focused on communicating up and across the project • Customer-focused behavior toward other team members, project managers, executives, citizens, and other stakeholders
Project Manager	• Specialist in the subject area for the projects they manage; a shift away from the project manager as "generalist" • Has basic business planning skills (e.g., resource management, budgeting, and procurement) • Participates on steering groups with sponsors and executives to foster cross-project coordination and communication • Adept communicator using a wide variety of methods and media
Program and Portfolio Manager	• Has strong analytical and decision-making skills; able to process a high volume of information from a multitude of sources • Shows flexibility and improvisation in allocating resources and addressing issues across projects • Has experience with various management and implementation methodologies and techniques, including coaching project managers • Applies appropriate project review, selection, and prioritization methodologies; has fortitude to identify and terminate "bad" projects • Ensures alignment of organization's strategy with operations, programs, and projects
Executive Sponsor	• Actively participates in setting the organization's strategy • Is a skilled communicator, motivating members of the organization toward implementing strategy through their operational and project-based work • Facilitates change, clearing the path for the changes resulting from executing projects • Identifies business opportunities and initiates associated projects or programs

Project Management Specialist	• Individuals with specialization, certification, or advanced degrees in a particular project management area
	• Deployed across multiple projects or assigned to focus on large, multi-year enterprise-wide projects
	• Likely area of specialization on projects in 2025:
	  • Risk Management
	  • Scheduling
	  • Budgeting
	  • Procurement/Contracting
	  • Change Management
	  • Organizational/Industrial Psychology

Certification and Training

The emergence of new skills and competencies for project managers, along with the increasingly important role of program manager and the need for greater executive participation in projects are reflected in the growth of project management oriented training and certifications. This trend toward increasing individual specialization will continue, adding to the certifications currently available from the Project Management Institute (see Figure 7).

A likely next phase in specialization is for industry or content-oriented project management certification. Some already exist, like the Certified Construction Manager (CCM) from the Construction Manager Certification Institute, administered by the Construction Management Association of America. How does this relate to project management in the government sector? The pressure on government to improve efficiency and deliver the best services at the lowest cost to its citizens will push agencies to build or hire specialized expertise. With the availability of formal certification or degrees from various non-profit and for-profit organizations in the areas of healthcare, IT, transportation, and manufacturing, state governments will increasingly employ personnel who have obtained these qualifications.

For government personnel without formal education, state governments are moving toward building an internal capability, outsourcing, or sending individuals to obtain training, certification, or degrees. A number of states already have implemented full-scale project management training and certification programs. Many of these education programs are aligned with newly established "title series" or formal career paths for project managers employed by state governments. Outside the government, a quick search of "degrees in project management" on the Web yields over a dozen colleges and universities that offer graduate degrees.

How Does Project Management Get Done in 2025?

Flying cars, self-aware computers and robots, and freeze-dried lunches are not likely, though greater reliance on expert, specialized project management is nearly guaranteed. Throughout the chapter we endeavored to use trends and our direct experience

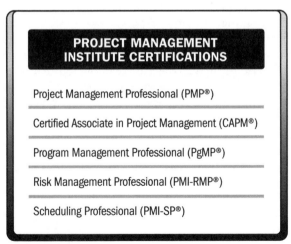

PROJECT MANAGEMENT INSTITUTE CERTIFICATIONS

Project Management Professional (PMP®)

Certified Associate in Project Management (CAPM®)

Program Management Professional (PgMP®)

Risk Management Professional (PMI-RMP®)

Scheduling Professional (PMI-SP®)

Figure 7:   Current PMI certifications.

with state government to inform our description of project management in 2025 in this environment. Taking a bit of a leap in prognosticating, what will project managers be doing in 2025?

- *Tools* – "Sticky notes," pens, and good-old paper will still be in wide-use. However, in addition, project managers will be using predictive planning software to build project plans, schedules, and budgets automatically from actual data from real projects that are similar in scale and scope. Imagine completing a "wizard"-like interview and having a comprehensive project plan, based on the results of hundreds or even thousands of other projects. Everyone from the governor to the taxpayer will have access to real-time reporting and information using Web-based dashboards that are the interface to complex business intelligence systems pulling data on projects across the state.
- *Communication* – The significance of communication in relation to a project's success is not likely to wane by 2025. In fact, the variety and complexity of communication is likely to increase. Project managers will employ a mixed variety of methods, including traditional written and oral presentation, supplemented with pithy and rapid "blog"-like communications. Broadcasting, podcasting, and other Web-based technologies yet to be invented or put into widespread use, are additional means project managers will utilize to reach various stakeholders. Project managers are likely to having an increased level of participation in communication with the press, in coordination with public information officers. The proliferation of informal "press" via blogs, and the increased expectations of citizens to have access to information may thrust project managers into an unwanted spotlight, requiring strong communication skills and diplomatic acumen.
- *Meetings* – As much as we'd love to see meetings go the way of the dinosaur, they're not going anywhere. Continuing attempts to promote teleconferencing, online communications (i.e., e-mail, project portals), and other meeting-avoidance techniques just reinforce that meetings are an essential part of project management and effective communication. Improving the efficiency and effectiveness of meetings is clearly an area of opportunity for organizations. Project managers should seek to build this capability by improving their facilitation, public speaking, and organizational skills. Making strides in these areas will enable project managers to take full advantage of the continuing maturity of the technologies that support meetings. For sure, 2025 will see a marked increase in the use of virtual meetings conducted over the desktop with full video, audio, and data flowing among all participants across the geography. Ultimately, the use of technology may allow meetings to be conducted more informally, in short, focused bursts as needed, leading to fewer formal and lengthier gatherings.
- *Transparent Borders* – The combination of more scarce resources and advances in business technology may push state governments in to regional consortiums or more public-private partnerships involving large, complex projects. Teams of project managers that go across geographical, political, or organizational boundaries will be formed to address the challenges that we will face in 2025. Similarly, increasing specialization of project management is likely to lead to the integration of communities of practice (COPs) across state lines. The for-

mation of functional project management-related COPs in the public sector around cross-border issues such as welfare, healthcare, transportation, and the environment will be an essential complement to major regional projects.

7.0 Conclusion

Like the concept car you see at an auto show, the future of project management looks quite different than it does today. When you see that car, you are excited about the prospects it presents–faster, more efficient, more comfortable, easier to drive, and sexy! You would buy that car right then and there. Sadly, the chances of the concept car hitting the showrooms any time soon are near zero. Over time, different features will start to appear in other, well-established cars until, many years later, everyone is driving the car you saw years back at the auto show. This chapter provides a picture of the future of project management in state government much the same as a concept car. The understanding is that the resulting environment will look quite different from what we currently project.

State government leaders in project management would do well to consider their current capabilities and processes for executing projects, and conduct futuring exercises for their own benefit. Project management is on the rise in state governments, and will continue to increase in visibility and value delivery until a new way of creating unique products and services comes along. State governments have a vital role to play in the coming years–a fact that project management can only help make better.

Bibliography

Jaques, T. (2008). The suite life: Enterprise project management in government. Gantthead.com, April 28, 2008.

National Association of State CIOs (NASCIO). (2006). Report "Looking to the future: Challenges & Opportunities for Government IT PMOs." October 2006.

State Government of Victoria (Australia). (2006). The future of the public sector in 2025," Report by the State Services Authority, 2006.

Blomquist, T., & Müller, R. (2006). *Middle managers in program and project portfolio management: Practices, roles and responsibilities.* Newtown Square, PA: Project Management Institute.

Project Management Institute. "Project Management Body of Knowledge; Government Extension 2006

Project Management Institute.(2008). Program Management Professional (PgMP) Credential Handbook. www.pmi.org, March 2008.

Project Management Institute. (2008). Project Management Professional (PMP) Credential Handbook. www.pmi.org, March 2008.

Project Management Institute.(2008). PMI Scheduling Professional Credential Handbook. www.pmi.org, March 2008.

Project Management Institute (2008). Certified Associate in Project Management (CAPM) Credential Handbook. www.pmi.org, March 2008

PART 5

Likely Growth of Project Management

CHAPTER 22

The Future of Team Leadership in Complex Project Environments

Hans J. Thamhain
Bentley University, Waltham, Massachusetts

Abstract

Team leadership has become critically important to project performance. The twenty-first century brings new technologies, social innovations, and a closely-linked world; but also constant change, uncertainty, and disruption. This provides great business opportunities, but also enormous managerial challenges. With increasing project complexity, globalization and linkages to broader enterprise issues, team leaders of the future must understand the dynamics of people and organizations at all levels. They must be capable of dealing with people across diverse organizational and cultural boundaries and manage working relations with support functions, suppliers, sponsors, and partners. This chapter provides an insight into the changing social processes and organizational environments that drive team performance. It suggests managerial actions for building the organizational environment, work processes, and leadership skills necessary for effective role performance in the years to come.

Teamwork – The New Managerial Frontier

Teamwork has been around for thousands of years to leverage human efforts. Awesome monuments, infrastructure, governance and military campaigns are vivid testimony of impressive results that have been achieved via teamwork throughout history. For a long time, teamwork has fascinated leaders in business and society as a powerful and robust management tool. It's a process that looks straightforward and does not seem to require exotic methods, strategies, or technology. Yet, throughout the ages, and into our current era of digitization and nano-technology, teamwork remains one of the vastly underutilized managerial resources (Thamhain & Skelton, 2007). While human resource policies and managerial practices often emphasize individual expertise and skill sets, performance is ultimately determined by collective efforts. This fact is increasingly recognized in today's world of highly complex projects and global business ventures[1], and supported by billions of dollars spent by companies each year for assessing organizational environments, work processes, and leadership style toward improved team effectiveness.

Does this contradict the description of teamwork as a robust management tool? Not necessarily. But, it points at the subtle and intricate nature of teamwork that involves many sets of variables from the work environment and its organizational, social, political, and project subsystems. These variables are often difficult to observe, measure, and integrate, often sending mixed signals regarding best practices for team leadership. In fact, field research shows that building and sustaining high-performing project teams in our dynamic and culturally diverse environment is a daunting task.

Most challenged seem to be managers in complex and technology-intensive project situations, such as R&D, high-tech product and system endeavors as pointed out by field researchers for many years (Guo, 2008; Page & Schirr, 2008). The summary in Table 1 shows that these projects span numerous organizational lines, connecting a broad spectrum of personnel, support groups, contractors, partners, and customers, creating a business environment characterized by high speed, high change, and high uncertainty.[2] Their team leaders must be both technically and socially competent, an argument supported by an increasing number of managers and researchers who point at the human side as the most challenging part. In fact, research shows consistently that performance problems on complex projects involve largely management, behavioral and organizational issues, rather than technical problems (Belassi & Tukel, 1996; Groysberg & Abrahams, 2005; Hartman & Ashrafi, 2002; Hoffman, 2009; Whitten, 1995).

Critical success factors (CSF) span across a wide spectrum of technological, organizational and interpersonal issues that involve technology transfer, multi-functional integration, commitment, self-direction, rapid change, resource limitations, innovation, and demands for flexibility and speedy implementation (Thamhain, 2008a, b). In such contemporary business environments, traditional models of management and team leadership are often not effective, and can be even counter-productive. As a result of this changing organizational landscape, *teamwork has moved to a new frontier,* prompting many changes of managerial principals and practices.

Evolution of Modern Team Management and Beyond

Teamwork is not a new idea. The basic concepts of organizing and managing teams go back in history to biblical times. However, it was not before the beginning of the Twentieth Century that work teams were formally recognized as critically important to the organizational process and its performance. Henry Ford's statement, "Getting together is a beginning, keeping together is progress, working together is success," shows a strong

---

[1] Because of its central role to business operations, teamwork has been studied by many in virtually all enterprise areas of industry, government and institutional environments, with little argument over the importance of teamwork to project success. For more detailed discussions see Ferrante, Green, & Foster (2006), Groysberg and Abrahams (2006), Keller, 2001, Nellore & Balachandra (2001), Page & Schirr and Shim & Lee (2001).

[2] For additional discussion on the challenges of teamwork and team-building in complex work environments see Cutler & Smith (2007), Shim & Lee (2001), and Zhang, Keil, Rai, & Mann (2003)

Table 1.   Characteristics of Complex Team Environments

In our highly connected, hyper-competitive world, most project teams must function in an environment that interacts with joint ventures, alliances, multinational sourcing, and intricate vendor relations. Projects are complex in nature and imbedded in lots of technology. We find these operationally complex team environments in virtually every segment of industry and government. They include computer, pharmaceutical, automotive, health care, transportation, and financial businesses, just to name a few. New technologies, especially computers and communications, have radically changed the workplace and transformed our global economy, with focus on effectiveness, value and speed. These techniques offer more sophisticated capabilities for cross-functional integration, resources mobility, effectiveness, and market responsiveness, but they also require more sophisticated skills both technically and socially, dealing effectively with a broad spectrum of contemporary challenges, including higher levels of conflict, change, risks, and uncertainty, and a shifting attention from functional efficiency to process integration effectiveness, emphasizing organizational interfaces, human factors and the overall business process.

Characteristics and Challenges:
- Strong need for innovation and creativity
- High task complexities, risks, and uncertainties
- Well-educated and skilled personnel, broad skill spectrum
- Specific technical job knowledge and IT competency
- Fast changing markets, technology, regulations
- High levels of creativity and innovation
- Intense competition, open global markets
- Multinational joint ventures, alliances and partnerships; need for dealing across different organizational cultures, values, and politics
- Virtual organizations, markets and support systems
- Resource constraint, tough performance requirements
- Tight, end-date driven schedules
- Total project life-cycle considerations
- Complex organizations and cross-functional linkages
- Complex business processes and stakeholder communities
- Need for continues improvements, upgrades, and enhancements
- Need for sophisticated people skills, ability to deal with organizational conflict, power and politics
- Increasing need for leveraging IT and other technologies
- Need for integrated approach of business management with particular attention to organizational interfaces, human factors, and the business process
- Need for alignment of projects with enterprise strategy.

endorsement of teamwork as an important management tool, already 100 years ago. More formally, the classic Hawthorne studies by Roethlingsberger & Dickinson (1939) led to new insight on group behavior and the benefits of work group identity and cohesion to performance (Dyer, 1977). However, it was not until the 1980s that the group reemerged in importance as the *project team* (Fisher 1993; Nurick & Thamhain, 2006; Thamhain & Wilemon, 1999), and gained in importance with an increasingly complex multinational and technologically sophisticated environment. In today's contemporary setting, team-building can be defined as

> *the process of taking a collection of individuals with different needs, backgrounds, and expertise and transforming them into an integrated, effective work unit.*

In this transformation process, the goals and energies of individual contributors merge and focus on specific objectives and desired results. Supported by modern information and communication technologies, and consistent with the concepts of stakeholder management (Newell & Rogers, 2002; Zhang, Tremaine, Egan, Milewski, Plotnick, O'Sullivan, & Fjermestad, 2009) and learning organizations (Senge & Carstedt, 2001; Senge, Smith, Krushwitch, Laur, & Schley, 2008), the roles and boundaries of teams have been expanding toward self-direction, within more open and organizationally transparent processes. Work teams play an important role not only in traditional projects, such as new product developments, systems design, and construction, but also in implementing organizational change, transferring technology concepts, and in running election campaigns. Whether Yahoo! creates a new search engine, Sony develops a new laptop computer, or the World Health Organization rolls out a new information system, success depends to a large degree on effective interactions among the team members responsible for the new development. This includes support groups, subcontractors, vendors, partners, government agencies, customer organizations, and other project stakeholders (Armstrong, 2000; Barkema, Baum & Mannix, 2002; Dillon, 2001; Gray & Larson, 2000; Karlsen & Gottschalk, 2004; Thamhain, 2005; Zanoni & Audy, 2004).

A Changing Environment

Globalization, privatization, digitization, and rapidly changing technologies have transformed our economies into a hyper-competitive enterprise system where virtually every organization is under pressure to do more things faster, better, and cheaper. Effective teamwork is seen as a key success factor in deriving competitive advantages from these developments. At the same time, the process of team-building has become more complex and requires more sophisticated management skills as bureaucratic hierarchies and support systems decline.

All of this has strong implications for organizational process and leadership. Not too long ago, project managers *could* ensure successful integration of their projects by focusing on properly defining the work, timing, and resources (known as *triple constraint*), and by following established procedures for project tracking and control. Today, these factors are still crucial. However, they have become threshold competencies, critically important, but unlikely to guarantee by themselves project success. Today's complex business world requires fast and flexible *project teams* that can work dynamically and creatively toward established objectives in a changing environment (Bhatnager, 1999; Hax & Wilde, 2001; Jasswalla & Sashittal, 1999; Thamhain, 2002, 2009). This requires effective networking and cooperation among people from different organizations, support groups, subcontractors, vendors, government agencies, and customer communities. It also includes the ability to deal with uncertainties and risks caused by technological, economic, political, social, and regulatory factors. In addition, project leaders have to organize and manage their teams across organizational lines. Dealing with resource sharing, multiple reporting relationships, and broadly based alliances is as common in today's business environment as e-mail, flex-time and home offices (Keller 2001; Sarin & O'Connor 2009).

Because of these complexities and uncertainties (cf. Table 1), traditional forms of hierarchical team structure and leadership are seldom effective and are being replaced by self-directed, self-managed team concepts (Barner, 1997; Nohria, Groysberg, & Lee, 2008; Prusak, 2009; Thamhain & Wilemon, 1999). The project manager becomes a social architect who understands the *interaction of organizational and behavioral variables*, inspires team members, facilitates the work process, and provides overall project leadership for developing multidisciplinary task groups into unified teams, hence fostering a climate conducive to involvement, commitment, and conflict resolution.

The Driving Forces toward New Managerial Focus and Team Leadership

We have been experiencing a shift in managerial thinking for some decades. The multitudes and complexities of variables involved in teamwork have led to a paradigm shift that relies to an increasing extend on *systems thinking* as a conceptual framework. This shift is also reflected in the language of managers who describe teamwork in terms of interdependencies, networks, relationships, collaboration, and integration, and the recognition of infrastructure and work process as important influences on overall team performance (Crothier-Laurin, 2008; Graen, Hiu, & Taylor, 2006; Manley, 2008).

Seven major shifts in our business environment have created changes and affected the way we work in teams. These paradigm shifts must be understood for managing and leading effectively in team-based organizations:

#1: Shift from Linear Processes to Dynamic Systems. While in the past, team management was based predominately on linear models, typically exemplified by sequential product developments, scheduled services, and discovery-oriented R&D, today's teams have to operate in a much more dynamic and interactive way, involving complex sets of interrelated, non-linear, and often difficult to define processes which require agile teamwork, strategic alignment, spiral processes, and open innovation. These situations involve high levels of group dynamics and more sophisticated management style which relies strongly on group interaction, resource and power sharing, individual accountability, commitment, self-direction, and control. Consequently, team management today relies to a considerable extent on member-generated performance norms and evaluations, rather than on hierarchical guidelines, policies, and procedures. While this paradigm shift is driven by changing organizational complexities, capabilities, demands, and cultures, it also leads to a radical departure from traditional management philosophy on organizational structure, motivation, leadership, and project control. As a result, traditional "hard-wired" organizations and processes are being replaced by more flexible and nimble networks that are most likely derivatives of the conventional matrix organization. However, these networks have more permeable boundaries, more power and resource sharing, and more concurrent operational processes.

#2: Shift from Efficiency toward Effectiveness. Many organizations have expanded their management focus from *efficient* execution of their operations and projects to include *organizational effectiveness* as part of their key performance measures (KPM). That is, in addition to emphasizing job skills, teamwork, communications, and resource optimization at the operational level, management aims for integration of ongoing activities and projects into the overall enterprise, making sure that we are not falling into the activity trap. In other words, not just "doing it right," but most importantly, "doing the right thing." As an example, companies are leveraging project management as a core competency, and integrating project-oriented activities closely with other functions, such as marketing, R&D, field services and strategic business planning. While this shift is enhancing the status and value of certain business functions within the enterprise, it raises the overall level of responsibil-

ity and accountability, and puts higher demands on previously more autonomous functions, such as R&D and product development, to perform as a full partner within the integrated enterprise system.

#3: Shift from Executing Projects to Enterprise-Wide Project Management. Many companies use project management extensively today to leverage the full capabilities of project teams enterprise-wide as a core competency, achieving accelerated product developments, higher levels of innovation, better quality, and better overall resource utilization. To accomplish this level of competency, project operations must be integrated with the strategic planning system and business processes throughout the entire enterprise. Managerial focus has shifted from the mechanics of controlling projects according to established schedules and budgets, to optimizing desired results across a wide spectrum of performance measures that span across the total enterprise.

#4: Shift from Managing Information to Fully Utilizing Information Technology. Today's technology provides managers in any part of the enterprise with push-button access to critical information on operational status and performance. The availability and promise of technology has led to the development of an enormous variety of powerful IT-based tools and techniques which support many aspects of teamwork, ranging from data sharing on websites to virtual team environments supported by groupware. With the powerful promise for increasing operational effectiveness, managers are eager to use these tools to support team decision-making and to manage teamwork, especially in geographically dispersed projects. While modern information technology (IT) has already helped in creating new methods of communications and work structures, and in facilitated project integration among global partners, the future focus is toward an even more optimized IT utilization at the enterprise level, aiming at an organizationally fully integrated management system . The challenge is for managers to look beyond the immediate application, such as information sharing, project planning and tracking, and to integrate and *apply* IT within the firm's business processes, solving operating problems *and* increasing business efficiency, rather than just replacing traditional forms of communications, interactions and problem solving.

#5: Shift from Managerial Control to Self-Direction and Accountability. With increasing business complexities, advances in information technology, changing organizational cultures, and new market structures, companies look *beyond* traditional managerial control for effective execution of their projects, operations, and missions. Top-down controls, based on centralized command and communications, have limited effectiveness. While still critically important as part of the enterprise's central management system, they are no longer sufficient as primary control for generating satisfactory results. Organizational activities are increasing project-oriented, relying on technology, innovation, cross-functional teamwork and decision-making, intricate multi-company alliances, and highly complex forms of work integration. The dynamics of these environments foster to a considerable extent member-generated performance norms and work processes, and a shift toward more team ownership, empowerment and self-control. All of this has a profound impact on the way managers must manage and lead, and analyze the work environment for effective intervention. The methods of communication, decision-making, soliciting commitment, and risk-sharing are shifting constantly away from a centralized, autocratic management style to a team-centered, more self-directed form of control where managers have to earn authority, trust, and respect.

#6: Shift from Focusing on Narrowly Defined Project Performance to Broader Measures Including Sustainability. Companies have steadily broadened the KPMs for their projects and programs to include more than the traditional time-budget-delivery measures, defined as the triple constraint. The shift is toward a broader set of measures or indicators that include a wide spectrum of factors critical to project success, including stakeholder satisfaction and sustainable development. Especially sustainable development, with its focus on social equity, economic efficiency, and environmental performance, has become an important measure of project performance and is expected to drive the design of future work process designs and team-building practices.

#7: Shift from Managing Teams as Part of a Functional Specialty to Team Management as an Integrated Part of Project Management with Distinct Skill Sets and Professional Status. Over the past decades, team leadership emerged from a common managerial skill set to a distinctly separate discipline with its own body of knowledge, norms, and standards. As an evolving discipline, team leadership benefitted especially from its *association with project management.* With its own body of knowledge, professional certification, and formal education programs, project management established itself firmly across virtually all industries and around the globe, and provides a systemic framework for modern team leadership and team management practice.

All of these shifts contribute to the enormous dynamics of our business environment. Yet understanding these shifts is just a starting point for understanding the interaction of organizational, behavioral, technical, and social variables that create the dynamics of this continuously changing landscape, driving the massive challenges that lie ahead for managers in the future.

Working with Teams in a Contemporary Business World

In response to the challenges created by the transformation of our business environment, many companies had to broaden their resource base via alliances, mergers, acquisitions, and joint ventures, to achieve operational results and market reach. They also have explored alternate organizational designs, business processes, and leadership styles. Traditional forms of organizational structure and leadership have often been found ineffective in this environment and are gradually being replaced by self-directed, self-managed team concepts (Barner, 1997; Thamhain & Wilemon, 1999; Thamhain, 2009). Managing these contemporary team organizations requires great understanding of the enterprise and its environment.

Strong Multidisciplinary Focus.

Project success in an increasingly complex world is not the result of a few brilliant people or any one group of specialists, but is determined by multidisciplinary efforts across all areas of the enterprise and its business interfaces (Keller, 2001; Nellonore & Balachandra, 2001). Project teams must cross many different types of functional, geographic, and cultural boundaries to reach into collaborating organizations with their customers, partners, vendors, and consultants, as well as cooperate with regulators and special interests. In such a complex and dynamic environment, team leaders must be able to unify these diverse teams and focus their efforts on desired results within the established constraints. A significant side benefit of this multidisciplinary involvement is enhanced collaboration and *distributed knowledge* throughout the enterprise, forming the basis for the much talked-about learning organization (Senge, 1994).

Self-Direction and Commitment

The evolution of contemporary organizations, such as the matrix, brought a decline of traditional bureaucratic hierarchies and a diminishing role of the team leader as supervisor. Instead, horizontally oriented teams and work units have become increasingly important. To function effectively, managers of these project teams must rely on *self-direction* and *empowerment*, as defined in Table 2. They also must be able to obtain and sustain team member commitment and accountability. Gaining the collective commitment of the team to the project objectives requires strong persuasion and negotiation skills, supported by the team leader's credibility, trust, and mutual respect with the team. Building a committed, high-performance team is a complex process that involves many organizational, behavioral, and project-related issues (Eisenstat, Beer, Foote, Fredberg, & Norrgren, 2008). It is also strongly influenced by the leader's ability to create a professionally stimulating environment that is low on organizational conflict, anxieties, and fear of the unknown (Nurick & Thamhain, 2006; Stum, 2001; Thamhain, 1996, 2002, 2009).

Multinational and Virtual Teams

As globalization and trans-nationalization continues to move forward with ever-increasing speed (Hofmeister & Breitenstein, 2008) and global outsourcing becomes the norm for virtually every enterprise, the changing business landscape ushers in new challenges and opportunities. Increasing competitive pressures force companies

Table 2. Self-Directed Teams

Definition: A group of people chartered with specific responsibilities for managing themselves and their work, with minimal reliance on group-external supervision, bureaucracy and control. Team structure, task responsibilities, work plans, and team leadership often evolve based on needs and situational dynamics.
Benefits: Ability to handle complex assignments, requiring evolving and innovative solutions that cannot be easily directed via top-down supervision. Widely shared goals, values, information, and risks. Flexibility toward needed changes. Capacity for conflict resolution, team building and self-development. Effective cross-functional communications and work integration. High degree of self-control, accountability, ownership, and commitment toward established objectives.
Challenges: A unified, mature team does not just happen, but must be carefully organized and developed by management. A high degree of self-motivation, and sufficient job, administrative and people skills must exist among the team members. Empowerment and self-control might lead to unintended results and consequences. *Self-directed* teams are *not* necessarily *self-managed,* they often require *more* sophisticated external guidance and leadership than conventionally structured teams.

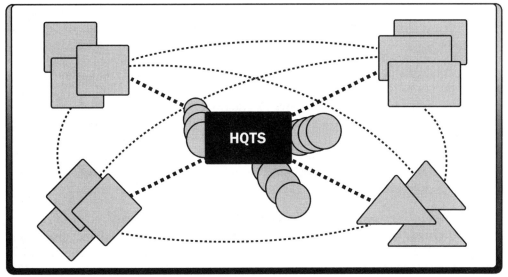

Figure 1.   Multinational Team Environment (Showing connections among partners and project headquarters, HQTS)

to search continuously for ways to perform better, cheaper, and faster. This results in alliances across the globe, ranging from R&D to manufacturing, customer relations, and field services. While these realities hold for most organizations in today's work environment, they are especially pronounced and challenging for team efforts that are associated with risk, uncertainty, creativity, and team diversity, such as high-technology and/or multinational projects. These are also the work environments that first departed from traditional hierarchical team structures and tried more self-directed and network-based virtual concepts (Fisher, 1993). Leading these geographically dispersed workgroups involves complex management issues of work process, integration, unified control, and systemic networking.

From the strategic side, guidelines and unified direction toward project objectives, technology transfer, and project integration must be "synthesized" centrally and translated across borders into the cultures of local operations. Furthermore, linkages among individual work components need to be developed and effectively "managed" across geographic areas and organizational cultures as shown in Figure 1 (Kruglianskas & Thamhain, 2000; Nurick & Thamhain, 2006; Wegryn & Wegryn, 2006). Therefore, multinational project teams need to be integrated not only across the miles, but also be unified among different business processes, management styles, operational support systems, and organizational cultures (Bahrami, 1992; DeMaio, 1994; Deschamps & Nayak, 1995).

What makes these geographically dispersed work groups feasible, are advances in collaborative, enabling technology, such as groupware and general telecommunications. Hence, dispersed work groups can work together as *virtual teams* connecting from anywhere in the world. Much attention has been paid in recent years to virtual teams in distributed environments, and the role of technology for creating a shared virtual world where interactions can take place irrespective of physical proximity. Whether an organization has 100,000 employees or just 10 people, it is interconnected with the rest of the world, and can work with any person from any enterprise in any place at any time. This opens up great opportunities and flexibilities of conducting business, including co-developments, partnering, joint ventures, strategic alliances, outsourcing, as well as customer and supplier relations management. In addition, company management itself, including its top executives, are often distributed geographically, separated by distance, time zones, and organizational cultures (Stoddard & Donnellon, 1997). As companies engage in more multinational joint developments, outsourcing and global expansion, virtual teams, as defined in Table 3, promise the flexibility, responsiveness, and improved resource utilization necessary to survive and prosper in our ultra-competitive environment that will be with us for years to come (Shim & Lee, 2001; Thamhain, 2009; Zhang, Keil, Rai & Mann, 2003).

Characteristics of High-Performing Team Environments

When describing an effective project team, managers in the field and researchers agree on two sets of performance indicators: *Team output,* measured as the quality of desirable results, plus time and budget performance, and team performance is associated with specific *traits which characterize a team* as a social entity. This association was measured in several of my field studies (Thamhain 2002, 2003, 2008a, b) and is graphically summarized in Figure 2. These findings are also consistent with other research (Ammeter & Dukerich, 2002; Bhatnager, 1999; Hacker, 2000; Robins, 2007). These traits can be used to profile work teams as a basis for establishing performance norms and identifying development need.

Table 3   Virtual Teams Defined

Definition: A group of (project) team members, physically separated but linked via information technology, to each other and various project partners, such as contractors, customers and regulators, to overcome differences in time and geography. The concept implies permeable interfaces and boundaries (Wegryn & Wegryn, 2006; Mowshowitz, 2002); therefore project teams can rapidly form and reorganize as needed. Supported by their technology links, these individuals can share information and operate as a unified project team across their physical boundaries. An example of a virtual team is a web-supported project review conducted among the team members, contractors and customer. The virtual team concept often overlaps with notions of virtual communities, networked organization, e-commerce and teleworking.
Benefits: Ability to share information and communicate among team members and organizational entities of geographically dispersed projects. Ability to share and communicate information in a synchronous and asynchronous mode (application: communication across time-zones, holidays and shared work spaces). Creating unified visibility of project status and performance. Virtual teams, to some degree, bridge and neutralize the culture and value differences that exist among different task teams of a project organization.
Challenges: The effectiveness of the virtual team depends on the team members' ability to work with the given technology. Information flow and access is not necessarily equal for all team members. Information may not be processed uniformly throughout the team. The virtual team concept does not fit the culture and value system of all members and organizations. Project tracking, performance assessment, and managerial control of project activities is often very difficult. Risks, contingencies, and problems are difficult to detect and assess. Virtual organizations often do not provide effective methods for dealing with conflict, power, candor, feedback and resource issues (Cutler & Smith, 2007). Because of the many limitations, more traditional team processes and communications are often needed to augment virtual teams.

Figure 2.   Characteristics of High-Performing Team

Measuring and Benchmarking Team Performance

Leading teams requires understanding of their culture and environment, and the value of their contribution. In addition to the ability of assessing project output, we must also understand what drives desirable team behavior and performance. We know from research that team performance is influenced by organizational ambience and leadership (Thamhain, 2004, 2005, 2009). This encompasses four components: (1) physical environment, (2) psychological environment, (3) skills, values, and culture of the team members and the team as a whole, and (4) team leadership. These influences can be seen as exogenous variables, affecting team characteristics and, ultimately, team performance. These linkages of *work environment, team characteristics,* and *team performance* suggest a simple model, as shown in Figure 3, which can be used as a framework for examining the influences of the team environment on team characteristics and project performance, allowing some lessons to be gleaned for effective project management and team leadership. It can also be used in combination with the characteristics of high-performance teams identified in Figure 2 of the previous section to benchmark work group performance, define needs and mutual expectations, or to develop teams on an ongoing basis.

Building and Sustaining High-Performing Teams

With steadily growing global competition, increasing access to global resources and advancing technology, many project teams of the future will be geographically dispersed, working independently and self-directed across organizational boundaries, time and space. Building these multidisciplinary teams across a wide range of cultural and organizational boundaries is not an easy task. Yet, it is at the heart of the project leader's job.

In fact, team-building is the art and science of resolving the tension between the objectives of the people and the enterprise without sacrificing either one. What have we learned? What can project managers do to create a work environment conducive to high team per-

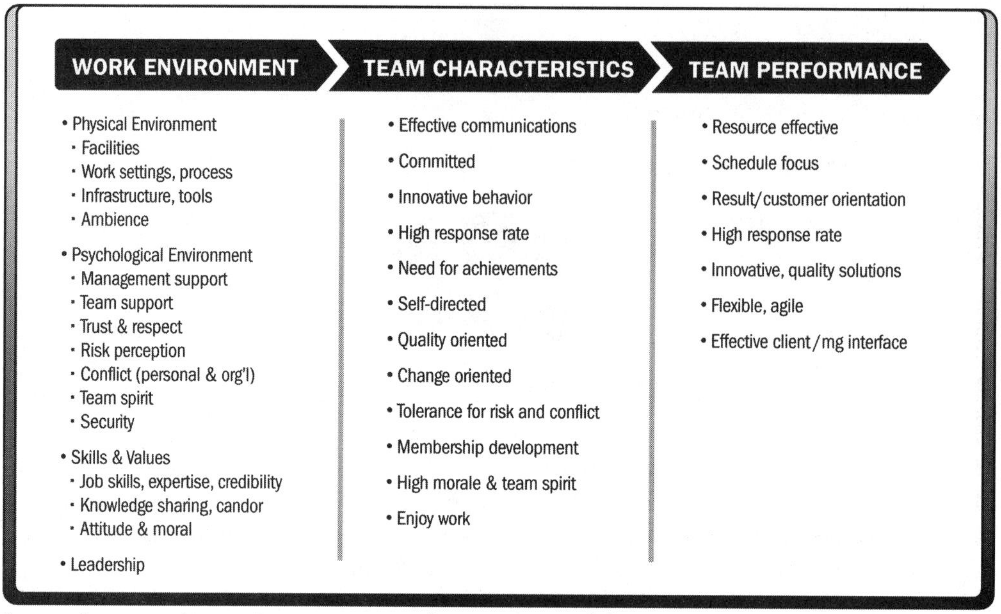

WORK ENVIRONMENT	TEAM CHARACTERISTICS	TEAM PERFORMANCE

• Physical Environment
  · Facilities
  · Work settings, process
  · Infrastructure, tools
  · Ambience
 	
• Psychological Environment
  · Management support
  · Team support
  · Trust & respect
  · Risk perception
  · Conflict (personal & org'l)
  · Team spirit
  · Security
 	
• Skills & Values
  · Job skills, expertise, credibility
  · Knowledge sharing, candor
  · Attitude & moral
 	
• Leadership
	• Effective communications
	• Committed
	• Innovative behavior
	• High response rate
	• Need for achievements
	• Self-directed
	• Quality oriented
	• Change oriented
	• Tolerance for risk and conflict
	• Membership development
	• High morale & team spirit
	• Enjoy work
		• Resource effective
		• Schedule focus
		• Result/customer orientation
		• High response rate
		• Innovative, quality solutions
		• Flexible, agile
		• Effective client/mg interface

Figure 3.   Team Environment-Performance Model

formance? How can they create a shared purpose, therefore linking the needs and wants of the people who do the work with the enterprise objectives? Observations of managerial practices and formal field research provide us with considerable insight into the conditions critical to high team performance. Part of this is summarized in the *research snapshot* of Table 4. It shows that many of the strongest influences originate in the project environment itself. Specifically, the organizational conditions that satisfy personal and professional needs seem to have the strongest effect on commitment, the ability to deal with risk and contingencies, and overall team performance. Most significant are those influences that derive from the work itself. Interestingly, people who find their assignments professionally stimulating, leading to accomplishments, recognition, and professional growth, also seem to function more effectively in a complex and technology-challenging team environment. Such a professionally exhilarating ambience also lowers communication barriers, increases the tolerance for conflict and risk-taking, and enhances the desire to succeed. Other influences to project team performance are derived from organizational processes, which have their locus outside the project organization, and are controlled by senior management. These processes affect the team in terms of organizational stability, availability of resources, management involvement and support, personal rewards, stability of organizational goals, objectives, and priorities. To be effective, project leaders must work with senior management to ensure an organizational ambience supportive to effective teamwork.

A clear lesson is that managers must foster a work environment supportive to their team members. One of the consistent and most striking findings from field studies, such as summarized in Table 4, is the importance of intrinsic motivators. These influences, such as recognition and work challenge, support *professional needs* and correlate most favorably to team performance, and seem to serve as bridging mechanisms, helpful in en-

Table 4.   A Snapshot of Field Research

The results of several field studies[a] provide an immediate snapshot of team performance as a function of the project environment and its dynamics. It highlights the critical importance of both human factors and traditional project management techniques to team performance. The most significant associations point at the importance of professional esteem needs and managerial leadership as particularly favorable influences. Listed in order of significance, the field research identifies the following conditions as critical to overall team performance:

1. Professionally stimulating and challenging work environments
2. Opportunity for accomplishments and recognition
3. Clearly defined organizational objectives relevant to the project
4. Relevant job skills and expertise of the team members
5. Overall directions and team leadership
6. Trust, respect, and credibility among team members and their leaders
7. Effective business process, cross-functional cooperation, and support
8. Clear project plans
9. Well-defined authority relations
10. Autonomy and freedom of actions aligned with the managerial expectations and accountabilities
11. Opportunities for career development and advancement
12. Job security

While many of these factors, such as clear objectives, skill sets, and effective business process deal with conventional project management practices, they also relate to the human side, conditioning the work environment for success. Hence in a complex project environment that relies on commitment, buy-in, and personal drive for success, these influences appear to deal effectively with the integration of goals and needs between the team member and the organization. They also become catalysts for cross-functional communication, information sharing, and ultimate integration of the project team with focus on desired results.

It is interesting to note that the same conditions, which are conducive to overall team performance, also lead to (i) innovation and creative problem solving, (ii) change orientation and high response rate of the team, (iii) self-directed teams with minimum supervision, (iv) effective customer and client interface, (v) effective conflict resolution among team members, (vi) ability to deal with risk and uncertainty, (vii) stronger personal effort and commitment to established objectives, (vii) more effective communications within the team and its interfaces, and (viii) favorable schedule and budget performance.

Furthermore, the research results provide a model for "performance projection." Project teams that are perceived by their management as *effective* in any one of these seven categories, such as innovation, change orientation, etc., are also seen as effective in many of the other seven categories, including efficiently utilizing time and resources, and leading to high overall project performance. While this finding is not surprising, it is interesting to see it statically validated. This was tested via Kruskal-Wallis analysis of variance by rank which shows that managers who rate their team's performance high in any one of the performance variables are likely to give high ratings also to the other variables.

It is interesting to note that many characteristics of the work environment, that were identified (perceived) by managers as important and influential to team performance *did not pass the test of statistical significance*. Examples are (i) financial compensation, (ii) compensatory time off, (iii) project complexity, size, or duration, (iv) stability of customer requirements, and (v) organizational stability and business processes.

This type of investigation helps researchers and practicing managers to understand the nuances and intricate nature of team performance in complex project environments. It also helps in developing new models for team development that might be needed in the changing organizations and business environments of the future.

---

[a] This ongoing eight-year field research includes data from 32 technology-based organizations, mostly part of *Fortune* 500 companies or government agencies involved in complex development projects. The results have been published in five journal articles and 14 conference papers (Thamhain 2001, 2002, 2005, 2008b, 2009).

hancing team performance, especially in complex and technology-based project environments. On the other side, "extrinsic motivators or influences," such as salary increases, bonuses, and time off, show a much weaker association to performance. This is in spite of the fact that all influences were perceived by most managers as critically important to team performance. These finding suggests that managers are more accurate in their perception of team members' intrinsic, rather than extrinsic needs. It also seems to be more difficult to assess the performance impact and influence of project parameters, such as size, duration, and complexity, than the impact of human factors on project performance.

Creating a climate and culture conducive to quality teamwork involves multi-faceted management challenges which increase with the complexities of the project and its organizational environment. For the complex, technology-based projects undertaken today and in the future, success is no longer the result of a few expert contributors and skilled project leaders. Rather, project success depends on effective multidisciplinary efforts, involving teams of people and support organizations interacting in a highly complex, intricate, and sometimes even chaotic way. The process requires experiential learning, involving a great deal of trial and error and risk-taking, as well as the cross-functional coordination and integration of technical knowledge, information, and components. This requires excellence across a broad range of skills, and sophisticated organizational support is required to manage project teams effectively. Hence, it is critically important for project leaders to understand, identify, and minimize the potential barriers to team development. Such team development can rarely be done "top-down," but requires a great deal of interactive team management skills and senior management support. Tools such as a project maturity model, the Six Sigma project management process, and focus groups can serve as a framework for analyzing and fine-tuning the team development and management processes needed to survive and prosper in a changing world.

Succeeding in our ultra-competitive word of business and preparing for the future is not an easy feat. No single set of broad guidelines guarantees performance. However, project success is not random! A better understanding of the criteria and organizational dynamics that drive project team performance can help managers in effectively integrating project teams with the enterprise. Effective team leaders are social architects who understand the interaction of organizational and behavioral variables and can foster a climate of active participation, accountability, and results-orientation. They can create a link between the people who do the work and the project objectives. They can focus their teams on desired results. This requires sophisticated skills in leadership, administration, organization and technical expertise, and a solid understanding of the organizational environment, its people, work processes, and infrastructure.

References

Ammeter, A., & Dukerich, J. (2002). Leadership, team building, and team member characteristics in high performance project teams. *Engineering Management Journal*, *14*(4).

Armstrong, D. (2000). Building teams across borders. *Executive Excellence, 17*(3), 10.

Bahrami, H. (1992). The emerging flexible organization: Perspectives from Silicon Valley. *California Management Review, 34*(4), 33–52.

Barkema, H., Baum, J., & Mannix, E. (2002). Management challenges in a new time. *Academy of Management Journal, 45*(5), 916–930.

Barner, R. (1997). The new millennium workplace. *Engineering Management Review (IEEE), 25*(3), 114–119.

Belassi, W., & Tukel, O. (1996). A new framework for determining critical success/failure factors in projects. *International Journal of Project Management, 14*(3), 141–151.

Bhatnager, A. (1999). Great teams. *The Academy of Management Executive, 13*(3), 50–63.

Crothier-Laurin, C. (2008). Effective teams: A symptom of healthy leadership. *IEEE Engineering Management Review, 36*(1), 140–143.

Cutler, G., & Smith R. (2007). Mike leads his first virtual team. *Research Technology Management, 50*(1), 66–69.

DeMaio, A. (1994). A multi-project management framework for new product development, *European Journal of Operational Management, 78*(2), 178–191.

Deschamps, J. & Nayak, R. (1995). Implementing world-class process. *Product Juggernauts*, Chap. 5, Cambridge: Harvard Press.

Dillon, P., A global challenge. *Forbes Magazine, 168* (Sept. 10, 2001), 73.

Dyer, W.G. (1977). *Team building: Issues and alternatives*. Reading, MA: Addison-Wesley.

Eisenstat, R., Beer, M., Foote, N., Fredberg, T., & Norrgren, F. (2008). The uncompromising Leader. *Harvard Business Review, 86*(7/8), 78–84.

Fisher, K. (1993). *Leading Self-Directed Work Teams*. New York: Irwin/McGraw-Hill.

Graen, G., Hiu, C., & Taylor, E. (2006). Experience-based learning about lmx leadership and fairness in project teams: A dyadic directional approach. *Academy of Management Learning & Education, 5*(4), 448–456.

Gray, C., & Larson, E. (2000). *Project Management*. New York: Irwin McGraw-Hill.

Groysberg, B., & Abrahams, R. (2006). Lift outs: How to acquire a high-functioning team. *Harvard Business Review, 84*(12), 133–143.

Guo, L. (2008). Perspective: An analysis of 22 years of research in JPIM. *Journal of Product Innovation Management, 25*(3), 249–260.

Hacker, M. (2000). The impact of top performers on project teams. *Team Performance Management, 6*(5/6), 85–90.

Hartman, F., & Ashrafi, R. (2002). Project management in the information systems and technologies industries. *Project Management Journal, 33*(3), 5–15.

Hax, A., & Wilde, D. (2001). *The delta project*. New York: Palgrave.

Hoffman, E. (2009). Multidisciplinary project leadership. *Ask Academic Sharing Knowledge Magazine* (NASA), Winter 2009, 54–55.

Hofmeister, H., & Breitenstein, A. P. (2008). *Contemporary processes of transnationalization and globalization*. International Sociology, 23(4), 480–487.

Jassawalla, A.R., & Sashittal, H. C. (1999). Building collaborate cross-functional new product teams. *The Academy of Management Executive, 13*(3), 50–63.

Karlsen, J., & Gottschalk, P. (2004). Factors affecting knowledge transfer in IT projects. *Engineering Management Journal, 16*, 1.

Keller, R. (2001). Cross-functional project groups in research and new product development. *Academy of Management Journal, 44*(3), 547–556.

Kruglianskas, I., & Thamhain, H. (2000). Managing technology-based projects in multinational environments. *IEEE Transactions on Engineering Management, 47*(1), 55–64.

Manley, T. (2008). Some thoughts on the evolution of work teams in organizations. *IEEE Engineering Management Review, 36*(1), 3–4.

Mowshowitz, A. (2002). *Virtual Organization: Toward a Theory of Societal Transformation Stimulated by Information Technology*. Westport, CT: Quorum Books.

Nellore, R., & Balachandra, R. (2001). Factors influencing success in integrated product development (IPD) projects. *IEEE Transactions on Engineering Management, 48*(2), 164–173

Newell, F., & Rogers, M. (2002). *Loyalty.com: Relationship management in the era of internet marketing*. New York: McGraw-Hill.

Nohria, N., Groysberg, B., and Lee, L. (2008). Employee motivation: A powerful new model. *Harvard Business Review, 86*(7-8) (Jul-Aug), 78–84.

Nurick, A. & Thamhain, H. (2006). Team leadership in global project environments. In David I. Cleland (Ed.), *Global Project Management Handbook* (Ch. 38). New York: McGraw-Hill.

Page, A., & Schirr, G. (2008). Growth and development of a body of knowledge: 16 years of product development research, 1989–2004. *Journal of Product Innovation Management, 25*(3), 233–248.

Prusak, L. (2009). Leadership knowledge. *Ask Academic Sharing Knowledge Magazine* (NASA), Winter 2009, 54–55.

Robins, H.C. Jr. (2007). Program and project management improvement initiatives. *Academy Sharing Knowledge, Ask Magazine (NASA)*, Issue 26 (Spring 2007), 50–55.

Roethlingsberger, F., & Dickerson, W (1939). *Management and the worker*. Cambridge, MA: Harvard University Press.

Sarin, S., & O'Connor, G. (2009). First among equals: The effect of team leader characteristics on international dynamics of cross-functional product development teams. *Journal of Product Innovation Management, 26*(2), 188–205.

Senge, P. (1994). *The fifth discipline: The art and practice of the learning organization*. New York: Doubleday/Currency.

Senge, P., & Carstedt, G. (2001) Innovating our way to the next industrial revolution. *Sloan Management Review, 42*(2), 24–38.

Senge, P., Smith, B., Krushwitch, N., Laur, J., & Schley, S. (2008). *The necessary revolution*. New York: Random House/Doubleday Publishing.

Shim, D., & Lee, M. (2001). Upward influence styles of R&D project leaders. *IEEE Transactions on Engineering Management, 48*(4), 394–413.

Stoddard, D., & Donnellon, A., (1997). *Verifone (The Nature of Work for Employees in a Virtual Organization)*. Boston: Harvard Business School Publishing,

Stum, D. (2001). Maslow revisited: Building the employee commitment pyramid. *Strategy and Leadership, 29*(4), 4–9.

Thamhain, H. (1996). Managing self-directed teams toward innovative results. *Engineering Management Journal, 8*(3), 31–39.

Thamhain, H. J. (2002). Criteria for effective leadership in technology-oriented project teams. In D. P. Slevin, D. I. Cleland, & J. K. Pinto (Eds.), *The frontiers of project management research* (Ch. 16), Newtown Square, PA: Project Management Institute, 259–270.

Thamhain, H. J. (2003). Managing innovative R&D teams. *R&D Management, 33*(3), 297–312.

Thamhain, H. J. (2005). Team leadership effectiveness in technology-based project environments. *IEEE Engineering Management Review. 33*(2), 11-25.

Thamhain, H. J. (2008a). Managing globally dispersed R&D teams. *International Journal of Information Technology and Management (IJITM), 7*(2), 36–47.

Thamhain, H. J. (2008b). Team leadership effectiveness in technology-based project environments. *IEEE Engineering Management Review, 36*(1), 165–180.

Thamhain, H. J. (2009). Leadership lessons from managing technology-intensive teams. *International Journal of Innovation and Technology Management. 6*(2), 1–16.

Thamhain, Hans, & Skelton, T. (2007). Success factors for effective R&D risk management. *International Journal of Technology Intelligence and Planning (IJTIP), 3*(4), 376–386.

Thamhain, H. & Wilemon, D.L. (1996). Building high performing engineering project teams. In R. Katz (Ed.), *The human side of managing technological innovation.* London: Oxford University Press.

Thamhain, H.J., & Wilemon, D.L. (1998). Building effective teams in complex project environments. *Technology Management, 5*(2), 203-212.

Wegryn, C. & Wegryn, K. (2006). *Managing without walls: Maximize Success with Virtual, Global, and Cross-Cultural Teams.* Lewisville, TX: MC Press.

Whitten, N. (1995). *Managing software development projects* (2nd Ed.). New York: John Wiley & Sons,

Zanoni, R., & Audy, J. (2004). Project management model for physically distributed software development environment. *Engineering Management Journal, 16*(1), 28-34.

Zhang, P., Keil, M., Rai, A., & Mann, J. (2003). Predicting information technology project escalation. *Journal of Operations Research, 146*(1), 115–129.

Zhang, S., Tremaine, M., Egan, R., Milewski, A., Plotnick, L., O'Sullivan, P., & Fjermestad, J. (2009). Occurence and effects of leader deligation in virtual software teams, *International Journal of e-Collaboration, 5*(1), 47–69.

CHAPTER 23

Global Trends in Project Management

Storm Cunningham

This Century of Restoration Will Move Project Management to the Fore: *The confluence of seven trends will put more power and money in the hands of project and program managers...**if** the profession rises to the challenge of global renewal.*

The 21ˢᵗ century will be the century of restoration.

—Historian Stephen Ambrose (January 7, 2001, lecture at National Geographic Society's Explorer Hall in Washington, DC)

Unless you've just returned from an extended vacation on Uranus, you've probably noticed that our planet ended the 20ᵗʰ century covered in decrepit infrastructure, derelict buildings, contaminated properties, dying fisheries, drying watersheds, exhausted farmlands, and a host of other factors that have been impeding economic growth and reducing quality of life.

A recent shift, powered by the convergence of seven trends, is turning those "problems" into a global inventory of restorable assets conservatively valued at $100 trillion. Far from impeding economic expansion, that catalog of problems now comprises the raw ingredients of revitalization. A reliable "recipe" for turning those ingredients into rapid, resilient renewal has recently been documented, and it's based on harnessing the seven trends. This author believes that the project management profession is well-positioned to be that recipe's "chef".

Turning our damaged natural, built, and socioeconomic assets into revitalization is now the world's most complex and urgent challenge. The case can be made—and will be in this chapter—that project and program managers can and should be the lead profession for the revitalization of our communities and the restoration of our natural resources. Planetary renewal, in other words. Grand words, granted. But true nonetheless.

This chapter has three goals:

1. To document rapidly-growing trends—already generating at least US$2 trillion worth of projects worldwide annually—that are renewing our world economically, socially, and environmentally.

2. To show how these trends are increasing the challenges to—and demand for—project management, and why they will do so even more powerfully in the near future.
3. To reveal a strategy by which PMI could exploit these trends to dramatically enhance the prestige, power, and pay of project and program managers.

The Seven Trends & Their Effects on Project Management

Six current global trends—plus one trend-in-the-making—are opening a vast gap between today's project management disciplines and tools, and those that that will be increasingly required as this century progresses. The need to close this gap is already urgent; it also presents the most promise for students just entering the field.

By 2025, these trends will have established new norms for projects related to revitalizing communities and regions and restoring natural resources. Project managers who aren't intimately familiar with the technical, legal, and managerial challenges of all these trends will find themselves increasingly obsolete. The good news is that the confluence of these trends will likely trigger the ascendancy of project management as the best path to the highest levels of executive leadership.

The seven trends are 1) restorative development (which creates "*rewealth*"); 2) *integration* of asset renewal; 3) stakeholder *engagement* in renewal efforts; 4) creating shared renewal visions (*visioning*); 5) creating renewal cultures (*culturing*); 6) renewal project/program *partnering*; and 7) creating *renewal engines* (the organizational model). The confluence of these trends creates a need for more and better project management to guide all of this renewal.

In re*Wealth* (this author, McGraw-Hill, 2008), these seven trends were examined from the standpoint of creating tools to more effectively put them to work. It revealed that the most spectacular community revitalization successes have effectively applied these trends to their benefit. These tools were divided into three categories: *rules* for decisions, *processes* for solutions, and a *model* for organization. Taken together as a system of tools, they are referred to as the *re*solution.

The first three trends (rewealth, integration, and engagement) translated into three "universal" *renewal rules*: a basic set of decision-making guidelines that—especially when combined—almost infallibly put communities on a revitalizing trajectory.

The next three trends (visioning, culturing, and partnering) manifested as three "universal" *renewal processes* that—again, especially when all three were applied together—created winning solutions (plans, policies, and projects).

The last trend (the standardized model) is the only trend that's nascent, rather than well underway. This "universal" model was dubbed a "renewal engine," as it seems to be the ideal way of organizing and powering revitalization activities. It's a nascent trend because—although first invented some two decades ago—it was never before documented. Now that it has been revealed, communities worldwide will likely adopt it and adapt it to their needs. This will help them escape the stop-start, project-by-project approach to renewal that has hamstrung so many efforts. It shifts them into a more sustainable, resilient, programmatic mode of renewal.

While all of these trends will profoundly affect project management in coming years, it's the last one—the renewal engine model—that promises to be the most valuable tool for program managers. Let's now take a look at each of these trends/tools in a bit more detail.

The first two goals of this chapter—documenting the trends and describing their effect on project management—will be combined in this first section. The second section will address the third goal of identifying opportunities to dramatically expand the influence (and compensation!) of the project management profession.

Trend #1: From Development to Redevelopment (dewealth vs. rewealth)

The restorative development trend was first revealed in *The Restoration Economy* (this author, Berrett-Koehler, 2002). It refers to the global shift away from a 5,000-year-old development model based on sprawling into "raw" land and on extraction of virgin resources. We're rapidly moving towards basing our economic growth instead on renewing the places we've already built, while repairing the damage we did to our natural resources along the way.

For the first time in five millennia, the basis of wealth creation is making a fundamental shift from development to redevelopment, from depletion to replenishment, and from degradation to restoration—from "dewealth" to "rewealth," in other words. We're moving from economic growth that undermines quality of life in the long run, to economic growth that leaves the world healthier, wealthier, and more beautiful with each passing year. Rewealth currently accounts for some $2 trillion of annual activity worldwide, and is tapping a global inventory of restorable assets worth at least $100 trillion. The global backlog of infrastructure restoration alone has been estimated by Booz Allen Hamilton (2007) at $43 trillion, and infrastructure is just one of twelve sectors of restorable assets.

Figure 1 illustrates our 5,000-year-old model of economic growth, which is based primarily on the extraction of virgin resources and the conquering of raw lands. This "dewealth" mode works fine with low population densities, but large and increasing

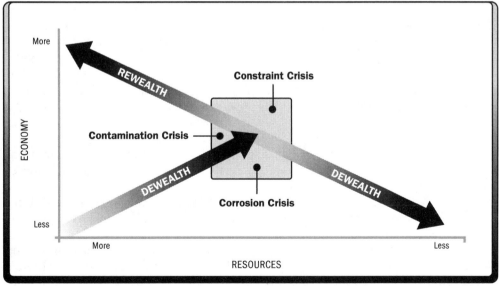

Figure 1:   The dewealth-to-rewealth transition.

human populations on a planet of finite size trigger three crises: contamination (of the natural and built environments), corrosion (an aging, decrepit, and/or obsolete built environment), and constraint (being forced to destroy treasured, often irreplaceable, cultural and natural resources to accommodate sprawl).

Figure 1 also shows how perpetuating this dewealth model after the three crises hit results in a decline of both the economy and the resource base. The solution is already happening: shifting to a "reconomy," which is based primarily on the renewal of all assets. This is as opposed to our dying "deconomy," which was based primarily on developing new built assets, on depleting natural assets, and on maintaining socioeconomic assets. The latter has been increasingly unsuccessful due to the unsustainable nature of the two former activities.

In *The Restoration Economy* (and as described in the cover story of the October 2003 issue of *PM Network*), restorative development was grouped into eight categories of projects. Four are primarily in the realm of the natural environment: ecosystem restoration, watershed restoration, fishery restoration, and agricultural land restoration. Another four project categories focused primarily on the built environment: brownfields remediation and redevelopment, infrastructure renewal/replacement; historic structure restoration, and catastrophe recovery.

re*Wealth* added a third category of restorable socioeconomic assets: education, community services/security, healthcare, and commerce. Together, these 12 categories comprise the key ingredients of community and regional revitalization.

But ingredients alone do not a cake make. A recipe is necessary, and there's the rub: until very recently, a reliable, proven recipe for revitalization (or regeneration, as it's referred to in the United Kingdom) hasn't existed. Managing each of those 12 categories of restorative projects is relatively straightforward, and many best practices have been defined. But managing an ongoing program of community or regional revitalization that includes *all* of those forms of renewal is another matter.

Therein awaits a huge opportunity. After all, what community doesn't want renewal? It's a universal goal. Even when a community is quite vibrant, people always want more: more quality of life, more jobs, a healthier natural environment, better transportation, etc. Actually, the universal goal of intelligent, well-run communities is more specific than just renewal. What they want is *rapid, resilient renewal.*

They want renewal, and they want it now. The need for speed is partly driven by election cycles, partly by a need to garner public support, and partly by the need to inspire confidence in the community's future among redevelopers, investors, and employers. But they also want resilience; they want that renewal to last (rather than just a brief flash of revitalization from an isolated high-profile project like a convention center or sports stadium).

The universal goal of rapid, resilient renewal is the primary driver of the shift from project-based to program-based renewal. Achieving rapid, resilient renewal requires more than effective management of the component projects: it demands program management of the first caliber. That kind of program management, to be successful, requires a reliable recipe for revitalization: rules for decision-making, processes for creating solutions, and a model for organizing and funding it.

Rewealth is the most important and fundamental of the trends we're discussing here. But other trends are greatly magnifying the power of that renewal, and they directly relate to effective project management. Let's look at them now.

Trend #2: From Silos to Integration

"Integration" refers to designing and managing projects and programs in a way that effectively addresses the natural, built, and socioeconomic environments together, as a whole.

The restoration trend has been a primary catalyst of this integration trend.   Take civil engineering, for example: For the past few centuries, civil engineering has largely been about the conquest of nature: constructing dams and levees, straightening rivers, and draining swamps. Now, the biggest trend in civil work is tearing down the dams, unstraightening the rivers, and refilling the swamps. Environmental restoration, in other words. Almost half the U.S. Army Corps of Engineers' budget is now restoration, and it's the fastest-growing portion of the budget. It would be growing even faster if so much of it didn't involve undoing their proud accomplishments of yesteryear: more retirements will be needed before the move to restoration hits full speed at the Corps.

There's a hitch, though. Civil engineering alone cannot undo the effects of civil engineering. Pure civil engineering is all one needs to kill an ecosystem (such as by impeding or altering the flow of water). But civil engineering is only one of many disciplines needed to bring those same ecosystems back to life: it's seldom as simple as just turning the water back on. An entire new science of restoration ecology has emerged. One of the discipline's greatest challenges is working with engineers from the old school, where everything should be mechanical and predictable, and where they demand complete control.

Large-scale (such as regional) ecological restoration ups the ante further, requiring a plethora of "soft" issues to be addressed. The engineering work of previous centuries was usually driven by a single issue, such as draining wetlands for agriculture, or making rivers more navigable so the products of that agriculture could get to market. That land is now inhabited (often densely) by people who can't be ignored or summarily displaced, as Western settlers did to the indigenous peoples. Restoring those same wetlands now involves dealing with diverse social, economic, regulatory, and political issues.

Restoration usually involves stopping or altering human activity on the land. That's a far trickier proposition than simply getting a permit to initiate human activity, or to continue an activity (such as mining or lumbering) that's been done on that land for decades or centuries. This brings us to the next trend: stakeholder engagement.

Project and program managers who understand the vocabulary, tools, and dynamics of asset integration find themselves in great demand today. Tomorrow, they won't be able to get hired without competence in renewing the natural, built, and socioeconomic environments together. Doing so triggers efficiencies and synergies that can greatly magnify both the public and private return on investment. Not doing so risks damaging one of more of those environments—taking one or two steps back for every one forward.

Trend #3: From Decree to Engagement

The push toward more integrated renewal is global, and affects virtually all disciplines. Urban redevelopers—especially when funded by public-private partnerships—must effectively address issues related to heritage, contamination, watershed, education, commerce, and all forms of infrastructure (water, power, transportation, sewer, etc.), just to name a few.

Long gone are the days of redevelopment based solely on knocking down and erecting buildings. Urban redevelopment program managers must now work with neighborhood groups, non-governmental organizations, planners, economic development agencies, schools, and a bevy of scientific disciplines, along with the usual cadre of engineers, architects, and contractors. The rewealth trend helped spawn the integration trend, which is—in turn—accelerating the stakeholder engagement trend.

Project and program managers who understand the vocabulary, tools, and dynamics of stakeholder engagement find themselves in great demand today. Tomorrow, they won't be able to get hired without being competent in effectively involving the business, academic, government, non-profit, and citizen realms. [A fifth category of "stakeholder" exists whose engagement is often crucial to success: the news media.]

Demanding engagement is much easier than doing it, of course. A model for efficient, effective engagement—the renewal engine—will be revealed momentarily.

Integration and engagement are two of the world's great challenges, and great trends. Maybe nowhere do we see the challenge more plainly than in China. Civil engineers dominate Chinese governance to a degree not seen in any other country. This makes the nation lean toward excessive control. Engineers hate uncertainty with a passion, and that's a fine trait when designing bridges and tunnels. But healthy human, economic, and wildlife systems are inherently complex, and thus unpredictable. Attempts at excessive control damages them—even kills them.

The engineering style of government also makes China lean towards doing projects in silos: look at the phenomenal levels of human suffering, and long-term damage done to their economy, their communities, and their natural resources by the Three Gorges Dam, which will be silted beyond usefulness in just a few decades. Lastly, government-by-engineers makes China lean towards management by decree: civil engineering as a discipline has a reputation for being quite poor at engaging other disciplines and stakeholders.

Dealing with a vast diversity of players requires tremendous people skills. All of this presents a huge opportunity for project managers. Someone has to tackle the opportunities posed by enhanced integration, increased stakeholder engagement, with the shift from "de" to "re," and—as we'll see momentarily—a greater dependence on partnering. project and program managers—program managers in particular—are best positioned to take leadership in coordinating all of the people who are restoring our world for a living.

Trend #4: From Flying Blind to Envisioning Renewal

Community revitalization and regional renewal processes usually bear a striking resemblance to voodoo, minus the dead chickens. Many highly-trained professionals from rigorous disciplines are usually involved. But what happens then they are all thrown together and asked to bring a dead or dying place back to life? The rigor disappears, replaced by blind faith that—if they all make good individual efforts—it will somehow result in neighborhoods or cities rising from the grave.

The reality is that most professionally-planned revitalization efforts in the past 50 years have failed, often miserably. Many have actually done grievous harm to their client communities. Detroit and Philadelphia are among many cities still trying to recover from the damage inflicted by earlier attempts at urban renewal. Unfortunately, the planning profession (like the architectural and medical professions) largely eschews forensic analysis, and resists providing prospective clients with effective ways to compare the track records of planning firms. It's nearly impossible to ascertain actual success or failure rates, much less the causes of either. Thus, the same mistakes keep getting made.

Most heritage preservation groups (historic and natural) that have arisen in the past few decades did so to protect the community from their own government and/or planners. The planning profession is getting much better these days, and some truly wonderful ones most certainly exist. But the basic deficiency persists: a relative lack of rigor. There's been no real underlying theory, and few reliable, replicable "universal" processes upon which a community could base their revitalization. It's very much been a matter of doing lots of stuff, and hoping something magical results...more a matter of art and faith than science. All that being said, failures are often not the planners' fault.

A key factor in the poor track record of renewal efforts has been that communities tend to abuse their planners. A plan is how one executes a strategy. A strategy is how one executes a vision. But most communities don't bother to create a shared vision of their future, on which to base a strategy and a plan. Asking a planner to plan in the absence of a vision and strategy is asking them to work in a vacuum...to fly blind. The resulting plan is unlikely to succeed. If it does succeed by certain limited measures, that success is likely to make many people unhappy. And that will be the community's fault. It's not the planner's job to invent a vision for the citizens. That's like hiring someone to invent your life's dream...to determine your goals and passions.

Now, communities worldwide are taking more control of their destiny, and are recognizing the vital role that a shared renewal vision has in doing so. Professional visioning facilitators (not necessarily using that title) are now ubiquitous. But, as they say at the U.S. Department of Defense, a vision without resources is a hallucination.

Trend #5: From Dewealth Defaults to Renewal Cultures (policymaking)

Despite the current economic woes wreaked by irresponsible (possibly criminal) lending practices, mushrooming oil prices, and war, there's no shortage of money in the world. Every community or nation that needs to be revitalized could be revitalized. One key is attracting investment, and the way to do that is to inspire confidence in their future.

Investors don't care much about current conditions: what they care about are future values. If they are convinced a community is coming back to life (or is about to), they will purchase and redevelop the most god-forsaken properties. What does it take to inspire such confidence? A shared vision is a great place to start: restorative investors and redevelopers prefer communities that know what they want, and that have a broad consensus on their path forward.

What really drives redevelopers crazy is being forced to jump through frustrating regulatory hoops and over code barriers to accomplish what the city says it wants. Redevelopers work on borrowed money, so delays are deadly. Why are so many communities difficult to redevelop? Because of vestigial incentives, regulations, and building codes that were designed for the old sprawl-based deconomy. Renovating a city's, region's, or nation's policy environment is a major factor in attracting and nurturing regeneration.

The goal is to create a renewal culture that attracts and nurtures rewealth. How best to do that? By embedding the three renewal rules—rewealth, integration, and engagement—into public policy. Making those rules the defaults for decisions affecting a community's future is the surest way to it on the path to revitalization. This doesn't mean that the community will never sprawl, never extract virgin resources, never operate in silos, or never make unilateral decisions. It just means that those will become the exceptions: they will no longer be the default modes of operation.

Trend #6: From Going It Alone to Partnering

The most important of the three renewal processes is partnering. Partnering for renewal takes three basic forms: public-public, public-private, and private-private. Such "renewal partnerships" now account for the vast majority of regeneration activity worldwide, especially in Europe and the Americas.

For the most part, only relatively small projects "go it alone" these days: virtually all billion-dollar-plus projects are partnerships, as are most 8-and-9-digit projects. The partnering trend has spawned a plethora of multi-billion-dollar restoration and redevelopment projects worldwide. The sheer size of these initiatives is increasing dependence on the project management profession, even without the additional challenges of integration and engagement.

Project and program managers who understand the vocabulary, tools, and dynamics of partnering find themselves in great demand today. Tomorrow, they probably won't be able to get an interview—much less hired—without such competence.

Trend #7: From Project-based to Programmatic Revitalization Using Renewal Engines

The three rules and three processes all derive power from being based on existing trends. The world is already shifting rapidly from dewealth to rewealth. Integrated solutions are already in great demand, as are projects that effectively engage the stakeholders. Communities are already well-aware of the power of having a shared vision of their future, and they are quickly realizing the importance of creating a culture (policies, legislation, incentives, etc.) that supports that vision. Partnering is already the default mode for large renewal projects, since the public nor the private sectors alone seldom have all the necessary resources.

Given all that progress and activity, why is the world still in such rough shape? Why have problems that used to be strictly local gone global? Maybe the key factor is that global solutions—like global problems—are based on the actions of individuals, and people's actions are primarily based on decisions that affect their immediate environment. That is, their community.

Revitalize the world's communities—including their natural, built, and socioeconomic environments—and perform that revitalization in a way that engages and benefits all stakeholders, and you revitalize the world. So, what's needed is a replicable, scalable, universal model for organizing, funding, and sustaining rapid, resilient renewal. We now have that. It's called a renewal engine.

The creation of renewal engines (such as that shown in Figure 2) is a trend-in-the-making. Renewal engines have been evolving independently in many cities around the world over the past two decades, but weren't recognized or documented until 2008, with the publication of reWealth. That formal recognition—that blueprint for forming successful renewal engines—means that the renewal engine model should soon join the three renewal rules and three renewal processes as *bona fide* global trends.

A renewal engine is a permanent, public-private entity, which can be not-for-profit, for-profit, or governmental. It's defined by its three functions: visioning, culturing, and

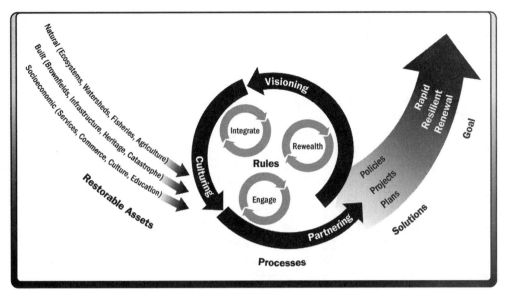

Figure 2:   A renewal engine.

partnering. The graphic above illustrates the essential workings of a renewal engine. The raw ingredients of renewal (restorable assets) feed into the engine, which has engaged all the stakeholders to create a shared vision of their renewed future.

The members of the renewal engine then make decisions based on the three renewal rules, which makes high-level audits of their actions quick and easy. They work to imbed these rules into public policy, which produces legislation and incentives that attract and nurture redevelopment, thus creating a culture of renewal. Potential projects are analyzed by task forces comprising potential project partners. The visioning, culturing, and partnering processes produce solutions: plans, policies, and projects, which lead to the universal goal: rapid, resilient renewal.

The renewal engine model was pioneered in cities like Chattanooga and Bilbao, but—as mentioned earlier—has never before been documented. As a result, each city has had to invent theirs largely from scratch. re*Wealth* identified the best features of these pioneering efforts to create a blueprint for an ideal renewal engine. With that "universal" model as a starting point, communities of almost any size, anywhere in the world can create their own—modified to their own customs and legal/financial/political environment—and start building their renewal capacity. What profession is better positioned to create and sustain renewal engines than project management?

In the U.S., the "smart growth" movement has made the best progress towards reorienting state and community policies towards restoration, reuse, remediation, and all the other "re" words. The smart growth movement has some serious fundamental flaws, though: by trying to be all things to all people, it often misses the revitalization target by a wide margin. Smart growth is a wonderful collection of intelligent practices that lacks a rigorous system for applying them.

Smart growth was a wonderful dialog and—again, in the U.S.—a necessary transitional process away from dewealth. Thus, if one already has a well-established smart growth group, it can be a great seed for a renewal engine. The kinds of people attracted to smart growth are the kinds that will embrace the more rigorous approach of "the *re*solution": again, that's what this holistic system of renewal rules, renewal processes, and renewal model is called. That calls for specialized program management, not just better tools and policies.

How Our World Is Suffering Due to the Lack of "Renewal Project Management"

Again, this trend towards renewal is as much about natural resources as it is about cities, and professional planners are seldom involved in restoring nature. As governments from Iraq to Florida to Russia to Israel recently have been discovering—and as mentioned earlier—the process of restoring nature is vastly more complex than the process of destroying it. The former requires a host of scientific and engineering skills, along with significant funding and all the political ramifications that accompany large expenditures and changing land uses. The latter requires only a bulldozer. The same can be said of cities that were bulldozed by so-called "urban renewal" last century.

The shift from a property-based, project-by-project approach to revitalization to a community-based, programmatic approach means longer-term employment. Integrated approaches tend to increase the lifespan of projects, often to the point where the line between project and program is blurred.

Look at the $10.5 billion Everglades restoration project, or the budding $2 billion Los Angeles River revitalization master plan. Both involve (or will involve) literally hundreds of legal entities: agencies, communities, tribes, companies, universities, and not-for-profits. Both comprise hundreds of projects. Both will go on for decades. Are they projects or programs? They are usually called projects, but sound more like programs.

The distinction is important, because the ongoing nature of a program forces people to think differently about management, and about the nature of engagement. You'll remember that renewal engines are permanent, non-profit entities. People don't create permanent organizations for projects, but they do for programs.

What a difference a renewal engine could have made in the Everglades, where the U.S. government's ecological restoration agenda was shanghaied by influential developers in the state during the previous governor's administration, turning it primarily into a project to supply water for sprawl and agriculture. This was made easier by a White House that refused to cough-up the promised 50% federal funding, making the project overly dependent on the state.

Creating a renewal engine for the Everglades restoration would have protected the shared vision and plan of the project against such machinations, and would have helped create a supportive policy environment. It would have effectively engaged all the stakeholders and partners needed to keep it on track.

It's not just politics that can doom a project, of course. Take the multi-billion-dollar restoration efforts focused on Chesapeake Bay, Long Island Sound, or the Great Lakes (if readers from elsewhere will excuse such North American centricity). Great amounts of time, effort, and money are being expended by citizen volunteers, communities, government agencies, and non-profits, but not much progress is being made.

The basic problems are insufficient integration and insufficient engagement. These deficiencies have led to insufficient funding, and inefficient expenditures of existing funding. Restoring all three of those bodies of water requires the restoration of watersheds, the renewal of sewage infrastructure, the remediation of brownfields, and the application of restorative agricultural techniques, to name just a few of the most basic challenges. But getting the money to do all of that requires engaging and partnering with all the affected communities and landowners.

Integrating the restoration of a lake or bay with the revitalization of the communities that affect it and/or depend on it requires a renewal engine: no other organizational model that I know of could handle such a challenge. Program managers who understand the process of creating and managing such a regional renewal engine will find themselves in the catbird seat. They will be able to write their own ticket.

Maybe the ultimate example of a failure to put the *re*solution (or any of its components) to use was post-Katrina New Orleans. Forget factors like political malfeasance at the local, state, and federal levels: just look at how most proposals failed to focus on *restoring* existing assets, concentrating on creating something new. Catastrophe often offers legitimate opportunities to undo past mistakes and create new functions, but the default mode should always be on asset renewal, for a number of reasons we don't have the space to go into here.

It took years for plans to start emerging that made a serious attempt to *integrate* the renewal of New Orleans' historic assets and infrastructure with the restoration of coastal wetlands and the surrounding agricultural economy. Likewise, it took years before the New Orleans neighborhoods were *engaged* in that planning process to any significant degree. So, the three renewal rules were largely ignored.

Creating a shared *vision* of renewal went by the wayside, as one expensive "expert" or private developer after another attempted to impose their own vision. Enhancing a renewal *culture* should have been an easier job, since New Orleans was in many ways the birthplace of the historic preservation movement in the U.S., but that, too, was ignored. Politicians at every level kept talking about reliance on the private sector, but were never a responsible *partner* in those prospective public-private ventures. The three renewal processes thus fared no better than the renewal rules.

Lastly, if there was any place on Earth that had a greater need for a *renewal engine*—or that provided a more perfect opportunity to create one—I'd love to know where that was. A renewal engine is probably the only way to create rapid, resilient renewal in such a tragic vacuum of political leadership.

How PMI Can Use These Seven Trends to Enhance Demand, Compensation and Status for Project Management Professionals

Project and program managers will increasingly be expected to know how to integrate the renewal of the natural, built, and socioeconomic environments. They will be expected to know how to effectively engage all the stakeholders in that renewal, and how to help foster renewal visions, renewal cultures, and renewal partnerships. They will be expected to know how to create renewal engines to organize, fund, and perpetuate these initiatives. Few of these vital functions are being taught to today's architects, engineers, or even planners.

It will remain the responsibility of the design and planning team to craft a project that integrates the renewal of the natural, built, and socioeconomic environments, but these trends mean that designers will need to involve the project manager at the earliest stages of that design process. Being involved earlier in the process automatically increases the project manager's control, status, and influence.

It will remain the responsibility of the project executives to craft strategy, communicate with stakeholders, and identify appropriate partners, but these trends mean that executives will need to involve the project manager throughout that entire process if they expect the project manager to be successful. Being involved in strategy, public relations, and partnering will move the project manager from a hired gun during one part of the project lifecycle to an executive function involved in the full lifecycle.

Again, what other discipline could hope to deal with such complexity? Architecture? Too focused within the building envelope to deal with the world at large, and too project-focused. Engineering? Too addicted to certainty to handle the messy complexities of human and wildlife communities, and too project-focused. Economic development? Too superficial, mostly focused on discredited strategies like wooing employers with tax incentives. Public policy? Give me a break.

Not even the planning profession is equipped to deal with such a challenge, though they are best-positioned to compete with project management for the honor of heading-up the regeneration of our cities and resources. Professional planners are essential to the success of revitalization efforts, but they are not project or program managers.

Planning associations might initially resist a trend toward project managers rising above their members in terms of control. Some might liken it to the long-standing jockeying of the architectural and engineering professions: for decades, each has lobbied government agencies and policy makers to have their profession recognized as the rightful leader of projects. But that's not an accurate comparison. Architects, engineers, and planners are all primarily designers: only project management is truly a management profession. In all other activities and institutions, those who manage the full lifecycle of an enterprise or place are higher in the pecking order than those whose input is more isolated or transient.

It will always be essential for a project manager to speak the language of architecture, engineering, planning, etc. However, actually *being* an architect, engineer, or planner will likely come to be seen as a *detriment* to being a good project manager; it often reduces one's ability to appreciate—or be trusted by—the other disciplines. Project management must emerge as the integrative, engaging discipline that fills—and adds value from—the interstitial spaces among the other disciplines.

This integrative/engaging role is obviously needed in all three modes of the socioeconomic lifecycle: development/depletion (dewealth), maintenance/preservation (prewealth), and redevelopment/restoration (rewealth). But rewealth is where the growth and solutions reside. Putting more of the project management profession's emphasis on the "re" projects and programs will assure project management's ascendancy as the discipline that can save and revitalize our world.

To supercharge that rise, proficiency in the three renewal processes—visioning, culturing, and partnering—is essential. Playing a vital role in visioning inserts the project manager into the formative stages of the community renewal process. Playing an essential role in the culturing process keeps the project manager involved in the policy decisions that shape that renewal. Playing a crucial role in the partnering process puts the project manager at the heart of the deal flow, where money and other resources meet the opportunities, and where all the players come together to get things done.

Project and program management in general has so far failed to achieve the status and compensation of disciplines such as architecture, engineering, and planning. From this outsider's perspective, there are three reasons for this:

1. *Youth.* The relative newness of the discipline, combined with the territoriality of other disciplines: one of the chief roles of professional associations is to protect their members from incursions by other professions, new or old;

2. *Perception.* Industry mostly sees project management as a secondary discipline. One is primarily an architect, engineer, planner, or whatever…project management is often seen as merely a role one takes on; and,
3. *Timing.* The confluence of the seven trends documented in this chapter means the time has come for project management to emerge as a distinct profession; the only profession that can tackle many of the greatest challenges faced by the modern world.

Turning this formative moment in the project management profession's emergence from opportunity to reality requires four things: academic support, owner support, technological support, and association support.

Owner Support

Private firms and public agencies have the greatest ability to accelerate project management ascendance as the go-to people for renewing the world, one community at a time. Property owners can bypass the inertia of the status quo by putting project management in the lead in reality—as a *fait accompli*—ignoring how project management is now perceived in the order of things. Eventually, perception will catch up with reality. "Private firms" refers primarily to property owners, rather than design and planning firms.

It's the owners of projects—private *and public*—who have the greatest need for the most efficient lifecycle management of their assets. It is they who will drive change, but they must first be made aware of this "better way." Public policy needs to recognize the essential role of project management in addressing complex community, national, and global problems and support its emergence as the lead discipline. Simply removing policy and regulatory barriers to that emergence might be all that's needed, but well-designed incentives can also play an important role.

Outreach is essential to ensure that employers are aware of the need for project management that effectively copes with the trends towards renewal, integration, engagement, and partnering. It's also essential that policymakers are brought up to speed: When policies—and resulting legislation and incentives—specify integrated, engaged, and partnered renewal projects, the ascendancy of project management will be assured.

Technological Support

The level of project management complexity described in this chapter is beyond the capacity of today's software tools to manage. That sounds like bad news, but in the business world, identifying such a need is considered great news: it offers an opportunity to stake out a market with very high "barriers to entry" for subsequent competition. New and/or enhanced software is necessary to help us cope with the vast complexity inherent in renewing all three environments together while engaging all of the stakeholders and meeting all of the partners' goals.

Better integrating existing tools will be a challenge, but it's essential to managing the full life cycle of a community's assets. Standardization of data tagging, formats, and taxonomies is also essential to allow renewal programs to be integrated with those of neighboring communities to achieve regionalization (yet another global trend).

Most of these new tools will either modify or integrate (mash-up) existing tools, such as project management software, asset management, and GIS. Many of the fixes needed are fairly superficial and non-capital-intensive, such as tagging according to the

12-sector taxonomy of restorable assets, and tagging them as to their place in the development lifecycle: new development (dewealth), maintenance/preservation (prewealth), and restorative development (rewealth). There is a "renewal project management" software initiative just getting underway at Revitalization Institute (see below) as this is written, so the timing is propitious.

Academic Support

Academia is far behind the curve regarding the restorative development trend in general and the integration trend in particular. The chasm between the $2 trillion per year of rewealth activities and the amount of research and curricula supporting the component professions is huge. In fact, design-related curricula at most universities are still focused primarily on dewealth projects: today's graduates are being prepared for yesterday's world.

Research and curriculum development must focus on these seven trends to maximize project management's relevance to current and emerging needs. While the research and graduate programs will take place at the university level, the critical role of two- and four-year institutions shouldn't be ignored.

Project management's emergence as a discipline that's no longer in the shadow of architecture, engineering, and planning presents a wonderful opportunity for community colleges, polytechnic schools, and undergraduate institutions to carve out a critically important role for themselves in the project management career path. While the non-graduate institutions are usually happy to partner with universities, academic arrogance usually stifles partnering in the other direction. Project management faculty in prestigious institutions can thus practice their integrating, engaging, and partnering skills in forming leading-edge alliances.

Research is needed to identify and fill the yawning gaps in our knowledge of how to design and manage revitalization. Both new and modified curricula is needed to turn out project and program managers who are familiar with the unique challenges and opportunities of rewealth (vs. dewealth) projects; who are skilled in integrating the renewal of our natural, built, and socioeconomic environments; who are adept at engaging all of the stakeholders; and who are proficient at the visioning, culturing, and partnering processes of such endeavors.

Association Support

PMI is obviously the critical enabler in this equation, and they've taken the first major step in publishing *Project Management Circa 2025*. PMI staff and members must now follow through. Internally supporting the research, training, and outreach initiatives of members is the obvious role. But "external" support is also needed. 501(c)(3) organizations are severely limited in their ability to lobby. There are many other ways in which PMI can help create a better environment for the emergence of project management as the premier profession in the revitalization of our economy and the renewal of our planet.

Not all project managers will work on renewal efforts, of course. Traditional development projects won't disappear: they are just on a downward trend *vis a vis* renewal projects. The demands of renewal programs are unique.

The best way for the project management profession to embed these seven trends/tools into its culture and practice would be to actually use them in the creation of an initiative to create a "renewal project management" discipline (or "revitalization project management", or "regeneration project management"). Such an initiative would use the three renewal *rules* to make decisions, ensuring that fully addresses the demand for integrated, engaged renewal.

The three renewal *processes* would be at the heart of the initiative's activities. Members would have a shared *vision*, such as making renewal project management the go-to discipline for the delivery of rapid, resilient renewal. The initiative should review the *culture* of project management, weeding out vestiges of the "deconomy" that inhibit the profession from fully embracing the "reconomy." The initiative should encourage—and provide a forum for—effective *partnering*, which would accelerate the accumulation of necessary resources, and provide ready paths to implementation.

In this practice-what-you-preach manner, the initiative might even be structured like a *renewal engine* for the profession. It's beyond the scope of this short chapter to go into detail as to what a renewal project management certification course might comprise, content-wise, but here's one idea: rather than competing with the planning profession for status and control, partner with them instead to solve what might be that profession's greatest challenge or deficiency.

> *While planners do manage projects, it not very common for them to have formal project management training, much less certification. This is something that has been raised in-house as an issue here at WRT, with the suggestion that we should seek project management certification for some of our planners.*
>
> —David Rouse, ASLA, AICP, WRT Planning & Design
> (e-mail to author, July 2008)

[Mr. Rouse greatly assisted this author in the planning-related insights that follow.]

Despite having their fingers in so many pies, the planning function often operates in a silo. In many cities, for instance, economic development and planning are almost totally disconnected from each other. Most people think of planners as being primarily designers, basically seeing them as architects of cities, rather than buildings. There's a lot of truth to that, but it's not so easy to categorize what planners do.

Private-sector planning consultants work with communities to develop plans that include implementation strategies, including designs, policies, regulations, programming, and partnerships. Public-sector planners work directly for the "owner" full-time, so they typically are more involved in managing the implementation of the plan. But they participate in the development of the plan as well (which could be seen as a form of public-private partnering).

It's true, however, that design is the star of the planning show: the city's capacity for plan implementation is often overlooked to a startling degree. A major part of the problem is that—as revealed in the David Rouse quote above—planners are trained in the design phase, but not the management phase. Whereas architects and engineers tend to take project management certification seriously, most planners manage without formal training. The solution to this situation has two major components, and project management is crucial to both.

The first approach would be to create a new discipline that designs and implements revitalization programs for communities and regions. Training and/or work experience in planning could be a prerequisite of such "renewal project management" certification. Creating such a discipline would ideally involve a three-way wedding: planning + project management + the *re*solution. There's little to be gained from ignoring the relevant skills that a certified planner brings to the party. On the other hand, the project management portion of the program must be very strong, to give proper weight to implementation. But implementation isn't the whole problem: revitalization plans are often seriously deficient on the design side as well. The *re*solution should thus guide all aspects of the curriculum.

The second way to resolve the problem would be via partnering. The effectiveness of both public and private planners could be enhanced through more effective public-private partnering in general, and renewal partnerships in particular. This would include private developers/redevelopers, with whom public-sector planners sometimes have an adversarial relationship. The ideal vehicle for creating and maintaining such partnerships is the renewal engine, so both planners and project managers should become proficient in the creation and operation of such organizations.

Public sector planners—and private sector planners retained as consultants to the public sector—are often accused by private developers of not understanding what it takes to do development, and of creating unnecessary obstacles to it. They are also subject to criticism (particularly from citizens and not-in-my-backyard (NIMBY) groups) that they are too friendly with developers, and that planning as a profession promotes development. And, of course, many private sector planners work as advocates for developers. Such complexities often catch planners in the middle, putting them more in the role of facilitators and consensus builders. Stakeholder engagement, in other words.

The renewal engine model is already being hailed by some planners as the best way to create such effective, long-term planning partnerships. It has the advantage of having a rigorous structure that can be audited from time to time for integrity, while at the same time being eminently customizable to meet the specific needs, goals, and character of each community.

An exciting new initiative was announced in February 2009 that also offers tremendous opportunities for PMI: the world's first metric for renewal capacity. Just as individuals can have their IQ (intelligence quotient) measured, so too can communities now have their RQ (renewal quotient) measured. This will give real estate investors and redevelopers their first indicator of which communities are most likely to turn restorative projects into actual revitalization. A rigorous RQ Test will be created during 2010 and 2011 by a network of planners, academics, and 20 selected communities around the world. We invite participation from the project management profession. You can learn more about this initiative at http://www.resolutionfund.com/RQ.html. The RQ scores will drive a database and annual "Top Ten Cities" media report called Places To Invest, which will first appear in 2012.

> *The nation behaves well if it treats the natural resources as assets which it must turn over to the next generation INCREASED . . . in value.* (emphasis added)
>
> —Theodore Roosevelt, from "The New Nationalism" (1910)

PMI doesn't really have to do anything for the project management profession to benefit from the trends described here. But the increases in demand, compensation, and status for such "renewal project management" will accrue more quickly with some conscious effort on the association's part.

The shift to more integrated approaches for renewal projects takes the complexity inherent in restoration and magnifies it manifold. Restoring an ecosystem, remediating and redeveloping a large brownfield, or renovating a subway system are all complex enough, even when done as silo projects. Require the work to integrate with the renewal of all 12 asset sectors in the natural, built, and socioeconomic environments, and the complexity goes through the roof. Add the need to engage all the government, academic, not-for-profit, business, and citizen stakeholders, and most professionals will run in terror.

Who can possibly rise to this challenge, if not project managers?

[**Note to PMI members from author:** I firmly believe that project management is the profession that is best-positioned to facilitate the renewal of Planet Earth, along with its human and wildlife communities. I extend an invitation to PMI chapters and colleges/ universities all over the world to work with us to make that happen. You can reach this author in Washington, DC, USA at storm@resolutionfund.com.]

CHAPTER 24

New Frontiers for Project Management: Nanotechnology and Future Energy

David L. Pells

Professional project management continues to grow rapidly in usage and demand worldwide, in most organizations and across all industries. This is especially true in high technology and information technology (IT) organizations, but in many other industries as well. The world is also rapidly changing, due to the global economy, climate change and other factors. What do these changes mean to project-based organizations and project management professionals? Most of these changes will require information technologies, offering new challenges and opportunities for both traditional and IT-related project management.

I believe there will be some significant new industries, and major changes in existing industries, that will offer "new frontiers" for projects and project management around the world in the next 15-20 years. Some of these new areas of project management application have been emerging slowly over the last decade, but are now expanding rapidly due to other forces and converging influences. Other new frontiers are in traditional industries and sectors, but based on new global information, perspectives and awareness that are leading to new and massive investments in infrastructure. And some frontiers are growing apparent based on changing demographics and more interconnected, urban and global human populations and civil society.

These trends are generating new and growing industries with significant future impact. Trillions of dollars will be invested in these industries in coming decades. Each of these emerging sectors will also have a significant impact on our society, personal lives and professional careers. The demand for project managers, and IT project management in particular, should increase dramatically in these fields.

This paper reviews two such emerging "frontiers," nanotechnology and future energy. These are industries that will grow rapidly in coming decades, will include thousands of programs and projects, and represent huge potential application areas for modern project management. Just as importantly, these are sectors with significant potential impact on the entire world. There will be other new industries and fields of application, however, and project management will continue to expand in current and traditional fields and industries. This paper is intended to drive interest and research related to project management applications in the new industries and fields of application.

Nanotechnology

According to Wikipedia, "Nanotechnology refers broadly to a field of applied science and technology whose unifying theme is the control of matter on the atomic and molecular scale, normally 1 to 100 nanometers, and the fabrication of devices with critical dimensions that lie within that size range. One nanometer (nm) is one billionth, or 10^{-9} of a meter. To put that scale into context, the comparative size of a nanometer to a meter is the same as that of a marble to the size of the earth." [1]

According to Dr. Ralph Merkel, "In the future, nanotechnology will let us ... snap together the fundamental building blocks of nature easily, inexpensively and in most of the ways permitted by the laws of physics. This will be essential if we are to continue the revolution in computer hardware beyond about the next decade, and will also let us fabricate an entire new generation of products that are cleaner, stronger, lighter, and more precise."

He adds in the same paper, "If we are to continue these trends we will have to develop a new manufacturing technology which will let us inexpensively build computer systems with quantities of logic elements that are molecular in both size and precision and are interconnected in complex and highly idiosyncratic patterns. Nanotechnology will let us do this." [2]

According to one investment company, "...more than 600 companies worldwide are already involved in nanotechnology. In the last year alone, corporations and governments worldwide have pumped over $4 billion into research and development in this exciting new sector. More importantly, companies have already applied this technology to a variety of consumer products, including automobile parts, semiconductors, clothing, sports equipment and toys, to name just a few." [3]

Nanotechnology Manufacturing

The manufacturing of semiconductors is one area that is rapidly embracing nanotechnology, with huge repercussions in many areas. On March 2, 2008, Intel announced "The Intel® Atom™ processor will be the name for a new family of low-power processors designed specifically for mobile Internet devices (MIDs) and a new class of simple and affordable Internet-centric computers arriving later this year. Together, these new market segments represent a significant new opportunity to grow the overall market ... a chip that measures less than 25 mm², making it Intel's smallest and lowest-power processor yet. Up to 11 Intel Atom processor die -- the tiny slivers of silicon packed with 47 million transistors each -- would fit in an area the size of an American penny." [4]

According to the National Center for Environmental Research (U.S. Environmental Protection Agency), "Nanotechnology offers the possibility of changing the manufacturing process in 2 ways: Incorporating nanotechnology for efficient, controlled manufacturing would drastically reduce waste products; and the use of nanomaterials as catalysts for greater efficiency in current manufacturing processes by minimizing or eliminating the use of toxic materials and the generation of undesirable by-products and effluents." [5] In other words, nanotechnology can also contribute to "green manufacturing."

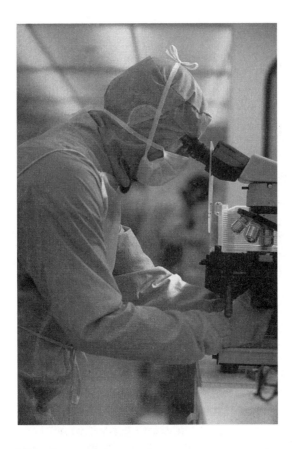

Governmental Involvement

Governments are seriously interested in nanotechnology. For example, in the United States, the federal government's nanotechnology research programs generally fall under the National Nanotechnology Initiative (NNI). Coordination of research in the field takes place through the Nanoscale Science, Engineering, and Technology (NSET) Subcommittee of the National Science and Technology Council. The National Nanotechnology Coordination Office provides technical and administrative support to the NSET Subcommittee and serves as a central point of contact for the NNI. On February 14, 2008, the NSET Subcommittee announced the release of a document describing the NNI strategy for addressing priority research on the environmental, health, and safety (EHS) aspects of nanomaterials.

According to the press release, "Strategy for Nanotechnology-Related Environmental, Health, and Safety Research presents a path for coordinated interagency implementation of research to address the needs identified in earlier reports. It is based in part on a detailed analysis of the Federal Government's FY 2006 nanotechnology-related EHS research portfolio, a $68 million investment in 246 projects. Experts from the NEHI Working Group analyzed how these activities addressed the priority research needs and then proposed emphasis and sequencing for future research efforts. Agency-specific research and regulatory needs, public comments on the prior documents, and considerations of the state of EHS research in the national and international nanotechnology communities all played an important role in shaping the strategy." [6]

Also on February 14, 2008, a summary of the NNI Fiscal Year 2009 Budget was released by the NSET Subcommittee of the U.S. government. The report was a supplement to the President's Budget for Fiscal Year 2009, providing additional details on the NNI budget request, as well as highlights of planned activities to be conducted under that budget. According to that press release, "Described in the report are the programs and activities taking place across all 25 of the Federal agencies participating in the NNI. The 2009 budget request provides $1.5 billion for the NNI, reflecting steady growth in the NNI investment." This sustained investment in nanotechnology R&D across the Federal Government over the past nine fiscal years of the NNI reflects the broad support of the Administration and of Congress for this program. [7]

In the European Union (EU), nanotechnology represents an important area of research, funding and political support. According to European Commissioner for Science & Research, Janez Potonik, "Nanotechnology is an area which has highly promising prospects for turning fundamental research into successful innovations. Not only to boost the competitiveness of our industry but also to create new products that will make positive changes in the lives of our citizens, be it in medicine, environment, electronics or any other field." [8]

Some of the nanotechnology projects being funded by the EU include [9]:

- Life sciences, genomics and biotechnology for health;
- Aeronautics and space;
- Food quality and safety;
- Sustainable development, global change, and ecosystems;
- Industrial and materials technologies; and
- Biomedicines and science.

In China, according to a report found on Azonano.com, "The rapid development of China's nanotech industry is due in large part to the intervention of the central government. Apparently added to a list of priority technologies at the end of the 1990s, nanotech has enjoyed state funding since then through National 863 Hi-Tech R&D Plan. The plan provided huge investments for nanotech projects from both the central and local governments. It seems that the Chinese leadership had plans to transform their nanotech industry by 2010 - with the hope of making it comparable to China's microelectronics, telecom, and other high-tech industries." [10]

According to this same report, "At the present time, some thirty institutions are engaged in basic nanotech research. These include CAS Physical Institute, CAS Chemical Institute, CAS Solid Physics Institute (Hefei), Tsinghua University (Beijing), Beijing University, Hangzhou University, Nanjing University, and several universities in Shanghai. In addition, Shanghai, Beijing, and Shenzhen have each created their own Nanotech Centers, uniting local R&D structures. In terms of basic nanotech R&D, China has reached the most advanced levels in the world, rivaling even the capacities of the United States." [10]

Future Impact

Rather than delving further into the political, scientific and technical aspects of nanotechnology, let me suggest that nanotechnology will transform the world we live in, also allowing for the manufacture of smart products with embedded computers. While we are used to computer chips embedded in smart cards, they will now be embedded in nearly everything, including construction materials, clothing, machinery and equipment, and end products, ranging from everyday appliances to mobile electronics and industrial equipment.

The implications are significant for project management, as nearly every industry and manufacturing sector will be affected in the future. Not only will new products be manufactured, but manufacturing processes, machinery and knowledge must be updated. In addition, the markets for all of the products and services will change and grow, offering additional opportunities for projects and project management in such nontraditional industries as advertising, marketing, publicity and in government and science.

The most obvious impact on project management is that there will be a huge number of new programs and projects launched based on nanotechnology and its impact. This will lead to an increase in the use of modern project management in the industries and organizations affected, and an increased demand for project management professionals.

Nanoengineered products for the food sector -- including a smart RFID nano sensor -- took centre stage at a two day conference held 20-21 November 2007 in Braga, Portugal to discuss the science of the miniscule. Hosted by the European Commission the conference targeted the commercialisation of products derived from techniques associated with science of the miniscule. Scientists and developers at the conference revealed some of the developments that could be important to the food sector if these are commercialised. Nanotechnology is championed by several manufacturers for use in packaging to extend shelf life, or more controversially, for improving the nutritional content and impact of foods. [11]

But there are other implications as well. Many of these projects will involve basic and applied science. Most will be complex projects, involving "new science". Most will involve scientists in lead roles on project teams. And most will involve short time frames – technology and markets are changing so rapidly that most new products must be developed within 12 months. These projects also involve global teams, virtual communications and massive data transfer needs.

New and better project management applications and tools are needed for these types of projects, and new experiences will be revealed. This is an area that deserves attention and research in the project management field.

Impact Today

Meanwhile, nanotechnology is already creating projects that need project management. Take for example, the National Institute of Nanotechnology (NINT) in Canada. NINT is a collaborative project of the National Research Council of Canada (NRC), the University of Alberta, and the Province of Alberta. This facility is a world-class center for nanotechnology research that will attract a core of the world's best minds in a field expected to revolutionize everything from computing and communications to medicine, energy, and manufacturing. Completed in 2006 and constructed on the campus of the University of Alberta, the project included 21,086 square meters (7 stories

nanotechnology

with a penthouse) and had a budget of $52,000,000. The project managers were Gordon Driedger and Jim Hinger. [12]

According to the Nanotechnology Research Center of the Research Institute of Petroleum Industry of Iran, "Nanotechnology is perhaps today's most advanced manufacturing technology. It is so rapidly emerging that most thinkers and scientists working on this field predict that nano will change our world in the next 100 years more than all the changes that we have seen in the last half of a millennium.

"Nanotechnology is the design, characterization, production, and application of structures, devices, and systems by controlling the shape and size at the nanometer scale. Since at nano-scale, the properties of materials differ in fundamental and valuable ways from the properties of individual atoms and molecules or bulk matter, nanotechnology has a wide range of applications in different fields such as electronics, pharmaceuticals, materials, polymers, chemical, and petroleum industry.

"In the petroleum industry, nanotechnology can affect both the upstream and downstream sectors. For example, in the upstream sector nanotechnology can help improve oil and gas production through improved understanding of processes at the molecular level. It can also help develop new metering techniques with tiny sensors to provide improved information about the reservoir. Moreover, applying nano-materials such as nano-particles and hydro-gel nano-composites could enhance the recovery rate of oil." [13]

Future Energy

New and future energy sources and supplies have been a hot topic for the last 10 years. In recent few months, however, it has frequently been front page news due to the combined influences of rapid demand growth (especially in emerging economies), oil and gas supply limits, rising prices, the global economy, and climate change. While prices for oil and gas fluctuate based on economic factors, most people (and governments) now recognize that there are no more than a few more decades of petroleum reserves underground and that our reliance on petroleum products for energy must end.

New reliable and economic sources of energy must be found to satisfy future energy needs. In addition, as populations and economies continue to grow, future energy requirements will increase. Solutions to this problem is not only an economic issue but a social imperative. This will lead to massive new investment into alternative, sustainable, and technology-based energy solutions. This sector represents enormous potential demand for project management and project managers, as we can easily anticipate thousands of programs and projects in the energy sector – and in all those industries and organizations connected to energy.

Current Primary Sources of Energy

The US Department of Energy (DOE) has information related to the following primary energy sources on the agency's website [14]:

- Bioenergy
- Coal
- Electric Power
- Fossil Fuels
- Fusion
- Geothermal
- Hydrogen
- Hydropower
- Natural Gas
- Nuclear
- Oil
- Renewables
- Solar
- Wind

Most of us know something about some of these energy sources, less about others. It is significant to note that the above list includes 14 important sources of energy, all of which represent project-oriented industries full of project-based organizations, project managers, and project management. While all of these do not represent "new frontiers" for project management, the changes and expansion of some of these energy sectors will, in fact, represent new and growing opportunities for projects and project management, especially as investments increase. Examples include bio-fuels, hydrogen, nuclear, solar, wind, and other renewable energy sources.

Future Energy Sources & Technologies

According to www.alternative-energy-news.info, "In the future, civilization will be forced to research and develop alternative energy sources. Our current rate of fossil fuel usage will lead to an energy crisis this century. In order to survive the energy crisis many companies in the energy industry are inventing new ways to extract energy from renewable sources. While the rate of development is slow, mainstream awareness and government pressures are growing." [15]

Some of the future energy projects and topics described on this website include:

- Biotechnology – growing energy
- Wind-powered rotating skyscraper
- Personal rapid transit by JPod
- Solar space heaters
- Ocean renewable energies
- Water fuel converters
- Ocean energy bionics
- Tidal energy
- Ambient energy technology generator
- Green steam engine (energy)
- Energy from pollution and waste
- New batter technology for hybrid vehicles

- Hydrogen fuel cells and automobiles
- Wind shade roof (pictured)

According to Wikipedia, "A key limit to the development of any particular energy source is availability of the underlying resource. Most of the world's main energy sources are based on the consumption of non-renewable resources (petroleum, coal, natural gas, and uranium). While still a small segment of the energy supply, renewable sources such as wind power and solar power are growing rapidly in market share. Closely linked to energy development are concerns about the possible environmental effects of energy use, such as climate changes. Energy development issues are part of the much debated sustainable development problem." [16]

Rather than discuss all possible sources of future energy, I want to focus on a few with significant potential.

Hydrogen & Hydrogen Fuel Cells

According to EnergyQuest [17], a Canadian government website, "Hydrogen is a colorless, odorless gas that accounts for 75 percent of the entire universe's mass. Hydrogen is found on Earth only in combination with other elements such as oxygen, carbon and nitrogen. To use hydrogen, it must be separated from these other elements."

As pointed out on that website, hydrogen is used today in NASA's space program as fuel for the space shuttles, and in fuel cells that provide heat, electricity and drinking water for astronauts. Fuel cells are devices that directly convert hydrogen into electricity. In the future, hydrogen could be used to fuel vehicles (such as the DaimlerChrysler NeCar 4 shown in the picture to the right) and aircraft, and provide power for our homes and offices.

Hydrogen can be made from molecules called hydrocarbons by applying heat, a process known as "reforming" hydrogen. This process makes hydrogen from natural gas. An electrical current can also be used to separate water into its components of oxygen and hydrogen in a process called electrolysis. Hydrogen as a fuel is high in energy, yet a machine that burns pure hydrogen produces almost zero pollution. NASA has used liquid hydrogen since the 1970s to propel rockets and now the space shuttle into orbit. Hydrogen fuel cells power the shuttle's electrical systems, producing a clean by-product - pure water, which the crew drinks.

Hydrogen fuel cells are a promising technology for use as a source of heat and electricity in buildings, and as an electrical power source for vehicles. Auto companies are already developing cars and trucks that use fuel cells. In a fuel cell vehicle, an electrochemical device converts hydrogen (stored on board) and oxygen from the air into electricity, to drive an electric motor and power the vehicle.

Although these applications would ideally run off pure hydrogen, in the near term they are likely to be fueled with natural gas, methanol or even gasoline. Reforming these fuels to create hydrogen will allow the use of much of our current energy infrastructure - gas stations, natural gas pipelines, etc. - while fuel cells are phased in. In the future, hydrogen could also join electricity as an important energy carrier. An energy carrier stores, moves and delivers energy in a usable form to consumers.

Some experts think that hydrogen will form the basic energy infrastructure to power future societies, replacing today's natural gas, oil, coal, and electricity infrastructures. Other scientists and economists are not convinced for a variety of reasons, primarily associated with economic challenges.

Nuclear Power returns

Another rapidly growing industry is nuclear energy, with new nuclear power plants now underway or being planned worldwide. In the United States, major research and development is underway on "next generation" nuclear energy, power stations using low-level radioactive fuel, more efficient technologies, and generating less radioactive waste. Trillions of dollars are now budgeted for nuclear power plants around the world, representing thousands of projects and a huge growing market for project management.

Here are some interesting nuclear energy facts from www.our-energy.com [18]:

- Nuclear energy is a non-renewable energy source. Nuclear energy is energy that is released either by splitting atomic nuclei or by forcing the nuclei of atoms together.
- Nuclear energy comes from mass-to-energy conversions that occur in the splitting of atoms. Albert Einstein's famous mathematical formula $E = mc2$ explains this. The equation says: E [energy] equals m [mass] times c2 [c stands for the speed or velocity of light]. This means that it is mass multiplied by the square of the velocity of light.
- Nuclear energy is produced by a controlled nuclear chain reaction and creates heat—which is used to boil water, produce steam, and drive a steam turbine.
- Nuclear power can come from the fission of uranium, plutonium or thorium or the fusion of hydrogen into helium. Today it is almost all uranium. The basic energy fact is that the fission of an atom of uranium produces 10 million times the energy produced by the combustion of an atom of carbon from coal.
- Nuclear power plants need less fuel than ones which burn fossil fuels. One ton of uranium produces more energy than is produced by several million tons of coal or several million barrels of oil.
- In France, nuclear power is the most widespread, supplying 80 percent of the country's electricity.
- As of 2004, nuclear power provided 6.5% of the world's energy and 15.7% of the world's electricity, with the U.S., France, and Japan together accounting for 57% of nuclear generated electricity.

(photo: nuclear plant near Cattenom, France)

- Nuclear energy (nuclear power) accounts for about 19 percent of the total electricity generated in the United States. There are 104 commercial nuclear generating units that are fully licensed by the U.S. Nuclear Regulatory Commission (NRC) to operate in the United States. Of these 104 reactors, 69 are categorized a pressurized water reactors totaling 65.100 net megawatts (electric) and 35 units are boiling water reactors totaling 32.300 net megawatts (electric).
- Russia has begun building floating nuclear power plants. The £100 million ($204.9 million) vessel, the Lomonosov, to be completed in 2010, is the first of seven plants that Moscow says will bring vital energy resources to remote Russian regions.
- Nuclear energy is now making a comeback because nuclear energy has virtually no greenhouse gas emissions and therefore isn't causing global warming like some other energy sources.
- Compared to other non-carbon-based and carbon-neutral energy options, nuclear power plants require far less land area. For a 1000 MW plant, site requirements are estimated as follows: nuclear, 1-4 km^2; solar or photovoltaic park, 20-50 km^2; a wind field, 50-150 km^2; and biomass, 4,000-6,000 km^2.

The Global Nuclear Energy Partnership (GNEP) is an initiative sponsored by the U.S. government to work with other nations to develop and deploy advanced nuclear recycling and reactor technologies. This initiative will help provide reliable, emission-free energy with less of the waste burden of older technologies and without making available separated plutonium that could be used by rogue states or terrorists for nuclear weapons. These new technologies will make possible a dramatic expansion of safe, clean nuclear energy to help meet the growing global energy demand. [26]

GNEP seeks to bring about a significant, wide-scale use of nuclear energy, and to take actions now that will allow that vision to be achieved while decreasing the risk of nuclear weapons proliferation and effectively addressing the challenge of nuclear waste disposal. GNEP will advance the nonproliferation and national security interests of the United States by reinforcing its nonproliferation policies and reducing the spread of

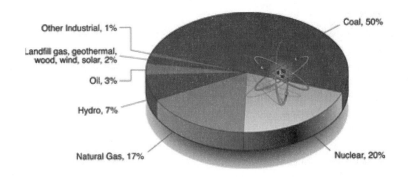

Other Industrial, 1%

Landfill gas, geothermal,
wood, wind, solar, 2%

Oil, 3%

Hydro, 7%

Natural Gas, 17%

Coal, 50%

Nuclear, 20%

enrichment and reprocessing technologies, and eventually eliminating excess civilian plutonium stocks that have accumulated.

The GNEP will build on the recent advances to stimulate new nuclear plant construction in the U.S. This will be accomplished by demonstrating the success of the streamlined regulations for siting, constructing and operating new nuclear plants through the Nuclear Power 2010 program, and by implementing incentives enacted through the Energy Policy Act of 2005.

At 20 percent of the total electricity supply in the United States, nuclear power is the second-largest source of domestic electricity, while 70 percent comes from fossil-burning fuels (coal, natural gas, and oil).

The GNEP also calls for an expanded program to design, build, and export nuclear reactors that are cost-effective and well-suited to conditions in developing nations. This is expected to allow for safely expanding nuclear energy in developing nations and small-grid markets without increasing proliferation concerns. Grid-appropriate reactors may be the best choice for expanding the use of nuclear energy in these markets. These reactors will be safe, simple to operate, more proliferation-resistant and highly secure.

Historically, the requirements of large national markets with big electricity grids have driven the development of nuclear power reactors, resulting in commercial units of about 1,000 megawatts. Markets with much smaller grids and less well-developed technical infrastructures have not had much impact on power reactor designs and technologies. A different reactor design approach, tailored to this developing market segment, will help meet the rising power demands associated with economic growth and urbanization, while avoiding the use of fossil fuels. It will also lead to more projects and a rapidly growing nuclear energy export and construction industry.

Japan has 53 nuclear units that can produce 42,369 MWe distributed on the home islands. Electric utilities with nuclear plants include Hokkaido, Shikoku, Chubu, Tokyo, Tohoku, Hokuriku, Chugoku, Kansai, and Kyushu. Two other organizations with nuclear facilities are Japan Atomic Power Company and Japan Nuclear Cycle Development Institute. [20]

Nuclear power is growing again in France, India, Japan, and Russia, where the technology is well developed and the public has long accepted nuclear power. The U.K. government has recently embraced nuclear power as a national energy strategy, with a number of new facilities now under development. And Russia is exporting and building nuclear power plants in Africa, Eastern Europe, the Middle East, and Asia, representing many billions of dollars of engineering and construction projects.

Hydroelectricity

Hydropower is using water to power machinery or make electricity. Water constantly moves through a vast global cycle, evaporating from lakes and oceans, forming clouds, precipitating as rain or snow, then flowing back down to the ocean. The energy of this water cycle, which is driven by the sun, can be tapped to produce electricity or for mechanical tasks like grinding grain. Hydropower uses a fuel—water—that is not reduced or used up in the process. Because the water cycle is an endless, constantly recharging system, hydropower is a renewable energy.

When flowing water is captured and turned into electricity, it is called hydroelectric power or hydropower. There are several types of hydroelectric facilities; they are all powered by the kinetic energy of flowing water as it moves downstream. Turbines and generators convert the energy into electricity, which is then fed into the electrical grid to be used in homes, businesses, and by industry.

Hydropower has many advantages. It is fueled by water, so it's a clean fuel source, it does not pollute the air like power plants that burn fossil fuels, and it is a renewable power source. Hydropower is generally available as needed; engineers can control the flow of water through the turbines to produce electricity on demand. Hydropower plants also provide recreational opportunities, notably fishing, swimming, and boating, and normally improve water supply and flood control.

Disadvantages of hydroelectric plants include possible negative impacts on fish populations, water quality, water flow, and especially on the environment immediately affected by the project and resulting reservoirs. Also, hydroelectricity depends on rainfall and can be adversely affected by droughts and weather patterns.

According to the U.S. Department of Energy (DOE) website [24], hydroelectric power facilities in the United States can generate enough power to supply 28 million households with electricity, the equivalent of nearly 500 million barrels of oil. The total U.S. hydropower capacity—including pumped storage facilities—is about 95,000 megawatts. Researchers are working on advanced turbine technologies that will not only help maximize the use of hydropower, but also minimize adverse environmental effects. DOE has completed a resource assessment has identified 5,677 sites in the United States with undeveloped capacity of about 30,000 MW. By comparison, today there is about 80,000 MW of hydroelectric generating plants in the United States.

Hydroelectric power projects in other countries, however, are either coming on line, in the planning stage or already under development. The most famous recent hydro project is the Three Gorges Dam in China. However, a massive and even larger hydro project on the Congo River in Africa is now under discussion among possible sources of finance in London.

And a number of hydro projects are either underway or in the planning stages in several South American countries, including Brazil and Peru. As the demand for energy

increases in developing countries, more hydroelectric projects can be anticipated. [23] Like nuclear energy, hydro-electric facilities normally involve huge investment and major engineering and construction projects, employing thousands of workers.

Solar Power

Solar technology isn't new. It probably started some time in the 7th Century B.C., when people learned how to use glass and sunlight to light a fire. But today's sophisticated solar technologies include everything from solar-powered lights and buildings to solar-powered vehicles. Examples of solar energy technologies being developed by the U.S. DOE and industry are photovoltaic cells, concentrating solar power technologies and low-temperature solar collectors.

Photovoltaic cells convert sunlight directly into electricity and are made of semiconductors such as crystalline silicon or various thin-film materials. Photovoltaics can provide tiny amounts of power for watches, large amounts for the electric grid, and everything in between. Concentrating solar power technologies use reflective materials to concentrate the sun's heat energy, which ultimately drives a generator to produce electricity. These technologies include dish/engine systems, parabolic troughs, and central power towers. Low-temperature solar collectors also absorb the sun's heat energy, but the heat is used directly for hot water or space heating for residential, commercial, and industrial facilities.

The DOE's Solar Energy Technologies program is developing cost-effective solar-energy technologies that have the greatest potential to benefit citizens of the United States and the world. Solar technologies diversify the energy supply, reduce dependence on imported fuels, improve air quality, and offset greenhouse gas emissions. A growing solar industry also stimulates the economy by creating jobs in solar manufacturing and installation. (More projects!)

According to the US Department of Energy [21], some things we can expect in the future from solar technologies include the following:

- All our buildings will feature energy-efficient design, construction, and materials as well as renewable energy technologies. In effect, each building will both conserve energy and produce its own supply, to be one of a new generation of cost-effective "zero-energy buildings" that have no net annual need for nonrenewable energy.

- In photovoltaic research and development, there will be more breakthroughs in new materials, cell designs, and novel approaches to product development. In a solar future, your mode of transportation—and even the clothes you wear—could produce clean, safe electric power.
- With today's technology roadmaps to lead the way, concentrating solar power will be fully competitive with conventional power-generating technologies within a decade. Concentrating solar power, or solar thermal electricity, could harness enough of the sun's energy to provide large-scale, domestically secure, and environmentally friendly electricity, especially in the southwestern United States.
- The enormous solar power potential of the southwestern United States —comparable in scale to the huge hydropower resource of the Northwest—will be realized. A desert area 10 miles by 15 miles could provide 20,000 megawatts of power, and the electricity needs of the entire United States could theoretically be met by a photovoltaic array within an area 100 miles on a side. *(photo: example of solar arrays at desert power station)*
- Within 10 years, photovoltaic power will be competitive in price with traditional sources of electricity.
- Solar electricity will be used in an electrolysis process that separates the hydrogen and oxygen in water so the hydrogen can be used in fuel cells for transportation and in buildings.

An example of a solar power facility is shown at left, the world's largest solar power facility — near Kramer Junction, California—consists of five solar electric generating stations with a combined capacity of 150 megawatts. At capacity, this is usually enough power for about 150,000 homes. The facility covers more than 1000 acres and has a collector surface area of more than a million square meters.

This solar dish-engine system (shown below right) is an electric generator that "burns" sunlight instead of gas or coal to produce electricity. The dish, a concentrator, is the primary solar component of the system, collecting the energy coming directly

from the sun and concentrating it on a small area. A thermal receiver absorbs the concentrated beam of solar energy, converts it to heat, and transfers the heat to the engine/generator. (Credit: Sandia National Laboratories)

According to PowerPedia.com [22], Solar Energy covers the various solar innovations that increase collection efficiency and reduce costs. The term "solar power" is used to describe a number of methods of harnessing energy from the light of the Sun. It has been used in many traditional technologies for centuries and has come into widespread use where other power supplies are absent, such as in remote locations and in space. Its use is spreading as the environmental costs and limited supply of fossil fuels are realized. Some of the solar power technologies discussed on the peswiki.com/PowerPedia Solar Energy website (9) include the following:

- Energy towers and solar updraft towers
- Space-based solar collectors
- Nanotechnology-based solar collectors
- Solar fibers
- Concentrated solar stirling engine
- Photovoltaics (solar cells)
- Quantum dot solar cell materials
- Full spectrum solar cell
- Solar chemicals
- Total spectrum solar concentrator
- Solar thermal electric power plants
- Concentrated solar power plants
- Solar power towers
- Solar dishes *(pictured below)*
- Linear fresnel reflector power plants
- Solar ponds

In some areas of the United States, solar electric systems are already competitive with utility systems. As of 2005, there is a list of technical conditions that factor into the economic feasibility of going solar: the amount of sunlight that the area receives; the purchase cost of the system; the ability of the system owner to sell power back to the electric grid; and most important, the competing power prices from the local utility. For example, a photovoltaic system installed in Boston, Massachusetts, produces 25% less electricity than it would in Albuquerque, New Mexico, but yields roughly the same savings on utility bills since electricity costs more in Boston.

The world's largest solar power plant is located in the Mojave Desert. Solel, an Israeli company, operates the plant, which consists of 1,000 acres (4 km²) of solar reflectors. This plant produces 90% of the world's commercially produced solar power (excluding photovoltaics). On January 12, 2006, the California Public Utilities Commission approved the California Solar Incentive Program, a comprehensive $2.8 billion program that provides incentives toward solar development over 11 years. These systems — to be installed on a 4,500 acre (18 km²) solar farm — will use mirrors to direct and concentrate sunlight onto the engines which will drive generators.

Africa is home to the over 9 million km² Sahara desert, who's overall capacity — assuming 50 MW/km² day/night/cloud average with 15% efficient photovoltaic panels — is over 450 TW, or over 4,000,000 terawatt-hours per year. The current global energy consumption by humans, including all oil, natural gas, coal, nuclear, and hydroelectric, is pegged at about 13 TW.

The largest solar power station in Australia is the 400kWp array at Singleton, New South Wales. Other significant solar arrays include the 220 kWp array on the Anangu Pitjantjatjara Lands in South Australia, the 200kWp array at Queen Victoria Market in Melbourne and the 160kWp array at Kogarah Town Square in Sydney. A building-integrated photo voltaic (BIPV) installation of 60kW in Brisbane (at the Hall-Chadwick building) has an uninterruptible power supply (UPS) which gives around 10-15 minutes worth of emergency power in the event of the loss of electricity supply. Numerous smaller arrays have been established, mainly in remote areas where solar power is cost-competitive with diesel power.

Japan currently consumes about half of worldwide production of solar modules, mostly for grid-connected residential applications. As of 2004, Japan had 1200 MWe installed. In terms of overall installed PV capacity, India comes fourth after Japan, Ger-

many, and the United States. India's long-term solar potential may be unparalleled in the world because it is one of the few places with an ideal combination of both high solar power reception and a large consumer base in the same place. India's theoretical solar potential is about 5,000 TW·h per year (i.e., 600 GW), far more than its current total consumption.

In 2005, the Israeli government announced an international contract for building a 100 MW solar power plant to supply the electricity needs of more than 200,000 Israelis living in southern Israel. The plan may eventually allow the creation of a gigantic 500 MW power plant, making Israel a leader in solar power production.

The 10 megawatt Bavaria Solarpark in Germany *(pictured above)* is one of the world's largest solar electric system, covering 25 hectares (62 acres) with 57,600 photovoltaic panels. A large solar PV plant is planned for the island of Crete. Another site is the Loser in Austria. The Plataforma Solar de Almería (PSA) in Spain, part of the Center for Energy, Environment and Technological Research (CIEMAT), is the largest center for research, development, and testing of concentrating solar technologies in Europe.

In the United Kingdom, the second tallest building in Manchester, the CIS Tower, was clad in photovoltaic panels at a cost of £5.5 million and started feeding electricity to the national grid in November 2005. On April 27, 2006, GE Energy Financial Services, PowerLight Corporation and Catavento Lda announced that they will build the world's largest solar photovoltaic power project. The 11-megawatt solar power plant, comprising 52,000 photovoltaic modules, will be built at a single site in Serpa, Portugal, 200 kilometers (124 miles) southeast of Lisbon in one of Europe's sunniest areas. [21]

This is probably more than any of you wanted to know about solar energy, but the point it that this field is growing rapidly, with significant projected investments and many, many projects. It is another growing field where project managers and project management is needed, worldwide. As economies and technologies improve, the opportunities and potential are multiplying in this area.

Tidal Power

Tidal energy is produced through the use of tidal energy generators. These large underwater turbines are placed in areas with high tidal movements, and are designed to capture the kinetic motion of the ebbing and surging of ocean tides in order to produce electricity. Tidal power has great potential for future power and electricity generation because of the massive size of the oceans. [18]

Tidal energy is produced through the use of tidal energy generators. These large underwater turbines are placed in areas with high tidal movements, and are designed to capture the kinetic motion of the ebbing and surging of ocean tides in order to produce electricity. Tidal power has great potential for future power and electricity generation because of the massive size of the oceans. [31] Here are some recent developments described on www.alternative-energy-news.info/.

- RWE Innogy has submitted a planning application to the relevant authorities for one of the world's first wave power stations off the Scottish coast. The pilot plant with an output of four megawatts will be installed in Siadar Bay on the Isle of Lewis. If everything goes to plan, construction work could begin in 2009. (April 24, 2008 news release)
- Hydro Green Energy, which wants to plumb U.S. waterways for electricity, has received $2.6 million in funding. The company wants to create somewhat small, modular turbines and then set them down in arrays in waterways. Each turbine would be capable of harvesting 250 kilowatts of power. The size of the array would then depend on the size and power of the waterway. It hopes to plant these arrays in Minnesota, Louisiana, Mississippi, and other states. (April 16, 2008 news release)
- Companies such as Ireland's OpenHydro are building large machines that look like oil derricks for harvesting power. These large machines go in the ocean. Tidal power has a number of advantages over other renewables. For one thing, it's predictable. Computer simulations can calculate the amount of electricity that can be generated from tides decades in advance. Besides being predictable, tides are also constant, unlike wind or solar.
- The world's first commercial-scale tidal stream turbine set to be installed. Bristol-based Marine Current Turbines (MCT) is set to deploy its 1.2MW SeaGen Tidal System in Strangford Narrows, Northern Ireland on Easter Monday. Producing enough clean energy for 1,000 homes (when fully operational), this will be the first, commercial scale, tidal stream turbine installed and operating anywhere in the world. It will generate one of the most environmentally friendly forms of energy - it makes no noise, is almost completely below the surface, never runs out and has zero emissions. (March 12, 2008)
- Marine Current Turbines confirmed that installation of its SeaGen commercial tidal energy system will commence during the week of August 20, 2007 in Northern Ireland's Strangford Lough. At 1.2MW capacity, SeaGen will be the world's largest-ever tidal current device by a significant margin, and will generate clean and sustainable electricity for approximately 1,000 homes. It is also a world first in being a prototype for commercial technology to be replicated on a large scale over the next few years. (June 6, 2008) *(photo: SeaGen tide farm, next page)*
- BioPower Systems is developing a new ocean energy technology in Australia that will use bionics to mimic natural systems in order to produce energy. Both bioSTREAM and bioWAVE technologies use biomimicry, which refers to the adaptation of biological traits in engineered systems. BioPower Systems has copied many of the beneficial traits from natural systems in the development of the new ocean energy conversion systems. The company is researching this new

technology for application. Laboratory testing will be completed in 2007, and full-scale ocean-based prototypes will be tested in 2008. Commercial units are expected to reach the market by the end of 2009. (November 2006)

- Tidal power proponents liken the technology to little wind turbines on steroids, turning like windmills in the current. Water's greater density means fewer and smaller turbines are needed to produce the same amount of electricity as wind turbines. After more than two decades of experimenting, the technology has advanced enough to make business sense, said Carolyn Elefant, co-founder of the Ocean Renewable Energy Coalition, a marine energy lobbying group formed in May 2005. (May 2006)

- With 12,380 miles of coastline, the U.S. may seem like a wide-open frontier for the fledgling industry, but experts believe only a few will prove profitable. The ideal sites are close to a power grid and have large amounts of fast-moving water with enough room to build on the sea floor while staying clear of boat traffic. "There are thousands of sites, but only a handful of really, really good ones," said Roger Bedard of the Electric Power Research Institute, a nonprofit organization in Palo Alto, Calif., that researches energy and the environment.

- Government and the private sector in Europe, Canada and Asia have moved faster than their U.S. counterparts to support tidal energy research. As of June 2006, there were small facilities in Russia, Nova Scotia and China, as well as a 30-year-old plant in France, according to a report by EPRI. *(photo: tidal power plant in South Korea, next page)*

- Ocean energy will be functioning in tandem with other renewable resources and supplement other sea-based technologies. In the United States, wave energy technology is less advanced than tidal and will need more government subsidies. However, the number of good wave sites far exceeds that of tidal. Wave power collection involves cork or serpent-like devices that absorb energy from swells on the ocean's surface, whereas tidal machines sit on the sea floor.

- Tidal energy technology has been able to build on lessons learned from wind power development, while wave engineers have had to start from scratch. A few companies are working aggressively to usher wave power into the energy industry. Aqua Energy started building a wave energy plant at Makah Bay in Washington state in 2007. Another wave plant, whose backers include major Norwegian energy company Norsk Hydro ASA, is under construction off the coast of Portugal.
- The Ocean Renewable Energy Coalition (OREC) is the national trade association for the marine renewable energy industry in the United States. Founded in 2005, OREC was formed to promote the advancement and commercialization of marine renewables and provide a unified voice for the marine renewables industry. The organization embraces a wide range of renewable technologies, including wave, tidal, current, offshore wind, ocean thermal, marine biomass and all other technologies that utilize renewable resources from oceans, tidal areas, and other unimpounded water bodies. [32]

The above provide a good indication of some of the interest and developments now occurring in the tidal energy field. Based on the size of the oceans and the latent power and energy there, this is an area that is bound to become a major energy source in the future, as technology advances and economics converge. The result will be more projects, needing more project management.

Wind Power

The following introductory information is from the U.S. DOE's website [33]. Wind energy uses the energy in the wind for practical purposes like generating electricity, charging batteries, pumping water, or grinding grain. Wind turbines convert the kinetic energy of the wind into other forms of energy. Large, modern wind turbines operate together in wind farms to produce electricity for utilities. Small turbines are used by homeowners and remote villages to help meet energy needs.

Winds are created by uneven heating of the atmosphere by the sun, irregularities of the Earth's surface, and the rotation of the Earth. As a result, winds are strongly influenced and modified by local terrain, bodies of water, weather patterns, vegetative

cover, and other factors. The wind flow, or motion of energy when harvested by wind turbines, can be used to generate electricity. Wind-based electricity generating capacity has increased markedly in the United States since 1970, although it remains a small faction of total electric capacity.

Modern wind turbines fall into two basic groups: the horizontal-axis variety, as shown in the photo, and the vertical-axis design, like the eggbeater-style Darrieus model, named after its French inventor. Horizontal-axis wind turbines typically either have two or three blades. These three-bladed wind turbines are operated "upwind," with the blades facing into the wind.

Utility-scale turbines range in size from 100 kilowatts to as large as several megawatts. Larger turbines are grouped together into wind farms, which provide bulk power to the electrical grid. Single small turbines, below 100 kilowatts, are used for homes, telecommunications dishes, or water pumping. Small turbines are sometimes used in connection with diesel generators, batteries, and photovoltaic systems. These systems are called hybrid wind systems and are typically used in remote, off-grid locations, where a connection to the utility grid is not available.

Wind energy offers many advantages, which explains why it's the fastest-growing energy source in the world. Wind energy is fueled by the wind, so it's a clean fuel source. Wind energy doesn't pollute the air or produce acid rain or greenhouse gasses. Wind energy relies on the renewable power of the wind, which can't be used up.

Wind energy is one of the lowest-priced renewable energy technologies available today. Wind turbines can be built in rural areas, where most of the best wind sites are found. People can continue to work the land because wind turbines use only a fraction of the land. Wind power plant owners make rent payments to the land owner for use of the land.

Disadvantages include a higher initial investment than fossil-fueled generators. The major challenge to using wind as a source of power, however, is that the wind is intermittent and does not always blow when electricity is needed. Wind energy cannot be stored

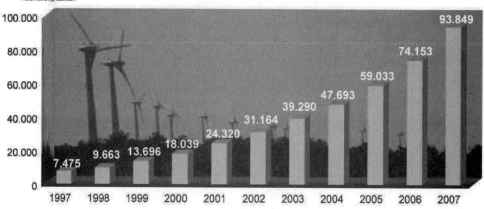

WWEA World Wind Energy - Total Installed Capacity [MW] 1997-2007

World Wind Energy Association

Year	Capacity
1997	7.475
1998	9.663
1999	13.696
2000	18.039
2001	24.320
2002	31.164
2003	39.290
2004	47.693
2005	59.033
2006	74.153
2007	93.849

(unless batteries are used); and not all winds can be harnessed to meet the timing of electricity demands. Good wind sites are often located in remote locations, far from cities where the electricity is needed. Wind resource development may compete with other uses for the land and those alternative uses may be more highly valued than electricity generation. Although wind power plants have relatively little impact on the environment compared to other conventional power plants, there is concern over the noise produced by the rotor blades, aesthetic (visual) impacts, and birds killed by flying into the rotors.

In the year 2007, 19,696 MW of new wind energy capacity were added summing up to a global installed capacity of 93,849 MW by the end of December 2007. The added capacity equals a growth rate of 26.6 %, after 25.6 % in 2006. The currently installed wind power capacity generates 200 TWh per year, equaling 1.3 % of the global electricity consumption – in some countries and regions, wind energy already contributes 40% and more. The wind industry employs today 350,000 people worldwide, after 300,000 employees in the year 2006. Based on the accelerated development, World Wind Energy Association has increased its prediction for 2010 and expects now 170,000 MW to be installed by the end of the year 2010. [33]

According to Wikipedia [35], At the end of 2007, worldwide capacity of wind-powered generators was 94.1 gigawatts. Although wind currently produces just over 1% of world-wide electricity use, it accounts for approximately 19% of electricity production in Denmark, 9% in Spain and Portugal, and 6% in Germany and the Republic of Ireland (2007 data). Globally, wind power generation increased more than fivefold between 2000 and 2007. *(photo: North Hoyle wind farm in the Irish Sea, next page)*

By 2010, the World Wind Energy Association expects 160GW of capacity to be installed worldwide, up from 73.9 GW at the end of 2006, implying an anticipated net growth rate of more than 21% per year. By 2025, it will be much greater.

Denmark generates nearly one-fifth of its electricity with wind turbines -- the highest percentage of any country -- and is fifth in the world in total wind power generation. Denmark is prominent in the manufacturing and use of wind turbines, with a commitment made in the 1970s to eventually produce half of the country's power by wind. *(photo: Horns Rev wind farm in Denmark, next page below)*

Germany is the leading producer of wind power, with 28% of the total world capacity in 2006 and a total output of 38.5 TWh in 2007 (6.3% of German electricity); the official target is for renewable energy to meet 12.5% of German electricity needs by 2010 — this target may be reached ahead of schedule. Germany has 18,600 wind turbines, mostly in the north of the country — including three of the biggest in the world, constructed by the companies Enercon (6 MW), Multibrid (5 MW), and Repower (5 MW).

Germany's Schleswig-Holstein province generates 36% of its power with wind turbines. In 2005, the government of Spain approved a new national goal for installed wind power capacity of 20,000 MW in 2010. With installation of 3,515 MW in 2007 (for a total figure of 15,145 MW), this target will probably be reached ahead of schedule. A significant acceleration of the bureaucratic proceedings and connections to grid, and the legislative change occurred during 2007 (with Royal Decree 661/2007), have accelerated the developing of many wind parks, so that they could still run under the previous more favorable conditions.

In recent years, the United States has added more wind energy to its grid than any other country; U.S. wind power capacity grew by 45% to 16.8 gigawatts in 2007. Texas has become the largest wind energy producing state, surpassing California. In 2007, the state expects to add 2 gigawatts to its existing capacity of approximately 4.5 gigawatts. Wind power generation in the U.S. was up 31.8% in February, 2007 from February, 2006. According to the American Wind Energy Association, wind will generate enough electricity in 2008 to power just over 1% (4.5 million households) of total electricity in the United States, up from less than 0.1% in 1999. U.S. DOE studies have concluded that wind harvested in just three of the 50 U.S. states could provide enough electricity to power the entire nation, and that offshore wind farms could do the same job.

India ranks 4th in the world with a total wind power capacity of 6,270 MW in 2006, or 3% of all electricity produced in India. The World Wind Energy Conference in New Delhi in November 2006 has given additional impetus to the Indian wind industry. The wind farm near Muppandal, Tamil Nadu, India, provides an impoverished village with energy. India-based Suzlon Energy is one of the world's largest wind turbine manufacturers. [35]

Bio-Fuels

The term "biomass" means any plant-derived organic matter available on a renewable basis, including dedicated energy crops and trees, agricultural food and feed crops, agricultural crop wastes and residues, wood wastes and residues, aquatic plants, animal wastes, municipal wastes, and other waste materials. Biomass offers U.S. tremendous opportunity to use domestic and sustainable resources to provide its fuel, power, and chemical needs from plants and plant-derived materials. The U.S. DOE's Renewable Energy Biomass Program includes major programs for developing and improving technology for biomass power, and for making biofuels such as ethanol (from biomass residues as well as grain) and renewable diesel.

Bioenergy technologies use renewable biomass resources to produce an array of energy related products including electricity, liquid, solid, and gaseous fuels, heat, chemicals, and other materials. Bioenergy ranks second (to hydropower) in renewable U.S. primary energy production and accounts for three percent of the primary energy production in the United States. [24]

Biomass is the only clean, renewable energy source that can help to significantly diversify transportation fuels. Biomass is any organic material made from plants or animals. Domestic biomass resources include agricultural and forestry residues, municipal solid wastes, industrial wastes, and terrestrial and aquatic crops grown solely for energy purposes.

Biomass can be converted to other usable forms of energy and is an attractive petroleum alternative for a number of reasons. First, it is a renewable resource that is more evenly distributed over the Earth's surface than are finite energy sources, and may be exploited using more environmentally friendly technologies. Agriculture and forestry residues, and in particular residues from paper mills, are the most common biomass resources used for generating electricity and power, including industrial process heat and steam, as well as for a variety of biobased products. Use of liquid transportation fuels such as ethanol and biodiesel, however, currently derived primarily from agricultural crops, is increasing dramatically.

Biofuels are any fuel derived from biomass. Agricultural products specifically grown for conversion to biofuels include corn and soybeans. R&D is currently being conducted to improve the conversion of non-grain crops, such as switch grass and a variety of woody crops, to biofuels. The energy in biomass can be accessed by turning the raw materials of the feedstock, such as starch and cellulose, into a usable form.

Transportation fuels are made from biomass through biochemical or thermochemical processes. Known as biofuels, these include ethanol, methanol, biodiesel, biocrude, and methane. Ethanol is the most widely used biofuel. Also known as ethyl alcohol or grain alcohol, it can be used either as an alternative fuel or as an octane-boosting, pollution-reducing additive to gasoline. It is an alcohol fuel made from sugars and starch found in plants. In the United States, ethanol is primarily produced from the starch

contained in grains such as corn, grain sorghum, and wheat through a fermentation and distillation process that converts starch to sugar and then to alcohol.

Currently, a majority of ethanol is made from corn, but new technologies are being developed to make ethanol from other agricultural and forestry resources such as:

- corn stover (stalks and residues left over after harvest);
- grain straw;
- switchgrass;
- quick growing tree varieties, such as poplar or willow; and
- municipal wastes.

Ethanol can be blended with gasoline in varying quantities to reduce the consumption of petroleum fuels, as well as to reduce air pollution. It is increasingly used as an oxygenate additive for standard gasoline, as a replacement for methyl t-butyl ether (MTBE), which is responsible for groundwater and soil contamination.

Biopower, or biomass power, is the use of biomass to generate electricity, or heat and steam required for the operation of a refinery. Biopower system technologies include direct-firing, cofiring, gasification, pyrolysis, and anaerobic digestion.

Most biopower plants use direct-fired systems. They burn biomass feedstocks directly to produce steam. This steam drives a turbine, which turns a generator that converts the power into electricity. In some biomass industries, the spent steam from the power plant is also used for manufacturing processes or to heat buildings. Such combined heat and power systems greatly increase overall energy efficiency. Paper mills, the largest current producers of biomass power, generate electricity or process heat as part of the process for recovering pulping chemicals.

Biomass for power production comes from four different sources: agriculture waste, forestry waste, municipal and industrial solid waste, and energy crops. Each year, agriculture production in the United States produces millions of tons of waste that could be utilized for energy production. Similarly, the forest products industry produces millions of tons of waste that could be used for the same purpose. Forestry waste includes residue left over from logging, saw mills, and paper production.

In addition, a significant amount of biomass residue is generated when non-commercial tree species are thinned from the forest to allow more valuable tree species to grow to maturity. Much of the waste generated by municipalities and industry consists of plant and organic waste that could be removed from the solid waste stream and used as a source of fuel in a biomass power plant. Finally, energy crops can be grown specifically for the purpose of producing electricity. In the quest to identify suitable energy crops, researchers are experimenting with fast-growing trees, shrubs, and grasses, such as hybrid poplars, willows, and switchgrass. Each year millions of acres of agricultural land are idle, making them available for growing energy crops. [25]

Biomass offers great potential to replace existing fossil fuel power plants. The United States currently relies on bioenergy for about 1.4 percent of the nation's electricity. Bioenergy is generally cost-competitive with fossil-fuel-generated electricity when biomass residue prices are very low or negative. Given that transportation costs are key to the price, biomass power plants must be sited near an ongoing, reliable biomass source. Given the prevalence of the forest product industry in the Northeastern United States, several biomass power plants are located in northern New England. There remains a significant untapped potential in the Northeast, given the fact that only a small portion of the plant and organic waste generated in the region is currently used for power production.

Most analysts believe that the economics of bioenergy will improve as larger plants are constructed with higher efficiencies. Increasing efficiency is the key to lowering the overall costs of bioenergy. The gasification process discussed above offers the potential to significantly enhance the economics of bioenergy, given that significantly higher efficiencies are achieved using modern turbine technology.

Biofuels have been commercially successful in Brazil (ethanol) and Germany (biodiesel). In Brazil, "Eighty percent of 2005 production (ethanol) is anticipated to meet national demands (transportation fuels)." In Germany, in the last 10 years, consumption and production of biodiesel has increased several fold. In 2004, 1.18 million tons were produced, up 45 percent from 2003, with an additional 500,000 tonnes produced in 2005.

An unintended consequence of the rapid increase in the use of agricultural products for ethanol and biofuels in the United States and other countries may be food shortages and increased food prices. This should be a temporary condition, as there is no question that biofuels production and usage will continue to rise due to the rising prices of oil.

Five Top Renewable Energy Sources in the UK

According to a 2006 article published on www.smartplanet.com [27], the top renewable energy sources for the United Kingdom were:

(1) Wind
(2) Hydroelectric
(3) Biofuels
(4) Wave and Tidal Streams
(5) Photovoltaic

According to that article, the U.K. was still lagging well behind other countries in renewable energy generation. In Spain over a weekend in March, according to the AEE (Spanish Wind Energy Association), wind power accounted for an average of 28 per cent of Spain's entire power demand. But renewables are growing and will continue to do so, as necessity dictates.

The Promise of Nanotechnology

Perhaps more than any other existing technology, the field of nanotechnology may hold the most promise for solving future energy needs and for moving society away from the carbon-based economy. Many researchers around the world are working in this field now, with exciting new developments being announced recently at several research institutions.

For example, on April 24, 2008, an article on NanoTechWire.com [28] was entitled "University of Queensland nanotechnology powering green energy future." According to the article, "One of Australia's leading nanotechnology researchers has been recognised for his work at The University of Queensland (UQ) on sustainable energy with a second Federation Fellowship... Professor Max Lu, from UQ's Australian Institute for Bioengineering and Nanotechnology, is developing a new type of solar material that is more efficient in harvesting sunlight and costs less to produce... He said his research had the potential to transform Australia's energy and environmental industries and to speed up our transition from a fossil fuel economy to a renewable energy economy."

Professor Lu is Chair of Nanotechnology in Chemical Engineering at UQ and Director of the ARC Centre of Excellence for Functional Nanomaterials.

At the University of California at Berkeley in California, serious research efforts are also underway. A cornerstone of the Berkeley Lab energy initiative is The Helios Project, a new energy/nano research building that will be central to a major scientific initiative: The conversion of solar energy into carbon-neutral form of energy that could sustain our world in an environmentally friendly manner.

According to the Berkeley Lab website, "The Helios Project proposal, led by Laboratory Associate Director Paul Alivisatos and Physical Biosciences Director Jay Keasling, will cut across divisions and programs in profound ways to produce transforming technologies in synthetic biology and nanotechnology, and will fuse our core strengths in biological, chemical, and physical sciences in the search for a sustainable carbon-neutral source of energy. Now is the time to consider how new research at the interface of basic energy sciences and applied fields of energy technology can increase our future energy options. A well-conceived program put in place now has the potential to provide the people of the United States with renewable energy security and economic growth in the decades to come." [29]

The following other equally exciting potential energy solutions based on nanotechnology are also mentioned on the Berkely Lab's website:

- Synthetic biology: Biologically inspired systems for biomass-to-fuel and solar-to-chemical solutions
- Engineered systems: Hybrid nanomaterials and biomimetic systems for solar-to-fuel conversion
- Nanomaterials and nanostructured assemblies for photochemical conversion (solar-to-electric and solar-to-fuel conversion)
- Photoelectrochemistry

These are fascinating programs. Each of these areas of research could result in new sources and supplies of energy in the future. While scientists worldwide are studying the secrets of matter at the molecular level, however, others are turning to space for possible solutions.

Space-Based Energy

The Space Solar Alliance for Future Energy (SSAFE), a new organization advocating investment in space-based solar power technologies to address the planet's future energy needs, was announced on October 10, 2007 in the United States. The coalition of 13 leading research organizations and space advocacy groups focused their inaugural event on the announcement of a new study of space-based solar power led by the National Security Space Office (NSSO).

The study concluded that space-based solar power deserves substantial national investment as a path towards addressing future U.S. energy needs via a renewable energy source with no carbon emissions or hazardous waste. In the Space Solar Power concept, developed in the late 1960s by Dr. Peter Glaser, energy from sunlight is collected in space and transmitted wirelessly for use on Earth. [30]

According to Air Force Colonel-Select M.V. 'Coyote' Smith, the leader of the study, "When we started this work I had my doubts about the technology. But as the facts poured in, it became obvious that my initial assessment was wrong. Not only is this possible, but space-based solar power is probably the greatest opportunity to develop a safe, clean source of energy that can readily be shared with all of humanity."

According to Mark Hopkins, Senior Vice President of the National Space Society, "As the United States makes decisions now to answer the energy challenges of the next 50 years, space-based solar power must be a part of the answer. The NSSO-led study charts the path forward. While the technical challenges are real, significant investment now can build Space Solar Power into the ultimate energy source: clean, green, renewable, and capable of providing the vast amounts of power that the world will need. Congress, federal agencies and the business community should begin that investment immediately."

The founding members of SSAFE are the National Space Society, Space Frontier Foundation, Space Power Association, Aerospace Technology Working Group, Marshall Institute, Moon Society, ShareSpace Foundation, Space Studies Institute, Spaceward Foundation, AIAA Space Colonization Technical Committee, ProSpace, Space Enterprise Council, and Space Generation Foundation.

The Near Future

For the next 20-30 years, the world will continue to rely on coal, natural gas and oil for public energy supplies. This means that, in fact, for many years to come the coal, oil, gas, hydro-electric, nuclear and other current energy sources will incur massive investments and represent thousands of projects requiring project managers and project management. New investments and new technologies will be applied in these traditional energy industries and market to lengthen the lives of those supplies and businesses. Examples include the oil sands extraction and oil shale conversion projects in Canada, coal gasification projects in the United States and similar projects in Australia.

However, as fossil fuel supplies dwindle and prices rise, investment in alternative and renewable energy will continue to increase. Use of biofuels will increase. Science and technology breakthroughs will lead to even more options, including those resulting from nanotechnology. By 2025, a majority of energy supplies may be from renewable sources or solutions based on new science.

Possible Unintended Consequences

As we all well know by now, many energy sources have negative consequences, some of which are unforeseen. The negative impact on the environment of carbon-based energy is well documented, with more governments taking steps to limit, penalize, and reduce those consequences. The massive shift to ethanol and biofuels in the United States over the last five years, and the resulting impact on food prices and supplies this year, were almost completely unforeseen.

This is an area where project management can both make a contribution and learn some lessons. Risk management is a well-established aspect of project planning and project management today; projects related to new energy sources and technologies would be well served in applying greater emphasis on risk management. Just as importantly, project and program executives must consider the potential consequences of each project, including business, economic, environmental and social costs. This suggests a broader project planning model with longer horizons and more external considerations than most models and standards now include. In my opinion, this represents an area for more research and development within the project management field.

Broad Implications for Project Management

The broad implications of all of the above for project management should be obvious. Literally everything occurring in the alternative and future energy sectors will be via programs and projects. Every organization involved in any aspect of these technologies and projects will need project management; the larger ones will employ professional project managers and harness professional project management. This is clearly a growing market for project management products and services, and for employment. Governmental and public pressures to harness alternative and sustainable energy supplies are also propelling this sector.

This discussion was not intended to be a comprehensive assessment of future energy, or even the opportunities in this sector for project management. It was, however, intended to suggest future energy as a new frontier, where increased need and demand for professional project management should be robust in the years ahead. By 2025, these energy fields should all represent major users of project management.

Conclusion

This paper was not intended to identify or describe all potential new frontiers for projects and project management. Rather it was intended to suggest that some exciting new areas of project management application are emerging, where new methods and systems may be needed, and where attention by the project management professional community is warranted. By 2025, many of these new industries will be well established, especially those associated with solving global problems, requiring global cooperation, and involving global applications of science and technology.

The potential for modern project management to help the world solve local, regional and global problems is significant and must not be downplayed. It is exciting to think that project managers and project management will and can be so useful to so many people, organizations, and societies. For these and other reasons, by 2025 project management will be one of the most visible and most important management fields in the world. Finally!

Good luck with your projects,
David L. Pells

References:

1. http://en.wikipedia.org/wiki/Nanotechnology
2. http://www.zyvex.com/nano/
3. http://www.investmentu.net/ppc/t4nanotech.cfm?kw=X300H228
4. http://www.intel.com/pressroom/archive/releases/20080302comp.htm?iid=pr1_releasepri_20080302m
5. http://es.epa.gov/ncer/nano/research/nano_green.html
6. http://www.nano.gov/html/news/releases/20080214_NNI_Releases_EHS_Research_Strategy.html
7. http://www.nano.gov/html/news/releases/20080214_NNI_Releases_FY09_Budget_Highlights.html
8. http://cordis.europa.eu/nanotechnology/home.html
9. http://cordis.europa.eu/nanotechnology/src/fp_funded_projects.htm
10. http://www.azonano.com/details.asp?ArticleID=1202#_How_the_Chinese_Central%20Government
11. http://www.foodproductiondaily.com/news/ng.asp?n=81618-nanotechnology-rfid-sensor
12. http://www.uofaweb.ualberta.ca/pi/nav03.cfm?nav03=25622&nav02=23447&nav01=22192
13. http://www.ripi.ir/en/Default.asp
14. http://www.energy.gov/energysources/index.htm
15. http://www.alternative-energy-news.info/technology/future-energy/
16. http://en.wikipedia.org/wiki/Energy_development
17. http://www.energyquest.ca.gov/story/chapter20.html
18. http://www.futureenergy.com/
19. http://www.dw-world.de/dw/article/0,2144,2306337,00.html
20. http://www.nucleartourist.com/world/plant4.htm
21. http://www1.eere.energy.gov/solar/csp.html
22. http://peswiki.com/index.php/PowerPedia:Solar_Energy
23. http://www.alternative-energy-news.info/technology/hydro/tidal-power/
24. http://www.energy.gov/energysources/bioenergy.htm
25. http://www.nesea.org/energy/info/biopower.html
26. http://www.gnep.energy.gov/
27. http://www.smartplanet.com/news/tech/10000995/top-five-uk-renewable-electricity-technologies.htm
28. http://www.nanotechwire.com/news.asp?nid=5883
29. http://pbd.lbl.gov/energy/research.html
30. http://ssafe.wordpress.com/
31. http://www.alternative-energy-news.info/technology/hydro/tidal-power/
32. http://www.oceanrenewable.com/
33. http://www.solcomhouse.com/windpower.htm

34. http://www.energy.gov/energysources/wind.htm
35. http://en.wikipedia.org/wiki/Wind_power
36. Pells, David L., *New Frontiers for Project Management: Nanotechnology*, project management World Today eJournal, March 2008 - http://www.pmworldtoday.net/editorials/2008/mar.htm
37. Pells, David L., *New Frontiers for Project Management: Future Energy*, project management World Today eJournal, May 2008 - http://www.pmworldtoday.net/editorials/2008/may.htm

CHAPTER 25

New Frontiers for Project Management: Earth Sciences, Monitoring of the Planet, Extreme Weather Response & Climate Control

David L. Pells

Professional project management continues to grow rapidly in usage and demand worldwide, in most organizations and across all industries. This is especially true in high technology and information technology (IT) organizations, but in many other industries as well. The world is also rapidly changing, due to the global economy, climate change and other factors. What do these changes mean to project-based organizations and project management professionals? Most of these changes will results in more programs and projects, and the need for professional project management.

I believe there will be some significant new industries, and major changes in existing industries, that will offer "new frontiers" for projects and project management around the world in the next 15-20 years. Some of these new areas of project management application have been emerging slowly over the last decade, but are now expanding rapidly due to other forces and converging influences. Other new frontiers are in traditional industries and sectors, but based on new global information, perspectives and awareness that are leading to new and massive investments in infrastructure. And some frontiers are growing apparent based on changing demographics and more connected and urban human populations.

These trends are generating new and growing industries with significant future impact. Trillions of dollars will be invested in these industries in coming decades. Each of these emerging sectors will also have a significant impact on our society, personal lives and professional careers. The demand for project managers, and IT project management in particular, should increase dramatically in these fields.

This paper reviews the generally related fields of earth sciences, monitoring of the planet, responding to extreme weather and, eventually, climate control. These are industries and application areas that will grow rapidly in coming decades, will include thousands of programs and projects, and represent huge potential application areas for modern project management. Just as importantly, these are sectors with significant potential impact on the entire world. This paper is intended to drive interest and research related to project management applications in these growing and important fields of application.

Planetary Change

Over the last decade, climate change, global warming, severe weather and natural disasters, food shortages and other issues have focused global attention on the need to better understand the Earth, mankind's impact on the planet, and future options for improving both forecasting technologies and outcomes. Many scientific projects and programs have been launched in the last few years to study climate change, changes in the polar ice caps, changes in the ocean and ocean currents, weather patterns, the ozone, and other related topics. At the same time, earthquakes, hurricanes, floods, tornadoes, tsunamis, fires and other several weather causing huge natural disasters have focused attention on climatology, meteorology, oceanography, seismology and other "earth sciences" – as well as preparation for and responses to extreme weather.

Another new frontier for project management is future climate control, based on current trends related to earth sciences, monitoring of the planet, and climate/weather management. Climate control is the stuff of science fiction, or is it? I think it is still several decades away. But over the coming years, mankind must invest in a better understanding of the planet, and better tools and methods for predicting and preparing for extreme weather. Let us examine a few areas where this is already occurring, and some implications for the project management profession. By 2025, this field will be well established, will include hundreds of programs and projects, will employ thousands of project managers, and will affect everyone on the planet.

Earth Sciences – Learning more about the Earth

The Earth is a complex, dynamic system that mankind does not yet fully understand. The Earth system is comprised of diverse components that interact in complex ways.

We need to understand the Earth's atmosphere, lithosphere, hydrosphere, cryosphere, and biosphere as a single connected system. Our planet is changing on all spatial and temporal scales. [4]

According to Wikipedia, Earth science (also known as geoscience, the geosciences or the Earth Sciences), is an all-embracing term for the sciences related to the planet Earth. There are four major disciplines in earth sciences, namely geography, geology, geophysics and geodesy... Earth science generally recognizes 4 spheres, the lithosphere, the hydrosphere, the atmosphere, and the biosphere. These correspond to rocks, water, air, and life. Some practitioners include the cryosphere (ice) as a distinct portion of the hydrosphere and the pedosphere (soil) as an active, intermixed sphere as part of Earth's spheres. [1]

It is worth repeating here this additional information from the Wikipedia webpage on Earth Science, describing disciplines and sub-disciplines in this general topic:

- Geology describes the rocky parts of the Earth's crust (or lithosphere) and its historic development. Major subdisciplines are mineralogy and petrology, geochemistry, geomorphology, paleontology, stratigraphy, structural geology, engineering geology and sedimentology.
- Geophysics and Geodesy investigate the figure of the Earth, its reaction to forces and its magnetic and gravity fields. Geophysicists explore the Earth's core and mantle as well as the tectonic and seismic activity of the lithosphere.
- Soil science covers the outermost layer of the Earth's crust that is subject to soil formation processes (or pedosphere). Major subdisciplines include edaphology and pedology.
- Oceanography and hydrology (includes limnology) describe the marine and freshwater domains of the watery parts of the Earth (or hydrosphere). Major subdisciplines include hydrogeology and physical, chemical, and biological oceanography.
- Glaciology covers the icy parts of the Earth (or cryosphere).
- Atmospheric sciences cover the gaseous parts of the Earth (or atmosphere) between the surface and the exosphere (~1000 km). Major subdisciplines are meteorology, climatology, atmospheric chemistry and atmospheric physics.
- A very important linking sphere is the biosphere, the study of which is biology. The biosphere consists of all forms of life, from single-celled organisms to pine trees to people. The interactions of Earth's other spheres - lithosphere/geosphere, hydrosphere, atmosphere and/or cryosphere and pedosphere - create the conditions that can support life. [1]

Just this small introduction to Earth Sciences provides an idea of just how many topics Earth Science covers, and how many projects might be underway in these fields. Especially interesting is the list of organizations around the world dealing with the various geosciences, including geology, geophysics, oceanography, and related fields [2] Included on the list are organizations based in most large and developed countries.

In addition, the list of topics and subtopics within the Earth Sciences field reveals a huge number of scientific topics, [3] most of which are also the subject of study, research and projects at leading universities around the world.

There are many national and international programs and projects underway related to earth science research. In the United States, NASA has established an Earth

Science Directorate to conduct and sponsor research, collect new observations from space, develop technologies and extend science and technology education to learners of all ages. NASA works closely with global partners in government, industry, and the public to conduct and sponsor research to answer fundamental science questions about the changes we see in climate, weather, and natural hazards, and help decision-makers make informed decisions. The purpose of NASA's Earth science program is to develop a scientific understanding of Earth's system and its response to natural or human-induced changes, and to improve prediction of climate, weather, and natural hazards. [4]

Some Big Questions

Again referring to NASA, the agency describes some "big questions" that are driving humans to invest in earth sciences, and space-based earth observation systems. Here are the big questions posed by NASA [5]:

- How is the global earth system changing? - Earth is currently in a period of warming. In the last two decades, the rate of our world's warming accelerated and scientists predict that the globe will continue to warm over the course of the 21st century.
- What are the primary forcings of the earth system? - The Sun is the primary forcing of Earth's climate system, driving almost every aspect of our world's climate system and making possible life as we know it. According to scientists' models of Earth's orbit and orientation toward the Sun, our world should be just beginning to enter a new period of cooling -- perhaps the next ice age. Humans, however, are also a new force of change affecting earth systems. Other important forcings of Earth's climate system include such "variables" as clouds, airborne particulate matter, and surface brightness.
- How does the earth system respond to natural and human-induced changes? - The second law of thermodynamics compels Earth's climate system to seek equilibrium so that, over the course of a year the amount of energy received equals the amount of energy lost to space. The equilibrium can be affected by three things: a change in the amount of incoming solar radiation; change in the abundance of greenhouse gases in Earth's atmosphere; and change in Earth's reflective features. Humans can influence only the latter two

- What are the consequences of change in the earth system for human civilization? - the temperature is rising faster now than at any other time in the history of human civilization and such rapid climate change is likely to seriously stress some populations.
- How will the Earth system change in the future? - As the world consumes ever more fossil fuel energy, greenhouse gas concentrations will continue to rise and Earth's average temperature will rise with them. Earth's average surface temperature could rise between 2°C and 6°C by the end of the 21st century. [5]

According to NASA's website, these big questions are now driving programs and projects in space. In other words, NASA is funding projects and using project management to answer these questions. Some examples of NASA projects in the Earth Sciences directorate are mentioned below.

Monitoring the Planet

There are many good reasons to study the planet, and especially the weather and climate change. According to NASA, over the past 50 years, world population has doubled, grain yields have tripled and economic output has grown sevenfold. Earth science research can ascertain whether and how the Earth can sustain this growth in the future. Also, over a third of the US economy - $3 trillion annually - is influenced by climate, weather, space weather, and natural hazards. [4]

Earth Science Data Centers: NASA uses Distributed Active Archive Centers (DAACs), the data management and user services arm of NASA's EOSDIS, to store and maintain earth science data. The data centers process, archive, document, and distribute data from NASA's past and current Earth-observing satellites and field measurement programs. Each center serves a specific Earth system science discipline. NASA's current list of DAACs includes the following [6]:

- Alaska Satellite Facility DAAC (ASF DAAC)
- GSFC Earth Sciences Data and Information Services Center (GES DISC
- Global Hydrology and Resource Center (GHRC)
- Langley Research Center DAAC
- Land Processes DAAC (LP DAAC)
- National Snow and Ice Data Center DAAC (NSIDC DAAC)
- Oak Ridge National Laboratory DAAC (ORNL DAAC)
- Physical Oceanography DAAC (PO.DAAC)
- Socioeconomic Data and Applications Center (SEDAC)

Each of these centers has hundreds of data processing and database related programs and projects, involving hundreds of professionals and scientists around the world..

Again, quoting a NASA website: In the area of community preparedness for disaster management, NASA satellite missions make significant contributions in the area of hurricane and flood prediction. National Oceanic and Atmospheric Administration (NOAA) combines satellite-derived estimates of precipitation from the Special Sensor Microwave Imager (SSM/I) and from the Tropical Rainfall Measuring Mission (TRMM), with winds from QuikSCAT. Doing so substantially improves the accuracy of forecasts for landfall, track and intensity of hurricanes, and increases the lead-time for warnings for both hurricanes and floods. More accurate forecasts, in turn, enable improved decision-making leading to more enhanced community preparedness for these types of events.

The potential socioeconomic benefits of many of these applications are significant. For instance, by minimizing unnecessary emergency evacuation measures, improved hurricane forecasts save as much as $40 million for each event. Similarly, improved weather forecasting can save millions by enabling utilities to better plan for anticipated energy requirements.

For agricultural efficiency, NASA is working with the US Department of Agriculture (USDA) to explore the benefit of predictions of El Niño and La Niña events for management of farmlands. Systems used to monitor and assess the health and condition of crops and forests around the globe are being improved. The value to US agriculture industry of a "perfect" El Niño forecast is reported to be $320 million per year.

To compete in the global economy of the 21st Century, a healthy and vibrant aviation infrastructure is also needed. NASA and other space agencies work to ensure a safe, secure, efficient, and environmentally friendly air transportation system through enhancements to aviation weather forecasting. Weather is a contributing factor in approximately 30% of all aviation accidents and accounts for over 60% of all delays experienced in the air transportation system. Incorporating new, more frequent, and more precise satellite observations into weather forecasts leads to more accurate, dependable, and useful forecasts of threats to aviation including icing, turbulence, convection, and volcanic ash. [7]

According to the US Environmental Protection Agency on their Climate Change website, "the Intergovernmental Panel on Climate Change (IPCC) has stated "Most of the observed increase in global average temperatures since the mid-20th century is very likely due to the observed increase in anthropogenic greenhouse gas concentrations" (IPCC, 2007). In short, a growing number of scientific analyses indicate, but cannot prove, that rising levels of greenhouse gases in the atmosphere are contributing to climate change (as theory predicts). In the coming decades, scientists anticipate that as atmospheric concentrations of greenhouse gases continue to rise, average global temperatures and sea levels will continue to rise as a result and precipitation patterns will change." [8]

Important scientific questions remain about how much warming will occur, how fast it will occur, and how the warming will affect the rest of the climate system including precipitation patterns and storms. Answering these questions will require advances in scientific knowledge in a number of areas:

- Improving understanding of natural climatic variations, changes in the sun's energy, land-use changes, the warming or cooling effects of pollutant aerosols, and the impacts of changing humidity and cloud cover.
- Determining the relative contribution to climate change of human activities and natural causes.
- Projecting future greenhouse emissions and how the climate system will respond within a narrow range.
- Improving understanding of the potential for *rapid or abrupt climate change.*

Addressing these and other areas of scientific uncertainty is a major priority of the U.S. Climate Change Science Program (CCSP). The CCSP is developing twenty-one Synthesis and Assessment products to advance scientific understanding of these uncertainty areas by the end of 2008. [8]

Examples of Programs & Projects

There are now thousands of projects underway in the Earth Sciences field. Here are just a few examples:

ESA – The European Space Agency (ESA) sponsors and coordinates a wide variety of international programs and projects aimed at better understanding the earth, the atmosphere, climate change and other important issues affecting the planet. For example, GENESI-DR (Ground European Network for Earth Science Interoperations - Digital Repositories), an ESA-led, European Commission (EC)-funded two-year project, is taking the lead in providing reliable, easy, long-term access to Earth Science data via the Internet. [12]

ESF – The European Science Foundation (ESF) is an association of 77 member organisations devoted to scientific research in 30 European countries. Since we were established in 1974, we have coordinated a wide range of pan-European scientific initiatives, and our flexible organisation structure means we can respond quickly to new developments. ESF's core purpose is to promote high quality science at a European level. The ESF is committed to facilitating cooperation and collaboration in European science on behalf of its principal stakeholders (Member Organisations and Europe's scientific community). This cross-border activity combines both 'top-down' and 'bottom-up' approaches in the long-term development of science. ESF provides grants, sponsors projects, organizes conferences and promotes international cooperation on scientific research. [13]

IPY – The International Polar Year (IPY) 2007-2009 is organized through the International Council for Science (ICSU) and the World Meteorological Organization (WMO), and is actually the fourth polar year, following those in 1882-3, 1932-3, and 1957-8. In order to have full and equal coverage of both the Arctic and the Antarctic, IPY 2007-8 covers two full annual cycles from March 2007 to March 2009 and will  involve over 200 projects, with thousands of scientists from over 60 nations examining a wide range of physical, biological and social research topics. It is also an unprecedented opportunity to demonstrate, follow, and get involved with, cutting edge science in real-time. [11]

NASA – According to the NASA Earth Science 2007 Senior Review, the NASA Earth Science Division (ESD) of the Science Mission Directorate (SMD) is supporting 11 Earth observing missions that are, or soon will be, operating beyond their prime mission lifetimes... data from several of these research missions are being used routinely by U.S. and international operational agencies in support of important Earth system prediction and monitoring tasks. Those 11 missions include Aqua, Jason, QuickSCAT, Terra, MODIS, TRMM, CloudSat, GRACE, SORCE, ICESat, and EO-1. Each mission includes dozens of projects. The FY 2009 budget for the Earth Sciences Division at NASA is $1.4 billion. [9]

  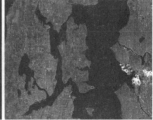

NEESPI – The Northern Eurasia Earth Science Partnership Initiative (NEESPI) is a program based on cooperation between NASA in the United States and the Russian Academy of Science (RAS) that began in 2002. It is composed of scientists from the United States, European Union, Russia, Japan, Ukraine, Kazakhstan, and Mongolia, totally more than 90 individuals representing a broad academic community and a variety Earth Science disciplines. Scientists from 11 countries are now participating; it is envisioned that many projects will be organized or sponsored by this group. [14]

NOAA – The National Oceanographic and Atmospheric Administration (NOAA), a division of the US Department of Commerce, sponsors and finances major projects. NOAA is organized in the following divisions, each of which sponsors many projects related to studying the earth, oceans and atmosphere: National Environmental Satellite, Data, and Information Service; National Marine Fisheries Service; National Ocean Service; National Weather Service; Office of Marine and Aviation Operations; Office of Oceanic and Atmospheric Research; and Office of Program Planning and Integration. [10]

NSF – The National Science Foundation (NSF) in the United States funds research and education in most fields of science and engineering. It does this through grants, and cooperative agreements to more than 2,000 colleges, universities, K-12 school systems, businesses, informal science organizations and other research organizations throughout the United States. The Foundation accounts for about one-fourth of federal support to academic institutions for basic research. NSF receives approximately 40,000 proposals each year for research, education and training projects, of which approximately 11,000 are funded. In addition, the Foundation receives several thousand applications for graduate and postdoctoral fellowships. [15]

UNESCO - International Geoscience Programme (IGCP): Geoscience in the service of society - The IGCP is a cooperative enterprise of UNESCO and the International Union of Geological Sciences (IUGS) and has been stimulating comparative studies in the Earth Sciences since 1972. After three decades of successful work, the "International Geological Correlation Programme" continued, as "International Geoscience Programme". Up to this day, IGCP has made research results available to a huge number of scientists around the world with about 400 projects. Visit http://www.unesco.org/science/earth/igcp.shtml

Predicting & Responding to Extreme Weather

According to a special report recently published by the NSF in the United States, Large-scale weather patterns which occur in various locations around the Earth, from the El Niño-Southern Oscillation (ENSO) in the tropics to the high latitude Arctic Oscillation (AO) play a significant part in controlling the weather on a seasonal time scale. Knowing the condition of these atmospheric oscillations in advance would greatly improve long-range weather predictions. Scientists search for clues in the earth's surface conditions such as tropical sea surface temperatures and snow cover at higher latitudes. Reliable and accurate weather prediction is vitally important in numerous areas of society, particularly agriculture and water management and weather risks are evaluated by a wide range of businesses, including power distributors who make fewer sales during cool summers and more sales during cold winters. [16]

According to Wikipedia, weather forecasting is the application of science and technology to predict the state of the atmosphere for a future time and a given location. Human beings have attempted to predict the weather informally for millennia, and formally since at least the nineteenth century. Weather forecasts are made by collecting quantitative data about the current state of the atmosphere and using scientific understanding of atmospheric processes to project how the atmosphere will evolve. Forecast models are now used to determine future conditions. The chaotic nature of the atmosphere, the massive computational power required to solve equations that describe the atmosphere, errors involved in measuring initial conditions, and an incomplete understanding of atmospheric processes mean that forecasts become less accurate as the difference in current time and the time for which the forecast is being made (the range of the forecast) increases. The use of ensembles and model consensus help narrow the error and pick the most likely outcome. [17]

A major part of modern weather forecasting is the severe weather alerts and advisories which weather services issue when severe or hazardous weather is expected. This is done to protect life and property. Some of the most commonly known of severe weather advisories are the severe thunderstorm and tornado warning, as well as the severe weather or the tornado watch. Other forms of these advisories include winter weather, high wind, flood, tropical cyclone, and fog. Severe weather advisories and alerts are broadcast through the media, including radio, using emergency systems as the Emergency Alert System which breaks into regular programming. [17]

Some of the major users of weather predictions are the aviation industry and air traffic controllers, those in marine related industries and activities, utility companies, the military, news services, governmental agencies and the general public. For extreme weather, of course emergency readiness and response organizations pay attention. Ultimately, every local, regional and national community and governmental organization has an interest in weather prediction. Suppliers of technologies, tools and services for these processes cover a wide range of hardware, software and information services entities, both public and private.

Meteorological organizations around the world provides a good list of organization most likely to have projects underway associated with weather prediction. [18]

Natural Disasters Affect Us All

Over the last two years, we have seen natural disasters strike around the world, including earthquakes, fires and floods. In addition to the human lives lost and affected, these events have also had significant impacts on local and regional economies and on the projects and project management profession in those places. This month, as we pass the two year anniversary of Hurricane Katrina's devastation in the United States, we find that thousands of Louisiana and Mississippi residents have not returned to their homes, cities and towns have not been rebuilt, and local and regional economies have not recovered.

It has become increasing clear to me that an important area of application for modern project management must be in the fields of emergency response (ER) and disaster recovery (DR). This is true for several obvious reasons. Due to climate changes, population growth and demographic changes around the world, natural disasters are increasing in both frequency and impact (in both human and economic terms). In addition, regional conflicts have continued and based on global communications, globally interconnected economies, and population migrations (including refugees), we are all aware of and affected by them. Accidents and industrial emergencies also occur on a regular basis, often leading to evacuations or significant damage. Finally, terrorism may be a semi-permanent phenomenon, with international criminals causing harm in countries worldwide on a regular basis.

These trends create the need for ER/DR programs and projects. I believe it is time for the project management profession to get serious about the need for better program and project management in these areas. Just as more and better project management is needed for economic development, so is it needed to save lives in emergencies and to rebuild homes, cities, infrastructure and regions hit by disasters, be they created by other humans or by the weather.

A Reminder – recent natural disasters [19]

As PMForum has added International Correspondents and Advisors around the world, we have been directly affected by accidents and disasters. We have learned immediately and through first person accounts about the impact and results of emergencies in those countries, have seen the need for ER/DR program and project management increase. Here are a few natural disasters that we are familiar with:

Fires in Greece (August 2007) – According to news media, and reports filed by our correspondent in Athens **Theofanis Giotis**, extreme heat in southern Europe led to more than 200 forest fires across the Greek countryside in August. According to the Washington Post on 2 September, "Fires have destroyed an estimated 469,000 acres of mostly forest and farmland over the past 10 days, prompting a massive relief effort but also criticism of Greece's government for allegedly responding to the crisis slowly and failing to safely evacuate villages before they were burned. The death toll rose to 65 Sunday…" According to Theofanis, "The title "Project Manager" as a career path does not exist for the Greek Government and local agencies. Project Management and proactive risk management are terms that have been introduced very lately in Greece. Project planning for dealing with fires in Greece was inadequate."

Earthquake in Peru (August 2007) – A magnitude 7.9 earthquake hit the coast of Peru just south of Lima on Wednesday, 16 August. At least 540 people were killed in towns along Peru's southern coast, with another 1,500 people injured and 80,000 suffering the quake's impact through the loss of loved ones or destroyed and damaged homes.

Peru's president, Alan Garcia, who flew to the region to take charge of response operations personally, vowed to rebuild the south-

Devastation in Peru

ern city of Pisco that was devastated by the deadly earthquake. According to PMForum International Correspondent **Jose Machicao** in Lima, disaster recovery teams were being formed and he had been invited to help.

Floods in the UK (July 2007) – According to an article in the Telegraph on 27 July, Britain's worst floods in modern history are likely to leave 350,000 homes without drinking water, while 50,000 are without power as levels in two major rivers continue to rise. "We have not seen flooding of this magnitude before," said Anthony Perry, an Environment Agency flood risk official. "The benchmark was 1947 and this has already exceeded it." In

Oxfordshire and Berkshire, where 700 homes have been flooded last night, 1,500 people were evacuated to Oxford United's football stadium.

Since Friday, almost 1,000 people - including 40 elderly residents at a care home in the rural village Hampton Bishop - have been rescued from flooded properties or cars in Herefordshire and Worcestershire. The Army this morning ferried food parcels to Upton-upon-Severn, Worcs, which is completely cut off by flood water on all sides. The cost of the summer floods could top £2 billion, making 2007 one of the worst years for insurers. According to **Miles Shepherd**, PMForum's International Correspondent in the UK, "these floods will have a major impact on projects and the economy for months!"

Monsoon rains & Floods in Southeast Asia (August 2007) - Weeks of continuous monsoon rains and severe flooding have wreaked havoc across South Asia, including Bangladesh, Nepal, India, and Pakistan. According to the UN OCHA Regional Office for Asia Pacific, over 40 million people have been affected. Flood waters have submerged entire villages, devastated over a million acres of agricultural crops, and left people stranded on river embankments and rooftops. There is a severe shortage of food, drinking water, and shelter, and outbreaks of waterborne diseases pose a significant public health threat. Concern Worldwide provided immediate disaster relief in Pakistan, Bangladesh and India, and is currently scaling up its response in all three countries. Concern has launched an emergency appeal to meet the urgent and ongoing survival needs of flood victims in the affected areas.

Floods in China (June – August 2007) - Parts of China, especially along the eastern Huai River, have had some of the heaviest rainfalls in 50 years. Continuous rain since mid-June has resulted in widespread flooding, affecting over 119 million people. Anhui, Sichuan and Hubei are the worst-hit provinces. At least 3.6 million people have been evacuated, over one million houses have been damaged and another 452,000 destroyed.

It is estimated that at least 7.87 million hectares of farmland have been ruined. Economic losses are estimated at $US 6.9 billion, but are expected to rise. More than 650 people have been killed so far this flood season. Last weekend alone, storms killed 17 in four provinces. Last Wednesday, a three-hour rainstorm in Jinan, the capital of Shangdon province, killed at least 34 people. Many died from electric shocks or drowned in cars that were swept away. Meanwhile, in Henan province, 69 coal miners were trapped underground when rainwater flooded a pit. (source: http://www.wsws.org/articles/2007/aug2007/)

Floods in the United States – In August 2007, after a week of powerful storms and record flooding in the United States, Governor Ted Strickland on Sunday called on the Bush administration to declare north central Ohio a major disaster area and provide emergency relief. The damage caused by the flooding is of devastating, historic proportions. Severe storms and flooding throughout the central US Plains and Midwest have displaced thousands of people and left hundreds of thousands without power. At least 26 deaths have been attributed to two storm systems that moved through the area in the past week. Emergencies were declared in five states in the upper Midwest and Plains states. Heavy flooding has damaged or destroyed at least 6,000 homes throughout Iowa, Wisconsin, Illinois, Indiana, and Ohio—states not historically known for flood problems. Consequently, many residences were not insured for flood damage. In flood-stricken southwest Wisconsin, for example, only 5 to

10 percent of homeowners, about 1,400, had flood insurance. Flooding was so severe in Findlay, Ohio, after the Blanchard River rose 7 feet above flood stage, that at least 500 residents were forced to evacuate and hundreds sought sanctuary in emergency shelters. Earlier in the summer, Texas, Oklahoma and Arkansas were hit with severe flooding as well. (source: www.wsws.org).

Floods & Extreme Heat in Romania (July – August 2007) – In July at least seven people died in floods following days of torrential rain in Romania. Thousands of people were evacuated from their homes, as flood water rose to 3m (9ft) in places. Dozens of roads were closed and many areas left without electricity or gas. Romanian Prime Minister Calin Popescu Tariceanu said the damage was so bad he was considering appealing for international help. In the eastern village of Ivesti, residents were stranded on rooftops, while the nearby city of Galati was put on alert as the River Siret reached record levels. A few weeks later, extreme hot weather hit southeastern Europe where heat was blamed for 30 deaths in Romania and several elsewhere in the region.

The record-breaking heat has also been blamed for widespread forest fires. According to PMForum correspondent in Bucharest, **Florin Gheorghiu**, "disaster recovery projects should be subject to project risk management methodology." (Sources: http://news.bbc.co.uk/)

Whether in rich countries or poor, we all suffer now from natural disasters and periodic emergencies. The project management profession will begin to promote project management experience, knowledge and expertise in order to minimize the impact of those events and to help with response, recovery and rebuilding projects. Over coming decades, disaster response projects will be recognized as a critical application area for modern project management, where good planning and preparedness will also save lives.

Managing the Earth's Climate

Faced with the specter of a warming planet and frustrated by the lack of progress, some scientists have begun researching ways to give humanity direct control over

Earth's thermostat. Proposals run the gamut from space mirrors deflecting a portion of the sun's energy to promoting vast marine algal blooms to suck carbon out of the atmosphere. The schemes have sparked a debate over the ethics of climate manipulation, especially when the uncertainties are vast and the stakes so high. For many scientists, the technology is less an issue than the decision-making process that may lead to its implementation.

Environmental policy driven purely by cost-benefit analyses cannot, they say, effectively point the way on large issues like climate change. But even as many scientists caution against unintended, even catastrophic consequences of tinkering with climate, they concede that the more tools humankind has to confront a serious problem, the better. Others wonder if the mere hint of a quick-fix solution will only provide a false sense of security and hamper efforts to address the root problem: carbon emissions from a fossil fuel-based economy. And then there's the trillion-dollar question: In a politically fractured world, how will technologies that affect everyone be implemented by the few, the rich, and the tech-savvy?

When scientists talk about geo-engineering, they generally mean subtracting a fraction of the sun's energy from the earth equal to that trapped by human-emitted greenhouse gases. It is not a new idea, but only recently has it moved toward the scientific mainstream. In 2006, Nobel Laureate Paul Crutzen of the Max Planck Institute for Chemistry in Mainz, Germany, published a paper on injecting particles into the upper atmosphere to reflect incoming sunlight and cool the earth. Climate scientists have since run scenarios on climate models and first reports found that it might work. In November 2006, NASA co-hosted a conference on the topic. [20]

Planetary climate control, or at least attempts to manage extreme weather, is a topic that is "on the table" now. It may have been the subject of science fiction a few years ago, but it is a serious discussion today. I believe that programs and projects will soon be launched to explore or even implement new approaches to affecting the weather. I believe these programs will involve massive funds, global cooperation, and professional project management. Just as nations are now spending billions on astronomy and space exploration, so too will we all be spending public funds on better meteorology, weather prediction and climate management.

The Potential Impact

The potential impact of a better understanding of the earth, our atmosphere and climate is significant, on many fronts. While climate change and extreme weather have become highly visible topics in the media in recent years, this year agriculture and food supplies has entered a near crisis stage, primarily due to high energy costs. According to the United Nations (UN), upgrading and improving weather services will play an important role in helping ensure food security in poorer countries at risk from the impact of climate change and natural disasters.

Speaking at a round-table discussion on food security in late June at the Global Humanitarian

Forum in Geneva, World Meteorological Organization (WMO) Secretary-General **Michel Jarraud** (pictured at left) said enhanced preparation and awareness of meteorological problems and challenges would allow policymakers to respond better once a disaster strikes.

Mr. Jarraud said WMO was working, through its regional climate centres and other agencies, to improve prevention and preparedness measures, including risk assessment, early-warning systems and emergency planning.

Natural disasters such as floods and droughts are among the biggest causes of what is known as "transitory hunger," compared to poverty-induced "chronic hunger." Although natural hazards cannot be avoided, capacity-building and prevention measures can greatly reduce their impact and ensure that people have enough food stocks to last them through a crisis. [21] Both the UN and the World Bank have committed recently to investing in improving meteorological services and weather forecasting capabilities in Africa.

Some Resources

Here are some useful and interesting resources related to Earth Sciences, monitoring the planet and weather management.

The American Geological Institute is a nonprofit federation of 44 geo-scientific and professional associations that represents more than 100,000 geologists, geophysicists, and other earth scientists. Founded in 1948, AGI provides information services to geoscientists, serves as a voice of shared interests in our profession, plays a major role in strengthening geoscience education, and strives to increase public awareness of the vital role the geosciences play in society's use of resources and interaction with the environment. http://www.agiweb.org/index.html

The Center for International Earth Science Information Network (CIESIN) is a center within the Earth Institute at Columbia University in New York. CIESIN works at the intersection of the social, natural, and information sciences, and specializes in on-line data and information management, spatial data integration and training, and interdisciplinary research related to human interactions in the environment. http://www.ciesin.org/

Earth Science Directory - a directory of earth science resources on the World-Wide Web - is built from a database which is constantly being expanded and updated. It is strongest in oceanography and meteorology and now contains 979 different links! http://www.datasync.com/~farrar/earth_sci.html

Implications for Project Management

The broad implications of all of the above for project management should be obvious. Thousands of projects costing billions of dollars are being launched today to better understand the planet, to predict the weather and future climate change, to prepare for respond to natural disasters, and to develop models, technology and information that can help humans better manage the planet in the future.

Every organization involved in any aspect of these technologies and projects will need project management; the larger ones (the government contractors, for example) will employ professional project managers and harness professional project management. This is clearly a growing market for project management products and services, and for employment. Public pressures to provide better weather predictions and to prepare for extreme weather are also propelling this sector. And if extreme weather or climate change can be "managed", the pressure will only increase.

This discussion was not intended to be a comprehensive assessment of climate change, earth sciences or related issues, or even the opportunities in this sector for project management. It was, however, intended to suggest these fields as a new frontier, where increased need and demand for professional project management should be robust in the years ahead. In any case, I am optimistic, actually excited to see another important area of human activity where modern project management can make significant contributions.

Conclusion

This paper was not intended to identify or describe all potential new frontiers for projects and project management. Rather it was intended to suggest that some exciting new areas of project management application are emerging, where new methods and systems may be needed, and where attention by the project management professional community is warranted. By 2025, these new industries will be well established, especially those associated with solving global problems, requiring global cooperation, and involving global applications of science and technology.

The potential for modern project management to help the world solve local, regional and global problems is significant – and must not be downplayed. It is exciting to think that project managers and project management will and can be so useful to so many people, organizations and societies. For these and other reasons, by 2025 project management will be one of the most visible and most important management fields in the world. Finally! [22]

Good luck with your projects

David L. Pells

References:

1. http://en.wikipedia.org/wiki/Earth_science
2. http://en.wikipedia.org/wiki/List_of_geoscience_organizations
3. http://en.wikipedia.org/wiki/List_of_basic_earth_science_topics
4. http://nasascience.nasa.gov/earth-science
5. http://nasascience.nasa.gov/earth-science/big_question_list
6. http://nasascience.nasa.gov/earth-science/earth-science-data-centers
7. http://nasascience.nasa.gov/earth-science/applied-sciences/approach-1
8. http://www.epa.gov/climatechange/
9. http://nasascience.nasa.gov/earth-science/mission_list
10. http://www.noaa.gov/organizations.html
11. http://www.ipy.org/
12. http://www.esa.int/esaEO/SEMDFQK26DF_index_0.html

13. http://www.esf.org/home.html
14. http://neespi.org/
15. http://www.nsf.gov/funding/aboutfunding.jsp
16. http://www.nsf.gov/news/special_reports/autumnwinter/intro.jsp
17. http://en.wikipedia.org/wiki/Weather_forecasting
18. http://en.wikipedia.org/wiki/List_of_meteorology_institutions
19. http://www.pmworldtoday.net/editorials/2007/sep.htm
20. http://www.csmonitor.com/2007/0329/p13s02-sten.html?page=1
21. UN News Digest, June 25, 2008
22. Pells, David L., *New Frontiers for Project Management: Earth Sciences, Monitoring the Planet & Change Control*, PMWorld Today eJournal, July 2008 - http://www.pmworldtoday.net/editorials/2008/jul.htm

CHAPTER 26

Why Are We Still Conducting Risky Business?

Rebecca A. Winston, Esq.

The initiating points for this chapter are the business communication drivers that will be operable in the year 2025 that will drive risk management in our projects. The exploration will begin from the first strategic decisions regarding risk on our projects to how we will disseminate communications about the risk(s) that exist on or touch our projects. The focus will be on profit and not-for-profit corporations as well as government operations.

The connection between business communication drivers and how risk management communication should be conducted and will continue to be conducted will be explored through the use of scenarios and business communication principles interlaced with the risk management process. The chapter will highlight those areas and the impact on the whole [the net bottom line] when one does not holistically view the impact of the connection between business communication drivers and risk management communication within project management.

"477 years ago, Niccolo Machiavelli in giving history's most famous advice to 'management,' said:

> ... for knowing afar off (which is only given a prudent man to do) the evils that are brewing, they are easily cured. But when, for want of such knowledge, they are allowed to grow until everyone can recognize them, there is no longer any remedy to be found" (Lesly, 1991, p. 20).

Imagine the boardroom 477 years ago in which this message was received about risk communication and how revolutionary the statement might have appeared; now imagine the boardroom of 2025 receiving the same message without the date or name of Machiavelli attached to the statement. Is it still as revolutionary? Will we have finally recognized that the risk management model needs to be modified to include the process step of risk communication, which includes all aspects of communication from reporting, documenting in general and for specific needs, external and internal stakeholder communication, and a continuous feedback process? Or will we still be conducting risky business? The thesis of this chapter is that we will be on the verge of the risk communication revolution because business will no longer be able to afford to ignore this risk process step, the documentation and communication of risk. The cost of ignoring the risk documentation and communication process step will have finally become too high for international organizations whether one is speaking in terms of for profit, non-for-profit, or government organizations.

In the year 2025, terms that were once confined to the public relations office of the organization will become commonplace in the project management office or in the meeting room of the project management team. Terms such as influence, attribution, reduction of uncertainty in message statement, framing, fire prevention, and fact versus speculation will become common lexicon for the project manager. A new team member may emerge within larger project teams. This new team member may not be a full-time member of the team depending upon the size of the project or the organization, but the team will be reaching out to use the skills of communication specialists. Project management in 2025 will be buzzing with outreach both internal to the organization and externally to outside stakeholders.

As Figure 1 illustrates, the inclusion of risk documentation and communication in the process makes a more complete process by providing a mechanism in fact for the continuous feedback process often highlighted by leading risk management experts such as Edmund H. Conrow, in *Effective Risk Management: Some Keys to Success* (Conrow, 2003, p. 22).

In the business communication textbook *Handbook of Public Relations and Communications*, Philip Lesly noted from a business management perspective the need for risk communication without calling it risk communication (Lesly, 1991, p. 22). If one can recognize that such communication must occur in the flow of standard business operations in regard to organizational risks, why are project risks treated differently?

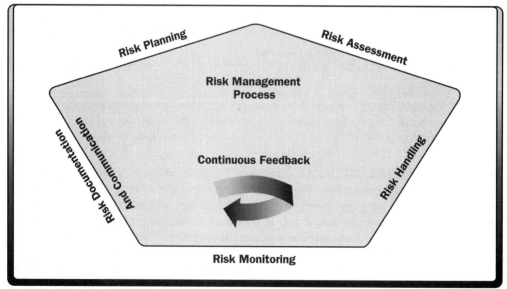

Figure 1   Risk Management Process in the Year 2025

The answer has been an historic separation of the operational risk and crisis management from the management of risks on the various projects undertaken by an organization. Risks on projects have been viewed as separate from the general workflow of the organization. Some of this separation may be reinforced by the status of projects as unique undertakings. However, the financial consequences of a risk realized even in part may not be confined to the boundaries of the project if the risk documentation and communication was ill conceived, poorly executed, or not done at all.

The answer to whether we will continue to conduct risky business in the area of risk documentation and communication is in the boardroom of the future, in the stakeholder meeting of the future, and in the project team meeting of future. For it is in these situational forums that we will begin to see and hear a shift in how we handle risk communication. These forums will be the arenas to demand the change in our process models because of the need to maintain the bottom line.

If one adopts the revised risk management process model, no longer will the risk register (along with the rest of the risk management plan) sit on the shelf behind the desk of the project manager collecting office dust. They will become part of the risk documentation for the communication of risk. What will transpire is what has occurred in business operations under standard business communication principles, an " . . . incorporating of the consideration of public [and private] issues and opportunities in all deliberations of management" (Lesley, 1991, p. 22). However, instead of handling the selected business issue or the crisis of the hour, risks will be handled along with the standard business communication, with the various stakeholders to become part of the handling strategy for the risk.

The basic tenets of business communication state that one should endeavor to perform "fire prevention." Generally, fire prevention is accomplished by engaging in activities that achieve:

- Continuous fact-finding;
- Attentive listening;
- Providing feedback; and
- Research of the publics or target audiences (Center & Cutlip, 1971, p. 195).

A communications effort with risk management at its core that is focused either internally or externally is not much different in its planning and execution than the typical business communication, which is a planned effort for public relations. It also must be a matter of fact collection and collation, with extensive listening and planning. The communication is directed toward a targeted audience through either established channels or channels that are developed for the specific purpose of the communication. This is followed by feedback and further communication and research. In other words, as with all processes in risk management, the documentation and communication process is iterative and continuous.

Incorporating this process step means that the project manager will most likely have a communication specialist on his or her integrated project team. Why? Because one has a choice of how to present material, and what works internally may or may not work externally or for every stakeholder group. Further, what works with one segment internally may not work with another segment of the internal organization or with the board of directors. One of the purposes of the presentation style of a bad-news message is to present it in the most pleasant format and tone as possible. The tone is dependent upon the audience and timing of the message as well as the severity of the message itself. Even an opportunity, the positive form of a risk, can sound onerous, so it is important to have the "you" emphasis in the message. In 2025, the risk communicator for the project will be crafting messages that will not only be incorporating the "you" message, but they will be capturing the "you" as a proponent of the handling strategy for the risk, whether it be how to avoid or mitigate the threat, or how to enhance or exploit opportunities. No longer will reports be handed or tossed over the transom to the management team. An active engagement of the management team and the stakeholders will occur to avoid the surprise or the risk that occurs when the inevitable statement comes that says "Why didn't I or we know this?"

Why in 2025 will this incorporation of a communication specialist become imperative to a well-run project? "The human climate has become vital in determining the operation of business [or a project] as the natural climate is for the farmer. Just as weather patterns bring storms that can destroy all the farmer's best work, so failure to detect and deal with emerging human climate patterns can devastate the best management of an organization [or project]" (Lesly, 1991, p. 22). While the project manager and the project team predict the risks that the project may encounter, the communication specialist and the team will engage in developing the profile of the human climate within which the risks will be communicated. The message should be crafted to enable it to be received within the anticipated or predicted human climate by the targeted audience. Imagine project team meetings in which the risk register is used to discuss how certain risks will be communicated to avoid the "surprise." It will no longer be paramount how does one downplay the significance of the risk or ensure the management team can handle the risk without going into specifics. Instead, the exercise will be how the project team can engage the management team in the thinking about the risk, making them aware, and making the management team:

- part of the solution process;
- part of the project communication process; and
- part of the project itself.

Now imagine the meetings with the management team as engaging interactions instead of one-way communication channels. No longer will the meetings be rooms filled with faces glazed over by slides on projector screens. Instead, interactions will be occurring over discussions about the risks facing the projects before the organization. Senior management will be engaged determining whether or not there is an opportunity to be shared among the projects in their new product research portfolio. The management team will now be engaged and have direct ownership of their portfolio. Risk communication will be at the heart of this change.

To complete the cycle, the communication plan will also be incorporated into the handling strategy of the risk or risks being communicated. Part of avoiding or mitigating a risk is to alert those impacted about the potential for the risk to occur, what the proposed handling strategy is, and the planned implementation for the strategy. The importance of this communication will increase as more corporations and government agencies or ministries continue to trim their workforces, and more electronic communication becomes the norm.

For numerous reasons, more corporations and government entities are doing their work efforts with fewer employees. Whatever the drivers are, this business reality will not change in the year 2025. The impact of fewer human resources on risk management in the risk communication arena is significant:

- Fewer human resources to devise options to handle risks;
- Fewer human resources to raise issues of latent risks related to those identified;
- Fewer human resources to identify opportunities related to identified threats; and
- Fewer human resources to continue the communication beyond the current meeting format.

The use of business communication principles and communication specialists for risk documentation and communication will lead the project manager to " . . . the establishment of common *frames of reference* [emphasis in text] about topics or issues of mutual concern is a necessary condition for effective relations to be established (Hallahan, 2007, p. 207). Project managers have begun to frame risks in terms of cause, risk, and effect, as captured in many textbooks on project management. Framing of a slightly different sort needs to occur for the purposes of communicating to a broader audience. The information must be organized to provide the appropriate contextual meaning for the target audience. Framing by a communication specialist teamed with the risk management specialist on the integrated project team or the project manager and his or her subject matter experts will, "Capture[s] the language struggle that can result in the 'knowledge gap'" (Ihlen & Nitz, 2008, p. 13). The article cited stated that professional communicators ignore the importance of framing at their own peril, but for years the project managers and their teams have ignored the framing of risk for the project stakeholders at their and their projects peril. (Ihlen & Nitz, p. 15). The inability to properly frame risk often led to a crisis in communication, which was most often highlighted on environmental projects in the United States, where the National Environmental Policy Act of 1969 required information be made public. A public hearing process was established by most agencies before major actions could be taken. While legislation will not be enacted to force the communication necessary to bring the discussion of project risk to the stakeholders in most cases, the discussion will be brought to the stakeholder as they take the place of the trimmed workforce, the missing voice at the team table, or the necessary input that often was heard too late to be of value in the handling strategy or before the risk became a crisis because the stakeholder was not involved or ignored. On very small scales, new-product companies have been seeking inputs to a greater extent through surveys and in-house product testing, but the inputs will now be directly sought on identified risks.

Let us open the door to a meeting where a company that is considering launching a new product has a group of testers from the general public assembled. These testers are ones they normally use to test the actual product, but instead of finding the product before them, they are hearing from the new product project team about the risks of changing a material for one that is more biodegradable. The project team has used its communication specialist to assist in framing the questions before the panel in a manner that they do not see as threatening but as seeking their input as specialist in their stakeholder realm. The project team uses the input in much the same manner as they would any of the other subject matter experts for the handling strategies for the identified risks regarding the introduction of the new material in the proposed changed product. Not only does the project team acquire information necessary for the handling strategy, but the stakeholders have an ownership proposition in the project, an understanding of the risks regarding the introduction of new material to a product even if it is more biodegradable, as well as a position that is less confrontational and more cooperative. In other words, another potential threat has been transformed into an opportunity by using the proper human resources on the project team and by expanding the risk management process to include risk documentation and communication. Opportunities, unlike threat risks, are not monetary sinks to the project, although there is usually a cost to take advantage of the benefit they afford the project.

"The techniques of communication are vastly important, but mere mastery of these techniques does not ensure effective communication. If the thoughts we are trying to communicate are not based on a sound background of information and understanding, then expert expression is of little value." (Malera, 1989, p. 101). Figure 2 shows just a sampling of the issues, concepts, and subjects that face a project manager and his or her team on a daily basis in regard to risk documentation and communication.

Central to all of these concepts is the idea of influence. Influence is central to the issue of " . . . strategic communication, . . . (i.e., 'the power or capacity of causing an effect in indirect or intangible ways')" (Hallahan, Holzhausen, van Ruler, Vercic, & Sriramesh, 2007, p. 24). Influence, rather than what occurs at the time of crisis communication, is what is desired in risk communication. "Crises are exactly the type of event that will trigger attributions, crises are sudden and negative. It follows that people will make attributions about the cause of the crises. Was the crises something the organization could control?" (Coombs, 2004, p. 267).

"The term strategic is often associated with practice and the tactics used to implement strategy" (Hallahan et al., 2007, p. 14). Within the practice of the implementation of the risk handling strategy that has been developed and refined over time by the project team is the need for a true understanding of the element of influence. Influence is defined by elements of "the act or power of producing an effect without apparent exer-

Communication Juggle

Past Crises Communications		Reducing Uncertainty
Influencers		Innovation, Leadership in Strategic Communication
Framing the Questions and the Answers		Hierarchy of Communication
	Fire Prevention Handling Attribution	

Figure 2   Just a few of the items the Project Manager and the Team must juggle.

tion of force or direct exercise of command" (Merriam-Webster On-Line, June 2008). Most project managers understand the concept of influence internal to the organization in which they function (e.g., for the purpose of acquiring human resources), but communicating risk is not one on those areas in which the concept of influence is used very often and not strategically. In the year 2025, the risk management process will include the combination of teaming the strategically prepared risk-handling strategy with a strategically prepared communication strategy and delivering it within a sphere of influence. It will be an iterative and continuous process that the project manager and his or her team will engage the communication specialist, if one is available. The risk-handling strategies will reflect a more thorough planned communication piece to the strategy.

Organizations will bring to bear all segments of their communication machinery. "Six relevant disciplines are involved in the development, implementation, and assessment of communications by organizations: management [including project management], marketing, public relations [including communications specialist on the project team], technical communication, political communication, and information/social marketing campaigns."[15] (Hallahan et al., 2007, p. 3) How much this statement sounds like the norm for project management—the use of available subject matter experts. In fact, in the year 2025 it will be a broader interdisciplinary organization that will be working to communicate risk to the organization and to external stakeholders, especially the external stakeholder. All segments of the project team will be involved, and the tentacles of the project team will have great reach when unleashed and used effectively. Generally represented on a project team are internal organizations such as safety, quality, human resources, engineering, legal, etc. In 2025, the project team will also have reach to the public relations department through a communications specialist. 2025 will be part of the movement toward the fully integrated project team for the purpose of risk documentation and communication. One could not achieve far-reaching influence without the myriad of disciplines and voices represented by the integrated project team that allows the range of stakeholders to be involved in the communications regarding the risks that the project may face and the extent of the cost and/or schedule consequences that these risks bring.

As Coombs noted, crises are exactly the type of events that will trigger attributions because they are sudden and negative (Coombs, 2004, p. 267). Unfortunately, once those attributions are set with a past crisis, they are nearly impossible to eradicate. In 2025, risk documentation and communication will mean being aware of what has gone before the project and considering prior crises and means and modes of handling those crises as part of the risk communication environment. Communication experts such as Coombs note this concept in business communications as "Situation Crisis Communication Theory." Part of the theory states, " . . . to adequately protect an organization's reputation, management must adjust their communication to account for possible past crises about which relevant publics are aware" (Coombs, 2004, p. 265). In project management, those relevant publics are the project stakeholders. The stakeholders will be aware or will make themselves aware of the past crises and what was or was not communicated. They will make attributions to the project team and its management, even though the project may or may not have existed at the time of the crisis in question. The issue will be one of control or at its core—responsibility. Through risk documentation and communication, the project manager and his or her team will need to communicate responsibility, thus control of the aspects of the consequences of the risk or risks being communicated, by allowing the past to inform future communications. Even if the risk occurs, the stakeholder will want to know the knowledge was shared in a manner that was informative, open to the extent possible, timely, and done in a responsible manner. Further, in meeting those criteria, the communication will need to be framed in the context that will meet the communication needs of the stakeholder audience as discussed previously.

The bottom line, however, is that "No matter how skillfully we write or speak, this attempt at communication is not effective unless it is based on a sound knowledge of what we are writing about. It has been said that 'You can't write writing.' Neither can we 'communicate communication.' We communicate facts, ideas, and opinions" (Malera, 1989, p. 101). In other words, it takes the team. The project manager cannot produce the communication alone. The subject matter expert alone cannot produce the communication alone. The communication specialist alone cannot produce the communication alone. In 2025, the project management team doing the "communication juggle" (Figure 2) will produce the risk documentation and communication, and the juggle will be a continuous and iterative process to meet the continuous needs of all the stakeholders of the project through the variety of media available to them (Figure 3).

There Are Always Choices of How to Communicate

Figure 3   The project manager in 2025 does not have to face the decision of which method is appropriate alone.

Currently, what we find in many organizations are reports being written, and management taking the reports 30 or more days after the fact and reviewing them. The internal risk documentation activity if done outside of the risk management plan has become an automated reporting function rather than a communication opportunity. Interface with external stakeholders is done as a have-to activity and often only when prescribed by law or when a risk has been realized. Such an approach leaves us with what Andreas Schwarz notes as, " . . . people … continuously making inferences about their social environment because of its ambiguity. They search for a feeling of control or even predictability of what will happen around them" (Schwarz, 2008, p. 36). This statement applies equally to internal as well as external stakeholders. However, internal stakeholders can request more reports or project reviews, both of which are financial drains on the project—and in the case of project reviews, are large financial drains on projects, especially in most governmental organizations, given the multi-layers of reviews that occur before the actual requested review. External stakeholders can cause greater financial issues for the organization if lawsuits are available, through boycotting, or via developing their own negative communication.

Now let us listen and look in on a project management meeting in 2025. Around the table in the meeting room, we find the project manager and her team. The team at the time we are viewing them consists of a safety engineer, a quality engineer, a chemical engineer, a mechanical engineer, a systems engineer, an administrative assistant, an electrical engineer, a computer scientist/engineer, a process engineer, a waste management specialist, a communication specialist, an environmental engineer, and today a liaison from the procurement management office. When we join the meeting, the project manager is reviewing the risk register for the month by highlighting those risks for which the trigger metric is highlighted for the reporting period. She is discussing the issue of permitting the off-gas stack for the thermal destruction process for the plant her team is designing. The risk is a delay in the approval of the air permit. She has noted three risks on the register dealing with this item. One of the issues is how to communicate with the external stakeholders about the thermal destruction process to gain acceptance prior to the public hearing on the permit. Several of the technical staff speak, with the communication specialist taking notes and asking questions.

The communication specialist asks several questions, as he is getting ready for a session to prepare various team members and executive management for the public hearing. The communication specialist notes that prior to the meeting, he handed out several articles that appeared in the local papers about a similar plant in a nearby state, and spoke about issues of attribution. The project manager requested a white paper be prepared for executive management that highlighted what they should be aware and how to respond to questions in regard to those items. The communication specialist stated that he would be contacting several of the subject matter experts around the table to appropriately and accurately prepare that paper. The communication specialist went on to note that the public hearing is the opportunity for the project team to frame the communication in their terms. Those terms should be positive and forward-looking and should avoid items that will be highlighted in the white paper he will be drafting. One he noted that they would be faced with is the issue of the risk of the past history of incineration and its reflection on thermal destruction. Several of the technical staff volunteered to assist with that item. The project manager reviewed the schedule to complete the actions and assigned due dates to the team. She stated she would establish a face-to-face meeting to brief as many of the necessary senior management staff as she could gather within the next three weeks. Therefore, it would be imperative that the initial white paper be completed within the next week for review by the full project team. The face-to-face meetings would be to answer questions and would not be a slide presentation, but to initiate the preparation for the public hearings that the organization would face on this project.

We leave the project team knowing that they are not just filing reports on a quarterly basis or updating risk registers only when required by a procedure, but actively engaging in documentation and communication about risk. Risk communication is a focus and the communication of that risk is the primary focus of the meeting and not in a crisis mode, but in a preparatory mode.

But let us ask ourselves what we heard as we closed the door before leaving the project meeting. We heard the words, "What was the latest word on the project blog?" Yes, the project blog was the topic being discussed. Stakeholders will be able to log into the project blog and be heard. We will not be discussing whether this item is the right way to conduct project input in many organizations. It will just be the way project input will be gathered. Stakeholders will be demanding the instantaneous mode of input to the organization.

As of 2007, Charles S. Catalano stated, "During the next five years, blogging will not render traditional tools of communication obsolete nor will it usher in a new era of corporate communications; however, it will become a permanent, fully integrated, and vital part of the media landscape" (Catalano, 2007, p. 254). For many product development projects, the blog is becoming a part of the landscape, and for many others, it is on the horizon. As more and more communication becomes electronic and the demographics skew more towards those who have grown up with the electronic age, blogging will seem like a norm for providing input to any system, including into a project as a stakeholder.

For organizations and projects, it is essential that guidelines be established for the development and management of those blogs, even before entering the blogosphere (Catalano, 2007, p. 254). Projects will need to decide how to establish the site, which staff member will manage it, how to respond to the input received, how to configure the input and responses, and what tier of information to the project this constitutes. These guidelines will determine whether the project and its organization will participate in an opportunity for stakeholder interaction, whether it will be internal and/or external, or whether it will be a reactive and potentially destructive communication disaster. Remember—not all communication is good communication. " . . . The well-established Merriman Formula (used to measure the impact of publicity) argues the effect of negative information is four times greater than the effect of positive information" (Shaia and Gonzenbach, 2007, p. 140).

The bottom line is the best risk management communication is controlled by the project as a well-framed, directed piece of communication to stakeholders. 2025 with its resource crunch, changing dynamics, and outreach to new expertise, is a year of change. Project management and in particular risk management will situate itself strategically in the organization. "The term *strategic* is also increasingly used in conjunction with change management [as is project management] to describe the role of communication practitioners in the organizational change" (Hallahan et al., 2007, p. 13). 2025 will see the marriage for change management of the communication specialist or practitioner to the project team to ensure that risk handling strategies capture documentation and communication as well as technical steps to avoid or reduce the risk.

The CEO looks across her boardroom table and asks, "Why are we still conducting risky business?"

The change will be that at least one or two of the executive staff will respond that we are conducting risky business in regard to our project risk communication. We have fully integrated our risk communication strategy and documented not only within our risk management plan and its risk communication plan, but it is within all of our risk handling strategies, which have been also fully integrated into our strategic communication plan. We are executing against those integrated strategies as our communication team is integrated with our project teams. This risk management process is reflected in our bottom line today as we sit here—2025.

References

Catalano, C. S. (2007). Megaphones to the internet and the world: The role of blogs in corporate communications. *International Journal of Strategic Communication, 1*(4), 247-262.

Center, A. H., & Cutlip, S. M. (1971). *Effective public relation*— 4ᵗʰ ed. Englewood Cliffs, NJ: Prentice Hall.

Conrow, E. H. (2003). *Effective management: Some keys to success*—2ⁿᵈ ed. Reston, VA: Institute of Aeronautics and Astronautics.

Coombs, W. T. (July 2004). Impact of Past Crises on Current Crises Communication: Insights from Situational Crisis Communication Theory. *Journal of Business Communication, 41*(3), 265-289.

Hallahan, K. (2007). Seven models of framing: implications for public relations. *Journal of Public Relations Research, 11*(3), 205-242.

Hallahan, K., Holzhausen, D., van Ruler, B., Vercic, D., & Sriramesh, K. (2007). Defining strategic communication. *International Journal of Strategic Communication, 1*(1), 3-35.

Ihlen, O., & Nitz, M. (2008). Framing contests in environmental disputes paying attention to media and cultural master frames. *International Journal of Strategic Communication, 2*, 1-18.

Lesly, P. (Ed.). (1991). *Lesly's handbook of public relations and communication*—4ᵗʰ ed. New York, NY: AMACom.

Malera, T. (1989). *Communication for business and the professions*—4ᵗʰ ed. Boston, MA: Allyn and Bacon.

Merriam-Webster On-Line. (June 2008). http://www.merriam-webster.com/dictionary/influence

Schwarz, A. (2008). Covariation-based causal attributions during organizational crises: suggestions for extending situational crisis communication theory (SCCT). *International Journal of Strategic Communication, 2*, 31-53.

Shaia, J. S. & Gonzenbach, W. J. (2007). Communications with management in times of difficulty and crisis: Silence explained. *International Journal Strategic Communication, 1*(3) 139-150.

CHAPTER 27

Sustainable Manufacturing and Project Management Circa 2025

Guiping Hu, Iowa State University, Ames, Iowa
Lizhi Wang, Iowa State University, Ames, Iowa
Bopaya Bidanda, University of Pittsburgh, Pittsburgh PA

The concept of "sustainability" and its impacts on the environment have gained popularity in a broad spectrum of societal sectors. Sustainable manufacturing can loosely be defined as production processes that utilize "green" concepts as far as possible. The development of a plan for sustainable manufacturing can be viewed as the conceptualization and implementation of a series of interrelated projects through the evolution of a product's lifecycle. In this chapter, we will discuss how to implement and manage sustainability-based projects, especially in the manufacturing sector. Case vignettes are utilized for demonstration. In addition, quantitative models will also be discussed to assist decision-making problems for stakeholders. We will also look ahead and discuss the implications of sustainability/sustainable manufacturing on project management in the next 15 years.

1.1 Introduction: The Movement Towards Sustainability

As part of the societal development process, informed economic growth and social equity have evolved into a major concern in both government and corporate sectors (Dyllick & Hockert, 2002, p. 130-141). Concerns about the environment started in the late 1960s in the U.S. and quickly spread worldwide (Caldwell, 1989, p. 6-11, 25-28). Interconnections between the environment, economy, and social well-being were also recognized. The concept of "Triple Bottom Line: People, Planet, Profit" (Wikipedia) defines the criteria of organizational and societal success. It is used widely to describe the ultimate goal of sustainability and sustainable development.

The terms "sustainability and sustainable development" were first acknowledged at the 1987 World Commission on Environment and Development (WCED) (Brundtland, 1987). Since then, the concept has made great impacts in the political, economic, and social sectors (Lancaster, 1999).With the growing concern about the global warming and environmental issues, sustainable manufacturing and the related efficient utilization of resources are gaining popularity, with significant potential in industrial applications and the further development of theoretical constructs.

Sustainable development has been defined as "passing on to the future generations a stock of capital (as in the assets of the earth) that is at least as big as the one that our own generation inherited from the previous generations" (The Times 100). These assets also include tangible assets (such as money, buildings, and natural resources) and intangible assets (such as intelligence, skills, and social systems). Approximately 6 billion people reside on the Earth nowadays; without a cure for AIDS which has caused more deaths than any other pandemic in history or a solution to the rapid population growth, there will be 8 billion people living on this planet by 2020 (Berry, 2004). Therefore, moving towards the goal of sustainable development is important and urgent for every societal sector.

The definition of sustainable development also acknowledges that the development in the social, environmental, and economic dimensions are of equal importance in the development of society (Azapagic & Perdan, 2000, p. 243-261). This aligns well with the "Triple Bottom Line" concept from the three aspects of human capital, resource capital, and economic benefits. From this perspective, sustainable development is also about pursuing a better life quality for both the current and the future generations. The achievement of the goal of sustainable development requires supportive actions from all of the three aspects: economic prosperity, environmental sustainability, and social equity. The scope and relationship of the three aspects are shown in figure 1.

Since the resources are limited, the studies on sustainable utilization of the available resources have been prolific. There is now an extensive collection of literature on how to achieve the goal of sustainable development in various societal sectors. Otterpohl,

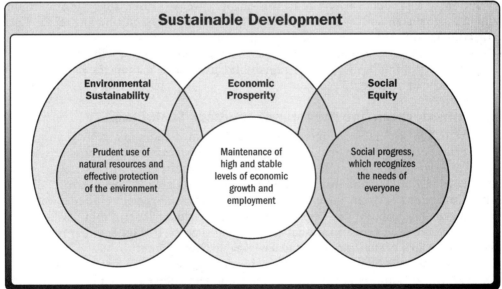

Figure 1:   Scope of sustainable development (Cornwall Government).

Grottker and Lange (1997, p. 121-133) completed a study on the sustainable water and waste management in urban areas. They proposed various realistic methods of using water and treating waste in a sustainable manner in the urban environment. Angell and Klassen (1999, p. 575-598) proposed an agenda for research on integrating environmental issues into the mainstream in operations management. Operations management issues in the environmental management area are summarized in the paper, and two distinct perspectives (the constraint and component perspectives) are identified to characterize the study and present the importance of sustainable development for the whole society.

From the perspective of a project manager and a consumer, manufacturing and construction industries are moving toward incorporating sustainability concepts without compromising profits. The manufacturing industry is one of the most important sectors in the sustainable development process in terms of material consumption, energy utilization, and human resources.

1.2 What is Sustainable Manufacturing?

The United States Department of Commerce defines sustainable manufacturing as "the creation of manufactured products that use processes that are non-polluting, conserve energy and natural resources, and are economically sound and safe for employees, communities, and consumers" (U.S. Department of Commerce International Trade Commission). Sustainable manufacturing concepts have slowly been extended along the entire product lifecycle. Extensions of sustainable manufacturing concepts beyond the design and manufacturing lifecycle phases are typically implemented as corporate-wide initiatives or as special projects. For example, many small and medium-sized manufacturers are now seeking ways to reduce their consumption of metalworking fluids–these are somewhat toxic and difficult to isolate and dispose. Most solutions tend to be customized and tend to be plant-level projects with goals and milestones.

The state of California's green building initiatives include a goal of reducing energy use in state-owned buildings by 20 percent by 2015 (from a 2003 baseline) with incentives to encourage the private commercial sector to set the same goal (California Energy Commission). In the power/energy sector, the U.S. Department of Energy has launched many green initiatives to improve energy efficiency and introduce renewable and clean energy in various states (U.S. Department of Energy, Energy, Efficiency and Renewable Energy). Two of the goals are 5% of U.S. electricity will be generated from renewable and clean resources by 2020, and tripling the U.S. use of bio-based products and bioenergy by 2010.

In addition, the pressure on companies to incorporate the principles of sustainable development into their decision-making is growing. The concept of "3R: reduce, reuse, and recycle" is a result of this impetus. Many countries in Europe require their manufacturers to take back their used products and dispose them properly (without adverse effects to the environment). In addition, we have witnessed a growth in remanufacturing companies that is likely to continue. These organizations take used products from customers, then refurbish, recycle, and resell them. These companies are typically either a separate entity or part of the original manufacturer. This process is sometimes referred to as reverse logistics or a closed-loop supply chain.

Lifecycle analysis/assessment/closed-loop product lifecycle management are all tools that examine the lifecycle of a product in detail to assist in decision making. This lifecycle analysis was brought out largely due to the increased environmental awareness on the part of the public, industry, and governments (Global Development Research Center). It has proved to be a powerful tool to assist manufacturers to analyze the processes and improve products, help government and regulators develop legislation, and inform consumers so that they can make better choices. One of the more popular tools is lifecycle costing analysis (Pesonen, 2001), under which environmental issues and green values are taken into account.

Traditional analysis methods in sustainable product lifecycle management are often conceptual. Labuschagne and Brent (2007) point out that current project management and engineering economic frameworks do not effectively address the three goals of sustainable development (i.e., social equity, economic efficiency, and environmental performance). They outline the needs of sustainable development and propose several ways to achieve the true sustainable lifecycle management in the manufacturing sector.

Most existing studies on sustainable manufacturing have been statistical summaries and case studies. Sperling et al. (2004) analyzed the impact of regulations on automobile industry and the consumers' choices. This study provides insights into the impacts of governmental regulation and they found that the cost imposed on vehicles due to regulations have been significant. Wiser and Fang (1999) carried out an assessment on green power market in real competition. Pilot programs in four states (California, Massachusetts, Rhode Island, and Pennsylvania) have shown that green power marketing is an effective way of attracting customers in the retail residential sector.

The "end-of-life" stage of a product is critical from the perspective of sustainability, and much of the research conducted in field is often termed "reverse logistics" or "closed-loop supply chains" since the product is recycled and reused. Blackburn, Debo, Dekker, Flapper, Fleischmann Guide, and Van Wassenhove (various) have conducted seminal studies in the area and conclude that remanufacturing, if implemented properly, can be beneficial for both the company and the entire society. In addition, quantitative supports are needed for decision-making in the reverse logistics and closed-loop supply chain systems.

There is, however, a dearth of studies that enable decision-makers to make rational decision in critical aspects of the product lifecycle such as:

- Whether to design a "green" or "traditional" product;
- The maximum cost differential between "green" and "traditional" products that will allow green products to flourish;
- How best to establish the green footprint of a product; and
- "End of life" incentives to encourage consumers to return used products to the manufacturer, etc.

It is evident that there exists a great need to make rational decisions in sustainable manufacturing. Developing a quantitative framework is essential to make the rational decisions. It is therefore the opinion of the authors that sustainable manufacturing in the next 15 years will involve a great deal of quantitative decision-making as part of the project management process. Quantitative models are timely and necessary to assist decision makers to make the "right" decisions at different stages in the product lifecycle. A detailed introduction with sample decision-making models in the project management process will be discussed in section 1.3.

1.3 Decision-Making Models In Sustainable Manufacturing

Decisions are made in corporations frequently at strategic, tactical, and operational levels. In the process of achieving sustainability in the manufacturing sector, it is important to have quantitative decision support tools to assist the decision-making process. As mentioned in the previous section, it is necessary to consider the whole product lifecycle evolution process when making decisions. Product lifecycle theory has been a key principle in the studies of technology innovation and has been recognized by leading management theorists as a useful tool for strategic decision-making (Windrum & Birchenhall,1998). Product lifecycle decision-making systems involve multiple stakeholders, including manufacturers, distributors, consumers, service providers, the regulatory agencies, etc.

Making the "right" decisions at each stage of a product's lifecycle is important to the healthy, sustainable development of the manufacturing industry. There is no single tool that can fulfill the different requirements at different lifecycle stages; therefore, a decision support system that considers the decision making process throughout the whole lifecycle is timely and necessary. Figure 2 portrays the relationship among different stakeholders and demonstrates current decision-making tools discussed in the literature.

In this section, we will introduce three representative quantitative decision-making models that can be utilized by corporate decision-maker in the sustainable manufacturing process. The linkage between these segments loosely follows the evolution of the product lifecycle.

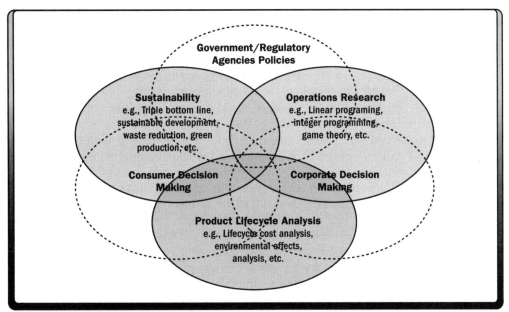

Figure 2:   Sustainable manufacturing decision making system.

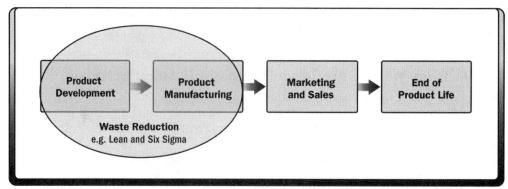

Figure 3:   Relationship between model 1 and product lifecycle.

1.3.1 Model 1: Project Portfolio Selection Model to Implement Lean and Six Sigma Manufacturing

This model focuses on identifying the optimal decisions in waste reduction in the product design and manufacturing phase, as shown in Figure 3.

The application of Lean and Six Sigma has made significant impacts in both academic research and industry over the last two decades. One of the complex decisions in the lean and waste reduction methodology is project portfolio selection with a limited amount of available resources. In the Lean and Six Sigma project-selection process, there are various objectives that need to be considered. Therefore, the first model which considers both product design and manufacturing lifecycle phases, is a multi-objective decision-making model with a Pareto frontier chart. This model formulation provides a new and better mechanism for project portfolio selection. It can assist the decision makers in identifying the optimal project portfolio for implementation of Lean and Six Sigma concepts. This model can be extended to other industrial applications where trade-off decisions have to be made among multiple objectives (Hu, Wang, Bidanda & Fetch, 2008).

1.3.2 Model 2: Game Theoretical Models for Market Competition Analysis in Green Production

This model concentrates on the market analysis for green products. It is related to the product manufacturing and marketing lifecycle phases.

As global awareness and concern for the environment increase, many policy makers, stakeholders, and business leaders have begun to call on the business community to play a major role in moving the global economy development toward sustainable manufacturing. Market competitiveness is an important factor for corporate strategic decision-making. Game theoretic models are developed to analyze the market competition between "green" and "traditional" products. The game theoretic models can provide detailed engineering and managerial insights on how to help green production survive in fierce market competition. In addition, the effects of the government and regulatory organization interventions are considered, such as tax reduction or subsidy for green products, standards on carbon dioxide emission, and education for public awareness. The game theory model can provide a new perspective to analyze the market competition between green and ordinary production industries, and engineering and managerial insights can be derived for the manufacturers, consumers, and the government regulatory departments (Hu, Wang, & Bidanda, 2007).

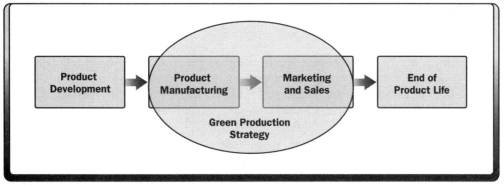

Figure 4:   Relationship between model 2 and product lifecycle.

1.3.3 Model 3: Long-Term Profit-Driven Decision Making in Product Market Lifecycle Management

The third model focuses on identifying the best investment decision at each phase of a product's lifecycle after it has been released to the market. This is one of the key elements in product upgrade and marketing strategies.

This mathematical model considers a sequential decision making process through each stage of the product lifecycle after its release to the competitive market. This problem is formulated as a Markov decision process (MDP) model where optimal sequential investment decisions are made based on the product lifecycle phases and market demand fluctuations so as to maximize the long-term profit. Managerial insights can be derived from the model and help decision makers identify best strategies. It is a general model formulation that can be adapted for a multitude of industries and products (Hu, Wang, Wang, & Bidanda, 2007).

1.4 Case Vignettes of Sustainable Manufacturing Projects

Product lifecycle evolution generally follows the process shown in figure 6. First, products are designed and developed and then the companies manufacture the products. After the production, the products are then released to the competitive market and face

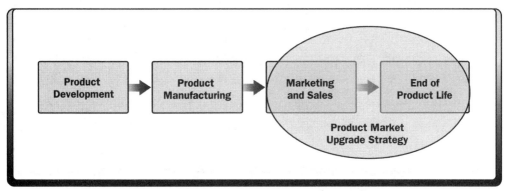

Figure 5:   Relationship between model 3 and product lifecycle.

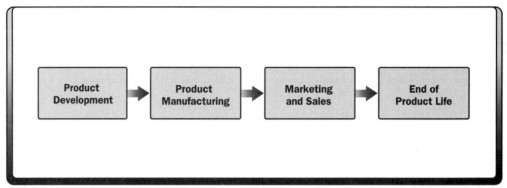

Figure 6:   Product lifecycle evolution.

fierce competition. After the product finishes its usage, it will eventually and inevitably reach its end-of-life stage.

In this process, series of projects are implemented. In order to achieve the goal of sustainable manufacturing, project management has to incorporate the sustainability concepts along the product lifecycle evolution process. The concept of "product stewardship" is brought out. It bears the idea that everyone involved in the lifespan of the product is called upon to take up the responsibilities to reduce its environmental impacts throughout its lifecycle evolution process (Environmental Protection Agency).

In this section, we will discuss how sustainability concepts are integrated into real-life applications in different project implementations and management along the product lifecycle evolution process. Case vignettes from diverse industries are utilized to demonstrate the approaches. The discussion on the case vignettes will follow the lifecycle evolution process introduced in Figure 6.

Product design phase:

The design for the environment (DfE) concept has been promoted in the sustainable manufacturing since the 1970s. This concept focuses on social and ethnical issues, together with corporate responsibilities and economical and environmental issues at the product design phase.

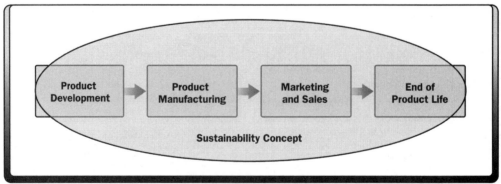

Figure 7:   Product lifecycle evolution with sustainability concept.

To be more specific, design process has to consider minimization of adverse health, safety, and environmental impacts. In addition, for the production, consumption, and disposal of the products, the product design project management has to consider the cost to effectively service, repair, and recycle the products at the "end-of-life" stage. In order words, product design should be as environmentally friendly as possible by considering, at the beginning of product innovation and design phase, disassembly and recycling.

Case vignette 1: Philips Vision and Sound System Design (Cramer, 1997)

The major driving force behind the Philips vision and sound system innovative design with sustainable manufacturing concept was legislative pressure and rules concerning industrial licensing.

In the Philips vision and sound system sustainable design project, a manual on environment-oriented product development was produced for designers, which emphasized avoiding banned material for production. In the material utilization management, weight reduction and reduction on the hazardous waste was the focus. In this process, material data information was studied and criteria for material utilization were specified.

Case vignette 2: Compaq Product Design (Dillon, 1997)

World competitiveness has enforced a lot of pressure on the product design process. Product design is critical to achievement of a sustainable manufacturing goal, especially due to short lifecycles and the rate of new product introduction to the market. In addition, customer needs and regulatory trends have made the sustainable manufacturing concept more urgent at the product design phase.

In 1994, Compaq completed a project that developed a comprehensive environmental design guideline, in which the whole lifecycle perspective was adopted in the design phase. The focuses were material selection with particular emphasis on recyclability, design for disassembly, design for reuse, and upgradeability.

Case vignette 3: Texas Instruments (Texas Instruments a)

At Texas Instruments, a program with "product stewardship" concept was launched to consider the lifecycle evolution process. They viewed product environmental responsibility and marketability as complementary values in the process. At the product design phase, they continued to seek to reduce or eliminate hazardous chemical usage. Custom-manufacture products were introduced to meet the individual product requirements and green criteria.

Case vignette 4: Patagonia Garment and Textile (Brown & Wilmanns, 1997)

Patagonia had been a long-time leader in sustainable manufacturing in the apparel industry. It was founded by an environmentalist Yvon Chouinard in 1973. At Patagonia, a lifecycle assessment product rating system named "ideal garment" was developed to setup guidelines for each product lifecycle stage.

At product design phase, the project focus was on choice of materials, features, performance levels. Specified performance criteria and product lifespan requirements were brought up. It was required that the garments only use organically grown cotton, natural fibers produced in a sustainable manner, biopolymers, and recycled content.

Case vignette 5: Kambium Kitchen Design (Tischner, 1997)

Kambium Furniture Inc. was a small/medium-sized German company. The company executive decided to go green and commit to environmental principles. The Kambium Kitchen project was for the high end market. It was designed specifically for individual customers. In the kitchen design, no pre-processed mass panels were used and all were handmade. The wood used was from European sustainably managed forests. The surfaces in the kitchen were designed to avoid toxic varnishes. With these environmentally conscious design concepts, the Kambium Kitchen was extremely ecological and long-lasting.

Product manufacturing phase:

After the products have been designed, the manufacturing phase is one of the most important product lifecycle phases in order to achieve sustainable manufacturing. The following case vignettes concentrate on the product manufacturing stage. They demonstrate how companies incorporated sustainable manufacturing concepts into the project management process.

Case vignette 1: Philips Vision and Sound System (Cramer, 1997)

In the Philips vision and sound system project, the focus was on the improvements to the industrial processes and production techniques. In the manufacturing process, projects are implemented to eliminate or reduce the production line processes that utilized materials and chemicals that were environmentally unfriendly.

Case vignette 2: Hewlett-Packard and Compaq (Dillon, 1997)

At Hewlett-Packard, one project was to manage the material supplier to the production. The company added environmental issues to supplier management along with the quality and cost concerns. In addition, energy consumption of the production process was almost recognized with high priority among the project management process.

In the Compaq production system, energy conservation in the manufacturing phase was also one of the focuses in the sustainable manufacturing implementation process. In addition, the project used standard screw heads, which helped with the repair and recycles process. The modular components concept helped with the minimization of number of parts in the final product.

Case vignette 3: Texas Instruments (Texas Instruments b)

At Texas Instruments, the "product stewardship" program shifted its focuses to energy consumption and pollution control in the manufacturing processes at the product manufacturing lifecycle phase.

Projects included improving energy efficiency to reduce electric use, installing air emission control systems, scrubbing corrosive and caustic exhaust, installing "cool" white roofs on buildings, and improving the indoor environment by using low-emitting adhesives, sealants, paint, carpet and composite wood.

Case vignette 4: Patagonia Garment and Textile (Brown & Wilmanns, 1997)

In the product manufacturing phase, the Patagonia sustainable development department implemented projects to improve efficiency of material, energy, and water use.

Energy from solar-based and other sustainable sources were recommended. Production defects were required to meet the three sigma level (97% of the products are defects free). The focuses of the sustainable development projects in the manufacturing processes were cutting, sewing, and garment finishing.

Marketing and sales phase:

The case vignettes in this section focus on the marketing and sales phase. This is the lifecycle phase that is often overlooked by the decision makers in terms of sustainability. For example, the layout of the store can have a big impact on space-saving and making the products easy to find in the store. In addition, inventory reduction can help bring down holding cost and save storage space for both the distributor and retailer.

Case vignette 1: Philips Vision and Sound (Cramer, 1997)

In the Philips vision and sound system project, the focus was on the packaging material and packaging process. Plastic compatibility rules were designed to regulate the plastics material usage in the packaging process.

Case vignette 2: Hewlett-Packard and Compaq (Dillon, 1997)

In the Compaq packaging process, the packaging materials had to be at least 35% recycled content. There was no heavy metal in packaging inks. The paperboards were 100% kraft paperboard with no bleach, and used recyclable materials only. Projects were launched to use only recyclable thermoplastics. At Hewlett-Packard, one of the main sustainable marketing projects was the eco-label initiative.

Case vignette 3: Texas Instruments (Texas Instruments c)

At Texas Instruments, product packaging and distribution was the focus of sustainable project implementation at the marketing and sales lifecycle phase. These projects worked to reduce environmental impacts and maintain compliance with international regulations.

Product labeling and responsible packaging were among the projects implemented. The packing materials were systematically reviewed throughout the sales process to assure regulation compliance. TI has significantly reduced the amount of packing materials. This resulted in lower shipping weights, shipping costs, and fuel consumption. One project involved shipping DLP® chip products to customers in non-toxic, reusable plastic packages. These packages are reused continuously until the end of useful life and eventually recycled. In 2008, TI launched a project to evaluate whether alternative greener packaging could be used for education technology products without compromising the function of protecting the products during transportation and in retail stores.

Case vignette 4: Patagonia Garment and Textile (Fast Company)

Patagonia has been one of the industrial pioneers in the environmental assessment and improvements. In order to go further in the green direction, the company launched an initiative named "footprint chronicles" which focused on the marketing and sales product lifecycle phase. It was an initiative to document and share with consumers the information (good or bad) on environmental effects of the products through its supply chain lifecycle. In this project, only primary materials are traced. They were considering tracking labeling and packaging process as well in the future.

End-of-life phase:

The end-of-life stage (how to dispose the end-of-life products) is a most important stage in sustainable manufacturing. There have also been many regulations enacted recently. Examples include the Waste from Electrical and Electronic Equipment (WEEE) Directive, the Restriction of Certain Substances Hazardous to Health (ROS) Directive, Electrical and Electronic Equipment (EEE) Directive and Home Appliance Recycling Law (HARL) (Charter, Billet, Boyce, Grinyer, & Simmonds, 2002).

A typical manufacturing and supply chain logistics system follows the typically open-loop path shown in Figure 8.

In recent times, the "3R: reduce, reuse, and recycle" process is gradually being accepted. Manufacturing companies are also starting to adopt the closed-loop logistics system displayed in Figure 9.

Case vignette 1: Philips Vision and Sound (Cramer, 1997)

In the Philips vision and sound system project, information on various costs was collected and profit for end-of-life product processing/remanufacturing were studied. This helped the decision-makers better make rational decisions on remanufacturing and recycling. In the project implementation process, rules for environment related disposal were released. These guidelines can help responsibly dispose end-of-life products.

Case vignette 2: Hewlett-Packard

At Hewlett-Packard, projects which require companies engage in collection of the products after consumers' use were implemented (Dillon, 1997). Product recovery centers were established in Roseville, California, USA, and Grenoble, France.

In addition, analyses were conducted on the recyclability of an inkjet printer such as the HP 855c. The implementation and management of the project included analyses of a variety of disassembly and recycling process scenarios (Lee and Ishii, 1998).

Case vignette 3: Texas Instruments (Texas Instruments d)

At the end-of-life stage, Texas Instruments launched projects in collecting, recycling, and reusing water. Due to unique material used at TI, projects on segregating and recycling solvents and metal-based solutions were implemented. In addition, wastewa-

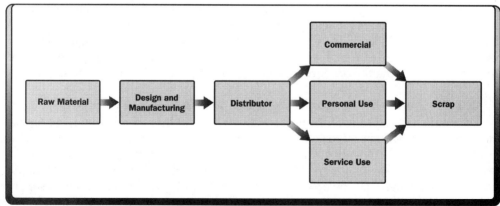

Figure 8:   Open-loop logistics system.

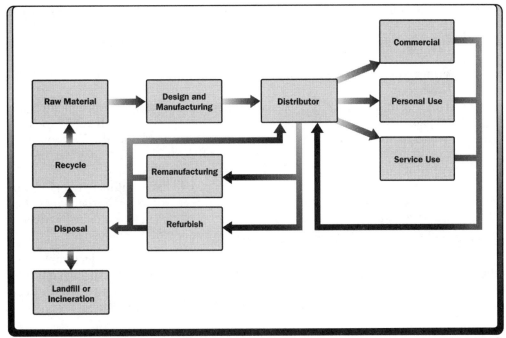

Figure 9:   Closed-loop logistics system.

ter systems were built to treat industrial wastewater. To further implement the sustainability concepts, scrap paper, metal, cardboard, wood, plastics and silicon were collected and recycled.

Case vignette 4: Patagonia Garment and Textile (Brown & Wilmanns, 1997)

At the end-of-life stage, projects on sustainable development focused on potential recyclability, components reusability, and remanufacturability. At Patagonia, restrictions on disposal were established. Consumers were urged to keep and use the products if they were still useful. Products could be returned to the company if consumers did not want to dispose of it. Management systems were launched on disassembling noncompostable products, material recycling, and remanufacturing.

1.5 Implication of Sustainable Manufacturing by the Year 2025

The following conclusions were developed, and are presented to help the project manager looking to the future:

- Sustainable manufacturing is a popular area in both academia and industry due to the growing concern about energy and environmental issues as well as cost effectiveness. Sustainability in the manufacturing industry is one of the essential elements in the achievement of the goal for sustainable societal development. In the past 50 years, many manufacturing companies have taken steps to improve the production efficiency and quality with initiatives in areas such as lean production, six sigma, and total quality management. In the next 20 years, a significant portion of new manufacturing projects and initiatives will involve sustainability.

- "Green" or sustainable products now command a cost premium because of a lack of the economies of scale. As sustainability concepts become more important, this cost differential will tend to diminish and market share will increase.
- Many organizations utilize "sustainability officers" at the corporate, division and plant-level. This hiring will accelerate. These personnel will need to possess a depth of knowledge in their domain of sustainability and also be good project managers, since much of their efforts will be directed within a matrix-type organization.
- The move towards sustainable manufacturing will have multiple drivers. Traditionally, increased legislation and associated regulations are initiated by policy makers. However, increased consumer awareness and new, ecologically friendly product designs and processes will provide additional momentum.

Looking ahead to 2025, we envision that almost every step in the project implementation and management process will incorporate sustainable manufacturing concepts. New project management tools and decision models will be developed to assist the decision makers make "greener" and more rational decisions at the operational level.

References

Angell, L., & Klassen, R. Integrating environmental issues into the mainstream: An agenda for research in operations management. *Journal of Operations Management, 17*(5).

Azapagic, A., & Perdan, S. (2000). Indicators for sustainable development for industry: A general framework. *Trans IChemE*, Vol. 78, Part B, July.

Berry, M. (2004). The importance of sustainable development. *Columbia Spectator*, September.

Blackburn, J. D., Guide, V.D.R., Van Wassenhove, L. N., & Souza, G.C. (2004). Reverse supply chains for commercial returns. *California Management Review, (46)*, 6-22.

Brown, M.S., & Eric Wilmanns, E. Quick and dirty environmental analyses for garments: what do we need to know. *Journal of Sustainable Product Design, April 1997.*

Brundtland, G. (1987). *Our common future: The world commission on environment and development.* Oxford: Oxford University Press.

Caldwell, L. (1989). A constitutional law for the environment: 20 years with NEPA indicates the need. *Environment, 31*(10).

California Energy Commission, http://www.energy.ca.gov/greenbuilding/index.html (Accessed January, 2009)

Charter, M., Billet, E., Boyce, J., Grinyer C., & Simmonds J. (2002). The state of the art in eco-design in the Japanese electronics sector, Research Report, The Center for Sustainable Design, The Surrey Institute of Art & Design, Univeristy College.

Cornwall Government, http://www.cornwall.gov.uk/media/image/6/4/strat721_2_.gif (Accessed January, 2009)

Cramer, C. (1997). Towards innovative, more eco-efficient product design strategies. *The Journal of Sustainable Product Design, April 1997.*

Debo, L.G., Toktay, L.B., Van Wassenhove, L.N. (2005). Market segmentation and product technology selection for remanufacturable products. *Management Science, (51)*8, 1193-1205.

Dekker, R., Fleischmann, M., Inderfurth, K., & Van Wassenhove, L.N. (2004). *Reverse logistics: Quantitative models for closed loop supply chains.* Berlin, Germany: Springer.

Dillon, P.S. Improving the life cycle of electronic products: case studies from the US electronics industry. *The Journal of Sustainable Product Design, July 1997.*

Dyllick, T., & Hockert, K. (2002). Beyond the business case for corporate sustainability. *Business strategy and the environment, 11*(2).

Environmental Protection Agency, http://www.epa.gov/epawaste/partnerships/stewardship/index.htm (Accessed January, 2009)

Fast Company, http://www.fastcompany.com/magazine/124/measuring-footprints.html (Accessed January, 2009)

Flapper, S. D. P., van Nunen, J.A.E.E., & Van Wassenhove, L.N. (2005). *Managing closed-loop supply chains.* Berlin, Germany: Springer.

Fleischmann, M., Bloemhof-Ruwaard, J., Dekker, R., van der Laan, E., van Nunen, J.A.E.E., & Van Wassenhove, L. N. (1997). Quantitative models for reverse logistics: A review. *Eur. J. Oper. Res., (103),* 1-17.

Global Development Research Center, http://www.gdrc.org/uem/lca/life-cycle.html (Accessed January, 2009)

Guide, V.D.R. & Van Wassenhove, L.N. (2001). Managing product returns for remanufacturing. *Production Oper. Management, (10),* 142-154.

Guide, V.D.R. (2000). Production planning and control for remanufacturing: Industry practice and research needs. *J. Oper. Management, (18),* 467-483.

Guide, V.D.R., Harrison, T.P., & Van Wassenhove, L.N. (2003). The challenge of closed-loop supply chains. *Interfaces, (33)*6, 3-6.

Guide, V.D.R., Teunter, R.H., & Van Wassenhove, L.N. (2003). Matching demand and supply to maximize profits from remanufacturing. *Manufacturing & Service Operations Management, (5)*4, 303-316.

Hu, G., Wang, L., & Bidanda, B. (2007). A game theoretic model of the market competition between green and ordinary products. Nashville: *Proceedings of the 2007 Industrial Engineering Research Conference.*

Hu, G., Wang, L., Bidanda, B., & Fetch, S. (2008). A multi-objective approach to project selection with six sigma criteria. In Press. *International Journal of Production Research.*

Hu, G., Wang, L., Wang, Y., & Bidanda, B. (2007). A new model for closed loop product lifecycle systems. Nashville: *Proceedings of the 2007 Industrial Engineering Research Conference.*

Labuschagne, C., & Brent, A. (2007). Sustainable project life cycle management: The need to integrate life cycles to manufacturing sector. *International Journal of Project Management, (23)*2, 159-168.

Lancaster, O. (1999). *Success and sustainability: A guide to sustainable development for owners and managers of small and medium sized business.* Edinburgh: Midlothian Enterprise Trust.

Lee, B.H., & Ishii, K. (1998). The recyclability map: Application of remanufacturing complexity metrics to design for recyclability. *The Journal of Sustainable Product Design, April 1998.*

Otterpohl R., Grottker M., & Lange J. (1997). Sustainable water and waste management in urban areas. *Water Science and Technology, 35*(9).

Pesonen, L. (2001). Implementation of design to profit in a complex and dynamic business context. Thesis, Department of Process and Environmental Engineering, University of Oulu.

Sperling, D., Bunch, D., Burke, A., Abeles, E., Chen, B., Kurani, K., & Turrentine, T. (2004). Analysis of auto industry and consumer response to regulations and technological change, and customization of consumer response models in support of AB 1493 rulemaking. Research Report UCD – ITS – RR – 4 - 17, Institute of Transportation Studies, University of California, Davis.

Texas Instruments a, http://www.ti.com/corp/docs/csr/prodstewardship/GreenProductDesign.shtml (Accessed January, 2009)

Texas Instruments b, http://www.ti.com/corp/docs/csr/prodstewardship/Sustainable-Manufacturing.shtml (Accessed January, 2009)

Texas Instruments c, http://www.ti.com/corp/docs/csr/prodstewardship/ResponsiblePackagingandDistribution.shtml (Accessed January, 2009)

Texas Instruments d, http://www.ti.com/corp/docs/csr/prodstewardship/GreenProductDesign.shtml (Accessed January, 2009)

The Times 100, http://www.thetimes100.co.uk/case_study.php?cID=65&csID=211&pID=2 (Accessed January, 2009)

Tischner, U. (1997). Sustainability by design: new targets and new tools for designers. *The Journal of Sustainable Product Design, October 1997.*

U.S. Department of Commerce International Trade Commission, http://www.trade.gov/competitiveness/sustainablemanufacturing/how_doc_defines_SM.asp (Accessed January, 2009)

U.S. Department of Energy, Energy, Efficiency and Renewable Energy, http://www.eere.energy.gov/greenpower/conference/5gpmc00/dreicher.pdf (Accessed January, 2009)

Wikipedia. http://en.wikipedia.org/wiki/Triple_bottom_line (Accessed January, 2009)

Windrum, P., & Birchenhall, C. (1998). Is product life cycle theory a special case? Dominant designs and emergence of market niches through coevolutionary-learning. *Structural Change and Economic Dynamic, 1998,* 109-134.

Wiser, R., & Fang, J. (1999). Green power marketing in retail competition: An early assessment. Technical Report, National Renewable Energy Laboratory.

CHAPTER 28

Project Management in a
Flat World Circa 2025[1]

Ozlem Arisoy, Murat Azim, David Cleland, Bopaya Bidanda[2]

Outline

The growing offshoring trend forces companies to transfer their high-cost activities to low-labor rate countries. Offshoring often stands out as an attractive option to reduce cost. However such an initiative can provide a competitive advantage to an organization only if careful analyses are performed and sound projections are constructed. A systematic project management approach during the process of global sourcing decisions is usually the key driver to success and will likely grow in importance over the next few decades.

Offshoring decision-making processes can be considered as large-size projects that impact a company's strategies and future operations. Although these projects can be managed based on the classical project management principles, modifications and extensions are inevitable to support the wide scope of the growing globalization movement. In this chapter, we begin by detailing how these offshoring projects change the entire direction of the company. In the following sections, we analyze the project life cycle of offshoring decisions by reviewing recent projects from various industries. We anticipate a modification and/or refinement of these general project life cycle phases. Critical processes at each of these phases are detailed, including activities, managerial challenges, and milestones, as well as cost, schedule, and technical performance factors. Methodologies specifically related to offshoring projects such as risk management, stakeholder management, and contract management are also highlighted, along with

---

[1]This Chapter has been drawn (almost in entirety) and then further refined from the chapter titled "Project Management for Outsourcing Decisions" by B.Bidanda, O.Arisoy and M. Azim in The Global Project Management Handbook (2006), Editors D. I. Cleland and R. Gareis, with permission from Mc Graw Hill.
[2]Corresponding author: bidanda@pitt.edu

their practical applications. As a conclusion, the multiple outcomes of these projects are discussed. Failure and success indicators of future offshoring projects and their implications are justified.

1. Introduction

Offshoring can be defined as a means of obtaining supporting organizational services from outside suppliers usually in another country with a view to either reduce costs and/or increase productivity and quality. Embracing this concept causes major changes in the manner in which the organization is managed. Offshoring is now transforming the corporation. Global companies such as American Express, General Motors, and many other utilize some form of offshoring at an ever increasing pace. Support from offshore companies based in India and China has now become standard organizational practice. Outsourcing to domestic corporations such as IBM (for information technology) gives access to technical scale and expertise that few other companies have.

Offshoring is a growing trend that has been subject of many controversial discussions at multiple academic and media forums. For some, it is a globalization effort that creates opportunities for future innovation, contributing to the world economy. For others, offshoring is believed to have a destructive effect on the U.S. economy, increasing unemployment rates and weakening the industrial power of the country.

It must be recognized that offshoring is a consequence of several trends. Globalization is a result of the unification of world cultures led by progressive governments and through the rapid proliferation of inexpensive communication technologies. Political and economical developments around the world, such as the privatization of public sector organizations and the formation of European Union, have further accelerated the speed of globalization. On the other hand, the U.S. consumption market continued expanding. The development of new (and leaner) manufacturing processes, technological enhancements, and rising demand has resulted in a reduction in the product life cycles. The number of products on the market has also increased exponentially, with fewer product differentiation features. The subtle power shift from manufacturers to the big retailers such as Wal-Mart and Home Depot has allowed retailers to have the upper hand in tough price negotiations, forcing the manufacturers toward lower-cost alternatives[1]. As a result, lower prices have been a major driving force in the drive towards a larger percentage of market share. Globalization and the cost pressures have, therefore, forced companies to look beyond their borders.

In his book *The World is Flat*, Thomas Freidman makes a convincing case on how the Internet and resulting inexpensive communication technology has changed the world to equalize individual and organizational core competencies and moved competition to a truly global level[2].

Today, offshoring stands out as an attractive option for a growing number of companies to reduce costs of their operational activities to low-labor rate countries either by a direct investment in offshore subsidiaries or by developing strategic local alliances. From a financial point of view, companies also anticipate significant reductions in their capital requirements to give management the opportunity to get higher return on equity (ROE). Therefore, offshoring is a credible alternative way for managers to enhance shareholder satisfaction.

The existence of highly educated youth, government subsidies, tax reductions. and infrastructural improvements in the developing countries also motivates senior managers toward offshoring their high-cost activities. However, it must be recognized that offshoring initiatives provide a competitive advantage only if careful analyses are performed and sound projections are constructed. A systematic project management approach during the process of offshoring decisions is the key driver behind the success. The lack of careful project planning is usually the reason why expected cost savings are not realized.

Offshoring decisions are in large part based on organizational strategies. A wrong decision in terms of location and vendor selection may have disastrous effects on the competitiveness of the company. Many companies have support from outside consultants for their offshoring decision process. There are also ways to source globally utilizing internal staff and expertise. In both cases, the decision process must go through several phases that have defined beginning and end time points. An offshoring decision process intrinsically fits into the definition of a project: a combination of organizational resources integrated to create something that did not previously exist will usually provide a performance capability in the design and execution of organizational strategies[3].

Offshoring decisions are now an important component of management responsibilities. As the volume and criticality of offshoring decisions continue to grow for the next few decades, basic management processes—namely, planning, organizing, motivating, controlling, and directing—become more important during execution. Risk, multitasking, extensive documentation, and complexity are inevitable in global networks. The growth of project-based global initiatives and their strategic importance on the business practices will receive the highest priority in comparison with other projects.

Even though today offshoring of manufacturing and services may seem limited only to the big corporations, as the process of offshoring becomes easier and more evident we can expect corporations comparably smaller in size to join the trend of offshoring. Especially for the small-mid size corporations, the management of these decisions and later implementation and governance will be challenging and riskier.

Project management and strategic management are highly interdependent. Strategic management deals with the futurity of current decisions. In the process of strategic planning, alternative choices of the manner in which future resources will be utilized to accomplish the mission of the organization are identified and evaluated. These resources typically involve new or improved products, services or organizational processes such as marketing, production, finance, and research and development. It is at the beginning of the identification and use of these resources that the need for project management arises.

Projects are ad hoc, resource-consuming activities used to evaluate and implement organizational strategies, objectives, and goals, needed to contribute to the realization of the organization's mission. Projects thus become the means for coping with the changes that will likely impact the future use of resources to support the organization's mission, objectives and goals. Project management has taken on a new and vital function for the development of competitive strategies in the changing global marketplace.

2. Project Life Cyle

The model in Figure 1 describes a futuristic offshoring project within the context of a project life cycle. The duration of each life cycle phase is often lengthy and the processes within each phase will require cutting across organizational boundaries such as in matrix-type organizations.

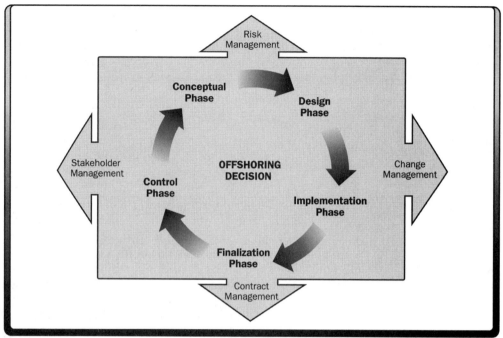

Figure 1:   Project life cycle.

The *conceptual phase* requires the alignment of the proposed global initiative with the company strategy. The role and the involvement of senior management is critical in order to achieve the desired outcome. The *design phase* involves investigation of alternatives, detailed financial analyses, and numerous negotiations. During the *implementation phase,* the appropriate offshoring practice is brought to fruition. In this period, the contractual meetings, cross-border distribution, and training are among the challenges faced by company personnel. After implementation, the offshored functionalities are carved out of the organization and divested to the offshore vendor/ captive center. The divestment consists of two phases, finalization and control. The *finalization phase* includes alteration of the organization, relocation of idle resources and final documentation, whereas the *control phase* is the continuous monitoring of the outsourced activities.

The conceptual and design phases of offshoring are critical to the offshoring deci-sion. In these phases, the functions in considerations should be analyzed from a process level. These phases also form a basis for implementation. If the concept and design are not well thought out, the implementation will not be successful.

The finalization phase is more about "knowledge transfer." In this phase the par-ent company needs to make sure that the functions are performed properly and service levels are met. The governance is the phase that is often ignored. As more and more companies establish offshore functions, in the future the "competitive edge" to an off-shoring process will be proper management during the governance phase. The compa-nies which are better in taking control will be the winners. Taking control means con-tinuously and diligently tracking the service quality and at the same time re-evaluating the concept and the design. The concept and design may change as the companies grow, shrink, experience organizational changes, and redirect their strategies. The offshore functions should be re-evaluated taking the project management cycle to the first phase, and necessary changes should be implemented. The re-evaluation may bring a small change, such as revising the service levels—or a big change, such as adding a new function. The governance and re-evaluation phase will be the most critical part of project management of offshoring in the future.

Conceptual Phase

The starting point in the new "flat world" often begins with the decision whether or not to source globally. The company management must recognize that offshoring is not the only choice. Although offshoring is attractive for cost reduction purposes, there are also many advantages of staying in-house. Maintaining control of core competencies and quality assurance are much easier in in-house operations. Concurrent teams and interdisciplinary projects can be performed more efficiently. Further, one does not have to be concerned about intellectual property protection.

On the other hand, offshoring may help a company gain competitive advantage by allowing it to focus on its core businesses and yet have access to external world class capabilities. It also reduces the capital expenditures and overhead, increasing the value of the company, which in most cases makes the company attractive in the stock market. Charles Gibbons of PricewaterhouseCoopers explains with the following statement:[4]

> "If I have a dollar to invest and can manage not to spend any portion of that investment dollar on my back office costs and put it instead in my real core business, that gives me a tenfold return. If my supplier partner will make investments in my back office, then I have that advantage as well. Then I have increased shareholder value."

A company should not decide on moving offshore just because other companies in the industry are offshoring. The advantages and disadvantages of global offshoring must be evaluated in detail to assure its appropriateness with the company's strategic direction. An offshoring decision project must be consistent with the company's mission statement and strategic objectives.

Cases: To Source Globally or Not?

Two opposite cases of offshoring decisions are the dilemmas seen by Huntington National Bank and Sears, Roebuck & Co [5].

Huntington National Bank Case:

In 2000, outsourcer CSC offered a business process offshoring (BPO) agreement that promised increased revenue streams in the future. The CIO was skeptical at first, but felt he could not reject it without further analysis. Huntington began its exploration of CSC's BPO offer by bringing in offshoring adviser TPI to assess the proposal. The company requested other proposals from different outsourcers in order to compare the economics the CSC offer. The CIO also hired Anderson Consulting to benchmark internal IT performance and costs.

The results showed that while the internal IT department had flaws, an outsourcer could not provide large cost savings due to built-in administrative and transaction costs. The CIO explained his concerns, "Can offshoring help us get better aligned with the business? We're a midsize company with one data center that's very limited in scope, and just saying, 'Hey let's out-source because some company argues that their economies of scale are better' didn't make sense for us." Cultural issues were also important. Huntington was positioning itself as an "essential partner" to external customers. It was felt, that keeping with this spirit, the IT department had to stay as an "essential partner" to the internal customers. So, the bank chose to keep IT in-house and support its enhancement.

Sears, Roebuck & Co.:

When offshoring was brought up within Sears, the company had not invested appropriately in its IT infrastructure for many years. Urgent improvement was needed for a more technically reliable infrastructure that would support company objectives. The CIO first asked, "Is this something my team could do?" And the major considerations, in his words, were "time, talent and treasure." How long would it take? Who would do it? And what would it cost?" Another consideration was Sears' mission. After all it was a retail company and expecting technological perfection would not be reasonable. Offshoring IT infrastructure stood up as a good alternative that would provide maximum value in a short period of time without the need for additional investment.

The CIO then brought in Transitions Partners, an IT offshoring consultancy, to develop a more thorough analysis. The consultants helped Sears see the major factors in an offshoring decision and guided them through possible choices. For nine months, they analyzed the different possibilities of transferring the business process. At the same time, they included probable impacts of offshoring on stakeholders such as employees, customers and investors. As a result, Sears decided that offshoring its IT operations would allow them to achieve their goal of a stable infrastructure faster without incurring high expenditures.

Conclusion:

Determining the right application to outsource is essential. Products or functions that have already reached maturity are less risky choices. These applications do not need big changes and can be managed without the need of direct control. The complexity of the offshored application is just as important. More effort is needed to outsource complex functions. The possibility of failure escalates as the complexity of the job grows. Operations will need close monitoring, which in turn will add to the transaction and communication costs. Most companies do not outsource their critical and strategically important applications to prevent the risk of losing intellectual property. Routine call centers and mass production operations are, therefore, the most popular processes that are outsourced.

Long-Range Planning for the Offshoring Decision:

A company that initiates and implements an offshoring strategy sets in motion an inexorable set of forces that foster change in the operational and strategic initiatives of the organization. The organizational culture of a company undergoing offshoring as a principal strategy must value and foster the use of project management philosophies and processes supported by the cultural elements of the company. The use of project teams as a means for the development and implementation of effective global sourcing can be strengthened by the following strategies:

- Keep project teams regularly informed on the status of the project, including both good and bad news. This should be done at regular project status reviews.
- Promote the sharing of ideas, problems, opportunities, and interests among the team members, particularly with those team members who are new to the project. This helps provide new team members with a sense of belonging to the mission of the offshoring project.
- Have social activities for the teams, such as informal lunches, coffee breaks, dinners, and, when possible, visits to the organizations providing offshoring support.
- Keep the team informed on what competitors are doing and the implications of competitor strategy.
- Work at creating a sense of importance and urgency to the offshoring project and its work. Make the most of having senior executives visit the project team and be briefed by the team members on their activities and accomplishments.
- Reduce the formality in dealing with team members.

Offshoring is a long-range decision. A structured long-range planning effort prevents unnecessary ad hoc decisions and provides an alignment of objectives within an organization[6].

Steiner[7] divides conceptual long-range planning into four stages. An offshoring decision may be also be conceptualized in the same framework:

1- Strategic Conceptualization:

The management should first assess whether an offshoring initiative is appropriate for the firm's future strategies. The market share, cost structure, product quality, good will and challenges in the organizational structure must be considered. Multidisciplinary teams are, therefore, needed to identify and analyze the strategic issues and report their consequences to the senior management. To support a make-or-buy decision on offshoring, the management can apply mathematical methods, such as linear programming, that will provide preliminary results on the financial consequences[8]. Subsequently, the management must assess the offshoring decision in terms of its strategic relevance, feasibility, criticality and urgency.

Many organizations have little experience with offshoring decisions. Though the value of internal assessment should not be minimized, if internal expertise is lacking, it is advisable to seek out a consultant with local experience. An outsider can objectively evaluate real costs, threats and opportunities by applying prior experience. An expert opinion is a wise contribution, especially while deciding whether or not to outsource.

2- Medium-range Conceptualization:

Once the strategic fit of an offshoring decision is reviewed, a preliminary analysis of the alternatives is necessary. A company can choose to invest in a low-cost country or continue its processes locally. Some companies need close correspondence and reliance in operations due to the nature of their business. These companies prefer to invest rather than choosing an international, contract partner. This investment can be made either in the form of acquiring an existing local company or by establishing a regional branch.

On the other hand, if the application does not require a long-term commitment and is not a critical function, a better choice is to have contractual agreement with a business partner in a low-cost country. Although the latter is more captivating in terms of cost savings, it may not always be feasible. The management needs to determine the best alternative based on the objective and limitations. Once a final decision is reached, the time and place are identified based on the economical, sociological and political environment, as well as the related business structure and availability of resources.

3- Short-term Conceptualization:

In this stage, the offshoring idea has already been conceived by the management, which in turn assigns a project team and project manager(s) to document the idea on paper. The project team can apply following measures in order to reduce the uncertainty the organization faces during the initial phases:

- Detailed market analysis and an investigation of the company's status versus external environment.
- A business survey to determine the standards of the market
- Benchmarking to provide a general view
- Proposals from vendors located in different regions of the world

4- Planning:

The final component of the conceptual phase is determination of the time line and budget constraints. The project team develops a preliminary schedule to the senior management for an approval before proceeding to the next stage. Due to their strategic importance, offshoring decisions are structured upon senior management approval. Even if there is a commitment from the highest level of the organization, effective communication through the organization is also crucial. If direct and unambiguous information is not provided, a chaotic environment may slowly develop among employees who perceive the offshoring motive from different points of views - some see it as a career opportunity while others fear from job insecurity. To mitigate the potentially adverse effects on the organization, the management can initiate face-to-face communication to create inter-team cooperation and trust. The frequency and quality of communication are major factors that facilitate the development of mutual understanding of goals[9].

Design Phase

The conceptual phase is the initiation point where the offshoring decision is evaluated in terms of its strategic fit, whereas the design phase is a long and challenging stage where decisions are structured within operational boundaries. In conceptualizing over the medium-term, the senior management reviews the location and contract/investment options before it reaches a decision on whether or not to invest, depending on the market transaction costs. There are various situations where a company may prefer a direct investment:

- For some operations, transaction costs such as negotiation, contract and monitoring costs are higher than administrative costs. If the transaction costs associated with organizing across markets are greater than the administrative costs of organizing within firms, we can expect the coordination of productive activity to be internalized within firms [10].

- Sometimes, investment may be the only alternative, because of extreme intellectual property security concerns.
- If the company wants to outsource some of its key functionalities, the management will require long-term commitments.

The business conditions and the company objectives will often determine the scope of offshoring. Linder divides offshoring into two categories, conventional and transformational[11]. Conventional offshoring is transferring non-core, simple interfaces to another entity, whereas transformational offshoring is offshoring to achieve a rapid, sustainable, step-change improve in enterprise-level performance. Conventional offshoring has little flexibility and involves well-understood processes, whereas transformational offshoring involves offshoring ongoing services that are critical to the performance of the business. Transformational offshoring is operated through by partnering or investments (do-it-yourself, merge/acquire or joint venture). Below is a case for conventional offshoring performed by Hewlett Packard. In this case, the primary benefit of offshoring was the cost savings obtained from reduced labor cost.

Case: Hewlett Packard

[12]Hewlett Packard was able to reduce total cost, increase cash flow, conserve capital and access markets by offshoring its test equipment products. By doing so, the management was able to focus on the core capabilities such as product design and marketing.

In early 1980s, its South Queensferry site had many manufacturing processes such as cables, transformers, plastic molding, sheet metal fabrication, precision machining, printed circuit board fabrication, printed circuit board assembly, subassembly build and final assembly and test. As a result of growing market, reduced life cycles and cost competitiveness, it became difficult for HP to continue to maintain a competitive advantage on all of its processes for a longer period of time. As a result, HP started to subcontract these activities one by one.

Activity Sub-Contracted	Year
Cables	1987
Wound components	1985
Plastics	1986
Sheetmetal	1987
PCB (Printed Circuit Boards)	1993
PCA (Printed Circuit Assemblies)	1994
Sub-assembly	1997

In 10 years, HP was able shift from vertical integration to horizontal integration. It learned many important lessons along the way:

- The decision to outsource a manufacturing process is fundamentally a business decision that affects a company's core business. Such a decision must be taken fully supported by senior management.

- The company must ensure that a competitive advantage should not be lost as a result of offshoring decision. The competitive advantage may be in logistics, supply chain management, or new product introduction.

Contract-Invest Decision:

If a company chooses to invest in a low-cost country, the size of the investment should be determined to evaluate whether it is within the scope of operational functions that will be outsourced. Investment is a key element that must be considered in the design stage where alternatives are analyzed in detail. On the other hand, if the company chooses contractual offshoring, the type of contract is a determining factor for the offshoring relationship. Figure 2 shows the content of four types of contractual offshoring proposed by Nam et al. [13] depending on the strategic impact and contract duration:

- *Support*:
  Non-core activities are outsourced with small short-term contracts.
  - Example: Contract programming, hardware maintenance
- *Reliance*
  Non-core activities are outsourced with large substitution. These are longer-term contracts.
  - Example: Contract programming with longer term contracts.
- *Alignment*
  There is a low amount of substitution. The contracts are smaller with short-term scopes. The strategic impact is considerable
  - Example: Consulting, technical supervision

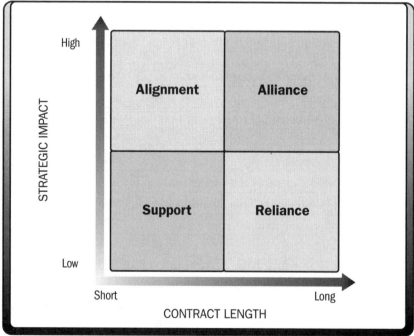

Figure 2:   Contract types.

- *Alliance –*
  There is a high amount of substitution. These are large contracts with important strategic impact.
  - Example: Complete transfer of information systems activities

Location Decision:

Typically, the analysis of location, time, and format of an offshoring initiative is performed concurrently. The objective is to find the optimum combination that will maximize the value and opportunities and minimize the risks and threats.

The Global Outsourcing Report 2005[14] assesses countries in terms of two indices: the Global Outsourcing Index (GOI) and the Future Outsourcing Rank (FOR). According to this report, India and China are the two distinct low-cost labor countries that head the list of locations that almost every company considers outsourcing to. China is mostly known for low-cost manual labor in manufacturing, whereas India has the advantage of an English speaking population and thus attracts a large amount of BPO contracts. Alternatively, Taiwan and Korea are known as the centers of the semi-conductor industry. Outside of these big players, countries such as Indonesia, the Philippines, and Malaysia also take their places in the offshoring business, with newly emerging economies like Vietnam are not far behind.

The number of location alternatives for offshoring is limited by constraints specific to each business sector. For instance, in the food processing industry, only certain regions with specific and favorable climatic conditions are an option for offshoring. The technical expertise and cultural environment also restrict the choices for a company determining the appropriate place to transfer operations.

Once location alternatives are determined, a systematic analysis is needed to identify the optimal choice in a way that encompasses the biggest cost reduction with minimum risk. Figure 3 shows the structure of a decision-support method for such an analysis.

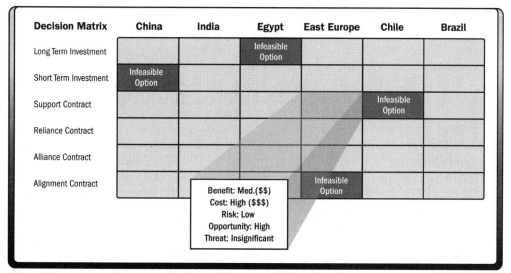

Figure 3:   Decision matrix.

The figure is an example of decision matrix created for a food processing company[15] where six countries are evaluated according to their costs, benefits, opportunities, risks, and threats. The alternatives represent the cells of the decision matrix, where the columns specify the country options and rows are the offshoring modes considered by the company. In case any of the combinations is economically infeasible, it is eliminated from further deliberation.

The analyst first gathers data about different alternatives, such as labor rates, energy prices, tax and duties, raw material prices, and transportation costs, which are relevant for a monetary comparison of countries in consideration. Using available quantitative data, the project team is able to examine the financial outcomes by performing benefit/cost analysis and return-on-asset calculations. The decision matrix is continuously updated according to the outcomes of the financial analysis. The decision matrix can also be used as a tool for what-if analysis in the proceeding stages of the offshoring project.

The challenge is that the real results are not based solely on financial outcomes, since the business environment is complex. The interactions between economical and sociological elements must be reflected in the dynamics of offshoring. Cultural differences, language capabilities, and time zones are some of the qualitative variables that determine the productivity of the offshoring processes[16]. There may be tradeoffs among decision variables such as cost, quality, ease of communication, transportation and reliability. For instance, the cost of food processing may be low in one country; however, if the agricultural practice is not very efficient, the desired quality cannot be achieved. In the manufacturing industry, the infrastructure of the country is as important as the technical skills and labor costs. Risk is another facet of the problem. Uncertainty must be considered explicit from the financial outcomes. Currency fluctuations, political transitions, flexibility, and cultural fit have substantial impact on the success of future operations.

The analyst's goal is to choose the best or optimal alternative; however, finding the optimum is not straightforward in a complex environment where variables are often stochastic and all variable cannot be captured. Monetary values such as cost can be expressed in terms of quantitative variables, but intangible values such as risks cannot be structured in numeric notations. In order to analyze the system, Fisher suggests that quantitative analysis should be utilized as much as possible but must be supplemented by qualitative analysis as well[17]. The key issue here is to use the quantitative analysis as a support for the final decision maker. Figure 4 shows a systematic approach towards the integration of quantitative and qualitative elements, where sensitivity analysis is performed as a feedback mechanism to control uncertainties.

Uncertainty is unavoidable in the global environment involving countries with different economies and politics. An explicit solution is to identify the risks associated with the uncertainties and mitigate their effects as much as feasible. There are several risk identification methodologies that have been used in the literature such as research, structured interviews and checklists. *Risk registration* is one of the practical tools to identify and control the uncertainties as a part of risk management effort. The same tool can be used for the purposes of offshoring decision, too[18]. Risks are first listed in a risk registration form that stores information such as risk number, risk description, ownership, probability, impact, risk factor, response, and status. Risks are divided into categories based on their characteristics. Then, the severity of impact and probability of occurrence are examined based on the risk categories. Response strategies follow the quantitative and qualitative uncertainty analyses thereafter. These response strategies can be used as a feedback mechanism during the analyses of alternatives for offshoring, while the behavior of outcomes is observed against a changing risk variable.

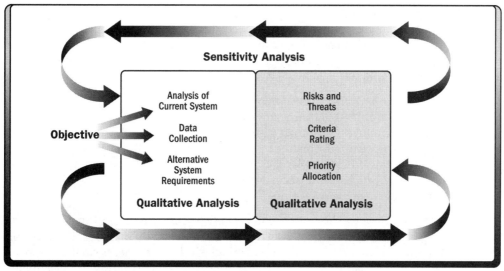

Figure 4:   Alternative analysis process.

IMPLEMENTATION PHASE

In the implementation phase, the offshoring decision is brought into life. Essential elements for a successful implementation are a comprehensive contract, an efficient relationship management, and a structural transition stage. Four basic management principles are applied—Change management, contract management, stakeholder management, and relationship management—as shown in Figure 5.

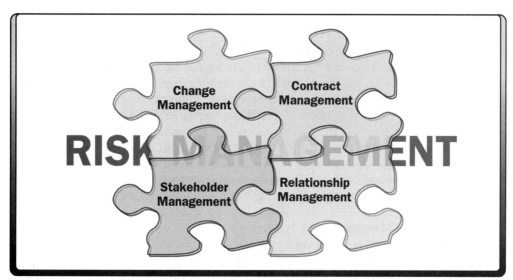

Figure 5:   Integration of management principles.

Change Management:

Change management principles are applied during the formation of contractual relationships and while controlling ongoing activities such as training and testing. For effective organizational change management, there are a few critical issues that must be identified a priori as follows[19] :

- Determining barriers to implementing change
- Change management planning and strategies
- Managing employee/ customer resistance
- Building executive sponsorship
- Creating communication plans
- Creating training and educational programs
- Maintaining business continuity

Project management can help effect change and begins with the multinational transition of operational projects such as contracts and investments. In this section, we will mainly talk about contractual relationships, though the basic elements can be practiced for "transformational offshoring" initiatives that begin with partnering or investment.

Contract Management:

There are two parties in an offshoring contract, the offshoring company and the vendor.

A contract consists of several documents[20]:

- *The contract agreement:* Identifies the parties, defines the scope of work, establishes the price and schedule
- *General specification and scope of work*: Describes the scope of work, the technical standards required and administrative procedures.
- *General conditions of the contract*: Includes details about the agreement and related issues such as bonds, safety, risks and disputes.
- *Special conditions of the contract:* Additions required by any of the parties.
- *Administrative and coordination procedures:* Includes procedural aspects.

The foundation of an offshoring contract is quality and productivity. The contract must include the definition of objectives, the structure of technology, historical data, scheduling and all of the other factors that may affect the implementation of the project. It should also reflect the size and the timeframe of the application and define standards as clearly as possible to prevent ambiguity. The contract should be comprehensive in determining the specification of the payment terms and expectations of each stakeholder. It is important that all parties play a role in providing input and also understand the full implication of how changes in the contract can affect their business processes. In addition to these basic principles, international contracts need to explicitly state which country's law will apply and specify the language of communication.

Stakeholder Management:

An offshoring initiative affects not only the company, but also all its stakeholders, including employees, managers, customers, and shareholders and perhaps the regional economy. In many cases, these benefits are contradictory depending on the stakeholder's perspective. Julius[21] studied stakeholder conflicts in the globalizing businesses and categorizes the stakeholders in four diverse groups: customers, employees, communities, and shareholders.

Customers:

The customers are always the primary stakeholders affected by changes in business structure. The consequences of an offshoring initiative are promptly reflected in products' prices. However, offshoring may not always result in higher customer satisfaction. While customers utilize the benefits of low-priced products and services, they may also be faced with lower product quality and inadequate service levels. A quality discrepancy will result in disappointment and motivate the customer to change products or brands. Thus, it is important for a company to be in contact with customers throughout the offshoring process and assure them of the continuation of the quality in their products and services.

Employees:

During the implementation stage, a company should not expect unanimous support from all employees. While employees understand the benefits of offshoring for shareholders and customers, they see their jobs migrating to low-cost countries. It is unreasonable to expect staff to share their knowledge when they know their jobs will eventually be lost. These projects are best implemented with management is transparent and establishes a supportive communications plan. Additional (re)training and education can open new opportunities in more strategic positions. It is imperative that management facilitate the realization of such outcomes to ensure employee enthusiasm during the transfer period.

Communities:

As the unemployment rises, offshoring is subject to more controversy in the home country. On the one hand, consumers cherish their increased purchasing power; On the other hand, a sizeable employee base loses jobs and security. In order to avoid disputes, companies are sometimes reluctant to pre-announce or publicize their offshoring decisions to avoid a loss of good will and trust.

Shareholders:

Shareholders that seek organizational profitability are often the driving forces behind offshoring initiatives. Stock prices often rise with offshoring project announcements in anticipation of an increasing return in the future. Even though the shareholder pressure cannot be neglected, it is important for the company management to remain objective and not take unnecessary risks in their decisions.

d) Relationship Management:

Four fundamental characteristics give shape to an offshoring relationship[22]:

- *The depth of the relationship:* Depends on the criticality of the outsourced job. As the job is gets closer to the core business process, greater depth is required.
- *The scope of the relationship:* Depends on the nature of the work outsourced.
- *The choice of asset to use:* Depends on the organization's ability to invest in asset development.

- *The choice of business culture to adopt and exploit:* Depends on how the ambiance is set for a culture that will ensure a smooth transition.

In order for an offshoring process to thrive, characteristics of the relationship should be defined before the transition starts at all organizational levels, since trust and communication among all parties is essential. Differences in style and culture are unavoidable, but as long as parties recognize such differences, they can agree to pursue common approaches. As a part of collaboration, both the outsourcer and the vendor should share responsibilities of the transition stage while setting goals and standards. A strong relationship will support the changes that the partner organizations will face in the next stages, and it is also an essential element for a long-term and productive business process, under which all parties maximize value with a win-win situation.

Problems during the implementation stages should not be neglected since even the smallest disagreements can grow into serious crises. The project team should treat these problems in an organized manner with confidence and reliability. Cheung presents a dispute resolution composed of six steps[23]: prevention, negotiation, standing neutral, nonbinding resolution, binding resolution, and litigation. These steps enhance the possibility of a binding resolution.

Clear and exhaustive documentation prevents ambiguity and serves as a reference for the management of future relationships, minimizing miscommunication between parties. All processes through the process must be documented in every detail. Comprehensive documentation not only supports a tight communication between vendors, but also helps to resolve disagreements that are likely to occur.

Smooth transition is vital for the success of an offshoring project, and the involvement of multiple stakeholders makes it more complex and fragile. While the changes are actually implemented, every stakeholder is concerned about his or her own situation. Some employees believe they are close to losing their job and resist the change, whereas executives and shareholders see it as a cost reduction effort and favor the change. Studies show that the reason behind most of the failed change projects is inadequate consideration of people and communication[24]. Miscommunication and lack of employee support causes prolong training and testing phases.

Today, a majority of workers are understandably sensitive to any kind of decision process which may lead an offshoring decision. Job security was a governing issue in 2004 elections and continues to be overriding in media. As a result, the employees who are in the process of transferring their jobs overseas are more reactive to the change and can resist one-to-one training. Overcoming the resistance barrier is not easy, but can be achieved by communicating with people, ensuring re-training programs and career development opportunities. During the offshoring process, the employees may go through several change management classes. Managers should also be encouraged to hold meeting with their people to keep in touch. Having employee counseling services available is also helpful.

A structured planning will lead to a structured transition. *Studies show that, when asked what they would do differently in structuring their offshoring relationships, both buyers and service providers respond that they would do more upfront planning for the transition phase.* A white paper published by SourceNet groups the pitfalls during the transition phase into five categories[25].

Pitfall #1: Inadequate Knowledge Transfer:

During the transfer of operations, as soon as the provider vendor is utilized, a drop in service levels is inevitable, even if the provider performs the work correctly and efficiently. There are valuable aspects lost beyond the mechanical transformation. Offshoring undermines some of the informal relationships that were developed over time with customers. A partial remedy to this pitfall is adequate transfer of knowledge. The first step is a detailed documentation of the business structure of the organization, including protocols and procedures. The actual process of developing job descriptions may not exactly align with the documented version. In this case, the best approach is to insert a validation step into the documentation, where the provider vendor's employees are trained in the physical environment while the business is conducted. By one-to-one training, knowledge transfer can be performed in a collaborative environment.

Pitfall #2: Inadequate Measurement of Service-Level Performance:

The host company may encounter problems with its customers when the provider vendor falls short in the performance levels that the company previously provided. The vendor may be meet the contractual service level specifications but may not concentrate on specific metrics. To prevent lack of satisfaction among customers, the host company can provide a baseline of performance level during the transition phase.

Pitfall #3: Lack of Response Scenario Planning:

Going into a transition with assumption that everything is planned is a common pitfall. Contingency plans must exist against potential disruptive events that can possibly appear during the transition phase. A scenario response plan, similar to disaster recovery plan, is the best approach. The company should know where to look for if extra resources are required during the transition phase and assign responsibilities for updating the organization and resolving pressures. A scenario response plan is beneficial to avoid chaos when unanticipated issues arise.

Pitfall #4: Lack of Executive Sponsorship and "Staying the Course":

The lack of sponsorship from a senior management champion is a serious pitfall. As a result, the transition stage is either hindered or ends with a breakdown due to vocal objections from the parties that disagree with the offshoring decision. Sometimes, the decision-making executive can announce the decision and leave the organization soon after. An effective approach is to have a senior executive lead the strategic changes. The executive should stress the commitment and responsibility towards the achievement of the objective. Weekly performance reviews by the executives and the people who are responsible for tactical execution, strengthens this process.

Pitfall #5: Lack of Flexibility:

Occasionally, the service level specifications and operational definitions in the contracts are based on assumptions. These assumptions may be wrong and calibration may be needed due to variations. Flexibility can be ensured by a review and tightening phase around the contractual service level specifications that lasts for a predefined period of time during the transition state. If calibration is needed, the contractual commitments can be refined upon mutual agreement.

Case: Infoworld Media Group

[26]InfoWorld Media Group is a division of International Data Group (IDG), a technology, media, research and event company. The company supports its customers by

providing IT news, technology comparisons, and focused research information. InfoWorld is not just a provider of technology but also a user of technology as well. In April 2001, InfoWorld hired a new chief technology officer (CTO). The CTO was faced with a broken IT infrastructure and dissatisfied users. InfoWorld considered business process virtualization to improve its current services. The CTO expressed his skepticism: "I wasn't a fan of offshoring at all before this particular experience. When your back is against the wall and you have X amount of dollars to accomplish a particular goal, then you just have to look at it differently and see what else is possible."

For six weeks prior to startup of the offshoring processing, InfoWorld evaluated its network to understand the operational structure. After the network evaluation, they performed testing for additional four weeks. Pilot rollouts were conducted during weekends due to the highly geographically distributed nature of the network environment.

Barriers to Implementation:

The biggest barrier was the lack of physical support. The employees had to solve the system problems via telephone calls without a physical contact.

Lessons Learned in the Testing Phase:

The company found many employees running applications that were not to be supported on a corporate network such as music and file-sharing. During the testing phase there were some legacy problems with Windows XP, which were solved soon afterwards. There were shortcomings in some of the services and the lack of monitoring in areas such as finance where the credit cards are cleared. The company was able to realize such shortcomings and implement more efficient processes. In general, the testing phase was an opportunity to review their business processes.

Unforeseen Benefits of Implementation:

At the end of the implementation, InfoWorld realized that the services they received were better than expectations. Secondary benefits were application awareness across the company and standardization of the applications.

Unforeseen Barriers of Implementation:

InfoWorld did not experience any unforeseen technical barriers to its desktop and server management virtualization. However there were difficulties in persuading people to change. It was hard to convince people in the benefits of the virtualization.

As a result, InfoWorld saved at least 30% in support costs in the first 12 months. It enabled flexibility toward changes in the business. If the company gets smaller, the cost will proportionally be reduced by the provider.

Finalization Phase

Once the transition phase is completed, resources become redundant. The idle resources may now be monetary as well as human assets. An organized plan for the relocation or elimination of idle resources is an important factor for the ongoing success of the offshoring project. In most cases, major alterations in the organizational structure are inevitable to cope with the new operational requirements.

The business environment goes through many changes and employees of the offshoring firm no longer perform the same jobs. Responsibilities and roles do not stay the same either. Nextel's transfer of IT operations can be given as an example of role changes. Nextel's vice president of customer billing services oversaw the expansion of its offshoring relationship with Amdocs in 2000[27]. Before offshoring, he led a group of 20 technicians who wrote the code for the billing system and eventually had the responsibility for technical assistance. They took orders from Nextel's business units. After offshoring, the vendor, Amdocs, took over the management of the technology of billing services. Nextel took responsibility for monitoring and controlling Amdocs service levels. Nextel allocated 20 people to manage this responsibility, but the vice president now began to manage 330-person organization for provision, messaging, and data management. At the same time, many employees were transferred to the vendors while Nextel outsourced its IT management. 4,500 employees were transferred to IBM as a result of their eight-year contract for the management of customer care services.

Unfortunately, many managers believed that the company is safe as long as the accounting books looked good. However, in long run, the dynamics of an organization does not solely depend on the monetary values. Without employee motivation, it is not possible to maintain efficient work. During an offshoring process, organizational change is inevitable, given that new employees will be hired, whereas some will lose jobs. The revolutionary changes may create a depressed psychology among the employees. Reorganization programs are very important to minimize the adverse effects assisting the continual success of an offshoring project. Necessary time and effort should be given to such programs.

[8]When the offshoring trend in manufacturing started, HP quickly recognized this phenomenon and outsourced its PCA and PCB activities. In the years that followed, when HP's competitors changed and expended significant effort in doing so, HP's management was flexible and could grow another business while closing one. The proactive movement of HP gave the company the time and opportunity to structure reorganization programs for their employees. During the finalization phase, HP managers were measured on the success of reorganization programs. This was done through the project milestones and employment-satisfaction surveys. As a result of shifting jobs overseas, a considerable amount of employees became redundant and were re-trained. In HP's case, the offshoring of manufacturing processes meant that there were fewer production labor jobs and more desk jobs. HP recognized this and made a significant investment in re-training, including career development education. Employees that were affected by the reorganization were given the priority for the open jobs. The hiring manager had to justify the reasons if a person from the reorganized area was not to be hired for the new position. The company also arranged early retirement programs and voluntary services for the employees who did not want to change their career paths.

Another natural consequence of offshoring is the exposure to new cultural and business styles. It is important to train both organizations' employees about the cultural differences in order to prevent misperceptions of one another. In a workshop held by B. Hurn and M. Jernkins at a large multinational company, Foseco, employees were asked to examine the cross-cultural issues involved in building and sustaining multinational teams and the problems of participating in multicultural meetings[28]. The major areas identified as part of the "cultural minefield" were greetings, degree of politeness, showing agreement and disagreement, use of interpreters, different approaches of time, gifts, status of women and body language. Linguistic barriers such as the use of complicated and idiomatic English were also mentioned. There was also discussion about different communication priorities in different cultures. For instance, U.S. relationship building is based on direct communication, whereas in Asia and Latin America, the "getting to know you" phase is emphasized.

The authors agree that that top management commitment is an essential prerequisite to develop the trust-building process. A technique for creating cultural synergy is adapted from a model by Adler[29]. In this technique, first the situation is described from one's own cultural perspective. The next stage is to determine the underlying cultural assumptions behind these situations. Then the cultural overlap is assessed by discovering the similarities. Then the participants identify culturally synergic alternatives based on the overlaps and differences. Finally, a culturally synergic solution is implemented by selecting the best alternative.

Control Phase

An offshoring project does not end until the outsourced operations are terminated. Experts suggest a continuous governance process to determine actual benefits derived from the joint work. The president and CEO of Robbins-Gioia, LLC, a leading program management consulting firm, states, "Just because you outsource something, it doesn't mean you can abdicate responsibility for it. The quality of management provided by the client is one of the most important factors in whether the relationship succeeds or not." [30].

A successful start does not always mean that anticipated benefits will continue. The loss of direct interactions, distributed supply networks and cultural differences challenge achievement of the objective. The complexity of environment necessitates continuous monitoring of the performance specifications. Any economic, sociological, or political alteration in the world can affect the business. Hidden costs behind the operations such as logistics and communication costs are likely to be higher than anticipated. Re-evaluation of offshoring decisions should be performed periodically based on the geopolitical and economic climate. There is always a possibility that cost-saving expectations may turn into negative incomes due to cost increases or performance reductions.

Periodic evaluation of performance by the customers and an internal review process is important. The customers in this case are the people who are directly in contact with the vendor. For instance, if a call center unit is outsourced to India, the satisfaction of consumers can be assessed by surveys and interviews. If an IT operation is outsourced, direct feedback from employees is useful. The results of these evaluations will confirm the present condition in the offshoring relationship. Both negative outcomes and positive feedbacks should be discussed with the parties. The process is everyone's responsibility, and common solutions can be derived in the presence of both parties. The assessment of drivers and consequences of the outcomes lead to reliability in the future.

For instance, customer feedback dramatically altered the offshoring practice of the computer giant, Dell, which employs about 44,300 people, with about 54% located outside of the U.S. As is the case with many other U.S. companies, its technical support center is in Bangalore, India. Sometime after the full transfer of operations, Dell found out that many U.S. costumers complained about the accents and scripted responses of Indian technical support representatives. As a result, the company terminated its technical support center in India for calls from its corporate customers that account for 85% of Dell's businesses. Since home PC owners were not a big chunk of the business and individual miscommunication did not have the potential to cause massive losses, calls from home PC owners continue to be directed to India[31].

There should be continual improvements even after the offshoring project is completed. It is also important to provide a continuing support system for the employees. Some keys to success[32] include the:

- Right applications
- Strong project management
- Smooth/planned transition
- Ongoing support
- Deliverables and scope which are agreed by both parties

Risks exist as long as an offshoring relationship continues. The challenge of controlling and managing risks is much bigger than the challenges faced in the implementation. In the 2004 issue of *The Marsh & McLennan Companies Journal, Viewpoint,* risk factors are classified by providing real-life examples[33]:

Loss of Strategic Control: JPMorgan Chase announced that it would retrieve major IT activities it had outsourced to IBM in a seven-year contract. After some experience, the managers realized that it was critical to manage and control IT directly to gain competitive advantage.

Hidden Costs: An AMR research study showed that 80% of offshoring deals did not meet targeted return on investment. Another study of by Gartner found that one-sixth of companies offshoring IT activities did not save any money.

Service Quality Problems: Lehman Brothers, Conseco, Capital One, and Dell have all experienced customer service disappointment from Indian call centers.

Lack of Scalability: A major airline found that its outsourced maintenance provider could not meet its needs for innovation and expansion.

Brand Damage: Nike was blamed for its offshoring relationships with China and Central America.

Weak Governance: At a leading high-tech company, a major function had been outsourced to the same provider independently, by three different divisions via eight contracts worth $100 million annually. Management realized the situation only when one of the divisions expressed its dissatisfaction.

The ability to notice the risks and react in a timely manner can be ensured by constant monitoring and documentation. As a general rule, a person or a team, depending on the size of the outsourced application, can be formed to monitor and evaluate the changes throughout the relationship. The three critical factors that require measurement and monitoring are reduced costs, rapid cycle times and responsiveness (3R's)[34]. Companies can expect cost savings starting in the first three months of an offshoring relationship. Costs adjusted for productivity need to be measured. New project initiatives should normally take shorter time periods as the relationship gets stronger. Indicators that can/should cause alarm include tardy operations and an inability to meet deadlines. Reduced costs and rapid cycle times cannot be realized without a rapid response time. In addition to the 3R's, evaluation of performance specifications and customer surveys should be included in periodical feedback reports to ensure continuous control over the offshoring relationship.

3. Conclusion:

Stiff competition, short product life cycles and increasing complexity of business structures drive the rise of the offshoring trend that began with manufacturing more than a decade ago. Recently offshoring projects began to receive attention for core competences such as design and R&D. The improvement of technological infrastructure and educational enhancements in developing countries facilitate the globalization efforts. While "cost reduction" is an attractive outcome in attracting companies from developed countries, procedures and results differ for each organization depending on the objective, the operational structure and the market the company is performing in. The steps toward an offshoring initiative are not the same and should not be the same for every company. For this reason, a project management approach is an effective tool in identifying, analyzing and assessing the actions needed to be taken throughout the decision-making and implementation stages.

The basic project management principles apply to offshoring decisions as well. The project life cycle phases of an offshoring decision undergo a similar rational supported by some modifications to classical project management structure. Scope and time objectives establish the basic structure of an offshoring decision. The drivers and results are examined according to their priorities in the conceptual, design, implementation, finalization and control phases. There are several aspects that influence the decisions and consequently the outcomes of the offshoring project. Cost is considered to be the major aspect but it is only one of the factors. Risk is also an important element that determines the faith of the project and it is an inevitable challenge which has to be mitigated in every period.

The success of an offshoring project depends on a number of critical factors (see Figure 6). The support of executive team and user community has the foremost criticality. Morale and productivity is hard to measure but plays an important role. Without support from the higher levels, the organization cannot achieve the targeted productiv-

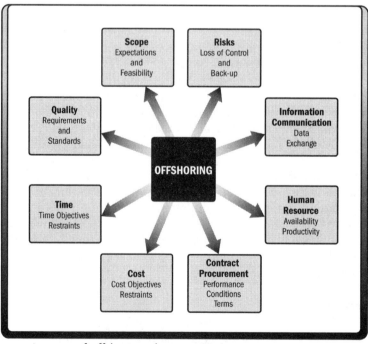

Figure 6:   Aspects of offshoring decisions[35].

ity. Long-range planning cannot be effective if there is weak or no support from the chief executive. He or she must be committed and the support must be visible to the other levels of organization. Style of management determines the actions of the executive in assuring the organization for the importance of the project. The executive must perceive the primary responsibility with an involvement starting from setting objectives and continuing with approval of strategies that lead to those objectives.

The qualities of the project manager and the executives play an important role in the success of an offshoring project. The project manager and the executive should have a basic knowledge of change management and risk management as well as contract management because outcome of offshoring project relies heavily on how the original contract is structured and how the transition is executed. If the contracts are made with good standards, offshoring can be a win-win situation both for the offshoring company and for the vendor. Moreover, communication and detailed documentation adds to the achievement by assuring an effective transition period. During the transition period, the first step is the transfer of intellectual capital from the client's organization to the offshoring firm. Ideally this process should be done one-to-one. For each employee from the vendor there needs to be a person from the offshoring firm. After they learn the basics, they should perform under the control of offshoring firm staff for some period of time.

An offshoring project does not end when the operation transfer is completed. A frequent failure is to discontinue the assessment of the offshoring decision once the process is set on track. An offshoring relationship is exposed to every economical, political and sociological alteration in the global environment. The key performance indicators must be monitored in continuous basis devoid of ignorance of hidden costs. Periodic feedback reports both from internal employees and from participating customers are useful tools to review the situation of the offshoring relationship.

Offshoring is an important decision that determines a company's operations and strategies. Offshoring decision and execution is an extensive project that affects the major strategies of a company. Today, a growing number of companies move to offshoring model either to remain competitive or to maintain existence in the market. A very dangerous rational is to decide and execute an offshoring initiative without a profound consideration. Thorough analyses of every factor should be performed by a systematic approach with a project management motivation. The goals can be achieved only if the project phases are successfully accomplished in a collaborative.

The future of offshoring requires project management qualifications that are more inter-disciplinary and multi-cultural compared to today's project management. Management of an offshoring project, and thereafter managing projects offshore, will inevitably be a part of the project management discipline. Future project managers will need to successfully interact, monitor, control, and enable processes that are required within an organization that is now established on many different shores.

The project management discipline is undergoing significant changes in its continued evolution over the last 60 years. These changes have included:

- Extension of the discipline to broader geographical and industry application;
- Continued growth of the discipline to management system and global industry applications;
- Broader use in organizational functional applications;
- Extension to other governmental applications beyond defense to include state and local governments; and

- Likely continued growth of the discipline in the improvement and depth of the theory and processes contained in the philosophy of project management.

The application of project management to the offshoring process has proved to be successful in preparing organizations to enter offshoring agreements with service provides and more broadly, a means to enter the new 'flat' world. It is abundantly clear that tomorrow's organizations will be able to enter these global networks with the help of project management to prepare them for such ventures.

References

[1]Frontline: "Is Walmart Good for America?", PBS Home Video, DVD 2004

[2]Freidman, Thomas, The World is Flat, Picador U.S.A., New York, NY, 2007.

[3]Cleland, I. D. Ireland, L.R. Project Management : Strategic Design and Implementation, 2002

[4]Woody, J. "Business Process Outsourcing- The New Market Trend", Morgen Group, White Papers, Series on Outsourcing and Business Process Outsourcing, -www.themorleygroup.com

[5]Overby, S. "One Outsources, The Other Doesn't", CIO Magazine, Nov.1.2004. -www.cio.com

[6]Steiner, G. A. " The Critical Role of Top Management in Long-Range Planning", Cleland, I. D. King, R.W. Systems, Organizations, Analysis, Management: A Book of Readings, p.132-139

[7]Steiner, G.A. "A Step by Step Guide Strategic Planning- What Every Manager Must Know", Free Press Paperbacks, First Edition 1997

[8]Balakrishnan, J. Cheng, C-H. " The Theory of Constraints and the Make-or-Buy Decision: An Update and Review", The Journal of Supply Chain, Winter 2005, p. 40-67

[9]Parker, D. W. Russel, K.A. " Outsourcing and Inter/Intra Supply Chain Dynamics: Strategic Management Issues" The Journal of Supply Chain Management, Fall 2004, p.56-68

[10]Grant, R.M. "Contemporary Strategy Analysis: Concepts, Techniques, Applications", Fourth Edition, p.390

[11]Linder, J.C. " Outsourcing for Radical Change", p: 28

[12]Reid, D. "Outsourcing for Competitive Advantage" , Bitici, U.S. Carrie, A.S. Strategic Management of the Manufacturing Value Chain, p. 631-643

[13]Nam, K. Rajgopalan, S. Rao, R. Chaudhury, A. " A Two Level Investigation of Information Systems Outsourcing", Communications of the ACM, Vol.39, No.7, 1996

[14]Minevich, M. D. Richter, F-J. " The Global Outsourcing Report" The CIO Insight Whiteboard 2005, Vol.55

[15]Arisoy,O. Bidanda, B. " The Logistics of Growing & Processing Tomatoes", IIE Annual Conference, 2005- Atlanta

[16]Wood, M. "Don't Be Sunk Offshore" Electronics Weekly, Sept 17,2003, p.4

[17]Fisher, G. H. " The Analytical Bases of Systems Analysis", Cleland ,I. D. King, R. W. Systems, Organizations, Analysis, Management: A Book of Readings, p.206-215

[18]Simister, S.J. "Qualitative and Quantitative Risk Management", The Wiley Guide to Managing Projects, Morris, P.W.G. Pinto, J.K. p.30-46

[19]"An Overview of Change Management"-http://www.change-management.com

[20]Lowe, D. "Contract Management" The Wiley Guide to Managing Projects, Morris, P.W.G. Pinto, J.K. p.678-707

[21]Julius, D. "Globalization and Stakeholder Conflicts: A Corporate Perspective" International Affairs (Royal Institute of International Affairs 1944-), Vol,73, No.3, Globalization and International Relations (Jul. 1997), 453-468

[22]Click, R.L. Duening, T.N. " Business Process Outsourcing: The Competitive Advantage" p.157

[23]Cheung, S. 1999. "Critical Factors Affecting the Use of Alternative Dispute Resolution Processes in Construction", International Journal of Project Management 5(4): 231-236

[24]Hammer, M. Stanton, S.A. " The Reengineering Revolution: A Handbook" Harper Business, January 1995

[25]"Change Without Pain – An Alternative Model for Year One of Outsourcing Agreements", White Papers, SourceNet Solutions, January 2003

[26]Young, M. Jude, M. " The Case for Virtual Business Processes: Reduce costs, improve efficiencies, and focus on your core business." p: 132-139

[27]Levinson,M. "Life After Outsourcing", Cover Story, CIO May.15 2004 issue

[28]Hurn, B.J. Jenkins, M. " International Peer Group Development", Industrial and Commercial Training, Vol.32 No.4 2004 p. 128-131

[29]Adler, N.J. "International Dimensions of Organisational Behavior (2nd edition),PWS-Kent Publishing Co. Boston, MA

[30]Santana, J. " Decision Support Part Two: Outsourcing Relationships Don't Stop at Negotiations", -http://www.insight.zdnet.co.uk

[31]CNN, November 25, 2003

[32]Clark,J. " Successfully Implementing a Global Applications Outsourcing Strategy", Nov.1998, DM Direct, -www.dmreview.com

[33]Bovet, D. Chadwick-Jones, A. "Outsourced But Not Out of Mind, Turning Contractors into Strategic Partners", The Marsh & McLennan Companies Journal, Viewpoint, Vol.33, No.2, 2004

[34]Chelikani,S. Polineni, V.K. "The 3 R's of Offshore Outsourcing" , Saven Technologies Inc. 2001, -www.saventech.com

[35]Naughton, I.E. " Outsourcing – Project Management Role", Institute of Project Management, Ireland, www.projectmanagement.ie/articles/outsourcing.htm

CHAPTER 29

"The Future of Project Management Education and Training Circa 2025"

Jang Ra

This chapter will focus on predicting the roles of project managers circa 2025 and use that knowledge to provide better education and training by reshaping the project management curriculum, teaching methods, delivery means, faculty and students. This approach is taken on the premise that future organizations will survive: (1) mainly through innovative and successful projects; (2) within a globally competitive environment representing many different cultures and time-zones; (3) by completing transformation cycles faster than their competitors.

1. Top tier organizations will find continued success through breakthrough innovations and continuous transformations. Organizations equipped with effective project management practices have outperformed their competition. However, without change it will be harder to maintain their leading status. Although the first change is always challenging, the second time is easier and faster. This trend will continue to be apparent and provide huge challenges to outdated and faltering organizations; moreover, by optimizing developmental processes and learning from predecessors' mistakes, second- and third-tier organizations can overtake the leading organizations. Good examples of these challenges are abundant in the automobile manufacturing industries in Japan, Korea, and the United States. [1,2]

2. In the future (circa 2025), global competition will be more prominent in aerospace, banking, defense, energy, environmental, IT, medical, and service industries, and we will continue seeing certain trends at an accelerating rate. Faster transportation and communication technologies will continue to make global environments closer. This will result in easier outsourcing of project resources available around the globe, but demand more integration and coordination by project management through effective communications – the exchange of information. The keys for

success here are to integrate project resources in multiple time zones and to communicate with and among multicultural project workforces.

3. Winning organizations will emphasize faster completion of new product development projects over operational cost-cutting efforts. In doing so, project life cycles should shrink to no more than a single fiscal cycle, thus preventing many multi-year project terminations and costly budgetary reassessments every fiscal turnover. Time reduction skills and techniques will be very much demanded over ones for cost reduction.

Organizations are groups of individuals. Winning organizations will be successful only through the efforts of their winning individuals. One might ask, who are those winning individuals, working effectively with multicultural project team members located in different time-zones? Who can accomplish the transformation cycle faster than their competitors? The answer lies in the project and program managers who have authority in the change and transformation processes. Their roles are further discussed in the next section.

Predicting the Roles of Project Managers Circa 2025

Predicting the future is never easy; project managers not only have to predict the future, but they have to do it well. Project managers have to visualize the roadmap leading to the final product delivery as well as its outcomes, and, in doing so, proactively identify, assess, monitor, and update project risks. It is worthy to predict the roles of the project managers who can visualize the future.

Let's start with the establishment of the project manager's status as shown in Figure 1. The project manager should be the focal point of the project management communication system, which facilitates information exchange and is comprised of three dimensions – accountability, supporting team, and information system.

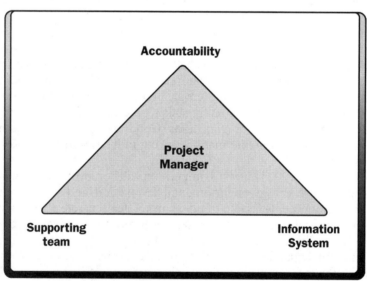

Figure 1:   Project management communication (information exchange) system

---

Every project should establish the project manager as the single point of contact throughout the project life cycle. The project manager should be accountable for the project work throughout the entire project life cycle, spanning from the business case to its delivery point. If necessary, the project life cycle could be extended to the beginning of the operation and maintenance period.

The project management team is needed to support the project manager when the project communication level is high enough. Supporting expertise might come from an administrative assistant, fiscal tech, IT support, scheduler, project controls, quality inspector, risk expert, etc. These project support professionals should be disciplined with globally standardized communication processes, since they will work with technical members outsourced globally.

A database system should be developed to capture all the project-related information. The database should be a subset of the organization's enterprise project management information system to allow for management at the project, program, portfolio, and organizational levels. In this way, limited resources within the organization can be utilized at an optimum level for multiple competing projects. Project management software like Microsoft Project and Primavera will become more popular and widely used, and additional and more advanced project management packages will be developed by Microsoft, Primavera, and other providers.

Given the fundamental role of the project manager as the focal communication point, four additional roles are worthy of mention. They are:

1) Project roadmap creator
2) Time reduction expert
3) Program manager
4) Project management trainer

1) Project Roadmap Creator

As illustrated in Figure 2, projects transform an organization from where it is to where it wants to be. In doing so, the project manager should be able to fully understand the current system of organization. The systems engineering discipline will play a critical role here. Goals and objectives should be clear through the strategic management discipline. After pinpointing the two systems (as-is and to-be), the project manager should establish the best roadmap to connect them through the project management discipline.

For large-scale transformations, a program management discipline or portfolio management discipline is necessary. A program is a series of similar projects for the same purpose. A portfolio is a combination of different projects and programs for diversifying and balancing the organization's assets and risks. The project roadmap (project schedule baseline) is developed by determining the start time and finish time for each project activity, with necessary and sufficient resources assigned and supporting details specified.

During the execution phase, progress is periodically monitored and controlled so that the project will achieve its planned value within budget and on time. Effective project managers not only know that the project roadmap leads just up to the product delivery, but they also extend the roadmap to the product operations and maintenance phase as indicated by the dotted axis in Figure 2. The project life cycle may even have to include the termination point. The cost of demolishing a nuclear power plant is about

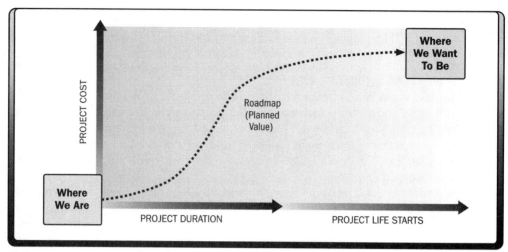

Figure 2:   Project roadmap for transforming the organization system

three times of the cost of building it. Seeing the big picture and visualizing the entire life cycle are the top skills that project managers should possess as part of their leadership skills.

At the working level, project managers have expertise in the five project process groups (Initiating, Planning, Executing, Monitoring and Controlling, and Closing) and their 42 processes listed in the *A Guide to the Project Management Body of Knowledge (PMBOK® Guide)*—Fourth Edition. [3] Using the process expertise, project managers achieve their established objectives with and through the actions of technical professionals spread around the globe.

2) Time Reduction Expert

The author strongly recommends that the project execution duration (not the entire project life cycle including the project planning phase) be no more than one year or fiscal cycle. In the case of large projects, the project should be broken down into smaller subprojects or phases. This will ensure that if the overall project is terminated, the subprojects will have salvage value rather than total project loss.

It is important to note that a project execution duration of less than one year is not simply obtained by dividing the project into shorter parts. Effective project managers know how to shorten the project duration by fully utilizing dependencies among project activities as well as their relationships with external factors. Future efforts on managing projects will focus on time reduction rather than cutting costs. This will result in a shorter time horizon of predictions as the project duration becomes shorter. Shorter durations mean fewer numbers and lower possibilities of changes, as well as less uncertainty to deal with.

As depicted in Figure 3, a project means extra work from an operational workload viewpoint. The extra work includes analyzing the current system to find the root causes of the problems, coming up with alternative solutions, and comparing the alternatives to select the best one. The project work starts with justifying the business case and ends with its desirable delivery, requiring less workload to do the same operations. However,

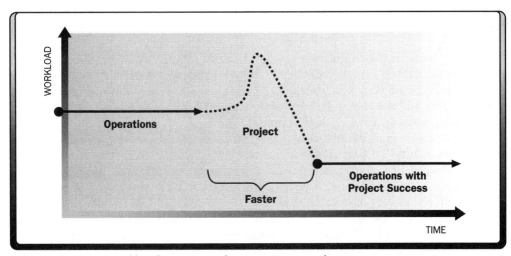

Figure 3:   Workload increases due to project work

the temporary increase in work will invite resistance from the existing workforce. Resistance to change is not an uncommon phenomenon. A lengthy or delayed project duration will further spur employees' resistance, resulting in a project failure. Project managers should have the necessary expertise to shorten project execution durations to support leaders' inspiration for a better future.

Additional cost is another important resistance in the time reduction effort. Cost increases as the project duration shortens. However, it is only true for the project direct cost, not for the total cost. As illustrated in the left side of Figure 4, the total project cost consists of direct and indirect costs. Oftentimes people do not see the benefit of time

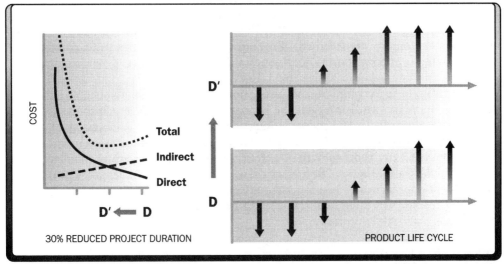

Figure 4:   Life cycle costs = project cost + fixed and indirect cost + product benefit

reduction as the fixed and indirect costs decrease. According to an experienced expert testimonial [4], projects with durations reduced up to 30 percent would lower the total project cost.

Furthermore, as shown in the right hand side of Figure 4, new products from the reduced project duration (D') will be available on the market earlier than ones from the normal duration (D), which means a shorter period of cash outflows and a longer period of cash inflows. Early delivery of new products leads to a larger market share than the competition. Speed kills the competition!

Many realistic practitioners also resist time reduction efforts due to an increasing risk of poor quality. This resistance is real when we do not exercise the proper project management practice. Many failed fast tracked projects were just pushing technical silos in the absence of necessary and proper coordination. It is very beneficial to remember that the reduced project duration means fewer scope changes, less frequent stakeholder turnover, and fewer possibilities of changes from external factors such as environmental, financial, market, political, regulatory, social, etc. The greatest challenge in managing a project is in managing changes which cause reworks and delays. Projects with fewer changes will guarantee faster delivery and better quality.

Better quality products delivered faster and at lower cost result in client and user satisfaction, which in turn stimulates the virtuous business cycle. Speedy and time-conscious projects will make organizations win! Winning organizations will be led by the winning professionals who know how to finish tasks in a shorter period.

3) Program Manager

In 1995, *Fortune* magazine predicted project managers would be the new corporate species to fill the gaps vacated from the business reengineering efforts that significantly reduced the number of middle managers. [5] In forthcoming years, a significant portion of professionals and managers born in the baby boomer generation will retire. This huge retirement will leave many corporate positions unfilled and delay major projects. [6] Is this a problem? Yes, it is. Is this an opportunity? That is not easy to answer right away. This problem is not limited to particular organizations. Winning organizations will be able to convert this problem into a competitive opportunity. This opportunity will stimulate organizations to come up with new survival strategy – projectization and integration – program management! Program management is the strategic discipline for optimizing limited resources to pursue multiple similar purpose projects without waste.

There is no time to complain about the shortage of professionals such as engineers, welders, and any technical workforce in local areas. We should search for an available workforce in other places in the world under the name of global outsourcing and/or by developing and adopting new technologies. Managing multicultural team members in a global and virtual environment will be extremely challenging. Program management is the only valuable asset that will be a practical solution for these challenges. The program management approach will lead to systematic solutions for utilizing limited resources within an enterprise system, whereas project management focuses on its own project resources as a sub-system solution.

The major focus of the program management approach is the alignment of a group of similar projects towards corporate strategic directions through coordinated efforts. Circa 2025, instead of this top-down approach, the time will come to practice agile strategies based on successful pioneering projects here and there. Setting strategies mainly based on the analyses of existing environments, technologies, and competitiveness will become soon ineffective. Winning organizations should put about 20% of their project efforts into exploring new opportunities such as new processes, new technologies, new products, new services, new markets, etc. Program management will be greatly required for those new endeavors. These risky but opportunistic project success rates have been very low so far and continue to be low—near 20%—whereas operation-improving projects will take 80% of the corporate efforts, with increasing success rate, around 80% circa 2025. Thus, the overall project success rate from both new product development projects and operation-improving projects circa 2025 is projected to be 68%, the sum of 4% (20% of 20%) from the former and 64% (80% of 80%) from the latter.

According to Standish Group's CHAOS reports [7], the IT project success rate was 16% in 1994 and 34% in 2003. In Figure 5, the two past project success rates are extended to the projected rate of 68% circa 2025.

IT stands for information technology. To the author, IT means transforming I-shape silo technical professionals to T-shape cross-functional project management professionals. In the project management environment, I-shape technical professionals work for the project under the T-shape project manager's leadership. Circa 2025, I-shape technical professionals will expand their capacity from a single expertise to multiple expertises (i.e., becoming II-shape technical professionals). Likewise, T-shape project management professionals will be coordinated by H-shape program managers. Program management capabilities will be in great demand for coordinating and integrating multiple projects as more professional work will be projectized. M-shape portfolio management professionals will be also working with T-shape project managers and H-shape program managers.

4) Project Management Trainer

The project success rate is expected to be significantly increased by academically educated and professionally trained project and program management professionals.

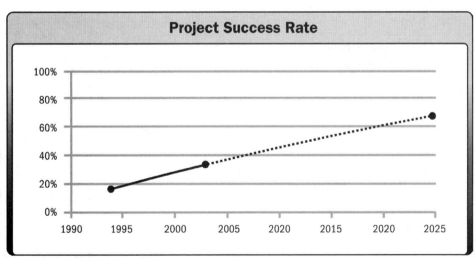

Figure 5:   Project success rate in 2025

According to GradSchools.com, as of November 2008, there are 240 universities world-wide (out of total 78,000 universities) offering project management programs: 89 certificate, 154 masters, or 17 doctorate degrees. From these universities, 18 are accredited by the Project Management Institute (PMI)'s Global Accreditation Center (GAC) and another 11 universities are candidates for accreditation. [8] Figure 6 shows the roughly projected numbers of total and GAC accredited project management programs to 2025. A few hundred universities are expected to be accredited by GAC out of thousands of universities worldwide offering project management programs.

The accelerating upward trend in Figure 6 is expected. However, the challenge will be the supply of qualified teachers and trainers. Project and program management are so practical that it will become harder to find a sufficient number of faculty who are qualified both in theory and practical performance. Project and program management is an excellent example of a subject for lifelong learning. Due to their continuous nature of learning, a significant portion of faculty should come from government and industry practitioners. Evening and weekend programs would be ideal for accommodating practitioners' professional life situations. Circa 2025, many good project and program management practitioners will be invited to classrooms as educators and trainers while also being expected to be role models and mentors in their workplace. Thus, it is desirable that all the post-graduate academic degree programs should contain "train the trainers" components in their curriculums, in which project and program management practitioners learn formal teaching skills as well as research capability.

As project and program management becomes more and more recognized as an indispensable discipline, project and program management professionals will have many different position titles. For example, single-expertise engineers such as civil, electrical, mechanical, or structural engineers have been entitled as project engineers. Likewise, process-oriented position titles will become common, such as project estimator, project scheduler, project controller, project auditor, etc. Higher-level positions will be filled

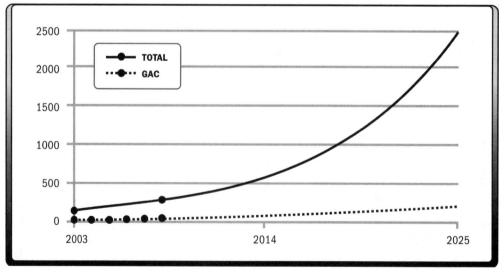

Figure 6:   The number of universities offering project management programs

with project directors, program managers, portfolio managers, PMO directors, chief program managers, etc.

In order to provide necessary and needed credentials, PMI will continue to offer more professional certificates such as PMP, CAPM, PgMP, PMI-SP, PMI-RMP, etc. while academic degrees such as BSPM, MSPM, MPM, MBA/PM, DPM, etc. will be offered by universities.

Practitioners will continue applying project and program management knowledge, skills, tools and techniques to their practical areas. Academics will advance them through research and teaching. The next section describes the project and program management curriculum to be reshaped circa 2025.

Project and Program Management Curriculum

PMI's *PMBOK® Guide* and *The Standard for Program Management* [9] contain essential and important areas to be covered in the education and training curriculum. Thus, this section does not try to rewrite them, but suggests a possible framework for developing the project and program management curriculum and introduces the Doctor in Program Management (DPM) curriculum being proposed at the University of Alaska Anchorage as an example.

1) Curriculum Development Framework

Professional responsibilities are required to become a PMI-certified Project Management Professional (PMP)®. Obtaining project authority is the main purpose of documenting a project charter. Both project authority and responsibility can be delegated to others, but project accountability cannot be separated from the project and program managers. The project management wheel in Figure 7 shows the five major elements for which project managers are accountable: project activities, data related with project activities, information from analyzing data, knowledge revealed from information, and wisdom improving next-generation project activities by utilizing knowledge from lessons learned.

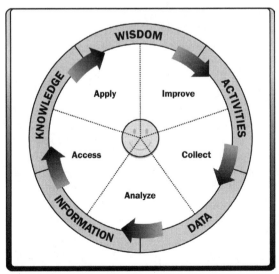

Figure 7:   Project management wheel

Project activities start with project initiation. They become the input for developing a project roadmap. Good project managers know how to create the project roadmap (the schedule baseline as in Figure 2) by identifying all the activities and only the activities and sequencing them in an efficient and effective manner.

Every project activity generates data as executed, but they are neither all nor always captured into a database. The project manager should be accountable for collecting data for maintaining and operating products as well as for improving the next generation of project activities. On the other hand, program managers should be accountable for collecting data from individual projects so that comparative analyses can be possible among the projects while optimizing limited resources. For those purposes, probability and statistics should be a prerequisite of the project and program management curriculum. Proper probability and statistical techniques produce essential and important information for decision-makers to reach informed decisions under uncertainty. These techniques also enable the measurement of project and program progress performance with the right data. An appropriate reward system is essential for a healthy management system.

Thanks to advanced information technologies and tools, real-time information exchanges (communications) are possible on a global scale. Compiling, retrieving, and disseminating the right information at the right time and to the right people will continue to be improved. Circa 2025, we will be arriving at the stage where all enterprise information systems will be linked to one common database for managing resources, finances, and projects.

Knowledge is power! The ability to find relevant information and to select the right information through Internet searches, literature reviews, interviews, seminars, and training is the new era of knowledge. Old knowledge is that which project and program managers already possess mainly through real experience and past education. Oftentimes, we blame project failures on the "unknown unknowns" that exist in the nature of project uncertainty. However, we can easily see that a good portion of the "unknown unknowns" can be classified as either "known unknowns" or "unknown knowns," leaving the pure "unknown unknowns" to a minimum or none. The "known unknowns" risk items (unknown likelihood and impact of known events) are continued to be analyzed through qualitative and quantitative tools and techniques listed in the *PMBOK® Guide*. It is interesting and significant to know that the "unknown knowns" are the "known to others, but "unknown to us" items. Knowledge management should be utilized in reducing these "unknown knowns" by sharing experience and information within the project management professional communities.

The final connection from knowledge to the next generation of project activities is the role of wisdom. The second time is always better than the first. However, the betterment should be achieved through the application of scientific theories, rather than of experience-only trials and errors. The execution of project activities for an uncertain future is project management's specialty. This will be possible only when project managers practice their specialties in a project management system built on logical processes and the culture of continuous lessons learned from the past professional activities, data analyses, information search, and knowledge applications.

The complete project management cycle, comprised of the five areas, can be used as an architectural framework for developing the future project and program management curriculum.

2) Doctor of Program Management

The need for project and program management education and training will increase at an accelerating rate like the predicted number of universities offering degree

Student	**66 Credits**	**30 Credits of Lecture Courses**	PM 650 (6)	Program and Portfolio Management	Fall	Year 1
			PM 652 (6)	Enterprise Program Management with Primavera	Spring	Year 1
			PM 654 (6)	Portfolio Finance	Summer	Year 1
			PM 656 (6)	Global Program Leadership and Innovation	Fall	Year 2
			PM 658 (6)	Program Governance and Group Decision Making	Spring	Year 2
		3 Credits Teaching	PM 660 (3)	Program Management Teaching and Training	Summer	Year 2
		3 Credits of Proposal	PM 695 (3)	Research Methods in Program Management	Summer	Year 2
		Qualification Exam			Summer	Year 2
Candidate		**30 Credits of Research Courses**	PM 699 (6)	Program Management Dissertation	Fall	Year 3
			PM 699 (6)	Program Management Dissertation	Spring	Year 3
			PM 699 (6)	Program Management Dissertation	Summer	Year 3
			PM 699 (6)	Program Management Dissertation	Fall	Year 4
			PM 699 (6)	Program Management Dissertation	Spring	Year 4

Figure 8: DPM curriculum at University of Alaska Anchorage

programs in Figure 7. Circa 2025 academics will receive increased pressure for advancing knowledge and developing better curricula. For this reason, universities will develop research-oriented doctoral programs.

Using the project management wheel's architectural framework in Figure 7, the University of Alaska Anchorage (UAA) is proposing a Doctor of Program Management (DPM) program. Its curriculum is summarized in Figure 8. The full DPM proposal can be found on the department website. [10]

Admission to the DPM program will generally require students to have earned their Master of Science in Project Management (MSPM) from UAA. The MSPM curriculum is built on the nine knowledge areas in the *PMBOK® Guide* - Fundamentals, Scope, Time, Cost, Quality, Human Resource, Communication, Risk, Procurement, and Master Project and Case Study.

The future project management curriculum will focus on the integration of project efforts with other projects as well as functional efforts within the organization. Program and portfolio management will be further advanced with contributions from systems engineering and strategic management disciplines, together with other management expertise such as finance, leadership, marketing, organizations, etc.

The DPM program prepares future leaders as academic faculty and professional practitioners in government and industrial fields. The DPM also prepares students for senior executive and consultancy roles, for careers at the frontiers of project, program, and portfolio management.

Teaching Methods and Delivery Means

Teaching methods and delivery means should be designed for educating and training the project managers who will be well prepared for working in a global market on a global scale. Actually, today's education is a global market. Utilizing every thriving communication technology available is critically correlated with communication speed.

It will greatly contribute to shortening project duration and facilitating coordination among multiple projects. Thus, project management education and training will not be effective without utilizing communication technology. This brings the crucial point that multicultural aspects of communication are also critical in project management education and training. Understanding project stakeholders' different cultures is one of the many vital pillars in project management education and training.

Figure 9 illustrates three levels of illiteracy. The first illiteracy step is the absence of the ability to read and write. The second illiteracy step is known as digital illiteracy, which causes one to not be able to use a computer. The tertiary illiteracy step was coined by Eckhardt and Keim [11] to relate lack of capability for using videoconferencing technology for communicating with multicultural team members located in multiple time zones.

It has become very popular for working professionals to complete a project management degree program through an online system. Online courses are convenient for working professionals to take anywhere and anytime. However, this mass delivery means limits to interactions between the student and faculty as well as among the students. In many cases, there is zero face-to-face interaction between faculty and students. This silo study method is the complete opposite of the spirit of educating and training T-, H- or M-shaped project and program management professionals. Professionals educated and trained through online courses will not be effective in practice in working with multicultural team members in multiple time zones. In other words, they can master the second illiteracy, but can't overcome the tertiary illiteracy.

On the other hand, teaching and learning project management in a local collocated classroom would prevent this silo environment, but would not explore the needs of using videoconferences. Thus, the combinations of local classroom with real-time videoconferencing for and by distance students (or even distance faculty) are very desirable. The program at the University of Alaska Anchorage has been delivering classes

Illiteracy Steps

Figure 9:   Illiteracy steps [12] Reprinted by permission of the author

to distant students in many places on the globe outside Alaska with local students. Distance students are able to see the exact same computer screen of the instructor, control the mouse for the class computer screen, and zoom in and out with the class camera. All the course materials and documents posted to blackboard are available without delay. In addition, students can review previous classes, recorded during class and available through blackboard, in the event of absences.

While traditional classroom teaching at local universities will continue to be the basic means of course delivery, faculty members will come to corporate conference rooms to teach cohort groups who come from the same organizations. Unlike the traditional classroom environment, cohort group members can express their personal situations in depth since they work in the same situations. These kinds of cohort teaching methods and customized curricula using actual corporate project cases will become more popular.

Faculty and Students

In global project management classes, it will be hard or at least obscure to distinguish teachers and students, since project management topics are so professional and so practical. Students with extensive experience will be sharing personal life situations with one another, while teachers cannot be effective teachers without significant practical experience unless they have unique specialties. Effective teachers will not only bring their practical experience to the classes, but also facilitate the learning environment by linking the students' expertise to the project management framework and processes.

Any subjects of project and program management can be taught by professional practitioners. This is especially true for professional faculty members with practical and competent backgrounds rather than purely academically oriented and based scholars. Oftentimes, academics are digging too much without balancing time and cost aspects. On the other hand, many practitioners are not well trained to behave well in the classroom environment. Thus, many university degree programs should develop the "train the trainers" programs. For example, the DPM program at UAA includes a course for teaching skills (See PM660 in Figure 8).

Even though excellent, competent, and qualified faculty members are teaching the courses, not all the students will become good project and program managers. It shows when the student possessing operational characteristics tries to be a project or program manager. It is desirable to choose their career options between operational professions and project management as early as possible. It is recommended to develop indicative scores in differentiating them. Typical characteristics between the project management-inclined and operations-inclined are contrasted in Figure 10.

It would be ideal for project-inclined faculty and students to work together in a global and virtual education environment using videoconferencing technologies.

Conclusions

This chapter has tried to predict the roles of project managers circa 2025 in order to reshape the project management curriculum, teaching methods, delivery means, faculty, and students for better education and training. This chapter concludes by emphasizing the importance of project management education to three other groups of people beside the project and program management professionals: The first group is top executives who have not received project, program, and portfolio management education, thus

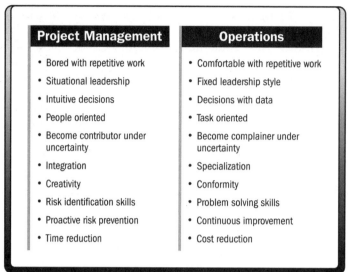

Figure 10: Characteristics between project management versus operational professionals

are not competent in the applications. The second group is non-project management professionals working either in the operations and maintenance areas, or in general areas but supporting project management work. The third group is K-12 students and college students studying an education curriculum without project management subjects.

One of the top executive effectiveness competencies is in appointing good project, program, and portfolio management professionals. However, executives' efficiency and competency will not be complete until they are fully competent by themselves with project, program and portfolio management expertise through proper education, training and practice. Circa 2025, the project, program, and portfolio management professions will be in the fastest track for becoming executives of top-tier organizations.

Project and program management professionals cannot be effective without the support of non-project management professionals and general supporting people. Thus, organizations should invest significant time and effort on educating these groups. It is very sad to observe that training is the first item to be cut by corporations experiencing financial crises, while those same organizations cannot afford to find training time for their employees when they are busy during profitable periods.

Fundamental project management principles should be taught and practiced as early as possible in the K-12 education. There are very promising movements toward this. The PMI Education Foundation has been working on this [13] and project managers in Japan are experimenting with project management education in their high schools. [14]

Project management education itself is a global market. Speed will be the ultimate winning strategy in a global competitive market. In education, PMI GAC-accredited universities will lead the advancement of the project and program management education and their contributing values and rewards will be beyond any imagination.

The world has overcome major challenges despite their difficult appearance. Revolutionary breakthroughs were made for agricultural, industrial, political, and informational challenging periods. We are facing environmental, financial, and managerial challenges. Project and program management are managerial revolutions. The way we are working will be further projectized to meet and exceed the triple constraint – completing a project on time, within budget and to the satisfaction of technical performance aspects of scope and quality. More project and program management professionals should be produced and educated. Academically trained project and program management professionals will help society advance through the uncertain future by successfully managing innovative projects and programs.

References

[1] The Toyota Product Development System: Integrating People, Process and Technology, James M. Morgan and Jeffrey K. Liker, Productivity Press, 2006

[2] The Global Korean Motor Industry (The Hyundai Motor Company's Global Strategy), Russell D. Lansbury, Chung-Sok Suh and Seung-Ho Kwon, London: Routledge, 2007

[3] A Guide to the Project Management Body of Knowledge, Project Management Institute, 2008

[4] Interview with Frank Weiss, President of Alaska Anvil Corporation, 2002

[5] The Corporate Jungle Spawns a New Species: The Project Manager, Fortune, July 10, 1995, pp179-180.

[6] "The Real Cost of Corporate Amnesia," Jason Kopschinsky, *Practicing Oil Analysis Magazine.* July 2006

[7] "Latest Standish Group CHAOS Report Shows Project Success Rates Have Improved by 50%". Business Wire. FindArticles.com. 22 Nov. 2008. http://findarticles. com/p/articles/mi_m0EIN/is_2003_March_25/ai_99169967

[8] Project Management Institute Global Accreditation Center http://www.pmi.org/ CareerDevelopment/Pages/Degree-Directory.aspx

[9] The Standard of Program Management, Project Management Institute, 2008

[10] Engineering, Science and Project Management Department at University of Alaska Anchorage, www.uaa.alaska.edu/espm

[11] "Conflicts and Conflict Resolution Mechanisms in Remote Collaboration via Videoconferencing," Andreas Eckhardt and Tobias Keim, System Sciences, 2007. HICSS 2007. 40th Annual Hawaii International Conference on, Volume, Issue, Jan. 2007 Page(s): 43 – 43

[12] "Glovirtualization – Managing a Golovirtual Project Team in Global Economy," Ki Pyung Kim, The Proceedings of the fourth International Conference on Project Management, 2008. Page #

[13] Empowering Kids through Project Skills, Kim Liegel, PMI Education Foundation, http://www.pmi.org/pmief/learningzone/PL-EmpoweringKidsThrough ProjectSkills.pdf

[14] "Web-based Practical Guidebook for Elementary Project Management Education," Toshihiro Ioi et al., The Proceedings of the fourth International Conference on Project Management, 2008. Page #